京戲三昧操釋　許謝經芸

The Chinese Conception of the Theatre

The Chinese Conception
of the
Theatre

Tao-Ching Hsü 許道經

UNIVERSITY OF WASHINGTON PRESS
SEATTLE AND LONDON

Library of Congress Cataloging in Publication Data
Hsü, Tao-Ching
The Chinese Conception of the Theatre
Bibliography: p. 669.
Includes indexes.
1. Theatre — China. 1. Title.

PN2874.H778 1984 792'.0951 83-5964
ISBN 0-295-96034-5

To

my friend

Dr. Chen Chie-Yuan

without whose

continued interest and patient generosity

this book

could not have been

published

PREFACE

This book records, on the personal level, the author's lifelong interest in the Chinese theatre, and the journeys of its manuscript, during many years, in and out of the offices of publishing and academic establishments, reflect the author's circumstances through wars and revolutions. The manuscript, first completed in 1955, was revised in 1979, the revision consisting mostly of the correction of errors and the addition of new references.

My original motive to make the long and intermittent study leading to this book was due to an initial sudden contact with the Peking dramas. To be introduced to an art through its greatest works can be an unforgettable experience and in this case previous scepticism made the psychological impact all the greater. Since then the Chinese theatre has intrigued me with its apparently crude *mise-en-scène* and its highly sophisticated style of acting and I have had the desire to make, for myself, an articulate statement of its aims and ideals. That desire led to the writing of this book and accounts for the theoretical outlook with which this book differs from those previously written on the subject.

Between the first completion of the manuscript and the definite news of its eventual publication, the manuscript of this book subsisted through a series of abortive attempts at publication, some short and uncomplicated, and some long and full of vicissitudes. Such experience is commonplace among writers. When, at the end of unfruitful negotiations, publication is eventually in sight, the prospect is usually accompanied by an umitigated sense of gratification and delight. In the present case, however, elation is mixed with sadness, partly owing to the changes in the author's personal life and partly due to what has befallen the subject matter of the book, namely, the classical Chinese theatre.

A book, on which one has spent a part of one's life and into which one has put something of oneself, is like one's own child. Re-reading one's own book after a long interval is, however, quite unlike meeting one's child after a long separation. When seeing one's child after a separation, one always imagines that he himself has remained unchanged, and is surprised to see how much the child has grown; but when one re-reads one's own book the reverse happens, one knows that the book has not changed and sees in it, as in a mirror, all the effects of aging on oneself. It is said that, if a book is to be revised, it must be done within five years after it is written, otherwise it is too late. Such perception comes only from experience. After twenty-odd years, I see in my youthful efforts a different person; he is recognizably myself, but not at all what I am now. Revision is no longer possible; either one starts writing another book on the same subject, or one leaves the early effort alone. Within five years of its writing, an author can perhaps look upon his book as a parent trying to bring up a child in his own image, and after five years the author becomes like the same parent who eventually realizes that his child is a different person from himself and gives up trying to mould the child's personality. Present circumstances, some of which will be explained presently, do not favour the writing of a new book on the same subject, and I am content to publish this book substantially as it was written over twenty years ago.

Some readers, deeply interested in the Chinese theatre and in my understanding of it, may wish to enquire what happens to the difference between this book and the one that I could have written now. Is there some additional material left out of this book? Perhaps the difference between this book and the one I could have written now is more than a difference in tone and emphasis. If so, what may be called additional material has mostly gone into two books in Chinese written in 1977 and 1978, of which a few copies were privately reproduced and bound and distributed to a few interested friends. Those two books are probably even more difficult to publish than this one, owing to the small and fast dwindling readership. Of course, if they are of real permanent value, some people will preserve them assiduously for posterity.

My information on the conditions of the modern Chinese theatre is based on direct observations but in the preparation of the first part of this book I have freely consulted Prof. Ch'i Ju-Shan's (齊如山) systematic documentation in his many publications. In the matter of appreciation with which the second part of this book is concerned I have tried to take into account the ideas of other Chinese writers, but it is inevitable that my own feelings have some effect on my views and to this extent this part of the book may be considered as a personal interpretation. In the history of the Chinese theatre I follow as a whole Prof. Wang Kuo-Wei's *History of Drama in Sung and Yüan Dynasties* (王國維, 宋元戲曲史) and for the periods after the Yüan dynasty, which are not covered by Prof. Wang's book, I have found Fung Yüan-Chün's *Studies in Ancient Drama* (馮沅君, 古劇說彙) and Aoki Masaru's *Modern History of the Chinese Drama* (青本正兒, 中國近世戲曲史) very useful. The connection between the theatrical practices of to-day and the history of the Chinese theatre is my own work and the sources of the historical data used in this part of the book are indicated in the footnotes. Comparison between the Chinese and the European theatres which forms the last part of this book has not, to my knowledge, been seriously attempted before. The typology of the Chinese and the European theatres is a vast subject which lies outside the scope of this work but part of the comparative study here attempted may be considered as a nibbling start in that field. The historical information on European theatres is derived from books on the various periods of European theatrical history among which I have been particularly benefited by those by A. E. Haigh, R. C. Flickinger, B. F. Allen, A. Pickard-Cambridge and M. Bieber on the Greek theatre, K. M. Lea on the *Commedia dell'arte,* and E. K. Chambers, W. J. Lawrence, A. H. Thorndike, G. F. Reynolds and M. C. Bradbrook on the Elizabethan theatre.

Most writers, I suppose, are, like artists, haunted by anxieties over real and imaginary defects in their works. In my case the anxiety is worsened by the fact that the writing of this book was spread over many years for the most part of which my daily occupation was remote from art or history and my access to Chinese reference books was limited in duration. To be able to wait for inspiration, to search every likely source and to polish the finished product in leisure does not fall to the lot of every writer. In spite of my efforts towards completeness and accuracy, there may yet be faults in this book which I would wish to see corrected, but as it is unlikely that I can spend more time on it, much as I wish to, I will leave it as it is, with the hope of possible future revision and of being followed by more able workers in this field.

In the twenty four years that have elapsed since this book was written, I have received, from one source or another, a number of criticisms. These criticisms are all helpful, but I cannot act on all of them, sometimes because of my limited scholarship, and sometimes because if I follow them I would have to change my book into another one, of a different nature and for a different purpose. Thus, the changes that I have made in the typescript are confined to correcting mistakes, especially bad mistakes. Naturally, I share with all serious writers the perennial apprehension that there may be some mistakes left uncorrected, an apprehension which starts as soon as one undertakes to write a book of any reasonable size. In this particular case, the apprehension has often grown into an anxiety because I am positive that there are mistakes left uncorrected and my only hope is that they do not invalidate the views and the conclusions in this book. Many subjects border on the matter of this book, for example, music, phonetics, literature, social history and architecture, in both China and Europe. As explained above, I am hardly ever in the position to indulge in exhaustive research, not has my profession allowed me ready access to the specialists. As I look back on these early literary efforts, I feel a kind of relief for the courage I then had to start writing this book, because without the partial ignorance of what was involved exactly, the worry over not knowing enough yet would have sapped that courage and paralysed the will permanently. Many writers must have also felt grateful for the initial dash of boldness without which an idea would not have been brought into fruition. With that gratitude in mind, it would be peevish to moan about one's imperfect preparation for the task. The writing of this book was an adventure and, as in any adventure, its lure, if not the credit for it, lies precisely in the unknown territory, pitfalls and all. The subject matter of this book being what, in scientific circles, is called interdisciplinary regions, those who till such land are like frontiers-men, eager to reap what they can without the fastidious pre-requisite for expertise in agronomy, horticulture, hydrology, animal husbandry and other agricultural technologies. From my readers I ask only for the same tolerance for rough workmanship that they would allot to the frontiers-men.

One possible amendment may warrant a special mention and that is, the abridgement of Part V on the comparison with western theatres. I had, at one time, in fact agreed to a drastic compression of this part for the sake of the prospective publication then, because it was thought to be disproportionately long, to contain nothing new and to be common knowledge to the specialist scholars. Curiously, on this issue, time has altered my views in my favour because now I have a second chance to abridge it, I see no reason to do so. The book is meant for western readers most of whom will read it for the information it contains on the Chinese theatre. However, the Chinese theatre is neither a building, nor does it consist of the visual and aural components of a performance. It is an institution and a tradition, based on a concept. To explain such a tradition and such a concept to western readers most of whom have seen little, if anything, of the Chinese theatrical performance, it is as important to show how the Chinese audience would consider and understand the various forms of the European theatre, as to describe what the Chinese theatre is like just as, when a professor is introducing a school of literature, it is as helpful to quote and analyse passages from that school, as to show how certain literary themes are likely to be treated by the exponents of that school. As for new materials, this book is far from being a report on newly unearthed sources. Information on the Chinese theatre is almost entirely, and that on the western theatres is completely, derived from known sources anyway.

The period from 1955 until now has revealed how unhappy the fate of the Chinese theatre has been. When the book was first written, I was teaching in the United States and news from mainland China indicated that the government there was a sincere champion for and an efficient preserver of the Chinese cultural heritage. A research institute was established for the Chinese theatre, excellent theatrical companies were formed and special care was exercised to preserve local theatrical skills and traditions. In 1957-58, I was able to witness in Peking and elsewhere, the preservation, if not the expansion, of the theatrical traditions, especially the local theatres, which had had a precarious existence. However, the government pronounced soon afterwards the need to reform and "improve" the traditional theatre and then, in the Cultural Revolution, its thorough destruction in spite of its popularity among the people. Within a few years, nobody dared speak for the classical theatre, let alone produce any plays. The artists retired, died, sank into disgrace and obscurity or committed suicide. At the time of writing this preface, one hears that the Chinese government has now understood its past mistakes. The change of policy came too late; because the Cultural Revolution had been most efficient, and there were not enough artists left to revive and rebuild the classical theatre.

The tacit understanding of the basic instability of the Party line, the ubiquitous fear of ideological mistakes which may become incriminating later, the exclusively autocratic decision on what the masses want and the lack of personal rewards, all make it very unlikely indeed that the past glories of the Peking opera will emerge again. Besides, the connoisseurs, who were effectively the guardians of the standards of excellence, are either dead or very old, and there is no discerning audience to replace them, as my recent visit to China has confirmed. Throughout history, artistic traditions rose and perished, like the biological species throughout geological times, but in the Cultural Revolution we witness a rare historical specimen of a virile form of art destroyed by deliberate government policy.

After the Cultural Revolution on the mainland, the classical Chinese theatre subsists precariously in Taiwan. Precarious existence is all that it can have because the population of Taiwan is a mixture of the Chinese from all parts of mainland China, whereas the classical theatre, called Peking Theatre, has served mainly, if not exclusively, the audience around Peking and Tientsin. Refugee artists from the mainland, like Ku Chen-ch'iu 顧正秋, tried running commercial theatrical companies and found that there was insufficient audience. The continued existence of the classical Chinese theatre in Taiwan is due in fact to the accident of the then commander-in-chief of the Chinese Air Force there, General Wang Shu-Ming 王叔銘, being an enthusiast for that theatrical tradition. He established the first government supported theatrical company attached to the Air Force, for the entertainment of the Air Force personnel, and soon the other branches of the armed forces followed suit. At present four theatre companies live on heavy government subsidies and prolong their own existence by each running a training school. There is another "experimental" theatrical academy, financed by the Ministry of Education, which also stages performances.

It has been the official policy of the Chinese government in Taiwan to serve as the guardian of the Chinese cultural heritage which is being destroyed on the mainland. Some measures have been taken to preserve the classical theatre, such as explanations of the theatrical conventions on television, the compulsory attendance by school children at special performances and the occasional use of the theatrical masks as motifs on postage stamps. Meanwhile, the existing companies play to an average 40 percent house in an 800 seat theatre and every few years in the rise in the average age of the audience becomes visible. The classical theatre is a subtle and sophisticated art which must derive its support from the educated class. The intellectual climate among the younger generation in Taiwan is, however, permeated by an uncritical admiration of the western culture. In addition to the lack of adequate support, the classical theatre has to compete with television and various forms of popular entertainment through cassettes and records and, like the traditional arts elsewhere, such as the flamenco in Spain and the *kabuki* in Japan it has been showing signs of succumbing to these attacks. Thus, like a sick man kept alive only by intensive medical care, the classical theatre in Taiwan has lost its commercial viability and social foundation. The surprise, as well as the pity, is that it still exhibits a robust *artistic* life. In spite of the usually inadequate supporting staff, the imperfect orchestra, the insufficient rehearsals and the general lack of money, within the last generation the theatrical training schools in Taiwan managed to produce at least one artist of the same calibre, if not of the same achievements, as the greatest on the mainland, like Mei Lan-fang 梅蘭芳 and Ma Lien-liang 馬連良. The decline of the Chinese theatre in Taiwan is therefore like the gradual wilting of a healthy plant transplanted to an alien soil and an unsuitable climate.

This book deals with the form of the Chinese theatre before the second World War, not with its contemporary changes, hence I do not have to make alterations in the text on account of the recent upheavals in China. However, the relationship between this book and its author has changed between the time when it was written and the time when it is published, because what was then undertaken as a paean and a celebration has turned almost into an obituary, and may, before long, be a memorial. Whether the obituary is more or less important than the paean is arguable. For my part, this book has been a labour of love and my love remains unchanged for the Chinese theatre, dead or alive.

Part of the study connected with this book was made in the British Museum Library in 1949-50 and in the East Asiatic Library of the University of California in 1954 and 1955, and I am grateful to their directors for the kind permission they gave me to use their libraries and to the staff in both places for their unfailing help. To Mr. Albert E. Dien of the East Asiatic Library of the University of California I am particularly grateful for his kind help in sending me information by correspondence. I cannot forget my debt of gratitude to my early mentors in the Chinese theatre, Mr. Hsü Hsi-Hsiang (許錫祥) and Mr. Ch'ai Ping-Chiu (蔡秉久) with whom I spent many happy hours and many rapturous moments of appreciation, and to my friend Mr. Hsu Mou-Chun (許懋淳) who kindly read an early outline of this book and gave me many valuable suggestions and who also collected for me material intended to be some of the illustrations in this book. I wish to thank my friends Dr.

Chang Hsin-Ts'ang (張心滄), Dr. P'an Huo-Hsi (潘和西) and Dr. P'an Huo-P'ing (潘和平) who have helped me in various ways. I am also deeply grateful to Mr. Liu Yang-Hui (劉揚暉) for his generous help in preparing the charts. To Dr. Ch'en Shih-Yi (陳士怡) I am indebted for the bibliographical information he collected for me in Paris in 1950. For the kindness shown to me by my friends Mr. and Mrs. Yen Chen-Hua (閻振華) no acknowledgement is adequate. I wish also to thank my sister Dr. Hsü Yin-Ming (許引明) who made it possible for me to devote myself entirely to this work for a period in 1949-50 and in the summers of 1954 and 1955.

The publication of this book is connected, in one way and another, with my visit to Taiwan for one year in 1976-77. Before and during that year, many of my friends in Taiwan have helped me in the collection of materials and among them I wish particularly to thank Mr. Chou Shih-Chuang 周石泉 and Mr. Wang Ts'e Hsi 王策禧. I also owe much to those friends who gave me general encouragement, lent me books and cassettes and introduced me to people of similar interests and of these I wish particularly to name Professor Wu K'uang 吳匡, Professor Yang Ching Mai 楊景邁 and Mr. Ch'ien Yün Yuan 錢運元. To Dr. Yang Lien-Sheng 楊聯陞 of Harvard-Yenching Institute I owe the indication of some deficiences in my treatment of early Chinese theatre which I have done my best to remove. Whatever defects have remained are due to my limitations alone. Mr. Hsing Ch'iu-T'an 幸秋潭 and Miss Chiang Chu-Hua 姜竹華 have both generously given me some photographs to be selected for the illustrations in this book. It was my good fortune to make the acquaintance of Professor Wang Ch'i-Hsiang 王企祥 and his talented and famous wife Madame Hsü Lu 徐露. They have both given me great encouragement and I am also deeply indebted to Madame Hsü Lu who trusted me with the loan of her large collection of photographic negatives for the purpose of choosing the illustrations included in this book. Among the many telling signs of decline and decay in the theatrical circles in Taiwan, the experience of watching her on stage never failed to revive my spirits and raise my hopes for the Chinese theatre, as it must have done for many others.

My greatest debt of gratitude I owe to my friend Dr. Chen Chie-Yuan 陳棨元 whose interest in this book, though the theatre is not his hobby, accused me of my own pessimism and whose unfailing help, while living a busy life of great responsibilities, has made this publication possible. Anyone finding information or entertainment here owes a similar debt to him.

I take pleasure also to acknowledge my gratitude to my publisher, the University of Washington Press, for the invaluable help I received in matters related to the publication of this book.

Birmingham, England

January 1984

CONTENTS

Part III   THE HISTORY OF THE CHINESE THEATRE

Part IV   THE HERITAGE OF THE CHINESE THEATRE

Part V THE CHINESE AND THE EUROPEAN THEATRE

ILLUSTRATIONS

(Figures 9-21 and 44-55 are in colour)

TABLES

SCORES

INTRODUCTION

(1)

The first European writer to be seriously interested in the Chinese drama was probably Joseph Prémare, a Jesuit missionary in China, who translated a drama of Yüan dynasty (1277-1367) into French, called *L'Orphelin de la Maison de Tchao* (1731) [1] from which Voltaire derived his tragedy *L'Orphelin de la Chine* (1755). [2] It was not, however, until 1838 that the first book in a European language on the Chinese theatre, Bazin's *Théâtre Chinois,* was published. At this time the interest of the translators and sinologues was in Chinese literature rather than in the Chinese theatre: in the first half of the nineteenth century alone, nine classical dramas, according to Henri Cordier's *Bibliotheca Sinica,* were translated into English and French. Bazin's *Théâtre Chinois* was, in spite of the title, a collection of four translated plays with an introduction concerned mainly with literary matters and his *Le Siècle des Youên* (1850) contained the synopses of all the hundred-odd classical dramas of the Yüan dynasty with extracts from some of them.

In the eighteen-eighties a drama of Ming dynasty (1368-1643), *Le Pi-Pa-Ki ou L'Histoire du Luth* [3] translated by Bazin in 1841, was produced at the theatre Port-Saint-Denis in Paris. This experiment was mentioned in Général Tcheng Ki-Tong's *Le Théâtre des Chinois* (1886), (published as one of the series *Les Chinois peints par eux-mêmes*), the first effort on the part of the Chinese to explain their form of theatre to the Europeans. It contains interesting comparisons between the contemporary Chinese and French theatre. At the end of the century appeared two German books on the subject: von Gottschall's *Das Theater und Drama der Chinesen* (1887), an attempt to read the Chinese mind through the Chinese theatre, and v. Minnigerode's *Über Chinesisches Theater* (1888), a descriptive work based on observations made in San Francisco. English writings at the turn of the century such

---

[1] 紀君祥，趙氏孤兒
[2] Adapted into English as *The Orphan of China* (1759) by Arthur Murphy.
[3] 琵琶記

1

as W. Stanton's *The Chinese Drama* (1899) and H. A. Giles' *History of Chinese Literature* (1901) reverted back to the emphasis on literature. Since then many books in European languages have been written on the subject both by Chinese writers visiting foreign countries and by European writers staying in China. R. F. Johnston's *The Chinese Drama* (1921) is a short but very elegant essay; Tchou Kia-Kien's *Théâtre Chinois* (1922) is more or less a collection of comprehensive notes on A. Jacovleff's drawings which illustrate it; A. E. Zucker's *The Chinese Theatre* (1925) is partly a historical survey and contains an interesting chapter on the analogies between the Chinese and the Elizabethan theatre, but it vacillates between dramatic literature and theatrical conditions and, on historical matters, is not always accurate in the quotations from Prof. Wang Kuo-Wei's works (see below); B. S. Allen's *Chinese Theatre Handbook* (1925), though brief, is probably the best, because it is the most appreciative, guide for foreigners; George Soulié de Morant's *Théâtre et Musique modernes en Chine* (1926) is a carefully written account even though the music in western notations by André Gailhard represents a westerner's impression rather than accurate documentation; L. C. Arlington's *The Chinese Drama from the Earliest Times until To-day* (1930) is less historical than its title suggests but contains numerous illustrations of costume, masks, musical instruments and properties; Mien Tcheng's *Le Théâtre Chinois Moderne* (1929) is another general description of the Chinese theatre of to-day; Camille Poupeye's *Le Théâtre Chinois* (1933) deals also with individual actors and dramas and contains some account of the history of the Chinese theatre; of specialized interest are Tsiang Un-Kai's *K'ouen K'iu Le Théâtre Chinois Ancien* (1932) and Wang Kwang-Ch'i's *Über die Chinesische Klassische Oper* (1934) both dealing with a particular type of the Chinese theatre; *Secrets of the Chinese Drama* (1937) by Ch'eng Hsiu-Ling (Cecilia S. L. Zung), a lawyer and an amateur actress, is a book on the Chinese style of acting particularly interesting for its profuse illustrations; Chiao Cheng-Chih's *Le Théâtre Chinois d'aujourd'hui* (1938) is a well-informed and penetrating work by the ex-director of the Academy of Theatrical Arts in Peking with emphasis on problems of training and reform and Jack Chen's *The Chinese Theatre* (1949) is a short essay written from the communists' critical point of view. The sympathetic introduction in L. C. Arlington and H. Acton's *Famous Chinese Plays* (1937) and the articles on Chinese drama in the *Encyclopaedia Britannica* (eleventh edition) and *Oxford Companion to the Theatre* (1951) should also be mentioned as accurate and succinct accounts on the subject.

The Chinese public has a demand for books on criticism and appreciation but hardly any for general descriptions of the modern Chinese theatre, for understandable reasons. Information on theatrical matters is normally scattered among the introductions to collections of modern dramas (戲考), collections of the scores of the arias, books on theatrical music written for the amateurs, newspaper articles on particular aspects of the theatre, reminiscences of great actors and other miscellaneous writings. The first book in Chinese on the Chinese theatre is by Tsuji Takeo, a Japanese enthusiast (聽花, 中國劇, 1925 also in Japanese 辻武雄, 支那芝居, 大正十三年) and this was followed by Prof. Ch'i Ju-Shan's *The Structure of the Chinese Drama* (齊如山, 國劇之組織, 1928) which covers the same ground. Both these books are authoritative, but neither has been translated into any European language although an abridged translation into English is said to have been attempted for the latter. Among the other important books on the subject may be mentioned *Studies on the Theatre* by Ling Shan-Ch'ing and others (凌善清等, 戲學彙考), which is concerned mainly with technicalities and *Chats on the Pear Garden* by Wang Meng-Sheng (王夢生, 梨園佳話) a book of criticisms and appreciation addressed to connoisseurs. The detailed and systematic treatises on the individual elements of the theatre such as masks, costume, music, management, acting, conventions, etc., compiled by Prof. Ch'i Ju-Shan and others in the *Theatre Series* (戲劇叢書) and elsewhere (see Bibliography) constitute an encyclopaedic account of the Chinese theatre, but they are hardly suitable for foreigners. [4]

There is as yet no book in a European language on the history of the Chinese theatre; historical information in the general works in English and French is usually brief and fragmentary. [5] The main source of both the inspiration and the information for the many books on the subject now available is Prof. Wang Kuo-Wei's *History of Drama in Sung and Yüan Dynasties* 王國維, 宋元戲曲史 which, together with the various studies in theatrical history in his *Collected Works,* still stands as the most important reference literature in this field. Of other original contributions may be mentioned Aoki Masaru's *Modern History of the Chinese Drama* 青木正兒, 中國近世戲曲史 designed as a sequel to Prof. Wang's book, bringing the account up to the present time, and Miss Feng Yüan-Chün's *Studies in Ancient Drama* 馮沅君, 古劇說彙 a collection of various findings on ancient theatrical conditions. [6]

---

[4] Note added in 1979: After Professor Ch'i's death, these books became part of his privately printed *Collected Works*.

[5] In *The Survey of the Chinese Theatre* by Lu Chi-Yeh 盧冀野, 中國戲劇概論 the author mentions in the preface "a short work" in English on the history of the Chinese theatre by Ch'en Fu-Ch'ing 陳紱卿 (家麟) which he had not seen. This appears to be an essay rather than a book.

[6] Note added in 1984: William Dolby's *History of Chinese Drama,* 1976, is a carefully researched book apparently based entirely on Chinese books, including documents from communist China, and contains a large bibliography. Other serious studies include: C. Mackerras, *The Chinese Theatre in Modern Times: From 1840 to the Present Day,* Amherst, 1975, and *The Rise of the Peking Opera,*

Lack of understanding in the West of Chinese fine arts, especially of music, calligraphy and theatre, is probably partly due to the difficulty of acquiring new tastes and accepting new standards and partly to the lack of an equivalent form in the western culture — for instance, in calligraphy, as the Chinese understand it — which could serve as a point of reference for western students. The wide difference between the Chinese and the European theatre of to-day is a case in point.

The Chinese have not shown much eagerness to advertise their theatre to the West: those who know western languages and are interested in the western peoples are often unappreciative of their own culture including the theatre and those who understand the Chinese theatre are mostly unfamiliar with western arts and tend to remain silent with cynical complacency. The difficulty of transporting the theatre physically over large distances further widens the gulf between the East and the West in this sphere. Foreigners in China who are interested in cultural matters can be easily discouraged by the forbidding approach to the Chinese arts which, as compared with the western, are more for the connoisseur. Those who are undaunted tend to be over-confident and too often judge the Chinese theatre with western standards and thereby overlook its distinctive merits.

The emphasis of the earliest European writings on the Chinese theatre was, as can be expected, placed on its strangeness. This point of view was that of the traveller for whom anything different from his own land is worth recording. Such writings are exemplified by Antonio Paglicci Brozzi's *Teatri e Spettacoli dei Popoli Orientali* (1887), Henry Borel's *Weisheit und Schönheit aus China* (1898) as well as Karl Mantzius' *A History of Theatrical Art* (1903) (translated by Louise von Cossel and C. Archer) in which the information on the Chinese theatre is apparently based on travellers' reports. Among the later works by European writers, although many are distinguished by the earnestness in purpose not all of them are free from misconceptions due to lack of genuine appreciation. It appears that in art even though an observer may be conscientious he does not *see* accurately without a

1770-1870: Social Aspects of the Theatre in Manchu China, Oxford, 1972, by the same author. A. C. Scott, *The Classical Theatre of China,* London, 1957, is a lighter book. C. W. Shih, *The Golden Age of Chinese Drama: Yüan Tsa-chü,* Princeton, 1976, and S. H. West, *Vaudeville and Narrative: Aspects of Chin Theatre,* Wiesbaden, 1977, treat specialized topics in more detail than the general reader can enjoy and are based on sound and well known sources. Colin Mackerras (ed.), *Chinese Theatre from its Origin to the Present Day,* Hawaii, 1984, seems to be the latest addition to the books on this topic. Some western bibliographies on the Chinese Theatre: Henri Cordier, *Bibliotheca Sinica,* Vols. 1-4, (1904-08), *Supplement* (1922-24). William Hu, *A Bibliography for Yüan Opera,* Ann Arbor, 1962. Daniel S. P. Yang, *An Annotated Bibliography of Materials for the Study of the Peking Theatre,* Madison, 1967.

certain degree of sympathy with the object of his observation. [7] Western writers who have no direct knowledge of the Chinese theatre rely on the secondary information which these first-hand observers provide, and thus misunderstandings and distortions filter through the more popular, but by no means the most reliable, references into histories of World Theatre and World Drama and even into encyclopaedias.

It is doubtful whether a foreigner's appreciation of a Chinese art can ever be the same as the natives'. However, to understand a new style in art it is usually necessary to leave one's preconceptions first, to unlearn one's taste, to give up one's unconscious aesthetics. This statement applies with special force to the Europeans interested in the Chinese theatre, because the characteristics of the Chinese and the modern western theatre are not only different but mostly opposite, and any attempt, deliberate or unconscious, to fit the former into the standards of the latter is doomed to failure. To those unfamiliar with the Chinese theatrical conventions watching Chinese dramas is like listening to music in a different scale, and just as the only way to understand such music is to learn the new scale, so the only way to learn to understand Chinese dramas is to try to appreciate them as the Chinese do. Adjustments of basic concepts, admittedly difficult, have to be made, otherwise appreciation, which could start in a small area, will remain crippled and become eventually smothered.

Most people are inclined to think that only one form of theatre — the form they know — is natural because their appreciation of that form appears to be effortless and natural. The ability to appreciate art is of course acquired, though in most cases the process of learning is so gradual as to be hardly perceptible even to the learner himself especially if the greater part of it is accomplished in childhood. By the time appreciation has become a habit, the process of acquiring it is forgotten. When confronted with a form of theatre belonging to a different period or country which one has not learned to enjoy, the mental adjustment for new ways of appreciation is usually so great and the success at the beginning so small that one is tempted to feel convinced that it is awkward and stylized, though to its own audience it appears perfectly natural.

In the European theatre itself dramatic values have by no means been stable: what was natural to the audience of the seventeenth century is not considered as natural now. Even the theatrical practices a century ago appear absurd now. Historians of the theatre realize that the mental habits of the theatregoers of the past

---

[7] For reports by baffled observers see *Theatre Arts,* Vol. XXIX, No. 5, May 1945 and *Journal of the North China Branch of the Royal Asiatic Society,* Vol. XX, 1885. "Chinese Theatricals and Theatrical Plots". In the latter one author said that the value of the Chinese dramas as compared with the European is like the value of a Chinese painting beside a western oil painting. At that time the merit of Chinese painting was apparently not recognized by members of the Society.

are vastly different from those of to-day and that reconstructions of theatrical conditions based on modern ideas of propriety in theatrical matters can lead to serious mistakes. [8] As the study of the European theatrical history is now being freed from that of dramatic literature [9] and as it is being recognized now that the modern European theatre is only one of many possible forms of theatre [10] the study of the Chinese stage should become less forbidding and more significant, less forbidding because it is no more different from the European theatre of to-day than, for example, the Greek theatre and more significant because it can add a geographical dimension to the historical breadth of view. [11]

Perfect appreciation of the Chinese theatre by western people is by no means impossible and should not be difficult under favourable conditions. For some years before the recent Sino-Japanese war a German woman, known in China only by her Chinese name 雍竹君, who grew up in Peking, performed in Chinese theatres as a guest artist and was highly acclaimed by the public. The sensation created might be due to the novelty but as the audiences in Peking are the most fastidious in the country her ability to appear in public represents in itself a high degree of proficiency. The western public has little opportunity of direct contact with the Chinese theatre, visits of Chinese actors to foreign countries being few and far between. Mei Lan-Fang 梅蘭芳, acclaimed by many as the greatest living Chinese actor, visited Japan in 1919 and 1924, the United States in 1930 and Russia in 1935, and Ch'eng Yen-Ch'iu 程硯秋 who is also a female impersonator, and is well known for his improvised ornamentation in the arias, visited Paris in 1931. It is difficult to estimate the effects of these visits on western theatres: Mei's tour of the United States was financially a success and Ch'eng is said to have impressed the Parisian costume designers, but so far as the dramatic art is concerned, there does

---

(8) cf. G. F. Reynolds, *The Staging of Elizabethan Plays at the Red Bull Theatre 1605-1625* (1940). p. 49; "Thirty years ago scholars were mainly anxious to find a place in the Elizabethan theatre for a front curtain; they seemed unable to imagine any stage without one". Other scholars wanted to see a front curtain in the open air theatre of ancient Greece — see R. C. Flickinger, *The Greek Theatre and Its Drama,* p. 243 *et seq.*

(9) *Vide* Preface to *The Oxford Companion to the Theatre* (1951) and Nagler, *Sources of Theatrical History* (1952), p. xx f.

(10) cf. W. Beare, *The Roman Stage,* p. vii, "It might have been well to pay more attention to the music, the art and drama of India and Java, of China and Japan, if only to remind ourselves that our western notions are not valid for all mankind, even at the present day".

(11) Artistic standards vary widely in different ages and in different countries. At the present it is considered a defect for a European painting to have little formal beauty but a great deal of social and emotional interest. The Chinese painters put different relative values on these elements of the graphic arts. In the modern European dramas great importance is attached to the intellectual content, and little to the spectacle but in the Chinese theatre formal beauty is one of the main attractions.

not seem to be any noticeable influence, except perhaps in Russia where some directors incorporated some elements of the Chinese theatre into their theory. [12] In recent years, an Amateur Theatre Society produced some Chinese plays at the Cambridge Theatre in London in 1946 and a company of Chinese players from Peking performed at Théâtre Sarah Bernhardt in Paris in the spring of 1955 and visited London in October of the same year. [13]

Several films, some in documentary form, have been made of the Chinese dramas and one technicolor film was made by Mei Lan-Fang and Chiang Miao-Hsiang 姜妙香 in 1947. Since the earliest days of the gramophone, records have been made of the Chinese dramas, mostly for short arias and of poor acoustic quality, but recent recordings of complete dramas (e.g. 馬連良, 武家坡; 譚富英, 四郎探母) are excellent in both their technical and artistic qualities. [14] One may venture to hope that through the media of films and sound recordings the western audience may, some time in the future, gain access to Chinese theatrical art.

---

[12] cf. L. C. Arlington and H. Acton, *Famous Chinese Plays,* p. xiii *supra.*

[13] Note added in 1979: In the last twenty years, artists from Taiwan have also toured Europe and North and South America several times.

[14] Decca's samples of Chinese music, Decca 20122-3, identical with Parlophone's *Musik des Orients* compiled by Erich M. von Hornbostel, are not of the highest musical standards nor are the explanatory introductions always correct. A complete reference book for the Chinese records is yet to be written. Western readers can find a short list of records in Cecilia S. L. Zung's *Secrets of the Chinese Drama.*

Part I

The Chinese Theatre of To-day

CHAPTER I

GENERAL CONDITIONS OF THEATRICAL ENTERTAINMENT IN CHINA

Dramatic performances in China to-day fall into two distinct types: the traditional Chinese theatre, an indigenous product developed in the twelfth century and continued with few changes till the present, and the modern drama, modelled on the western naturalistic theatre and introduced into the country at the beginning of this century. The aims and techniques of these two theatres are widely different and the attempts at combining them into one form have so far produced no noticeable effect.

The traditional Chinese theatre is characterized by the freedom of the audience and the lack of realism in the performance. The audience not only watch the performance but also smoke, drink, eat and talk. There is no scenery on the stage which projects into the auditorium and is surrounded by the audience. The musicians sit on the stage fully visible to the audience and the stage hands move freely among the actors during the performance. The dialogue is partly sung and partly spoken in stylish declamation and the acting, conventionalized and accompanied by music, is akin to dance. Contemporary events are rarely represented and the costume, rich and colourful, is quite unlike the modern Chinese dress, so that the world of the drama is remote from that of the audience.

Owing to the difference in the Chinese spoken language from district to district which is such that people of different provinces cannot understand each other, and owing to the hitherto relative rarity of communication between different parts of the country, there are many types of the traditional Chinese theatre each serving a locality in which the dialect is wholly or partially understood. These local types of the traditional theatre differ from each other not only in dialect but also in music and repertoire. They all, however, share the characteristics mentioned above, of the freedom enjoyed by the audience and the unrealistic staging. Roughly speaking each province has its own type of theatre, although in some cases one dialect and one type of theatre serve two or three provinces. In cosmopolitan cities like Shanghai with a

11

large population consisting of people from many provinces one naturally finds several types of local theatres.

The artistic quality of these local types of the Chinese theatre depends on the economic status of the area: if the economic conditions remain good for a period of time the theatrical profession enjoys an unbroken tradition and, encouraged by the well-to-do section of the community, who alone have the leisure for cultivating their taste, often develops the theatre towards a high level of artistic achievement. On the other hand, with war or natural calamities the people cannot afford such luxuries as theatrical entertainment, theatrical companies are broken up and the accumulated knowledge and experience wasted and trained talents lost. Occasionally a great actor enriches a local theatre with his art but his achievements usually die with him. It is the relatively sporadic nature of the theatrical activities in many parts of China which accounts for the comparatively poor quality of many local types of the traditional theatre.

There are however two types of the traditional theatre which do not suffer from the instability of local economic conditions and which through long continuous development attain a high artistic standard. They are the *K'un* dramas 崑曲 and the Peking dramas 京戲 and these, in order to distinguish them from the less stable and generally less meritorious local types, will be referred to as the classical Chinese theatre. The classical Chinese theatre is free from the disturbance of local economic conditions because with its high artistic standard it appeals to a nationwide audience. The *K'un* dramas, sung in the dialect of Soochow (near Shanghai) have an unbroken tradition of about three hundred years and although their popularity declined after the middle of the nineteenth century, they are by no means extinct. The Peking dramas are sung in the Peking dialect, also the official language in imperial times and the standard national language since the Republic, hence it is taught in schools everywhere in the country and spoken, with a reasonable degree of accuracy, by all educated people in China. The home of *K'un* dramas, before their decline, was in Soochow but the companies, like those of the Peking dramas to-day, toured many parts of China. The popularity of *K'un* dramas would probably have been greater than it was if the knowledge of the dialect were more prevalent — outside the provinces of Kiangsu and Chekiang, except for the habitual theatre-goers, they were only partially understood. Nevertheless, amateur societies of *K'un* dramas, like those of Peking dramas, are even now a widespread pursuit in China. The home of the Peking dramas is Peking but the larger Chinese cities like Tientsin and Shanghai also have companies playing them. [1]

The modern drama, on the other hand, is performed on a stage equipped with

---

[1] In 1935 there were about twenty players' companies in Peking alone. The social conditions described in this book are, unless otherwise specified, those of the period before 1937, when the Sino-Japanese war started. Since then vast changes have occurred in the country and it is difficult to say whether new stability has been reached.

front curtain, scenery, realistic stage effects and modern stage lighting. The properties and costume are, as far as possible, authentic and historically correct and the acting and elocution are naturalistic, in fact it is a copy of the western naturalistic theatre. [2]

The earliest dramatic performances in the western style, that is, with naturalistic acting and delivery, were given by the students of missionary schools as part of their study in foreign languages. It is difficult to ascertain which performance was the earliest, because owing to the foreign language used, few people outside the schools were interested, but according to one account [3] the performance in St. John's University in November 1902 was the first. The event appears to have had little effect on the public as the production was a western drama which they could not understand but several high schools and the Y.M.C.A. soon started producing plays based on current events with moralizing passages for the edification of the public and these productions proved highly popular, so that some were used to raise charity funds. It was not however until 1907 that serious literary purpose was attached to the movement by a group of Chinese students in Tokyo who, dissatisfied with the paucity of modern Chinese dramatic literature, formed an amateur dramatic society and produced Dumas' *Camille* which was highly commended by the Japanese press. The success led to further translation and production of European plays in Tokyo, and, through students returned from Japan, to several dramatic societies and many performances in Shanghai. Among those active at this time were Li Shu-T'ung 李叔同 now better known as Hung-I-Fa-Shih 弘一法師, the name he adopted after he became a Buddhist monk, and Ou-Yang Yü-Ch'ien 歐陽予倩 the well known dramatist. The experiment in Shanghai was not however uniformly encouraging, nor was the appeal purely through naturalism, because ancient costume and adaptations from the traditional plays were employed to attract the audience, but as a whole the movement may be considered to have taken root in China at this time. It lies outside the purpose of this book to trace the spasmodic existence of the many early dramatic societies and the fortunes of the pioneers, [4] suffice it to add that the movement was then confined to Shanghai and the neighbouring towns and was introduced into Peking only in 1908. At this time the Chinese revolution was brewing and the movement of modern drama was in no small way connected with it, in fact in the first years of the Republic (from 1911) many of the leaders in this dramatic movement were members

---

[2] The modern drama in China is in every respect a copy of the western naturalistic theatre except one: in its early days, owing to the oriental social convention, there were no actresses and men played the female parts. In *wen-ming-hsi* which came afterwards (see below), however, there were all women companies with women playing men's parts — see 周貽白, 中國戲劇小史, 頁七七.

[3] 朱雙雲, 新劇史

[4] For details see 朱雙雲, 新劇史.

13

of the revolutionary party and many of the dramas were overtly propaganda pieces. Nevertheless even at this early stage both amateur and professional actors seized the opportunity to fame and fortune and adapted the technique to please the public, even to the extent of incorporating in it dance and singing from the traditional stage. It may be added that the early exuberance of the modern drama is at least partially due to the relatively little training required to become an actor in it.

Since then the modern drama has spread to every part of China, especially during the Sino-Japanese war when it was extensively used for war propaganda in the army and in remote towns and villages. Its popularity however has been confined to the educated Chinese, especially in schools and colleges, and that is why the few permanent companies can only survive in the largest cities and there only with difficulty.

Judging by contemporary accounts the modern drama was first introduced to the public as a novelty, and though it was then as such a success, it has never established itself as stable entertainment for the general public. It has been kept alive more by the efforts of the producers than by the demand of the audience, more for its propaganda value than for its merits as entertainment. It is difficult to estimate its effect on patriotism and social reform for which it has almost always been a mouthpiece, but its effect on modern Chinese literature must not be overlooked: apart from the many translations of European dramas covering practically every country in the western world, a large number of modern dramas in the vernacular and conversational style have been written by native authors.

The movement of modern drama has, as a whole, been in the hands of conscientious producers and playwrights, hence it has been free from vulgarity and sensationalism. However the commercialization of the modern drama following its early success has produced a type of drama known as *wen-ming-hsi* 文明戲 or "new culture drama" in which the dialogue is entirely improvised and adjusted to the momentary appreciation of the audience. At first the modern dramas were produced by amateurs, sometimes for the edification of the audience and sometimes to raise funds, but by 1914 several professional companies were competing with each other in Shanghai and in order to attract audiences with new plays some of these, notably the Min-Ming Society 民鳴社 and the Min-Hsing Society 民興社 partially improvised their stage dialogue to cover inadequate rehearsal. Within a year the production became further simplified so that no script was necessary: the plot was explained to the actors who, following the table of exits and entrances posted in the green room, improvised the entire dialogue and stage business. The dialogue soon became rude and banal, fit only for the lowest of tastes and stock situations were repeated in every play. It lingered for a while in fair grounds but is now fortunately practically extinct.

Since the communist revolution yet another type of drama called *yang-ko* 秧歌

14

has become prevalent. This is derived from the peasants' dance in Shensi province 陝西 in northwestern China where the communist army was at one time stationed. The original dance, in simple steps and with recurring twistings of the body, was accompanied by singing and simple dramatization, but the obscene element in it and the name (literally "rice plant song") suggest strongly the derivation from primitive fertility rites. The steps have now become more complicated and dramatic plots have been grafted into the dance. It is as yet too early to evaluate the importance of this form of theatre. [5]

At this point mention may be made of the attempts to modify the form of the traditional theatre, mostly by grafting some realistic features to it, with the view of either improving the traditional form or meeting the popular demand for spectacle, and of the wholesale imitation of western opera and ballet as well as the numerous experimental forms of theatre with various mixtures of old and new or Chinese and western elements. All these new forms, except those already dead, are too young and unstable as yet to warrant classification. [6]

Theatre in China differs from that in the western world in one important respect: only a small portion of the Chinese theatre is commmercialized. In the western world, in order to see a professional performance of either opera or ballet or drama, one has only to go to the commercial theatres where a more or less constant supply of theatrical fare is offered and where one can buy the privilege of watching the performance at any time. This is true in China only in the cities. For the majority of the Chinese people living in villages where no commercial theatres are available the only opportunities of watching plays are the festivals and celebrations which occur only a few times a year and to which, in most cases, everyone is invited. The social function of theatrical performances in China is based on the fact that they are considered to be appropriate presents to man and god, [7] for example, to hire a professional company to give private performances at birthday parties is one of the best birthday presents one can give and amateur societies often offer their own performances as birthday presents. Religious festivals, usually in honour of local gods, are more often than not accompanied by theatrical activities in front of the images of the gods, so much so that most Chinese temple buildings have a stage facing the main hall. Theatrical performances for the benefit of the whole village can also stand for the fine for certain public offences or a token of apology for personal insult. New year celebrations, weddings, important anniversaries, opening ceremonies of public buildings and so forth are usually also occasions for dramatic

---

[5] Jack Chen's *The Chinese Theatre,* Ch. 3 contains an account of this type of drama.

[6] No attempts are made in this book to describe the various forms of entertainment allied to the theatre, such as shadow plays, hand puppets, rod puppets, marionettes, farcical duologue 相聲 recitation of narrative poems, etc.

[7] cf. similar custom in ancient Rome — Gibbon, *Decline and Fall of the Roman Empire,* Ch. XV. Abhorrence of the Christians for idolatry.

performances which would take place either in the temples for local gods or in the ancestral temples or guild halls or on temporary stages in the village squares.

Except in Peking and its vicinities, commercial theatres present both the local type of dramas and the classical dramas, the latter when touring companies are available, whereas the village performances and private performances are mainly, though not exclusively, of the local types of theatre.

As regards the quality of performance, classical theatre and the local types of theatre overlap to a certain extent but as a whole the former is artistically better than the latter. It is necessary to distinguish between classical taste and popular appeal because between extreme cases, such as between the best companies of the classical theatre and the local companies in remote districts or the vulgarized theatres in the cities, there exists not only difference but also opposition in the characteristics. As this book is primarily concerned with the classical theatre, to avoid misunderstanding, the differences between classical and popular theatres will be explained forthwith.

It is often said that the Chinese theatre is allied to moral instruction. This is true only of the popular theatres, especially those in country districts. Moral ideas are reflected in the theatre in China, as elsewhere, but in the classical theatre the emphasis is on artistic achievement rather than moral instruction. In the popular theatre, which, roughly speaking, consists of local types of the traditional theatre, the wicked is invariably punished in the end either by human or by supernatural agencies and the good and just are rewarded with what are desirable in the eyes of the Chinese people. This is true only to a minor degree in the classical theatre. Indeed, the customary form of performance of the classical theatre makes it unsuitable for moral instruction because, whereas in the popular theatre more or less complete stories are represented, in the classical theatre one performance comprises a large number of separate dramatic episodes, each of which is a part of a different story. Thus even if virtue is rewarded in the end, the performance does not normally reach that part of the stories.

The difference in moral content together with others which may be grouped under the general heading of artistic quality, is due directly to the difference in the taste of the audiences. On the one hand, for the popular theatre, we have mostly illiterate peasants who have seldom been outside their own village, coming to the temple for amusement a few times a year or the less educated part of urban population visiting cheap theatres for easy entertainment; and on the other hand, for the classical theatre, we have a class of leisured bourgeoisie who visit the theatre frequently and who have a cultivated taste. The two kinds of audience differ in degree of education, intelligence, sensitivity and seriousness towards the theatrical art. The one comes to the theatre for excitement, the other for artistic experience. Therefore in the classical theatre the repertoire is stable and the audience, like those of the European operas, know the plays well because they have seen them many times before but in the popular theatre the plays are new to the audience and the appeal of the unfolding plot is often exploited. [8]

[8]   In China, in the cinema the cheaper seats are sold out first but in the classical theatre the most expensive seats are the most difficult to get. Since theatre in China is not as much a social event as opera in Europe and the element of snobbery can have only a minor role in it, this fact is significant of the ample financial support for good theatrical art.

CHAPTER II

THE THEATRE BUILDING, THE AUDIENCE AND THE PROGRAMME

The most prominent and important feature of the Chinese theatre is the protruding stage, open at the sides as well as in the front and surrounded on three sides by the audience. All Chinese theatres have such a stage. However, there are two standard types of theatre building: the tea-house theatre and the temple theatre.

The main hall of a Chinese temple or guild hall faces an open yard and is connected with it through a few steps. In the temple yard, which is normally walled but not roofed, there is usually a stage, about five or six feet high, facing the hall. In some temples the yard is flanked by two narrow roofed galleries, one on each side. The roof over the stage, supported partly by the two pillars (PP in Fig. 2) at the front corners of the stage, is separate from that of the main building. At the back of the stage are two doors (SS) or rather door openings leading from the stage to the simple green room behind it, and at the front and side edges is a low rail. The audience, except those in the galleries, stand in the yard and in the front portion of the hall. The galleries, with seats and attendants, are reserved for the women folk of wealthy patrons of the festival or the guests to the private birthday party that finance the performance, the yard being usually so closely packed that it would be indecorous for women to be there.

Free-to-all theatrical performances in the villages without a temple are presented on temporary stages in the village squares or any open space facing the streets which are then closed to traffic during the performance. The temporary stage and green room, built with bamboo poles, heavy planks, mats and thatched roof are erected in a matter of hours and the performance is nicknamed "straw mat plays" 草台戲.

In Canton boats are also used as stages by the players travelling up and down the river. When the boat is moored to the shore, the deck serves as the stage, the space below deck as dressing rooms and the shore as the auditorium with the spectators standing.

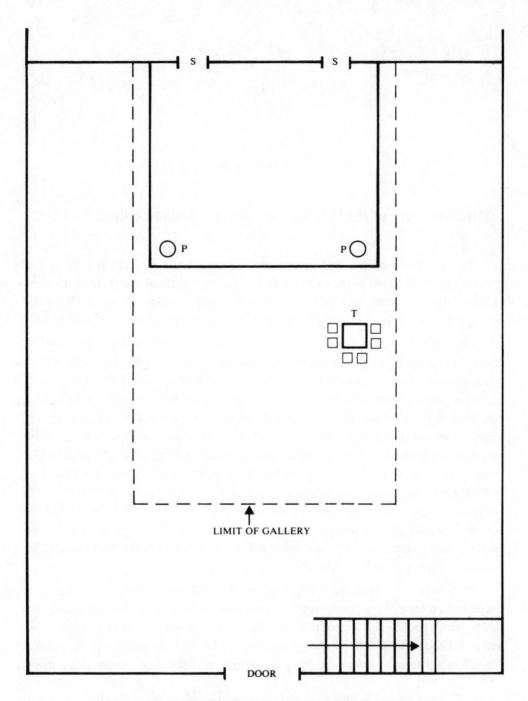

Fig. 1 Schematic Plan of Typical "Tea-House Theatre".

SS — stage doors
PP — pillars
T — tea table and stools

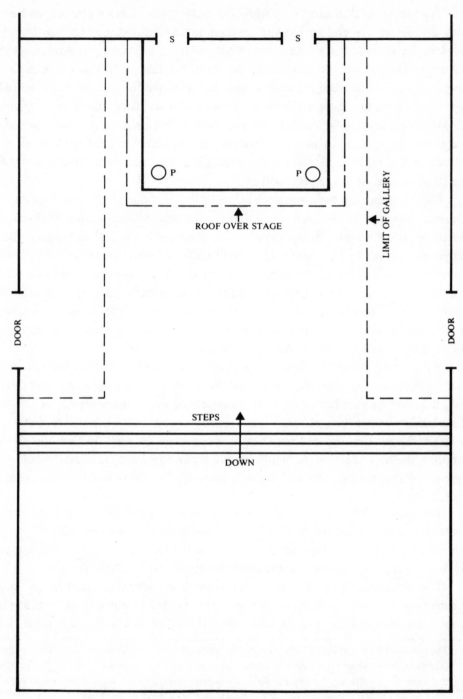

Fig. 2 Schematic Plan of Typical "Temple Theatre".
SS — stage doors
PP — pillars

21

The commercial theatres vary widely in architecture: from a genuine tea-house with a stage at one end to modern theatres in the European style, that is, with receding stage, front curtain and tiers of balconies. In this book, however, only the tea-house theatre will be described, not only because it still occupies a large proportion of commercial theatres to-day, but also because, having been the only type of commercial theatre in China for some time, it is closely related to the manner of production and the attitude of the audience. When traditional dramas are now sometimes performed in modern theatres, the building is used as if it were a tea-house theatre, for example, the front curtain is not used and the musicians sit on the stage instead of in the orchestra pit.

Before discussing the commercial theatre it is not out of place to explain the Chinese tea-house first because it is unfamiliar to most western people. Perhaps the closest approach to the Chinese tea-house in the West is the café in France, where people go not only to drink and eat but also to talk and read and loaf. The tea-house is an institution for the leisure class who go to it with no particular object in mind, least of all to quench thirst. They sit in the comfortable chairs, sip the tea, and spend hours enjoying unadulterated leisure. They may meet friends, discuss business, gossip, read the papers, eat snacks, smoke pipes, eat fruits or nuts, or listen to the singer or story-teller at the corner of the hall.

A tea-house theatre is simply a tea-house modified for theatrical performances and the modification generally consists of the provision of a stage at one end of the hall, the addition of a balcony and such alterations as are necessary to provide the management with a box office, some dressing rooms and so forth. A theatre is generally larger than an ordinary tea-house, and to increase further the sitting capacity, the easy chairs in the tea-house are replaced by smaller chairs, stools and benches so that they can be more closely packed. The entire building is of course roofed over.

The stage, from two to three feet high, depending on the size of the theatre, protrudes as in the temple theatre into the auditorium and is surrounded by the audience on three sides. There are two pillars at the front corners, two doors at the back and rail at the sides and in the front exactly as in the temple theatre. [1]

The arrangement of the seats vary from one theatre to another. In some theatres the stall area is occupied by tables surrounded on three sides by chairs or stools, as shown in Fig. 1 and the whole table is booked as a unit, and in others it is

---

[1] The essential features of the Chinese stage to-day appear to have been developed in the T'ang dynasty (618-906). In a contemporary memoir about court musicians 一崔令欽, 教坊記, 七段一 the stage 舞臺 (literally "dance platform") was mentioned, and the stage doors called, in Sung dynasty (960-1276), "ghost doors" 鬼門, were first mentioned by Su Tung-P'o, a poet of the eleventh century. 蘇軾詩 「搬演古人事, 出入鬼門道」, 見太和正音譜, 詞林須知, 末款, "Acting ancient events, Coming and going through ghost doors". The etymology of the latter term is obscure.

occupied by long tables *running towards the stage* with stools or benches at the sides (so that the audience do not face the stage but the sides of the auditorium). Some theatres have rows of seats facing the stage, with long ledges behind them to hold the tea cups. Usually the arrangement of seats is a combination of the above, with the square tables in the gallery facing the stage and the long tables and benches in the stall area and in the side gallery.

It should be stressed at this point that there is no standard size or proportion for either the temple or the tea-house theatre. For an average theatre, the stage is about twenty to sixty feet square. Roughly speaking, the capacity of the majority of tea-house theatres is from two hundred to a thousand and that of most of the temple theatres, owing to the dense crowd of standing audience, one to five thousand. It may be noticed that the floor is level in both types of theatre therefore the sight lines for the back seats are necessarily poor. The floor is raised at the back of the gallery of tea-house theatres to make the stage visible at all, but the sight lines in the gallery are usually spoiled by roof supports and cannot be much improved by the level of the floor.

Day-time performance depends on the day-light which in the temple theatres and on the open air temporary stage is adequate on bright days but in the tea-house theatres is hardly sufficient by western standards. At night the stage is lit with a row of oil or kerosene lamps in front of the stage or by electric lights when available, but the lights are not controlled as in the modern western theatre. Chinese theatres being wooden buildings, the acoustics is usually excellent in so far as there is little echo, but in some large theatres the voice of the weaker singers does not reach the back of the auditorium. It should be obvious from the above descriptions that even the tea-house theatre lacks the physical comfort of western theatres: apart from the hard seats, the theatre is not heated in winter nor ventilated in summer; hence those who are not accustomed to the Chinese dress and Chinese endurance may find it hard to enjoy the dramas in such an environment.

About the audience and the programme, it is again convenient to deal with the temple theatre and the tea-house theatre separately.

In commercial theatres where a programme consists of a number of separate dramatic episodes, the audience come at various times in the course of the performance, so that the theatre is nearly empty at the beginning and is full only after a greater part of the programme is over. During the former half of the programme when the theatre is half empty the audience act in about the same way as in any tea-house: they drink tea, crack nuts, eat candies, talk with each other and joke and laugh among themselves, besides looking at the players. The spectators in a Chinese theatre contrast sharply with those in a modern western theatre: the auditorium of a Chinese theatre is fully lit all the time and silence is not imposed on the spectators. The place is all the time full of life with people coming to their seats,

23

attendants bringing hot towels for the patrons to clean their faces and hands and throwing them to their assistants after they are used, friends greeting each other, boys selling cigarettes and candies and people shouting sincere or sarcastic *"hao"* ("bravo") to the actors. These activities die down in the later half of the programme when the theatre is full and the best part of the performance has begun, except tea-drinking, which goes on until the end.

In the temple theatres the audience come earlier, partly because the only way to reserve a good standing position is to occupy it and partly because the programme here consists of one or two complete dramas, which, as pointed out before, are new to the audience, and have to be seen from the beginning in order that the plot can be understood. Those who are in the centre of the standing space cannot help seeing the complete programme because the dense crowd makes it next to impossible for them to get out before the end; at the fringe of the crowd, however, many people come late or leave early. In the days when a performance takes place, the theatre is surrounded by temporary open-air restaurants and peddlers of all kinds, sometimes with gambling tables among them. The adjoining lanes and open spaces are then transformed into a busy market of fruits, toys, sweets, drinks, cakes, trinkets and so on.

One reason for the late arrivals in the tea-house theatre and indeed in the temple theatre as well is the great length of the performance and the lack of interval: in both places the matinée is from about one o'clock to six o'clock and the evening performance from seven o'clock to midnight. Matinées are not common in commercial theatres but the village performance is normally reckoned and paid by days, a day's performance consisting of the afternoon and the evening performance.

Writings of the nineteenth century show that the tea-house theatre has remained practically unchanged in the last hundred years, if not longer:

"The auditorium is divided into the stalls and the gallery. Upstairs, near the stage, the space is partitioned into three or four boxes on each side called 'gentlemen's seats' and the second box near the stage exit is considered the best, because when the actors are about to leave the stage this is where they cast their telling glances, as the popular ditty has it, 'The bewitching glances cast sidewise and up promise rendezvous after supper'. Next to the gentlemen's seats are scattered tables, and these are cheaper the further they are from the stage. Downstairs are long tables at which the audience sit next to each other and near the walls these seats are raised. The spectators downstairs are servants, labourers and such like. The seats near the stage exit are considered better because on the other side the orchestra is too loud".

（清）楊懋建, 夢華瑣薄, 十九款, 參, 三款, 二十一款.

"All tea-houses have galleries where seats are sold by tables, called 'gentlemen's seats'. The right side of the theatre is called 'the side of the entrance door' and the left, 'the side of the exit door' and those who make acquaintance with the female impersonators try to take the seats near the exit door. Downstairs there are seats at the two sides of the stage as well as in front of it, but children's half price seats are confined to the former. Once the musicians are on the stage, no tickets can be returned. Admission is called 'tea ticket' and for the 'gentlemen's seats' each table is about seven times the single seat downstairs. Of the two seats at the table one is left empty for the female impersonators to come and chat during the interval. Servants of the patrons upstairs are admitted free into the theatre to watch the performance standing and those who do not want to pay for the admission can stand among them''.

（淸　）華胥大夫, 金臺殘淚記, 卷三.

Theatre has never been a congenial place to the Chinese women and ladies of perfect decorum never went to it until the recent emancipation. Emperor Ch'ien-Lung (reigned 1736-1796) on the recommendation of Lang Su-Men 郞蘇門 once prohibited all women to visit theatres but at other times those women who were not fastidious could and did go to them. [2] They were however, at first segregated from the men.

---

[2]　齊如山, 京戲之變遷, 頁七.

CHAPTER III

THE CHINESE STAGE

In the temple theatre the stage is not decorated for the performance except for the permanent decorations on the structure such as the carvings near the eaves of the roof and the painted colour patterns on the ceiling. A couplet in gilded characters which moralizes theatrical entertainment as a whole, is carved either on the pillars on the stage or on wooden boards hanging in front of them. In the tea-house theatre, however, the back of the stage is covered by a large piece of tapestry with bold designs and sometimes, when there is available space, the same wall is also covered with silk banners and pennons bearing eulogies for the company given to it by its friends. The two door openings at the back of the stage are covered with flaps which form parts of the tapestry. (See Fig. 3).

In both types of theatre as the performance is about to begin, the five or six musicians take their position at the rear corner of the stage on stage right, called "Nine Dragons Point" 九龍口, [1] and at the other corner, on stage left, the property man arranges the properties that will soon be used. At the centre of the stage stands a table about two by four feet and about three feet high with the longer edge facing the audience and the front covered with a red satin curtain embroidered with the name of the company in large Chinese characters in gold. As dramatic performances often form part of private and public celebrations, it is customary for the players' companies to choose auspicious names, such as Pervading Happiness or Heaven's Blessings, which, shown on the stage, add to the festivity of the occasions.

Beside the musicians and the property man the rear portion of the stage is also lined with a small portion of the audience smuggled to the stage through connections with the back stage personnel to watch the plays free of charge. Thus, strictly speaking, the stage is surrounded by spectators on all four sides.

---

[1] According to tradition, the name is derived from the symbol of royalty — dragons — which became attached to the place when Emperor Ming-Huang 明皇 of T'ang dynasty (reigned A.D. 713-756) played the leader of his own court orchestra.

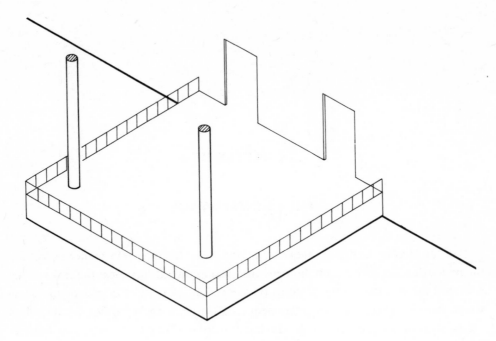

Fig. 3 The Chinese Stage

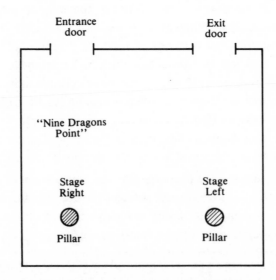

Fig. 4 Positions on the Chinese Stage

The acting space, for most of the time, is limited to the front half of the stage and the actors act towards the audience on their sides as well as those in their front, but the latter necessarily get the greater share of the actors' attention.

One of the functions of scenery is to specify what the stage represents. Since there is no scenery on the Chinese stage, some device is obviously needed to indicate the locality represented by the stage. The location is in fact defined in a number of ways: it may be obvious from the title of the play or the context of the dramatic action, it may be specified by dialogue, or by special miming, or by arrangement of tables and chairs or by special properties, or by the characters appearing on the stage: usually it is by a combination of these. For example, the action of the entire drama called *Libation at the Pagoda* 祭塔 takes place in front of the Pagoda of the Thunder Peak where a high official comes to invoke the spirit of his mother imprisoned in it. The stage in this case, as is obvious from the title, represents the ground near the pagoda. In other cases, the action, such as two armies fighting, or a fisherman rowing a boat, makes it obvious that the stage is supposed to be a battlefield or a river. If a man stops walking, looks up and says, "Ah, this is his house" and then goes through the motion of knocking at the door, he makes it clear that part of the stage is the street and part of it is the house. The host then comes towards the visitor and goes through the movement of pulling the bolts, opening the door and leaning forward to look in one direction and then the other and, seeing his friend, invites him into the house (the visitor lifting his feet high to cross the imaginary threshold) and closes and bolts the door. As will be explained later, the profession of a character is clearly shown by the costume: for example, a hotel keeper or the emperor can easily be recognized as such. When the hotel keeper answers a call, the stage is naturally the hotel or when the emperor and his entourage appear, it can only be the palace hall; similarly with boatswains and apothecaries. The arrangement of tables and chairs can indicate the type of building the stage represents because in China, their arrangement in different types of rooms is more or less standardized by custom. In the main hall of the private residence or public buildings, for example, the table is at the back of the room, with a row of chairs on each side of the hall, the chairs near the table being the honoured seats, and these halls are represented on the stage accordingly. The palace hall, where only the emperor sits and all other people stand, is represented by a chair and a table at the back of the stage without chairs on the two sides because such is the arrangement approximately in the palace. Special properties, such as a miniature city wall made of cloth or plaques with clouds painted on them, are sometimes used to transform the stage into the approaches to a city or the abode of deities, respectively. The nearest approach to scenery on the Chinese stage is a plaque called "rock and mountain plaque" 石山片 with symbolic drawings of rocks and hills on it which is placed on the stage when the scene is the open country.

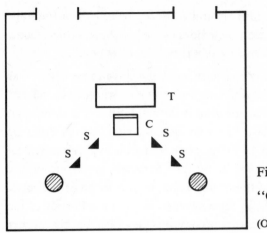

T — Table
C — Chair
S — Servant
▶— Actor, facing this way →

Fig. 5A Setting for Sitting Room — I

"Outer Seat" 外場椅

(One master sitting and servants standing at the sides).

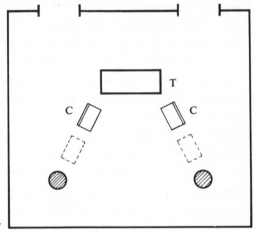

Fig. 5B Setting for Sitting Room — II

"Outer Seats" 外場椅

(For host and guest or husband and wife.
More chairs may be added).

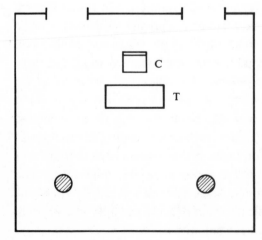

Fig. 6 Setting for Hall in Public Buildings

"Inner Seat" 內場椅

(For emperor's throne, judge's bench,
official's desk — also scholar's desk).

30

In many scenes it is in fact unnecessary to know the location of the scene, for example, when a servant finds his master and passes on a message or when a man meets a fairy in a dream, and, in other cases, a general indication of the location is all that is necessary, as in the play *Li-Ling's Monument* 李陵碑 when the starving general of the besieged army leaves his tent and tries to shoot a wild duck, it is clear that he is in the battlefield but it is immaterial whether he is in the hills or on the plain. When the location has a special dramatic significance, however, it is precisely indicated by special properties, as, for instance, towards the end of the drama just mentioned when the general, having abandoned all hope, kills himself at Li-Ling's Monument, the monument is placed on the stage, because, being erected for a warrior who surrendered to the enemy, it adds poignancy to the scene.

It is understood by the Chinese audience that when all the actors have left the stage the particular scene is ended and as the actors appear again, which marks the beginning of the next scene, the locality of the stage has to be defined. (The reverse, it is to be noticed, is not true: the scene can change with the actors remaining on the stage). This apparently raises the difficulty of representing characters coming back to the same scene, but, with the convention for the two doors at the back of the stage, this difficulty does not arise: the actors normally enter by the door on stage right and leave by that on stage left. This simple convention solves many problems of dramatic representation which would otherwise have been difficult and facilitates the understanding of the action. Thus, suppose in the story a man forgets something and goes back to fetch it, he would enter first by the right door, discover his omission, and exit and enter by the same door again and by this the audience understand that he has gone back to wherever he came from. Similarly after leaving the stage if he wants to return to the same scene for some action or remark, he re-enters by the left door and exits through it again. Such hesitant actions, are, however, momentary deviations from the general rule, so that in general no doubt occurs in the mind of the audience whether a scene has ended or not.

An apparent violation of the rule which occurs in *P'ing-Kuei's Return* 武家坡 where the hero enters by the exit door at the beginning of the scene is in fact an effective application of this convention. In a previous scene he left China and was prisoner among the Hsi-Liang tribe for eighteen years and when he left China he made his exit by the left door. Now he is coming back and the scene starts with off-stage singing "My horse leaving Hsi-Liang border . . ." which means that the back stage represents a foreign country where he has gone in a previous scene.

Using one door as entrance and another as exit defines, in effect, the locality of the space beyond them and with definite locality, it may be used as acting space. In the scene of *P'ing-Kuei's Return* the hero goes to the door on stage right (entrance door) and asks for direction to his wife's hut. A voice off-stage answering him represents someone near the hut. The voice shouts to his wife who, being nearby,

31

answers it off-stage. When the wife at last enters, she sings a long aria on the right side (entrance side) of the stage while her husband stands and waits on the left side (exit side): here the wife is supposed to be still near the hut and is too far to see her husband, until the aria is over when the hero comes forth to meet her.

There are cases in which the doors cannot possibly represent passages leading to different places, as, for example, when the stage represents the inside of a boat. In such cases although the characters enter by the entrance door to begin the scene, they are understood to be already on the scene when it starts, and similarly for the end of the scene. These are the scenes where in modern western theatres the curtain would rise or fall on actors on the stage. Many indoors scenes in the Chinese theatre are to be understood in this way. At the beginning of *The Clandestine Visit*四郎探母, for example, the hero, although entering the stage from the entrance door is to be considered as discovered on the stage, because in the opening aria he says he is "sitting in the palace", but, when later his wife, the foreign princess, enters to join him she is coming from her own room, bringing the baby.

In short, the entrance on the Chinese stage, as well as the exit, can have two different meanings according to whether it is a *theatric entrance* or a *dramatic entrance*. A theatric entrance or exit is a movement by the *actor* on the stage, a dramatic entrance or exit is that of the *character* in the scene; the former is the actor taking or leaving his position and the latter is the character coming to or going from the scene; in the former the locality of the back stage is understood to be the same as that of the stage itself and the characters are supposed to be in the scene before the entrance and after the exit, but in the latter the space beyond the stage doors has different localities and the stage is where the characters *pass through*. Action and dialogue make it clear to the audience which type of entrance or exit is intended. A clear idea of the localities represented is sometimes essential to the understanding of the plot as, for example, in the battle scenes of historical plays, hence the importance and precision of the conventions.

In the case of a journey, which is indicated by the travelling characters walking round the stage, the Chinese stage can further represent a shifting instead of a stationary locality. This is analogous to the movie screen representing a shifting scene when the backgrounds move across it. The stage may represent a room upstairs if the actors perform the miming of going up the steps. Convention also allows the stationary and the shifting locality to combine, so that an indefinite portion of the stage represents the one and the remaining portion the other, as when a thief hiding behind an obstruction (crouching beside a chair) is not seen by his pursuer, or when a family already on the stage is supposed to be in their house and the visitor does not see them until he enters the house, or when some characters who have mimicked going up steps are supposed to be upstairs and others not having so acted are supposed to be downstairs until they have. One common scene is a man

32

taking leave of his family and going on a journey: during the farewell scene the stage is his house, then when the family leave the stage, one has to imagine that the house goes with them and the stage become the road. By the use of this convention it is possible to make one scene run directly into another without a break, for, if the traveller leaves the stage for his journey in the farewell scene the family would have to clear the stage so that it can represent the road when the traveller enters again and there would be a break between the two scenes. One should imagine a movie camera following the man from his house to his journey, or, to follow the usage of the western theatre, the curtain being lowered after the farewell scene and the traveller now acts in front of the curtain.

On the Chinese stage, not only are distances compressed, but straight paths are curved into small circles. When a servant or a son is summoned he advances downstage, turns to face the master or parent and lifts his feet to cross the imaginary threshold (at point △ in Fig. 7) but he does not bow and greet the master or parent sitting in the chair until he has made another turn and stopped walking (see Fig. 7). In this movement, the path after entering the imaginary room is understood to be

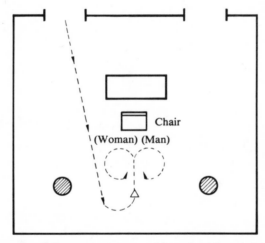

Fig. 7 Movement of Servants Approaching the Master (△ — Threshold)

the distance between the door and the place where the master is sitting and when the servant first faces the master (at △) he supposedly does not see him. If he greets the master immediately after he crosses the threshold the audience will get the impression that the chair is placed right behind the door, or else, if the chair is placed far upstage, the subsequent action will be unnecessarily far removed from the audience, making it more realistic perhaps, but less effective as theatre.

Movements of the stage properties, sometimes to indicate change of scene and sometimes to meet the requirements of the action, are naturally carried out in full view of the audience, both between scenes when the stage is empty of actors and when action is in progress. Except when assistance is required, there is only one property man to handle the movements and there is inevitably a certain amount of intermingling between him and the actors. When an actor, especially one with elaborate headgear, is about to enter or exit, stage hands lift the flap on the stage doors for him to pass and when an actor is about to kneel, the property man throws a cushion in front of him to protect the costume. In scenes of fainting and death, the property man places a chair behind the actor in anticipation or with a small pillow in hand, he waits behind the actor about to fall backwards and carries the weight of the actor until he reaches the floor. Sometimes the make-up man also comes on the stage to help the property man adjust the ruffled clothes of a warrior after a vigorous fight and change costume on stage when the dramatic action requires it. During the instrumental passages of a long aria the personal attendant of the singer also comes on to the stage to serve tea and retreats with his tea pot just before the singing is resumed. [2]

---

[2] This is usually, but not always, done discreetly and inconspicuously. Prof. Ch'i Ju-Shan deplores the practice of some actors letting their attendants enter the acting area with great flourish, carrying thermos flasks strapped to their sides. Some warriors drink tea even in the middle of a fight, holding their weapons till they have been served and then continue the combat. 齊如山, 京戲之變遷, 頁二八.

CHAPTER IV

THE STAGE CONVENTIONS

All dramatic representation involves conventions but some of them, being universally accepted, are not recognized as such, for example, that the stage is one place in one scene and a different place in the next, and that the events in the drama are supposed to cover a longer time than it actually takes to perform the drama. In this chapter only those conventions which are peculiar to the Chinese theatre will be discussed. They may be conveniently divided into conventions of entrances and exits, conventions of speech, conventions of action and conventions of properties, to be treated in the following in this order.

Entrances are often accompanied by music, therefore a cue for the orchestra is usually required. As there is no prompter in the Chinese theatre the cue is supplied by the entering actor before he emerges from the entrance door and it may take the form of a line like "Let us go!" or "Lead on" 走呀 sometimes followed by a phrase sung *ad libitum* 倒板, off stage. When it is appropriate to the character, a stylized cough or laugh off stage is used for the same purpose. After the entrance, actors normally proceed quietly down the stage, but clowns have the licence sometimes to talk to themselves while walking into the scene. If actors after entering stand on chairs and then come down again, they are understood to be riding the clouds if they are supernatural beings, or going over a hill if they are mortals. (Clouds are also represented by the "cloud plaques" held by pages walking in front of the actor). An actor may also enter walking backwards, indicating some centre of interest in front of him, or enter facing the audience but stepping to the side suggesting walking in the dark or on tiptoe (走邊). If an actor is led by a stage hand holding the "water flag" or "wind flag" he is understood to be washed by waves or lost in a wind storm, respectively. Two armies meeting on the stage enter either simultaneously by the two doors, the one entering by the exit door being understood to be stationary and the other entering by the entrance door, the moving forces coming to meet them; or successively by the entrance door, in which case they are supposed to be both moving and meeting on the battlefield.

35

All entrances and exits — those representing movements of the characters in the drama as well as those of actors taking or leaving their positions — are formalized: they follow a pattern calculated to attract the attention of the audience. Actors who start an aria immediately after their entrance pause at the "Nine Dragons Point" and proceed, while singing, slowly down the stage, but normally all characters, including those summoned in the course of the action, advance silently to the stage front, assume a pose, and address the audience before partaking in any action.

In all dramas the *dramatis personae,* especially those who start the action, have to be introduced to the audience. A character in the Chinese drama would, upon entering the first time, state for the audience his name, his place of birth, his age, his profession and his motives together with other information relevant to the subsequent action, such as family relations, financial status and so forth. This speech of self-introduction usually ends with the statement of his intentions which he proceeds to carry out forthwith. Such soliloquy does not represent what happens in the drama but is understood to be the actors taking the audience, so to speak, into their confidence. Sometimes the introductory speech runs directly into a real soliloquy, as at the opening of *The Clandestine Visit* 探母 when the hero, after introducing himself, begins to bewail his fate. In all cases there is no attempt to disguise the convention; in fact, it is parallel to the formal parade of the warrior after his first entrance so that the audience can have a good look at him.

Rhymed couplets or short poems are spoken at the beginning and the end of some scenes, either by one character alone or, when more than one character enter and exit at the same time, spoken by them in turn. These are taken by the audience to be comments on the scene which do not form part of the action. Occasionally they may be considered as part of the dialogue as, for example, when at the end of a scene, the poem is connected to the preceding dialogue with "Indeed . . ." 正是 in which case one can think of the characters in the drama as commenting on the situation among themselves.[1]

In cases where etiquette or action precludes formal entrance, as in eavesdropping scenes and servants entering while the master is speaking, a silent entrance 暗上 is used.

In a place like the Chinese theatre where the audience are engaged in pleasurable activities other than watching the drama, the formal entrances and exits serve to emphasize the outline of the action. Their main purposes are to facilitate the understanding of the plot and to add model commentary to the drama but they also serve to attract the attention of the audience to the beginning and end of the scenes.

---

[1] Technically the introductory passages are differentiated into the following types. They are used in different combinations according to the needs of the particular scenes.

    (1) Introduction 引子 — a passage of varying length in verse and sung *ad libitum* at the beginning of a drama or a prominent section of it. It is usually a commentary on the theme of the drama or on the characters and events in it.

36

The relation between the entrance and exit and the change of locality has been explained in the last chapter. A special style of entrance which suggests scattered locality will be explained below as a special convention. In this the actor enters by the entrance door, stands on a chair half-facing the audience and speaks a few lines, he then exits through the same door and comes out from the exit door, repeats the mime, leaves by the exit door, and enters in the normal way by the entrance door. (See Fig. 8.) In this convention the backstage represents places adjacent to the scene, for example, grounds outside the city, and the actor is supposed to be speaking to people unseen by the audience in one place and another. [2]

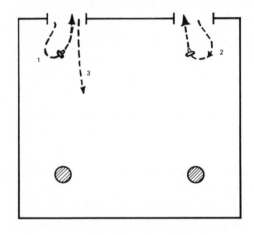

Fig. 8
Style of Entrance to
Suggest Scattered Localities.

---

(2) Couplet 上場聯 — lines apposite to the character speaking them used most often by the clowns, for example, "Without grass on the roadside a horse will starve; without extra income a man cannot become rich" (spoken by a thief.)

(3) Poem 坐場詩, 定場詩 — similar in content and form to the "introduction" it is declaimed without musical accompaniment. Military officials sing it, alone or in unison, according to whether it is a single or multiple entrance. The only tune used is fixed by convention (點絳唇). For multiple entrances of non-military characters the lines are spoken by the characters in turn. (Prof. Ch'i Ju-Shan thinks that the reason why the military officials are required to cover their faces with their sleeves when they sing this poem is that they thereby indicate speaking not as characters in the drama but as prologue, 一齊如山, 中國戲劇之組織, 頁十一 — however the use of sleeves may be aimed at the effect of sudden discovery).

(4) Self-introduction 通名 — the passage which begins with "I am so-and-so of such-and-such city . . ." and in which the characters tell the audience their age, profession, family relations and so forth. In multiple entrances one character introduces the others after he does himself.

(5) Opening Speech 定場白 — similar to "self-introduction" except it is a longer and fuller statement of the background and past development of the drama.

The names of the different types of introductory lines have not been used by the dramatists of the past with perfect consistency. The above represents modern practice.

(2) For the music accompanying the entrances of different types of dramatic characters and that used on various types of scenes, forty-eight styles in all, see 齊如山, 上下場, 頁十一, 十二.

Since at the end of a scene all the actors must leave the stage, an excuse has often to be found for their exit. The last character on the stage may be asked by another who is leaving to go with him, or one may be chasing the other off the scene, or one may be dragged along by another if the action requires it, or one may be forced to leave as when one clown pushes another with the hand, or a character may be leading the horses away, or a woman may be embarrassed and retreats. Occasionally actors leave severally by both doors, as at the end of a meeting, indicating that they go to different places. Exit by walking on the knees means that the character is weakened by terror or grief, exit in quick and small steps means either leaving against the will of other characters who are holding his sleeve or leaving in a hurry under a shattering emotion and exit on hands and knees means that the character is wounded or in extreme humiliation. Some warriors exit by a somersault and they are understood to leave the scene in a jump, as in avoiding an enemy in combat. As in entrances, actors may be led away by stage hands holding the "water flag" or "wind flag" when there is a storm or flood. When a man is killed by fire or by an enemy or by his own hands he either falls on the stage and later leaves quietly in which case the exit is ignored by the audience, or he could combine the two actions into one, and with proper mime indicate that he is dead before he leaves the stage. When he is supposed to jump into a river or well, he jumps down from a chair and then walks into the stage door. [3]

Difficulties occasionally arise in finding a suitable excuse for exits. When at the end of *P'ing Kuei's Return* the wife, supposedly going to another room in the hut, asks the husband to follow her, it appears perfectly natural, but in *The Son's Lesson* when the lady of the house acts similarly towards the servant the device has unwanted implications.

The aside, which is freely used in the Chinese drama, is marked by lifting the sleeve to shield the speaker's face from the rest of the actors. Spontaneous comments on the action by the characters are rarely, if ever, used; the asides in the Chinese dramas are the audible thoughts of the characters before they make decisions, thus showing the audience their motives.

In relation to the mime, the most frequently used convention is the horse, represented by the whip, a stick about two feet long with tufts of tassels at regular intervals. Holding the whip vertically and pointing upwards is leading the horse to the rider, holding it so that it points downwards, leading the horse away. The mime for mounting and dismounting cannot, of course, be realistic, but in the conventional pantomime, which is strictly codified, the action, for instance, of putting the foot in the stirrup, mounting and sitting down on the saddle can still be traced. To simulate riding, the rider walks about on the stage, shaking the whip behind him as if beating the horse. Dropping the whip at the side of the stage after acting as if

---

[3] See 齊如山，上下塲，頁二四 for nineteen types of musical accompaniment for exits.

38

tying a knot means tying the reins and leaving the horse at a post or in a stable.

The boat is represented by one or two oars. Walking round the stage in a group with one member paddling means people being ferried in a boat. The mime at the departure and the arrival is meticulous: the boatswain holds the (real) oar to serve as hand rail for the passengers walking over the plank, puts down the oar, goes to the shore himself, unties the imaginary rope, throws the imaginary plank to the boat, jumps into the boat himself, collects the rope and pushes the boat from the shore with the oar. A corresponding series of mimings in the reverse order is performed at the end of the journey.

The Chinese carriage, by which women travelled in ancient China, is like a canopied and curtained chair with wheels at the sides and is pushed from behind. On the stage it is represented by two flags with wheels painted on them. When a footman holds the flags in front of him so that they nearly touch the floor, they are an empty carriage. To ride in it an actor or actress stoops and steps in between the flags while the maid lifts the imaginary curtain. The sedan chair is represented by a long curtain parted at the middle and supported on bamboo sticks. To ride in it an actor or actress goes through the curtain from the front and walks behind it with the boy holding the curtain by the bamboo sticks walking behind the actor supposed to be in the sedan chair.

Entering the door is indicated by lifting the feet high to cross the threshold (which in Chinese houses is about a foot high). Great care is taken to make the mime appropriate to the particular situations, for example, for small doors such as those of bedrooms, two persons cannot enter together but must pass through them one after the other. Appropriate gestures are used for opening the door, closing it, locking it, bolting it and knocking on it.

Eating and drinking are considered unattractive hence drinking on the stage (from empty cups) is done with the sleeve covering the mouth and eating, as at banquets, is represented by drinking. Lying on one's back is considered unsightly. Sleep, except for clowns, is represented by sitting at a table and leaning the head on one hand.

The city wall is a piece of cloth about four feet high and six feet long rolled on two vertical bamboo sticks sewed to the ends. Stage hands hold it by the sticks such that the side painted with masonry patterns faces the audience and actors in front of it are supposed to be at the city gate and those standing on a chair or table behind it are on the top of the wall. For stationary scenes it is left leaning against a table. However, the same piece of property can also represent the city gate, because its middle portion, except for a narrow strip at the top, can be folded towards the ends so that it looks like an arch and as such it can be lifted for the actors to pass through as if through a gate.

As mentioned previously, the small table on the Chinese stage stands for different types of furniture according to the type of room as indicated by the arrangement of the stage: it is the throne if the emperor sits behind it, it is the judges' bench if it is in a court room, and so forth. It can, however, be more than a piece of furniture: with a chair at each end and actors walking over it it is a bridge, against the back wall of the stage with actors standing on it it is a hill or rampart as the case may be and at the centre of the stage with candles and incense on it it is an altar. Sometimes when the representation of special tall structures is important, as the mound and altar in *Conjuring the East Wind* 祭東風 several tables are used to support the one representing the altar. (Three or four tables are put one on top of another in the purely acrobatic scenes which battle scenes sometimes temporarily become, but in such cases the tables do not stand for any real objects.)

When a chair is placed on the stage in an abnormal position, as with the back facing the audience or lying sidewise on the floor, it represents something other than a chair. In *P'ing Kuei's Return* 武家坡 it is the low door of his wife's hut and, placed at the centre of the stage, divides it into two parts, the hut and the ground in front of its door. When the wife is persuaded to let the hero into the hut she simulates opening the door by tilting the chair and he stoops and steps forward beside it. A pole attached to a chair makes it into a tree or a pillar on which an actor can act hanging himself. With its back towards the audience and a piece of cloth hanging on it as in *The Son's Lesson* 教子 it is a loom.

Night time is indicated by bringing in lamps and candles and by striking the hour on the drum and the gong in the orchestra in the same manner as it used to be done in Chinese cities from the city watch tower. The lights on the stage, however, are not dimmed: if the scene is supposed to be dark, the darkness is entirely conveyed by mime. The bed is a curtain supported by two bamboo poles attached to the chairs and is, the chairs apart, a slightly under-sized replica of the front of a Chinese bed. Unless the scene involves looking from out of the bed, in which case the sleeper, without undressing, goes through the curtain and sits in a chair behind it, the bed is merely a property to indicate the locality of the scene. Dreams are limited to the meeting with gods and spirits without much dramatic action and the representation does not differ from that of apparitions except that it occurs in a sleeping scene. The gods and spirits are distinguished from human beings by costume. A burglar on the eaves waiting to enter the house is an actor standing on a chair at the front corner of the stage and when he jumps down from the chair he is near the house. While he is breaking the imaginary door or window and entering the house, groping around all the time, the people in the house, even if awake, do not see him because the scene is supposed to be dark.

Weather conditions, except the storm, are not often required in Chinese dramas. Thunder is imitated by a roll on the drum and simultaneously those who are caught in the storm put their sleeves over their heads and stagger. Storm in indoor scenes or with an empty stage is unknown in the Chinese theatre. Wind, fire and flood are indicated by flags which a supernumerary, who is to be considered a stage hand, carries across the stage: the wind by a black flag and the fire and the flood, by red flags or those with waves or flames painted on them. [4] In these conventions there is hardly any element of imitation; the flags may indeed be considered as entirely symbolic. [5]

The street crowd seldom occurs in Chinese dramas but when the story requires it, four or five actors are to be taken as a large crowd. Armies, however, are often involved in battle scenes and an army is represented by twenty-odd officers and men with a few for each rank. When two armies meet, the Chinese stage, never very large, becomes very crowded indeed. The whole stage is then a mass of elaborate costume, horse-whips, flags, banners, spears and swords. The battle scene usually begins with two armies approaching each other, that is, each army parading round half of the stage. While they literally rub shoulders with each other, they are understood to be so far apart that they do not see each other, until they meet, when the stage is cleared for single and group combats.

The conventions came into being through long usage rather than deliberate codification. Although theorists can find system in them, the audience do not know its consistency, they understand their dramatic significance without knowing the details of the codes. A general standing on a chair upstage is on a prominence discussing or watching the battle but the exact nature of the prominence is immaterial. Conventional stage business, such as the horse-riding and the boat-sailing, though essentially abbreviated representations, are to the audience means of dramatic expression, like good acting. Though conventional, they can be very effective because the force of established convention is amazingly great — witness the feeling aroused by a hat worn at the dinner table. Force of convention coupled with trained imagination make the audience astute observers: actors who forgot to spit out the end of the imaginary threads they had bitten have been disgraced by spontaneous and unanimous laughter. It is this ability on the part of the audience to see more than is actually shown on the stage that makes the platform stage self-sufficient.

Proprietors of Chinese theatres, unlike those of the western theatres, do not own any stage properties. The players either carry their own properties and costume or hire them from the special shops. It is therefore inconvenient to use large properties in the plays and when needed they are represented by substitute articles specified by convention. The audience do not demand realistic properties because

---

[4] "Wind flags" carried in front of an actor sometimes mean that the actor is a ghost riding the wind.

[5] In western theatres, the thunder and lightning at dramatic moments have a special poignancy which borders on religious implications; in the Chinese theatre thunder and lightning under such circumstances appear on the stage as gods who come to mete out punishment personally.

the style of the symbolic acting makes them incongruous with the other elements of the Chinese drama and real properties are only used for comic effects, as the real donkey in the farce *Visit of the In-laws* 探親 . [6] A tradition is thus established in which realistic properties are deliberately avoided and when some theatres introduce them for sensationalism they are considered as signs of bad taste. Some of the substitute properties may be described: the severed head — red flag wrapped around the hat-mould; soldiers — a long bench standing on end with soldiers' clothes on it; meat — red hat; cakes — round pieces of paper; large stone (for lifting) — flag wrapped on a hat; fish — rolled flag on a tray; severed leg — rolled flag stuck in a boot; and blacksmith's shop — a bench, an overturned chair in front of it and a sword (bellows) on the chair. [7] For some properties, one realistic piece is available and when two or more are required, a substitute is used with the realistic one, for example, there is normally only one oar, and the long-handled war knife is used for the second and there is one doll for the baby, the second baby is a bundle of clothes. One piece of property can also be used for two purposes, for instance, the red flag, which is the ''fire flag'', is also used for the parade of the prize-winner of the official examinations 狀元 . There are two curtains among the properties, the larger one is used for the bed, the curtains of boudoirs and the military tent and the smaller one, for the judges' bench and the inspection booth on military grounds.

Properties which add to the colour of the pageantry are, on the other hand, beautifully made, for example, all the larger weapons, flags, standards, generals' personal flags, pennons, official umbrellas, ceremonial staffs 符節 , the imperial mandate (a rectangular piece of silk), token arrows and token flags 令旗 . Small properties like lamps, candles, pens, ink slabs, cups, letters, etc., are also real objects.

Conventions do not always satisfy the needs of dramatic representation. In the murder scene of *The Strange Retribution* 奇冤報 the Avenging God 判官 standing on a chair at the back of the stage is a picture of the god whose eyes embarrass the murderers cutting the bodies to pieces and are cut out of the picture by the criminals. After the mutilated bodies have been removed, the god jumps out of the picture and performs a weird dance. In such cases the dialogue helps the audience to understand what is represented.

The conventionality of the Chinese stage is a mixture of arbitrary rules and trained imagination. The audience is at first initiated into some of the basic rules, such as those governing the entrance and the exit, then having grasped the spirit of the conventional stage, they can guess the meaning of the other symbolic properties and gestures. What they apprehend is the conventionalism rather than the individual conventions.

---

[6] cf. the real fish in Act I of Puccini's *La Boheme*.

[7] Sixty such articles are listed in 齊如山, 戲班, 頁十九至二三．

CHAPTER V

THE TYPES OF CHARACTERS AND THE COSTUME

(1)

In the Chinese theatre the sex of the players bears no relation to the sex of the characters they play: both actors and actresses can take male or female roles. This is possible because the style of acting is sophisticated and the professional players are highly trained. The impersonation is so well done that even for the experienced theatregoer it is seldom possible to tell the sex of the player on the stage. As a whole, however, the best players for both male and female roles are men. The small build of Chinese men and the exiguous growth of beard make female impersonation easier than it would be for western actors.

The characters in the Chinese dramas are divided into four distinct categories: the male characters in general (*sheng* 生), the female characters (*tan* 旦), the masked characters (*ching* 淨) and the comedians (*ch'ou* 丑). These types differ from each other primarily in the style of acting, including singing and elocution but the masked characters and the comedians are also distinguished by the use of mask and heavy make-up. The removable type of mask is seldom used in the Chinese theatre; the mask is normally painted on the actor's face, hence the name "painted face" for *ching*. It is distinct from heavy make-up because the colour and pattern of the paint is unlike any human face. Roughly speaking, all awe-inspiring characters belong to this category, thus chiefs of bandits, gods and spirits, obdurate judges, uncouth warriors and cold-blooded officials are cast as this type. The colour and pattern of the masks for particular characters are standardized and records are carefully kept of them, hence the audience can often recognize the masked characters individually as soon as they appear. [1] The make-up of the comedian's face, consisting of a white patch in the middle of it, is also contrary to the natural appearance of the human face, hence it cannot be considered as make-up in the ordinary sense of the term.

---

[1] cf. the Greek audience recognizing Hercules and Cassandra by their appearance.

43

Each of the four categories is sub-divided into several types. For the male characters in general *(sheng)* there are: the old man 老生, the middle-aged man 鬚生, 正生, the young man 小生, the child 娃娃生 and the warrior 武生. Some of these types are further differentiated by special styles of acting: thus among the middle-aged men 鬚生 is the man with short beard 鬚子生, among the young men are the young warrior with pheasant feathers 雉尾生 (a general or strategist) and the young man with the fan 扇子生 (gay scholar) and among the old men 老生 is the red-faced warrior 紅生 (a majestic warrior). The female characters are divided into: the lady 正旦, the old lady 老旦, the gay woman 花旦 (among which are the termagent type 潑辣旦 and the playful type 玩笑旦), the ugly (and pretentious) woman 搽旦 and the "sword-and-steed" type 刀馬旦 (the female warrior). [2] Of the masked characters the black-face 黑頭, the white face 粉臉 and the masked warrior 武淨 are special types. The comedians are divided into the witty 文丑 and the acrobatic type 武丑.

Apart from the trained players, supernumeraries are employed for footmen and flag-bearers. These do not speak and hardly act at all.

Since the style of singing and acting differ not only between the four main categories but also between many of the sub-divisions, players are trained only for a limited range of characters. For example, an actor trained to play the middle-aged man can also play the old man but he cannot play the young man or the warrior. Professional players never take any part for which they are not trained, except in jest at private performances.

Owing to the fact that the *dramatis personae* in Chinese dramas must fall into one of the four types of characters, there cannot be all shades and combinations of personal characteristics among them. Two characters are either more or less alike or differ widely from each other, depending on whether they belong to the same type of character or not. A man is either very old or middle-aged or very young; a woman is either a well-bred one or a gay woman or one of the other types. Certain types, such as the adolescent and the little girl, never appear on the Chinese stage. Training the players according to the character-types results in the concentration of certain types of stage business in certain characters, for example, a character not cast as a warrior cannot fight under any circumstances and all characters are serious all the time except those played by the comedians who do little else than jest.

(2)

Costume is an important part of the Chinese theatricals because it is standardized so that at one glance the audience can recognize the social status and

---

(2) According to 王夢生（梨園佳話）第三章 "余莊" female warriors are of three types: those skilful with the weapons, the contortionists and those noted for their beauty.

temperament of the characters in the dramas, thereby making it easier to understand the action, and also because its rich colours add to the visual pleasures of the Chinese theatre. The standardized theatrical costume is a self-contained system of garments, head-gear, foot wear and other personal ornaments which is a mixture of Chinese dress ranging from T'ang (618-906) to Ch'ing dynasty (1644-1911) and does not conform in details to any particular period. No contemporary costume is used in the classical theatre. [3] Garments belonging to different periods are not only worn in the same drama but also by the same person. [4] The anachronism is however noticeable only to experts; the audience in general, who are not equipped with sufficient knowledge to discern historical accuracy, look upon the costume purely as a part of the Chinese theatre without connections to real dress. [5]

Even if the costume were historically correct, it would still not be realistic because it is uniformly rich and beautiful. The material is mainly silk and most of the garments are embroidered, some in gold. It is true that the shops which hire out theatrical costumes usually make them of glossy material and with rough needle work because under the lights and viewed from the distance the defects are not noticeable, yet, they are luxurious garments, so much so that the cost of the more expensive pieces would be prohibitive if they could not be used over long periods as they always are. The style, but not the richness, of the dress depends on the social status of the character who wears it. No actor ever looks shabby on the stage: the beggar wears a black gown with neat patches of different shape and colours; a man in ruffled conditions has his hat tilted and the skirt of his gown tucked behind his belt; a sick man has the tails of his cap tied round his head and leans on a servant and a mad woman has two coats on, the outer one worn by one sleeve. [6]

The Chinese theatrical costume is differentiated with respect to age, social status and nationality (Chinese or foreign) but not with respect to district, seasons and historical periods. Of the more than seventy types of garments that have been

---

[3] Except in periods of national mourning when actors were not allowed to perform in costume. It would have been then little more than recitals. See 齊如山, 京劇之變遷, 頁十四.

[4] For details on the incongruity of costume and forms of address see 王夢生, 梨園佳話, 四章 "戲之劣處".

[5] The inaccuracy of the costume is no doubt due to the ignorance of the players in the past, but apparently there was at times danger in historical accuracy: Prof. Ch'i Ju-Shan relates how at a private performance before Manchu officials two clowns wore the correct official caps which some of the audience took as an insult so that the manager of the company was given twenty strokes. 齊如山, 京劇之變遷, 頁十八.

[6] There is a general tendency to make the theatrical costume richer and more elaborate, which, if unguided by good taste, can lead to vulgarization. Wealthy families who own private companies of players vie with each other in the splendour of the costume, actors who own their costume try to augment their talents with the aid of good appearance and stores from which it is normally hired compete with each other. 齊如山, 中國劇之組織, 三章頁五十八至五十九.

listed (齊如山, 行頭盔頭, 上, 頁一至二一) a few of the most commonly used may be mentioned here:

    (1) *Mang* 蟒   — a formal gown of Ming dynasty (1368-1643) worn by both men and women on ceremonial occasions. (Figs. 9A and 9B). It is always richly embroidered, often in gold.

    (2) *P'ei* 帔   — semi-formal gown worn by men and women in meetings and minor official occasions. (Figs. 9C and 9D).

    (3) *Tieh-tzu* 褶子 — informal dress worn by men and women at home. (Fig. 9E).

    (4) *K'ao* 靠   — armour worn by military officials in inspections. It always has a mirror on the breast-plate and a tiger's head below the mirror. (Fig. 9F).

    (5) *K'ai-ch'ang* 開氅 — similar to *tieh-tzu,* worn by military officials as semi-formal dress. (Fig. 9G).

    (6) *Ch'ün* 裙   — petticoat, which can be cream or red, plain or embroidered. (Figs. 17B and 21). Women wear it on all occasions, except foreigners, woman warriors, prisoners and some serving maids.

The colour of the dress has special significance to the audience because in real life the Chinese do have a convention for the colour of their dresses. In the theatrical practice, which follows roughly the social convention, there are five basic colours: red for formal and happy occasions, green for virtuous people, yellow for royalty, black for uncouth characters, servants and foot soldiers and white for young people. For informal dresses, in order to vary the colour-scheme of a large assembly of characters on the stage, five other colours are used: purple, pink, blue, light green and scarlet.

The majority of the important roles in the Chinese dramas belong to the middle class and the aristocracies and they wear the dress mentioned above. Other characters have their special costume, so that they can be readily recognized by the audience, for example, eunuchs, Taoists, people in mourning, beggars, royal attendants, servants, flag-bearers, soldiers, gaolers (Fig. 20), nuns, monks, Manchurians, pugilists, waiters, executioners, bawds, goblins, gods, giants, spirits, etc. The costume of gods and spirits is often based on the descriptions in the popular novels and the images in the temples. [7]

A few items of the Chinese theatrical wardrobe deserve special mention because

---

[7] Properties also help to distinguish particular types of characters, for example, the horse-tail switch carried by fairies and nuns and the feather fan by Taoists.

Mang (Men's)

Mang (Women's)

P'ei

P'ei

Tieh-tzu

K'ao

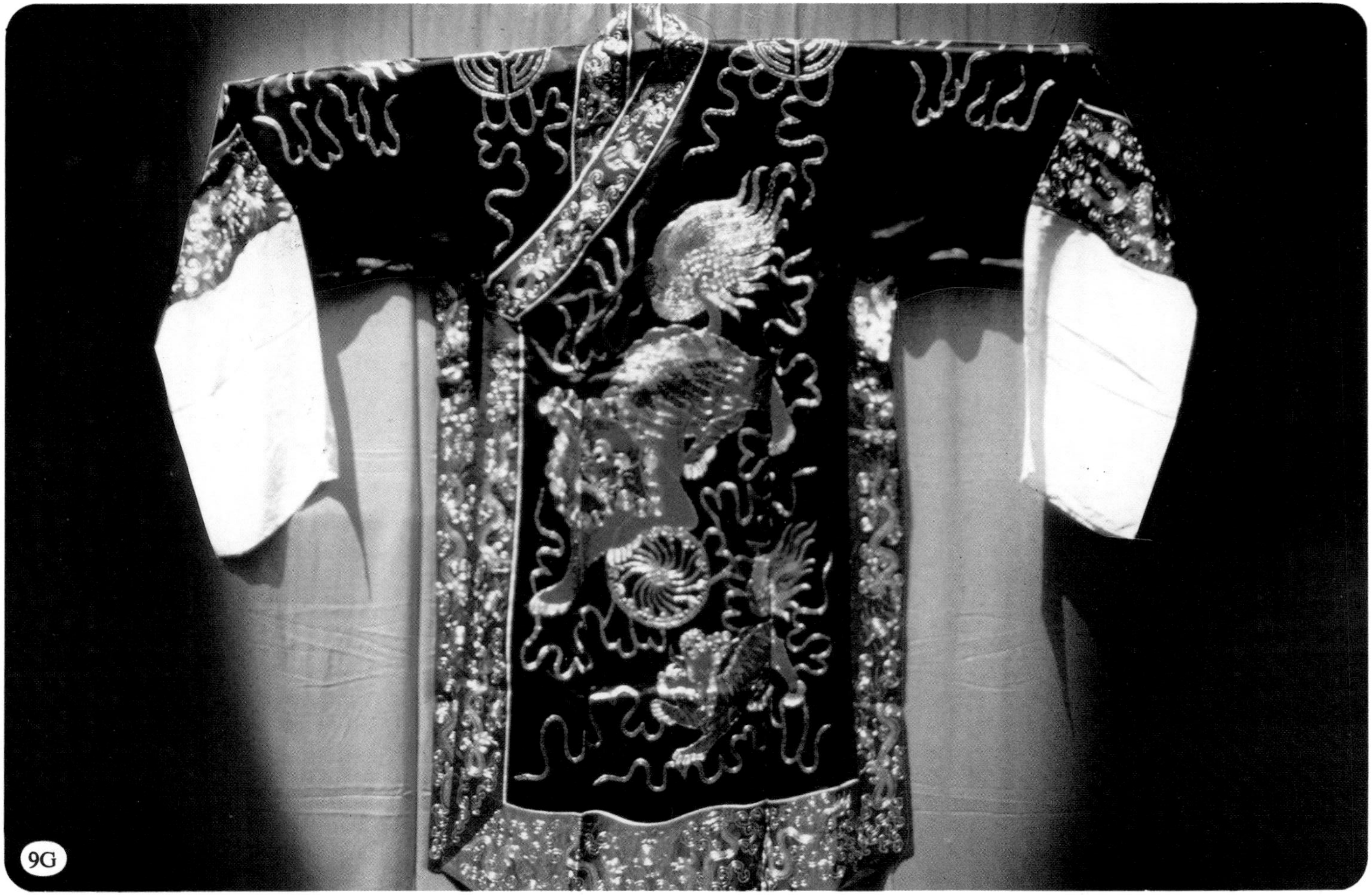

K'ai ch'ang

Emperor's crown (left), warrior's helmet (right)

Official's hat and jade belt

9J

Empress's crown

10A

A royal consort

10B

A lady in humble circumstances

11A

A scholar

11B

A scholar

12A

A foreign princess

12B

A foreign princess

13A

An old man without official rank

An old man without official rank

A servant girl

A servant girl

A young man

A young official

16A

A young warrior

16B

A female warrior

17A

A goddess

17B

A lady

18A

A high official

18B

A prime minister

A fisherman and his daughter

A woman prisoner and her guard

A prince and his consort

of their relation to the Chinese style of acting. A distinctive feature of the gowns mentioned above is the "tab-sleeve" 水袖, a piece of white silk, slit at the lower side, more than a foot long which forms the extension of the sleeve (Figs. 10B, 11A, 11B, 13A, 13B, 15A, 15B, 16A, 17B, 18A, 18B and 21). The main body of the sleeve reaches the finger tips, therefore the end of the "tab-sleeve" reaches the floor when the arm is stretched downwards. Underneath the gown the Chinese actor wears a cotton shirt 水衣 partly to protect the gown from perspiration and partly to make the long and soft sleeves easier to manipulate. Warriors also wear a padded jacket 胖襖 to augment the stature (Fig. 21). For purely decorative purposes are the "jade belt" 玉帶, a stiff and loose belt worn by high officials (Figs. 9I, 18A and 18B) and the "armour flags" 靠旗, four small pennons worn on the back of warriors (Fig. 16A, said to have originated from the practice of warriors carrying small flags for tokens of authority to accompany messages). When travelling, women of the working class sometimes wear, over the regular petticoat, the "waist petticoat" 腰裙, a short and pleated skirt worn high up in the waist and reaching only the knees.

There are more than a hundred different types of head gear in the Chinese theatre [8] of which the following are the types most commonly seen:

(1) The *helmet* 盔 and the *crown* 冠 look very much alike, being hats bristling with pompons (Figs. 9H, 16A and 16B). The emperor's crown is distinguished by the two long tassels at the side which hang in front of the shoulders, and the crown of the rebel or foreign king has two long pheasant feathers on the top and two fox tails on the back. There are more than ten different types of helmets.

(2) *Hats* 帽 worn by civil officials on formal occasions have two wings 翅 at the sides (Figs. 9I, 15A, 18A and 18B), the shape of the wings varying according to the rank. Warriors' hats are larger, usually hexagonal and have pompons on the top but are without the wings. The pompons and some of the wings are mounted on springs, so that they quiver and sway as the actor struts across the stage.

(3) Men's *hats for informal wear* 巾 have no wings but some have tails at the back (Figs. 11A and 11B). The shape varies with age and social status. Young men's hats are decorated with tassels at the sides or pompons on the top (Fig. 15B).

There are special hats for children, old men (Figs. 13A and 13B), fishermen, monks, etc. Women do not wear hat or cap except when women of the poorer classes wear straw hats when travelling. They normally wear a tall bun at the back of the head with the front part of the coiffure heavily decorated with studs and pins

---

[8] See 齊如山, 行頭盔頭, 下, 頁一至一三.

(Figs. 10A, 10B, 14A, 14B, 17A, 17B and 20). The empress wears a crown bristling with pearls on the top and numerous tassels at the sides (Fig. 9J). When a man becomes a prisoner or is in otherwise abject conditions he does not wear a hat but a tuft of hair about two feet long tied together at the top of his head and hanging down the side of his head甩髮. Women wear two small tufts of hair, each about half inch wide and three inches long, pasted to the sides of the cheeks鬢髮. They make the face look narrower and less flat (Figs. 10A, 10B, 12A, 12B, 14A, 14B, 16B, 17A, 17B, 19, 20 and 21). The two long pheasant feathers翎子 worn by warriors (six or seven feet long) were originally exaggerated features of authentic decorations on foreign warriors but are now worn also by native military officials (Figs. 16A and 16B).

With formal and semi-formal dress men wear boots with soles two or three inches thick (Figs. 15A, 16A, 18A and 18B); only in very informal occasions, as when a man is ill, does a man wear shoes. Monks, boatswains and servants wear their own types of shoes without the thick soles. The thickness of the sole increases the height of the actors, changes the apparent length of their legs and modifies their gait and posture. In the past, female impersonators simulated the small feet of the Chinese women by wearing small shoes and bandaging their feet so that in effect they walked on tiptoe (Fig. 14B). [9] This theatrical practice which was started by the notorious female impersonator Wei San魏三 of Ch'ien Lung's reign (1736-1796) who was also the first to use realistic coiffure, has been admired by several generations of connoisseurs but is now replaced by flat soled shoes and an appropriate gait.

Beards and moustaches on the Chinese stage may be black, grey, white or red, the last for foreigners, thieves and ghosts. They vary widely in size and shape but the most common types on the dignified characters are: the "full beard" 滿髯 about one and half feet long, covering the mouth (Figs. 13A, 13B, 18B and 21) and the "three tufts" 三髯 which is similar to the "full beard" but slightly thinner (Figs. 11A, 11B, 18A, 19 and 20). On clowns and characters of low social status the beard or moustache is usually much thinner and can take rather unrealistic shapes, such as a single tuft pointing upwards. The beards are attached to wire frames worn on the ears and owing to the poor fitting of the wire frame they are usually visibly at a distance from the actor's face (Figs. 11A, 11B, 13A, 13B, 18A, 18B and 20) and even when they are well fitted, they are usually too opulent or bizarre to be realistic. [10]

---

[9] For details of the device see Arlington, *The Chinese Drama,* pl. 65; and A. C. Scott, Some Chinese Theatrical Costumes and their Accessories, *World Theatre,* (UNESCO), Vol. II, No. 4. (1953), 30-34.

[10] The full list of the types of beards: (1) 滿髯, full beard, more than a foot long, covering the mouth. (2) 三髯, similar to the above but in three tufts. (3) 扎髯, similar to the full beard but with the mouth visible, used on warriors and uncouth characters. (4)二濤髯, like the full beard but much

Chinese players, like western actors, wear stage make-up. Young male and female roles use both powder and rouge, the rouge mainly as shade, to change the apparent contour of the face (Figs. 10A, 10B, 12A, 12B, 14A, 14B, 15A, 15B, 16A, 16B, 17A, 17B, 19 and 20). The outer ends of the eyes and eyebrows of both male and female roles are lifted by bandages in order to make the face look more handsome (Figs. 10A, 10B, 12A, 12B, 14B, 15B, 16A, 16B, 17B and 20). Some actors drop chemicals into their eyes to make the pupils look larger. Monks, eunuchs and old men wear special make-up to accentuate their characteristic features.

The mask or "painted face" differs from heavy make-up in that its purpose is not to accentuate the natural features but to *replace them* with colour patterns which usually in no way resemble the human face (Figs. 18B, 20 and 21). The form nearest to make-up is the "powder face" 粉臉, a completely whitewashed face with artificial wrinkles worn by arch traitors and Machiavels (Fig. 18B). The powder is applied with the fingers, hence it is also called "smeared face" 揉臉. Other types of the painted face are drawn on the face with grease colours, either with a brush or with fingers, and leave a shiny surface 勾臉. The simpler masks are of one uniform colour such as red or black sometimes with huge eyebrows added but the number of colours and the complexity of the patterns can increase in various degrees till in the extreme cases the whole face is one mass of multi-coloured figures with only the eyes barely discernible among them. Sometimes, to make the mask more grotesque, the natural eyes are obliterated by colours on the eyelids and false eyes painted elsewhere (see illustrations in Ch. XVII). [11]

shorter, used on soldiers and old men of lower social ranks, (5) 加嘴髯, like the preceding but with the mouth shown. (6)丑三髯, three slender tufts, used on comedians. (7)八字髯, two short tufts at the sides, used on comedians; sometimes pointing upwards, called 二挑髯. (8)一字髯, short beard round the face, used on men of low social rank; when a short beard is added below it, it is called 二字髯 (9)吊塔髯, whiskers and short beard on chin; two tufts added at the sides of the face — 五嘴髯; without the beard on the chin 一四喜髯. (10) 虬髯, curled beard round the face. (11)一戳髯, single tuft on the upper lip, pointing upwards, used on comedians only. 齊如山, 中國劇之組織, 五章. Types of beard and moustache are also associated with temperament and character in the western mind, but they are not as thoroughly exploited in the western theatre as in the Chinese.

[11] Technically the masks are divided into the following types: (1) The "smeared face" 揉臉 white powder applied to the face with fingers. (2) "Mask of uniform colour" 整臉, only one colour, red or black, used. (3) "Three piece mask" 三塊瓦臉, the mask is of one colour but divided into three prominent pieces by two hugh eyebrows reaching upwards to the edge of the forehead. (4) "Three piece multi-coloured mask" 花三塊瓦臉 same as the preceding except there are more than one colour. (5) "Three piece variegated mask" 碎三塊瓦臉 same as the preceding except the patches of colours are smaller and more complicated. (6) "Multi-coloured mask" 花臉, with large colour patches but no prominent eyebrows. (7) "Variegated mask" 碎臉 complicated figures of many colours, without eyebrows. The design of the mask is broken down into the following elements by Prof. Ch'i Ju-Shan (齊如山, 臉譜, 五至九章,): eyebrows — twenty-two types, eye sockets — more than sixteen types, mouths — six types, brow — fifteen types and nose — (not listed, actually it is either the extension of the cheeks or that of the brow) .

49

As a rule actors paint their own faces, and spend a long time to make the pattern expressive [12] and the borders between the colour patches sharp, but some actors can do it with extreme speed, with fingers, in a matter of seconds, the result may not be neat, but can be very expressive. Actors wearing the "painted face" shave their foreheads to make the face look larger and to facilitate the adjustment of the colour pattern to the existing features of the face.

To summarize, the costume, beards and masks in the Chinese theatre are all standardized into a number of types so that when a new drama is written a choice can be made among the standard types for each of the characters in the drama. New types are rarely created, and when they are, they do not survive long. For a character in the old dramas, the mask is fixed and record is kept of it so that all actors playing him wear the same mask. The choice of costume and ornaments for him is limited to a narrow range. [13]

---

[12] In theatrical slang, *ch'u hsiang* 出像.

[13] For details about the material covered in this chapter see: Arlington, *The Chinese Drama;* Cecilia S. L. Zung, *Secrets of the Chinese Drama;* and Ch'i Ju-Shan, *Répertoire des masquillages de théâtre avec une traduction française par André d'Hormon, 1932.*

齊如山，行頭盔頭.

齊如山，臉譜.

張笑俠，臉譜.

齊如山，戲劇脚色名詞考.

國立台灣藝術館，國劇臉譜，民四九.

國立台灣藝術館，國劇行頭，民五十.

張伯謹，國劇之臉譜，台灣美亞書版股份有限公司，民五九.

CHAPTER VI

THE MUSIC

The Chinese theatre is, strictly speaking, light opera rather than drama. Although the greater part of the dialogue is spoken, the music in it is not incidental music: it accompanies all the action and part of the dialogue and is closely related to the style of acting and singing. It is true that in some farces characters in the play are explicitly represented as singing to entertain themselves [1] and what they sing has no connection with the action, yet in general passages that are sung are parts of the dialogue, and are therefore arias instead of incidental songs. Even though in some farces there is almost no aria and what is sung may be substituted with spoken passages, yet the style of acting is dependent on musical accompaniment, hence in such cases music must be considered as an integral part of the performance.

The Chinese theatre, however, differs from the opera in several ways. One can enjoy listening to the music of the western opera without seeing the stage performance because it is, apart from its dramatic function, interesting music. In the Chinese plays, however, except the arias, the music cannot stand on its own feet, no one would think of listening to the orchestral part alone. Again, in western operas the music is played according to the score which contains all the details of the music but in the Chinese theatre the conductor (the drummer) has no score, the musicians in the orchestra memorize the standard passages which accompany each type of action and synchronize the music to the action. The connection between the action and the music is much closer than that in western operas, in fact the acting is like dance and at any particular moment, has the same rhythm as the accompanying music. There are frequent pauses of indefinite length in the music as, for example, when the actor is speaking or when he is singing without accompaniment, so that, unlike the western opera, the music is not played continuously from beginning to end.

The music of the Chinese theatre in its present form is derived from several

---

[1] e.g. 紡棉花，拾黃金 .

51

local theatres and from the classical *K'un* dramas 崑曲 which it displaced. By far the greatest part of the musical material is, however, taken from the two styles of music know as *Hsi-p'i* 西皮 and *Erh-huang* 二黄 . The small extent to which the auxiliary schools of music are used in the Chinese theatre of to-day does not justify discussing their technicalities, but their general characteristics will be explained in the following.

(1) *Kao* tunes 高腔 (literally "high tunes") — sung in high *falsetto* with shimmering accompaniments. It can be traced to a school of southern dramas called *I-yang* tunes 弋陽腔 which flourished in Kiangsi province in early Ming dynasty (1368-1643). Plays with this school of music were staged in towns near Peking within living memory but, like the several other local schools of music of Ming dynasty, they are now extinct.

(2) *Ch'in* tunes 秦腔 . Originated in the north-western part of China, in the province of Kansu, which was the ancient kingdom of Ch'in 秦 , it is accompanied by the fiddle and the gong, and is still used in the theatres in that district. It was introduced into Peking about the middle of the eighteenth century.

(3) *Pang-tzu* tunes (literally "wooden-block tunes") 梆子腔 . It is accompanied by the wooden block and probably originated in Kiangsi province. In Ch'ing dynasty (1644-1911) it was popular in several provinces in east China. In the late eighteenth century it was a favourite style in Peking and at one time almost monopolized the classical theatre. A tune called "Southern Pang-tzu" 南梆子 often played in the theatre to-day, is believed to come from this school.

(4) *Shansi Pang-tzu* tunes 山西梆子 . This is a separate school from the *Pang-tzu* tunes, being of more recent origin and probably perfected in Shansi province and introduced into Peking at the end of Ch'ing dynasty. It is accompanied by the flute and hurried percussions, in the mood of *appassionata*.

(5) *K'un* tunes 崑腔 . This is the innovation in the sixteenth century by the musician Wei Liang-Fu 魏良輔 who "after ten years of study to improve the contemporary music, created a new style of singing". It is based on two local styles, *Hai-yen* 海鹽 and *I-yang* 弋陽 and is accompanied by flutes. The name is derived from the town of K'un-shan 崑山 , the early centre of this style. Following its immediate popularity among the audience it soon won over the playwrights who started to write for this particular type of music and it went on to monopolize the

classical theatre for three centuries until it was displaced by the *P'i-huang* style about the middle of the last century. Amateur societies to-day try to keep the tradition alive but the general public consider it as being too formal. Some classical plays are still being performed completely in *K'un* tunes but the style of acting has changed from the original. [2]

The origin of the two styles of music, *Hsi-p'i* and *Erh-huang,* which form the basis of the classical theatre to-day, is still a controversial subject. It is however fairly well established that the *Erh-huang* style had its beginning in two neighbouring cities, Huang Kang 黃岡 and Huang Pi 黃陂, in Hupei province in central China. Before it was adopted in the classical theatre it had spread into and was modified in many provinces in central and south China. The *Hsi-p'i* style may have originated in the same locality or it may have come from Shensi, but as it is sung and played now it sounds similar to the *Erh-huang* style to the untrained ear. Actually, the *Hsi-p'i* tunes are based on the diatonic scale starting with F (FGABCDEF') and the *Erh-huang* tunes on that starting with G (GABCDEFG'). [3] In any case it is certain that both have been modified during their rising popularity in Peking because it is known that at one time *Erh-huang* tunes were accompanied by flutes, not fiddles, as they are now. [4]

The orchestra in the Chinese theatre is much smaller than the western counterpart because, harmony being unknown in China, all instruments are played in unison so that no large bodies of instruments can be used to exploit the harmonic resources. The total range of the orchestra is about two octaves. The orchestra is divided, according to its function, into two sections: the percussion group which accompanies most of the action and the strings and the woodwinds which support the singer. In the western symphony orchestra the combination of the instruments is constantly being changed for variation in colour, but in the Chinese theatre this is hardly done at all, the music is played by the same small group of instruments until the script indicates another style of music which requires different accompaniment. The Chinese musicians cannot, therefore, change the orchestral colour without using a different style of music and since most plays are written for one style only there is normally no variation in orchestral colour within a play. Difference in tempo and mood of the music helps the musicians to fit the music to the different scenes in the dramas.

---

[2] The history of the local theatres is still obscure; for detailed discussions see 青木正兒, 中國近世戲曲史, 十二章一節.

[3] See 王光祈, 中國音樂史, p. 185 台灣版, 1974.

[4] It is said that emperor T'ung Chih 同治 (reigned 1862-1875) considered the flutes as unsuitable "for developing the tunes" (perhaps because they lack *glissando*) hence they were changed to fiddles. 齊如山, 京劇之變遷, 二四.

In the percussion group, the instruments in more or less constant use are:

1. The gong 鑼 , smaller than the tam-tam in symphony orchestras, about one foot in diameter, sounding like a large dinner gong.

2. The cymbals 鈸 , of which there are two sets, the larger one about ten inches in diameter, and the smaller, about eight inches. The two halves are crashed against each other.

3. The "small gong" 小鑼 (Fig. 22) which differs from the gong just mentioned in construction — its face, about eight inches in diameter, is convex. It is struck at the centre with the edge of a thin splinter and has a high pitch.

4. The "T'ang drum" 唐鼓 , a tall and barrel-shaped drum, with faces about eight inches in diameter.

5. "Single-face drum" 單皮鼓 (Fig. 23) which is like a drum in construction but sounds like a wooden block. It is made with leather tautly stretched over a convex wooden base about ten inches in diameter, with a round hole of about two inches in diameter at the centre. It is played with small bamboo sticks like chopsticks.

6. The Chinese castanets 夾板 (Fig. 25) which are more sonorous than the Spanish castanets and are different in construction: two pieces of wood, each about one by three by eleven inches are tied loosely together near the top with ribbons: and are played by holding one piece in the left hand and swinging the other to hit it.

Some of the percussion instruments are used only occasionally for special effects or for special types of music. They are:

7. The "large drum" 大鼓 , larger and of lower pitch than the "T'ang drum", with faces about eighteen inches in diameter.

8. *Hsing* 星 (Fig. 24) , two small brass cups, about one and a half inches in diameter, held by the string attached to the bottom and struck against each other.

9. *Yün-lo* 雲鑼 (Fig. 26), ten small gongs, each about four inches in diameter, tuned to the notes of the scale suspended in a frame.

10. The wooden blocks 梆子 sound like the Chinese castanets but more sonorous.

It should be added that the shape and size of the instruments are not standardized and vary between the makers and, to a greater extent, between different localities.

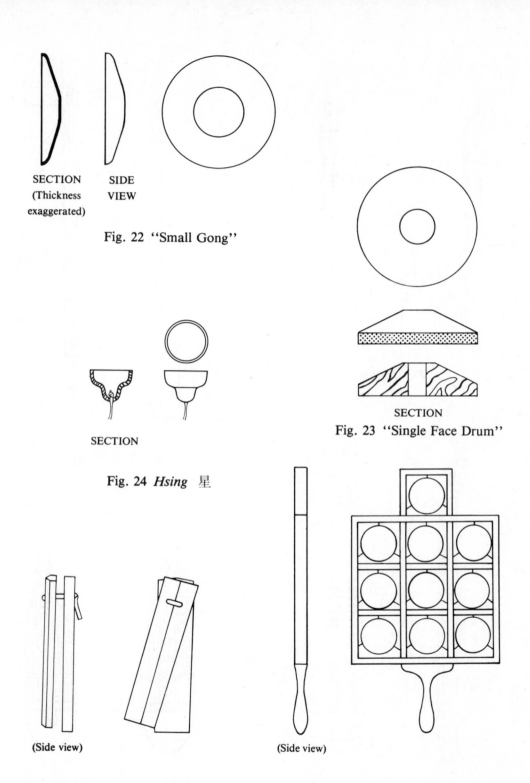

SECTION
(Thickness
exaggerated)

SIDE
VIEW

Fig. 22 "Small Gong"

SECTION

Fig. 24 *Hsing* 星

SECTION
Fig. 23 "Single Face Drum"

(Side view)

(Side view)

Fig. 25 The Chinese Castanets

Fig. 26 *Yün-lo*

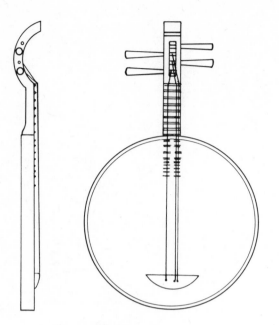

Fig. 27 "Moon Lute"

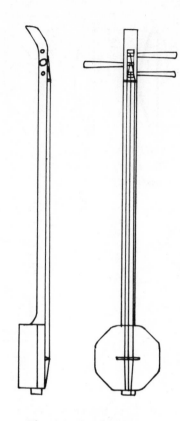

Fig. 29 *San-hsien*

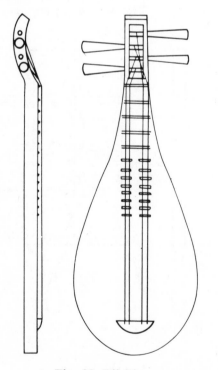

Fig. 28 *P'i P'a*

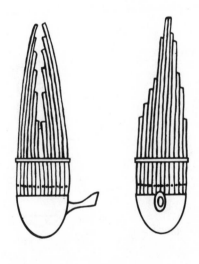

Fig. 30 *Sheng*

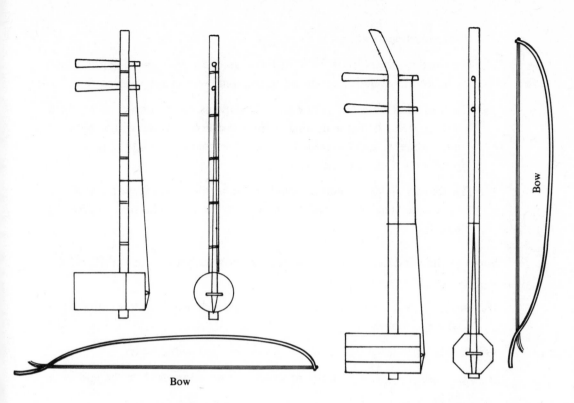

Fig. 31 *Hu-ch'in*   Fig. 32 *Erh-hu*

The string instruments are:

11. The "moon lute" 月琴 (Fig. 27), a four-string instrument with a large round sound box about eighteen inches in diameter.

12. The "three strings" 三弦 (Fig. 29), a three-string banjo with a long neck without frets and a sound box faced with snake skin about seven inches in diameter.

13. The fiddle 胡琴 (Fig. 31), a two-string instrument with a small cylindrical sound box, about two inches in diameter, faced with snake skin. The hair of the bow is between the strings. It is played by resting it on the knee, with the left hand for stopping and the right hand for bowing. It has a piercing tone.

14. The "second fiddle" 二胡 (Fig. 32), similar to the above but with a slightly larger sound box and considerably milder tone. (There are many variations of the fiddle of which this is the most often used).

The wind instruments are:

15. The vertical flute 簫 is held like the recorder but, being without the whistle, the sound is produced in the same way as the western flute.

16. The horizonal flute 笛, very much the same as the western flute except it has no keys. A distinguishing feature is a hole covered with a bamboo membrane which is wrinkled so that it resonates with all the notes thus producing a more tender tone.

17. The shawm 哨吶, similar in construction to the oboe except there are no keys and there is a large bell-mouth at the end. The tone is like the bagpipe.

Some of the wind and string instruments occasionally used for special effects are:

18. *Sheng* 笙 (Fig. 30), a small reed organ about fourteen inches high played with the mouth.

19. *P'i-p'a* 琵琶 (Fig. 28), a lute with pear-shaped sound box.

20. *Hao-t'ung* 號筒, a trumpet of crude construction used at the end of a play.

The number of players in the orchestra is much smaller than the number of different instruments might suggest because there is only one instrument of each kind and not all the instruments are played at the same time. No member of the orchestra is idle at any time, because most of the musicians can play more than one instrument. For any style of music the instruments used are only more or less fixed and when the music is changed the same players take up new instruments as necessary. [5] The drummer, who is also the conductor, is in charge of three instruments, the "T'ang drum", the "single-face drum" and the castanets, often playing the last two at the same time, one with each hand. He and two cymbalists and two gong-players form the normal basic orchestral accompaniment. When there is singing, wind and string instruments are added and among them the chief flautist or fiddler is the most important, the others, playing softer instruments in unison, are sometimes omitted and even when they are present their composition and number depend on the resources of the company. The chief accompanist employed by the star singer plays only when he sings and is expected to be a musician of some calibre, because the instrumental introduction and bridge passages are considered integral parts of the aria and most players add improvised ornaments to them.

---

[5] For the variations in the instruments used in each style of music and the different instruments each member of the orchestra can normally play see 齊如山, 戲劇脚色名詞考, 八章.

Generally speaking, unless there is singing only the percussion group accompanies the action, but certain scenes which involve a long stretch of stage business without dialogue such as offerings, libations, banquets, assemblage of the royal court, etc., are accompanied by special music played by the strings or winds or both. [6] When the actors speak the orchestra punctuates rather than accompanies them. When a singer pauses for his tea (which is served on the stage) or when an actor changes his costume in the scene, the orchestra plays long muted notes to indicate that the action is temporarily suspended.

Probably owing to the smaller orchestra and simpler music, the quality of performance, in so far as timing is concerned, is noticeably higher than in western symphony orchestras. The ensemble of the Chinese orchestra is always extremely neat and precise.

The Chinese theorists have known several systems of temperament since ancient times — in fact, this is the favourite subject of authors of the histories of Chinese music — and the even-tempered scale since early Ming dynasty. The scale used now is the major diatonic scale but with notes other than C as the tonic. The construction of the holes on the flutes and the frets on the string instruments show that the musicians are not clearly aware of the details of the diatonic scale, for example, the half tone between the leading note and the tonic. This is probably due to the lack of musical knowledge among the players of the local theatres. It is said that some musicians can vary the pitch of a note by half a tone on a single hole on the flute. [7] Perhaps their musical sense ensures accurate pitch in the notes actually played.[8]

---

[6] 曲牌子.

[7] 齊如山, 京劇之變遷, 頁十三.

[8] Two excellent studies by non-practitioners and based on western musicology have been published: F. Kornfeld, *Die Tonale Struktur chinesischer Musik,* Mödling bei Wien, 1955; G. Schonfelder, *Die Musik der Peking-Oper,* Leipzig, 1972.

CHAPTER VII

THE STYLE OF SINGING

The vocal music of the Chinese theatre differs from that of the western opera for two reasons: the lack of harmony in the Chinese music and the relation between singing and phonology in the Chinese language.

Lack of harmony probably limits the size of the Chinese orchestra and confines the vocal music practically to the solo. The nearest approach to the duet in Chinese music is two singers singing alternate phrases, and choruses, which are sung in unison, are usually omitted from the commercial performances. [1]

In order to understand the characteristics of the singing in the Chinese theatre it is necessary to have some basic knowledge of the pronunciation of Chinese words.

An important difference between the pronunciation of the Chinese language and that of European languages is that whereas in the latter inflexion is used for expressions, in the former it is used to differentiate one word from another. To illustrate, the English word "ma" means "mother" both in "Ma! (please don't)" where the tone falls and in "Ma (where are you?)" where the tone is high and even. In Chinese the word 馬 which means "horse" is pronouced as "ma" with an upward inflexion and the word 罵 meaning "to abuse by words" is also pronounced "ma" but with a downward inflexion (similar to "Ma! (please don't)"). As shown in the following table, in the standard pronunciation of the Chinese language there are five different inflexions. To pronounce a Chinese word correctly one should know not only the consonant and the vowel involved but also the particular inflexion the word belongs to. When the word *"ch'ing"* is inflected in the five ways, the first inflexion may mean either "blue" or "clean", the second either "affection" or "clear weather", and so on. In other words, *"ch'ing"* has not

---

[1] Choruses sung by marching soldiers can still be heard in the public performances of the Schools of Dramatic Art in Shanghai in which all the parts are played by the students. In commercial theatres, the flag-bearers are supernumeraries hired temporarily and they cannot sing.

Inflexions in the pronunciation of Chinese words	陰平	陽平	上	去	入
Approximate rendering					
Different expressions for the English word "No."	"No?" (genuine doubt)	"No?" (incredulous)	"No?" ("Won't you please?")	"N-O" (emphatic)	"Nope" (curt)
Chinese words pronounced "ch'ing"	青 blue 清 clean	情 affection 晴 clear weather	請 invite 頃 a moment	慶 celebrate 磬 a musical instrument	(ch'i) 乞 beg 泣 sob

TABLE I Tones in the Chinese pronunciation.

only five meanings corresponding to the five inflexions but several meanings in each inflexion. [2]

Since correct pronunciation in the Chinese language is a matter of regulating the pitch or speaking as a *staccato* musical note is sung, a Chinese poem, when read aloud or declaimed, has a pronounced melodic quality. In fact, Chinese prosody is based, not on accents, but on the inflexions: the rules specify the type of inflexion each or some of the words in a line should have and the basic principle of versification is the pleasurable combination of the different inflexions. To declaim a Chinese poem is merely to sustain the sound of each word longer than in the ordinary way of reading. When the pitch of the voice is now held constant and now varied for correct pronunciation and when one syllable is connected to the next by sustaining the voice the result is very near to a melody. To read a Chinese poem or stylized prose slowly and expressively is almost to sing it, as those who have heard a

---

[2] It is inevitable that inflexions are used in a monosyllabic language to increase the number of distinguishable words. In European languages the number of different monosyllabic sounds may be few, but by combining them with each other a great number of polysyllabic words are formed. Suppose there are 200 monosyllabic combinations of consonants and vowels: by using five inflexions there can be 1,000 words, but by combining them into words of two syllables there can be 40,000 words. This is why even with the inflexions the Chinese are inconvenienced by numerous homophones in the language. In the written language there can be no possibility of mistaking one word for its homophone — because the shape of the characters is different — in the spoken language the context helps to determine which of the homophones is meant.

Chinese school teacher reading a lesson will agree. The vocalization is continuous, the pitch is varied and the accents occur at regular intervals by the inherent rhythm of the poem; to make the declamation into a musical melody all that is needed is to constrain the pitch of the voice to the notes of a scale. Poems which are similar phonologically would, when set to music, sound similar, because the melodies cannot be too far removed from the phonological pattern, and conversely, if several poems are to be set to one melody, they have to be phonologically similar. [3] If a poem is sung to a tune which does not fit its words, the words become mispronounced and the poem becomes unintelligible. To illustrate the last point let the words of a poem be set to music according to correct pronunciation: [4]

（去）年（今）日此（門）中
（人）面桃（花）相映紅
（人）面不知何處（去）
（桃）（花）依（舊）笑東風

---

[3] The correspondence between melody and the phonological pattern is not, of course, absolute: some variations are possible by shifting the position of the words with respect to the tune and by adding musical ornaments.

[4] This simple melody is formed merely by choosing the musical progressions to conform with the inflexions and adding cadences to the ends of the lines, hence it is akin to the poem being declaimed. The construction of many folk songs in China suggests that their origin is in poem reading, as the following:

More complicated melodies may of course be fitted to the poem, for example, a word may be sung to a florid musical phrase and the time value of each word may not be uniform.

Below the original poem is written a second poem which has the same number of lines and the same number of words in each line and the words in the second poem which are mispronounced if sung to the tune are put in parentheses. (5)

This close relationship between language and music which lends the expressiveness of speech to the arias puts heavy burdens on the dramatist and the singer. A Chinese dramatist must understand not only how to write dramatic poetry but also how poetry is set to music and the Chinese singer must know something of phonology. (6) In the past, Chinese dramatists chose traditional tunes for the arias and in spite of the restrictions imposed on poetic creation were able to produce some excellent dramatic poetry. The practice in the Chinese theatre of to-day is that the players write the dramas and improvise the music to fit the words. The lack of education in theatrical circles and the restrictions imposed by music on the text result in the low literary quality of the contemporary Chinese dramas.

The music in the Chinese theatre differs from the European opera in yet another respect: in the western operas though the style of singing may change the melody is fixed by the composer's score, but in China, even when there is a score, the singer takes the liberty to change it, indeed he takes pride in doing so. In order to understand the source of the music in the Chinese theatre it is necessary to deal with some of its technicalities.

As has been mentioned before, the music of the theatre of to-day is derived mainly from two types of local music called *Hsi-p'i* and *Erh-huang* but is supplemented by the music in *K'un* dramas as well as some other local theatres.

In *K'un* dramas a system of musical notation was used and scores have been carefully kept both by the players and by the patrons. Even though singers take liberty with the score, the deviations are not accumulative and therefore not serious. (7) Strictly speaking, the *K'un* tunes have no composers, they are traditional. (8) In the

---

(5) Western hymn tunes used in Chinese churches do not fit the translated text of the hymns which sound painfully wrong to people familiar with the Chinese theatre. The problem appears to have been encountered by Chinese musicians in the past: "When the poems are sung to music of the Nü-Chen 女眞 style [foreign tribe] the words, sung in the tone of the Nü-Chen people, are often mispronounced; yet, so long as they do not depart too far from the principles of phonology there is no harm done". （元）周德清, 中原音韻, 小引.

(6) For rules for setting Chinese poems to music see 王季烈, 集成曲譜, 玉集附論, 三章, 項衡方, 曲韻探驪, 上, 七章, 楊蔭瀏, 中國音樂史綱 （一九五二） 頁二四二至二六三. Books on music and singing usually contain substantial sections on the subject. Probably owing to the monosyllabic nature of the language there are more vowels in the Chinese language than in the English and together with diphthongs, they make rhyming a complicated subject. Dramatists have to master these studies before they can start writing dramas.

(7) For the musical notation used see Wang Kwang-Ch'i, *Ueber die chinesische klassische Oper*. The earliest score was published in 1792 — 葉廣明, 納書楹曲譜. According to Wang Kwang-Ch'i *(ibid.)* modern gramophone records differ by about ten per cent from a score published

sixteenth century, a musician, called Wei Liang-Fu, is said to have modified the contemporary tunes into "water mill tunes" 水磨調 which were later called *K'un* tunes. One may say that the music of the *K'un* dramas is the result of Wei Liang-Fu's modification on the then traditional tunes which were composed by unknown musicians of the imperial court and the people.

The *Hsi-p'i* and *Erh-huang* tunes as we know them now come mostly from the great singers of the nineteenth century [9] who created the Chinese theatre of to-day out of comparatively rudimentary materials. They took the tunes from the local theatres and modified them to suit the dramatic purpose at hand and when they sang in new dramas they derived new tunes out of those they already improvised. Since then the tunes were taught by successive generations of teachers and pupils and partially preserved in the score used by them, but as a singer changes the tunes even within his own lifetime one can realize how much they must have changed since they were first used in the classical theatre. The local theatres from which the music was derived have also changed since the rise of the modern Chinese theatre hence there is no means of telling how many or how much of the present tunes were taken from the original local theatres or to what extent the style of singing has changed. Judging by the way great singers graft phrases into their tunes [10] when the tunes were first created the musical material from the local theatres were probably very freely used and much new material was added.

The melodies in the Chinese theatre are therefore in a constant state of flux, which is why in the popular editions of the scores a tune is identified not only by the scene and the drama in which it occurs but also by the singer. This is necessary because no two singers render the same aria in exactly the same notes. In fact, even records of the same arias made by the same singer at an interval of a few years are different from each other.

That the music in the Chinese theatre should be constantly changing is probably inevitable and neither score nor gramophone can stop the change although they may

in 1881 王季烈, 集成曲譜 which in turn differs by the same amount from a score published in 1792 葉廣明, 納書楹曲譜.

[8] *K'un* tunes can be traced ultimately to the music of the southern dramas of Sung dynasty (960-1276). Beyond that, whether the tunes used in the local theatre in Kiangsu and Chekiang provinces, the domain of the southern dramas, were derived from folk music, or from the northern dramas, or from court music, it is now difficult to say — see 青木正兒, 中國近世戲曲史, 七章一節 — they were probably a mixture of all these, in that case, the original composers were anonymous court musicians and the unknown authors of folk tunes. How much the music had changed between Sung and Ming dynasties is a mystery which will probably never be solved because there was no workable system of notation in Sung dynasty and only a few fragments of the musical score have survived, from which modern musicologists are still attempting reconstructions.

[9] e.g. 程長庚, 余三勝, 孫菊仙, 譚鑫培.

[10] e.g. Mei Lan-Fang's aria in *The Joint Court* 三堂會審 in which a phrase from *Southern Pang-tzu* 南梆子 is grafted.

slow it. Unlike western operas, the music in the Chinese theatre is more predominantly the singer's art as opposed to the composer's art; its beauty lies less in the basic shape of the melody than in the singer's execution, especially his improvisations. By Chinese standards it would be harmful to constrain him to the exact notes if he feels he can interpret the words of the aria better by a different musical phrase.

In the *K'un* dramas, therefore, the score is used as the basis of the music in much the same way as in European operas, but in the Peking dramas the exact details of the melodies are not recorded but are known only to the singer and the key musicians in the orchestra. Agreement between the musicians taking part in the performance is achieved in the following manner. In the text, which does not contain the score, the music of the arias is indicated by the school and the type of "rhythm" to be used [11] and by these specifications the musicians know the tempo, the time, the general construction of the text, the instruments used in the accompaniment and the introduction and the bridge passages, because these are fixed by convention. [12] The chief fiddler, who always works closely with the singer, knows the melodies by heart, and follows the singer in unison and the other fiddlers and lute-players follow the chief fiddler. The percussion group, led by the drummer, play the standard accompaniment for each type of "rhythm" and are unaffected by the exact details of the melody because the singer has to conform to the tempo and general structure of the particular "rhythm" he has chosen. An aria in the Peking drama is identified not, as western operas, by the first or the most prominent phrase, but by the name of the play and the "rhythm", thus, "The slow rhythm in *The Stratagem of the Empty City*", and since a play rarely contains two arias worth identifying, this method, though not perfect, is workable.[13]

The table, which represents most of the tempi and rhythms used in the Chinese theatre, shows that the technical resources of the music are, as compared with the European opera, very limited. Only the duple and the quadruple times are used and the latter may be said to be a derivative of the former. With the lack of harmony, modulation, which is done by harmonic devices in western music, is unknown; an aria, however long, remains in one key. The tempi cover a wide range, but they are coupled rigidly to the time and the general construction of the text and many

---

[11] There are about a dozen conventionally fixed "rhythms" in each of the *Hsi-p'i* and *Erh-huang* styles; see table. The table includes only those "rhythms" that are very often used; the so-called "reversed tunes" 反調 in both *Hsi-p'i* and *Erh-huang* used in sad arias are not included. See 傅玉賢, 元曲與皮簧之比較, 文學年報, 六期（一九四〇）.

[12] Except in the choice between the longer and the shorter introduction in some cases. The key of the arias is not specified in the script; each singer chooses his own and directs his accompanist to play accordingly.

[13] cf. "Andante from Symphony No. 3" etc.

Chinese name	Literal translation	Approximate tempo	Time	General construction	Basic number of syllables in the verse	Uses
慢板	"Slow rhythm"	Lento	Quadruple	Long aria in regular verses	7 or 10	Lament, prayer, invocation, meditation, recollection
原板 正板	"Basic rhythm" "Moderate rhythm"	Adagio	Duple	do.	7 or 10	Soliloquy, narrative, testimony
快板 流水板	"Quick rhythm" "Running rhythm"	Presto	Duple	do.	7	* Agitated narrative and all dialogue in haste
二六	("Erh-liu")	Allegro	Duple	do.	7	* Narrative, explanation, farewell.
搖板	"Swaying rhythm"	Andante	(No regular accents)	A couplet or any number of verses	7 or 10	Couplet at exit, reproof, angry remarks
散板	"Diffused rhythm"	Andante	(No regular accents in the voice, quick accompaniment)	Generally two or four verses	7	After fainting, being haunted
倒板	"Inverted rhythm"	Adagio	(No regular rhythm)	One or two verses	7	Introduction to arias
廻龍	"Dragon curl"	Adagio	Quadruple	Usually only one phrase	Indefinite	Bridge between "inverted rhythm" and "basic rhythm"

TABLE II Types of rhythm and tempo most often used in *Hsi-p'i* and *Erh-huang* tunes

* (Note: These are not used in the *Erh-huang* tunes).

possible combinations of tempo, time and rhythm are unknown to the Chinese musicians. Owing to the close relationship between the text and the melody, the small number of meters used in the verse passages further limits the variety of the arias, in fact, all passages sung to the same "rhythm" in the same style of music (e.g. *Hsi-p'i* moderate rhythm) have the same general metrical shape.

Apart from *Hsi-p'i* and *Erh-huang* music, some tunes are taken from various local theatres and the ultimate origin of many of them is now difficult to trace. Like the other melodies, they are modified by the singers and vary in details from one singer to another. Of these perhaps the most often used are the *Southern Pang-tzu* 南梆子 a gay and effeminate tune and the *Ssu-p'ing tune* 四平調 , a carefree and sometimes mischievous tune.

Owing to the practice of actors playing the female parts, the female voice, both in singing and in speech, is simulated by *falsetto* [14] except the old woman 老旦 who sings within the natural range but in an affected hard tone. [15] The masked characters sing in approximately the baritone range but with a resonant voice using the chest and head register extensively. [16] The most curious case of vocalization is that of the young man 小生 who speaks in what is called "double voice" 陰陽嗓 oscillating between high voice in *falsetto* and the natural voice, an exaggerated version, perhaps, of the changing voice at puberty; he sings in *falsetto,* but with a more masculine tone than the female characters. The other types of male characters all sing in the "natural tone" 本嗓 but the naturalness is only relative (no singing voice is really "natural"), the tone is akin to tenor but the range is somewhat below it. Actresses playing female parts do not of course have to sing in *falsetto* but as the tradition of the tone quality was established by male players the actresses try to sing in the tone of the male *falsetto*. Actresses cannot sing the male parts or the part of the old woman unless their voice is unusually low.

A peculiarity of the voice in the Chinese theatre is that like all the other features, it is not natural. Very few actors can, like Mei Lan-Fang, sound natural in the *falsetto,* the affectation is usually quite noticeable. The speaking voice of the young man cannot be reconciled with any type of voice one normally hears and the masked characters sound like bulls speaking human language.

---

[14] cf. seventeenth century European theatre and church music using *castrati.*

[15] The Chinese name *chia-sang* 假嗓 means exactly "false voice" .

[16] 寬嗓 , literally "broad tone" .

CHAPTER VIII

THE SCRIPT

The text of the Chinese plays of to-day differs from that of modern European dramas in the following respects: the authorship is practically always anonymous, [1] it has little or no literary value, it is constantly being modified by the players and it is considered to be a relatively unimportant part of the Chinese theatricals. These characteristics are due to the theatrical conditions in China, especially in the local theatres from which the present form of the classical theatre was derived. For centuries players have been adapting the text of old dramas to suit their particular needs so that the present versions of a particular play represent many layers of modifications and replacements, hence it is difficult to ascertain the authorship. [2] If it is remembered that these players are semi-literate artisans trying to eke out a living by hook or by crook it will not seem surprising that literary value is not respected or indeed recognized, and that the text was plagiarized and mangled in the most ruthless manner for the smallest financial gains. [3] [4] New plays are written by the players themselves for the sole purpose of the performance, and naturally they, like

---

[1] cf. some French dramas of the seventeenth century.

[2] For the relation between the different versions of the same plays see 周貽白， 中國戲劇史， 附錄 where successive derivations are traced back to the Yüan dynasty. For the present Chinese theatre, the earliest copies of the script are probably the hand-written copies in the Theatre Art Museum in Peking, and they are anonymous — see 北平戲劇學會圖書館書目，上， 二十三，中，十三．

[3] Obscenities would have been exploited by the Chinese players if law and public opinion had allowed it. In the seventeen-eighties one players' company scandalized Peking with a play based on the twenty-seventh chapter of *Chin P'ing Mei*. (In Egerton's translation of this novel, called *The Golden Lotus,* the passages referred to are clothed in the obscurity of Latin). [4] [Note added in 1979: These passages are in English in the 1972 edition]. The play and its many imitations were soon banned — see 青本正兒， 中國近世戲曲史， 十二章二節．The Chinese censor, however, is by western standards over-sensitive in these matters: a scene of a man disguised as a bride was once banned — see 齊如山， 京戲之變遷， 頁三六．

the older plays, contain many mistakes of grammar and wording. Modern Chinese plays are not meant to be published and read and no one reads them as literature, indeed they would never have been published if the music had not attracted a large number of amateur players throughout the country. European dramas are preserved in the published texts and can be revived at any time but the preservation of the Chinese dramas depends on the players and many of them have carried their favourite plays to their graves.

The ultimate sources of the majority of Chinese dramas are the popular legends, perpetuated and propagated by the popular novels and collections of stories. [5] In some of the Chinese romances based on history, as the famous *Romance of the Three Kingdoms* 三國志演義 some attempt is made towards historical accuracy, but most Chinese novels, historical or otherwise, are pure fiction tagged to some historical incident of dubious authenticity. The length of the Chinese novels accounts for the episodic construction of the Chinese plays: the stories are usually so long that a drama can only cover a very small portion of it. The Chinese audience, unlike the western audience, know the stories of the dramas before they see them.

The lack of publication and the existence of variant versions make it difficult to find the exact number of plays in the Chinese theatre of to-day. The total number has been estimated to be more than a thousand, of which four to five hundred are in the "standard repertoire", [6] but only about one hundred and fifty plays are regularly produced in the theatres. In a Japanese collection of the synopses of six hundred Chinese plays [7] four hundred and seven are traced to eighty different novels and ancient dramas, but the percentage of dramas of which the audience know the stories is actually greater, because the study does not include cheap novels which do not enter the libraries. The number of plays based on some of the best known novels may be listed below:

三國志演義　*Romance of the Three Kingdoms* 90

水滸傳　*Water Margin* 20

紅樓夢　*Red Chamber Dream* 9

今古奇觀　*Chin Ku Ch'i Kuan* 6

---

[5] In this discussion the farces and the dramatic dances among the Chinese plays are excluded, because the former, being constantly modified by the comedians, have no stable text and the latter contain only lyrical verse which cannot pass as dramatic dialogue. This does not mean however that some farces are not considered great plays; in fact some farces occupy the honoured position of the last play in a programme（大軸子），齊如山，京劇之變遷，頁五二．

[6] 波多野乾一，支那劇大觀（昭和十九年）一篇四章；青木正兒，中國近世戲曲史，十三章二節．

[7] 波多野乾一，支那劇大觀．

Before discussing the language used in the Chinese dramatic text it is necessary to explain that there are two different styles of written language in China, the "literary" style, an archaic language which has changed little for some two thousand years and which has long been divorced from the spoken Chinese, and the vernacular style, used by popular novelists and ballad-writers. Before the literary "renascence" in the nineteen-twenties led by Hu Shih 胡適 and Ch'en Tu-Hsiu 陳獨秀 all orthodox Chinese literature was written in the literary style, but the Chinese dramas, first written in late Sung dynasty, have always been a popular art, and considered by the *literati* as unworthy of the name of literature, hence the dramas have been written in the vernacular style. Some vestige of the literary style can be found in the verse passages, and in the dialogue for formal occasions in which the Chinese would, in real life, use a mixture of vernacular and literary language, but as a whole the dialogue is in the vernacular style.

Theatre, like other arts, inevitably reflects the morality and the emotional life of its audience. Dramas often bear a moralizing tone because moralization brings comfortable feelings after emotional disturbances. The tendency to moralize is strengthened in China by Confucianism, in which everything from history to divination is given an ethical interpretation. In popular theatres, the edification taught in dramas takes the form of punishment of the wicked and reward of the good, which end the dramas happily, but in the classical dramas moralization is more subtle and sometimes non-existent. Foreigners unfamiliar with the Chinese way of life, however, can easily mistake the moral precepts which govern Chinese life, especially those connected with the sanctity of the family, to be social propaganda, but to the natives the respect for the family has become second nature and the sentiments expressed in the dramas in relation to the family are, to them, natural feelings. In terms of human emotions, the subject matter of all dramas is extremely simple and is the same all over the world: it is the love and hatred, the joys and sorrows and the hopes and fears of man. It is the difference in the social conditions and moral ideas in which these emotions occur that make dramas

---

(8) Some of the Chinese novels which are the sources of Chinese dramas have been translated into European languages: 金瓶梅 *The Golden Lotus,* by Clement Egerton, London, 1939; 封神榜 *Fêng-shên-yen-i, die Metamorphosen der Götter, historisch-mythologischer Roman aus dem chinesischen.* Leiden, E. J. Brill, 1912; 西遊記 *Monkey,* by Arthur Waley, London, 1942; 三國志演義 *Die drei Reiche, Roman aus dem alten China.* G. Kiepenheuer, Berlin, 1940; 水滸傳 *All Men Are Brothers,* by Pearl Buck, New York, 1933; 聊齋志異 *Strange Stories from a Chinese Studio,* by H. A. Giles, Kelly & Walsh, Shanghai, 1908. There are also more recent translations. See M. Davidson, *A List of Published Translations from Chinese into English, French and German,* Ann Arbor, 1952-57.

difficult to understand for foreigners. [9] Moral pre-conceptions naturally influence the relative emphasis placed on the different dramatic themes and, as can be expected, much stress is placed on family obligations in the Chinese dramas. One of the dramas based on such a theme is *A Son Abandoned* 桑園寄子 , in which the hero, while a fugitive in a war, lost contact with his widowed sister-in-law and had to take care of both his own son and his brother's child. In one journey, the two children, who had to be carried, slowed down the progress dangerously and the hero tied his own son to a tree with a letter on him asking whoever might find the son to take pity on him. This he did because he could have another son but his late brother could not and the Chinese audience admired the respect for the brother's memory. Much of the emotional appeal of this play is lost to a European owing to the difference in moral ideas. Next to the family, religion absorbs the serious interests of the Chinese people. There are numerous plays containing elements of popular religion but curiously there have been few dramas on Confucius. [10] Heroism, both in warriors and in great statesmen, is a favourite subject, as shown by the numerous plays of court intrigue and military exploits based on popular novels. The love interest which exists in practically every modern European drama and novel, has, however, only a small place in the Chinese drama. Few plays are devoted to it entirely and in most cases what could be romantic love is absorbed into the family and becomes the less exciting conjugal love.

Attempts to classify the Chinese plays into tragedies and comedies have not been, or are not likely to be, successful, for the simple reason that the Chinese drama was developed under conditions very different from those of the Greek

---

[9] Among the social conditions which make the Chinese way of life and Chinese dramas unfamiliar to the Europeans may be mentioned: the loyalty and the often considerate treatment of the household slaves, the official examinations which give the scholars chances of sudden social distinction, the eagerness of the people to avoid lawsuits and to settle their differences in councils of family elders, the ideal of practical wisdom in Confucianism, the popular belief in ghosts and spirits, the respect for ancestors, the Confucian pacifistic code of conduct, the obligations to parents, the elements of Taoist and Buddhist ideals in the Chinese life, the seclusion of women, the system of marriage by arrangement and the permission of concubinage.

[10] One obscure play on the subject is mentioned in a book on theatrical history:無名氏,顯聖公, 見, 姚燮, 復道人今樂考證, 著錄五, 明院本, 頁十一. The Chinese consider the stage representation of great men as disrespectful to their memory. In Chin dynasty (1115-1234) actors were not permitted to act emperors of the past — 金史, 樂志, 上, "散樂". In 1410, in the reign of Yung Lo, a public notice prohibited representing emperors in the plays. 周貽白, 中國戲劇史, 五章十四節, 頁三二六. This was, in all probability, a political measure at the time when the dynasty was newly changed. In Europe it was also at one time thought that the dignity of kingship was offended when kings were being played by actors — Chambers, *Eliz. Stage*, I. 251. At one time plays on Kuan Yü, a deified warrior of the third century A.D., were banned and actors were arrested for having played him. 齊如山, 京劇之變遷, 頁二一, 十八.

drama and has not been influenced by European dramatic theories. [11] Few of the Chinese plays can be said even to approach the European idea of tragedy, but many would, by western standards, be classified as melodramas. The small dimensions of the plays do not always allow the development towards a climax and a *denouement*; the main interest in them lies, not in the flow of events, but in the deeper apprehension of single dramatic situations. There is usually a crisis in a play, but the dramatic conflict, built up slowly as in the European dramas, is lacking. [12] Dramatic construction and analysis of motives are not the strong points of the Chinese dramatists. The psychology of the characters and the emotions involved in the plays are often simplified and exaggerated. It is the intensely vivid emotions expressed *in the actual performance* that make them deeply moving in spite of the meagre plot.

In order to show the construction of Chinese dramas the play *Li-Ling's Monument* 李陵碑 is outlined as follows:

Scene 1

Four ghosts (mute) lead the spirit of Ch'i-Lang.

Ch'i-Lang, after telling the audience his name, explains that his father who is besieged by the Mongols [13] has sent him for succour, but the commander-in-chief, instead of sending relief, has killed him for some private grievance in the past, and that he is now to warn his father in a dream. He then sings a short aria of more or less the same purport. *Exeunt omnes.*

Scene 2

Stage effect: striking the first hour of the night.

Enter Ling-Kung. He tells (sings) about his anxiety for his son whom he has sent for succour and complains of the cold. (Sleeps).

Stage effect: second hour of the night.

Enter Liu-Lang with a lantern: He (singing) tells the audience that he has been keeping watch. He sees his father asleep and takes off his coat to cover his father.

Stage effect: third hour of the night.

---

[11] cf. the less clear-cut distinction between tragedies and comedies in the Elizabethan dramas.

[12] e.g. in *The Gathering of the Heroes* 羣英會 the crisis is the jealous young general's scheme to kill the strategist K'ung Ming; in *The Joint Court* 三堂會審 it is the prisoner's attempt to move the presiding judge who is her former lover and in *Hsin An Station* 辛安驛 it is the danger of the bridegroom being discovered as a woman disguised.

[13] In this book all the northern foreign tribes will be called Mongolians. It is not worth while to enter the by no means clear-cut classifications of the different tribes.

Enter spirit of Ch'i-Lang. He says (singing) he must wake his father up.

The father, waking, asks (singing) why he looks so sad and wants to embrace him but he stops his father and (singing) explains what happened. He adds that he wants to ask his brother Liu-Lang to be good to his mother now that he has no chance to repay her love but as the dawn is breaking he must leave.   Exit spirit.

The father tells (singing) how he has seen his son in a dream and wakes up Liu-Lang who has fallen asleep.

Liu-Lang, waking, tells (singing) his father that he saw his brother covered with blood in a dream.

The father explains (speaking) that he had the same dream and that he believes it must be Ch'i-Lang's spirit. He sends Liu-Lang to find out what has happened.

Liu-Lang (speaking) refuses to go, because he does not want to leave his father alone but his father (speaking) persuades him in the end to go.

Liu-Lang (singing) warns his father that he should stay in the camp if the Mongols come to challenge him.   Exit Liu-Lang.

The father, after seeing Liu-Lang away, curses (singing) his son's murderer.   Exit the father.

Scene 3

Enter Mongol soldiers and a lieutenant. The lieutenant tells (speaking) his name and says he is on patrol duty, and (enter Liu-Lang) seeing Liu-Lang asks who is coming.

Liu-Lang (speaking) reveals his identity and a fight follows.

Ch'i-Lang's spirit appears to frighten away the Mongols who while retreating say that they will report the apparition to their queen.   *Exeunt omnes.*

Scene 4

Enter Liu-Lang. He says (speaking) he is going to seek relief for his father.   Exit.

Scene 5

Enter Ling-Kung and four soldiers. In a long aria, which is the most important part of the play, the old general tells (singing in *lento*) how though his family have served the country well, in the present war a traitor is made commander-in-chief

74

and he and his sons were sent to the front without proper supporting forces, *(presto)* how his eldest and second sons died in the battles and his third son was crushed to death under a horse, how his fourth and eighth sons were taken prisoners by the Mongols and no news has come from them, how his fifth son took orders in a monastery, how his seventh son (Ch'i-Lang) was murdered and how his sixth son (Liu-Lang) was sent to bring relief. Then *(adagio)* he tells how the commander of the army had led him into a trap, how he found himself surrounded and outnumbered by the Mongols, how fortunately one of his sons came at this time, how they fought a pitched battle, how he thus retreated to this hill, how he has neither food for his soldiers nor grass for his horses and how he has despaired of seeing his son and the relief army.

An old soldier (speaking) complains of the hunger. The general (continues singing) suggests killing the horse.

Second soldier (speaking) complains of the cold. The general suggests burning the tent.

Third soldier sees a wild duck. The general tries to shoot it but the bow breaks; he sighs and (singing) regrets this last piece of bad luck.

Enter messenger to report (speaking) that the horse has died. The general (singing) says he has nothing left and can only seek shelter from the cold. *Exeunt omnes.*

Scene 6

Enter spirit of Su-Wu (a Chinese official of Han dynasty who was kept by the Mongols) who (speaking) tells that he is to receive the spirit of Ling-Kung but first he must show him (Ling-Kung) a phantom temple and monument.

Enter Ling-Kung. He recollects (singing) that once a monk told him he was to die in a siege.

A spoken dialogue with the spirit of Su-Wu follows in which the latter hints that he (Ling-Kung) is near the end of his life.

Ling-Kung, incensed by the suggestion, tries to strike Su-Wu's spirit but both his weapon and the spirit disappear. He says (speaking) that he sees a temple and monument. Finding that the monument is one erected in honour of Li-Ling (also a Chinese who was captured by the Mongols) he makes up his mind (speaking) that he is not to betray his country and that rather than being starved to death, he will dash his brains out there.   Dies.

Enter Mongol lieutenant who (speaking) discovers the dead body and goes to report it.   Exit.

In this play, as in some others (e.g. *The Fisherman's Revenge* 打魚殺家), the mood of the dramas is quickly set in the first few scenes. The economy and effectiveness of the construction is more obvious in watching the actual performance than in reading the script.

CHAPTER IX

THE ACTORS' TRAINING AND PROFESSIONAL LIFE

A Chinese actor is called professional not only because he earns his living by acting but also because he has completed a long and rigorous course of training and apprenticeship. An amateur performing as guest artist (票友) is clearly labelled as such in the bill and the audience make concessions for his lack of acrobatic skill. Amateurs of exceptional talents do sometimes enter the theatrical profession but their lack of formal apprenticeship is remembered throughout their career.

In the local theatres, actors are trained in the players' companies and training starts at the age of eight or ten and lasts about five years. In this period the pupils live in the compounds where the companies are stationed and the companies provide both their keep and their education. When the training is completed the new actors play in the company without salary until the expenses involved in their training are liquidated. In Peking there were two guild schools, Fu Lien Ch'eng富連成 and Jung Ch'un She蓉春社which, before they closed, trained many Chinese actors and did much to preserve the tradition of the Chinese theatre. [1] Both the players' companies and the guild schools have absolute control over the daily conduct of the pupils, in and out of classes, and discipline is strict and punishment heavy. All pupils receive the same instruction in the general stage technicalities but they specialize in particular types of characters or are trained to be musicians according to their individual capabilities. The life of these trainees is hard; for example, they rise before daybreak and even in winter have to practice singing and declamation in early morning against the city wall which they use as a sounding board. [2] Most of the actors trained in this way do not know how to read, they learn the dialogue of the

---

[1] Of the two Fu Lien Ch'eng was the greater and better known. Before it was disbanded in 1943 it had a history of forty-two years and graduated seven classes of actors, musicians and backstage personnel, totalling more than seven hundred people. 梅蘭花，舞台生活四十年（一九五三）五章二.

[2] There are two hours of practice in declamation and one hour in "stage steps" — deportment — every day. 齊如山，京劇之變遷，頁二三.

plays by rote. They must also remember thoroughly the music and the acting that go with the dialogue because there are no prompters in the Chinese theatre. Pupils are better treated and receive better instruction if they can obtain private tutorship from the great actors and in such cases they live in the house of their master, the expenses being then matters decided by mutual agreement in individual cases. Actors who have completed their training sometimes get advanced instructions from great actors, but such instructions are given only to special friends and the master is considered to be doing a great favour in receiving a pupil. The master-and-pupil relationship lasts for the whole lifetime, and there is mutual loyalty between them. The initiation ceremony, with the touching of the forehead on the floor in front of witnesses, is solemn and impressive. Distinct styles of singing are handed down through generations of masters and pupils in this way and students of the theatre keep records of the genealogy. [3] In recent years attempts have been made both in Peking and in Shanghai to maintain dramatic academies more or less along the lines of modern schools but their existence has been sporadic.

The players' companies are organized in several ways but the majority of them are financed and organized by the star actors (hence the form of address "Proprietor so-and-so" usually applied to the great actors). There is often close comradeship between the star and his fellow actors, many of whom may have been fellow students in his training days and have played with him for a long time. In difficult times the stars, who usually have investments elsewhere, help the company. In some cases the company is financed by either patrons, or amateurs, or managers, or proprietors who are experienced in the business but are not actors themselves and sometimes are several financiers may be the joint proprietors of a company.

A company is normally organized as follows:

The Proprietor (1) 承班人 is the highest executive of the company and usually supplies the capital. Important matters of the company, such as the employment of great actors and change of place of performance are, however, decided in a council of proprietor and managers.

The Leader (1) 領班人 the official head of the company who is responsible to the police for the company and is usually chosen for his resourcefulness in legal matters. He is free from internal affairs so that in case of arrest the company need not cease to function.

The General Manager (1) 總管事人 who is in charge of choosing the plays for particular performances and casting. He must have a good knowledge of the capabilities of all the actors and remember the parts each has played in the past few performances in order to avoid unequal load. He has to

---

[3] See 徐慕雲, 梨園影事 charts following the "masks".

78

arrange the programmes with consideration for the wishes of the star actors and the capabilities of the minor actors, as well as the programmes in other theatres on or near the same day and possible similarities between the plays in the same programme. Care has also to be taken that two dramas connected with the same story do not appear in the same programme in the reverse order.

The Assistant Managers (4 to 8) 小管事 who are in charge of separate types of actors such as those who play masked characters, those who play female parts, etc. Whenever necessary they take parts in the performances or give last minute instructions to other actors. They are usually busy in getting the players ready for the plays.

The Controller (1) 催場人 usually one of the assistant managers. His duty is to adjust the time of performance by curtailing and padding the plays.

The Master of Revels (1) 抱牙笏人 who passes the list of plays among the guests at private performances for them to choose.

First Class Actors: 頭等脚

Old men	2
Virtuous women	2
Beautiful women	2
Comedians	2
Masked characters	1 or 2
Warriors	1 or 2
Young men	1 or 2

Second Class Actors: 二路脚

Old men	2 or 3
Virtuous women	1 or 2
Old women	1 or 2
Young men	1 or 2
Masked characters	2 or 3
Comedians	8 or 9
Warriors	2 or 3

Third Class Actors: 三路脚

Male characters in general	7 or 8
Female characters in general	10 or more
Masked characters	6 to 9
Young men	2 or 3
Old women	1 or 2
Comedians	4 or 5
Male warriors	2 or 3
Female warriors	2 or 3

Animals and gods, being mute, are distributed among the minor actors and there is a custom of which type of actors play which gods. Unsavoury parts, such as pigs, dogs, snakes, ghosts, etc., get extra pay.

The Acrobats (8) 上下手 for the acrobatic parts in military plays. One of the eight is the leader and spokesman.

The Minor Warriors (20 to 30)武行 for military plays.

The Flag-bearers龍套. These are mute and are divided into teams of four. The two leaders in each team know the stage business and the rest follow them. There is a system whereby a sub-contractor takes so much wages from the company and is responsible for supplying all the supernumeraries needed. He may hire ordinary porters and train them on the spot [4] or in an emergency ask some of the third-class actors to play the flag-bearers for him. [5]

Unpaid Actors 效力之脚 who play for practice.

Guest Actors 外折脚 from other companies for special parts.

Pupils 學生 to play children without pay.

The Musicians: 場面(They play in three shifts in a day's performance).

    The Percussion players: 武場

Drummers	3 or 4
Gong players	2
"Small Gong" players	2

    The String and Wind players: 文場

Fiddlers	3 or 4
Lute players	2
Flautists	2
Sheng players	2

    (Most of the musicians can play more than one instrument).

The Stage Hand (1) 監場人 who shifts properties on the stage. He has to know the plays thoroughly.

The Wardrobe Men (6 or more) 管衣箱人 who take care of the costume and keep it ready for use. They also help in dressing.

The Head-gear Men (2) 管盔箱人 to take care of hats and caps.

---

[4] cf. "When the man cried to the boys, 'Who will go and be a devil, and he shall see the play for nothing?' then he [Killigrew] would go in, and be a devil upon the stage, and so get to see plays." Pepys, *Diary,* quoted in Lawrence, *Those Nut-Cracking Elizabethans,* 46 .

[5] Originally these were played by minor actors. 清逸, 戲中角色舊規矩, 戲劇叢刊, 三期.

The Property Man (1) 管旗包箱人 to take care of large properties. He also blows the trumpet at the end of the play.

Small Properties Man (1) 管後塲棹人 to take care of cups, pens, etc.

Stage Hands at the Stage Doors (2) 打門簾人 to lift the flaps on the entrance and exit door.

Grease Paint Man (1)管彩匣人. He is usually a contractor.

The Messengers (2 or 3) 催戲人 mainly for calling the actors at their homes and getting them to come to the theatre in time.

Other personnel in the company are: man in charge of tea and wash basins, labourers for moving large properties, accountant and men for checking the "take" at the box office (against possible fraud by the owners of the theatre).

Great actors have their own hairdresser, personal manager and wardrobe manager all of whom are paid by the company.

Companies are not always as large as the above list would suggest because many minor actors can take roles other than what they normally play, for example, old women can play eunuchs, middle-aged men can play masked characters, etc. In 1864 the personnel for the San Ch'ing Company 三慶班 was as follows:

Old men	20
Young men	9
Masked characters	11
Comedians	8
Warriors	8
Old women	5
Musicians	16
Wardrobe man, etc.......................	7 [6]

When an actor joins a company he gives the General Manager a list of the parts in standard dramas that he can play. [7] He is obliged to play any of the parts on the list when he is cast in it, but he need not play a part not on the list and if he does one of the assistant managers would teach it to him. Before the performance of a play there is a "reading rehearsal" 對戲 in which actors check their version of the dialogue against each other (see the preceding chapter on the lack of uniformity of text) and the principal actor decides which version to use. There are no other

---

[6] 齊如山, 戲班, 五三至五四.

[7] In the Chinese theatre to be able to play a part means to be able to play it without rehearsal and at short notice. Each company has a list of plays from which guests at private performances may choose those they would like to see. In 1900 the T'ung Ch'ing Company 同慶班 listed one hundred and twenty-six plays in their repertoire.

rehearsals. One of the most important persons in the company is the "bag of plays" 戲包袱 who can play almost any part in any play equally indifferently.

Plays to be performed in the coming day are written on a thin tablet [8] on the Manager's desk [9] in the green room and the plays being performed are written on a notice board. [10] When the performance is about to begin the percussion group of the orchestra play a long and loud introduction by which the actors, wardrobe manager and hairdressers, etc., can get ready. This introduction may sound monotonous to the uninitiated but it is musically quite interesting because it consists of a series of different "tunes". There were at one time more than a hundred different percussion "tunes" but some of them have been lost.

The "take" at the box office is divided between the theatre and the company, the latter getting from seventy to eighty percent according to relative prestige. [11] This may be augmented, for particularly good companies, by a small percentage from the box office for the "special expenses" 加錢 of the company with the remainder to be divided according to the agreed percentage or by "guarantee fee" 定籤 which is paid when the contract is accepted by the company. Theatre owners on their part can charge the "tea money" 茶錢 over and above the usual admission and this is not divided with the players. In busy seasons the players can make extra money by playing in two or three theatres at the same time. Amateurs who want to appear as guest artists pay the company a small amount for admittance and this money is used on the incense and candles for the Patron God or a feast for the whole company. In some private performances specially high fees are paid in order to provide for the best possible performance. [12] A representative of the company is first sent to discuss the programme and the cast with the patron and great actors from other companies are invited to join in the performance. Such performances are sometimes arranged for trade guilds and guilds of merchants from the same province. A bonus can be expected from the patron and tips from the appreciative or vain guests when the performance is connected with celebrations and one way of getting these is to dance, at strategic moments, the "promotion dance" 跳加官, a mute dance by a masked actor which stands for the compliments of the company. Command performances in palaces for royalty and the nobility were tipped; there was no agreed price.

An actor who joins a company temporarily, as when on tour, is paid a sum for the period he plays with it, but the regular member of the company is paid his daily

[8] 牙笏.

[9] 帳棹.

[10] 戲圭.

[11] In Ch'ing dynasty owners of theatres were not allowed to be proprietors of the players' companies. 齊如山, 戲班, 頁六七.

[12] 堂會.

salary for those days in which the company is employed. [13] Great actors get, besides their own salaries, what are nominally travelling expenses and salaries for their personal assistants and the most popular actors may even demand a percentage from the box office "take" over and above their salaries. Old actors and those who have lost their popularity for one reason or another do not accept salaries lower than they used to get but instead agree to take a percentage of the nominal pay according to the percentage of seats sold. Actors invited from other companies for emergencies do not work for an agreed salary but are always presented with a handsome "gift" afterwards. When business is bad and the proprietor is unable to pay all hands, he still pays the smaller salaries in full because in the Chinese theatre those who earn them live from hand to mouth, but he keeps what is left with the agreement of the first and second class actors because if distributed it would amount to only a small fraction of the large salaries. [14]

Although some companies own their costumes, most hire them from special stores and this constitutes a considerable expense for the proprietor. Apart from costumes and salaries he also has to pay for the replacement or hire of stage properties, advertisement (if that is agreed upon between him and the theatre-owners), make-up, paints (for masks) and musical instruments, the last three items usually through sub-contractors.

The actors' life in the theatre is regulated by many religious duties and taboos. Some of the taboos are obviously sensible rules based on common sense but others may have a religious origin. To ensure orderliness in the green room there is an established rule that the different types of actors, when resting, sit on different specified boxes. The contents of the different boxes are strictly standardized and there are definite places for small properties, grease paint, combs, jewellery, powder, rouge, etc. It is forbidden for actors on stage to look at the green room at any time and for those in the green room to applaud. Actors taking female parts are not allowed to take off their clothes after they have completed their coiffure. While on stage actors must cover the mistakes made by others in the same play (those who have a bad reputation in this respect cannot easily get a job) and they must not laugh, or change details of the dialogue and stage business, especially in the "self-introduction", thereby making it difficult for the other players to follow. If the musicians make some mistake the players may not look at the orchestra or stamp their foot but must wait till the play is over and then complain to the manager. The drummer must be the last to leave the stage, unless he is relieved by a new drummer, because he is the conductor and the orchestra cannot play without him. In case of

---

[13] This is new practice which allows the actor to change companies often; the old custom was to pay a yearly salary and to add "travelling expenses" whenever the company is engaged. Actors then remain with the company for at least one year.

[14] In such cases the proprietor has to say something nice to those who are not paid, and in stage slang it is called "making others stick (to him) with his mouth water" 吐沫黏人 .

dispute on mistakes in the performance, the drummer is the most important witness in the council of managers set up to deal with grievances.

It is easy to see the reasons for the regulations just mentioned but there are others which can not be easily explained, for example, the emperor's crown must not be exposed to or put together with the crowns of foreign and rebel kings; when they are both in the green room one is covered with red cloth; otherwise, it is believed, there would be quarrels in the company. Weapons belonging to deities; including deified warriors, and the ensign 大纛旗 , the severed head, the beard of the God of Fire, the three-pronged spear 叉 and other tabooed objects may not be handled in the green room except being taken to and from the stage. The umbrella must never be seen in the green room, when required it is assembled on the stage (like the taboo for the three-pronged spear this is based on a pun, the Chinese word for "umbrella" sounds similar to that for "disbanding"). (15) The actors observe these taboos for religious awe and, in cases where the religious basis is not apparent, for "auspiciousness".

The patron god of the theatre is called *Lao Lang Shen* 老郎神 (Old Lord God) or *Tsu Shih* 祖師 (The Founder) whom Arlington suspected to be Emperor Ming Huang but Prof. Ch'i Ju-Shan has traced to an ancient god of music. (16) His image is placed in the green room and joss-sticks are constantly burned in front of it. Actors entering and leaving the theatre each day bow to him and important actors burn new joss-sticks just before they start their performance. Second in importance to him is the doll used for the baby in the plays, called The God of Happiness 喜神. On stage he may be treated in whatever way the action requires such as being pinched and thrown about, but in the green room he is treated as a god. When he is in the property trunk and if there is no image of the patron god (as when the company is on tour) the actors bow to the trunk containing him. He is always placed with his face downward, otherwise actors would have to bow each time they pass him. Actors playing warriors also worship a god of war called Wu Ch'ang 武猖神 (17) and the acrobats worship the Monkey God 孫悟空 . Beside these the profession also worship the twelve gods of music whose images flank the Old Lord God on two sides (they are deified musicians of Chinese history and legends), the Nine Emperors (legendary inventors of clothes, houses, etc.) the deified Emperor Ming Huang, Kuan Kung 關公 (an ancient warrior; the actors call him Lord 老爺), Yüeh Fei 岳飛 (an ancient patriot); Pao Cheng 包拯 (a legendary judge) and a god called *Erh Lang* 二郎神 .

The actors' annual holiday is the eighteenth day of the third lunar month. On

---

(15) For other taboos, see 齊如山, 戲班, 頁三四至四十·

(16) See Arlington, *The Chinese Drama*, p. 54., 齊如山, 戲班, 頁二八·

(17) Originally consisting of five war-gods, see 齊如山, 戲班, 頁二九·

this day the image of the patron god of the theatre is taken, amid music, to a large restaurant where the company is assembled for worship and feasting. It is also on this day that raises in salary, new additions to the company, resignations, etc., are decided upon. (Back stage personnel, such as wardrobe managers, hair-dressers, etc., have their holiday the third day of the fifth lunar month). About the twentieth day of the last month of the year each company give a special performance, with temporary additions from other companies, and from that performance until the New Year there will be no performances.

On New Year's Day a ritual is performed on the stage at the beginning of a special performance as follows:

Four gods 靈官, each with a whip, perform a dance on the stage and before their exit burn the whips, which contain fireworks, at the four corners of the stage.

Four pages with sweeps enter and clean the stage by sweeping upstage.

The "Promotion Dance" 跳加官 follows during which a table is brought in, with two trays of gold and silver billets on it (the billets are made of paper) and two red paper scrolls which are sealed. The dancer opens one scroll which shows "Auspicious Beginning of the Year's Business" written on it.

The god of wealth enters in green gown, wearing gold mask and gold ornaments on the crown, and holding a huge gold billet, dances towards the table, sees the paper scrolls and acts as if he regrets that he has come too late, then he puts the gold billet on the table and opens the other scroll showing "Good Luck in All Our Endeavours" on it.

The trays are then passed by stage hands to two attendants in the auditorium who take them to the main gallery and post the red paper scrolls on the pillars. [18]

The extensive religious belief among theatrical circles is probably due to the low intellectual level and the unstable and often precarious living which makes the actors seek consolation in faith. The worship of the doll, for example, appears to be due to primitive awe for images, because no satisfactory explanation has been found for it. [19] The actors apparently believe in their partial metamorphosis when they play the parts of gods and deified warriors and take precautions so that the change of identity is not complete. When wearing a removable mask (only worn by deities) they do not look at the mirror or speak, and before they change into the costume they must take a bath. The mask itself is never exposed except when worn: the actor takes it off as he leaves the stage and covers it with his sleeve as he enters the green room. No masks may be handled except by the actors using them. There is also a

[18] 齊如山, 戲班, 頁三四, 三五.
[19] See 齊如山, 戲班, 頁三十 for three possible explanations.

religious awe for dreams, and actors never say the word "dream" but use a substitute term when they must say it. [20]

The low intellectual level of the actors together with a certain amount of loose morality among them make the social status of the theatrical profession in China very low. [21] The tendency towards laxity is probably present among the actors in every country in the world, being a natural trend under the combined pressure of precarious livelihood and temporary fame. In China the stigmatization and the low moral standard form a vicious circle. [22] The actors are therefore considered a class separate from the rest of the society and as a result they develop a jealous solidarity among themselves. Amateurs do not enter the profession unless they are quite sure of public acclaim and even then they would seek connections in the profession first. To enter the profession is always a serious step to take and once in it it is very difficult to seek other work. It is to be remembered that the position of the fine arts in the Chinese culture is very different from that in the European culture. The Chinese *literati,* whose taste had an important influence on the classical theatre, consider the fine arts as elegant pastime and take them as vocations only under extreme pressure of circumstances. All Chinese poets, calligraphists and painters are amateurs who are either officials in the government or scholars of independent means. Musicians and actors are considered as artisans rather than artists, and self-respecting Chinese scholars do not even associate with them.

It is difficult to believe that the actors are by nature any worse than the rest of the Chinese people. Their hard life must have made what is called respectability appear unimportant to them and short termed fame and fortune would add to the temptation to reckless enjoyment. They do not know how to choose vices which are less disapproved by society and their work makes their vices as well as their merits more conspicuous. There can be little doubt, however, that many of them are drug addicts and some of them catamites, and that most of them are by character more artisans than artists.

The private lives of some of the great actors in recent times may be related here:

---

[20] Theatre seems to be a fertile place for slang because theatrical slang was also common in T'ang dynasty — see 崔令欽，教坊記，七段.

[21] In the application for the licence to form new companies there has to be the clause, ". . . there are no criminals or people of unknown past among us". In Ch'ing dynasty Manchus were not permitted to become actors 齊如山，戲班，頁六十.

[22] For the custom of calling young female impersonators to attend at dinner parties (often connected with further associations) see Arlington, *op. cit.,* p. 39 ff. According to Prof. Ch'i Ju-Shan the custom started in this way: In the early days of Peking dramas, players live in compounds and apprentices normally live with them, but some good actors have their own homes and favoured apprentices live with them for greater comfort and better education. When the master had friends for dinner some of the pupils would join the party because they were practically members of the family. 齊如山，戲班，頁四二至四三.

"Wang Kuei-Fen 汪桂芬 lost his singing voice at fifteen and later became the fiddler for the famous Ch'eng Ch'ang Keng 程長庚. After Ch'eng's death he was persuaded to try singing and much to his own surprise found he had his voice again. Having followed Ch'eng's singing with the fiddle for many years he was the only singer who could imitate Ch'eng's style. He, like Ch'eng, was admired for his simplicity of melody and beauty of tone. His interest in the theatre was, however, mainly in what he could get out of it, for he sang only when his purse dictated it and whenever he had more than sufficient for his livelihood, he would spend his time among courtezans. Neither wealth nor the sense of duty could move him. He constantly ignored the offers of the nobility some of whom had to resort to threats of force in order to persuade him to a performance and even then he sometimes slipped away without performing. He died of dissipation". 王夢生，梨園佳話，三章.

"Ho Kuei-Shan 何桂山, called the 'steel throat', not only had a powerful voice but was also the innovator of many details of the dance of supernatural characters. By nature impatient and fond of wine and women, he would not wait long in the theatre for his part and usually demanded immediate work when he arrived at the theatre to work. Sometimes he was fitted into the earlier part of the programme to play among inferior actors but he did not mind. With the money he got, he disappeared with young female impersonators into the notorious deserted park in the city". 王夢生，梨園佳話，三章.

"Ch'eng Ch'ang Keng 程長庚 was honoured as the founder of the Peking drama because of his purity of style. He was the proprietor of a company, but took a small salary so that lesser actors could not ask for more and thereby ruin the company financially. When business was bad he would sing twice in a programme and this never failed to attract a crowd. He helped the aged and destitute in the profession and taught the young as if they were his own relations. At a performance in the palace, the Empress Dowager was pleased and wanted to give him an official rank. When the eunuch came to fetch him he said, I thought actors are not allowed to have official ranks', but the eunuch answered, 'This is royal command; you better go to thank her'. Since then other actors have obtained official ranks but they got them through application and spent sums of money to get them". 王夢生，梨園佳話，三章；齊如山，京劇之變遷，頁五四.

"Yang San 楊三 and Ko Ssu 葛四 were both good comedians and there was no room for both of them in Peking. At the suggestion of the former Ko, who was the better comedian, left Peking and made a name for himself in Honan and Shantung. In his old age Ko was blind and continued to act but he would not enter Peking because of his promise to his friend. Even after he became blind, his skill was much acclaimed. He could carry another player on his back and run about on the stage and few in the audience knew he was blind. People who knew his history often offered him employment when they knew he needed work and would tip him handsomely". [23] 王夢生, 梨園佳話, 三章.

The low status of actors and musicians has a long tradition in China; musicians were not better treated in T'ang dynasty than they are now:

"A retired official had a villa outside the city and near a river. While fishing he saw something about five or six feet long in the water with a piece of silk around it and asked his servants to pull it to the shore. It turned out to be a coffin. He opened it and found a girl in rich clothes with a silk scarf on her neck. When the scarf was removed the girl could breathe. He took her home and had to nurse her for ten days before she could speak. She said, amid tears of gratitude, that she was a court musician but having displeased the emperor was ordered to be strangled to death. The silk on the coffin was in fact the gift of her fellow musicians. The retired official wanted to marry her but she said she was a lutist and would serve him as a household musician. She told him how he could buy her lute, he bought it and would enjoy her performances late at night to avoid discovery. One fine evening, after having too much wine, she played loud in the garden and was overheard by a court attendant who recognized the virtuosity and he went to report to the emperor. The emperor Wen Tsung 文宗 (reigned 827-841) repented and was glad to have her back in his court". 段安節, 樂府雜錄, "琵琶" 四款.

"Emperor Hsuan Tsung 宣宗 (reigned 847-860) was fond of the wind instruments and composed a tune himself. There were several places at which the rhythm was not right. When the emperor first tried it himself on an instrument he ordered a musician to play the beats [on a percussion instrument]. The beats went wrong and the emperor looked angrily at the musician. That night the musician died of fear". [24]

Of recent times,

"An actress named Yü Chuang 余莊 who played woman warriors had a beautiful face and exquisite skill but was proud and unsociable. She was much loved by the public for her portrayal of heroic womanhood. After a royal command performance in the palace in the reign of Te Tsung 德宗 (1875-1909) she arranged to have herself reported dead and never

---

[23] It is possible that Ko was only partially blind.

[24] *Ibid.*

appeared again". 王夢生, 梨園佳話, 三章.

In 1917, T'an Hsin-P'ei 譚鑫培, then retired, declined the offer to play in a private performance ordered by a military governor then in the city. After the second refusal the governor went to his house and used violence to force him to go to the governor's house and there insulted and abused him and threatened to kill him if he did not play. When he played many in the audience wept for pity. He died soon afterwards. He was one of the greatest singers of the Chinese theatre. (*Asia* — Journal of the American Asiatic Association — Vol. XVIII, No. 4, April, 1918. F. S. Williams, "The Chinese Theatre").

All in all, the actor's lot is a hard one. As the critic Wang Meng-Sheng said of their life from their apprenticeship onwards:

> "Every morning he has to get up early to train his voice by singing and declaiming loudly; at midday, he has the dramas read to him so that he can learn the dialogue by heart and at night he deliberately sleeps in damp beds in order to catch a minor skin disease which would make his body itchy and would keep him awake so that he can learn the dialogue by heart. Then the musician will teach him to sing by leading him with the tune on the fiddle and teachers will instruct him, behind closed doors, on acting, in small details, like laughs, arm movements, etc. When he makes mistakes he is whipped. After three months he is to try on the stage and after six years he is graduated, but for lack of a good voice or musical sense, there are not five pupils who become actors out of ten. Those who fail become supplementary players, the whole lot of text learned by heart wasted, or become back-stage personnel, or personal attendants of great actors, or stage hands". 王夢生, 梨園佳話, 一章, "科班各項名色"

There is a Theatre Guild in Peking. It was originally housed in the Temple of Loyalty 精忠廟 and was financed by the players' companies. Its purpose was to help the players in their applications for licences which were required for the formation of new companies and the dissolution of old ones. In 1914 the guild was called Society of Musical Culture 正樂育化會 and was financed by a small tax on the tickets. In 1928 it was replaced by the Society of Mutual Help in the Pear Garden 梨園公益會 financed by subscriptions and special performances and later by one dearest ticket from each performance.

Part II

The Artistry of the Chinese Theatre

CHAPTER X

CONVENTIONS AND THE DRAMATIC ILLUSION

In this and the following eight chapters an attempt is made to *explain* the Chinese theatre to the western readers. From what it said in the preface and the introduction, it should already be obvious that the object of this book is not mere documentation. Indeed, it is doubtful whether even a book written expressly with documentation in view would be read with such a pure purpose, because the readers, having all had some experience of theatrical appreciation in one form or another, are bound to try to understand the particular theatre described in the book.

The tone of these explanatory chapters is influenced by two considerations: that they must be written with a certain type of readers in view and that a modicum of sympathy is the pre-requisite for even the basic understanding. It will be helpful to discuss these two considerations first.

The full spectrum of the readers of this book can range from scholars expertly knowledgeable in the history of the western theatre and the diversity of the modern movements in it, to the casually curious reader, intelligent but not necessarily well informed on the western theatrical traditions. The tone and the contents of this and the following chapters depend critically on which part of this spectrum of readers the author chooses to address his explanations to. Once the choice is made, the interests of those on both sides of the band of model readers are inevitably sacrificed. Those of a more catholic taste and a more panoramic view will have to put up with what appears pedestrian to them, and those insufficiently informed on the history of the western theatre may feel inconvenienced by certain tacit assumptions and undefended assertions.

Since the majority of those who read this book are unlikely to be specialists, this and the few chapters that follow are written against the background of the popular western conception of the theatre. The historian may be aware of the fact that, strictly speaking, naturalism is an out-of-date movement which occurred in the last century and that the modern developments in the West have surpassed it with a virile diversity of style and objective; nevertheless, for the ordinary reader, the habit of theatrical enjoyment is predominently influenced by naturalism. If for nothing else, the popularization of theatrical entertainment through the cinema and television has most effectively brought about a universal and probably subconscious expectation of realism. Such a tendency is really inevitable, considering how popularization of the theatre must depend on the instant appreciation of a massive audience too impatient to learn any conventions and unequipped for sophisticated rhetoric. The Chinese theatre is, unfortunately, at the opposite extreme of naturalism. Hence, in the course of explaining the Chinese theatre to the western readers, doubts are unavoidably cast on and limitations shown in the naturalistic tradition. To those whose understanding and taste have outgrown naturalism, such doubts and exposé are of course quite superfluous.

The appreciation of art always involves mental habits. One does not realize this until one is suddenly confronted with unfamiliar works of a foreign country or of a hitherto unknown period. The experienced art-lover knows how to suspend his judgement and admit ignorance; the inquisitive would search for a link with the past experience; but the over-confident would measure them with what he has accepted as the standards of value and, when he finds the unfamiliar works incompatible with these standards, reject them.

The aims of an art vary from time to time and from one country to another. Whether or not the aims of a particular school appeal to one depends on individual temperament and upbringing: many people are indifferent to one school of poetry or another, but one cannot be sure of one's love or indifference until some understanding of the art has been acquired. In order to understand it one has to learn its idioms, and to become thoroughly familiar with them.

Learning artistic appreciation requires direct experience but understanding the artistry first would facilitate appreciation.

Those who approach the Chinese theatre with no knowledge of theatrical traditions other than realism are tempted to think that it is crude and primitive. Both Chinese and foreigners have been severely critical of it. It is not surprising that they have, seeing that in practically every respect the Chinese theatre is opposite to the realistic theatre and that they judged it by the standards of realism. In the realistic theatre a programme consists of only one self-contained and self-explanatory drama with a beginning and an end which the audience see for the first time, but in the Chinese theatre several separate dramatic episodes well known to the audience are presented together and each of them belongs to a different story. In the former, the subject is often based on contemporary life and even if it is not the characters act and speak as the audience would do, but in the latter contemporary life is rarely, if ever, dramatized and the characters act and speak in a way completely different from the manners of the audience. In the former, if a certain action such as death or lunacy cannot be reproduced, it is convincingly imitated but in the latter such action is indicated rather than imitated and there is little effort to disguise the pretence.

The realistic theatre to-day has the quality of a magic lantern and peep show. It is a darkened hall with an opening on a wall covered by a curtain. When the performance begins, the curtain, which functions like a shutter, is raised revealing a well lit box built, decorated and furnished to resemble a specific locality, often a room. At the same time absolute silence is imposed on the audience who keep very still in their seats. The actors and actresses move and speak among themselves in the well lit box, but never speak to the audience whose presence they ostensibly do not notice. Some events are supposed to have happened in the box and the audience come to watch and overhear them by removing the shutter at the end of the auditorium. Intrusion of the magic box by audience or stage hands during performance is unthinkable and almost sacrilegious and to show any part of the unadorned stage is considered unforgivable. The uncanny stillness of the audience and the absolute isolation of the actors would suggest to an ignorant observer that the audience are partaking an occult rite and that the performance is a conjured vision. Only after the performance is over when the audience applaud the actors and when the actors bow to the audience is there any indication that the drama is mere pretence, that the space behind the curtain is a stage and that the actors belong to the same world as the audience.

All dramatic representation involves conventions, and the realistic theatre is no exception. Convention is merely the understood allowable disparity between the dramatic representation and reality and it is ineradicable because no theatre can be exactly like real life. There are many conventions in the realistic theatre which are so common that one does not notice them. The lighting, for instance, is seldom, if ever, realistic. Most theatres employ foot lights but one can hardly think of any place where such lighting is naturally used. The stage is normally lit by a complicated system of lights capable of flexible control, but no such lighting systems can be found outside theatres. The apparatus is no doubt used to imitate the lighting condition in different times of the day and at different places, but the disparity between the stage and the place represented is usually quite conspicuous if one looks for the difference, for one thing, the light intensity is usually greater than in ordinary rooms in order that the spectators far from the stage can see it well. The reason why people do not look for the difference is that they have tacitly agreed to ignore it, in other words, they have accepted the convention. Again, the voice and the movements of the actors are far from being natural; if they are, actors should need no training. In real life people normally talk so as to be heard by a few people only, but actors on stage, wherever they are supposed to be, must talk so loud that the whole theatre can hear them clearly. In real life people often remain silent for long periods of time; on stage, periods of complete silence, if any, must be short. In

95

real life people sit or stand in every direction; on stage they mostly face the audience. There are many other unrealistic details that one can, but normally does not try to find in the realistic theatre but they are slight in comparison with the basic convention involved in the front curtain and the stage. When the stage is sealed off by the curtain its locality may change and long periods of time are sometimes supposed to pass before the curtain is lifted again. These conventions are so deeply ingrained in most people's minds that to question their realism sounds facetious. However, conventions become noticeable when realism is pushed to the extreme. When a death scene is acted with uncomfortable realism, as is sometimes done, the whole effort is contradicted a few minutes later when the supposedly dead person walks to the front of the curtain to take the bow. If the illusion that the drama is real is the object, such convention should be considered as the most wasteful way of undoing in a few seconds what takes hours to create. Taking the bow is not absolutely necessary, and it is done because the convention of the front curtain is so thoroughly accepted that no incongruity is felt. The boundary between the stage and the auditorium, the line dividing the world of the drama and the world of the audience, is a convention which no effort has as yet been successful in evading. When the stage is set for a room, this boundary is the notorious "missing fourth wall", which Evreinov cynically suggested building at all costs. The suggestion seems to have been taken in earnest because sometimes a mutilated fire place is built on it, presumably to establish its presence, with the unfortunate effect of underlining its absence or at best establishing its transparence. The inconsistency of the "missing fourth wall" always exists: if the stage is a street the houses on the side nearer to the audience are missing, if it is a court yard, either the entrance or a wall has to be counted as missing, and so on. An attempt was once made to intensify realism when the stage represented the waterfront by flooding the orchestra pit to represent the river, but at least those in the front rows must be keenly aware of the fact that all the scenic designer did was to push the boundary a few feet towards the audience. Even supposing this boundary can somehow be effaced, the fact remains that a room or a street is never connected to rows of seats filled with silent spectators. The presence of the spectators, which is the basic feature of the theatre, is itself unrealistic.

Even the cinema, perhaps the most convincing mode of representation, involves many conventions. Few people notice them, but those who deliberately direct their attention to them can find the films to be "documentaries of movie stars at work" as some critic put it. All the conventions peculiar to the film become recognizable when one watches the reaction of people who see it for the first time. They not only cannot follow the story but are also surprised and amused by the peculiarities of the camera eye. To them a close-up shot of a face is not a closer look but a bigger head like those one sees in the circus and the carnival and when the camera moves towards the object they see the object moving towards them. It is not clear to them that an aeroplane flying or a ship sailing means some one (but who?) has travelled from one place to another (but where?) and that pages of a calendar dropping by themselves means time has passed. They do not understand how some consecutive shots mean simultaneous events, as in a chase, whereas others are supposed to be a long time apart, or the why and wherefrom of the music in love and battle scenes, or the juxtaposition of music, sound effect and conversation at the same time. In fact most camera positions, camera angles and movements are unrealistic: no real spectator can move steadily beside a galloping horse or be just in front of its legs or be in front of the wind shield of a moving car, or be at one spot in one moment and several yards away in the next, or safely see a building falling down on him, and so on.[1]

Even if the representation can be made to look exactly like real events, by using, for instance, actual sites and real people, as has been tried, no audience with a healthy mind can be convinced. When one goes to see drama one knows it is mere pretence; theatre is, by its own nature, artificial. Even for a perfectly realistic theatre one convention is still necessary, namely, the "suspension of disbelief".

So far as convention is concerned, the only difference between the various types of theatre is the difference of degree. To a certain extent the disparity between reality and its representation can be lessened and conventions accordingly decreased. To those accustomed to the realistic theatre any disparity above the customary amount is disturbing and can ruin, to them, the merit of the theatre, but to those who are used to less exact reproductions, the essential pretence involved in all drama is so far-reaching in its implications that unrealistic details hardly matter at all. Conventions, once accepted, are no longer felt to be such; they appear natural and do not distract the mind from other matters in the play. It is just a matter of habits. Those who accept the fundamental pretence involved in the drama, as all theatre-lovers must, and yet object to unrealistic details in some types of theatre only need to extend their mental habits in order to feel satisfied.

When a character in the Chinese drama is killed by poison he struggles and twists in agony and then collapses to the floor but after a few seconds he gets up by himself and walks into the green room. The audience do not in the least think that there is anything incongruous in this, no more, at any rate, than the western audience would do when Hamlet, dead and borne away by the soldiers, stands in front of the curtain to acknowledge the applause. It is true that Chinese actors open imaginary doors and cannot see each other if they are separated by the imaginary wall, but to the mind of the Chinese audience the wall is real, though absent, like the "missing fourth wall" of the realistic stage. It is sufficient for a Chinese actor speaking an aside to hide behind his sleeve to make him inaudible to the other

---

[1] cf. R. Williams and M. Orrom, *Preface to Film* (1954), 59 ff.

actors. The Chinese audience accept the pretence unquestioningly that he is then not heard by the other actors on the stage just as the western audience would believe that the dialogue spoken on the realistic stage is not heard by actors off stage even though they know that some of these are waiting for their cue behind the scenery.

With a type of theatre in which scenery can be altogether dispensed with, the problem of the purpose of scenery becomes significant. Most people would perhaps say that it is for creating the dramatic illusion. The dramatic illusion, however, is never complete, however realistic the scenery may be: no one except the pathological is ever deceived by a realistic stage. The pathological, moreover, does not need any scenery to induce a delusion: in a village performance near Soochow a man once stabbed and killed an actor who was playing the villain. It would be unpleasant as well as unsafe if the audience were stirred to behave as if the drama were real; in any case, most people would affirm that that is not the object of the theatre. Either the audience believe in the reality of the staged events or they do not, and it is obvious that they do not. Dramatic illusion is in fact merely the willingness of the audience to pretend for the time being that what goes on in the drama is real. The pretence always requires imagination to support it, if one suppresses one's imagination one can see even the moving picture as a "documentary of film stars at work" and the most realistic stage will leave one cold. On the other hand, the barest stage can become transformed if the audience cooperate. The purpose of scenery is to help the imagination of those who are addicted to it. To an amazing degree, the Chinese audience can exercise their imagination practically unaided.

Besides, the more one pretends the more pretentious one becomes when the pretence fails. This is why mishaps on the naturalistic stage are more disconcerting than on the platform stage.

CHAPTER XI

THE MOOD OF THE UNADORNED STAGE

The lack of realism in the Chinese theatre is a legacy of the past, but it has been a characteristic of the Chinese theatre for so long that it has a profound effect on the artistic aims of the Chinese drama. The fact that Chinese actors often deliberately try to destroy the realistic illusion which some dialogue creates shows that realism is not merely alien to the aims of the Chinese theatre but is indeed opposed to them. The lack of realism is not an accidental vestige of the primitive theatre but is now an important means to achieve the aims which make the Chinese theatre distinctive.

In *The Story of the Black Pot* 烏盆記 [1] the murderer was leading his needy creditor through the new house built with the plunder. To impress the visitor, he pointed out each part of the house as they passed it: "You have just passed through the main gate; now you enter the courtyard; this is the portico; this is the flower veranda and now see the main hall". The visitor, lifting his head, replied, "I don't see anything, except a stage". The Chinese playwright, one may think, afraid that the names of the different parts of the house may conjure up in the mind of the audience a visual image, tries to nullify this effect by reminding them that what the actors are walking round and round on is only a stage. If this is an isolated case one would think that it is just a bad joke, but similar remarks occur again and again in the dramas. Only a few lines later in the same drama the murderer, not wishing to be reminded of his poorer days, denied that he owed the visitor any money and said, pointing to himself, "Look at me. What do I wear on my head, what do I wear on my back and on my feet? Do I look like one who owes *you* money?" To which the creditor answered, "Now don't you brag about it; you have to take it all off when you get in there", pointing to the green room.

Sometimes the actors make fun of the scanty properties, such as the city gate, a cloth arch so small that it has to be raised by the stage hands to let the actors pass. In the dramatic episode *The Pursuit in Anger* 趕三關 the Mongolian lady pursuing

---

[1] or *The Strange Retribution* 奇冤報 .

99

her husband who had escaped back to China had to go through a garrisoned pass. The officer in charge of the garrison, played by a clown, after a lot of nonsense and fun refused to let her through. The lady, annoyed by the delay, ordered her followers to attack, but upon hearing this the Chinese officer stopped her by saying, "Wait a minute, our gate is made of cloth and cannot stand any attack. Come, let us raise it" (for them to pass).

The actors' real identity is also sometimes used in gags. Thus, on a certain occasion an actor was playing the woman-prisoner in *Su San's Journey* 蘇三起解 and his brother happened to be a musician in the orchestra. In the play, in order to befriend the old jailer, the prisoner offered herself to be his god-daughter, which he accepted. On this occasion the jailer, before accepting, said, "But don't you have to ask your brother first?" pointing to the orchestra.

One can go on finding similar instances in the dramas but it would be tiresome, because there is hardly any drama that does not contain similar gags. It is true that only comedians have the licence for them, the other actors always have to maintain their serious attitude, but the fact that the audience not only tolerate them but find them amusing suggests that while they indulge in pretending the drama to be real events they remember, or do not object to being reminded, that it is a pretence after all. In the realistic theatre where greater effort is made to preserve the dramatic illusion such gags would be in bad taste.

Classical dramas have been produced in modern theatres in Shanghai where scenery, front curtain and the orchestra pit are available but the front curtain is not lowered, the scenery not used and the musicians sit on the stage as usual. If this is thought to be due to the conservatism of the particular companies rather than the basic incongruity between scenery and the Chinese drama then the failure of the various attempts to graft scenery into the traditional theatre, called "improved Peking dramas" 改良京戲 should leave little doubt that realism conflicts with something in the Chinese theatre.

In the realistic theatre scenery and stage property contribute towards the dramatic illusion, but in the Chinese theatre they have serious disadvantages, as has been shown by the attempts to employ them. Scenery limits the practicable number of scenes in a drama and breaks the continuous flow of the action because time is required to change it. The number of scenes is probably a matter of indifference to the Chinese audience but to wait in suspense several times during a performance is certainly not the Chinese idea of enjoying theatre. These are perhaps minor disadvantages as compared with that of the realistic property, which would ruin the Chinese style of acting. In general, elaborate property limits the scope of action and in the extreme case of a stage full of furniture the actors can hardly move. The Chinese stage is at the other extreme, it has normally only two or three pieces of property and often none at all. Apart from furniture, realistic representation such as that of the horse is out of the question on the Chinese stage for the simple reason that an actor riding it has to suspend all acting and singing, and in this instance the disadvantage is so great that it is avoided even in the realistic theatre. In the Chinese theatre the horse is theoretically represented but it is only imagined, not only because without it the playwright will either have to avoid practically all outdoor scenes (horses being the only means of land travel for man in old China) or to be grossly inaccurate in making all men walk, but also because without it the studied grace of actors mounting and dismounting the horse would be lost. With all the historical inaccuracies in the Chinese theatre the audience would hardly notice one further instance of inaccurate representation, but they would not easily put up with mutilated acting. Similarly for the boat, which is often required but can never, on the Chinese stage, be real; similarly for the house: if it is real one cannot see, for instance, the dainty movements of the hands of a young woman pulling the cross bars, opening and closing the doors. In studying the Chinese theatre one cannot help being led to the conclusion that scenery and property tend to enrich the acting, especially acting in the Chinese style, if they are imaginary, but are handicaps if they are real. The variety of scenes in the realistic theatre is much smaller than in the Chinese theatre: in the latter one sees cities, rivers, hills and battlefields in practically every performance whereas in the former one rarely, if ever, sees them. In both types of theatre the disadvantage of elaborate scenery and property is avoided, each in its own way: in the realistic theatre by avoiding the scenes in which they are required and in the Chinese theatre by omitting them in such scenes.

Even the most conscientious producer would probably agree that stage property does not have to be correct down to the smallest detail, but most producers in the realistic theatre would allow only very limited omissions. The needle and thread, for example, are sometimes omitted even in realistic productions, because they cannot be seen by the audience in any case and with good acting the audience would think they did see them; the wine glass however has to be filled with water even though good acting could certainly make the glass appear to contain wine. The lack of property in the Chinese theatre may be considered as the extreme case of substituting property with acting. The horse is created by its rider's movements; through them the audience see the horse in their mind's eye. The actor can never create an illusion of the horse as he can that of the thread, but to the Chinese audience the physical existence of the thread is unimportant *even if the thread is really there,* hence the physical absence of the horse is unobjectional to them. The audience of the realistic theatre must be sure that the thread is there even if it is not but the Chinese audience are not interested in the thread even if it is there, and this is probably the difference which makes it possible to omit the thread but not the horse in one case and permissible to omit both in the other.

Even in the realistic theatre movements are sometimes abbreviated as, for instance, in writing letters. Obviously it serves no purpose to write a letter on stage truthfully and the delay would bore the audience. Following such reasoning to its logical consequences, one can accept that the actors travel hundreds of miles by walking around the stage twice, as they are supposed to do in the Chinese theatre.

There are properties which can be realistic without any inconvenience to the actors and yet they are represented by unrealistic copies. Here realism is deliberately suppressed because it would make the scene undesirable in one way or another. For example, in *The City of Chi Chou* 冀州城 the general, who should be defending a city, fell into the trap of the attacking warrior who lured him to a futile pursuit by night and in the morning, the general came back to the city to find it taken by the enemy and the bodies of his wife and children thrown down from the city wall. This last scene if realistic would be intolerably gruesome, and the Chinese audience of the classical theatre would not like to be shocked. In this scene, the bodies are slender bundles of clothes which do not look like bodies at all but which are, for the audience, sufficient indication of why the returning general expresses so much grief, the lamentations being what the audience watch and enjoy.

Refined taste requires higher sensitivity and for high sensitivity violent emotional expressions are painful. Suggestion is enough.

Perhaps few dramatists of the realistic theatre would choose the scene in the Chinese drama *Inspection of the Head* 審頭 in which a court room scene is solely concerned with the identity of the man whose head is exhibited and examined. A realistic human head or any convincing expression by the actors who see it would be nauseating. In the actual case, however, the head is a wrapping of red cloth as in all cases when the head is shown on the stage.

Another scene which could be gruesome is in *The Story of the Black Pot* 烏盆記 when the merchant and his servant are murdered by the kiln-keeper. After the poison in the wine has taken effect, the merchant staggers to the door and tries to open it but can only manage a few desperate pulls. A long struggle in agony follows, then he dies in the room and his servant also falls to the floor soon afterwards. The kiln-keeper and his wife then come in with large carving knives to chop the bodies into smaller parts so that they can be more easily taken to the kiln to be burnt. On stage the couple beat the knives on the floor near the merchant who rises and goes to the green room quietly. When they come near the servant however, he stands up, shakes his clothes and starts to walk away comfortably. The kiln-keeper shouts to him, "Hey, you can't walk away like that". "I can walk in whatever manner I like", the servant answers, "mind your own business". The kiln-keeper retorts, "But this *is* my business; you are dead and I am cutting up your body", at which the servant pretends to look shocked and says, "Oh, I am dead, in that case I better play the spook", and he makes a few squeaks and jumps away.

The actors continually make fun of the dramatic illusion and the audience can share the fun because they do not indulge in the autohypnotic effort towards a real delusion, they are in every moment clearly aware of the pretence involved in the theatre. That such gags often occur when the scene tends to become uncomfortably vivid due either to its gloominess or to lively description in the dialogue may be because they are then more effective but the general characteristics of the Chinese theatre suggest that there is also a deliberate effort to alleviate the effects of the scene on the imagination. In the classical theatre there is never any attempt to excite the audience by realistic details, pleasant or otherwise. The female form is never exploited and amorous scenes hardly ever go beyond the verbal stage. When some one is beaten with a whip or slapped in the face, this is done so that it is obviously a sham. Swoons and weeping are conventionalized and accompanied by music, while shrieks, groans, screams and sighs are rendered with poetic style, and are often semi-musical passages leading into an aria. There are many delicate bedroom scenes in standard classical dramas. In *The Jade Pin* 碧玉簪 the bridegroom would not go near the bride because he suspected her having a lover at the time she married him and in *Hsin An Station* 辛安驛 the bridegroom could not comply with the bride's requests to retire because "he" was really a woman in disguise. Such scenes are handled with the utmost discretion, the actors are fully dressed and the sleeping party merely leans on a table or the back of a chair.

There are many opportunities in the stories of the Chinese dramas for crude sentimentality: in *Fire on the Mien Hill* 焚棉山 a man and his mother are burned to death in a tree trunk; in *The Capture and Escape of Ts'ao* 捉放曹 a whole family and servants are put to the sword; in *The Assassination of T'ang* 刺湯 an unwilling bride stabs the husband in the bridal bed; in *The Dream of Butterflies* 蝴蝶夢 a coffin is opened for the brain of the dead man who is found to be still alive; in *Li Ling's Monument* 李陵碑 an old man dashes his brains out on the stone monument; and in *Death in the Chapel* 斬經堂 the wife cuts her own throat with the sword and the mother hangs herself at the same time. It cannot but be significant that in spite of such subjects no concession is made to realism, on the contrary, the audience is frequently reminded of the unreality of the representation. Everything that might shock and excite the audience is concealed from them. In *The Son's Lesson* 三娘敎子 when the step-mother cuts the threads on her loom in despair she merely pushes a small towel from the back of a chair which stands for the loom.

There are two types of scenes the sight of which, without any artistry, can arouse strong emotions, namely, scenes of violence and sex. In the Chinese theatre all passionate love scenes are avoided and all acts of violence scrupulously camouflaged by conventional acting. That certain love scenes are not acted is partly because the Chinese do not see them in real life, they never kiss or embrace in public. When the husband in *The Clandestine Visit* 探母 meets his wife after years of separation there is no passionate embrace, they kneel to each other and wipe their own tears.

Here we find one of the features of the Chinese classical theatre with which realism is incompatible: emotional agitation through the realistic details of strongly dramatic scenes is contrary to the taste of the Chinese audience.

Men are born with the potentiality for all emotions, but practical considerations make it unwise to indulge in all of them. Religion teaches forgiveness when nature dictates hatred, and morality forbids love except between certain people under certain conditions. Individual and collective security requires a strict code of behaviour which allows only narrow emotional experience and most of the natural capacities to love and hate, to assert one's pride and to taste danger are suppressed and frustrated. We exercise our muscles and sinews to keep them healthy, but our emotional faculties have little opportunity for exercise. Thus there is a thirst for strong emotions, we instinctively know that a hearty laugh and a good cry will alike do us good, and thus we go to the theatre, to watch something which though false appears real and can, if we will cooperate by banishing our disbelief, make us anxious or angry or pitiful or sad. The more real it looks the more easily and strongly our emotions are aroused, and the more they are aroused the more satisfying the experience is. As such, theatre is mental gymnasium.

In order to understand the classical Chinese theatre it is essential to realize that it does not aim at such mental exercises.

One may say that art can excite two different kinds of emotions, the primary and the secondary. By primary emotions are meant the above-mentioned exercise of the emotional capacities and in the dramas this is usually accomplished by the imitation of realistic and intensified emotional situations. Art can also exite secondary emotions, that is, feelings *about* the emotions of the drama and these pre-suppose a contemplative mood. This type of emotion is one step removed from the direct excitation of the passions and differs widely from that towards real events. The sophisticated audience of the Chinese theatre remain emotionally aloof. They understand but do not share the passions of the characters in the drama; they remain spectators to the drama in the fullest sense of the word. They do not feel involved in the drama, the distress and suspense due to dramatic illusion is altogether absent and there is always a psychological distance between the world of the drama and the world of the audience.

Realism is however admired by Chinese audiences in rural districts, and to them the "psychological distance" has of course no meaning:

"The drama *The Salvation of Mu-Lien's Mother* 目連救母 is a religious play performed in the villages in the southern part of Anhwei province . . . in some places, once in ten years, in others, once in five years . . . The length of the performance varies from one to seven nights . . . In the scene when the demons

104

are driven about . . . the lights on the stage are turned off and ghosts of those who drowned or hanged themselves jump about on the stage. When the Taoist priest points his steel wand, two ghosts jump down from the stage and run towards the altar, the priest running after them . . . Besides the drama there were comic scenes and acrobatic display . . . in the farce *Stealing the Cock* the actor dressed as an old woman comes to the seats of the women among the audience''. [2]

It is significant, though it may appear curious to westerners, that in China the exhibition of ghastly sights is considered, together with obscenities, as a matter of public morality. Prof. Ch'i Ju-Shan quotes from two government notices, one of 1864 and one of 1895, both prohibiting the exhibition of ''lewd and gruesome scenes'' in the theatres. [3] In 1897 another public notice prohibits the ''dramatization of such events in history as one cannot find it in one's heart to see'' and mentions, as an example, *The Relentless Search* 搜山（八義圖）in which a child is dashed to death. [4] The Chinese are perhaps by nature particularly sensitive to gruesome sights, because when Emperor Kao Tsung (reigned A.D. 650-684) of T'ang dynasty saw the magicians from T'ien Chu tribe 天竺 who could ''cut off their legs and arms and stab their stomachs with knives'' he issued an order that they be not allowed into China again ''lest they disturb the mind of the people''. [5]

[2]   周貽白,中國戲曲論叢 ,頁九, 引胡樸安等,中華風俗志,下篇, 卷五.
[3]   齊如山, 戲班, 六章 "禁演各戲".
[4]   *Ibid.*
[5]   惡其驚俗（新唐書, 禮樂志, 十二 ）.

CHAPTER XII

THE WORLD OF THE CHINESE DRAMA

Even if the actors can develop a style of acting suitable for elaborate sets and the audience accept gruesome and exciting details, realistic setting will still be out of place in the Chinese theatre because all the other elements of the stagecraft are unrealistic. Realism grafted to the Chinese theatre would not live. To inject realism into the Chinese theatre successfully it would be necessary to make the rest of the stagecraft consistent with it and that can only be brought about by changing everything of the traditional theatre and making the Chinese theatre disappear altogether. If that happens the aim and achievement of the classical Chinese theatre, to which every feature of it contributes, including the bare stage and the crude property, would be lost, for the artistic effects that it can produce cannot be achieved in the realistic theatre.

The whole Chinese stage is unreal. The characters never look like the audience; they are dressed in clothes which belong to the theatre only and are very different from what the audience wear. They use a stylish language. They do not talk but declaim and sing and they do not walk but strut and stalk and amble and glide. They do not sit, the men lean on the high cushions in the chair and the women perch on the edge of the seat. They do not fight, they clash their weapons, parade across the stage, spin on one leg, turn and jump and walk off the stage. They do not weep, they put their sleeve to the eye and start an aria in *lento*. They do not faint, they fall back into a chair, wipe their eyes with both hands one on each side and start another aria in *adagio*. They do not laugh, they utter sounds like laughing to strict rhythm. They do not get angry, they stamp their feet and then toss their long beards right and left. [1] The costume, the music, the singing, the declamation, the diction, the mime, the make-up and the mask all make the *dramatis personae* a different race of human beings, a race which lived in some bygone ages and of which we now see a few

---

[1] Some conventional stage actions, however, come from the actors' low life, such as dusting the chair with the sleeve and flicking the tears from the fingers.

surviving specimens in the theatre. This different race of human beings establishes the world of the Chinese drama.

The Chinese stage becomes an entirely different world not by isolating it with the barrier of the footlights and the curtain but by distinguishing it with the consistently unusual appearance, archaic language and quaint manners of the actors. In the realistic theatre the barrier of the footlights must be guarded religiously because on it depends the assumed identity of the actors. Once they mix with the audience they lose their status of dramatic characters because they can hardly be distinguished from the audience by appearance, and if spectators and stage hands appear on the realistic stage as they do on the Chinese stage, they can be mistaken to be some of the actors. The magic world of the drama, lying behind the proscenium arch which serves as a peep hole, is maintained by sheer physical segregation, and all the things inside the limits of the stage, though they look very much like the things in the world of the audience, belong, by convention, to a different world. Isolation is probably the only possible means of establishing a world of the drama which resembles but is distinct from the world of the audience and the meticulous care with which this separate world is guarded against intrusion and periodically sealed from sight for changes gives some idea of its precarious existence. The Chinese actors, however, are surrounded by spectators on three sides if not four and share the stage with spectators, stage hands and musicians. There is neither curtain nor footlights to serve as boundary for their world. When they are in the front portion of the stage that portion is the domain of the drama but when they require more acting space, the table is pushed back and spectators at the back of the stage make room for them. So far as space is concerned, the world of the drama is in the midst of that of the audience, and yet it is a remote world because its inhabitants are widely different from the audience. It is a world that can remain distinct and intact even though stage hands mix with the actors and the stage and the auditorium almost merge into each other.

The Chinese theatre is legend come to life. Historically, the rise of the Chinese drama was preceded by the formation and propagation of a large body of national legends in Sung dynasty (960-1276) through the agency of various forms of popular entertainment, such as story-telling, shadow play, puppets and ballads, and popular legends have, since then, been the most important raw materials for the Chinese dramas. The legend as subject matter determines the psychology of the Chinese audience: the heroes of the Chinese theatre are national heroes for whom the audience already have, not only sympathy, but admiration and reverence also. The emotional attachment to the dramas far exceeds what is possible in journalistic and sociological themes: there the story and the characters are hypothetical or common-place, but here they are objects of love and pride; there a good play thrills the audience and a bad one bores them but here a good play is an act of homage and a bad one is an insult.

In the mind of the Chinese audience, the historical characters in the dramas really looked like their stage versions:

"In the reign of Ch'ien Lung (1736-1796) there was an actor called Mi Hsi-Tzu 米喜子 who was famous for the role of Kuan Yü 關羽, a warrior in the period of Three Kingdoms (A.D. 220-277). At a private performance for high officials, this actor in his famous part entered, as is customary, with the sleeve in front of his face till he reached the front of the stage and then dropped his arm. The audience, all at once, stood up, thinking that they saw Kuan Yü himself. From then on, for a period of time, the play was banned, because Kuan Yü is a deified hero and realistic representations were felt to be sacrilegious". [2]

Even to-day the character Kuan Yü is treated with religious awe in the theatre: actors about to play the part burn incense in front of his image. The special style of music for his arias and the accompaniment by the Chinese hautboys instead of the usual fiddles add to the weird dignity of this role. The Empress Dowager Tz'u Hsi 慈禧太后, in her palace performances, would find an excuse to stand up whenever Kuan Yü appeared on the stage. [3]

Legend, and through it the world of the Chinese drama, is the product of collective imagination. The Chinese plays are not, like the modern western dramas, works of individual minds offered to and accepted or rejected by the audience, they are conceived by the whole people and reviewed by them, the real authors, over and over again. Among people who do not understand scientific accuracy, myth and history attract fiction. Around simple stories that excite the imagination of the people, fiction grows and changes according to some obscure law of mass psychology. Legends are parables told by the joint effort of the people; they form the expression of their psyche. The selection of the theme and the embellishments added to them are natural processes which, it may be believed, are dictated by some psychological purpose, but, whatever that psychological purpose may be, logic and historical accuracy do not serve it, nor is it conducive to static products, for legends have a life of their own, sometimes breaking into a multitude of different versions and sometimes transforming themselves through a series of variants. Drama and novel are the two literary forms which the popular entertainment of Sung dynasty produced and the formation and transformation of the legends that became the subjects of the novels and dramas can be partially traced, especially in the later stages. [4] Legends, like rumour, represent the diversity and even the self-

---

[2] 齊如山，京戲之變遷，頁五十． cf. modern Chinese films based on historical themes in which the theatrical costume is used — "tab-sleeve", anachronism and all.

[3] 同書頁五一．

[4] For example, in the case of *Shui Hu Chuan* 水滸傳, the story of the thirty-six robbers in Sung dynasty and the subject of one of the greatest Chinese novels. Modern scholarship has revealed several layers of embellishment in the novel. It is an amazing example of collective literary effort.

contradiction of the collective mind, hence in the various versions of one story the dramatists can explore its different dramatic possibilities. The Chinese theatre is therefore the testing ground of legends and, in cases where the dramatists break new ground, also their breeding place. The credulity, the naîveté and the simplicity of the popular intellect are all reflected in the legends and the dramas; the ideal and the actual merge into one, there is no sharp distinction between what the public wish the story to be and what they think actually happened. Characters are larger than life-size; both the small and the great are magnified. When the wronged are saved eventually or the innocent suffer till the end, it is only because the audience wish to see them so. The fact that the Chinese audience are still moved by dramatized legends show that the national legends are still a vital part of the Chinese life.

One of the reasons why the new Chinese intelligentsia, educated in the western tradition, cannot appreciate the Chinese theatre, is that they have lost touch with the national legends and another is that they mistake the rules of science and history to be applicable to drama. Truth in art is never empirical truth; the audience come to the theatre for a kind of satisfaction different from what they can derive from the museum. Intelligent people accept the supernatural elements in the dramas not because they are superstitious but because as part of the legend these elements reveal some psychological truth, they no more believe in the doings of the gods than the historical accuracy of the dialogue. Considered in this light, the complaint of inaccuracy in the costume is unnecessarily fastidious, especially as sartorial history is a subject on which few Chinese can hold convinced opinions. The pedagogue can always find something to criticize for historical inaccuracy, he can question whether the diction and idioms are historically correct, or the pronunciation or the manners. (5) When all details of a dramatic performance are historically correct, if that is possible, it is a documentary pageant, not a drama.

Contemporary life is too real for the subject of the theatre, there is always something drab about it and we know it too well to be able to beautify it. It is difficult to make legend out of contemporary life just as it is difficult to deify a contemporary person. The past, however, is to most of the audience happily indefinite, everything is possible in it. What to the historical mind are unchangeable facts to the audience of the theatre are plastic material capable of being moulded into a work of art. This is why the supernatural which is out of place in history is a legitimate element of the legends. Historical events are subject to the influence of a thousand accidents and their pattern is discernible only to experts; drama requires subject matter which has more prominent shape and form. Legends are often inspired by history but they never remain true to it. Only from a scientific point of view are the different versions of a legend contradictory, from the artistic point of

(5) cf. 齊如山，論戲詞不怕典在事後　戲劇叢刊第三期 which contains examples of anachronism in quotations in the Chinese dramas.

view they are mutually complementary. The audience may not be able to explain the appeal of legends in spite of the outraged logic, but they divine their meaning.

The pattern of legend-making in its cruder forms is probably the same all over the world. In the popular theatre in China it consists of parading the admirable and the despicable to provide opportunities for exercising envy and contempt, the sharp distinction of the good and the bad and the reward of the kind and punishment of the wicked to exercise the moral judgments of the audience. In the classical theatre, however, dramatic themes are more complicated. There drama becomes a commentary on life but is usually without a moral. The distinction of the good and the bad or the admirable and the contemptible is not always sharp, still less are the good always rewarded and the wicked punished. In the best dramas, a moral problem may be implied but it is left for the audience to solve. The very fact that the end of the story, happy or otherwise, is seldom reached in the classical dramas, shows that the audience is not anxious to see it.

When the legend is based on history the story usually has no beginning or end. The drama is then a small unit in a large network of interconnected events and retribution, if any, is too belated to be satisfying. The career of Ts'ao Ts'ao of the Three Kingdoms (A.D. 220-227) for example, is a long series of daring intrigues and precarious battles, and from his many adventures one small incident was chosen by the dramatist of *The Capture and Escape of Ts'ao* 捉放曹. At the time covered by the drama, a foreign general, Tung Cho, who had been welcomed into the capital to settle dangerous court intrigues, all but usurped the throne. Ts'ao Ts'ao, at this time loyal to the emperor, tried to assassinate Tung Cho but failed and was wanted in the capital. While a fugitive, Ts'ao Ts'ao was arrested and taken to Ch'en Kung, mayor of a small city and by arrogance and eloquence, Ts'ao persuaded Ch'en Kung to give up the office and follow him. On their way to Ts'ao Ts'ao's home they were met by a friend of Ts'ao Ts'ao's father who insisted on hospitality and who, after inviting them to his house, left them to buy some wine. Ts'ao Ts'ao, overhearing some conversation about killing, suspected that his host had gone to bring the police and in anger put the whole family and the servants to the sword, only to find afterwards that the conversation referred to a pig to be slaughtered for the feast. Running away from the house they met the host on his way back and after some embarrassment on one side and amazement on the other Ts'ao Ts'ao killed the host as well. That night, in an inn, Ch'en Kung, in grief and regret, had half a mind to kill Ts'ao Ts'ao while he was sleeping but hesitated and after leaving a derogatory poem, left him.

This episode is as history unimportant and as drama shapeless, but that does not prevent it from being the subject of a powerful play. It is the contrast of the egoism and self-possessedness of one character and the meekness and kindheartedness of the other which makes it interesting. "I would rather do wrong to the world" said Ts'ao Ts'ao, "than let the world do wrong to me". To the Chinese audience the climatic construction is not essential; whether a play is moving or not depends, rather, on whether the emotions are represented on the stage with sufficient truth to touch the audience. The conversation between Ch'en Kung and Ts'ao Ts'ao at the beginning of the play can be expanded into a long discussion on the problem of loyalty in times of political turmoil, the hasty killing by Ts'ao Ts'ao may raise the question of man's conduct in times of personal danger and the mercy killing near the end of the play and Ch'en's hesitation to kill Ts'ao Ts'ao in his sleep may lead to ethical issues as well, but the dramatist is entirely unconcerned with philosophical arguments, the situation and the characters are presented, the moral is left to the audience. It is the impersonal quality that brings home to the audience with particular force the irony of life.

Whether a drama makes one ponder over life depends on one's sensibility; as is said of *Hamlet,* to the simple-minded everything is simple. To the contemplative there is always much to think about life, especially when joy and sorrow are brought back to them by the drama with fresh impact.

In some Chinese dramas the meaning of the legend reaches the level of religious feelings. There are several dramas which, like Goethe's *Faust,* open with a scene in Heaven, and the deities partake in the action of many dramas. Supernatural intervention is often used purely as *deus ex machina,* as in many of the dramas about Judge Pao 包公, who possesses supernatural powers, but in some classical dramas it represents deeper thoughts. In *The Story of the Black Pot* so far as the development of the plot is concerned there is no need to introduce any deity, nevertheless, the Avenging God 判官 (in some versions Chung K'uei 鍾馗) is involved. At the beginning of the play the main characters are introduced to the audience separately in three short scenes: in the first the potter and his wife are shown making pottery, in the second, the merchant and his servant caught by the storm on their way home and in the third, which is mute, the Avenging God chasing demons. [6] In the fourth scene these principal characters meet; the merchant and his servant ask the potter for shelter in his hut and are both poisoned after their host has found that their baggage is heavy with silver. While discussing the murder with his wife the potter hesitates because, as he says, it would be doing evil, but he is re-assured by his wife when she says, "But if we do it only once it would not matter very much". In this murder scene the Avenging God stands on a table at the back of the stage, facing the wall and after the bodies have been cut to pieces and removed to the kiln to be burnt the Avenging God turns, jumps off the table and performs a weird but dignified dance. (In one version the Avenging God stands facing the audience, and is understood to be a picture hanging on the wall. While cutting up the

---

[6] cf. the witches at the gallows in *Faust* Pt. I.

bodies the potter feels uneasy when he notices the eyes of the god so he cuts them out of the paper with a knife).

The dance by the god divides the drama into two parts, closing the first and introducing the second.

The second part begins with the introduction of a new character, the old sandal-maker, who is going to collect the price of some sandals from the potter. In the first part of the drama, the potter is an ordinary working man except that he believes "it does not matter very much if we do it only once", but in the second part he is a snob and a miser; he must show his new house to his visitor, he must tell the shabby visitor to sit on the floor because "it would be inappropriate for him to use the richly decorated chairs" but those "blessed by the gods" may sit in them, he would not admit he ever bought sandals and after exhibiting "vases for kings and dukes" and "urns for the high and wealthy" he can only give the sandal-maker a black pot in lieu of payment, and in parting tells the visitor that he may look out for young boys and girls that can be useful in the house. The merchant now appears as a ghost, veiled and clothed in black, walking stiffly on to the stage as soon as the black pot made from his ashes is produced. The ghost, supposedly unseen by the sandal-maker, begins to tell him of the murder and begs him to file a suit at the magistrate's court for it. The sandal-maker is, however, one who cannot be persuaded to do anything, good or otherwise, without seeing immediate concrete reward and tries everything he knows to get rid of the ghost. He throws the pot away, he runs, he tries recipes for exorcising spirits but all without avail. At last he makes a supplication to the City God and promises to bring a sow and vegetables as offerings if the ghost is expelled. That proved potent but he remembers that he is too poor to buy any offering and reasons that if he makes an enemy of the City God he will be in even greater trouble, so he addresses the City God again saying that he did not go to see the potter for money and there was no black pot given to him and it did not talk and there is no need to exorcise the ghost, and so on, repeating at the end that he is not to bring any offering the next day.

The religious element which is added to the drama even though the plot does not require it strongly suggests that even without it the drama would point to religious thoughts. That an earthen pot, whatever its ingredients, can talk with a human voice is something that few, even among the Chinese, would whole-heartedly believe. Some may perhaps believe in the Avenging God, others not, but in whatever degree one accepts the literal truth of the drama its basic meaning is the same. So far as real action is concerned the play may be considered to end with the murder, and the second part, practically entirely occupied with the lament poured out by the ghost in singing, can be taken as a commentary on the first part. The audience are hardly interested in the punishment of the murderers because the court room scene is brief and is normally omitted. In the theatre the main interest of the

113

play lies in the long arias sung by the ghost, all the hatred and agony and bitterness of the wronged are in them. The contrast between the characters is significant: the ghost who is all sorrow and anguish, the potter who cannot miss the chance to get rich, the sandal-maker whose life is entirely based on immediate returns and above them all the Avenging God who witnesses the murder scene in silence. The Avenging God never appears again after the murder scene; one is led to think that the dramatist takes three samples of humanity to make a drama and adds the god to fix its key note.

All dramas are re-organized experience to carry new understanding and new visions of life. As compared to the journalistic dramas the Chinese theatre, being based on legends, has more freedom in the manner of the re-organization.

CHAPTER XIII

THE FUNCTION OF THE STORY

Chinese plays may be divided into four types: the *congratulatory play,* the *dramatic dance,* the *farce* and the *dramatic excerpt.*

The congratulatory play, although performed at the beginning of every theatrical performance, is taken seriously only in birthday and wedding celebrations in which it is looked upon not purely as entertainment but partially as a ceremony connected with the occasion, a formality which must be completed before entertainment can begin. It varies from the two simple and most often performed pieces, *Heavenly Official Bestowing Blessing* 天官賜福 and *The God of Wealth Presenting Treasures* 財神獻寶 both of which are symbolic solo dances, to slightly more elaborate and spectacular plays on some mythological subject involving supernatural favours on mortals. [1] In the commercial theatres, the congratulatory play is performed partly "for good omens" and partly as a polite gesture of the management towards the audience but in private celebrations it usually represents the good wishes of the guest who pays for the performance of the plays as a present to the host.

Some plays in the repertoire of the classical theatre are not dramas but dances. They are usually without any plot and scarcely connected with any story. For example, one such play, *Ch'ang O's Flight to the Moon* 嫦娥奔月 although based on the myth of an ancient archer whose wife took his magic pill, became a goddess and was chased by him to the moon, is, as performed, a solo dance by the goddess without any dramatic action. *Fairies Scattering Flowers* 天女散花 is another of these dances.

The farce is a short play with rudimentary action usually of sufficiently loose

---

[1] The Promotion Dance 跳加官 performed as compliments of the players, sometimes several times in a programme, is in fact an abridged version of the *Heavenly Official Bestowing Blessings* 齊如山, 京劇之變遷, 頁十二. The dance now performed under either name is mute, but it was originally accompanied by singing. 錢沛思, 綴白裘, 一編一卷 .

115

structure to allow the comedians to improvise gags and songs. In some farces an excuse is provided for indiscriminate singing, as in *Sudden Gold* 拾黃金 in which a beggar (or two in some versions) sings anything he chooses to entertain the audience because he has found a piece of gold and is too happy to be quiet, and in *Spinning Cotton* 紡棉花 in which a woman sings at the spinning wheel while waiting for her husband to come home. Often the singer would address the audience directly and announce the particular arias he would sing for them and ventriloquism and caricature are frequently exploited. Sometimes the excuse is disguised as in *The Cowherd and the Country Girl* 小放牛 in which a cowherd stops a country girl and will not let her pass until she dances and sings with him. Other farces are for showing off virtuosity in acting as *The Dragon's Amour with the Phoenix* 遊龍戲鳳 (flirtation of the emperor incognito with an inn-keeper's sister) and *Haunting Chang San* 活捉張三 (the ghost of a woman dragging her paramour to the abode of the dead) or *The Flower Grotto* 五花洞 (a farce of mixed identity between a travelling couple and two disguised goblins). The characters in the last two farces are from other dramas but the identity of the characters is not significant because there is no relation with the action of the other dramas hence they are to be considered as separate plays. [2]

The pure dance and the farce, though devoid of dramatic interests, can, with talented actors, be fascinating plays. It is difficult to convey in words what good actors can express in voice and gestures and the merits of these pieces can only be understood by those who have seen good performances of them.

By far the greatest majority of the classical dramas are, however, really dramatic excerpts. The construction of these plays deserves special consideration because it differs from what western people understand by dramatic construction and it determines a peculiar quality of the Chinese theatre.

Although the story-tellers of Sung dynasty (960-1276) had some influence on the rise of the Chinese drama — puppets, and possibly also human actors, being then actually used to illustrate the stories — the influence of dance and poetry has been so predominant in the Chinese theatre that the presentation of stories has not, as a whole, been its purpose. The audience know the story before they see the drama because the plays are mostly based on popular legends which the audience know well and because most of the plays are performed over and over again. Suspense is entirely absent in the Chinese dramas. The playwright cannot rely on the curiosity of the audience for sustained interest because they know exactly what is to happen next in the play. They watch the plays not because they are intrigued by the mystery in the

---

[2] A special type of farce, of adjustable length, is performed in the Chinese theatre when the company is waiting for late actors. cf. Carpenter's Scene in the English theatre which contains matters irrelevant to the development of the plot but is used in the Victorian theatre to allow time to build the scenes and is still used in the English pantomime.

gradually unfolding plot but because the performance by the actors is good. In the classical theatre, the plays hardly ever cover whole stories, but are, strictly speaking, scenes representing episodes in the stories. As the audience do not come to the theatre to learn the story, they do not demand a representation of it from beginning to end. What interests them is not the plot, but the treatment of the plot; not how the events turn out, but how they are presented; not the subsequent fate of the characters, but the present virtuosity of the actors. Thus, in order to hold the attention of the audience the plays have to be essays of concentrated histrionic art. The fact that one can scarcely find a single classical play which covers a whole story indicates that it is very difficult, if not impossible, to achieve uniform quality of performance for such a play. When a complete story is represented, as is sometimes done in the popular theatres, one finds that only one or two scenes in it are worth seeing.

The typical classical play is therefore a dramatic episode presented with the histrionic and musical resources of the Chinese stage. In many of the plays the interest is concentrated in one single scene and in some of them, in one aria. One gets a very poor idea of the play by reading its script and could be seriously mistaken if one tries to judge the performance by it, because as published a play is usually only a few pages long but the performance can last for an hour or two. There is no indication in the script of how long a mute dance is to take, or a battle scene, or an aria. The written dialogue in the Chinese drama is only a small and unimportant part of the play; it can be, and often is, changed by the actors without any damage to the total effect of the actual performance on the audience. It is well known that in the modern Chinese theatre the script has little, if any, literary value and that it would not be worthwhile preserving it if the tradition of the acting and music is lost. The players can however so enrich a play with their artistry that what makes dull reading can become a fascinating play on the stage.

Without seeing the play *The Son's Lesson* 三娘教子, for example, one would wonder what dramatic interest there could be in a single scene of a step-mother teaching a child to read. The play has hardly a plot: it is about a physician's concubine who remains in his house after he has been reported dead, in order to bring up his son whose mother has married again. The scene shows the step-mother checking the child's lessons after school and trying to cope with the progressive defiance of the child. At last she threatens punishment but the child taunts her by saying that she should have a child of her own to punish. Stunned and mortified she sits silently in despair, till the old servant teaches the child to ask for forgiveness on his knees and happiness is eventually restored. The content of this play is really the contrast between the loving care of the step-mother and the unknowing truculence of the child, but the theme is developed through many accessory details till what appears in print to be a simple melodramatic scene becomes on stage an exquisite

117

study of the characters and the situation, full of genuine pathos. It is not by virtue of what happens in the play that it is moving but by the truth of the expressions. The interest of plot and action is at its minimum; the value of the play lies entirely in the acting and singing.

The above play is based on a simple situation which, like a subject for a painting, hardly requires a story to make it understandable. Most classical plays, however, have a story for their background and cannot be fully appreciated without knowing the story. The play *Death in the Chapel* 斬經堂 , for example, is about a military officer in Han dynasty who was in charge of a certain pass at the time when the country was ruled by a usurper. His father, who was loyal to the true emperor, had been killed by the usurper but he was then too young to know it and his mother, who changed their name and allowed him to marry the new princess for the sake of their personal safety, did not tell him of the true cause of his father's death. During his office at the pass he captures a loyalist who was trying to recover the throne for the true emperor and when his mother knew it she told her son that his father was killed by his father-in-law, that the prisoner was a friend of his father and that he should give up his office, kill his wife and follow his father's friend. Of this story the play covers only the part where the hero met his wife in the chapel and told her what his mother had asked him to do. After much hesitation and grief on both sides, the wife tricked her husband to look away and killed herself with his sword before he could stop her. When the hero went back to tell his mother about it, he found that she too had committed suicide.

In this play, as in many others, a scene is chosen such that the emotions of the whole story can be focused on it. The situation is a familiar one of conflict between loyalty and love, and this is exploited in full, but in addition, the theme has for its overtones the family feud and the political upheaval. The audience know that the hero did follow his father's friend and the true emperor was restored to the throne. In the whole stream of events connected with the hero's family before and after the death of the wife, only the episode in the chapel is chosen to carry the emotions involved in the story. It is possible to read the life history of a tree in a cross section of its trunk; similarly, it is possible to illumine all the emotions in a story by presenting its central scene. This is, however, only possible if the audience know the story before they see the play because the play derives its interest not only from what had happened before the events in the play but also from what was to happen afterwards. As the expressions refer to the whole story, it is unnecessary to have the whole story represented. Even if the actors could play the scenes for the other parts of the story well they would find that the emotional significance of the theme had been exhausted and, as far as feelings are concerned, the other scenes would be redundant. This is why of the drama *Yü T'ang Ch'un* 玉堂春 about the ill-fated courtezan of that name, only one of the scenes is normally played: either *Su San's*

Journey 蘇三起解 or *The Joint Court* 三堂會審 , the former about the girl's journey to a higher court where she meets her former lover who is the judge and the latter, the trial scene. The Chinese dramaturgy is such that to see these plays together is, to a great extent, like to see the same play twice over. [3]

As long as a play contains all the emotions in a story it does not matter how much and which part of the story it covers. The usual scheme of a Chinese play is to introduce the audience to the background of the play in the opening passages and then proceed to embellish the chosen scene or scenes with singing and mime. Some plays, however, are entirely outside the story. A popular legend tells of the spirit of a white snake who, tired of her supernatual existence, changed herself into a young woman to seek adventure in the mundane world. Boating on the West Lake in Hangchow, she met a young scholar during a rainstorm and soon afterwards married him. A monk, friend to the young scholar, noticed in his manners some occult influence and persuaded him to leave his wife and stay in the monastery and when Lady White Snake found where her husband was she came to claim him but was driven away by the monk with supernatural weapons. When the wife was to have a baby, however, the young scholar, still ignorant of his wife's identity, came back to her. Unfortunately, during the Dragon Boat Festival the wife had too much to drink, and while intoxicated, took the shape of a snake. After this incident the husband was easily persuaded by the monk to help in a scheme to trap the spirit and this he did by casting a spell over his wife while she was dressing. In the classical play connected with this legend, *Libation at the Pagoda* 仕林祭塔 , the son, now a high official, comes to seek his mother's spirit at the Pagoda of the Thunder Peak where she is imprisoned and the story of the legend is told in a long aria sung by the imprisoned spirit. Here the story, instead of being the subject matter of the drama, is only its background and the play is more a recital of a narrative poem set to music than a drama. To the Chinese audience, however, the distinction is unimportant; it is enough for them that the simple action of the son meeting his mother's spirit contains the tragedy of the family.

The play just mentioned is outside the story in time. Sometimes the play is within the time span of the story but the characters in the play are not the main characters in the story. In Han dynasty a scholar, Ts'ai Yung, left his parents and his wife to seek officialdom in the capital and having distinguished himself there, married the daughter of the prime minister and stayed in the capital. At home his wife did her best under difficult circumstances to support her parents-in-law, but

---

[3] On the play *The Fisherman's Revenge* 打漁殺家 about a fisherman's forbearance under the outrages of the local bully and his subsequent revenge, even Ou-Yang Yü-Ch'ien, who is sometimes sweepingly critical of the traditional Chinese theatre, says that it is "a complete play in itself". "If the rest of the drama, covering other parts of the story, is produced with it, the final effect is dull". 歐陽予倩, 談二黃戲, 盧冀野, 中國戲劇概論, 頁二六五引.

when the district was struck with famine, they died. The young lady sold her hair for the funeral expenses and, dressed as a Taoist pilgrim, begged her way into the capital to meet her husband. The story is the subject of a long poetic drama in Ming dynasty, called *The Story of the Lute* 琵琶記 . In the modern classical play, *Messenger at the Tomb* 掃松下書 the scene is chosen at the tomb of the parents and the characters in it are an old villager who was entrusted with the care of the tomb and a messenger bearing a letter from the capital. The play contains some narrative of the story but it is at the same time a commentary on it. The two characters in it, like the audience, are not involved in the story: they do not share the emotions in it. In this particular play the story is twice removed from the audience and the psychological distance between the story and the audience is increased twofold. The characters in it may be considered as the model audience, who have no direct emotional relation with the main characters but who are moved by it as spectators.

The interest in the classical drama is always twofold: there is the play as such and there is its significance when seen against its background. The play as such, which one can enjoy without knowing the story, usually contains a contrast of characters: thus, in *Messenger at the Tomb* the encounter of the artless villager with the more politic messenger from the city may itself be enjoyed as a delightful character study; for those who know the background, however, the uninhibited and sincere reproaches of the old villager and the genuine and suppressed emotions of the messenger can be truly touching. *The Capture and Escape of Ts'ao* 捉放曹 , *The Son's Lesson* 三娘教子 , *Su San's Journey* 蘇三起解 , *The Prince's Farewell* 霸王別姬 and many others are all built on sharp contrast of characters, but in the emotional perspective of the story they acquire additional significance.

Owing to the knowledge of the entire story on the part of the audience, dialogue and acting become permeated with emotional significance. The audience always know more than the characters in the play. Many great classical dramas would be spoiled if the audience did not know the ending: the farewell of the prince and the suicide of his consort, for example, would not be so tragic if the audience did not know that the prince was to fight his way through the seige with dwindling guards and that when he was offered a ferry to his home town he refused to go back because, having lost all the men who followed him from there, he could not bear to see the elders again. There was a reward on his body, hence it was torn to several pieces after he was killed. In *The Capture and Escape of Ts'ao,* when Ch'en Kung quailed at his attempt to kill Ts'ao Ts'ao in the inn, he explained to himself that he should not put the innkeeper in jeopardy by leaving a dead body. The excuse loses much of its poignancy if the audience do not know that in another play, *The Loft of the White Gate* 白門樓 , Ch'en, then in the service of another warlord, was to be captured and executed by Ts'ao. In another story, Su San, the young courtezan, fell in love with her client Wang, and, after her keeper had sapped Wang's fortune, secretly helped him with funds for his journey into the capital. She herself was subsequently sold to be a concubine and was branded as a murderess when the wife, trying to poison her, killed the husband by mistake. One play based on this story is *Su San's Journey* 蘇三起解 about her travels with her gaoler to a higher court for trials. The journey would lose much of its interest if she was not known to be going to meet her former lover who was the presiding judge.

The audience can appreciate the acting only if they understand what is being expressed, but unless they know at least as much as the characters in the play are supposed to, they cannot understand what is being expressed. All the power and precision and subtlety of an expression are wasted if the audience do not know the feelings behind it, or know it, as in mystery dramas, only at the end of the play.

The interest in interconnected events which develop towards a culmination is exploited in China by the novelist and the story-teller, not by the dramatist. The classical Chinese drama does not aim at telling a story; indeed it is ineffective for the purpose. To the dramatist and his audience, the story is a means to an end: only from a plot can the drama derive its emotional content. The narrative function of the drama is subsidiary and the plot, when not told in the dialogue like a story, is represented in clear but brief scenes. [4] If the audience do not know the story of the drama, their interest can only be thin at the beginning and becomes deeper as the plot develops and they know more about the characters. Chinese dramas are constructed on the principle that the slight interest at the beginning should be avoided, hence the audience are told forthwith in the introductory poem what the drama is about, to strike the keynote of the drama so to speak, and then they are introduced to the characters with the narrative passages in the dialogue. It is like an essay that begins with a brief statement of the theme and then proceeds with the exposition. [5]

---

[4] Prof. Ch'i Ju-Shan points out that new plays which represent whole stories in a large number of scenes contain little singing, because the audience are eager to follow the development of the plot and cannot relish the elaboration of single scenes. When the audience know the story, they want to see only one good scene and the players add material to it till it contains all the interest in the drama 齊如山, 京劇之變遷, 頁六 , 十一．

[5] cf. 齊如山, 京劇之變遷, 頁十一, 十二．

CHAPTER XIV

THE COMPLETE THEATRICALISM

The Chinese theatre is overtly and thoroughly theatrical. It is necessary to make this statement clearly because the term "theatrical" is sometimes a derogatory term in theatrical matters.

Similarly, being "stagey" is considered a defect, owing to a long western tradition to disguise the stage so that it will look like something else. It constitutes a small short-cut to the understanding of the Chinese theatre to realize that "being theatrical" and "being stagey" are alike tautological to the Chinese theatre-goer. The style of the Chinese theatre is such that these terms cannot have any imaginable meaning at all.

The stage, of course, can only be disguised but can never be transformed. As a raised platform for the performance of dramas to be seen by a crowd of spectators, its characteristics remain unchanged whatever and however heavy the disguise may be. With all the paraphernalia of the modern realistic stage certain rules of stage performances have still to be observed, for example, that the actors should face the audience most of the time, that on a crowded stage effective entrance from the back can only be made at a higher level than the stage floor, etc. It has been a fashion in modern European theatres to conceal the stage as much as possible, as if the producer is ashamed of it, and to stage dramatic performances as if they are not aimed at maximum theatrical effect.

On the naked Chinese stage there is no attempt to conceal or evade its characteristics. The characteristics are not merely tolerated, they are exploited. When an actor entering for the first time, steps slowly downstage (towards the audience) to the rhythm of the music and pauses at the front of the stage to address the audience his movements on the stage are such as to put him slowly into the focus of the audience's attention. The effect of these conventional entrances is similar to that of the introduction in a piece of music: it is undesirable to start with the main themes. When there is a break in the action and when a scene ends with a couplet, to mark the break, the last actor to leave the stage in that scene would sing the first line of the couplet, move towards the exit while the orchestra plays the interlude and then turn and sing the second line — in doing this he is slowly withdrawing from the focus of attention of the audience. There is a cadence in both the music to which the couplet is sung and the dance steps accompanying the singing so that the sense of finality is aurally and visually emphasized. The dramatist and critic Li Yü analyzed the function of the introduction to a scene as follows:

"... there is always a long introduction 引子, followed by a couplet or a poem, the whole called 'speech to set the scene' 定場白, meaning that before the speech the audience do not know what the play is about, but after it they do and will settle down to listening". 李漁，笠翁偶集,·齊如山, 中國劇之組織, 頁九引.

The position and movement of the actors on the stage have their particular effects on the audience whatever the stage may represent and no matter whether scenery is used or not. [1] Thus an actor downstage (nearer the audience) is more conspicuous than one upstage and a moving or speaking one, more than a silent or stationary one and one near the centre of the stage, more than one at the side. An actor flanked by two rows of actors looks important whether there is scenery or not. A "scissor cross" (two actors crossing the stage in opposite directions) is clumsy because it is uncomfortable to try to follow them both at the same time, and is avoided even in the realistic theatre except when used intentionally for special effects. In the Chinese theatre the actors normally do not make the "scissor cross" but indication of wind or flood by flags is carried out by small boys in a "scissor cross" and the two mute couriers of the God of Literature (文昌二童) also make the "scissor cross" when they appear. The object here is to indicate that the stage hands carrying the flags or the visiting spirits are not among the characters in the drama and are supposed to be invisible to them.

Owing partly to the protrusion of the stage into the auditorium and partly to the explicit design in the movements of the actors, the Chinese audience are keenly aware of the depth of the stage. In modern European theatres the proscenium arch tends to make the stage a picture with the arch as a frame. The position of the stage and the mental habit of the audience together make it difficult to be aware of the actors' relative positions, so much so that when the pattern on the stage floor is important, as in Fokine's ballet *Les Sylphides* one had to be in the balcony to see the figures formed by the dancers. When the mind of the audience is absorbed by the acting or singing the movements on the stage may escape their notice, but when there is no interesting action, such as at the beginning of a scene or during a mute passage,

---

[1] Even on the modern European stage, strong visual illusions can be created without using scenery, for example, when an actor is near the edge of the stage and the curtain is dropped behind him, he appears to *move* nearer to the audience.

the actor's movements become particularly conspicuous, hence in these moments the formal beauty of the actors' movements becomes important. For a stage without the front curtain a scene can only start with the actors entering the stage, hence, in the case of a crowded scene such as the imperial court or a battle scene, it takes some time to assemble all the actors. Normally an actor upon entering introduces himself or announces his intentions before he takes part in any action but this procedure would be monotonous beyond one or two actors and tediously long for a crowded scene. Monotony is avoided in such cases by making the actors enter according to a dance-like pattern with musical accompaniment so that the audience are pleasantly occupied while waiting for the scene to be properly set. The guards and flag-bearers, played by supernumeraries, enter first. They advance straight to the front, pause to display their flag or weapon and turn, one in each direction, to take up their positions at the sides. The visual interest is kept up partly by the symmetrical movements of the actors and partly by the increasing splendour of the costume as officials of higher ranks appear. Introduction of the guards and officers is unnecessary because they are recognizable by their costume, and the main characters make their announcement after the whole scene has assembled. A moving army can exit simply in a file with one officer following another but large court scenes have to end in the same complicated way as they started, with the flag-bearers advancing to the front of the stage pair by pair before leaving the stage.

The pageantry on the Chinese stage has considerable choreographic interest. It

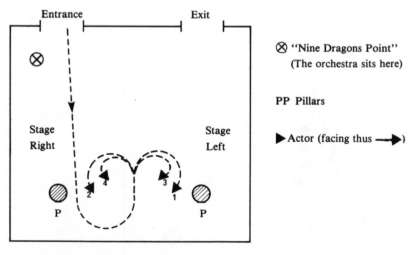

Entrance   Exit

⊗ "Nine Dragons Point"
(The orchestra sits here)

PP Pillars

▶ Actor (facing thus ⟶▶)

Stage Right   Stage Left

P   P

Fig. 33 Entrance Style — I

can be illustrated by a few examples of conventional styles of entrance and exit:

In stationary scenes (actors considered discovered), when the attendants enter, they must first come downstage to the front, pause, then turn and arrange themselves at the sides (Fig. 33). If there are four or more of them, they enter pair by pair, the second pair entering just before the first have taken their positions.

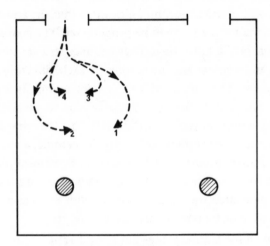

Fig. 34 Entrance Style — II

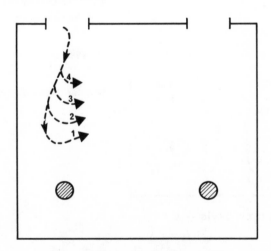

Fig. 35 Entrance Style — III

For moving scenes (journeys), the attendants stop near the entrance door (Fig. 34) and wait till the master enters, then stay at his sides and move with him only between the phrases in his aria, when the orchestra plays the bridge passages.

Variations of the moving scene are shown in Figs. 35 and 36 — here the attendants wait for their master in a line.

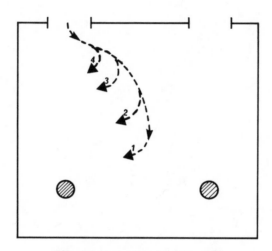

Fig. 36 Entrance Style — IV

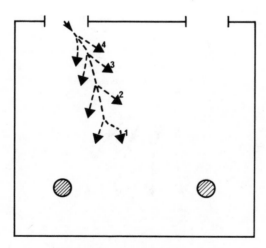

Fig. 37 Entrance Style — V

When there are eight attendants in a moving scene, as when a high official is travelling, they wait for their master in the position shown in Fig. 37.

Four warriors entering at the same time take the positions shown in Figs. 38 and 39, to announce themselves to the audience.

When two armies enter simultaneously, the attendants, foot soldiers and petty

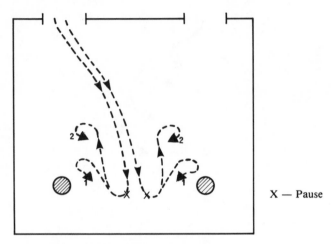

X — Pause

Fig. 38 Entrance Style — VI

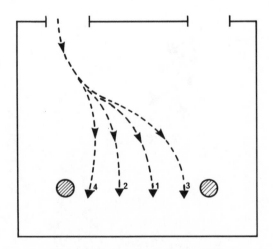

Fig. 39 Entrance Style — VII

128

officers are arranged as shown in Fig. 40. There are, of course, more than eight soldiers even in an army on the Chinese stage, and the officers of higher ranks stand in rows in front of the soldiers shown in the diagram. The generals on each side are the last to enter. After their entrance the two armies march around the stage.

At entrances, attendants and minor officers enter first, but at exits, the general or emperor leaves first. One form of exit is shown in Fig. 41.

If the attendants are in a row as shown in Fig. 42, the one furthest downstage exits first, walking backwards a few steps and the others move consecutively to the downstage position of the first attendant and leave as he does.

For short scenes, in which the characters pass through the locality represented by the stage, the attendants make their exit as shown in Fig. 43.

Some of the entrances and exits by single actors are also very beautiful to watch as, for example, the entrance of the heroine in *P'ing Kuei's Return* 武家坡 (Fig. 10B) when she appears in the middle of the instrumental introduction to her aria,

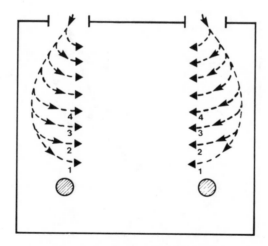

Fig. 40 Entrance Style — VIII

129

steps gingerly half way down the stage, puts down her vegetable basket, adjusts her hair and arranges her sleeves. In such cases, when the attention of the audience is focused on her entrance, the gait and poise, matched to the music, can produce a powerful effect.

The frank theatricalism of the Chinese stage is not, however, always used to decorate the unavoidable stage business, as in the entrances and exits, but is also used to embellish and beautify the action. Even the simple action of inviting the guest to take a seat becomes a series of dance steps on the Chinese stage. The Chinese are ceremonious to guests and would ask them to take the honour seats and wait till they are seated first before sitting down themselves but the stage version of the action based on the essential movements of pointing to the seat and the bows, is more rhythmic and intricate than it is in real life. A journey, normally represented by walking round the stage, becomes a graceful piece of stage business when it is accompanied with singing (圓塲). The action is most effective when there are two

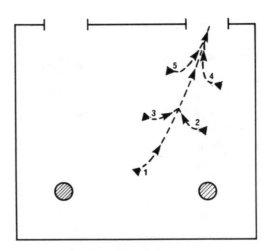

Fig. 41 Exit Style — I

130

actors moving diametrically apart along a circle, so that when one is coming downstage the other is going upstage and when one is moving to the right in the front of the stage the other is moving to the left at the back. When they pause to sing a line of the aria, strut slowly forward during the bridge passage and pause again, the movement, with the music, induces a mood of peacefulness and leisureliness

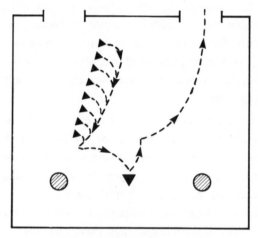

Fig. 42 Exit Style — II

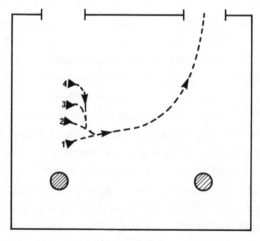

Fig. 43 Exit Style — III

which is difficult to describe. This is a case of a convention becoming an idiom; it is at once a piece of dramatic action and a dance figure.

In fact, much of the acting can be properly understood only when one sees it as dance. Messengers and supernumeraries apart, almost every movement of the actors is rhythmic and strictly timed, so that if they make a wrong move or take one step too many or too few, not only the orchestra but the other actors too have to make adjustments for it. Acting unaccompanied by music is rare on the Chinese stage. Stage movements tend to become dance when they are accompanied by music, because with music, they acquire rhythm, balance, accents and cadences. Rhythmic movements, which can be beautiful, cannot however be realistic, because movements in our daily life are regulated by considerations of utility and economy and are, as compared with dance, brief and irregular. It is the quality of dance in the Chinese style of acting that gives it its sensuous beauty which even those who do not understand the play can enjoy.

Taking the dramatic performance as a dance, one finds that many features of the Chinese stage are the natural accessories of the dance. The stage is in fact the dance floor and there is nothing strange in the dance floor being surrounded by spectators and used by the musicians. There have been attempts to banish the spectators and conceal the musicians, but if the spectators and musicians are successfully banished from the Chinese stage their absence would be a loss instead of a gain, especially the musicians, because they make the stage look unmistakably a dance floor. To a dance scenery is not essential and, even if employed, should not be realistic, because mimetic dance, considered as acting, is unrealistic and would not mix well with realistic decor. For the Chinese stage, where the mind of the audience is concentrated on the actors — as dancers — scenery is not only superfluous but positively undesirable. The best background for a dancer is the space around him. It is in a dance that the naked stage need not be ashamed of itself. Realistic property is of course incompatible with any type of dance and is minimized, if not dispensed with, on all dance floors. Masks and sumptuous costume, on the other hand, belong to the dance and dramatic dances lose much of their beauty when performed in ordinary clothes. Only in the dance is it normally considered justified to place so much importance on the performer's art and so little on the playwright's, and only because the Chinese play is a dance can one enjoy watching several separate episodes together in one performance and the same pieces in many different performances. It is the quality of the dance that makes the Chinese drama an art for the connoisseurs rather than for the general public, an art of which the appreciation has to be learned and on which its devotees spend years of training and study.

The different aims of Chinese and naturalistic acting are also reflected in the difference in technique. In the latter, actors try to excite the audience with replicas of the *dramatis personae* and some of them excite themselves first with the emotions in the drama. (2) The Chinese actor however, being a dancer, remains cool in the most passionate roles and all his moves are deliberately and carefully executed, and calculated to produce certain artistic effects. His mind is like the puppet player and his body like the puppet, in order that absolute control is maintained throughout the performance he, like the puppet master, must not become excited himself. It is this control that gives the Chinese actors their poise and bearing which makes it a pleasure to watch them even when they are standing still.

The Chinese play can best be understood as a long dance and the scenes in it as movements (in the musical sense) of the dance. It contains two elements, the mimetic dance which is related to the dramatic content, and the pure dance which is related to pure stage business; the former is part of the dramatic action but the latter is not. Each scene, or each movement of the dance, begins with an introductory passage of pure dance and closes with a coda. The relative amount of pure and mimetic dance varies from one play to another, but all Chinese plays contain some of both. (3) Special dances, like the sword dance in *Gathering of the Heroes,* are sometimes grafted into the action (4) and they form a homogeneous whole with the play. Most of the military plays can only be considered as military dances, (5) because they consist practically entirely of battle scenes, the scenes that precede and follow the battles being brief and sketchy. The action is only remotely like a battle: not even the most sensitive people can become concerned with the safety of the belligerents. When one warrior, for example, thrusts his spear repeatedly at another who ducks to avoid the weapon, the point of the spear is many inches from the opponent at any

---

(2) *Vide* T. Cole and H. K. Chinoy, *Actors on Acting, passim.*

(3) The Chinese style of acting is more mimetic than is often realized. The strut of the male characters, for example, is based on the dignified and affected "rectangular steps" 方步 which the Chinese used in ceremonial occasions. *Vide* L. C. Arlington, *The Chinese Drama,* 70 n.

(4) There are many special dances in the Chinese theatre, for example, the sword dance 劍舞 (羣英會), the truncheon dance 鐧舞 (當鐧), the hoe dance 花鋤舞 (嫦娥奔月), the sash dance 帶舞 (天女散花), the flask dance 壺舞 (獻壽) and the ring dance 圈舞 (乾坤圈) . Tableaux 堆花, 推鬼 are also often used.

(5) The different styles for handling the weapons and for bare-handed fighting have been enumerated in a list (said to be incomplete):

```
Somersaults . . . . . . . . . . . . . . . . . . . . . . . . . . . . . . . . . . .32 types
Spear against spear . . . . . . . . . . . . . . . . . . . . . . . . . . . . . .20 types
One long-handled knife against another . . . . . . . . . . . . . . . . . 9 types
Staff against staff . . . . . . . . . . . . . . . . . . . . . . . . . . . . . . . . .13 types
Spear against long-handled knife . . . . . . . . . . . . . . . . . . . . . 6 types
Long-handled knife against scimitars . . . . . . . . . . . . . . . . . .12 types
Long-handled knife against single scimitar . . . . . . . . . . . . . . 4 types
Spear against scimitar . . . . . . . . . . . . . . . . . . . . . . . . . . . . .11 types
Spear against two scimitars . . . . . . . . . . . . . . . . . . . . . . . . . 8 types
Bare hands against various weapons . . . . . . . . . . . . . . . . . . . 4 types
Bare-handed fighters . . . . . . . . . . . . . . . . . . . . . . . . . . . . . .19 types
```

尚和玉, 武工把子名詞, 戲劇叢刊, 第二期.

time. [6] At any rate, the real battles are not long sustained, they soon deteriorate into distinctly acrobatic acts, with tumblings, rollings, jumpings and sometimes even juggling with the weapons, in which all resemblance with any battle has disappeared. [7] It may appear incredible that such explicit acrobatic displays having nothing whatsoever to do with the drama have subsisted in the middle of Chinese plays but their existence becomes comprehensible when one sees them as virtuoso dances in which all dancers sometimes indulge. It is in fact a kind of *cadenza* of the dancers, which one not infrequently finds in European ballets especially with solo dancers, and like the musical *cadenza,* it is the part of the performance which, if the audience do not like, they have to suffer for the vanity of the performer. [8]

The pleasure of watching a good military play is complex. One appreciates the

---

[6] Some foreigners think that the skill lies in not touching each other! — B. S. Allen, *Chinese Theatre Handbook,* 29.

[7] The stage battle has its mimetic basis and cannot be considered as entirely acrobatic exhibition: In ancient warfare, when two armies met (players call the action 會陣) they arranged themselves at a visible distance from each other and the generals or their deputies fought personal combats (起打) in front of the soldiers. Thus two armies parade on the Chinese stage, each on one side, walking round and round, as if they are on the journey to meet each other and then they arrange themselves briefly on the two sides of the stage and all leave the stage except two warriors who stay to carry out the single combat. When they raise their weapons and pass each other (過合) they portray the charge and clash of weapons and when they raise their weapons and step back (拉開) they represent an approach in which neither can find a point of vantage. When they suddenly stop fighting (亮住) (the music also stops) they represent the mutual withdrawal for a pause before another charge and they should look at each other as if watching for surprise attack. When one army chases another from the entrance to the exit door (追過場) they represent one army routing another, and when a warrior, after victory, displays his skill, we can consider him as showing his pleasure (耍下場). When one warrior strikes another and the other makes a somersault (打搶背) he is striking him down from the horse or down to the ground if he is on foot. Several warriors may touch their weapons with each other and hold them still for a while (架住) — this means they cannot get the better of each other and thus have a pause in the scuffle. Sometimes two or three or four warriors from one side fight with an equal number on the other (幾股當) and sometimes one warrior is represented as fighting a gradually growing group (結攢) showing that he is a great fighter. Sometimes the first warrior on one side is represented as defeating the first warrior on the other but is in turn defeated by the second warrior from the enemy, etc. (連環). Sometimes warriors exchange their weapons (川手) — this is not impossible in scuffles, but is often used excessively. On entering a warrior usually displays his postures by gripping his wrists in turn, stretching his arms, etc. (起霸) — this means that he is making sure that his dress is properly fastened for action. 齊如山，中國劇之組織，頁三十四. According to some veteran connoisseurs, the style of acting in the military plays has deteriorated both in variety and in expression. 清逸，戲中角色舊規則，戲劇叢刊，三期.

[8] The Chinese drama has been criticized for the extraneous matter it contains. Turner, it is said, was once asked why he put colours in his landscapes which cannot be found in nature and answered, "Don't you wish they could?" The same answer should be given to the critics of the Chinese drama.

expression of masculine beauty — the prowess and pride of warriors — as well as the suppleness and control of the players' body which is acquired through years of training. It exhilarates the spectators as a fast dance does and gives them the joy over sheer dexterity. The precision with which the action and music fit into each other even in the fastest passages cannot be found in the western theatre, not even in the modern European ballet. The pleasure of watching such histrionic art is similar to that of a music-lover, who knows a concert piece well, watching a good orchestra playing it flawlessly and with ease. The palpitating poise of a warrior on the Chinese stage is difficult to describe. Only those who have watched a tropical fish with outspread fins and bright colours marshalling itself for a fight or a bird with exotic plumes taking position in front of an enemy, can have some idea of the majesty and grace.[9]

A foreigner, an appreciative audience of the Chinese theatre, went to the naturalistic theatre in China. Instead of finding himself more at home with the scenery he saw:

"... a sorry sight. All the old glamour and romance were gone and with them all the art. No splendid costume, no fine struttings and sweeping gestures, no proud posturing and graceful dancing! It was as if the light had gone out". [10]

---

[9] Some critics also value special skill for its dramatic effect. When the general in *Li Ling's Monument* is about to die his armour is supposed to be removed by supernatural means, hence the actor should doff it without visible movements. 王夢生，梨園佳話，一章，"戲必有技". The actor Ho Kuei-Shan 何桂山 is remembered for his role of God of Fire in which he could spit fire endlessly. *Ibid.* 三章 . In *Haunting Chang San* 活捉張三 the way the dying man falls is also considered an important piece of histrionics. 齊如山, 京劇之變遷, 頁五八 .

[10] B. S. Allen, *Chinese Theatre Handbook,* 46.

CHAPTER XV

A SCHOOL OF STYLISH ACTING

Theatre, as an art, is basically different from drama, as literature. A stage performance appeals to the audience by the combined visual and aural effects of the stage action but drama, when read, produces its effect entirely by words. The only possible connection between the two is the fact that the script of some plays is not only good for stage dialogue but also interesting to read. In by far the majority of cases in the Chinese theatre, however, the script has no literary value. The fact that literary works can be cast in dialogue form does not mean that theatre and literature are similar in aim or method. Only when the stage is practically devoid of histrionic art and the performance little more than dressed play-reading does it become easy for one to confuse the values of the theatre with those of the written play. Dull revivals of classical plays, for example, are, as theatre, entirely to be deprecated, however valuable the written drama may be, because no amount of literary value in the script can compensate for poor production and acting. Similarly, when a play as performed appeals to the audience, it is good theatre even if the script is boring to read. The relation between the theatrical value and the literary value of the script is analogous to that between the song and its text, a good poem may be the text of a poor song and a beautiful song may be based on a poor poem. It is not impossible for good music to be without words just as good theatre, as in the case of pure dance, can be without any script.

The expressiveness of language does not depend on context alone. When words are spoken, the human voice can attach to them a wide range of feelings and, if one sees the facial expression and gestures of the speaker as well, the overtones of feelings can be even further increased. When we hear the voice we habitually understand much more than the words by themselves can convey as shown by the fact that when we want to know a person well we prefer conversation and interview to exchange of letters. Sometimes, the voice is so important to the meaning of words that the same sentence can have entirely different meanings according to the way it is spoken. Thus, "I beg your pardon", can mean either "I am sorry that I stepped on

137

your toes", or "I did not hear what you said, please say it again", or "I don't agree with you at all; I am sure you are wrong". In fact, the meaning of a word can even be reversed by a slight difference in the tone, as in the Chinese theatre when the audience shout "Hao"! (bravo) to both exceptionally good and disappointing singers each with its particular tone. Although it is only in such extreme cases that one can put totally different meanings into the same words, one can hardly find any words or phrases into which one cannot put a wide range of implications. [1]

Dramatic literature differs from theatre in the way the script becomes expressive: in literature it is through the context and the imagination of the reader and in theatre it is through the voice and gestures of the actors. In the Chinese theatre of to-day the plays, as literature, are not only feeble but often puerile and indeed they are seldom, if ever, read for their own sake. The characteristics of the Chinese stage are such, however, that despite such literary defects, great theatrical achievements are accomplished. Good theatre depends on the expression *on the stage* and the Chinese theatre has a style of highly expressive acting and declamation. [2] It is, for example, the fascination of the stylish acting that conceals the monotony of the dialogue of *The Lotus Lamp* 寶蓮燈 in which there are about as many repetitions of the same verbal phrases as there are of musical phrases in a Beethoven rondo. We see the facial expressions and gestures and hear the voices of other people so constantly that we are all more or less experts in reading other people's thoughts by them. Voice and gesture are more direct means of communication for one's feelings than words: dogs and little children understand them even if they do not understand the words. One may need a few moments of reflection to recognize the exact meaning of words, but the effect of the tones in the voice and the shades in the gesture is immediate. In the Chinese theatre of to-day the dramatists' words are feeble but the players' voice and gestures are highly developed. [3]

The expressions we use in ordinary life, verbal or otherwise, are, by the standards of art, poor in power and range. From childhood onwards the expressions of our feelings are curbed to conform with the social conventions and what is rigorously taught us in early life soon becomes second nature as we grow older. Expressions which are spontaneous in early childhood become stereotyped and divorced from the emotions which are supposed to prompt them. We cultivate these conventional expressions, such as that of concern over other people's health and

---

[1] There is no theoretical reason why a system of signs — a language — cannot be developed on the fingerings, or movements of the limbs, but the economy of energy and the ease of control probably made the prehistoric man develop the language of voice.

[2] cf. The expressiveness of music makes the puerile quality of western libretti unnoticeable.

[3] cf. "In dramas of the northern school, the words are very expressive but the voice is not; in those of the southern school the words are not very expressive, but the voice is". 魏良輔, 曲律, 十節: "北則辭情多而聲情少, 南則辭情少而聲情多".

that of good wishes and perform them in the prescribed manner at appropriate moments with a complete lack of feelings. Even when the rules of good manners allow us free expressions we often voluntarily refrain from them because we want to remain sober for practical reasons and expression aggravates sudden emotional disturbance, or else our own modesty forbids public exhibition of our feelings. Again in most people's life the exciting moments are few and far between, fewer and milder at any rate than in dramas. What is not smothered by imposed and voluntary suppression withers through lack of exercise. In the end most of us become so inexpressive that when confronted with sudden humiliation or unexpected joy we cannot show any feelings at all; we are stunned: a situation faithfully reproduced in the realistic theatre. [4] Emotional expressions, in their simplest and most natural forms, as in children, have a physiological basis and are the same throughout the world. We learn their meanings in our babyhood hence their effects are felt directly and almost instinctively. Conventionalized expressions, on the other hand, are partially or wholly divorced from the emotions, they are partly arbitrary codes, hence they differ according to race, social class and historical period. We learn a set of them in childhood and have to learn other sets if we live among people of different customs and manners. In civilized societies the expressions in adult life are mostly conventionalized, hence to imitate them in the drama is to use, at the best, crude and restrained and, at the worst, awkward and false expressions. In the Chinese theatre the expressions used are derived from the natural and spontaneous manifestations of emotions but are developed beyond them to carry the more complicated emotions of adult life. Unlike the natural expressions of children, the Chinese style of acting cannot be automatically and universally understood, it is a language which has to be learned. The ceremoniousness of Chinese life makes the contrast between ordinary and stage expressions particularly striking, the one regulated by considerations of decorum and expediency and aimed at pleasant and advantageous social relationship, the other directed towards felicity and truth with the ultimate aim in a beautiful style of acting. The manners of everyday life are inexpressive because they evolved under the need to conceal feelings; only in the theatre can modes of expression be developed which can communicate feelings with maximum effectiveness.

We are all potential artists. Although our capabilities for emotional expression are undeveloped our understanding of expressions is sound. We can appreciate a greater range of emotions than we can or care to express and we become good audience more readily than we do good actors.

The effectiveness of the Chinese style of acting is primarily based on its

---

[4] The stifling feeling we have under strong emotions is probably due to this inability to express them. Even in everyday life, speech is often inadequate for the expression of our feelings. In south China, at the Tomb Festival, one can see women at the tombs wailing in a melodious chant.

complete disregard of realism. As people do not show much feeling in real life, for an actor to appear natural he must restrict his expressions to the range and force consistent with real life. In the naturalistic theatre, if the actor deviates noticeably from what ordinary people can be imagined to do, he is liable to be accused of being "theatrical". [5] Such limitation does not exist on the Chinese stage: the Chinese actors are free to express the emotions in tones and gestures far removed from the habits of the audience. If we think of the Chinese theatre as legend come to life, we can also think of the people that man the legends as curiously uninhibited. Even when they are stunned they do not remain inactive for long. In *The Capture and Escape of Ts'ao* when Ts'ao Ts'ao shouted rudely at Ch'en Kung, "Let's go!" (走吓) the latter for a moment could not answer but merely stammered after Ts'ao "Let's go", but later when Ch'en knelt beside the old man whom Ts'ao killed, he gave way to lamentations. If the scene is to be naturalistic the lamentations must be omitted and the sorrow expressed in silent tears.

In normal life, the use of the language and the speaking voice is, to a certain extent, governed by economy: we do not want to say more than is necessary to convey the information. In a theatre where realism is disregarded convenience need not be considered. [6] In the Chinese theatre where the plot is a means to build up scenes that are rich in feelings, the story is told with the utmost economy, in concise diction and simple voice, but as the emotional pitch of the action rises the language becomes more emotional, and the style of acting and delivery becomes more expressive. At the climax the dialogue becomes poetry, the acting becomes dance and speech becomes singing. The Chinese theatre is in fact a mixture of drama, opera and ballet. The dialogue is partly prose and partly poetry and it is sometimes more or less plainly spoken, sometimes declaimed and sometimes sung. When the action has little emotional content or when it is not chosen by the playwright for elaborate treatment, the conventions simplify the representation as, for example, in journeys and slumbers, but when the action is the centre of the emotional interest of the play as in lamentation, prayer, confession, etc., it is embellished by arias and mime so that the acting time is usually far longer than what it would take to do the same thing in real life. At one end one finds sketchy narration, simplified action, concise dialogue and plain voice and at the other poetic diction, singing and elaborate acting. The former, though it may occupy the greater part of the script, is a minor part of the performance both in time and the attention it receives from the audience who can, it is to be remembered, at any time be engaged in eating and

---

[5] cf. The naturalistic theatre has no clowns — those who represent subnormal intellect and emotions. They lie beyond the range of average humanity.

[6] There is a story of a troupe of Japanese actors playing reapers in a village who noticed that the audience, which contained real reapers, whispered disapproval of the actor's movements. The actors then watched and learned the reapers' movements, but the next performance, with the realistic movements, was a failure. A. Waley, *The Noh Plays of Japan,* Introduction p. 39.

drinking, but the latter, though it may be one monologue or incantation can occupy the greater part of the performance time, and is, in fact, the only thing in the Chinese theatre which can impose silence on the audience. [7]

The consistency with which dramatic action is graded according to its emotional content by the amount of the actors' effort and the audience's attention indicates that the interest of the Chinese theatre is not in the narration of events but in the expression of emotions and the form which the dialogue and the acting take in the most emotional and most interesting parts of the action suggests that ordinary means of expressing strong emotions are considered unsuitable for the purpose of the Chinese stage. Realistic acting, especially for highly emotional moments, is likely to excite and agitate the audience but that is what Chinese players try to avoid. The Chinese stage has a quality which, for want of a better term, one may call lyricism. The play is more a commentary on the plot than a narration of it; it is nearer to a poem than to a tale. The audience does not share the sentiments of the characters nor mentally take part in the action but contemplates the sentiments through the poetical form in which they are expressed. It is therefore important for them always to remain psychologically aloof. The stylized expression at highly emotional moments are not only for the lyrical effect but also for guarding against sentimentality. A cry or a shriek can induce a nervous tension but a melodious aria or a graceful dance cannot. The transition from declamation to singing in scenes of rising emotional pitch is particularly significant: the declaimed passage is usually connected to the aria by an ejaculation or sigh which is drawn out in a high tone, then the instrumental introduction to the aria follows. As the spoken passage becomes more excited the audience becomes more tense but the ejaculation is as far as it is safe to go, and when the orchestra starts the music there is a sense of relief, the audience are calmed by it and make themselves ready for the singing. Similarly the acting, though conventionalized, bears the mark of excitement during the spoken passages but as soon as an actor starts singing he generally puts all his expression into the voice. While singing he controls his voice to make good music, not to do vocal acting. Some Chinese singers have tried to simulate the voice being

---

[7] The script should be considered only as a skeleton scheme for the art of the actor. The length of the performance can be varied enormously, as shown by the following anecdote: "In the late nineteenth century T'an Hsin-P'ei 譚鑫培 was in the same company as T'ien Kuei-Feng 田桂鳳 who had the bad habit of being late so that T'an often had to dress and sing his play first, which is a great favour because the last item is by custom reserved for the best actor, and T'ien certainly was not better than T'an. One day T'ien was late again and when he arrived at the theatre T'an, who was already dressed, asked, 'Who shall sing first?' expecting an apology for the inconvenience of dressing and undressing, but T'ien answered, "Any way you like". From then on it became a custom for T'ien to sing last whenever he was late. T'an purposely acted slowly, so that by the time T'ien was on the stage it was dark (there were no lamps in the theatre in those days) and eventually T'ien lost the support of the public". 齊如山, 京劇之變遷, 頁五七.

choked with emotions, but this is considered to be bad form. The object of the Chinese theatre is a beautiful vision, not a nervous state. If nothing else, the concentration required to appreciate the subtleties of the singer's voice makes it undesirable for the audience to be emotionally excited. An audience carried away by the emotions of the play can hardly be at the same time sensitive to what is best in a singer's voice or a dancer's movements; to them the complex feelings the actors express are likely to appear simple, elusive feelings pass them unnoticed and subtle feelings they would misunderstand. No doubt, in village performances the uncultivated taste of the rustic audience demands nothing except crude and stirring expressions; but what is said in the preceding relates to the classical theatre, not the local theatres.

The lyrical quality of the Chinese stage is due to the combined effect of the richer resources of the histrionic art made possible by its departure from realism and the strict form in which they are cast. It is not impossible to imagine a style of acting developed beyond the restrictions of realism which is so powerful that many dramas would be physically unbearable. The Chinese style of acting and declamation, however, is clothed in a strict artistic form which takes away the impact of powerful expressions. The acting is like dance not only because it is accompanied by music but also because whatever the actor does, even in the most tragic scenes, he has to be graceful. [8] Standard conventions for simple action such as laughing, being angry, feeling contempt, etc., are developed and form a major part of the actors' training. [9] These conventionalized styles of acting are such that they can be stiff and dull in poor actors but can never be crude and violent. The actors' training is in fact similar to that of the dancers': the technique first and the expressions later. [10] An actor may or may not learn how to put emotional shadings into his acting and make it lively

[8] In the military plays the warriors, engaged in ferocious fighting would suddenly stop into a tableau with the staccato coda in the music. The object is to arrest the eyes of the audience in a calculated pose and leave a static impression of the warriors' postures. The Chinese style of acting always aims at giving pleasure as well as expressing emotions.

[9] In a book on Mei Lan-Fang 齊如山, 梅蘭芳藝術之一班 (民二四) 頁二至十一, laughs are differentiated into twenty-seven types. This however does not seem to be included in the regular training of the actors, because in its preface it is said that the book was written "especially for foreigners".

[10] The different types of movements and postures have been documented by Prof. Ch'i Ju-Shan. The numbers are as follows:

Sleeves .... 72 movements.
Hands .... 7 ways to hold the hand.
26 gestures of pointing (pointing in anger, pointing backwards, pointing to oneself, etc).
14 gestures for pointing at different parts of one's own body.
10 gestures for pointing with something one holds in one's hand.
3 gestures for pointing with a finger at something one holds oneself.

and precise but his training and the tradition of the theatre preclude the possibility of crude exaggerations. He may be stolid but he can never be blustering; he may be a slave to conventions but he cannot overact.

The movements of the Chinese actors are often specified in considerable detail, so that blind actors can act on the Chinese stage.

"In the early years of Kuang Hsü's reign (1875-1909) there was an actor Ting Hsiao-San 丁孝三 , then over seventy years old, who was blind but continued to act. He had to be led to the entrance door after which, following the music, he could perform on the stage. but when he reached the exit door, he had to be led again into the green room". 齊如山，京劇之變遷，頁五九. Presumably the blind actor could only manage simple action. Even so, it is significant that in the green room, where the movements of the other actors are not predictable, he needed help, but on the stage he could manage himself.

Through the formal quality of the acting what is agitating in an emotional expression is concealed and what is elegant brought out. For example, in the representation of slumber on the Chinese stage, the actor, instead of sprawling over the table or lying stretched out in bed, merely leans on his hand and closes his eyes, suggesting without reproducing the act of sleeping. In emotional expressions the audience see the emotions only through a veil of graceful movements and harmonious voice. In fact everything on the Chinese stage has the qualities of music: the predominance of form — rhythm, balance — and sensuous pleasure; hence the dialogue is in verse and the acting is akin to dance. Nothing is so contrary to the taste of the audience as to intensify the part of an expression that is frightful or harrowing and thus reap immediate and powerful effect. One wishes to be moved, even to tears, not by the emotions but by the beauty with which they are expressed.

There is a wide range of gestures and vocal acting but in it flourish and rhetoric predominate. Even a simple phrase like *"Lai-liao"*, 來了 (coming) can become highly embellished, as in *P'ing Kuei's Farewell* 從軍別窰 : the hero has joined the

---

Feet . . . . 46 different gaits (swimming steps, going upstairs, going downstairs, ghosts' steps, etc.)

9 styles for moving the foot (not in walking or running).

Leg . . . . 12 movements and postures.

Arm . . . . 8 movements.

Beard . . . . 39 styles of movements.

Pheasant feathers . . . . 11 styles of movements.

In *K'un* dramas 崑曲 and *Pang Tzu* dramas 梆子 there are more conventional movements and postures. 齊如山，國劇身段譜，三，四章 . See also Cecilia S. L. Zung, *Secrets of the Chinese Drama* for illustrations. It is to be noticed that a movement, for instance, pointing at an object far away, is different for different types of characters, one style for men, another for women, another for comedians, etc., so that the real number of different styles is even greater than shown above.

army and returns to the hut as an army officer to bid farewell to his wife and after knocking at the door waits uneasily; the wife inside the hut (off stage) answers, *"Lai-liao"*. In this scene the two words *"Lai-liao"*, are drawn out in a crescendo and a diminuendo totalling some six or eight seconds. Then in *P'ing Kuei's Return* 武家坡 the husband, having returned after many years as a captive in a foreign country, meets his wife at the roadside but, instead of presenting himself forthwith, he pretends to be a messenger from her husband. The wife, not very well dressed, does not care to disclose who she is to what she takes to be a stranger and, in order to get the letter the "messenger" says he is carrying, offered to deliver it for him. When he insists on delivering it in person, however, she has to reveal her identity but demureness keeps her from saying her own name, so she proposes to play a game of riddles with him and asks, "What is far away?" "Those whom we cannot see and meet", says her husband. "And the near — ?" (這近) she asks again, in a diminuendo cadence, with her head tilted away and looking at him from the corners of her eyes. This can be one of the most alluring expressions of a coy woman. Similarly the repeated shouts, in mounting force, of "Let's go!" in *The Capture and Escape of Ts'ao* 捉放曹 can be a piece of beautiful acting, expressive of the impatience of the callous statesman towards the meek and sorrow-stricken scholar. In *The Stratagem of the Empty City* 空城計 the attacking general desists from entering a city with wide open gates because he suspects ambush, though his son thinks it is truly empty, so he camps at a distance and sends reconnoitre parties to the surroundings. Meanwhile, the general in the city has sent for relief and is ready to fly as soon as he can afford to do so. The manner in which the deceived general receives reports, first of the true state of the city, then of the approach of the relief force and lastly of the flight of his enemy who, he knows now, was practically alone in the city, each time crying, "More patrol!" (再探) but with different intonation, well illustrates the fact that the voice can put a great deal of dramatic effect into comparatively simple phrases. When the prisoner in *The Joint Court* 三堂會審 cries "Your Honour!" (大人哪) just before she gives her testimony, the audience hears all her hopes and fears in one phrase; and when the unscrupulous statesman in *The Capture and Escape of Ts'ao* 捉放曹 cries, "Ah that —" (這個) when asked whether he ever thought how posterity would see him, it reveals, for one moment, what looks like conscience in a man of boundless egotism. In such cases it is not so much what the actor says as the way he says it that makes good theatre.

The possibility of using the long-drawn voice in the pronunciation of Chinese words may be an important factor in the style of declamation in the Chinese theatre. In normal life we do not always pronounce words with meticulous care because those who listen to us need not, and often do not in fact, hear every syllable we speak, what they do not hear their imagination, guided by the context, will supply. In the theatre, owing to the greater distances involved, the audience cannot hear intelligibly unless the players speak with particular clarity and force. In speaking the Chinese language, to speak clearly is to accentuate the inflexions of the tone. In fact the Chinese actors divide the word into the "head" 音頭, the "body" 音腹 and the "tail" 音尾 for purposes of training and practice. What in everyday life are short syllables are expanded by the players into long-drawn tones capable of subtle modulations.

The expression of feelings in the drama, not directly, but through an artistic form, has its secondary effects. Where there is form there is idiom and idiom has to be learned. Although little training is required to understand the realistic theatre, for the appreciation of the Chinese theatre a period of initiation is needed. For most Chinese people learning "the idiom of the stage" starts and finishes in childhood and the mental process is later forgotten but, for those who are not familiar with it, the particular type of acting and singing can appear forbidding even after they have accepted the lack of realism. Once appreciation is acquired, however, the dance-like acting and the singing are sources of rich sensuous, if not intellectual, delight. The Chinese theatre, like European classical ballet, is decorative and entertaining even when it is not inspired. This is why it is a pleasant adjunct to the tea-house; it is dramatic *divertimento*. This sensuous delight, which one also gets in concerts and pageants, is what a Chinese audience misses first in the realistic theatre where the mind is supposed to be feasted but the eye and ear are starved.

Theatrical poses of the masked character

Theatrical pose of the masked character

45A

Theatrical pose of the lady

45B

Theatrical pose of the lady

45C

Theatrical pose of the lady

46A

An officer in
travelling clothes

46B

A swashbuckler in fighting gear

A swashbuckler in formal dress

Theatrical pose of an old man

47B

*Theatrical pose of
a scholar
(contemplating cutting
off his own arm)*

47C

Theatrical pose of a high official

CHAPTER XVI

RELATION BETWEEN THE COSTUME AND THE ACTING

The Chinese players do not use realistic stage effects and dummies, because they want to avoid emotional agitation, but they employ rich costume and colourful masks in order to achieve the theatrical effects. The object of the Chinese drama is not to recount events but to express emotions and the object of the acting is not to reproduce action but to invoke feelings. What the Chinese audience want is not documentary accuracy, but felicity of expression, so the players minimize the utilitarian part of the movements and gestures and accentuate the expressive part.

A night scene on the Chinese stage is as bright as any other scene. What the players try to produce is the impression of darkness, not the physical fact. If the lights were dimmed, the audience would no doubt have greater difficulty in seeing the actors and it would be registered in their minds that the scene is dark, but unless the scene is skilfully acted the actors, who could of course see well enough to do their stage business, may appear to the audience as being in a bright place. The Chinese stage remains well lit in a night scene because it is important that the audience should see the acting clearly. The players evoke the feelings of moving about in the dark by portraying the awkwardness of groping at unseen objects, the ill directed efforts to avoid knocking over things, the reliance on fingers as feelers and guides and the loss of sense of direction and distance. Whether the stage is actually dark is uninteresting and unimportant, the success of the mime lies in reviving in the minds of the audience the experience of being in a dark place. When the conspirator in *The Gathering of the Heroes* 羣英會 plants a fake letter in the sleeping quarters of the spy, he enters the fully-lit stage with a candle in his hand but, through his timid steps, one can feel he is walking by the small circle of light from the candle. He puts the candle on the table, makes a last minute check on the letter, slips it under some article on the table, snuffs the candle-wick with his fingers, drops it on the floor and puts out the sparks with his foot. Then, leaving the candle on the table, he retreats, supposedly in total darkness. By shading the acting before and after the candle is

147

snuffed the actor makes the audience aware of the difference between the feeble light of the candle and total darkness.

If rain is faithfully reproduced on the stage the set and the actors will get wet and wet actors may not succeed in communicating the feelings we experience when we are caught in a rainstorm. The players can act more easily when they are dry. In *The Royal Monument* 御碑亭 the heroine, caught by a rainstorm in her ill-advised journey, passes the night in a pavilion which houses the royal monument. In the morning she comes out gingerly to see whether the stranger who has been standing under the eaves all night has gone and finding no one outside the pavilion she steps forward and is surprised by a water drop. She wipes her forehead, looks up and puts out her hand to make sure that there are no more. Then, finding that water has collected round the building she pauses. Finally, choosing one dry spot or stone after another, she crosses the puddle in zig-zag steps and resumes her journey. All this, done expressively on a bare stage, can conjure up the feelings of a morning after the storm better than a wet stage. Dark nights and rainstorms are common experience, the theatre would be rather pointless if it is to display artificial weather conditions. It is the keen feelings of moving in the dark and trying to avoid getting wet in the rain that only the art of a poet or an actor can revive.

Acting is the most important part of the Chinese theatre, stage effects and properties are only accessories. It is noticeable that in spite of the general paucity of the stage setting, some properties, such as the candle and the lantern in night scenes are completely realistic. The horse is imaginary but the whip is not only real but beautifully made and, similarly, the boat is only supposed to be on the stage but the oars are actually there. Whereas the carriage, the sedan-chair, the city wall, the bed and the throne are symbolic models, the spear, the flag, the military token (used both as a pass and a token of authenticity of a message), the imperial mandate (a silk scroll from which the royal orders are read) and most of the weapons are full-sized and exact copies. The contrast is so sharp and the tradition so constantly observed that they suggest a strong reason behind them. In fact if one traces the use of the properties one can find that all the properties used in acting are accurately made but those not so used are symbolic. Owing to the lack of interest in representation as such, it is sufficient merely to indicate certain properties, but as good acting is the predominant feature of the Chinese stage, what the players *act with* becomes important. This general rule applies to all properties even though details are sometimes modified by fortuitous considerations. That the sword has its scabbard but the bow has no arrow, even when used for shooting, would not seem odd when one takes safety into consideration. The halberd and the battle-axe are tasselled, for decorative effect, and the dart has a large cloth tail so that the audience can see it more clearly. (Real objects are sometimes produced on the Chinese stage for comic effects. The reason for the comic effect is: it is incongruous in the Chinese drama.

Surprise intensifies grief and joy but in this case the unexpectedness is not connected with any emotion. The incongruity implies burlesque, defiance of convention, sudden departure from the world of drama or a joke on the fundamental pretence involved in the drama — like topical allusion. It may also be taken as an expression of Harlequinish childishness and simple faith to take drama too literally).

That the costume should be elaborate and even luxurious but the scenery non-existent and stage properties meagre is also because the players do not act with the set but they do act with the costume. Nothing is spared to achieve beautiful acting but no more effort is spent on representation than is absolutely necessary.

No actor or dancer, unless he is in tights, can, strictly speaking, be dancing or acting with his body alone; all actors act with their costume as well. The effect of costume on acting is partly instinctive, for even in ordinary life both men and women carry themselves differently when they are in different types of clothes, such as athletic wear and evening dress. In the Chinese theatre both the costume and the style of acting are the result of centuries of tradition and development; no one can be said to have designed the one and directed the other, hence the present close relationship between costume and acting may be said to be the result of a long mutual influence. [1]

Dress is a foil or accompaniment to personal beauty. Close fitting dresses are suitable for showing the beauty of figure and loose dress, the beauty of movement and posture. Chinese stage costume is of the latter kind because Chinese garments are generally loose. [2] The stage costume is mainly made of soft silk and is particularly suitable for slow and dignified dances. Heavy disguise and elaborate embellishment are often used and though some personal ornaments are based on ancient customs they are usually exaggerated for theatrical effects.

The imitation of small feet, originally with the actual wearing of the small shoes and walking practically on the toes on the stage, is the basis of the carriage of female characters, hence it deserves special explanation. The feet of Chinese women were bound because the small and deformed feet were considered to be beautiful. Within living memory women took pride in possessing them and men were attracted to women by them. Whether the custom was healthy and ethical is one problem, whether the small feet are beautiful is another — there should not be confusion of categories. It is believed to originate in the imperial court of Southern T'ang dynasty (937-975 A.D.) when a style of dance with ample opportunity to display the feet was fashionable among the ladies of the court. The fact that the shoes worn on the small feet are called "bow shoes" (弓鞋) suggests that they were originally probably a

---

[1] When skill of the actor or dancer is valued above faithful reproduction, costume will not be historically correct. cf. European ballet.

[2] The gowns used on the Chinese stage are particularly loose because they are not made to fit individual actors but are made large for interchangeability.

kind of high heeled shoes worn on natural feet to make them appear shorter and more plump and to improve the gait. Then binding the feet to fit smaller shoes started a craze which led to its application to children. The unnatural size of the resultant adult feet, two inches or less in length, must be unattractive to modern taste, but the excess, like that of the corset, the bustle and the skirt in European fashions, was reached through a long period of competition and changing taste. To the Chinese of the older generation, the small feet, whose mystery is enhanced by the long skirt, have more fascination than their effect on women's carriage. Distortion of the female body has been practiced till now by many peoples, because what is natural is not always beautiful, and foot-binding was not the first or last instance of carrying it to excess.

So far as theatre is concerned, one can ignore the beauty of the small feet as part of the female body but deal only with their effect on the general appearance of Chinese women. The idea of feminine beauty is always connected in China with daintiness and frailty. The effect of having small feet is basically the same as that of wearing high-heeled shoes and that is, to lessen the area of support and make the body less stable. Even when a woman is standing still in long petticoat one can tell whether she has small feet or not, because, in order to balance herself on two points instead of four, she has to adjust her body so that its weight acts directly through the small soles and to move herself occasionally in order to maintain equilibrium. [3] This gives her the grace of a flower on a slender stalk, or that of ballet dancer *sur les pointes* in a tableau. When the ballet dancers stand on the soles of their feet their posture is static and stable, like a flask on a table, but when they are *sur les pointes* they are constantly in danger of falling, constantly balancing themselves and therefore look palpitating with loveliness. This kind of loveliness is what the Chinese audience look for in a female character. Even when she is standing she is on the border line of motion and stillness and when she is walking her frailty is aggravated, because though she can stand on two points, when walking she has to support her weight on one for the greater part of the time. She can therefore walk only in small steps and has to shift her body more frequently in order to maintain the balance. She automatically thrusts her pelvis backwards and her chest forwards and moves the shoulders in the opposite direction of her feet. The movement of the whole body is altogether more complicated. The feminine gait is, by Chinese standards, least attractive when most natural, as when walking barefooted, or with flat-heeled shoes, or in ballet shoes (in which case it is called, in European theatres, the "ballerina's wobble"). A woman is more beautiful on high-heeled shoes and even more so when *sur les pointes*. The gait of a Chinese woman with small feet, of which the theatre produces an enriched version, is somewhere between wearing high-heeled shoes and *sur les pointes*.

---

[3] cf. One can recognize dancing on bare feet or on high heeled shoes without seeing the feet.

This gait is acquired by painstaking training, sometimes with the disguise for small feet (in which the feet are bandaged against splints so that the actor practically walks on his toes) or, more often now, in ordinary shoes. The difference in the poise of the female impersonator due to the disguise is conspicuous and connoisseurs prefer the use of small shoes. [4] In both cases the feet, except for female warriors, are concealed on the stage by the long petticoat. When the actors wear the disguise they are expected to have complete control of their body and not to show the smallest sign of strain and they are trained in such exercises as running, while wearing the disguise, in circles on ice and standing still on the edge of large jars.

The bearing of the male characters, including the military types, is regulated by the thick soles, two or three inches, on their boots. It is impossible to walk in the natural way in these boots and the possible steps are limited to struts of various tempi. Except in military scenes, the gait is slow and dignified. The thick sole affects the appearance of the actors by making them taller and by changing the proportion between the legs and the rest of the body. As in the case of high-heeled shoes which increase the apparent length of the legs, the audience is conscious of the effect but not necessarily of the mechanism, especially as the actors are usually disguised in other ways at the same time. The thick soles are only part of a system of disguise: the spreading headgear of the military characters, the pennons they wear on their back, the painted masks made larger than the face by shaving the forehead and the temples, the heavy padding of the warriors' torso and the opulent beards worn by them would make them top heavy but for the apparent lengthening of the legs. The disguises, though keeping in general proportion, are carried to such extent at each point that the result does not look natural. The characters are legendary figures; so long as they look beautiful, their weird appearance fits them. Indeed they should, in appearance as well as in language and elocution, belong to another world.

Acting on stage, unlike acting in the moving picture, is based on movements that can be seen from a distance. On stage small details, however expressive, are lost to the majority of the audience. Although some Chinese actors have tried using facial expressions, generally speaking the acting is meant to be seen from a distance. [5] Posture and carriage are extensively used to express the personality and temperament of the characters and relatively inconspicuous action, such as laughing or weeping, is made more easily visible by the accompanying hand movements, for example, when a woman chuckles or cries she covers her face with the sleeve (a decorous Chinese woman cannot cry or laugh loud). As in the puppet theatre, many

---

[4] It is to be noticed that when the actor wears the disguise for small feet his height and the apparent length of his legs are increased.

[5] Most people in the theatre think that they see facial expressions when actually they do not. This is because we are so accustomed to the mutual accompaniment of facial expressions and gestures that when we see one, we imagine we also see the other.

151

feelings and emotions are expressed by the movement of the body: a man would wave his hand and turn his head in disgust and draw circles in the air with his finger when he is laying a scheme. [6] The transference of expression from the face to the

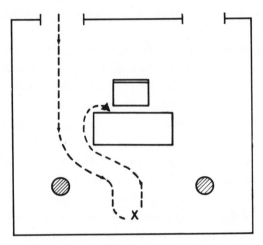

Fig. 48
Conventional Entrance — A (for Men)
X — Pause

---

[6] There is a certain similarity between the puppets and the Chinese style of acting — in both the accentuation is prominent. This similarity has been cited as evidence for the theory that the Chinese drama was derived from puppet plays — 孫楷第, · 近代戲曲原出宋傀儡戲影戲考, 輔仁學誌, 十一卷一二期. Prof. Ch'i Ju-Shan was told by an old actor that a certain convention of the Chinese stage, namely, male and female characters turn in different directions when they go upstage after addressing the audience at the front edge of the stage, was derived from the puppet play. 齊如山, 京劇之變遷, 頁七. The explanation was: if both puppets turned in the same direction their strings would be tangled (see Figs. 48-51). In the Chinese theatre when an actor makes a mistake in this convention he is said to "reverse the strings" (反線), apparently a term for marionettes. The similarity may, however, be due to the fact that both in the puppets and in the Chinese theatre accentuation is necessary, in the former to compensate for the small size of the figures and in the latter, to compensate for the large distances between the actors and the audience.

hands and the body is particularly noticeable in the masked characters who cannot have any facial expression at all, but even in the other characters the sensitive expressions in the eyes and the muscles of the face are impracticable on the stage and

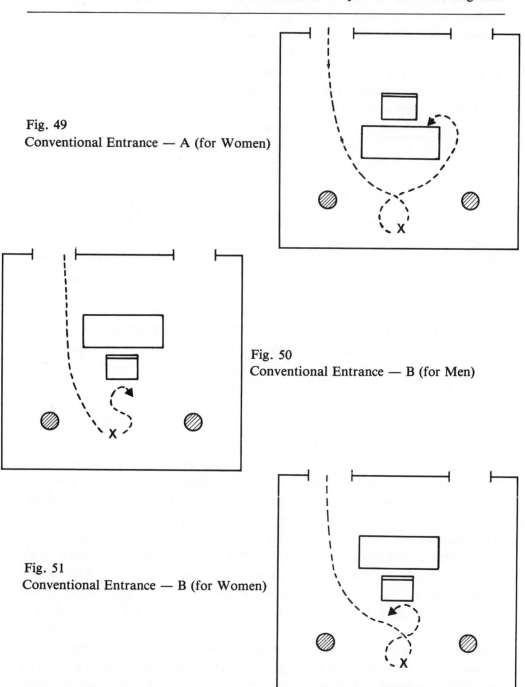

Fig. 49
Conventional Entrance — A (for Women)

Fig. 50
Conventional Entrance — B (for Men)

Fig. 51
Conventional Entrance — B (for Women)

have to be substituted by gestures. The inclination of the head and the movements of the hands, both of which are highly expressive and can cover a wide range of feelings, can only be used to a certain extent under normal conditions because nuance is lost to people looking at the stage from a distance and only the accentuated movements can be seen. Perhaps the most striking aspects of the Chinese theatrical costume are the two devices that enhance the expression of the head and the hands, namely, the large headgear and the "tab sleeve". The principle is very simple, as the movements are obscured by the distance they are magnified on the stage to compensate for lost clarity. Women wear a tall bun near the top of the head and men wear caps with pompons on the top or wings at the sides, the pompons and wings being mounted on elastic stalks. The effect of the large head dress is to magnify the movements of the head: a slight tilt produces a lurch of the pompons and wings and a shake sends tremors through them. The most sensitive headgear is that with the pheasant feathers, six or seven feet long, leaning backwards and slightly to the sides, worn by some military officials. With the resultant magnification the actor cannot move his head in the slightest degree without the whole theatre seeing it clearly; therefore wearing them properly requires special skill and this type of character is a class by itself called "pheasant feather roles" (雉尾生). The actors wearing them use head movements extensively, such as sending waves through them in suppressed anguish and tossing them to one side with a decisive turn of the head when they are suddenly aroused and they also act with them by holding the ends in their mouths in ferocious moods and bend them forward with their hands to let them spring back at a sudden change of mood. The long beards also serve to make the movements of the head more clearly visible but the actors also manipulate them with the hands and arms such as by lifting the whole with the forearm, holding it to one side with a hand, lifting a small tuft with two fingers near the root and passing them through its length, etc.

The "tab sleeves" may have been the overgrown sleeves of a shirt or the inaccurate copy of the long sleeves on ancient Chinese garments — whatever the origin, they are now purely a theatrical device. As they are made of white silk and hang about two feet from the end of the normal sleeves they can be seen clearly at a great distance and the lightness of the material and the absence of the seam on the lower side make them easy to manoeuvre. They can be carried in thin heaps on the wrists (Fig. 17B), they can be tossed to the front or the side, they can be stretched between the two hands, they can hang on the hand to shield the face and they can be caught by the hands after an upward jerk, etc. Both the male and female characters have many ways of acting with them ranging from the more obvious and specific expressions such as sending waves down them when the hands are trembling, to the more subtle and stylish, such as using one to balance a posture visually (Figs. 45A and 45C) and letting one fly above a woman's head like a pennon when she glides through a curve. [7] ''Tab sleeves'' make the arm movements so sensitive that no actor is allowed to stretch his arms straight downward, they must be slightly bent on all occasions, even for unimportant characters like serving maids, except for ghosts whose straight arms make them look like stiff corpses.

Only the warriors do not wear ''tab sleeves'' but they are expected to act more with their bodies. [8] Apart from the elaborate armour they wear they carry four pennons on their backs and dozens of pompons or some top knots on their caps. When they marshal themselves into position before a fight one may compare them to well plumed cocks. If they are to wear realistic and tight fitting clothes, the fight, like that of two plucked cocks, would lose all its splendour. Similarly with the other types of characters: when they strut or amble their gowns sway and the pompons and wings oscillate to the rhythm of the music. With sustained rhythm both in the music and in the dancing, the glittering figure on the stage can have an almost hypnotising fascination.

Of the other garments and properties specifically used in acting may be mentioned the fan — a symbol of frivolity — and the ''waist skirt'' (腰裙) — a thin plaited skirt slit in the front worn over the gown by women travelling on foot, with the top at the waist and the hem reaching to the knees. [9]

The cultivation of feminine charm is an art. In the western world only women cultivate that art (by going to the college of beauty culture, for example) but in the oriental countries actors also study it and, as in all arts, men excel women. In Japan the geisha girls, to whom seductiveness is a professional qualification, go to the theatres to learn from the female impersonators. In the Chinese theatre, the cultivation of feminine charm has reached a dangerous level. To experience lasting emotional disturbance in the theatre must be considered as a pathological condition, yet, both men and women in China have fallen for beautiful actors. The handsome actor Yü Chen-T'ing 俞振廷 who played the young warrior was admired by so many women that several of them became his concubines. [10] In the case of female impersonators the emotions are complicated by the fact that men played women. Actors who appeared as beautiful women in the dramas, and presumably retained some of that beauty off-stage, became favourite companions to admiring patrons. At one time, theatre was almost a secondary profession for the female impersonators, as the following conversation, taken from a novel of the eighteenth century, clearly shows:

---

[7] Seventy-two styles have been listed in 齊如山, 國劇身段譜, 三章一節.

[8] *Ibid.* 三章一節引言 : There are more conventional movements for the legs for male characters than for female characters but there are more movements of the hands and arms for the female characters.

[9] *Vide* A. C. Scott, Some Chinese Theatrical Costumes and their Accessories, *World Theatre* (UNESCO), Vol. II. No. 4 (1953). 30-34.

[10] 王夢生, 梨園佳話, 三章.

"I was told that these two troupes are the best, but when I went to see them there were only some old actors singing *K'un* dramas. All those coming in and out on the stage are like defeated soldiers, not a single good-looking *hsiang-kung* among them. I really can't see why they are supposed to be good".

"Ah — but what you don't know is: these two companies are engaged mostly in private performances, where you can find the good looking *hsiang-kung*. They don't come to the theatres at all . . ." 陳森書, 品花寶鑑, 四回.
The prevalence of such admiration is also shown by the innumerable panegyrics written for female impersonators, mostly of low literary quality, which deluge the *Sources of Theatrical History in Peking in Ch'ing Dynasty* 清代燕都梨園史料. On this subject the critic Wang Meng-Sheng has this to say:

"Appreciation of *hsiang-kung* is considered as romance of the highest order and those who can enjoy it claim to have exhausted all the erotic joys of the world; but owing to these few, everyone who comes near to actors is suspected of ulterior motives, and this is truly regrettable. In the past, government officials were strictly forbidden to visit pleasure houses hence some of them invited female impersonators to their dinners, partly for music and partly, judging by their rich clothes and their jests, for other types of appreciation. Whether or not it is romantic feeling of the highest order as is claimed, it is difficult for me to say, as the saying goes, 'Without trying horse liver one cannot judge its superior taste', but from Ming and Ch'ing dynasty till now many scholars who gave themselves to wine and poetry were the slaves of such passions. Near the end of the last century, there was a fashion for such pursuits in Peking and many young actors were famous for their agreeable company . . . In particular Pao-Shan (寶珊) who was handsome, though not particularly good in singing and acting, could fascinate the audience with his natural beauty alone. Whenever he entered or left the theatre, people like ants pressed forward to catch a glimpse of him . . . Although his profession was, strictly speaking, different from the theatrical, it was connected with it. To understand the taste one can consult the *Treatise on the Appreciation of Beauty* (品花寶鑑 a novel of the eighteenth century). Recently, real feminine beauty is by no means lacking in the city and the nobility are now free to enjoy themselves as much as they wish, therefore, even without prohibition, the male competitors of these female beauties will probably become extinct. Indeed, it is said that they have already established an agreement among themselves to abandon the trade and earn their living by theatre alone. If they succeeded, it would be a happy event". 王夢生, 梨園佳話, 四章 "像姑".
This was written in 1915; but they were apparently still active when Arlington wrote *The Chinese Drama* (published 1930).
The vogue of the admiration for feminine beauty in men has several causes. The

seclusion of women must have its effect on the sexual psychology of men and the official attitude towards homosexuality facilitated the propagation of such taste — "public quarters" of young boys were openly operated and patronized. In the theatre, owing to the low social status of the actors, the favours of powerful patrons would be both attractive and compelling. In the late eighteenth century, some of the most notorious female impersonators even staged obscene dramas. In particular, Ch'en Yin-Kuan 陳銀官 specialized in lewd plays; he would have a curtained bed on the stage before the play began and peep through the curtain in the most suggestive manner. [11] It was Ch'en's teacher, Wei San 魏三, who first used the coiffure and small shoes that have survived till to-day. [12]

[11] 青木正兒，中國近世戲曲史，十二章二節.

[12] （清）楊懋建　夢華瑣簿，二十五款.

CHAPTER XVII

PSYCHOLOGY OF THE MASK

The dramatic power of the mask is due not only to its effect on the spectators but also to that on the actor wearing it. It imposes the impersonation on the actor and makes him involuntarily act the role he thus assumes, to the extent, it is said, of pulling his face even though he knows that it is wasted effort. [1] A weird mask automatically makes its wearer assume weird gestures and movements, sometimes approaching dance, just as formal dress makes people change their deportment, and it is probably for this effect that primitive people believe in its magical power. In spite of our scientific knowledge, masks produce a reaction in us. The primitive people lived more by feelings, hence the psychological effect of masks on them must have been greater than that on us.

We read faces so much in our daily life that when they are substituted by false ones in the theatre we still allow them to affect us. The effect is twofold: on the one hand, through its concealment of the natural features it deprives us of the normal psychological contact with other people through their facial expressions and, on the other, its features, often very different from what we expect on a normal human face, give us the impression that the wearer has actually been so transformed — as if by sheer need for a face, our mind is ready to accept one which is unlikely. The latter effect may sometimes be vague or weak owing to the poor quality of the mask and the acting or dance that accompanies it, but the effect of the concealment is always felt; a mask may fail to terrify or to amuse but it never fails to mystify. We are instinctively afraid of the unknown hence even the most absurd mask can inspire religious awe. [2]

---

[1] *Vide* W. T. Benda, *Masks,* 1944.

[2] It is said that masks with enigmatic expression will appear to change when accompanied by gestures. This effect is not always noticeable in the Chinese mask, because it is mostly violently unrealistic and without emotional expression. The absence of facial expression is not, however, felt in the actual performance, because the common characteristic of the masked characters is a lack of expression and the expressionless mask contributes to the representation of the awe-inspiring, inscrutable type. The more realistic Chinese masks, however, accompanied by good acting, can induce this illusion of facial expression. *Vide* Benda, *op. cit.,* 3.

The masked characters or "painted faces" of the Chinese theatre form, to the Chinese audience, a class by themselves. They have a common psychological trait in spite of the difference in temperament, social level and moral qualities among them. This trait, which distinguishes them from all other characters, is related to the Chinese code of behaviour and cannot be easily understood apart from it. The Chinese have a long tradition of practical rules of conduct which in their social life is manifested in a general policy of avoiding conflict and violence — a policy necessitated also by the close contact in family life. To maintain this desired peaceful relationship every member of the society, from the highest officials to the meanest labourers, is expected to have the important quality of "reasonableness" which is in fact a combination of realistic outlook, respect for tradition and a readiness to compromise. Traditional ethical values are the foundation of all social relationships, but they are not enough, because, in particular situations conflict and danger cannot be avoided even though every one concerned respect the same ethical values and in such cases critical situations can be averted by being "reasonable". Compromise eliminates extremes in attitudes and ideals and realistic outlook makes all great suffering involved in conflicts appear futile. [3] In practical life, especially as a member of the family, the emotional habits of most Chinese are moulded by social conventions into a superficial character which veils their individual temperaments and gives them a certain degree of uniformity, at least in such public functions as concern only their acquired character. Most people, Chinese or otherwise, in conducting their lives do not follow a single ideal but are influenced by many considerations so that for the majority of mankind both noble and evil deeds are done in moderation. For the Chinese moderation is further encouraged through their obligation to be "reasonable". [4]

The common mental trait of the "painted faces" is the lack of this spirit of reasonableness. Since this spirit serves as the unwritten code of social behaviour, a person without it is not only difficult to deal with but also difficult to understand. Much of the individual visual effects of the masks are based on association and the masks are recognized because the audience are familiar with the personal history of the particular dramatic characters. These effects are lost to those new to the Chinese theatre, but their common mystifying effect should be evident to all. Masks, which break the normal psychological contact through natural facial expressions, deprive the masked characters, in the mind of the Chinese audience, of the "reasonableness" and moderation with which they understand each other in normal life. Therefore these characters, good or bad, are always extreme types. The noble

---

[3] cf. ". . . take note of the two extremes and apply the middle way to the people". 執其兩端用其中於民, 中庸, 六章.

[4] In fact, lack of the tragic ideal in the Chinese drama can also be traced to this system of ethics which makes moral conflicts impossible.

types are either resolute or impetuous or uncouth or dauntless, and the base
characters are callous or savage or treacherous or knavish. (5) They are never
balanced or temperate, hence, to the Chinese, they are baffling and, in extreme
cases, awe-inspiring; they are in fact freakish examples of men of singular virtues and
unmitigated evils either more, or less, than human. (6) The masks make them look
impenetrable and fearful like the supernatural beings, in the minds of the Chinese.
In some cases a character wears a mask in one drama but appears without it in
another. This is because in the latter his behaviour may be normal, and in the former
that side of his nature represented by the mask comes to light. (7)

The principles behind the design of various masks (or "painted faces") can be
most conveniently discussed in three different groups of masked characters: gods
and spirits, human characters, and goblins.

Powerful deities are painted in gold and minor gods in silver because their
statues are painted in this way in the temples. (8) Supernatural judges (判官) and
spirits (神怪) also wear masks similar to their statues. In this class the masks are, in
a way, realistic. Mute gods such as temple guards (金剛) and earth gods (土地)
wear detachable masks which they hold by their mouth. This type of mask is more
economical than the painted faces, but can only be a worn by those who do not
speak or sing.

For mortals, the colour denotes temperament and age, and the pattern, social
position or moral quality. White and pink are used for old men and grey for very old
men to represent the pallor of old people. Light red and dark red are used on old
warriors who in their youth wear bright red. The correspondence between colour of
the mask and the temperament of its wearer has been thought to be symbolic (9) or
conventional (10) but in fact it is not arbitrary. There is a popular belief in China that
a man's character can, to some extent, be read from the characteristics of his
physiognomy, including the complexion. Laymen judge their impressions of men

---

(5) 齊如山, 臉譜, 頁一.

(6) From the earliest days of the Chinese drama till to-day, there has been, according to Prof. Wang
Kuo-Wei, a shift in the significance of the classification of dramatic characters. 王國維,
古劇脚色考, 餘說一 . The criterion changed from social status to character and from
character to temperament. Character is partly acquired, temperament is entirely inherited; character
can be good or bad, temperament as such is neither good nor bad; character can only be known after
long acquaintance, temperament is often obvious at first sight; character can be changed by
education, temperament can never change. The immediate effect of the mask concerns temperament
and the symbolism in it concerns character.

(7) For examples see 齊如山, 臉譜, 頁一, 二 .

(8) Prof. Ch'i Ju-Shan believes that the gold may be derived from the "golden light" said to surround
Buddha in Buddhist scriptures. 齊如山, 臉譜, 第二章, 金色臉 .

(9) H. Acton, *Oxford Companion to the Theatre,* CHINA.

(10) L. C. Arlington, *The Chinese Drama,* 107.

more or less instinctively, but specialists have written on the detailed classification and analysis of the human face. For the present discussion whether or not there is correspondence between a man's face and his temperament is immaterial, the important thing is, the audience of the Chinese theatre believe there is and therefore to them the colour of the mask is significant. It is believed, for example, that full-blooded people are often single-minded and loyal, therefore the red face signifies steadfastness and, at the other extreme, an anaemic face (painted white with many wrinkles) means treachery. Similarly the black face is associated with uprightness, the yellow face with cunning, the blue face with conceit and viciousness and the green face with excitability.

The colour pattern of the masks varies from a pure colour for the whole face (整臉) to variegated spirals and streaks of many colours (碎臉), through various types of large eyebrows and broad streaks. For the more fantastic masks the eyebrows are twisted beyond recognition and the eyes are obliterated or transposed (false eyes painted). [11] In general the more complicated the pattern, the lower the social caste, probably based on the subjective impression that prominent people have more clear-cut features than the nondescripts. [12]

So far as make-up is concerned, the comedian 丑 forms a continuous series with the masked character of the treacherous type: they both wear white paint but the comedian only in small patches. The grand Machiavel wears white grease over his entire face with wrinkles called "treacherous-looking wrinkles" (奸紋), but his lesser brothers wear grease only from the forehead to the cheeks and have the lower part of their faces powdered (二花臉), the men of low cunning, really a hybrid between the masked character and the comedian, wear an oblong patch across the face, covering the nose and cheekbones, and the comedian wears a small patch across the nose.[13] For the type of clown specializing in acrobatics, there is only a dot at the end of the nose. Judging by the make-up, the Chinese audience understand the comedian as representing a type of petty and harmless craftiness. [14]

The definite effectiveness of the white patch across the comedian's face is

---

[11] Fantastical colours and patterns are by no means unknown on the faces of European clowns. *Vide* S. McKechnie, *Popular Entertainment Through the Ages,* (1931), Frontispiece, and illustrations opposite pp. 60, 114 and 220. These face paintings are not make-up because they are more than accentuated features, they are really masks.

[12] Some characters are painted in certain colours owing to misunderstanding through puns, analogies, etc., for example, a man named White is painted white. See 齊如山，臉譜，頁五，六．

[13] The grand Machiavel has small eyes. This is because we normally read other people's minds in their eyes, and a treacherous person does not show what he thinks.

[14] It is the custom for those who play minor masked characters to play comedians in case of need. 齊如山，戲班，頁六．The feeling of superiority must play an important part in the psychology of laughter, as in animals' unexpected show of intelligence and low human craftiness — if it is awkward enough the mischief has no offence.

difficult to explain. Its psychology may perhaps be clarified by some experiments on people unfamiliar with the Chinese theatre, because the comic effect on the Chinese audience may be due to association. [15] It may however be due to the fact that the middle of the face thus appears flat which, together with other touches on the eyelids and eyebrows, constitutes an expression of simian mischief, or it may be due to a change of the apparent contour of the face.

When the masks are used to convey special information to the audience they are entirely symbolic, as in the case of genii and goblins who are sometimes painted like the animals they are supposed to originate from and sometimes, when they can transform themselves to other shapes, painted with half of the face in the original and the other half in the form of the adopted animal. Gods of fire and gods of clouds wear symbolic flames and clouds on the face, respectively. Some foreigners are considered to be half-human and half-spirit (cf. "foreign devil" 洋鬼子) and therefore wear masks of no definite pattern. By convention, symmetrical faces are for people loyal to the Chinese emperor and asymmetrical ones for thieves and rebels. For characters in new dramas, masks are modified or copied from those of similar temperaments in existing dramas. However, records of the patterns for different characters have been kept since Ming dynasty and there are few occasions when the players have to draw new masks.

The theatrical mask is an emphatic statement of what is characteristic of the type. The masks are artistic creations which have outgrown the purpose of verisimilitude. It is doubtful that men can see faces as scientific instruments "see" them. In our perception of other people's faces there is always a subjective element and that is why photographs sometimes do not look like the sitter and why other people's faces appear to change with our own emotional states. The design of theatrical masks exploits this subjective element.

Painting the face is a skilful and specialized task. Records of the masks for different dramatic characters are printed or drawn on paper and the masks look flat but the actor's face is solid and varies in proportion and shape, hence it is necessary to adapt the printed pattern to the particular face so that the mask can be expressive. A badly fitted painted face may look good from the front but poor from the sides, for the expression of a mask changes according to the angle one looks at it [16] and the curvature of the actor's face can reveal serious defects when the head is turned.

Samples of the bare records of the patterns are shown in Figs. 52A and 52B.

---

[15] European circus clowns also powder their faces. The practice is said to be due to a Parisian tradition based on three bakers at the time of Molière's childhood who discovered their comic powers while throwing flour at each other — *Oxford Companion to the Theatre,* CLOWN. Whatever the origin, everything about a clown is accentuated, make-up is one part of the general accentuation.

[16] *Vide* Benda, *op. cit.*

The effect that these patterns can produce when they are transferred onto the human face can be partly seen in Figs. 53A and 53B, which are clay models. The toy-makers who painted the models shown in Figs. 53A and 53B are not artists and they cannot fully exploit the quality of a mask. The beauty of a well painted mask can be surmised in Figs. 54A, 54B and 54C, which are pictures of some masked characters painted by an artist.

52A

Masks drawn on paper (for record)

52B

Masks drawn on paper (for record)

53A

Mask drawn on clay model

Mask drawn on clay model

54A

Picture of masked character painted by an artist

54B

Picture of masked character painted by an artist

54C

Picture of masked character painted by an artist

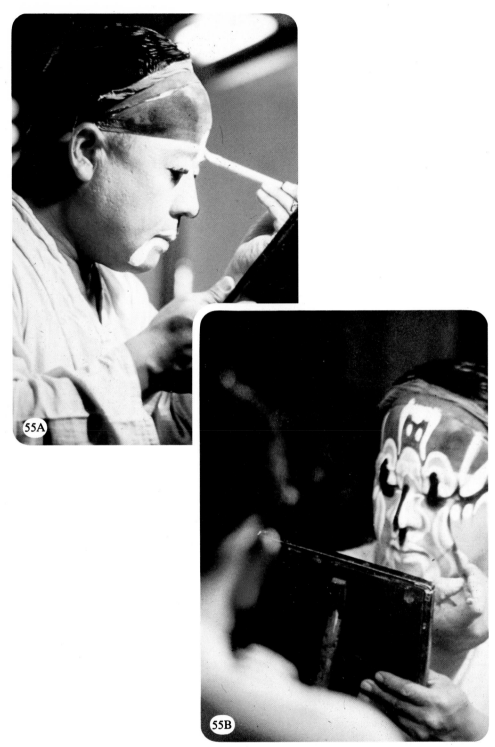

An actor painting a mask on himself

CHAPTER XVIII

THE ARIA AS VOCAL ACTING PAR EXCELLENCE

The many differences between the music in the Chinese theatre and its western counterpart, the opera, stem from the lack of harmony in the Chinese musical system. [1]

Although the classical European music generally known at the present is based on the principles of harmony and counterpoint, European music did not always have harmony. Before the eleventh century European music was monophonic but vocal parts, first in parallel and later as independent melodies, were slowly added to the main tune later. A method of musical composition based on the combination of notes and melodies was, however, fully developed by late fifteenth century and has dominated European music since. At the present, from chamber music to opera, composition is based on polyphony: even in the occasional unaccompanied works, the melodic structure is influenced by the principles of harmony. All this one cannot expect to find in the Chinese music. [2]

The use or absence of harmony had profound effects on the development of the European and the Chinese music. It determined the directions along which the two systems of music developed and the aesthetic ideals cherished by their devotees. Harmony and counterpoint lead to complex musical structures but single melodies can only develop in delicacy and nuance. In one style there is architectonic splendour, in the other, the quality of the line; the former is the beauty of the design, the latter, that of texture. In the European orchestral music there are frequent and abrupt changes in force, colour, tempo and rhythm but in the Chinese music, the tone colours are limited and the rhythm is usually uniform. There are variety and surprise in western music but in the Chinese music there is sustained mood.

---

[1]   "Multiple notes" 複音 are sometimes mentioned in Chinese books — e.g. 齊如山, 中國劇之組織, 頁一〇九. They are occasional chords on string instruments, not polyphony.

[2]   The architectonic quality of western music is sometimes beyond the comprehension of the Chinese musicians: the *canon rectus et inversus,* for example, is unthinkable in Chinese music.

The Chinese musicians divide the Chinese orchestra used in the theatre into two sections, the percussions (武場) and the winds and strings (文場). The nearest approach to the orchestral part of the European opera is the music played in stage weddings, religious ceremonies, royal entries and so forth, but they are really incidental music because the same tunes are played in every drama in the same way as the Wedding March would be played in the wedding scenes in European dramas. The only other use for the winds and strings is to accompany the arias in unison, with some of the percussion instruments marking the beats. The spoken dialogue and the acting are, in general, punctuated by the percussions and occasionally, as in night scenes and battle scenes, the appropriate moods are indicated by percussion music.

The best part of the music of the Chinese theatre is, however, the vocal music. As explained previously, owing to the inflexions in the pronunciation of Chinese words, there is much closer relation between speech and singing in the Chinese than in the European language. In the western operas music is composed to fit the words hence the disadvantage of translated libretti, but the relation between correct pronunciation and music is slight and a badly fitting score is still a workable score. In the Chinese theatre, there is a difference between a *correct* and an *incorrect* score. This close relationship between words and music is the foundation of the style of singing in the Chinese theatre.

There are several styles of delivery in the Chinese theatre. First, the comedians have the licence to use naturalistic delivery, speaking exactly as the audience speak in their everyday life. Secondly, for comic effects, they may also speak in strict rhythm to the accompaniment of the Chinese castanets and the "small drum", repeating the last line of the speech for cadence (乾唸). Thirdly, for all characters except the comedians, the normal way to speak the dialogue is to declaim it without regular rhythm. Fourthly, when reciting the poem or couplet at the beginning of a scene, the players declaim in drawn out voice in the rhythm of the verse; and lastly, some part of the dialogue is sung. From the technical point of view, stage delivery can deviate from natural speech in three ways: in adopting a regular rhythm, in sustained vowels with accentuated inflexions (declamation) and in regulating the voice to the definite pitch of the notes in a musical scale (singing). The several styles of delivery on the Chinese stage are based on the different combinations of these deviations: the Chinese players can speak, declaim or sing with or without regular rhythm. The transition from declamation to singing can be very gradual and, when well rendered, almost imperceptible, because, as has been previously explained, a Chinese poem declaimed suggests a melody. In the long soliloquy at the opening scene of *The Clandestine Visit* 四郎探母 , for example, as the voice becomes more impassioned, it lingers longer and longer over the words till at last it becomes wailing just before singing starts. Speech and singing are not two totally different forms of vocal expression; they differ not in kind, but only in degree. The style of vocalization can vary continuously from what we use in ordinary conversation to the highly musical delivery in the theatre. What we call speech and what we call singing cover two different ranges of vocalization — it is difficult to specify exactly at which point speech becomes declamation and at which point declamation becomes singing. An aria in a Chinese drama is not merely dialogue fitted with a tune, it is the extension of declamation. To sing on the Chinese stage is to declaim to the notes of a musical scale. [3] Expressions in the speaking voice depend on its tones and since the shape of the musical phrases has to conform to the inflexions of the voice in speaking the words, much of the expressions in speech passes automatically into the music. Through several centuries of this style of vocal music a tradition and an ideal become established for all music in the Chinese theatre that its progression and rhythm should be subordinate to the feelings of the words. An aria is thus merely a passage in the dialogue delivered at a high emotional level. [4]

It is due to this connection between singing and speech that the musical construction of the Chinese aria appears baffling to those brought up in the western musical tradition. In a Chinese aria one cannot find the type of tune which is made up of musical phrases arranged according to the principles of balance, contrast and echo and fitted with various types of cadences at regular intervals — the rhythm is altogether more complicated. [5] In the Chinese theatre the human voice is never used as an instrument, as in *coloratura* in which it often resembles, and is matched by the flute; or in choral passages of a symphony where it sometimes becomes one group of orchestral instruments.

It is the quality of articulate emotional expression that makes it a pleasure not only to listen to the Chinese aria but also to sing it. [6] There are few Chinese who cannot sing a few lines from some of the standard plays. [7]

All emotional passages in the dialogue are sung, but not all the passages set to music are impassioned. Singing is also used to relieve the monotony of long or repetitive dialogue, for example, in the single lines which are sung now and then in a

---

[3]   cf. Nicomachus (first century A.D.) in *Enchiridion:* "If the notes and intervals of the speaking voice are allowed to be separate and distinct, the form of utterance becomes singing". — quoted in D. B. Monro, *The Modes of Ancient Greek Music,* 115.

[4]   The importance of the audience understanding the words of stage-songs was fully recognized in the English theatre in Elizabethan times and later, when the words were read before they were sung. (cf. the opera). This might have been based on similar practice in real life. *Vide* Lawrence, *Those Nut-Cracking Elizabethans,* ch. XI. The Wedding of Poetry and Song.

[5]   Tunes of simple regular phrases occur in Chinese folk songs and are called by the players "small tunes" 小調. They are rarely used in the dramas.

[6]   cf. the pleasure of performing a dance.

[7]   Prof. Ch'i Ju-Shan mentions how, by listening to the snatches of arias sung in the streets of Peking, one can tell which plays are the most popular at the time. 齊如山, 京劇之變遷, 頁三.

long conversation between two characters and in the messages and narratives which have already been told to the audience and are repeated to some characters in the drama. The long and slow arias which form the centres of interest in many a Chinese play are practically always soliloquies and the moods involved may be those of bitterness, grief, melancholy, remembrance or joy. [8] Some dramatic characters also sing in order to relieve the boredom of work, but this is rare. Passages set to music are also inserted in the conversational dialogue at such moments as of surprise, anxiety, bitterness, joy, fright and love. [9] In most cases impassioned passages that are sung are introduced by an exclamation indicating rising emotions (叫板).

The Chinese players consider declamation as more difficult than singing, hence the saying: "Ten thousand catties of declamation to four ounces of singing". (千斤說白四兩唱) The explanation is that in singing the voice is guided by the music, but in declamation there is nothing except the players' artistic sense to guide them. This is a case of greater freedom making the art more difficult.

The Chinese plays are divided into the singers' plays 唱工戲 and the actors' plays 做工戲. Of the former the basic scheme is to develop the action with spoken passages interspersed with singing till an emotional climax is reached and then the central emotions of the play are expressed in an aria. [10] The aria, usually of great length and sung without interruption by the spoken passages, starts in the slower tempi, such as *lento* (慢板) or *adagio* (原板) and following the rise in excitement, becomes quicker towards the end. [11] Its length limits its use to such occasions as lamentation, prayer, ravings, self-reproach, and so forth. In the quickest passages the audience admire crisp and clear elocution; in the slower passages, the beauty of tone and the control of the voice. The best combination of musical and dramatic

---

[8] In this connection the length of the aria refers to the performance time, not to the length of the text. A slow aria on two lines is very much longer than a quick one on twenty lines.

[9] 齊如山, 中國劇之組織; 頁十四, 十五.

[10] e.g. *The Stratagem of the Empty City* 空城計, *The Capture and Escape of Ts'ao* 捉放曹, *Li Ling's Monument* 李陵碑, *Conjuring the East Wind* 祭東風; *The Clandestine Visit* 四郎探母 which begins with a long aria, is an exception.

[11] The predominant moods of the different styles of music have been described as follows:

      Erh-Huang 二黃 .... sad or dignified.

      Hsi-P'i 西皮 .... gay or light-hearted.

      Ssu-P'ing tiao 四平調 .... frivolous.

      Nan Pang-Tzu 南梆子 .... coy or melancholy.

           The moods of the various "rhythms" may be said to be:

      'Basic rhythm" 原板 .... strong feelings (but without emotional abandon).

      "Slow rhythm" 慢板 .... deep emotions.

      "Quick rhythm" 快板 .... anger or anxiety.

      "Erh-Liu" 二六 .... self-satisfaction.

齊如山; 中國劇之組織, 頁十六, 十七.

expressions is considered to be in the slowest arias. [12]

The technical resources of the Chinese musicians are, by European standards, very limited, yet a Chinese aria is a complicated piece of music in its own way. Chinese music has no harmony, but it can have the interplay of rhythms which, as in the case of the harmonic structures in western music, is lost to untrained ears. First of all, the words of the arias have their own rhythm. In the Chinese theatre of to-day, the lines set to music are of regular length with either seven or ten words in each, and as the Chinese words are monosyllabic the two basic rhythms are:

and

Unaccented words may be added to some of the lines so that the rhythms become:

and

or some other forms. These are of course the rhythms of the lines when they are read. The musical phrases in the quick and moderate tempi have rhythms roughly similar to those shown above, but in the slow arias, the musical rhythm is far removed from the metrical rhythm. Furthermore, in arias in *adagio* and *lento,* the melodies are such that the time (as 2/4 or 3/4) is not prominent and in order that the singer and the orchestra will agree, the beats are marked by the leader of the orchestra on percussion instruments. The vagueness of the time is also why Chinese musicians do not use *rubato*: all pieces are played in strict time except the *fermata* in the last notes of an aria. [13] If, however, every accented beat is marked by striking a percussion instrument the result would be unbearably monotonous, [14] hence the leader of the orchestra normally plays an impromptu florid variation on the basic rhythm. For example: If the music is in quadruple time as

---

[12] The art of singing is said to consist of five elements: 1. Tone of voice, 2. Melody, 3. Ornaments, 4. Rhythm, and 5. Elocution. All good singers use ornaments with discretion and some of the greatest singers do not use them at all — it is a matter of style. As in western music, timing is considered to be extremely important. When a singer starts making mistakes in timing the leader of the orchestra warns him by playing exceptionally loud, or by other visible means. 王夢生, 梨園佳話, 一章, 頁十七.

[13] When *ad libitum* passages are accompanied by the orchestra, the singer and the orchestra do not keep time, the instruments merely form a background for the voice.

[14] In western music too the accented beats are not marked regularly, except in the march and the waltz.

the percussions may play

(Chinese castanets)

("Small drum")

The fascinated look of the veteran Chinese playgoers who listen to the arias with closed eyes counting the beats by striking their fingers on the chair is due to the concentration required to be fully aware of the several layers of rhythms at the same time. [15] One of the keenest pleasures in the appreciation of music, one which sometimes transports the listener into pure rapture, lies in following the bold deviations of great singers from the original phrasing and rhythm, when the deviations compensate each other and constitute a harmonious whole in the end. [16] To the connoisseur, a great singer is full of surprises and inventions — the sheer dexterity is exhilarating — and if it is coupled with new emotional significance put into the phrases of the aria, the effect is overwhelming. A good player sings correctly and with good tones, [17] but a great singer treats an aria as a flexible melody, capable of changing into hundreds of different forms all equally interesting and beautiful. The audience never knows exactly what shape the next phrase is going to take. In western music there is a similar feeling of exhilaration when one listens to the fragments of a theme changed into numerous shapes and played on the different instruments of the orchestra yet each fitting closely into all the others.

The Chinese singer is not only free to change the length of the musical phrases by changing the time value of some of its notes but he is also free to change the notes themselves. Theoretically, since only the style of the music and the "rhythm" are specified in the script he can sing any melody of the proper time and tempo so long as it fits the pronunciation of the words. In practice, each singer learns the arias

(15) There is a system for counting the beats with the fingers in which the accented beats and the ends of the four-bar and eight-bar phrases are all distinguished. Those who cannot remember the words often listen to the arias with the libretto in hand. Libretti were at one time sold at the theatre at a few coppers each.

(16) "A melodic phrase is sometimes compressed so that its end does not reach the particular beat as it normally does, or sometimes expanded, so that its end passes the beat. All is adjusted, however, so that at the end of the musical sentence the notes are in the right place. The former device is called 'dodging the beat' 閃板 and the latter, 'racing the beat' 趕板" 王夢生, 梨園佳話, 一章頁十八 . This is not *rubato;* it is shortening or lengthening a musical phrase by changing the time value of some of the notes so that, for instance, a four-bar phrase becomes three-and-a-half bar or four-and-a-quarter bar. This musical device does not seem to have been used by western singers.

(17) The Chinese singers also know the "chest voice" 胸音 and the "head voice" 腦後音 like the western singers, but they have another mysterious "cloud on moon" voice 雲遮月 . Methods of training the voice include abstaining from wine and tobacco and drinking white of egg in the morning. Singers also take a pill called "steel flute pill" 鐵笛丸 王夢生, 梨園佳話, 一章頁十四 .

from his teacher and only when he has become proficient does he begin to modify the melodic line. The melodies of the Chinese arias are always in a state of flux; no two singers at the same time or one singer at different times sing the same notes. [18] In the Chinese musical system, it would be a sad state of affairs if the melodies were fixed in all details, because then the singers would not be able to be constantly putting new interpretations and new musical ideas into them.

It is doubtful however whether more prevalent use of the score can stop the gradual changes in the melodies. [19] The Chinese style of singing is such that the score can only be a record of the skeleton melody with the expressive details left out. The voice of the western singer moves deftly from one note to another, except in notes connected by slurs, and for the duration of a note, the voice is held steadily at the particular pitch. [20] A Chinese singer, however, rarely holds his voice at a constant pitch, he touches the main notes in the melody and either fills the space between them with other notes or moves from the first note to the second along a curve — in western music, called *portamento*. It would give a wrong impression to say that the Chinese singer uses embellishments extensively, because in the western musical system embellishments are mainly decorative and are mostly standardized, for example, it is either a trill, or a turn, or an inverted turn, and so on, but in the Chinese system the flexibility of the voice produces infinite shades of variations which are not ornaments but are part of the lyrical expression of the singer. For lack of a better term let them be called ornaments. The critic Wang Meng-Sheng defined them as follows:

"Ornaments are the notes that follow the words in a singer's voice. The singer may add his own notes before he reaches the next word, but he must not miss the beat or be out of tune. In the Peking dramas singers were at first admired for the tone of their voice, like Ch'eng Ch'ang-Keng and Chang Erh-K'uei (程長庚，張二奎) but later they were admired for their ornaments, like Yü San-Sheng and T'an Hsin-P'ei(于三勝，譚鑫培)" 王夢生，梨園佳話，一章，頁十六．

The difference between the voice of a Chinese singer and that of a western one is the difference between a dance in which one posture merges into another and one in which prominent postures are connected by quick movements, or that between calligraphy written with a brush and that engraved on a plate. The western singers

---

[18]   The fiddler must be able to follow the singer closely in all his arias, hence he has to work closely with the singer for a long time before he can accompany him in the theatre.

[19]   Wang Kwang-Ch'i *(Ueber die chinesische klassische Oper)* found by comparing the eighteenth-century scores of the *K'un* dramas with modern gramophone records that only about eighty per cent of the score is followed by modern singers.

[20]   cf. the "rectangles of notes" in western singing. Music is of course never played or sung anywhere with mechanical precision except in the music box. Nevertheless, as compared with the Chinese style of singing western music is more nearly precise.

follow the notes specified by the composer conscientiously and, for the purpose of expression, they employ slight and momentary changes in tempo and force; the Chinese singer, on the other hand, sings to strict time, but varies the force *and* the pitch of his voice freely. (21) To put such singing in notation is very difficult, if not impossible; either the score has to be covered with masses of auxiliary notes and expression marks or only the most important notes are written down and directions in words, such as *"vivace"*, *"tenero"* are added; in either case the score cannot fully record the music. (22) Singers in the Chinese theatre are taught orally without scores; the popular scores (using Arabic numerals) one finds in Chinese book stores are, even with the embellishments they contain, mere shadows of the real performances and they, for obvious reasons, never agree. If notations encourage a style of singing based on steady pitch and neat transitions from one note to another, it would be unwise for the Chinese singers to use them extensively.

Some Chinese actors have an astonishing ability to improvise:

"Yü San-Sheng 于三勝 once started a play without the supporting actor. He was playing a husband who, after a short soliloquy, was to be joined by his wife. The actor to play his wife had not come, but he was already singing on the stage, the aria in which there are four lines beginning with "Like the . . . I . . ." (我好比). He improvised seventy-four lines of the same construction while waiting. Every one in the company was wet with sweat, but the audience, who knew he was waiting for something, was not alarmed because they were charmed by his singing".王夢生 , 梨園佳話, 三章, 頁五九, 六十.

"On one occasion Yü San-Sheng 于三勝 was playing the emperor and the flag-bearers went wrong, so that there were three on one side and one on the other. Yü tried to direct them with his eyes but without avail. At last he improvised two lines and sang:

'There are three on one side and only one on the other,

We will have to pull one to the other side'.

and dragged the extra one to the correct position. The whole theatre roared with laughter and the erring supernumerary, who could not refrain from laughing himself, ran off the stage so that there was still only one attendant on that side". *(Ibid).*

To the mind of the Chinese audience the gist of the singer's art is the beauty of line. (23) A phrase sung by a great and a mediocre singer may sound exactly alike to

---

(21) cf. the actor Ch'eng Yen-Ch'iu 程硯秋 who is famous for his *diminuendo* passages crammed with ornaments, called "Ch'eng's style".

(22) cf. the hardly recognizable Chinese music in western notation in de Morant's *Théâtre et Musique modernes en Chine.*

(23) Hence Yü Shu-Yen 余叔岩 who, at the end of his career could not be heard beyond the fifth row, was still proclaimed the best singer of his time.

the layman but to the connoisseur there is a world of difference between them, just as a painting and a copy may look alike to the layman but are widely different in the eyes of the expert. Chinese music-lovers listen to their singers as art-lovers look at painters' sketches. In the sketches the quality of the line shows clearest and every stroke is telling; the artist, as it were, must take his audience more into his confidence. As in Chinese painting and calligraphy, where every brush stroke is a terse and vivid record of the force and speed of its execution, so in the solo voice all the imperfections as well as the perfections are exposed. As with ink on absorbent paper, so with the solo voice not supported by voluminous accompaniment, the power, the control, the ease with which a line is executed is grasped in an instant, not even the slightest falter could be concealed. Anything uniform would sound dead and mechanical but a supple voice can reveal the confidence and verve of the singer. Like the line of a draughtsman, the singer's voice can be either pedestrian, restrained and overworked, or bold, spirited and abandoned.

It can also be noticed that the Chinese style of singing is unsuitable for part-singing — harmony being based on steady pitch. It is not even suitable for chorus in unison, because to keep time with each other choral singers cannot enjoy the freedom to which Chinese singers are accustomed.

Such a style of singing is the performer's rather than the composer's art. The voice of an inspired singer has its own momentary tendencies and cannot be constrained by the score. Each performance of an aria, even by the same singer, is different from the last, hence the Chinese go to the same play over and over again. Since much of the beauty of the music lies in the delicate details, there is an immense difference between a good and a correct performance. Those who cannot see the subtle difference between a confident and a stolid line cannot enjoy good Chinese singing, hence it is a connoisseur's rather than a popular art. To appreciate it requires concentration as can be seen in the absolute silence in the often noisy Chinese theatre when a great singer starts to sing. The audience sharpen their senses to catch the finest nuance and many turn their eyes away from the stage to hear better.

The classical Chinese theatre is a school of refined entertainment accessible only to those with cultivated taste. For the survival of such an art a body of appreciative audience is necessary.

> "In Peking, even shopkeepers and labourers among the audience know every beat of every tune and they all, in one voice, cheer the good turns and boo the mistakes. When a favourite player enters, the whole theatre gives him welcome. Actors do not covet the favour of the nobility but seek the approval of the ordinary people, being careful never to make a mistake". 王夢生，梨園佳話，一章，頁九，十.

The conditions in Shanghai are different:

> "When T'an Hsin-P'ei came to Shanghai, the advertisement was un-

173

precedented in its lavish scale, and he was engaged to play for 12,000 dollars. The people of Shanghai, however, knew no music and applauded in the wrong places. T'an, disgusted, continued to play for the sake of the contract, but deliberately pronounced the words wrong and missed the beats in the music, out of spite. One man in the galleries shouted a sarcastic "Bravo" and was driven out of the theatre by a mob and severely beaten". (*Ibid.*, 73).

The fascination of good singing is illustrated by some of the writings by Chinese critics:

"Ch'eng Ch'ang-Keng (程長庚) is considered the best singer in the whole history of the Peking dramas. Actors who played with him and musicians who were supposed to be accompanying him are known to stop and listen to him in spite of themselves". (*Ibid.* 三章，頁五七).

"T'an Hsin-P'ei had the bad habit of being late, so that for matinee he might appear only in early evening and sometimes even only in the middle of the evening. Before he appeared the audience had to sit in the dark waiting for the lights to be turned on, but in spite of the discomfort no one left the theatre before he came. In 1909, there was the national mourning for the death of the emperor so that there were no dramatic performances, but when the period of mourning ended T'an was to perform again and people hurried to tell their friends and relatives in order to get their seats early as if a comet or some strange heavenly body was to appear. At a performance of *Retribution by Thunder* 天雷報 the whole theatre was packed so that there was hardly room to move, and by the time the old man in the drama had dashed his brains out it was about nine o'clock. The management, knowing that the audience being without dinner must have been very hungry, abridged drastically the scenes that followed the old man's death. By this time the audience were, however, too much enthralled by T'an's acting and everyone hated the adopted son as he would a personal enemy and they remained to see the end of this ungrateful man. The last part of the play was hurried through and as the audience poured out of the theatre a storm broke out so that they were all drenched from above and splashed at from below. They must have known that if they had left a little earlier they would have missed the rain but none of them seemed worried: they helped each other with outstretched garments, and held each other's arm, all the time talking about which passage was particularly moving, which scene was beautifully played, etc., laughing and talking while staggering through pools of water on slippery streets, as if it did not matter in the least that they were hungry inside and wet outside". (*Ibid.* 三章，頁七十).

The deepest aesthetic feelings are always difficult to describe in words. Those who share the same experience can understand each other, but to those without the experience descriptions sound obscure. The critic Wang Meng-Sheng's description of the aria in *Li Ling's Monument* 李陵碑 is as follows:

"At the lines 'And now surrounded on this hill without food for men or grass for horses, all hopes of reinforcement abandoned, and no news from my departed son, here, with my hair grey with age I shall end my life in desolation', it is as if the ten thousand valleys resound with the singer's voice, which one can only compare to a hundred rivers pouring into the sea; one feels the warm blood of the old warrior surging forth in the music. Every word is a drop of tear and every drop of tear as exquisite as a pearl. There is a touching pause after the word 'grass' in '. . . without food . . . or grass . . .' (外無草) and a sad even tone for the word 'life' in '. . . end my life . . .' (老殘生). Then, after the mourning for his son, the singer's voice flows out in absolute freedom, reaching the heavens and making one think of the currents of a powerful river, rushing through many turns to its destination. One feels like floating through clouds and mountains and suddenly reaching an open space. At this point one is lost in ecstasy — this is truly the supreme effect of music". (*Ibid*. 二章, 頁三五).

(Even though there is always restraint and control in a work of art, there should still be an element of abandon and freedom in it. Unless a song or a dance becomes, or appears to be, a free expression of over-abundant emotions, it cannot communicate the exaltation to its audience).

ARIA in Adagio — Andante from
The Story of the Black Pot
(Erh-huang Style)

As sung by Yen Chü-P'eng

言菊朋唱烏盆記

淚　　滿　　腮

僧　一　聲

老 大　細 聽　開

懷

Andante

家 住 在　　　　南 陽

178

城　　　關　外　離城
十　里　太　　平
街

179

劉世昌

祖居

有　數　代

務農　爲本頗有　　家財　奉母命

180

上京　　　做　　　買　賣　　販賣綢緞

倒也　　　生、財　　　前三　年　也曾

把　　　貨　　　賣　　　算清　賬目轉回

家來　　　行至　在　　趙大的　窖　門

以　外　　　借宿　一　宵惹

祸　灾　　　赵大夫妻将我谋

害　　把我的　尸骨未曾

葬　埋　烧作了乌盆窑

中　排　偶遇老丈讨　　赈

来　可怜我冤仇有　三载有三

載

老　丈呀

NOTE: The above score can only give a general idea of the shape of the melody and the way the accompaniment bridges the gaps in the tune. Owing to the comparatively few leading notes and subdominants and the peculiar forms of cadences, the melody may seem by western standards to lack colour and pattern and its original lyrical quality will not be apparent without the proper style of singing. Unfamiliar figures and the irregular rhythm will also add to its apparent strangeness. The aria, introduced by a standard instrumental passage, consists of two parts: the *adagio* in which the ghost implores the old man to listen to him and the *andante* in which he relates how he was murdered. It can be noticed that as the narration in the *andante* progresses, a gradual *accelerando* effect is obtained without actual change of tempo, by putting more words, on the average, into each bar. It can also be noticed that as compared with western operatic arias each syllable (or word) is sung to many notes and, as these notes vary from one singer to another they are to be considered as ornaments even though they never acquire standard forms such as shakes and turns.

Part III

The History of the Chinese Theatre

CHAPTER XIX

ON THE SOURCES OF CHINESE THEATRICAL HISTORY

Although the Chinese theatre has a long history it was ignored by the Chinese scholars before Yüan dynasty (1277-1367) owing to its lack of literary value. It was then considered as mere entertainment, of little importance to culture as the Confucian scholars understood it and of no value as historical data except in its connections with court activities and with poetry and music. In Yüan dynasty Chinese dramatic poetry reached the highest point of its development and its literary value soon became widely recognized so that Chinese critics who tried to find a distinctive literary form for each dynasty allotted the drama to the Yüan period. Nevertheless, conservatism in literary matters was such that this new form, for which there was no place in the traditional system of literary classification, was not considered to be orthodox literature, though perhaps it was taken to be a freakish gem. This attitude is well represented by the following passage from the Bibliographical Notes in *Ssu-K'u-Ch'üan-Shu,* an imperial collection of 79,339 volumes of Chinese books compiled in 1773-1783:

"Dramatic poetry (*ch'ü* 曲), lying between literature and entertainment, is of no literary value. Talented writers have vied with each other in the beauty of language, but they cannot be said to have achieved any genuine literary accomplishment . . . Hence, under the heading of dramatic poetry there will be no dramatic works, but reviews, criticisms and phonology will be included. That Wang Ch'i in his *Hsu-Wen-Hsien-T'ung-K'ao* (王圻, 續文獻通考) included the dramas *P'i-P'a-Chi* (琵琶記) and *Hsi-Hsiang-Chi* (西廂記) among the classics is hardly an example of judicious editorship". [1]

In the same book, referring to the dramatic poetry of Yüan dynasty, there is:

". . . these poets have become known through their works because they have no other use for their talents so that they put them to writing descriptive and lyrical poetry which may be counted as small accomplishments in the realm of songs, hence not entirely to be ignored". [2]

---

[1] 四庫全書總目, 集部, 卷一九八, 詞曲類, 引言.

[2] 四庫全書總目, 詞曲類, 卷二百, 七頁, 張小山小令注.

It is curious that those who wrote complete dramas should be ignored and those who wrote single poems in the style of dramatic poetry (*ch'ü* 曲) should be accepted. Those who are acquainted with the Yüan dramas will understand, if not sympathize, with the orthodox attitude: the fact that they, being for popular consumption, were written in the vernacular instead of the classical language was no doubt one reason for the rejection by the scholars and we cannot agree to this reason now, but the puerility of some of the themes and grossness of the language do not even now suit the refined taste. Dramas were not considered as healthy reading material for young scholars, especially for women. In *Hung-Lou-Meng* (紅樓夢), the hero, when a boy, read them in secret and the heroine, then a young girl, when discovered to have quoted from a play inadvertently during a rhyming game, was abjectly ashamed of herself. [3]

For this reason even the survival of the Yüan dynasty texts was precarious: but for the confidence of a few lone collectors who put the dramas into print, they would have also perished. Of the extant collections of Yüan dramas by far the most important is Tsang Chin-Shu's *Selections from Yüan Dramas* (臧晉叔, 元曲選) both for its early publication (in the reign of Wan-Li, 1573-1620. 明, 萬曆) and its scope (it contains one hundred dramas of which ninety-four are of Yüan period). Later discoveries from Japanese and Chinese libraries [4] added little to the existing knowledge of the Yüan dramas except perhaps the *Mo-Wang-Kuan* collection found in Shanghai in 1938 which is noteworthy for its unique account of properties and costume. [5] All these collections represent, however, only one school of Yüan dramas called the "northern school". Of the "southern dramas" probably of earlier and separate origin, thirty-three were selected in the *Yung-Lo-Ta-Tien* (永樂大典 an imperial collection of 22,877 volumes compiled in 1403-1406) but of these only three dramas survived. [6]

For information before the Yüan dynasty the modern student of the history of

---

[3] 曹雪芹, 紅樓夢, 四十二回

[4] 日本京都帝國大學影印: 覆元槧古今雜劇三十種; 南京圖書館影印: 元明雜劇;（明）息機子編刊, 元人雜劇選;（明）新安, 徐氏刊, 古名家雜劇。

[5] 上海涵芳樓印 : 脈望館孤本元明雜劇。

[6] There was originally only one hand copy of this collection but when it survived a palace fire in 1563 two more copies were made. There were attempts to print it, but the project was abandoned owing to the prohibitive cost. Two copies were later lost in fire and the third copy suffered gradual losses through the centuries till at the end of the nineteenth century less than five thousand volumes were left and of these only about three hundred survived the Boxer War. In 1920 Mr. Yeh Kung-Ch'o 葉恭綽 found in a small antique shop in London a volume from the collection. The thirty-three southern dramas were in volumes 13,965 — 13,991 and the volume found in London was volume 13,991. For other discoveries of Yüan dramas see 傅芸子, 中國戲曲研究之新趨勢, 戲劇叢刊, 第三期; 陸侃如, 馮沅君, 南戲拾遺, 燕京學報專號第十三; 錢南揚, 宋元南戲百一錄, 燕京學報專號之九.

Chinese theatre has to glean what data he can from books not primarily connected with the theatre, such as books on music, court records, memoirs, local history, books on customs and manners, ancient novels, and so forth. The result, as can be expected, is not a continuous account of theatrical development but a series of glimpses of the types of entertainment in various times. One of the most interesting periods in the history of Chinese theatre is that of the evolution of the drama from non-dramatic forms. To trace the evolution of the drama one needs to compare the earliest dramatic compositions with the quasi-dramatic works immediately preceding. Unfortunately the extant Yüan dramas represent the best rather than the earliest works, hence the beginnings of the drama can only be incompletely surveyed.

From Yüan dynasty onwards the text forms an important source of theatrical information and it can be supplemented by books on dramatic criticism and phonology, the latter for its connection with dramatic poetry. It is to be remembered however that Chinese scholars were interested in Yüan dramas as literature, not as theatre, therefore, among the considerable amount of writings on drama only a small part concerns the theatre.

The study of the history of the Chinese theatre may be said to have been started by Prof. Wanga Kuo-Wei's *History of Drama in Sung and Yüan Dynasties* (1915) [7] which, in spite of the title, is a compendious account from the earliest times to the end of Yüan dynasty. In its preface the author said: "I am the first to study the subject and this book is the greatest contribution in this field, not because of superior scholarship but because no one has done any similar work before". [8] The value of this book lies not only in the erudition and insight it represents but also in the widespread interest it has excited. Since then many articles and books have been written on the subject, some representing original research in specific problems and others treating the history of the Chinese theatre from slightly different points of view, but nothing has yet been written that is comparable in scope and originality to Prof. Wang's book.

The study of the Chinese theatre is still often appended to that of the Chinese drama, but now the drama has been recognized as a part of Chinese literature the theatre should in turn be accepted as a fine art on its own merits. Only when it is so considered can the many problems and gaps in the history of the Chinese theatre be solved and filled.

---

[7] 王國維, 宋元戲曲史 — before it appeared in book form it was published in *The Eastern Miscellany* 東方雜誌 in 1911.

[8] Since then the manuscript of *Fu-Tao-Jen's Study of Music and Drama* has been discovered and published (1936)北京大學出版, 姚鼐, 復道人今樂考證. This sketch, of the same intention as Prof. Wang's book and covering part of the same field, was written some seventy years before Prof. Wang's book. However, in its present form it is not as coherent an account and Prof. Wang did not know of its existence.

TABLE III

夏	HSIA	2205 — 1767 B.C.	. . . .
商	SHANG	1766 — 1122 B.C.	. . . .
周	CHOU	1122 — 255 B.C.	. . . .
秦	CH'IN	221 — 206 B.C	. . . .
漢	HAN	206 B.C. — A.D. 220	. . . .
	"Three Kingdoms"	A.D. 220 — 277	. . . .
	CHIN	A.D. 265 — 419	. . . .
南北朝	"North and South"	A.D. 402 — 588	. . . .
宋	SUNG	A.D. 420 — 478	. . . .
齊	CH'I	A.D. 479 — 501	. . . .
梁	LIANG	A.D. 502 — 556	. . . .
陳	CH'EN	A.D. 557 — 588	. . . .
隋	SUI	A.D. 589 — 617	. . . .
唐	T'ANG	A.D. 618 — 906	. . . .
五代	"Five Dynasties"	A.D. 907 — 959	. . . .
宋	SUNG	A.D. 960 — 1276	. . . .
元	YÜAN	A.D. 1277 — 1367	. . . .
明	MING	A.D. 1368 — 1643	. . . .
淸	CH'ING	A.D.1644 — 1911	. . . .
	REPUBLIC	1911 —	. . . .

so called YIN 殷 . The first dynasty for which there is substantial archaeological evidence.

e classical period of Chinese history. CH'UN-CH'IU period 春秋 722 — 481
C. in which the emperor's power dwindled and the dukes ruled autonomously.
EH-KUO period 列國 481 — 221 B.C. the dukedoms had become separate
tes. CHAN-KUO period 戰國 403 — 221 B.C. — period of "warring states".

-unified China.

e country was divided into three states, WEI 魏 in the north, WU 吳 in the east and SHU 蜀
the southwest.
om A.D. 304 barbarian kingdoms in north China. "Eastern CHIN" from A.D. 317.
lled "North and South" to distinguish the dynasties from others of the same names.

ese four dynasties were established in south China; the northern part of the country
s for most of the time the battleground of foreign tribes.

-unified China.

riod of transition with five rapidly succeeding dynasties each lasting a few years: LIANG,
ANG, CHIN, HAN and CHOU, called "Five Dynasties" to distinguish them from the other
nasties of the same names. Northern China invaded by Manchurians at one time.

rthern China under Mongols and Manchus from A.D. 1115 onwards. "Southern Sung"
er A.D. 1127.
reign rule (Mongol).

reign rule (Manchu).

Chinese history each dynasty represents the continuous rule of one family. When the
one, which is hereditary within the dynasty, is taken from the family either by revolution or
foreign invasion, the name of the dynasty is changed. In those periods when the country was
der divided rule with several states and names of dynasties simultaneously it is customary to
oose the leading native state for historical reckoning).

CHAPTER XX

ELEMENTS OF THE THEATRE IN ANCIENT LIFE

The beginning of the Chinese theatre has been variously traced to the impersonation involved in ancient religious rituals, to the ceremonial dances and to the musicians of the ancient courts.

The earliest form of dancing among the primitive Chinese is lost in the unrecorded times before the dawn of history. According to one theory, in primitive societies community dancing preceded the performance of specialized dancers; in the former everyone present was both dancer and spectator at the same time and the dancing was improvised but in the latter dancers and spectators were distinct and the performance was more expert. [1] Community dancing for courtship and worship can still be found among the aboriginal Miao tribes (苗) in southwestern China: the dance, called "moon dance" (跳月), is accompanied by pipes and bells and lasts all day. It is believed that several poems in the *Book of Odes* (詩經) describe this type of dancing. [2] The poems in question are from the folklore of south China, of an

---

[1] *Vide* Aoki Masaru, *Modern History of the Chinese Drama* 青木正兒, 中國近世戲曲史, 一章一節.

[2] 詩經, 陳風

The sound of the drums	At the elms by the east gate
At the foot of the hill,	At the oaks by the hill,
Summer and winter alike —	The daughter of *Tzu-Chung* —
Dancers holding the heron's feather.(宛丘第二)	Dancing under them.(東門之枌一)
The sound of the earthen vessel	In a fine morning
On the way to the hill,	On the plain in the south
Summer and winter alike —	She leaves twisting her hemp
Dancers holding the fan of heron's feather.(宛丘第三)	And goes a-dancing. (東門之枌二).

These passages quoted by Aoki Masaru refer, according to Prof. Wang Kuo-Wei, to the dance of the shamans. 一王國維, 宋元戲曲史, 一章 (一段). These odes are from the country of Ch'en (陳). In a history of Han dynasty (漢書, 地理志, 下, "陳") it is said that "among the women of the noble families in the district of Ch'en religious rituals and offerings were much in vogue, and these were officiated by shaman priests, hence superstition was prevalent there".

unknown date before Confucius (551-479 B.C.) and it has been argued that they may represent ancient folk dance similar to that now practiced by the isolated Miao tribes. [3]

So far as ancient records show the earliest specialized dancing appears to be that connected with shamanism, the popular religion of ancient China. The nature of shamanism was described in *Kuo-Yü* (國語) an ancient history book attributed to Tso Ch'iu-Ming (左丘明):

> "In ancient times priests were distinct from the laymen. Those among the people who were discerning and devout as well as serious and upright, and who could distinguish between right and wrong and benefit the people around them . . . were endowed by the gods with special powers and became shamans *(hsi* 覡) and shamanesses (*wu* 巫). Their duties were to provide the gods with shrines according to their degrees and to give them seasonal offerings . . . and to pray for those who come to worship them . . . After the reign of Shao-Hao (少皞), however, the tribes under his rule followed their evil ways, shamans and laymen were no longer separate and when people offered sacrifices they acted as their own priests". [4]

This is probably an idealized description of the religion, but as Shao-Hao is a legendary emperor who supposedly reigned from 2597 to 2513 B.C. one may conclude that even in the later part of Chou dynasty (1122-255 B.C.), when the above account was written, the beginning of shamanism was lost in the legendary past. Modern shamans among the Mongolian tribes correspond closely to the above description of the ancient priests: they act as the intermediary between men and gods, they exorcise daemons from the sick person and his household, and they wear special costume and use ceremonial swords, mirrors and drums in their dances and incantations. [5] The study of the oracle bones [6] and ancient texts of history books showed that shamans and shamanesses were also responsible for making rain, sometimes by dance and incantation [7] or supplicating cries [8] and sometimes by

---

[3] Aoki Masaru, *op. cit.*

[4] 國語, 楚語, 下, 第十八.

[5] Walter Heissig, Shamanen und Geisterbeschwörer im Küriye-Banner, *Folklore,* v. III. i., 1944. Publ. Catholic Univ. of Peking. Marco Polo, *Travels,* Ed. M. Komroff (1942), Bk. II. ch. 50 appears to be a description of shamans. European histories of medieval times also indicate that the Asiatic shamans used bells, drums, incense and incantation for exorcism — see Gibbon, *Decline and Fall of the Roman Empire,* ch. XLII. Embassies of the Turks and Romans, note by Dean Milman, quoting Niebuhr, *Byzantine History.*

[6] Ancient bones, first discovered in 1900, on which were carved the results of divination in ancient script. 甲骨文.

[7] For modern examples of the text of the incantations see Walter Heissig, *op. cit.*

[8] Ch'en Meng-Chia, Myths and Witchcraft during Shang Period, *Yenching Journal of Chinese Studies,* No. 20. Dec. 1936. 陳夢家, 商代之神話與巫術, 燕京學報, 第二十期. Part II of this article contains details of the various shamanist practices.

exposing themselves to the sun or fire. [9] They were also responsible for curing the sick, for divinations, for interpretation of dreams and for exorcism, especially of spirits of the epidemic. [10]

The relation of shamanism to the evolution of the theatre lies partly in the dancing. Dancing was so much a part of the shaman's ritual that in Han dynasty the etymology of the word for shamaness was thought to be connected with dancing. [11] In the script of Ch'in dynasty (221-206 B.C.) called the "small seal" (小篆) the ideogram for "shamaness" is 巫 which, according to the lexicographer Hsü Shen (許慎), means "women who served the spirits and could communicate with them by dance" — the character is shaped like a dancing woman with long sleeves, and for its meaning it contains the radical 工 for "doing". [12] In fact, since Ch'en Meng-Chia's paper was published, the ideogram for "shamaness" has been identified in the oracle bones to be 𢀳 which shows an awning in which two hands 𠂤 hold a piece of jade 玉, because it was the duty of the shamaness to officiate in offerings to the spirits. The ideogram for "dance" 㚤 went through another line of evolution. Nevertheless, Hsü Shen's mistaken etymology could only occur because shamanism was closely associated with dancing in people's minds.

That superstition was widespread in Shang dynasty is fully shown by the oracle bones, and that the shamans were also active then is shown by I Yin's (伊尹) warning of its excess:

> ". . . constantly dancing in the hall and singing abandonedly in the house . . ." [13]

In Chou dynasty religion was absorbed into the political system and shamans became government officials assigned to the duties of divination, of interpretation of dreams, of prayers, etc. [14] Nevertheless, unofficial shamans and shamanesses

---

[9] E. H. Schafer, Ritual Exposure in Ancient China, *Harvard Journal of Asiatic Studies,* v. 14, no. 1 & 2. 1951.

[10] Ch'en Meng-Chia, *op. cit.*

[11] It also appears that the shamaness preceded the shaman because the ideogram for "shaman" 覡 is a derivative form.

[12] 許慎，說文解字（第五）a dictionary compiled in Han dynasty (206 B.C. — A.D. 220). It has been thought that the ideogram for shamaness 巫 was in fact derived from that for "dance" which on the oracle bones was 㚤 or 㚤 with a man 大 holding yak tails 𠂉𠂉 which were commonly used in ancient dances. (Ch'en Meng-Chia, *op. cit.*). Thus,

$$㚤 \rightarrow \left[夾 \rightarrow 巫 \rightarrow 巫 \rightarrow 巫 \right] \rightarrow 巫$$

(intermediate forms conjectured).

[13] 商書，伊訓；墨子，非樂上 引，湯之官刑.

[14] Large bodies of shamans were employed as officials 儀禮，士虞禮. "Shamans countless" and "shamanesses innumerable" served under the government for divination, cleansing rituals, interpretation of dreams, prayers, rain-making, rituals for better crops, exorcising epidemics, etc., each as a separate group— 周禮，春官，宗伯.

were active at the end of the dynasty if not earlier, as shown by the numerous references to them in *Tso-Chuan*. [15]

In some of the official ceremonies of Chou dynasty remnants of primitive religion could still be found. Thus, after Tzu-Kung (子貢), a disciple of Confucius, saw the ceremony called *Pa-Cha* (八蜡 an offering at the end of the year to eight gods connected with agriculture) he reported that "the whole town appeared to have gone mad", referring probably to the abandoned dancing. [16] It was the duty of an official called *Fang-Hsiang-Shih* (方相氏) to

> "wear bear-skin, black jacket, red shirt and four golden eyes and, waving
> the halberd and shield, to lead the people into houses and tombs and by striking
> the halberd in the four corners to chase away spirits of the epidemic". [17]

This reference is of special interest because it is the earliest mention of mask in the Chinese literature. [18]

Towards the end of Chou dynasty (1122-255 B.C.), probably owing to the dwindled central control, unofficial shamanism flared up in the southern part of the country. According to writings of the second century A.D.:

> "In the southern part of Ch'u 楚 [now Hunan province] . . . the people
> believed in spirits and were addicted to rituals in which they had music, singing
> and dancing. Ch'ü Yüan 屈原 [332-295 B.C.] who saw their ceremonies and
> dances found their songs crude and vulgar and composed the *Nine Hymns*
> 九歌 for them". [19]

The *Nine Hymns* are extant and the text discloses several interesting points in the shamans' practice of this time. We know, for instance, that in the rituals swords decorated with jade were used, [20] there were libations, [21] string and wind instruments were played, [22] the dancers' dresses were colourful, [23] perfume or incense was used [24] and the descending cloud-spirit was supposed to be riding a dragon. [25]

---

[15] 左丘明, 左傳, (e.g. 成公十年, 襄公八年, 十八年, 二十九年) annals of late Chou dynasty written by Tso Ch'iu-Ming, a contemporary of Confucius.

[16] 蘇軾, 東坡志林, 卷二, 一款 "祭祀" (學津討原)

[17] 周禮, 夏官司馬.

[18] 周禮, 夏官司馬, 方相氏, 鄭玄註. Early commentators specifically pointed out that this was a mask.

[19] 王逸, 楚辭章句, 九歌.

[20] 撫長劍兮玉珥, 東皇太一.

[21] 奠桂酒兮椒漿, 東皇太一.

[22] 陳竽瑟兮浩倡, 東皇太一.

[23] 靈偃蹇兮姣服, 東皇太一; 靈衣兮被被, 大司命. Walter Heissig, *op. cit.* also mentions bright-coloured skirts.

[24] 芳菲菲兮滿堂, 東皇太一.

[25] 龍駕兮帝服........靈皇皇兮既降, 雲中君.

In the *Nine Hymns* the word *Ling* 靈 appears sometimes to denote the shaman or shamaness and sometimes god, [26] and this strongly suggests that among the cults of shamanism in this district the dancing shamans were believed to be possessed and were worshipped as gods. [27] Impersonation, later to be deliberate in the theatre, was at this time believed to be mystic transformation. [28]

Impersonation in ancient religious ceremonies was by no means confined to shamanism: in ancestral worship the deceased was impersonated by one of his children, in this capacity called *shih* (尸). [29] In one instance an impersonator was also used for the worship of Heaven. [30] *Shih* was however a mere image, there was no change of identity in the mind of the worshippers. [31] The ceremony was nevertheless mimetic:

> "Priest (祝) receives *shih* (尸) . . . *shih* enters gate . . . *shih* reaches steps . . . priest leads *shih, shih* mounts the steps . . . *shih* enters door . . . *shih* sits . . . *shih* takes the ceremonial cup . . . priest passes meat to *shih* . . . *shih* eats . . . *shih* drinks the wine . . . *shih* bows in return . . . *shih* goes out of the door".

The ceremony, with music and cries, must be rather theatrical and impressive. [32]

---

[26] 王國維, 宋元戲曲史, 一章.

[27] 靈之來兮蔽日 (東君); 靈之來兮如雲 (湘夫人); 靈連蜷兮既留, 靈皇皇兮既降 (雲中君).

[28] Modern scholars have argued that *Ch'u Tz'u* (楚辭), which contains the *Nine Hymns,* could not have been written before Han dynasty and some believe that the *Nine Hymns* were original songs used by the shamans, not the work of Ch'ü Yüan.胡適,胡適文存, 二集, 讀楚辭; 陸侃如, 屈原. The point is, however, immaterial here; shamanism must in any case have been prevalent in southern China at or shortly after the end of Chou dynasty. 何天放, 楚辭作 於漢代考; 徐中舒, 九歌九 㝬考, 中國文化研究所集刊,卷一,三號. In Han dynasty emperor Wu-Ti 武帝 (reigned 140-86 B.C.) believed in shamanism. Many shamans came to the capital and shamanesses were regular visitors to the palace. At first they taught protection against danger by worshipping wooden figures buried under the house but later they participated in secret curses and occult charms. "When the emperor was ill and suspected some secret curse on him he sent Chiang Ch'ung 江充 to stamp out shamanism. Chiang hated the crown prince and dug in his palace where he found some wooden figures". 漢書, 戾太子傳. Shamanesses were also mentioned as priestesses in offerings in the district of Ch'en 陳. 漢書,地理志, 下.

[29] 儀禮, 士虞禮.

[30] 國語, 晉語, 第十四, 鄭簡公使公孫成子來聘 (董伯為尸).

[31] 儀禮, 士虞禮 "哭從尸" 註.

[32] 儀禮, 士虞禮. The ritual was also mentioned in the *Book of Odes* 詩經小雅,谷風 之什, 楚茨.In Chinese religious ceremonies there are several types of offerings: *chi* 祭, is a communion — 孝經註疏, 卷二, "守其祭祀": 祭者...人神相接:*hsiang* 享 is a feast—周禮, 地官鼓人疏; 朱駿聲, 說文通訓定聲, 壯部十八, "享" 註, 詩, 商頌, 殷武, "莫敢不來享" "for men called *hsiang* 饗 and for spirits called *hsiang* 享 ...";and *tien* 奠 is offering — 說文解字, 第十四 "酒器" (to place food and wine before gods and spirits). Except in the last, action is implied in these names, hence the impersonator.

It is also possible that the exorcist *Fang-Hsiang-Shih* mentioned above was supposed to be a spirit [33] or it might be a remnant of primitive ritual dancers in which the animal impersonator was, judging by the primitive practices in other parts of the world, a usual feature. [34]

The dance formed an important part of the religious ceremonies of Chou dynasty and the *Book of Rituals* 禮記 contains the description of many types. Dances for worship were performed for Heaven and Earth, for gods of agriculture, for ancestors, for mountains and rivers, for stars, etc, and dances were also performed for the celebration of military and civil merits. According to one classification there were six types:

1. *Fu* 帗 — dance with wands fitted with whole feathers (for the worship of the gods of agriculture).
2. *Yü* 羽 — with wands fitted with divided feathers.
3. *Huang* 皇 — dancers in feather caps and garments of kingfisher's feathers (for rain-making).
4. *Mao* 旄 — with yak tails.
5. *Kan* 干 — with shields (military dance).
6. *Jen* 人 — with bare hands and sleeves. [35]

Ceremonial dances were invariably accompanied by music; in fact the same word *yüeh* 樂 referred to both the dance and the music. [36] Some of the songs sung during the dances, called *sung* 頌, are extant and may be found in the *Book of Odes*. It has been suggested [37] that *sung* really means "express" and that the dances were mimetic in nature [38] hence these ceremonial dances were the predecessor of drama. It has also been pointed out [39] that throughout the ancient dynasties musicians and dancers were kept in the imperial court for ceremonial purposes and that these might well have later been diverted into court entertainment which was instrumental in the development of the Chinese theatre. [40]

---

(33) Ch'en Meng-Chia, *op. cit.*

(34) *Vide* W. Ridgeway, *The Origin of Tragedy,* ch. 4.

(35) 周禮, 春官樂師; 參, 馬端臨, 文獻通考, 卷一四四.

(36) 禮記, 內則, 五十二節 "勺舞"; 詩經, 周南序; 樂記一節: "干戚羽旄謂之樂"

(37) 劉師培, 原戲, 國粹學報, 三卷九號.

(38) "Dances with shields and halberd are in the military manner; those with feathers and flutes are in the civil manner". 禮記, 文王世子注.

(39) 許之衡, 戲曲史.

(40) Ceremonial dances were performed in Chou dynasty not for magic, but rather for the expression of religious feelings. In shamanism the dance might become routine, the meaning of the steps might be obscure, but the purpose, which was the potency of the occult invocation, was always clear. In ceremonial dances, once the emotional meaning of the movements was lost there was hardly any sense in performing it. It was to the preservation and re-interpretation of the ritual that Confucius (551-479 B.C.) devoted himself at the end of Chou dynasty. If the ceremonial dances of Chou dynasty were originally mimetic, their mimetic quality must have become very obscure at the time of

It may be noticed that although the rituals of shamanism and the official religious ceremonies of Chou dynasty contain elements of the theatre — impersonation, music and dance — they are not entertainment. Some of the refined ceremonies were probably mere expressions of religious feelings, in nature widely different from the dances performed by the shamans for magical potency, and Confucius for one untiringly insisted on the educational value rather than the religious merit of the "ritual and music" (*Li-yüeh* 禮 樂). Dances were also used to solemnize a meeting or for celebration [41] and sometimes an originally ritual dance may be performed for recreation [42] but they were never performed for amusement.

Towards the end of the Chou dynasty, however, when the feudal system of Chou dynasty was gradually disintegrating, religious as well as political tradition was gradually ignored. Among the luxuries enjoyed by the autonomous dukes were court jesters [43] who entertained their masters with witticisms, songs and dances. Judging by what they were called: *ch'ang-yu* 倡優, they were musicians (倡) as well as jesters, and at least some of them were dwarfs. [44] Mainly through their connection with politics, some of them left their names in history books. Jester Shih 施, who was a dwarf, [45] was once sent by a lady to dance in front of her opponent and to win him to her schemes through a song with *double entendre*. [46] He once danced before the duke of Lu 魯, probably again as a tool, and was executed by Confucius because he "made fun of the head of the state". [47] Jester Meng (優 孟), in order to find favour for his friend Sun-Shu Ao's (孫 叔 敖) orphan, dressed in the dead man's clothes and after practicing his friend's manners for more than a year, appeared before the prince who thought Sun-Shu Ao had come to life. [48]

Music and dance formed no small part of the life of the ancient Chinese people. With the shamans they were to serve the spirits; in the temple ceremonies of Chou dynasty, they were to honour gods and perhaps also to provide an outlet to religious

---

Confucius, otherwise he would not have devoted so much of his energy to study the significance of the ceremonies. cf. Confucius: "When we talk of ritual do we mean the jade and the silk [ceremonial objects] and when we talk of music do we mean the bells and the drums?" 論 語, 陽 貨.

[41] *Vide* 論 語, 八 佾.

[42] 論 語, 先 進 where a rain-making dance was mentioned.

[43] 倡 優, 俳 優.

[44] 侏 儒 cf. "Although I am short ..." 史 記, 滑 稽 列 傳 (優 旃). Dwarfs were often employed in Chinese imperial courts. In T'ang dynasty dwarfs were annually drafted from a district to serve in the palace 舊 唐 書, 卷 一 九 二, 陽 城 傳.

[45] 孔 子 家 語, 相 魯; 何 休, 公 羊 解 詁, 定 公 十 年.

[46] 國 語, 晉 語, 第 七, 八.

[47] 春 秋 穀 梁 傳, 定 公 十 年.

[48] For witticisms of other jesters see 史 記, 滑 稽 列 傳 from which the above anecdote is taken. cf. Roper, *Life and Death of Sir Thomas More*: " ... would he at Christmas tyd sodenly sometymes stepp in among the players, and never stydinge for the matter, make a parte of his owne there presently amonge them". Chambers, *Med. Stage*, II. 193 n.

feelings and with the court jesters, they became means of entertainment. It was with the court jesters that we first learn of deliberate mimicry, although in the one example on record it had practical rather than theatrical purpose.

Rituals differ from the theatre in several respects. In the theatre men represent, for the most part, other men and neither the performers nor the spectators really believe that the actor *is* the character he plays; in primitive rituals men impersonate gods and the performers are believed to change their identity, as can be seen most clearly in the case of *ling* (靈). The aim of religious rites is the potency of an occult task, not the success of providing entertainment. The shamanesses worked on the spirits, not on the spectators; they tried to invoke gods, not to amuse men; in fact, in some cases there might not be any spectators at all, and if there were they did not concern the performers. What the possessed dancers did was therefore not necessarily interesting to watch because they were not necessarily meant to be seen.

CHAPTER XXI

COURT PAGEANTS AND SPECTACLES

In the dynasties that followed Chou dynasty, through a period covering about eight centuries, court entertainment became increasingly elaborate, first in masquers and circus and later in spectacles and pageants.

Various forms of amusement involving contests and physical feats first appeared in late Chou dynasty. Stilts and jumping through rings of swords were once presented as novelties [1] and one dwarf "played with the stem of the spear". [2] The second emperor of Ch'in 秦 (221-206 B.C.) once watched court jesters and wrestlers [3] and a history of Han dynasty indicated that "in the time of the Warring States (403-221 B.C.) military ceremonies were modified for amusements, which in Ch'in dynasty was called *chiao-ti* 角抵 [wrestling]". [4] Military contests probably formed a part of the social intercourse among the nobility of Chou; in any case, practice of archery, chariot-driving and wrestling was mentioned in the *Book of Rituals*. [5]

The court entertainment of later dynasties, with music and dance, was derived from the "secular music" (including dance) 散樂 of Chou dynasty [6] which, though distinguished from the "ceremonial music" 雅樂 for religious ceremonies, was nevertheless taught by special government officials. [7]

Contortionists and acrobats were also mentioned in early Han dynasty [8] sometimes in connection with entertainment presented at banquets:

"There were in attendance twenty or thirty women wearing powder and ink (ink for the eyebrows) and in embroidered clothes. Amid the music of drums and flutes, tumblers, masquers and dancers were presented for the

---

[1] 列子, 說符.
[2] 國語, 晉語, 第十.
[3] 史記, 卷八十七, 李斯傳.
[4] 漢書, 卷二十二, 刑法志.
[5] 禮記, 月令, 孟冬之月.
[6] 參, 舊唐書, 音樂志一.
[7] 周禮, 春官, 旄人.
[8] "... bend the body like a ring ..." 劉安, 淮南子, 卷十九, 脩務（鼓舞）.

201

amusement of the guests. After a short interval, puppets danced to the rhythm of the drums". [9]

In Han dynasty "worship of famous mountains and rivers involved musicians and dancing masquers", [10] and among the attendant musicians at state banquets in the palace, according to a history of this dynasty, were seven animal masquers. [11]

Circus, which was brought into China in 107 B.C. by a tributary tribe in West China, appears first to include only wrestling and conjuring. [12] It gradually became more elaborate: emperor Wu-Ti 武帝 (reign: 140-86 B.C.) entertained foreign envoys with "ponds of wine and forests of meat" together with pageants of "fish and dragons" and acrobatic shows. [13] In description of the second century A.D. there were "tripod-lifting, pole-climbing, jumping through rings of spears, somersaults, lying on pikes, juggling balls and knives, rope dancing, swallowing swords and spitting flames". [14] Animal masquers mixed with the acrobats and there were "dancing leopards and bears, tigers playing the zither, dragons playing the pipe", and "dwarfs and giants making fun together". Of stage machinery there were, according to another poem of the same period, "a fairy sitting on a bird", [15] and "goddess Nü-Wa 女媧 singing in the clouds with the legendary musician Hung-Yen conducting and when she finished, the clouds moved away and snow began to fall, at first lightly, growing gradually into a snowstorm". [16] Of stage effect there was "rolling stone to make thunder"; of built sets there were "tall mountains and rolling hills with trees, grass and fairy fruits" and of stage illusions there was a monster transformed into a fairy carriage. [17] A book of the first century B.C. said that the last emperor of Hsia dynasty (2205-1767 B.C.) "indulged in strange and spectacular shows staged by jesters and dwarfs" but the account is of doubtful authenticity, being more probably a description of the contemporary court entertainment. [18] To stage water pageants emperor Ming-Ti 明帝 (reigned A.D. 227-240) of Wei "flooded the front of a palace hall to stage the shows on water and in the New Year

---

[9] 賈誼, 賈子新書, 卷四, 匈奴篇.

[10] 桓寬, 鹽鐵論, 卷六, 散不足篇.

[11] 漢書, 禮樂志, 末二段.

[12] 史記, 大宛傳. Acrobatic displays were also known to be popular in Liao dynasty 遼 (A.D. 916-1125). They appear to have a continuous tradition among the foreign tribes. 王圻, 續文獻通考, 卷一一九.

[13] 漢書, 西域傳, 下, 讚.

[14] 張衡, 西京賦 (文選卷二).

[15] 李尤, 平樂觀賦 (藝文類聚, 卷六十三).

[16] 張衡, 西京賦 (文選卷二).

[17] *Ibid.* It is believed that the scenery changes were part of the conjuring tricks which came earlier as a tribute from the tribes in western China. 王國維, 宋元戲曲史, 一章.

[18] 劉向等, 列女傳, 卷七, 孽嬖傳, 一. For stone carvings of Han dynasty representing these spectacles see 聞宥, 四川漢代畫象選集, 戌, 九, 三十二, 七十五至七十七.

celebrations huge animals were built, fish and dragons [probably masquers] joined the games which included riding on horseback upside down''. [19] In the periods of Wei 魏 (A.D. 220-265) and Chin 晋 (A.D. 265-419) for pageants we hear of "dancing elephants and tortoises, rivers and islands, artificial trees and snow" and of circus, "tripod-lifting, walking on hands, contortionists and rope-dancing". [20] In the reign of emperor Ch'eng-Ti 成帝 (A.D. 326-343) minister Ku Chen 顧琛 suggested abolishing circus shows because they were unhealthy and they augmented the palace expenses unnecessarily [21] and some of the less decorous acts, based on repulsive episodes in Chinese history, were for a time stopped. [22]

In the reign of emperor Shih-Hu 石虎 (A.D. 335-349) of Later Chao dynasty 後趙, circus acts were described as: a pole on a man's forehead or teeth with another man climbing up and revolving on the top and a horse-drawn carriage with a twenty-foot vertical pole on it and a horizontal bar on top of the pole with acrobats flying or hanging upside down at the two ends of the bar. [23] In North Wei dynasty 北魏 (A.D. 386-534) emperor Tao-Wu-Ti 道武帝 summoned the chief musicians in A.D. 404 to "expand the pageants and spectacles and at a banquet in front of the palace hall were presented wrestling, rope-dancing, juggling and various animal masks", [24] and emperor Ming-Yüan-Ti 明元帝 (reigned A.D. 409-423) of the same dynasty "augmented the pageants and spectacles and supplemented them with music". [25] In Liang dynasty 梁 (A.D. 502-556) there were "juggling of balls and knives and rope-dancing", [26] and in the reign of Wu-P'ing 武平 (A.D. 570-576) of North Ch'i dynasty, apart from the familiar dwarfs and animal images, there were "killing the horse and skinning the donkey", apparently conjuring tricks. [27] Sometimes the spectators also joined the pageants, as in South Ch'i dynasty 南齊 (A.D. 479-501) when "dwarfs led the dance and spectators sang for the dancers". [28]

The pageants and circus shows grew increasingly extravagant: in North Chou dynasty 北周 emperor Hsüan-Ti 宣帝 (reigned A.D. 578-579) again summoned

---

[19] 陳壽, 三國志, 明帝紀, （三年）斐松之註 . In the third or fourth century A.D. a certain Phaedrus, governor of Attica, flooded the orchestra of the theatre of Dionysus in Athens for spectacles on water — see J. T. Allen, *Stage Antiquities of the Greeks and Romans and Their Influence* (1927), 86. This may be an indication of the similar workings of *blasé* minds.

[20] 晋書, 樂志, 下, 末二段 .

[21] *Ibid.*

[22] W. Arthur Cornaby, Notes on the Chinese Drama and Ancient Choral Dances, *The New China Review,* v.1. no. 1 March, 1919.

[23] Exactly the same act was seen in the Byzantine court — see Gibbon, *Decline and Fall of the Roman Empire,* ch. LIII. Note 51.

[24] 馬端臨, 文獻通考, 卷百四十七, 散樂百戲 .

[25] 魏書, 樂志（三段）.

[26] 馬端臨, 文獻通考, 卷百四十七, 六款 .

[27] 隋書, 音樂志, 下 .

[28] 南齊書, 樂志 .

musicians to expand the shows and the performances, which included young men selected for their handsome faces dressed and dancing as women, "lasted days and nights". [29] It was not, however, until Sui dynasty 隋 (A.D. 589-617) that pageants reached mammoth proportions. Emperor Yang-Ti 煬帝 (reign: A.D. 605-617), a pleasure-loving ruler whose court music included music for cock fights and dragon-boat races, [30] was supported in his love for revelry by an understanding minister who, "to satisfy his taste, summoned from all parts of the country professional and amateur musicians totalling more than three hundred people and placed them under the chief court musician". [31] The description of the pageants is as follows:

"In A.D. 607, in order to impress the Turk ambassadors then in the capital, the emperor assembled musicians from the four corners of the country for spectacles to entertain them. At first the performance took place at a lake in the imperial park and the emperor watched it with his ladies from a tent. At the beginning a fabulous bird entered and performed a dance but soon, splashing the water and drenching the grounds, fish, water spirits, reptiles and many kinds of tortoise appeared. While mist was coming out of a whale's mouth which darkened the sunlight, the whale was suddenly transformed into a yellow dragon, about eighty feet long, which crawled and jumped about. There were also two women dancing on a rope stretched between two poles a hundred feet apart, they met and passed each other without stopping the dance. Tripods were lifted and carriage wheels, stone mortars and big jars were juggled; two men danced with poles on their heads and could exchange their poles without the help of their hands. There were islands on huge tortoises and magicians spitting fire and thousands of other transformations never heard of before. The amazement of the foreigners pleased the emperor and from then on the performers were trained in the Ministry of Ceremonies and every year at the New Year the envoys of the tributary tribes, who generally came at this time, were invited to stay for fifteen days and the streets in front of the palace, for about eight *li* [approximately three miles] were closed to traffic for the spectacles. The nobility erected their own tents to watch the shows which lasted all night and the next day. Thirty thousand musicians and actors took part and all of them were dressed in silk and most of the singers and dancers were dressed as women, wearing rich jewelry". [32]

---

[29] 隋書, 音樂志, 中, 下.

[30] *Ibid* 下.

[31] 馬端臨, 文獻通考, 樂考二.

[32] 隋書, 音樂志, 下.　A very similar account is found in a history of Chin dynasty 晉 (A.D. 265-419), written in T'ang (A.D. 618-906): "In late Han dynasty when the emperor received visitors a fabulous bird would appear and dance in front of the palace and, after beating the water to produce a legendary fish and spitting water and mist to cover the sun, became a long dragon about ninety feet long playing above the water. Two women dancers danced on a rope stretched between two poles,

The initial provision for the costume of the pageant exhausted all the silk cloth in the district. [33] A poem written about the pageants mentioned also "lanterns on fish and candles in a dragon's mouth [probably floats in the parade] as well as foreign dances, masks, display of horsemanship and fairy mountains and islands complete with forest and animals". [34] "The sound of music reached the heavens and the whole area was lit by bright torches; all sorts of strange shapes and manners were found there", according to a letter to the emperor asking him to stop the extravagance. [35]

Large scale spectacles and pageants were still staged in T'ang dynasty: in the reign of emperor Kao-Tsu 高祖 (reigned A.D. 618-626) court musicians borrowed more than five hundred women's skirts from the public for pageants [36] and emperor Ming-Huang 明皇 (reigned A.D. 712-756) once summoned musicians within three hundred *li* for a contest in pageantry and a few hundred musicians in bright dress paraded in carriages with stuffed wild animals. [37] The pageants of Sung dynasty had great variety, including choral dancers, puppets [38] and "fish and dragon". [39] Wrestling, "fish and dragon", "lantern mountains" and ball games were indulged in also by the emperors of Liao 遼 (916-1125) and Chin 金 (1115-1234). [40] Spectacles and pageants can even now be seen in China in the tableaux and floats at religious festivals. [41]

they met and touched each other without falling" 晋書, 樂志, 下. This however does not mean that the pageant had acquired a standard programme through the ages; the explanation for the similarity of the two accounts lies rather in the fact that the same authors wrote the history of Sui 隋書 from which the above description of Yang-Ti's pageants is quoted.

[33] 隋書, 音樂志, 下.
[34] 隋, 薛道衡, 和許給事善心 場轉韵詩 (初學記, 卷十五, 雜樂第二, 詩).
[35] 隋書, 柳彧傳.
[36] 馬端臨, 文獻通考, 樂考, 二十.
[37] *Ibid.*
[38] 周密, 武林舊事, 卷二, 元夕; 卷三, 迎新, 歲除.
[39] 辛棄疾, 青玉案: "元夕一夜魚龍舞".
[40] 王圻, 續文獻通考, 卷一一九.
[41] For circus of later times see — 太平御覽, 卷五百六十九.

CHAPTER XXII

THE BEGINNINGS OF DRAMATIC REPRESENTATION

In the last two chapters it was shown that impersonation, at first a part of religious rituals, became, through the masquers, an element in court entertainment. In this chapter it will be shown how acting, which followed impersonation, gradually grew from mimicry to simple dramatic action and how it led to the topical farce and the dramatic dances, the predecessors of the Chinese drama.

Impersonation inevitably suggests mimicry. When the shamans of southern China impersonated gods and spirits in late Chou dynasty the songs they sang indicated the arrival and departure of the god or impersonator and similarly the impersonator in the ancestral worship ate and drank in the ceremony. In these as well as in the performance of the court jesters there were probably unrecorded cases of dramatic acting.

In Han dynasty the ceremony of exorcism may be said to contain rudimentary acting:

> "For exorcising epidemic spirits one hundred and twenty virgin boys from ten to twelve years old were chosen from the families of the palace guard to join the chief exorcist Fang-Hsiang-Shih 方相氏 in the ceremony. The children wore red turbans and black gowns and carried small drums fitted with handles and the chief exorcist wore golden mask with four eyes, black jacket, scarlet skirt and bear-skin and carried spear and shield. There were also twelve animals with fur and horns . . . who danced with the exorcist. All these together went over the grounds three times, shouting all the time, then with torches they chased the epidemic spirits out of the gate". [1]

In T'ang dynasty five hundred children accompanied the exorcist. They were all in masks and wore red jackets and white gowns. [2] The exorcist of Sung dynasty was less impressive: "Near the end of the year some poor people dressed as women and

---

[1] 後漢書, 禮儀志, 中, 大儺.
[2] 段安節, 樂府雜錄, 驅儺.

207

spirits went from door to door with torches, gongs and drums, asking for tips for their supposedly effective exorcism". [3]

In the pageants of Han dynasty some acting was involved in the tableaux of gods and fairies [4] but more explicit dramatic action was introduced through a wrestling act depicting the magician Huang Kung's 黃公 calamitously unsuccessful attempt to charm a tiger. The magician, according to a later account of this circus act, "tied his hair with red silk and carried a golden dagger as a charm. In his youth he was not only able to cast spells on snakes and tigers but also able to raise cloud and fog and move hills and rivers". At the end of Ch'in dynasty (秦), the same commentary says, he volunteered to subdue a white tiger but, being old and weak and excessively intoxicated, his magic failed to work and he was killed by the beast.[5]

Mimicry unconnected with pageant or acrobatic acts was recorded in connection with emperor Ts'ao Fang 曹芳 (reigned A.D. 240-254) of Wei 魏 who was said to have made his jesters "play wanton women in front of a palace tower with extreme indecency for which those who passed by covered their eyes". This was also the earliest record of men playing women. In the same period emperor Liu Pei 劉備 of Shu 蜀 (A.D. 221-263) once made his jesters mimic the manners of two of his councillors, who were always arguing with each other, for the amusement of his court. [6] In Chin dynasty, in the reign of emperor Ch'eng-Ti 成帝 (reigned A.D. 326-343) a memorandum to the emperor mentioned the performances of *The King of Ch'i* [齊] *Rolling Up His Clothes* as indecorous. [7] It may be assumed that, unlike the burlesque of the argumentative councillors, the representation of this historical episode was often repeated, otherwise there would have been no point in asking the emperor to suppress it as the writer of the memorandum did. In the same dynasty the musicians kept by a Minister of War named Yü Liang 庾亮 honoured the memory of their master, who died in A.D. 380, by impersonating him in a dance using his canopy and *a likeness of his face*. "The music used was later always played after the 'Nine Schools' ." [8] This is probably the earliest record of human mask in China. As in the case of jester Meng in Chou dynasty (Ch. XX) the impersonation served a purpose and had no entertainment value, hence only the music survived.

---

[3] 孟元老, 東京夢華錄, 卷十, 十二月. For exorcism in the palace see *ibid.*, 卷十, 除夕.

[4] See Ch. XXI — legendary musician conducting and goddess singing a song.

[5] (漢) 劉歆, 或, (晉) 葛洪, 西京雜記, 卷三, 一段. This circus act was among the spectacles of Han dynasty — 張衡, 西京賦.

[6] 陳壽, 三國志, 魏書, 齊王紀, 斐註, 引, 司馬師廢帝奏, 陳壽, 三國志, 蜀書, 許慈傳.

[7] 晉書, 樂志, 下, (末段). W. Arthur Cornaby, Notes on the Chinese Drama and Ancient Choral Dances, *The New China Review*, v.1. no. 1. March 1919.

[8] 隋書, 音樂志, 下, "禮畢". "Nine Schools" are the officially approved nine schools of music in Sui dynasty.

A scarf dance (巾舞) was said in Chin dynasty (晋) to be a mimetic dance based on the attempted assassination of the founder of Han dynasty [9] but in later times it was not recognized as such, apparently due to a gradual deterioration of the mimetic element. [10]

The *tableaux vivant* of the pageants could not be often staged because of their cost and the occasional mimicry of court jesters could not be repeated for the same audience because its effectiveness depended on topical allusion. If however the interest of music and dance was injected into a mimetic performance it could be repeatedly enjoyed. In this way the performance could acquire a stable form.

Between Chin (265-419) and T'ang dynasty (618-906), the mimetic dances, or ballets, were evolved. The origins of these dances are described in books written in T'ang dynasty when these dances had become very popular:

1. *Tai Mien* 代面 (literally "substitute face") or *Ta Mien* 大面 ("big face"). The dance was based on Prince Lan Ling 蘭陵王 of North Ch'i dynasty 北齊 (550-577) "a warrior of great prowess who was handicapped by his effeminate face and took to wearing a mask in battle to terrorize his enemies". [11] "In admiration for his valour, his people devised this dance representing him in battle and called it, and the music, *Prince Lan Ling in Battle*". [12] In T'ang dynasty he was represented as "wearing purple armour and golden belt, holding a truncheon", [13] and this may have been the earliest theatrical costume.

2. *T'a Yao Niang* 踏搖娘 (literally "stamping and swaying woman"). "A man of North Ch'i dynasty 北齊 (550-577) [14] who, though never in the government, gave himself an official rank, and was known to be fond of the bottle and cruel to his wife. When the lady got beaten by the drunken husband, she would complain to the neighbours of her sorrows. Based on this story, man dressed as woman trudged on the stage singing a lament and the audience joined in the chorus. Then the husband, with a turgid nose, entered and fought with the wife to the amusement of the spectators. The impersonated wife sang to the rhythm of her own slow steps, hence the name of the play". [15] Details of the performance appeared to be in a state of flux, because the *History of T'ang Dynasty* 唐書 said that "modern actors have changed the original

---

[9] 晋書, 樂志, 下 "公莫舞".

[10] 宋書, 樂志, 一.

[11] 崔令欽, 教坊記, 大面.

[12] 舊唐書, 音樂志, 二; (唐) 劉餗, 隋唐嘉話, 下, 六十一款.

[13] 段安節, 樂府雜錄, 鼓架部.

[14] Other sources give the date as late Sui dynasty 隋 (589-617) and North Chou dynasty 北周 (559-581) — 舊唐書, 音樂志, 二; 段安節, 樂府雜錄, 鼓架部.

[15] 崔令欽, 教坊記, 踏搖娘.

production". [16] At one time the music included "string and wind instruments" [17]; at another, "the ugliness of the husband, the beauty of the wife and her skill in singing" appeared to have been prominent features of the dance [18]; and at yet another, the drunkard was said to be "fond of dancing in public places" and the actor "wore scarlet hat and belt and made his face red to represent drunkenness". [19] The "red face" in the last reference may be the earliest mention of make-up.

3. *Po T'ou* 撥頭 "This dance is about a foreigner in a country west of China who was killed by a beast and his son who sought and slew the animal". [20] In the performance "the son, who assumed a rueful face, had his hair let down and wore white clothes [for mourning]. He was portrayed as climbing the mountain in search of his father's body and the eight verses of his song were supposed to correspond to the eight turns in his journey". [21] In the period of North and South (402-588) the foreign tribes who occupied part of China are known to have introduced their music into the country. It is likely that this dance was similarly brought into China at this time, especially as the name had several phonetically similar variants all of which are meaningless in Chinese, being probably phonetic equivalents of a foreign word. [22]

It can be noticed that along with the addition of music and dance to the mimetic performance was the development of make-up and costume, partly for simulation, for instance, the drunkard's red face and the orphan's mourning gown, and partly for theatrical effects, for instance, the turgid nose and the golden belt. [23]

What gave these dances their permanence was not the story, which was in no case dramatized in full, but the song and dance, which formed the essence of the performance. In one case the performance consisted of a military dance; in the

---

[16] 舊唐書, 音樂志, 二.

[17] *Ibid.*

[18] *Ibid.*

[19] 段安節, 樂府雜錄, 鼓架部.

[20] 舊唐書, 音樂志, 二.

[21] 段安節, 樂府雜錄, 鼓架部.

[22] The probable location of its geographical source has been discussed by Prof. Wang Kuo-Wei. 王國維, 宋元戲曲史, 一章. For the theory that the dancer originally imitated a horse see 田邊尚雄, 中國音樂史, 陳清泉譯, 頁七一至七八; 田邊尚雄, 日本音樂史, 三章三節 in which the author traces the dance to the folk tales of Asia Minor. The theory that *Po T'ou* was the imported original of which *Ta Mien* and *T'a Yao Niang* were native variants rests only on the common element of humiliation and violence. According to this theory *Ts'an Chün Hsi* 參軍戲 (see below) may also be a native variant. However, slapstick farce is so much a common element of the theatre that the argument for this theory is weak. 王國維, 宋元戲曲史, 一章.

[23] Some of these dances are extant in Japan: *Po T'ou* and *Prince Lan Ling* are both danced there with masks. 大槻如電, 舞樂圖說 (昭和二年), 二十五, 二十六, 七十四.

second a lament with slapstick comedy, in reality a human Punch and Judy and in the third, a lament and perhaps a fight with a beast. The plot merely supplied the background; the interest was theatrical rather than dramatic. Fidelity to the original story or early productions is hardly to be expected.

Dance and song can be repeated, jokes cannot. If therefore a short dramatic performance had its centre of interest not in the dance or song but in the farce, it would either have to be short-lived or else be such as to allow changeable action which can be loosely tagged to the story. Some time between Chin (265-419) and T'ang dynasty (618-906) a type of farce was developed around a story whose plot allowed variations in the comic action. It is called *Ts'an Chün Hsi* 參軍戲 so named because it concerns "an official of the *ts'an chün* rank in Chin dynasty (晉) who, convicted of larceny while in charge of a large quantity of cloth belonging to the government, was sent to prison but was later released. After this, at banquets the actors would make fun of him in the following manner: one of them, dressed in a yellow gown and wearing a special hat would impersonate the ex-official and another actor would ask him, "What is your rank that you come to be among us?" 'I was once an official of the *ts'an chün* rank', the first actor would answer, and lifting his gown said, 'but ruined by this, I am now one of you' ." [24] It may seem incredible that such simple farce can stand repetition. However, according to another account [25] "the emperor pardoned the larcener but made him wear a white gown at banquets and let the actors make fun of him for a year". [26] If this is true, the original ridicule was not only entertainment but a commuted punishment also, and the actors were in fact playing themselves, so to speak. By the end of the year a pattern of bullying must have been evolved by which the actors could continue to entertain their audience if one of them now impersonated the ex-official.

In T'ang dynasty, if not earlier, the name appeared to apply to a class of farce with variable content because on one occasion it was said to be "well played by two actors and the wife of one of them" and that "their singing voice pierced the clouds", [27] and in the reign of emperor Su Tsung 肅宗 (reigned 756-763) "an actress in green gown and holding a plaque acted the official" in the same play [28] yet in the original farce neither woman nor singing could have a place. The fact that when emperor Ming Huang (reigned 713-756) was pleased with a performance of it he granted the actor Li Hsien-Ho 李仙鶴 a real *ts'an chün* rank does not suggest either that it was then a simple farce. [29] By Sung dynasty the term *ts'an chün hsi*

---

[24] 李昉, 太平御覽, 卷五百六十九, 十一款, 引趙書.

[25] 段安節, 樂府雜錄, 俳優.

[26] This may be a true incident — for its probable date see 王國維, 宋元戲曲史, 一章.

[27] (稗海全書) 范攄, 雲溪友議, 卷九, 六款.

[28] 趙璘, 因話錄, 卷一, 四款.

[29] 段安節, 樂府雜錄, 俳優.

seemed to refer to slapstick comedy in general and *ts'an chün* meant the actor who played the butt.

"In the reign of Ch'ung Ning 崇寧 (1102-1106) when actors played before the emperor, a *ts'an chün* played the prime minister . . . and his assistant beat him on the back with a rod". [30]

"In A.D. 1146, at a banquet given by the prime minister . . . a *ts'an chün* came forward to make a complimentary speech to the host and another actor followed him with a chair . . . but when the *ts'an chün* was about to sit down he dropped his hat and the second actor beat him on the head with a stick". [31]

So far as can be seen from the dramatic dances and conventionalized farce described in the above, comedy in the early Chinese theatre was at first connected with derision, as in the case of the drunkard's appearance and pretentiousness, and ridicule, as in the punishment of the larcener, but involved afterwards molesting the clown, as in the conventionalized farce *ts'an chün hsi*.

Apart from the farce and dances mentioned above, a dramatic sketch, called *Fan K'uai's Rescue* (樊噲排君難劇) was produced in A.D. 902 in T'ang dynasty. It was about Liu Pang (劉邦) the founder of Han dynasty, who, in an attempt on his life, was saved by Fan K'uai, then in his service, and was produced by command of the emperor for the entertainment of a rebel general who had killed the rebel leader and joined the emperor's army. [32] The performance was not, however, known to have been repeated.

Meanwhile, dramatized joke was also developed and became popular in T'ang (618-906) and Sung dynasty (960-1276). [33] This was basically a performance by one actor though it sometimes required one or two assistants. The dialogue depended on the time and place and the composition of the audience, and normally could not be effective outside that particular occasion. Some of the texts, mostly those with political significance, have been preserved and may be quoted to exemplify the type. The earliest extant specimen is of T'ang dynasty:

"In early eighth century, chamberlain Sung Ching 宋璟 , impatient with those who appealed to the emperor through his office, handed all such cases to the judicial department with the instruction to detain those who wanted to appeal again and to release those who did not. At this time there happened to be a drought. An actor, dressed as the god of drought, played before the emperor and declared that he came on account of the emperor's officials and when asked

---

(30) 王國維, 古劇脚色考, 副淨條引（宋）洪邁, 夷堅志, 丁志, 卷四.

(31) （學津討原）程史, 卷七, 三則. For other examples of *ts'an chün* see 王國維, 古劇脚色考, 參軍.

(32) 陳暘, 樂書, 卷百八十六;（宋）王溥, 唐會要, 卷三十三, 諸樂, 末款.

(33) For undramatized witticisms of actors in the court, in the tradition of the earlier court jesters see 南卓, 羯鼓錄; 王國維, 優語錄.

for the reason answered, 'Those who appealed to the emperor are treated as if they try to break the jail, therefore I have to give a warning' ." [34]

"At a state banquet given by emperor Wen Tsung 文宗 (reigned 827-841) actors played Confucius. The emperor said, 'Confucius is the teacher of the nation, no one should make fun of him', and sent the actors away in disgrace". [35]

"A gentleman of Huai-Nan district employed musicians to teach theatricals to his young servants. When the instruction was reported complete, he ordered a private production and watched it with his wife. Knowing the jealous and termagant nature of their mistress the servants played a wife and several concubines and a hen-pecked husband being knocked about among them, always bowing and saying, 'Yes, madam'. At this point the master was pleased and ordered wine, but his wife did not notice anything. Later, the players began to simulate the manners of their mistress; she saw it, but believed it was coincidence thinking that the servants would not dare ridicule her. The players, who had their own plans, became more and more obvious, till at last the wife shouted to them, 'How dare you, I was never like that', at which one of the servants answered, pointing to her, 'Then what are you so excited about?" [36]

For the period of Five Dynasties (907-959) may be quoted the following examples:

[In China to over-tax the people and appropriate the surplus is called to "scrape the earth"]. "When the governor of Hsüan-Chou was at a royal banquet, an actor wearing a mask and a green gown played the earth-god of Hsüan-Chou district, and when asked how he came into the capital, said, 'our governor scrapes the earth so thoroughly that I too am among his belongings'." [37]

"When the governor of Lu Chou, notorious for his open disregard for public law, was summoned into the capital, his people, who had suffered much under him, talked with each other in the streets, saying, 'Let us hope that he never comes back'. On hearing this, the governor levied by families what he called 'tax of improper hope'. The next year, he was summoned again and the people, not daring to talk, stroked their beards and smiled to each other. When the governor returned, he levied 'beard-stroking tax'. Later, when he was staying outside his province, some actor played to him the soul of a man who after being taken to the underworld was allowed to go back to the body

(34) 司馬光, 資治通鑑, 卷二百十二, 玄宗八年.
(35) 舊唐書, 文宗紀, 六年.
(36) 說郛, 卷四十六, 唐, 無名氏, 玉泉子眞錄, 三款.
(37) 鄭文寶, 江南餘載, 卷上, 十九款.

'because he came from a district which knows of no laws in heaven and earth'."[38]

In Sung dynasty this type of farce remained unchanged, as shown by the following examples:

"In the reigns of Hsiang Fu (1008-1016) and T'ien Hsi (1017-1021) there was, among certain literary circles, a fashion for the poetry of Li I-Shan (李義山) and some would-be poets had no scruples in putting Li's lines bodily in their own poems. At a royal banquet, an actor dressed in tatters played Li I-Shan and said he had been relentlessly robbed". [39]

"In A.D. 1104 the smallest coin issued was ten cents and people were inconvenienced by the shortage of small change. At a royal banquet actors played a soup-vendor who sold soup for one cent a bowl and a customer who, for lack of change was persuaded to drink ten bowls. After five or six bowls he could drink no more and resigned himself to the thought that fortunately the smallest coin was not a hundred cents. After this smaller coins were issued". [40]

"At a royal banquet in the reign of Shao Hsing 紹興 (1131-1163) an actor played an astrologer who claimed to see only people's astrological stars when he looked at them through his special lens. The lens being unavailable, he asked for a coin as a working substitute and looking through it [the Chinese coin has a hole at the centre for stringing] he said he saw the emperor's star, the general's star and so forth, but when he looked at Chang Hsün Wang 張循王 [probably of inordinate wealth], he said he could not see any star, and when asked to try again, said, 'Honestly, there is no star — here is my money, it has a hole in it and my lord Chang is sitting inside the hole'."[41]

Actors playing in the farce had the

"... licence to jibe and to speak their mind, hence their nickname 'fools of no offence' (無過蟲). In state affairs when the ministers could not prevail upon the emperor, these players sometimes invented a story and put the matter in a play. In such cases the emperor was not angered". [42]

"In the reign of Hsi Ning 熙寧 (1068-1077) a great many new officials were presented to the emperor. In a farce an actor threatened to ride a donkey into the hall where the emperor was sitting and when he was stopped said, 'I

---

[38] *Ibid.*, 二十款.

[39] 劉攽, 中山詩話, 十六款.

[40] 曾敏行, 獨醒雜志, 卷九, 第二十二款.

[41] （明）田汝成, 西湖遊覽志餘, 卷二十二. For other examples see 王國維, 宋元戲曲史, 二章.

[42] 耐得翁, 都城紀勝, 瓦舍眾伎; 吳自牧, 夢粱錄, 卷二十, 妓樂 cf. Jester Shih (優施) recommending himself for a delicate piece of diplomacy, "I am a jester, my words cannot give offence". 國語, 晉語, 第八.

thought anything with legs may come here'." [43]

Farcical duologue (相聲) continues till to-day. Examples can also be found in various miscellaneous writings of Ming dynasty. [44]

[43] （宋）朱彧，萍洲可談，卷三，三十八款.

[44] 王國維，宋元戲曲史，二章.

CHAPTER XXIII

DEVELOPMENT OF FARCE

AND DRAMATIC DANCES IN SUNG DYNASTY

Sung dynasty (A.D. 960-1276), in spite of the danger and humiliation involved in the foreign occupation of northern China, is known for its dilettantism: it was in this dynasty that some of the best landscapes were painted, some of the most romantic poems written and a great many forms of popular entertainment were developed. In a book on the customs and manners of Sung dynasty, the different forms of popular entertainment are said to be : story-telling, humorous talks, shadow plays, ballads, songs, farce, impersonation of gods and spirits, recitation of saints' lives, minstrels, jokes, riddles, conjuring, jugglers, puppets, pole-climbing, rope-dancing, wrestling, mock fights, tumbling, skill with staff, weight lifting, football, bow and arrow, trained animals, trained birds and insects, snakes, fireworks, etc. [1] There were in contemporary writings endless festivals, street-dancing, parades, fairgrounds, lanterns and celebrations, all these activities lasting through the night. [2] Emperor Le Tsung 理宗 (reigned 1225-1264) made a boat with fragrant wood inlaid with gold and in the region of Ching Ting 景定 (1260-1264) the emperor's son-in-law went to sail in a specially luxurious boat on the West Lake in Hanchow and the whole city turned out to watch him so that the shops were all closed. [3] In this atmosphere of exuberant public amusement the dramatic dances, already existing in T'ang, multiplied and many farces acquired permanent form through the addition of music.

The development of popular theatre in Sung dynasty was partly due to the repeated abolishment, in 1162 and later, of *chiao fang* 教坊 (imperial music school)

---

[1] 周密, 武林舊事, 卷六, 諸色伎藝人, cf. forms of popular entertainment in medieval and Renaissance England: contortionist, equilibrist, trained animals, songs, ballads, story-telling, exotic beasts, dancing, juggling, tumbling, acrobatics, sword-swallowing, conjuring, rope-dancing, stilt-walking, puppets, freak humans, freak animals, etc. S. McKechnie, *Popular Entertainment Through the Ages, passim.*

[2] 周密, 武林舊事, 卷二, 元夕; 耐得翁, 都城紀勝, 井市; 吳自牧, 夢粱錄, 卷一, 元宵, 卷十三, 夜市, 卷四, 中秋.

[3] 周密, 武林舊事, 卷三, 西湖遊幸.

and the dispersal of musicians and actors. [4] *Chiao fang* included oboe players, drummers, castanet players, flautists, lutists, zither players, xylophone players, reed organ players, dancers, singers, actors and conductors. [5]

There are indications that plays were written early in Sung dynasty, but none of them have survived.

"Emperor Chen Tsung 眞宗 (reigned 998-1023) who did not like the current music, composed some plays himself, but these were not known outside the court". [6]

In a contemporary catalogue of books was mentioned two volumes of players' script in verse, of uncertain date. [7] It was also said that in the capital of North Sung (960-1127) a man in the *chiao fang* wrote script for the players. [8]

The standard theatrical programme in Sung dynasty consisted of a "short *introductory piece* [9] representing familiar scenes and two *main farces* [10] followed by *miscellaneous impersonation* [11] mostly of rustic clowns". [12] The nature of the farce was described as "making use of stories for comic effects" [13] and the "comic effects" were often rude, because it was recorded that "in the plays presented in the palace during festivals, actors did not dare go too far in jests because there were foreign envoys". [14] The script was sometimes composed by the actors. [15]

Whereas in the farces of T'ang dynasty the basic requirement of actors was the clown and an assistant with whom to carry on the dialogue, [16] the minimum number was now four and this was augmented by special characters as the occasion required. "A standard company of players varied from five to eight". [17] The stage duties of the four basic players were specified: "the first was to introduce [the situation and the characters] [18] the second was to arrange matters, [19] the third to make a feint [20]

---

[4] 宋史, 樂志, 十七.
[5] 耐得翁, 都城紀勝, 瓦舍衆伎條.
[6] 宋史, 樂志, 十七.
[7] （宋）崇文總目, 卷一, 樂類, 周優人曲辭.
[8] 吳自牧, 夢粱錄, 卷二十, 妓樂.
[9] "豔段"
[10] "正雜劇"
[11] "雜扮"
[12] 吳自牧, 夢粱錄, 卷二十, 妓樂; 耐得翁, 都城紀勝, 瓦舍衆伎.
[13] 吳自牧, 夢粱錄, 卷二十, 妓樂: "雜劇全用故事務在滑稽".
[14] 孟元老, 東京夢華錄, 卷九, 宰執親王宗室百官入內上壽.
[15] 耐得翁, 都城紀勝, 瓦舍衆伎條.
[16] cf. Even nowadays undramatized jokes are mostly in the form of a short dialogue often in questions and answers.
[17] 周密, 武林舊事, 卷四, 乾淳教坊樂部, 雜劇三甲.
[18] "主張"
[19] "分付"
[20] "發喬"

and the fourth to bring out the joke, [21] [22] and to these were added the "official" [23] or the "woman" [24] as required. It can be noticed that the farce had at first no woman in it; and this is one of the reasons why in the Chinese theatre men play women. In a contemporary painting there are five actors on the stage, and they have supposedly been identified as the four basic actors mentioned above and the "official". [25] It appears that the standard technique was for two actors to create a potentially comic situation and two clowns to exploit it. The usual manner of achieving the comic effect was described as "first to create an unexpected absurdity and then to solve it with a surprising joke". [26] The performance, however, also included "improvised speeches", [27] declamation, [28] somersaults [29] and stage business [30] [31].

To illustrate the method, a farce contained in a drama of Ming dynasty [32] may be outlined:

Four actors enter at the same time and the leader among them says, "To-day is the birthday of Master Shuang; let us each recite a poem of congratulation". *Each of the three actors recites a poem; at last the clown also recites one, but the assistant clown strikes him and says,* "Do you call this a poem? Say again". [33]

The leader says, "We should each give a present", *and the three actors produce various symbolic paintings of Prosperity, Longevity, etc. At last the clown comes forward impatiently, saying,* "Look at mine", *and lifts with*

---

(21) "打諢"

(22) 耐得翁, 都城紀勝, 瓦舍衆伎.

(23) 陶宗儀, 輟耕錄, 卷二十五, 院本名目; 耐得翁, 都城紀勝, 瓦舍衆伎.

(24) 周密, 武林舊事, 卷四, 乾淳教坊樂部, 雜劇三甲.

(25) 故宮博物院, (宋) 蘇漢臣五瑞圖; 李家端, 蘇漢臣五花爨弄圖說, 雲南大學學報, 一類一號.

(26) 王國維, 宋元戲曲史, 二章, 引, 呂本中, 童蒙訓: "打猛諢入 却打猛 諢出". cf. "I have taken the trouble now and then hurriedly to write down the conversation between the clowns in a circus, and to a great extent it resembles the conversations in Molière; in essentials the method is practically the same, but when recorded the result is anything but funny. The point made at the end is always the thing on which they are counting to convulse their hearers, and the rest is all preparation to get them into an expectant state of mind". E. G. Craig, *The Theatre Advancing* (1921), 25.

(27) 散說

(28) 道念

(29) 筋斗

(30) 科汎

(31) 陶宗儀, 輟耕錄, 卷二十五, 院本名目.

(32) (明) 朱有燉, 呂洞賓花月神仙會雜劇, 二折 (孤本元明雜劇).

(33) Note the remnant of the clown in *ts'an chün hsi.*

pompous pride a pornographic picture, and is again beaten by the assistant clown. (34)

The actors then one after another sing a congratulatory song with the same comic ending by the clown who is again beaten for it. This is followed by some trifling dialogue between the clown and his assistant who closes the play with two lines of poetry.

It may be noticed that the actors here did not impersonate any specific characters and that there was no plot involved. The minor importance of the story is a natural consequence of "making use of stories for comic effect".

The texts of the many farces which had attained permanent form in this period are unfortunately entirely lost, except for one or two farces quoted in other writings. (35) This is particularly regrettable, because these farces were the immediate predecessors of the Chinese drama and as there was probably great variation among the farces the two examples now known to us form a very inadequate sample of them. Two lists of titles have however survived, one containing two hundred and eighty titles of "Official Copies of Miscellaneous Plays" (36) presumably based on official records of Sung dynasty, is in *Wu Lin Chiu Shih* (37) a book of customs and manners and literary miscellany of Sung dynasty and a second, of six hundred and ninety titles of "House Copies of Chin dynasty" from the pleasure-houses, (38) is in *Cho Keng Lu,* (39) a similar book of Yüan dynasty. (40) The text of these plays being unavailable, one has to extract as much information as possible from the titles in these lists.

Of the two lists, the first is both older and purer; the two hundred and eighty plays were all of Sung dynasty and as the heading of the list suggests, they were plays. The second list contains products of Chin 金 (1115-1234) and Yüan 元 (1277-1367) as well as those of Sung dynasty and includes, beside plays, miscellaneous forms of entertainment such as recitals, humorous talks, etc. (41)

---

(34) Such pictures were prevalent in Sung dynasty and probably originated in earlier times. 辭海, 秘戲圖. In Ming dynasty pornographic literature was more in vogue and people "well informed in the art of love" became advisers to the emperor. 魯迅, 中國小説史略, 頁二二六.

(35) i.e. the example just quoted and another to be mentioned presently.

(36) 宋官本雜劇段數.

(37) 周密, 武林舊事, 卷十.

(38) 金院本名目.

(39) 陶宗儀, 輟耕錄.

(40) The original *tsa-chü-tuan-shu* 雜劇段數 means literally "miscellaneous plays, sections of" but *tuan-shu* refers to the shortness of the pieces, as the music hall artists would say at present, "turns". *Tsa-chü* 雜劇 in Sung dynasty referred, in the narrower sense, to farce and in the wider sense, to talks and non-farcical dramatic sketches as well. In T'ang dynasty the farce was generally referred to as *tsa-hsi* 雜戲; in Yüan dynasty *tsa-chü* 雜劇 meant dramas and in Ming dynasty, short dramas.

(41) From the very beginning of Sung dynasty (A.D. 960) China was menaced by the northern tribes, first by the Liao 遼 and later by the Chin 金, both Manchu tribes. In A.D. 1115 Chin, having

More than ten titles appear in both lists [42] but probably more of them are identical plays, because the difference in place and time would have caused variations in the names of plays.

The first characteristics noticeable in these titles are that most, if not all, of them were partly in verse and set to music, because most of the titles, especially of the "official copies of miscellaneous plays" were in two parts, the second part being the name of the music, for example, "Donkey Spirit *Liu-Yao*", [43] *liu-yao* being the name of the music. Owing to the close relationship between music and the Chinese libretto a tune regulates the prosody of the verses of the text, hence the name of a tune also indicates the type of verse in which the libretto was written. In this way, the types of verses used at least in most of the "official copies of miscellaneous plays" have been traced to those common in Sung dynasty. [44]

Judging by the intelligible part of the titles among the "official copies of miscellaneous plays" there was a great variety of themes, which may be divided into three groups, of diminishing dramatic content:

Group 1 A. History as *The Prince* [45] apparently based on the story of Hsiang Yü (項羽), an unsuccessful rival to the founder of Han dynasty, who died in a tragic defeat.

---

occupied a great part of north China, declared a separate dynasty and so jeopardized the safety of the capital of Sung that it was moved to the south of Yangtze river, hence the name South Sung from A.D. 1127 onwards. Later the Mongols, having been powerful for some time, conquered the Chin and ended their dynasty in 1234 and did the same to the Sung in A.D. 1279. Thus,

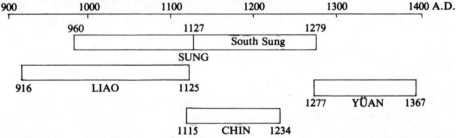

[42] 王國維，宋元戲曲史，六章，末段. There are foreign words in the "official copies" showing foreign influence from the Chin and Liao.

[43] 驢精六么

[44] 王國維，宋元戲曲史，六章. Of the two hundred and eighty "miscellaneous plays" the music of 153 titles have been identified; at least part of the difference were also set to music. Of the six hundred and ninety "house copies" only 61 titles have identifiable music, but some of the titles in this group, though without the name of the music, are identical with those in the "official copies of miscellaneous plays" 青木正兒，中國近世戲曲史，一章四節，二章，二節，丙. and it was probably the custom of omitting well-known musical names that deprived them of the second part of the title.

[45] 霸王劍器

221

B. Legend	as *The God of Exorcism* [46] apparently based on the story of the exorcising spirit whom emperor Ming Huang of T'ang dynasty met in his dream.
C. Fiction	as *Miss Ying-Ying* [47] based, judging by the name Ying-Ying, on the story of illicit love with unhappy ending, later dramatized in the famous *Hsi Hsiang Chi* (西廂記) [48]
Group 2 A. Comic Situations	as *Unpaid Rent* [49]
B. Character Sketches	as *The Cook* [50] and *Three-Religions Man* [51] the latter a quasi-religious ritual — it was not however ritual that had become theatre (as in the Greek theatre) but was a play, probably of farcical content, based on the customs and manners of the time. [52]
Group 3 A. Dance	as *Ya Ku* [53] a dance created by the commander of a garrison for his idle army, probably tattoo [54] and Choral Dance [55] with one tune repeatedly sung to several poems or two tunes alternating with each other.
B. "Talks"	as *Hundred Flowers* [56] probably a talk based on the names of flowers, with anecdotes, poems, jokes, etc., a form of entertainment popular at that time. Similar talks can be found in southern dramas, as the talk on the *Thousand-Word Essay* [57] and one on the *Three-Word Verses* [58] is used in the theatre to-day. [59]

---

[46] 鍾馗爨

[47] 鶯鶯六么

[48] It is impossible to tell how many and to what extent the legends suggested by the titles were dramatized, because it is known that the script for story-telling was definitely among the titles, e.g. 諸宮調霸王

[49] 賴房錢啄木兒

[50] 廚子六么

[51] 滿皇州打三敎

[52] See Ch. XXII for exorcism in Sung dynasty.

[53] 迓鼓熙州

[54] 王國維, 宋元戲曲史, 五章.

[55] 隊舞

[56] 百花爨

[57] 千字文

[58] 三字經

[59] 齊如山, 京劇之變遷, 頁三十.

The six hundred and ninety titles of "house copies" covered a similar range of subjects, except that there are among them titles for juggling acts or dramatic pieces including exhibitions of juggling. [60] There is also an abundance of "talks", such as on the names of stars, fruits, herbs, weapons, etc. (twenty-eight classes, as, one class for stars, another for herbs, etc.) and many groups of what appear to be character sketches (fourteen groups) as well as one group of riddles. The large amount of non-dramatic entertainment in this list can be more readily understood when one remembers the place and purpose of their performance. It also indicates that to the Chinese audience at that time dramatization was not an important criterion for the classification of types of entertainment; farces and juggling acts were, like the music hall programme of to-day, considered more or less the same thing. [61]

It has been pointed out that some of the titles of the "house copies" suggest longer plots than those in the two extant examples of farces of the Sung dynasty. [62] This may be due to the fact that the "house copies" represented later works than the "official copies" and dramatization had by then advanced beyond farce and simple plots. In any case there could be no doubt that many of the themes were material for the dramas of Yüan dynasty.

A short play, classified as "house copy", was recently found in *Chin P'ing Mei* [63] a pornographic novel written in Ming dynasty and based on earlier copies of the story-tellers' script. [64] It is one of the rare examples of the farce of Sung dynasty:

Enter Sergeant

Sergeant. (Recites an introductory poem of four lines). "I am the police sergeant of this district. Yesterday I bought a screen, with a poem on it which, I was told, was written by a certain Wang Po (王勃) of T'ang dynasty, a great literary genius less than three feet tall. I want to meet this genius, so why shouldn't I send a messenger to bring him here. Boy, where are you?"

Enter Footman

Footman. "Here I am. What is your order?"

---

(60) 雜砌

(61) Some of the titles in the "house copies" are unintelligible. "Some of the 'house copies' were named by the tune, some by the subject matter, some by persons' names, some by the first line of the poem, some by the type of character and some by a combination of musical terms and subject matter". 王國維, 曲錄, 卷一, 末段.

(62) 青木正兒, 中國近世戲曲史, 一章四. One reference may indicate the existence of long dramas in Sung dynasty: "From the seventh day of the seventh lunar month, the players produced the play *Mu-Lien's Rescue of His Mother's Soul,* which lasts till the fifteenth day of the month. Every day there were more spectators than the last". 孟元老, 東京夢華錄, 卷八, 中元節. This does not mean that the one play took more than a week to produce, nor could it be too short, otherwise there would be too many repeats in a day.

(63) 金瓶梅詞話, 三十一回.

(64) 馮沅君, 古劇說彙, 五章四, 頁一七九 (published 1947).

Sergeant. "I bought a screen yesterday and I like the poem on it. It was, I understand, written by Wang Po of T'ang dynasty, a genius less than three feet tall. Now here is a yard-stick, go and bring him to me soon. If you find him, I will tip you well; if not, twenty strokes on your back".

Footman. "Yes, sir". *(Turns)* "This stupid ass of a sergeant! Wang Po was of T'ang dynasty, he must have lived more than a thousand years ago, where can I find him? No matter, coming here, going there, here I have come to Confucius' temple and there comes a scholar toward me. I'll ask him. Sir, do you know by any chance the poet Wang Po who is less than three feet tall?"

Clown (as scholar). (Aside) "Wang Po lived in T'ang dynasty, how can this man find him now? Still, I will fool him. Yes, as a matter of fact, I am Wang Po, I wrote the famous poem *T'eng Wang Ke,* let me read it to you" (reads a few lines).

Footman. "My sergeant gave me this yard-stick to measure the poet with. He must be less than three feet, not a hair taller, how can you pass as he?"

Clown. "Nothing is impossible if you really want it. Look there is another Wang Po coming". (Crouching down as a dwarf). "Now come and measure me".

Footman. "A bit shorter yet".

Clown. "Now, will that do?"

Footman. "That will do".

Clown. "Just one thing: when you see your sergeant don't you forget to give me a low stool. This is important. Coming here, going there — here is the sergeant's house".

Footman. "You wait outside".

Clown. "Don't forget the low stool. Go on, announce me".

Sergeant. "Have you invited Wang Po?"

Footman. "Yes, he is waiting outside".

Sergeant. "I am going to meet him at the gate. Go and bring good tea and prepare a dinner".

Sergeant meets Clown

Sergeant. "Is this really the poet himself? I am most lucky to be able to meet you, sir. Let me kowtow once".

Clown (desperate). "Where is the stool?"

Sergeant. "From ancient times till the present day there is hardly a lucky occasion equal to this one. To meet a great man in person is indeed much better than just hearing about him. Let me kowtow again".

Clown (desperate). "Where is the stool?"

Footman slips away

Sergeant. "I have heard that you are a great genius, of incredible memory and fabulous knowledge. My humble self has thought of you as a hungry man of food, and as a thirsty man of water. Let me bow to you again".

Clown (angrily). "How is your father, how is your mother, how are your sisters, are your family all well?"

Sergeant. "All well, thank you".

Clown. "Damn it — your family are all well, don't you think you should let me stretch myself?"

Clown recites a poem which closes the play.

CHAPTER XXIV

DEVELOPMENT OF THE CHINESE DRAMA I —
THE INFLUENCE OF STORY-TELLING, PUPPETS AND SHADOW PLAYS

So far as we know, the "miscellaneous plays" of Sung dynasty were short and simple, and probably of low literary quality otherwise some would have been preserved. From T'ang to Sung dynasty, although the variety of themes and number of players increased and music was added, the basic nature of the farce remained unchanged — they were dramatized jokes, "to use the story for comic effects", as the Sung writer put it. Some time at the end of Sung dynasty, a new form of theatre emerged in China. It differed from the preceding forms of theatrical entertainment in broader emotional interests, longer plots, better poetry, richer music and fuller representation with the use of costume, make-up, properties and so forth. The story was no longer a means to exhibit the clown's talents or the singer's or dancer's skill, and the text was written rather than improvised.

The influence of the various forms of popular entertainment of Sung dynasty on the development of the Chinese drama can be traced in the intermediate forms between lyrical and dramatic poetry.

It is convenient to discuss the development of the Chinese drama in two parts: the influence of story-telling and the evolution of dramatic poetry, and these will be the subjects of this and the next chapter.

Story-telling probably had its beginnings in the practice of reciting saints' lives among the Buddhists of T'ang dynasty for religious instructions: among the manuscripts discovered in Tun Huang 燉煌 [1] were several Buddhist books in the vernacular style apparently for oral instruction. [2] These recitations in the Buddhist temples were, as early as in T'ang dynasty, embellished to enhance their

---

(1) A cave used for a secret store for books of T'ang dynasty, discovered in 1900.

(2) 魯迅, 中國小說史略, 第十二篇. There is no statement in ancient books that story-telling came from this Buddhist practice, but the form of the Buddhist text and the script of the story-tellers is very much the same — 向達, 唐代俗講考, 燕京學報, 十六期.

entertainment value. Passages in verse alternated with those in prose, presumably in order to hold the attention of the audience by refreshing their ear with alternating styles. The object was "rather to encourage donations than to disseminate Buddhist doctrines" [3] but it proved very popular among the uneducated [4] so that "those who came to listen filled the whole temple". [5] According to the documents from Tun Huang the ceremony was at first solemn and complicated [6] but it soon became almost a secular activity and by Sung dynasty it was entirely for popular entertainment. [7]

Meanwhile, Chinese fiction reached a new artistic level in T'ang dynasty: before T'ang dynasty Chinese fiction was little more than gossip with supernatural sensationalism as its favourite theme, only in T'ang dynasty did it begin to show artistry in description and narration and only then were longer stories written. [8] The better and longer stories of T'ang dynasty were soon recited in the same way as religious stories and story-telling, as a completely secularized form of entertainment, was thus established. This happened before the ninth century when "story-telling in the streets" was first mentioned in Chinese books. [9]

In Sung dynasty story-telling was one of the several forms of "talks", that is, entertaining talks.

---

(3) 司馬光, 資治通鑑, 唐紀, 敬宗, 寶曆二年, 胡三省註.

(4) （唐）段成式, 酉陽雜俎, 續集, 卷五, 大同坊, 平康坊.

(5) （唐）趙璘, 因話錄, 卷四, 七款.

(6) 向達, 唐代俗講考, 燕京學報, 十六期. There were even theatres at the monasteries for story-telling.

(7) Recitation of saints' lives by nuns became partly dramatized at some unknown date before Ming dynasty, probably through the influence of the theatre. It is described in *Chin P'ing Mei* 金瓶梅詞話, 三十七回, 五十一回, 七十三回 which represented conditions before Ming dynasty: the recitation (俗講) on Buddhist subjects was both in prose and in verse, partly sung and partly spoken. It had ostensibly a religious purpose but it was essentially entertainment to encourage donations. Sometimes there was dialogue between two tellers and refrains (佛號) were spoken by the audience or the acolytes.

(8) 魯迅, 中國小說史略. The term *hsiao shuo* (小說) was first used in Han dynasty, if not earlier, 漢書藝文志 but the nature of the writings referred to is not known. Prince Ts'ao Chih (曹植) was said to be "able to recite the players' *hsiao shuo* to the extent of several thousand words". 魏志, 王粲傳, 註引. In ancient China the term seemed to mean trivialities generally. 中國小說史略 (一九三五), 頁十九至二十一. In Chin and Sui dynasties (晋隋) it meant anecdotes told or recorded for moralization. True fiction started in T'ang and was called *ch'uan ch'i* (傳奇), literally, "propagating the strange", actually short tales. The influences of story-telling on the development of Chinese fiction may be said to be: (1) the use of the vernacular language, which makes it easier to write, (2) longer stories required by the listeners, (3) collection, embellishment, propagation and preservation of legends, and (4) development of the legends under the stimulation of competition. One similarity with drama may be said to be the need for immediate and sustained appeal in the story-telling, hence extraneous material was included in both forms.

(9) 段成式, 酉陽雜俎, 續集, 卷四, 貶誤, 三十八款.

"In the reign of emperor Jen Tsung 仁宗 (1038-1063) the country, after a long period of peace, was prosperous and in their leisure, people sought to entertain themselves with strange stories". [10]

Two types of "talks" are, however, not narrative: the "humorous talks" (說諢話) probably including humorous interpretations of well-known books by deliberate misreading and the "improvisations" (合生) probably of poems, couplets, puns, jokes, etc., on subjects chosen by the audience. [11] The narrative "talks" were divided into: "talks on Buddhist scriptures" [12] "talks on saints' lives" [13] "talks on histories" [14] and "trivial talks" [15] — the last is story-telling. [16] The "trivial talks" were subdivided into three classes: those on "beauties and spirits", "those on pugilism, swordsmanship, swashbucklers, sudden eminence and change of fortune", and "those on combats and warfare". [17] Of the "talks on histories" the period of Three Kingdoms (A.D. 220-227) and the Five Dynasties (A.D. 907-959) seemed to be the most popular and some story-tellers specialized in them, [18] but they took great liberty with facts, so that their talks "were half history and half fiction". [19]

Even the "talks on histories" had an irresistible appeal for children; at one time "a certain district was plagued by unruly children so the inhabitants hired a story-teller and let them sit around him to listen to the stories. In the history of the Three Kingdoms, when their hero was defeated some of the children would frown in disappointment and others would shed tears but when the hero was victorious, they shouted with joy". [20]

The story-telling of Sung dynasty served to organize and propagate popular legends and in doing so it influenced the formation of two literary genres, the novel

---

[10] (. 明) 郎瑛, 七脩類藳, 卷二十二, 九款, 小說.

[11] For examples see 李嘯倉, 宋元伎藝考, 合生考. This form of entertainment is not entirely unknown in Europe: in the eighteen thirties Sloman entertained the London music-hall audience with improvised topical rhymes.

[12] 說經

[13] 說參請

[14] 說史書

[15] 小說

[16] 孟元老, 東京夢華錄, 卷五, 京瓦伎藝; 吳自牧, 夢粱錄, 卷二十, 小說講經史; 耐得翁, 都城紀勝, 瓦舍眾伎; 周密, 武林舊事, 卷六, 諸色伎藝人.

[17] 吳自牧, 夢粱錄, 卷二十, 小說講經史; 耐得翁, 都城紀勝, 瓦舍眾伎.

[18] 孟元老, 東京夢華錄, 卷五, 京瓦伎藝.

[19] 吳自牧, 夢粱錄, 卷二十, 小說講經史; 耐得翁, 都城紀勝, 瓦舍眾伎.

[20] 蘇軾, 東坡志林, 卷六, 十七款.

and the drama. The earliest Chinese novels [21] on which some of the greatest Chinese novels were based, were in fact derived from the script of story-tellers. [22] In relation to the drama, apart from providing later dramatists with a large mass of subject material, story-telling left its marks in the form of the Chinese dramatic writings as it did in the novel and it stimulated the dramatization of longer stories, and thus brought about the transition from simple farce to full-length dramas.

A story, especially one with a large proportion of dialogue, is already partially dramatized. When it is told by the story-teller, he in fact impersonates the different characters in the story as he speaks the dialogue. It is known that in Ch'ing dynasty (1644-1911) the story-teller acted during his recitation, sometimes with great emphasis, as in the case of one who "when he came to the stirring part of Wu Sung killing the tiger bare-handed [23] shouted and roared till the house almost fell on him". [24] If the story-teller acted with both voice and gestures, as he seemed to have done, his performance would become a one-man dramatization of the story as he impersonated the characters in the story in turn. It is reasonable to believe that story-tellers in every age and country dramatize with their voice and facial expressions.

The tendency to dramatize stories when they are told found an outlet in puppets in Sung dynasty which were used to illustrate the stories.

Puppets had existed in China long before Sung dynasty. They originated in the wooden image used in burials [25] which was condemned as a hard-hearted practice by the Confucianists. [26] In Han dynasty (206 B.C.—A.D.220) "puppets could sing and dance and though originally only used in funerals, became purely for entertainment at the end of the dynasty". [27] In *Lieh Tzu,* a book by several writers, puppet making was attributed to an artisan in Chou dynasty:

"Emperor Mu Wang 穆王 (reigned 1001-946 B.C.) toured the western part of China beyond K'un Lun mountains . . . As he was returning and before he reached the central part of China an artisan named Yen Shih (偃師) was presented to him. The emperor asked Yen Shih, 'What can you do?' and Yen

---

[21] eg. 五代史平話, 宣和遺事.

[22] See, for example, R. G. Irwin, *The Evolution of a Chinese Novel* Shui-hu-chuan, 1953, Harvard Yenching Institute Studies X.

[23] A famous episode in *Shui Hu Chuan* 水滸傳.

[24] （清）張岱, 陶菴夢憶, 卷五, 柳敬亭說書.

[25] （宋）高承, 事物紀原, 卷九, 傀儡. It was perhaps a substitute for human sacrifice of pre-historic times.

[26] 禮記, 檀弓.

[27] （唐）杜佑, 通典, 卷一四六, 散樂. In fact they were acceptable as obsequial offering throughout Chinese history: in T'ang dynasty two tableaux, each representing a historical episode, were at one time presented at a funeral. （唐）封演, 封氏見聞記, 卷六, 道祭.

Shih answered that he would try to do whatever the emperor commanded but he had already made an object which he hoped the emperor would like to see. 'Bring it and show it to me some day', said the emperor. The next day Yen Shih came again. Mu Wang asked, 'Who is the man that comes with you to-day?' 'He is the musician your servant has made', answered Yen Shih. The emperor looked at the figure with amazement, for indeed it could walk and move about like a real man, and as the artisan turned its head it sang in perfect harmony and as he lifted its arms it danced in rhythmic steps. It could move in a thousand different ways and indeed in any way one may like to see it, and the emperor thought it was a real man. At the end of the exhibition the figure ogled at the ladies of the court who were watching it with the emperor. Greatly incensed, the emperor wanted to kill Yen Shih immediately for this offence but the frightened artisan took the figure to pieces and showed the emperor that it was all made of glue, paint, leather and splinters. The emperor examined it closely and found that it had heart, liver, gall, lungs, bladder, stomach, kidneys and intestines but like its bones, tendons, teeth, skin and hair, they were all artificial. The emperor took the heart out and it could not speak, the liver out and it could not see, and the kidneys out, and it could not walk. Greatly pleased, the emperor said, 'Can man be so clever that he can perhaps do the work of Nature?' and took the figure in his carriage back into China''. [28]

The historical accuracy of the book has been discredited; nevertheless, the above account shows that at the time the book was written — Han dynasty — puppet making was sufficiently advanced to carry the writer's imagination so far. The puppet described was not impossible: it could be an early prototype of the dummy used by ventriloquists nowadays, with movable eyes and eyebrows, and the artificial lungs and heart could easily be added. A book on the music of T'ang dynasty, however, said that the puppet was an invention by Ch'en P'ing (陳平), a strategist in the service of Liu Pang (劉邦) the founder of Han dynasty: [29]

"According to tradition the founder of Han dynasty was once besieged by the Mongolians in a city. On three sides he was surrounded by troops under the Mongolian chief and on the fourth side by those led by the wife of the foreigner. The garrison was threatened by dwindling supplies but Ch'en P'ing, who had discovered that the Mongolian had a jealous wife, made puppets and danced them on the side of the city facing her troops. When the Mongolian lady saw them she thought they were real women and, being apprehensive of her husband's probable interests if the city were taken, withdrew her troops. In history books Ch'en P'ing was said to evade the siege by secret strategy without explaining what the secret strategy was because the manoeuvre of puppets was

(28) 列子, 湯問.
(29) 段安節, 樂府雜錄, 傀儡子.

thought to be unworthy of him. In later times musicians used puppets for plays and there was a leader of song and dance, a comic character familiarly known as *The Fellow Kuo* (郭郎) who was distinguised by his baldness''. [30]
Though hardly a credible account it again pointed to the existence of puppets in Han dynasty.

In the period of Three Kingdoms (A.D. 220-277) the construction of activated figures was such as to allow them ''to play the flute, beat the drum, rope-dance, stand on their heads and, standing on a mound, juggle balls and knives''. [31] ''In North Ch'i dynasty 北齊 emperor Kao Wei 高緯 (reigned A.D. 565-576) was fond of puppets. Among the puppets then was a type called *Sir Kuo* (郭公) for which we now have the 'Song of Sir Kuo' (郭公歌)''. [32] This was probably the same puppet who ''in Sui dynasty (589-617) was less politely called *Kuo the Bald-pate* (郭禿) probably because there was once a clown of that name who was bald and afterwards a puppet was made in his likeness''. [33] Emperor Yang Ti 煬帝 (reigned 605-618) used puppets in his artificial water pageants which were on the same lavish scale as his human pageants:

''By royal command designs for decorations on water, filling fifteen volumes, were made, and when the construction was completed the emperor watched them with his court. There was the mythical tortoise with the Eight Divinatory Figures (八卦) on its back coming out of water to give it to emperor Fu Hsi (伏羲); there was the Yellow Dragon with the Magic Chart (河圖); there was the ancient turtle with its charm in its mouth and there was the legendary fish with its amulet . . . and there were beauties bathing in the stream. Also represented was Ch'ü Yüan (屈原) drowning himself in the river, a huge monster parting mountains, a large whale swallowing a boat, etc., seventy-two tableaux in all, entirely built of wood. The figures, more than two feet tall, were all dressed in silk and decorated with gold and jade and with them were fish, birds and many other kinds of animals all moving as if they were alive. Some of the people were represented as being in a boat, others on an island, others on a mound, or on rocks or in palaces. Among these silent tableaux were inserted twelve musicians' boats, each ten feet long and six feet wide, on which the wooden figures played melodies on bells and zithers in perfect harmony. There were also circus acts such as juggling knives, throwing rings, pole-climbing and rope-throwing, and they all looked real''. [34]

---

[30] cf. *Guignol,* the French marionette who also acquired a name. Originated in Lyons in the last years of the eighteenth century, he later became the symbol for theatres in which the taste for violence is served — *Théâtre du Grand Guignol.*

[31] 魏書, 杜夔傳, 斐註．

[32] 宋, 郭茂倩, 樂府詩集, 卷八十七, 雜歌謠辭, 五, 邯鄲郭公歌, 引, 樂府廣題.

[33] 顏之推, 家訓, 卷六, 書證篇, 第三十九款.

[34] 李昉等, 太平廣記, 卷二二六, 引, 大業拾遺.

Thus the development of the puppet theatre paralleled the human theatre: it had its own lavish pageant and its own favourite clown.

The marionette, a puppet moved by strings from above, was first described in T'ang dynasty. It was then apparently well made, which shows that it had existed for some time before T'ang. According to one poem, "carved wood suspended on strings" was the construction of "a puppet whose wrinkled skin and thin hair looked like those of a real old man". [35] In Sung dynasty puppets danced both singly and in groups and were part of the entertainment at royal banquets side by side with the human farce, [36] and they were once presented to emperor Li Tsung 理宗 (reigned 1225-1264) with actors and musicians. [37] In one city alone, there were twenty-four companies of puppet players [38] and at festivals rows of puppets "by the dozens" joined in the parades. [39] Of activated figures there was "a huge lantern fifty feet tall with figures activated by mechanisms powered by water wheels, the whole structure being so big that a special pavilion was constructed for it". [40]

The puppets of Sung dynasty were of six varieties. They are, in literal translation: [41]

> *Chemical-activated-puppets* 藥發傀儡
> *Water-puppets* 水傀儡
> *Puppets-walking-on-wire* 走線傀儡
> *Puppets-on-rods* 杖頭傀儡
> *Puppets-hanging-on-strings* 懸絲傀儡 *and*
> *Flesh-puppets.* 肉傀儡

Chemical-activated-puppets, judging by the fact that they were mentioned among fire-crackers, squibs, and other fireworks, must have been simple figures activated by squibs or rockets. [42]

Water-puppets were described in a contemporary book as follows:

"There was a boat which carried a decorated pavilion on the top with three little doors below it like those in puppet booths on land. The boat was moored opposite the musicians' boat, on which, at the beginning of the performance,

---

[35] （宋）計有功, 唐詩紀事, 卷二十九, 梁鍠, 明皇傀儡詩.
[36] 周密, 武林舊事, 卷一, 聖節.
[37] 宋季三朝政要, 卷三, 末段.
[38] 吳自牧, 夢粱錄, 卷一, 元宵；參, 周密, 武林舊事, 卷二, 舞隊, 卷六, 諸色伎藝人.
[39] 周密, 武林舊事, 卷二, 元夕.
[40] 周密, 武林舊事, 卷二（元夕, 燈品）.
[41] 周密, 武林舊事, 卷六, 諸色伎藝人；孟元老, 東京夢華錄, 卷五, 京瓦 伎藝, 卷七, 駕幸臨水殿觀爭標錫宴；吳自牧, 夢粱錄, 卷二十, 百戲 伎藝.
[42] 耐得翁, 都城紀勝, 瓦舍眾伎.

the conductor made an introductory speech. With the music that followed, the middle door on the decorated boat opened and a small boat sailed out, with a puppet man in white clothes angling in it and a puppet boy rowing behind him. The small boat sailed round a few times and then, amid music, a real fish was lifted out of the water, after which the small boat disappeared into the door. There were also puppets playing ball, dancing, making speeches and singing''. [43]

Water-puppets also performed circus acts in connection with transformation scenes. [44] These accounts show that there were activated figures of considerable ingenuity; the object of playing them on water was presumably to impress the audience of the absence of mechanical connections.

Of *puppets-on-rods* it was said that a famous performer "opened five shows every day; for the first show, of 'miscellaneous plays', one had to go early, or one missed it". [45] These are most probably what are now known as rod puppets, with the figure on the top of a rod and its limbs activated from below. They are still used in puppet dramas in China. [46]

Puppets-walking-on-wires were apparently auxiliary players for *puppets-hanging-on-strings,* which are obviously marionettes.

"When puppets played in stories of beauties and spirits, of combats and lawsuits and in stories of emperors and their generals in the various dynasties, the script used was the same as those in the 'trivial talks' and the 'talks on histories'. In marionettes there were two best performers [names omitted] and those performances incorporating *puppets-on-wires* are specially good". [47]

"*Flesh-puppets* were children playing as puppets". [48] As the construction of marionettes had already reached a high degree of perfection in T'ang dynasty in so far as realistic appearance is concerned, and as the activated figures called *water-puppets* and other types were repeatedly praised for their lifelike quality, it may be assumed that children playing as puppets marked the last stage of a race to make puppets more and more lifelike. [49]

The puppets, which had hitherto been imitative of human actors in pageants

---

[43] 孟元老, 東京夢華錄, 卷七, 駕幸臨水殿觀爭標錫宴. For water puppets of Ming dynasty see 劉若愚, 明宮史, 木集, 鐘鼓司.

[44] 吳自牧, 夢梁錄, 卷二十, 百戲伎藝.

[45] 孟元老, 東京夢華錄, 卷五, 京瓦伎藝.

[46] For construction see M. H. Batchelder, *Rod Puppets and the Human Theatre,* Plate XIX.

[47] 吳自牧, 夢梁錄, 卷二十, 百戲伎藝.

[48] 耐得翁, 都城紀勝, 瓦舍眾伎.

[49] In some Japanese textile exhibitions, mannequins were stationed among the dummies so that it was very difficult to tell which was alive and which was not. A similar effect could be achieved by including a few children among the puppets.

and circus acts, were now leading the human actors towards the development of longer dramas. When they were played to the script of the story-tellers they were the first actors to represent the unfolding plots in long stories and with their action the script, one can readily imagine, could not remain unchanged for long, especially as at the same time puppets also played in the fully dramatized, though short, contemporary farce. [50] Children acting as puppets marked a further step towards the dramatization of long stories in the human theatre.

Meanwhile, the marionette clown *Kuo* was still alive in Sung dynasty. According to a poem quoted in a book of the end of the eleventh century:

> "Pao Lao [51] laughed at the Fellow Kuo for the flappy sleeves of his dancing costume but if Pao Lao danced himself his sleeves were even longer and more flappy than Fellow Kuo's". [52]

Besides puppets, shadows were also used by story-tellers to illustrate their stories.

The origin of the shadow play was attributed to a magician called Hsiao Weng 少翁 in the reign of emperor Wu Ti 武帝 (reigned 140-86 B.C.) of Han dynasty.

> "The emperor (Wu Ti) had a favourite Madame Li for whose early death he was so disconsolate that he gladly accepted the offer of the magician Hsiao Weng to put him in communication with her spirit. The magician erected a curtain with lights behind it and the emperor, watching in front of the curtain, could see the shadow of the dead lady. In later times the same method was used in shadow plays". [53]

It has also been suggested that shadow plays originated in the custom of the story-tellers of T'ang dynasty and the Five Dynasties to hang up pictures. [54] Whatever the origin of the shadow play,

> "by the reign of emperor Jen Tsung 仁宗 (1022-1063) of Sung dynasty some popular story-tellers employed shadows to act in the wars between the Three Kingdoms, using the material from the 'talks on histories' but modifying it with embellishments". [55]

The modification was probably the expansion of battle scenes, but there may also have been partial dramatization.

> "The figures were at first cut from paper, but later they were made of tinted parchment for better wear. The text was similar to that of the 'trivial

---

[50] 耐得翁, 都城紀勝, 瓦舍衆伎.

[51] 鮑老 a fantastic masked dancer mentioned in a comic dance in *Shui Hu Chuan* 水滸傳（百回本）三十三回.

[52] 陳師道, 后山詩話, 十四款, 楊大年傀儡詩.

[53] 高承, 事物紀原, 卷九, 影戲.

[54] 孫楷第, 近代戲曲原出 宋傀儡戲影戲考, 輔仁學誌, 十一卷一二期.

[55] 高承, 事物紀原, 卷九, 影戲.

talks' [stories] and 'talks on histories', half fact half fiction''; and "the normal and good characters had fine features but abnormal and bad characters had ugly faces, so that the audience could understand the moral of the story easily''. (56)

It appears that the shadow plays then were very similar to what they are now. (57) Children were particularly fond of them and at one time they served as a kind of automatic nursery:

"In the fair ground many booths of shadow plays were provided among the other shows to attract the children so that they would not get lost''. (58)

There were also in Sung dynasty references, without explanation, to *hand-shadow-plays* which were probably shadows animated directly by disguised hands. The *impersonated-shadow-plays* (59) were in all probability men playing for shadows: (60)

"Some presented their shows in an elevated cabin, using men to produce the *big-shadow-play,* (61) and the shouts of the children could be heard all evening''. (62)

As in the case of puppets, the development of the shadow play, probably consciously towards greater realism, culminated in the use of human actors, thus bringing the shadow play very near to the drama. (63)

---

(56) 耐得翁, 都城紀勝, 瓦舍衆伎; 吳自牧, 夢梁錄, 卷二十, 百戲伎藝.

(57) It is now a form of technicolor moving picture because not only people but cloud, garden, sea, mountains, palaces, temples, sedan chairs, boats and even conflagrations are reproduced on the screen.

(58) 孟元老, 東京夢華錄, 卷六, 十六日.

(59) 喬影戲.

(60) 孟元老, 東京夢華錄, 卷五, 京瓦伎藝.

(61) 大影戲.

(62) 周密, 武林舊事, 卷二, 元夕.

(63) For Chinese puppets see 李家瑞, 傀儡戲小史, 文學季刊, 四期; 佟晶心, 中國傀儡戲考, 戲學月刊, 三卷十期. For Chinese shadow plays see: G. Wimsatt, *Chinese Shadow Plays* (1936); *Chinesische Schattenspiele, Uebersetzt von Wilhelm Grube, herausgegeben und eingeleitet von* Berthold Laufer, *Verlag der koeniglich bayerischen Akademie der Wissenschaften. Munchen,* 1915; G. Jacob and H. Jensen, *Das Chinesische Schattentheatre* (1933); B. March, *Chinese Shadow-figure Plays and their Making* (1938), and the bibliography in *Enciclopedia dello Spettacolo,* CINA, III. In the early part of the nineteenth century the Toy Theatre was constructed and played in British homes. It was a miniature stage decorated with scenery and manned with flat paper characters which could move only along slides. The scenery and figures were generally bought in a half-manufactured state and the Book of Words was the dialogue used by the children who played it. They provided material for history of the British theatre because they were derived from and were meant to be copies of it. (G. Speaight, *Juvenile Drama, The History of the English Toy Theatre,* 1946). The Chinese shadow play was a kind of toy theatre which preceded the real theatre. German scholars have suggested that in India puppets and shadow-plays were the sources of the Sanskrit drama — A. B. Keith, *The Sanskrit Drama* (1924), 52-57.

CHAPTER XXV

DEVELOPMENT OF THE CHINESE DRAMA II —
EVOLUTION OF THE DRAMATIC POETRY AND THE MUSIC

The importance of poetry in the development of the Chinese theatre is due to the fact that drama marks a stage in the history of Chinese poetry and is considered as one of its principal forms. Chinese dramatists were all poets because all dramas were written in a particular style of poetry. The development of the Chinese drama and the evolution of Chinese poetical styles are closely related to each other.

Poetry influenced the development of the drama in two ways: one, it entered the story-teller's script and attracted music into his performance so that story-telling became a form of minstrelsy and when the narrative form became dramatized, poetry and music became part of the Chinese drama; and two, lyrical poetry, which was sung in T'ang and Sung dynasties, sometimes derived its emotional background from well known stories and when the music induced dancing, the combination of dance and reference to stories is believed to have had some effect on dramatization and acting.

(a) Changes in Metrical Form

Changes in the metrical form of Chinese poetry and the reciprocal influence between it and music were intimately connected with the development of the Chinese drama, hence it is necessary to explain certain technicalities of Chinese prosody.

Although Chinese poems rhyme in much the same way as English poems, their rhythm is based on the sequence of different intonations rather than on that of accents, and this is partly because the Chinese monosyllabic words acquire accents only through the context but mainly because the sequence of intonations imparts a strong musical quality to Chinese verse which overshadows the sequence of accents. There are five standard intonations in most of the modern Chinese dialects and each Chinese word, as pronounced, belongs to one or another of them. The five types of

239

intonation are: [1]

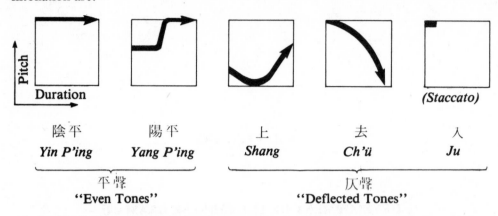

陰平	陽平	上	去	入
Yin P'ing	*Yang P'ing*	*Shang*	*Ch'ü*	*Ju*

平聲
"Even Tones"

仄聲
"Deflected Tones"

In T'ang dynasty poems were almost entirely written in verses of equal length, either of five words in the rhythm ♩ ♩ ' ♩ ♩ ♩ or seven words, ♩ ♩ ♩ ♩ ' ♩ ♩ ♩ and although the number of verses varied widely, by far the most popular forms were four- or eight- verse poems. The standard pattern for a poem of four seven-word verses is as follows:

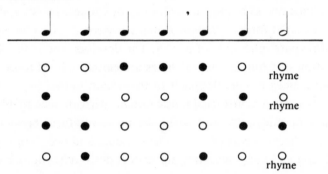

The circle ○ stands for a word of the "even tone" and the dot ● for one of the "deflected tone". If one reads the circle as "p'ing" and the dot as "tse", as "p'ing-p'ing-tse-tse-, -tse-p'ing-p'ing, etc.", in the indicated rhythm the pattern, read aloud, will give some idea of the musical quality of a Chinese poem. [2] The actual poems, with the different types of "even" and "deflected" tones, are of course phonetically more complex and poets not infrequently broke the rule of

---

[1] This distinction started in the period of North and South (402-588) though the difference had been in the Chinese language before then. For a brief historical review of the Chinese phonology see 張伯駒, 亂彈音韻輯要, 戲劇叢刊, 二期. The exact number and characteristics of the intonations vary from one dialect to another. For the present purpose it is hardly necessary to delve into the intricacies of the phonology of the Chinese dialects.

[2] A student of music will find that the rhythm is based on intricate contrasts and echoes and that the cadence at the end of each verse and the sharp variation at the end of the third verse are similar to the simple song form of many folk songs.

prosody by using an "even" tone at a place where it should be a "deflected" one or vice versa, but the basic rhythm is as shown above.

In the imperial court of T'ang dynasty, the poems were set to music for singing, called "entering the music department". [3] The music of that time is not at present known, but as the basic construction of the poem is akin to that of simple songs, it is probable that the music was similar in construction, that is, in four phrases of equal length with the third cadence, or the whole third phrase, in strong contrast with the rest. [4] It was necessary to "set the poem to music" because of the peculiarity of Chinese pronunciation: the musical progression in the tune should correspond to the way the words are intoned if the words are to be pronounced correctly when they are sung: it is not possible to sing a poem to any tune of the same length, as is often done with western hymns. [5]

Literary conservation, reinforced by the large volume of poems of high quality written in regular verses, caused the stability of this form of poetry throughout T'ang dynasty in spite of the occasional experiments of some poets in irregular rhythms. It is possible that in T'ang dynasty some of the tunes to which the poems were sung did not consist of musical phrases of equal length, that is, the musical phrasing might not have always been the same as the prosodical phrasing, in which case, there would have been a tendency to write poems with irregular verses, but the lack of information on the music of this period makes it impossible to tell with certainty whether this did happen in T'ang dynasty or, if it did, for how long the standard rule of versification resisted such influence. However, it is believed that by

---

(3)　入樂府

(4)　There are poems of the earlier part of Sung dynasty which have musical notations (in several different systems) written beside them — 姜夔 (?1150-?1230) 白石道人歌曲 (遼海叢書) — and several attempts have been made to decipher the music. Unfortunately there does not seem to be any indication of time in the notation. Prof. Ch'i Ju-Shan mentioned more than twenty different types of Chinese musical notations. 齊如山, 梅蘭芳遊美記, 頁十八.

(5)　The sad result in the hymns sung in Chinese churches is due to the indiscriminate grafting of western music on to the Chinese language. The native products, even the folk songs, have the words pronounced correctly, because singing is to primitive singers a natural extension of declamation, a kind of emotionalized delivery. The distinction has been made between singing with melody (曲) and singing without a melody (謠) both of which involve correct pronunciation. 劉復, 中國俗曲總目稿, 序. When the hermit of Ch'u *sang* a satirical poem to Confucius he was probably singing without a musical melody because he seemed to be improvising. 論語, 微子. Rules for fitting music to words have been formulated. 王季烈, 集成曲譜, 玉集附論三章; 項衡方, 曲韻探驪, 上, 七章. Roughly speaking the progression of the melody should be similar to that of the intonation of the words, but ornaments may, within limits, be added. There are other rules such as that the *ju* 入 intonation *(staccato)* has to be sung in a long note in slow-moving melodies and that the relative pitch of the preceding words may affect the apparent intonation of a word as sung.

late T'ang dynasty musical construction of the tunes began to break down the rigid form of the regular verses and this process continued throughout the Five Dynasties (907-959) and probably into the early part of Northern Sung (960-1127) as well. That the musical influence should become at this time strong enough to change the form of poetry was due to the introduction of foreign music and perhaps also the adoption of folk music of irregular rhythm especially of Wu district (Kiangsu province). [6] These styles of music, when used by the musicians for songs, could not fit the poems perfectly, so that the singer, for the sake of proper musical phrasing, had to add occasionally meaningless sounds such as "y-i-a-" or "do-do." If these were inserted at the proper places they could be considered by the audience as emotional interjections and as such they would not spoil the sense of the poems. [7] The necessity to insert these meaningless sounds, called "floating sounds" [8] was a symptom of the conflict between the musical and metrical constructions of the song and if the union of music and poetry, prevalent and well established in T'ang and Sung dynasty, was to continue some means had to be found to alleviate the incongruity. The insertion of meaningless sounds could only be limited both in quantity and in their possible positions, therefore, while it established workable congruity between the music and the words it must have at the same time made the conflict more conspicuous. It is generally agreed upon by modern scholars that poets writing poems to be sung, knowing the music well, began to put actual words where meaningless sounds were necessary or expedient for the singer and thus the form of regular verses was violated. Once the rule was broken [9] verse-forms multiplied in the new freedom by the combination of verses of different length, so that in Sung dynasty Chinese poetry flourished in a rich variety of metrical patterns. [10]

The rise of the irregular verses was described by ancient Chinese writers as follows:

" . . . The songs of T'ang dynasty were poems with five-word or seven-

---

(6) "Songs of Wu district" occupy a separate portion (吳聲歌) in a collection of poems compiled in Sung dynasty.(宋) 郭茂倩, 樂府詩集, 卷四十七, 清商曲辭, 四. The kinship between poems of Sung dynasty and the "songs of Wu district" was also indicated in more recent writings: 四庫全書總目提要, 集部, 詞曲類, 二, 御定歷代詩餘.

(7) Another possible reason for expletives: when a word is sung to many notes, the first few notes determine its intonation; if the rest are sung to the same word, the impression may be a different intonation. Hence the word terminates at the first few notes and the rest is sung in meaningless sounds.

(8) 泛聲 cf. "hey nonny-nonny" "tra-la-la".

(9) For example, by changing the seven-word phrase ♩♩♩ ' ♩♩♩ to six-word variant ♩♩♩♩♩.

(10) Whereas in T'ang dynasty, except long poems, the metrical patterns were in most poems confined to four types: poems of five- or seven-word verses either with four or eight lines, the number of different patterns after Sung dynasty has been estimated to be more than two thousand and three hundred. 王奕清等, 欽定詞譜; 參, 林大椿, 詞式 (一九三五).

word lines with *additional sounds* when sung. This poem resembles an eight-line poem of five words each with words added in the first three lines in place of the additional sounds mentioned above". [11]

"In singing it was an old practice to insert meaningless sounds such as *ho-ho-ho* or *whuo-whuo-whuo* and to write these among the words of the poems. In T'ang dynasty poets substituted these sounds with words". [12]

"Originally songs were written in verses of regular length but when the songs were sung there were 'floating sounds' added to them, and in later ages lest these 'floating sounds' be lost they were replaced by words, hence the irregular verses of the modern songs". [13]

"In T'ang dynasty people sang to poems with five- or seven- word verses and added, for musical expediency, meaningless refrains. Later words were put in their place, thus giving rise to the long-and-short verses". [14]

Music would not have influenced the metrical form to such an extent if poems were not set to music. The fact that some of the expletives were handed down with the words shows how much poems were written to be sung in those days. [15] The extent to which poems were set to music exceeded what the modern practice of writing poems to be read would lead us to think.

"When the musicians composed a new tune they would ask Liu Yung (柳永) to write a poem for it. Wherever there was a fountain or well, there one would hear his poems sung". [16]

"Li Ho (李賀) had several thousand poems to which the musicians had composed tunes to fit, and Li I (李益) whose fame was equal to Li Ho's, was also well known for his poems: as soon as he finished a poem the musicians all tried to get it so that they could set it to music for the emperor". [17]

Some poets changed old poems to fit the contemporary music [18] and it was sometimes a matter of regret that a poem could not be sung:

"For some time I have been attracted by the quiet beauty of this song created by Wu Meng-Ch'ɥang but have not been able to write another for the same tune . . . on the river, touched by the scenery, I wrote this stanza, unfortunately the old melody is forgotten and it can no longer be sung". [19]

---

[11] （清）全唐詩，十二函，十冊，詞部，元宗皇帝好時光詞註. Italics mine.

[12] （宋）沈括，夢溪筆談，卷五（第十段）.

[13] （宋）朱熹，朱子全書，卷六十五，五十七款.

[14] 方成培，香研居詞塵，卷一（首段）.

[15] For other details about the expletives see G. W. Baxter, Metrical Origins of the Tz'u, *Harvard Journal of Asiatic Studies,* Vol. 16, 1 and 2.

[16] 葉夢得，避暑錄話，卷下，三款.

[17] 王灼，碧雞漫志，卷一（九段）.

[18] **e.g.** 楊誠齋，歸去來辭引（陶潛，歸去來辭）.

[19] （宋）張炎 (1248-?) 西子壯慢序，見，山中白雲，卷二，（彊村叢書）.

The practice of singing in meaningless sounds is not unknown even in recent times:

"A friend told me that there is now a new style of singing in Szechuan which is accompanied, not by the reed organ and the flute but by the fiddle and the lute. There are no words, but the tunes are sung as if there were". [20]

In the theatres in Foochow in south China it is the practice for the musicians to sing meaningless refrains for the singers. [21]

Among the many consequences of the change to irregular verses was the fact that whereas in T'ang dynasty the usual process for writing a song was to set a poem to music, now in Sung dynasty, the poems (called *tz'u* 詞) the form of which was evolved by the pressure of musical technique, were written to fit the tunes. [22] In order to ensure correct pronunciation, the musicians of T'ang dynasty must not compose the tune of a song without knowing the words, nor could the poets of Sung dynasty write the words of a song without knowing the tune. [23] For this reason, a poet of Sung dynasty had more freedom in his choice of metrical forms than his predecessors in T'ang dynasty but he had much less freedom in his choice of words, because, in order that his poem could fit its music, the rules governing the intonations in his poems were more strict and more detailed than before.

"It is more difficult to write songs than to write poems [to be read] because for songs the words must fit the music, if they do not, the result is a poem of irregular verses, not a song". [24]

It can be noticed that in the poems of Sung dynasty the "deflected tones" were often differentiated whereas in T'ang dynasty they were not: the rhythm of the former is altogether more delicate.

It was the practice to attach the name of a musical air to every poem of Sung dynasty: the name of the tune might originally be for the convenience of the musician but was preserved also for the poet and the reader for ready reference to the metrical form connected with the tune. To write a poem a poet first chose a tune to which his unwritten poem could be sung and then followed the metrical form or "tone pattern" of the tune. [25] In spite of the restrictions many beautiful poems have

---

[20] （清）吳長元, 燕蘭小譜 （一七八六刊）卷五, 雜咏, 第十三.

[21] Called 馱嶺

[22] 王驥德, 曲律 （宮調）.

[23] It should be added that poems were later written to be read only but it was considered an irregular practice. "It is said that Su Tung-P'o's （蘇東坡） poems are often incompatible with the principles of music and can hardly be sung, but as he is a prolific poet and a genius, the principles of music cannot deter him". （宋）吳曾, 能改齋漫錄, 卷十六, 樂府 （首段）; 參, 沈義父, 樂府指迷, 十七款.

[24] （宋）沈義父, 樂府指迷, 一款.

[25] A "tone pattern" （詞譜) is a schematic diagram, often in circles and dots and other symbols, which indicates the number of verses in a poem, the number of words in each verse, the necessary or desirable intonations of each word and the positions of the rhymes. It is the work sheet for the

been written in this way. It was only when later poets lost contact with the principles of music and started following the established "tone patterns" blindly that the creative impulse died out.

In literary style the poems of Sung dynasty were distinguished from those of T'ang dynasty by their greater passion and freer use of imagery. This is not entirely unconnected with the greater variety of metrical forms.

Irregular verses are more suitable for the drama than the poems of T'ang dynasty both because their rhythms are more varied and because, as some poems of Sung dynasty show, they sometimes come nearer to speech. It is doubtful if drama of any length and artistic merit could be written on regular verses of seven words each. That form has proved effective in short lyrical and descriptive poems but it could hardly be used exclusively in dramas, because the consequent monotony and limited range of expression would make the drama excessively artificial.

The Chinese dramatic poetry, despite its different name, ch'ü (曲 literally "song") was technically of the same form as the poems of Sung dynasty, tz'u (詞): it was written to fit song-tunes and the poet-dramatist had to conform to "tone patterns". The dramatists, however, unlike the lyrical poets, were allowed to add words, called "fill-in words", [26] to those specified by the "tone patterns". [27] In the tune no corresponding musical notes were provided for these "fill-in words" and the singer had to add a corresponding musical ornament [28] without changing the time and the outline of the melody, hence only dramatists who understood the music well knew where to put these words and how many to use. [29]

In the dramas of Yüan dynasty the tunes used differed from those of Sung dynasty in the addition of foreign music and the use of folk tunes and the "tone patterns" for the poems multiplied accordingly.

"When the Chin people came into China they brought with them their own

---

student. The "tone patterns" are now still followed by the poets because they ensure the musical quality of the poem, a quality originally derived from the melody, but only partially retained in the reading voice.

[26] 襯字

[27] These "fill-in words" differed from those added to the T'ang poems and giving rise to irregular verses, in that whereas in the T'ang poems words were added for musical necessity, in dramatic poetry the option of inserting words was merely a permissible expediency for the dramatist. 王驥德, 曲律 (襯字). Colloquial expressions were sometimes used for the "fill-in words" — hence the liveliness of Yüan dramas.

[28] This may be a source of the improvised nature of modern Chinese dramatic music.

[29] As time passed, however, musicians made the mistake of allowing musical time for these "fill-in words" by shifting the musical accent (or as a music student would say, moving the bar lines). Then, just as the meaningless sounds added to the T'ang dynasty songs changed the metrical form of the poems, so these "fill-in words" in the dramas eventually changed the tunes. 王驥德, 曲律 (襯字).

music which had a quick tempo and the old way of singing the poems did not fit it, hence a new style of music came into fashion". [30]
In literary style the dramatic poetry of Yüan was more familiar in diction than the Sung poems and contained more vernacular elements.

The association of music with poetry at the rise of the Chinese drama determined the musical nature of the Chinese theatre: Chinese dramas as performed are in fact operas. The difficulty of writing dramatic dialogue to fit existing tunes owing to restrictions on the choice of individual words may be the reason why Chinese dramas were never completely sung, and certainly accounts for the short length of early Chinese dramas. The interdependence of Chinese music and the libretto due to the peculiarity of Chinese pronunciation explains, on the one hand, why the artistic quality sometimes of the music and sometimes of the text suffered, and on the other, the special kind of expressiveness — the quality of speech — in the Chinese style of singing.

(b) Poetry and Music in the Dance

The discussion of the relation between dance music and the Chinese theatre may conveniently start with the *suite*. The *suite* in Chinese music, called *Ta Ch'ü* (大曲 literally "long melody") was similar to the suite in the western music in that it was a group of dance music arranged in a studied order, but it differed from the European suite in that it was not only played but also partly sung and that it was for real dance performances. The earliest *suites* mentioned in history books were of the period of North and South (A.D. 402-588) [31] and at least as early as in T'ang dynasty it was a common form of court music: of the ten schools of music current at this time there were *suites* in nine schools. [32] At this time a *suite* consisted of three sections, each with several movements, and some of the poems sung to the music are extant. [33] In Sung dynasty (960-1276) the number of schools of music decreased, because indigenous music somehow lost its appeal and only music of foreign origin was preserved, so that only forty *suites* in eighteen combinations of keys and modes [34] were listed in history books [35] but the number of movements in each *suite*

---

[30]　(明) 王世貞, 藝苑巵言, 附錄一, 三十二款 .

[31]　王國維, 唐宋大曲考, 首段 .

[32]　舊唐書, 音樂志, 二 (十部樂); 王國維, 宋元戲曲史, 四章; 大唐六典, 卷十四, 協律郎條註 . A "school" of music meant a style of music, sometimes of different foreign origin. The modes and the instruments used differed between the "schools".

[33]　The names of the *suites* in foreign music (the majority of the ten schools of T'ang music were foreign) are in 崔令欽, 敎坊記 and some of the poems have been preserved in 郭茂倩, 樂府詩集 .

[34]　The Chinese term for key is *kung* 宮 and for mode, *tiao* 調 (See 楊蔭瀏, 中國音樂史, P.80. 台灣版 , 1976). Music lovers of T'ang dynasty were apparently sensitive to modes and the artistry of the music of T'ang and Sung dynasties was partially based on the shading of musical feelings through change of modes. This type of music, at one time also a part of European

increased, sometimes reaching a few dozens. [36]

The music of both T'ang and Sung *suites* being entirely lost, it is profitless to try to guess the meaning of the names of the movements which have come down to us. [37] Contemporary references indicated that the content of Sung *suites* was elastic, for instance, for a performance certain movements would be chosen from a standard work and played without the rest, and that the proportion of singing decreased but that of dancing increased. [38] In other words, the performance was now a combination of dance and vocal and instrumental recitals. Probably owing to its elasticity and hence comparative ease of poetical composition, poets of Sung dynasty sometimes used the form for lyrical poems based on stories which, as compared with short lyrical poems, were more difficult to write owing to the fixed subject matter and hence required a freer form. The performance of a *suite*, with instrumental music, songs and dances, appears to have reached a high artistic standard; the poet Yen Shu (晏殊 ? -1055) wrote:

"In one movement, the sonorous voice of the singer; in another, the form

---

music, is now lost to both the Chinese and the Europeans, in one case through lack of records and lost tradition, in the other, probably through the requirements of harmony (the harmony of modern European music is based on only two modes). Only in India are modes still being used as a means of musical expression.

(35) 宋史, 樂志, 十七, 教坊; 馬端臨, 文獻通考, 卷一四六.

(36) 王灼, 碧雞漫志, 卷三, 一段 (末); 沈括, 夢溪筆談, 卷五, 六段. Of the *suites* played in Sung dynasty about fifty names can be traced in various works on music and fragments of the poems are extant. 王國維, 唐宋大曲考, 四段.

(37) There are extant songs of T'ang dynasty complete with dance and music notation which may be connected with the music and dance of the *suites* but this has not yet been deciphered. 任二北, 敦煌曲初探 (一九五四), 四章. The *suites* of Sung dynasty were derived from those of T'ang dynasty and those of T'ang dynasty, from local folk music (hence they were named after the districts of their origin as I Chou 伊州 etc). *Vide* 王國維, 唐宋大曲考, *passim*. The gradual loss of the music, which probably started in Sung, appeared in contemporary books as continuous abridgement. "The score of *ta ch'ü* nowadays is abridged from the original; the codas are curtailed so that it is hardly possible to write words for them". — 王國維, 唐宋大曲考, 四段, 引, 陳暘, 樂書, 卷一八八. The nature of the *suites* was such that no musician or poet knew the whole work and as the survival of the music depended on memory, this state of affairs must have contributed considerably to the causes of the loss: "The players of wind and string instruments seldom play the *suites* from beginning to end, hence those who learn them do not learn the whole and poets who write poems for them really only write for part of the *suites*". — (宋) 王灼, 碧雞漫志, 卷三, 一段 (末). The guardians of the music were court musicians inaccessible to ordinary people, hence once the tradition was lost among them it could not be recovered from the people: "Owing to the fact that in T'ang and Sung dynasties the music of the *suites* was in the hands of *chiao fang* ordinary people only knew single movements". 王國維, 唐宋大曲考, 頁十六 (王忠愨公遺書); 參, 馬端臨, 文獻通考, 卷一四六, 樂考十九. 引, 兩朝史樂志論.

(38) 王國維, 宋元戲曲史, 四章.

247

of the dancer lost in whirling colours''. [39]

According to a contemporary account, the manner of the performance was as follows:

"In the early and last movements of the *suite* there is no dance; it is in the middle section when the three types of drums and the string and wind instruments are played together and when the tempo becomes quicker that the dancer enters and regulates his movements to match the rhythm of the music, in a hundred different gestures and poses. There is normally only one dancer, using his hands and sleeves for expression and stepping his feet in rhythm. Good dancers are faster than the galloping horse and the diving eagle''. [40]

Lyrical poems based each on a different subject or all on one story were sung to the same tune in Sung dynasty when the scholars entertained each other at dinner parties. [41] Similar poems were also part of the *choral dance* used for formal banquets, consisting of a *corps de ballet* which, unlike modern European ballet dancers, sang as they danced. [42] There is no evidence that the dance ever became

---

(39) 玉樓春：" 重頭歌韻響錚琮, 入破舞腰紅亂旋 ". The dancer's waist was mentioned again and again in the poems of this period probably indicative of the extensive posturing:

白樂天, 江樓宴別：" 舞腰歌袖莫辭勞 "

　　題山石榴花：" 風嫋舞腰香不盡 "

　　夜涼：" 舞腰歌袖拋何處 "

（梁）何遜, 旦夕望江山贈魚司馬：" 舞腰凝欲絕 "

　　蘇軾, 次韻王鞏顏復同泛舟 " 舞腰似雪金釵落 "

　　白樂天, 三月三日祓禊洛濱：" 舞急紅腰軟 "

　　洛橋寒食日十韻：" 舞腰那及柳 "

　　與牛家妓樂雨夜合宴：" 舞腰無力轉裙遲 "

These lines may give some idea of the style of dancing at that time.

(40) 陳暘, 樂書, 卷百八十五.

(41) 王國維, 宋元戲曲史, 四章.

(42) For details of the different types of *choral dances* 隊舞 both for boys and for girls, see 宋史, 樂志, 十七. The songs were called *chuan t'a* 傳踏（轉踏）. A more complicated form of song was used in popular entertainment and consisted of a poem as introduction and one as coda with either two alternating tunes (纏令) or a collection of tunes in between (纏達) — 吳自牧, 夢梁錄, 卷二十, 妓樂; 耐得翁, 都城紀勝, 瓦舍眾伎. With musical accompaniment it was called *chuan* 賺 and was probably used for ballads: "In the reign of Shao Hsing 紹興 (1131-1163) Chang Wu-Niu 張五牛, inspired by the section of the percussion music called *t'ai-p'ing-ling* 太平令, invented the *chuan* 賺 . . . It sometimes included romance and adventure". 吳自牧. 夢梁錄, 卷二十, 妓樂; 耐得翁, 都城紀勝, 瓦舍眾伎, 道賺, 覆賺, 賺詞, 唱賺 mean the same thing.

248

dramatic in nature, but the lyrical poems were similar both in construction and in style to those contained in later dramas, hence they formed a link in the development towards dramatic poetry. [43]

The combination of ballet dancing and poems based on stories did however show definite tendency towards dramatization in one example called Sword Dance (劍舞) in which a military dance (劍器) figured prominently:

THE SWORD DANCE

*Two dancers stand on the carpet facing the hall and start the military dance as the musicians sing the tune for it. (*劍器曲破*)*

After the dance, the two dancers sing a song of a different melody (a poem in forty-five words on swordsmanship and its ethical application).

The two dancers perform the military dance to the tune sung by the musicians.

*The dancers then stand on two sides and two mute actors in the costume of Han dynasty enter and sit opposite to each other at a banquet table. The conductor (*竹竿子*) recites* (a passage of stylized prose in ninety-four words praising the heroism of the founder of Han dynasty and tells how when an attempt was made on his life at a banquet he was saved by his bodyguard).

The two dancers perform the military dance as before.

At the end of the dance the dancer on the left advances towards the banquet table and makes a thrust at one of the men sitting at it and the other dancer shields him.

Exit the dancers and the mute actors.

Two mute actors, dressed in the costume of the T'ang dynasty enter and sit opposite each other at a desk with stationery on it. One of the dancers, now dressed as a woman, enters and the conductor recites (a passage of stylized prose in fifty-six words on the beauty and skill of a woman dancer and how her dance inspired a poem by Tu Fu (杜甫) and the style of the calligraphist Chang Hsü (張旭), both of T'ang dynasty). [44]

---

[43]　Thus the change from simple to complex musical structures:

Single poems set to music (詞)

Two tunes alternating (纏令)

Several tunes mixed (纏達)

Chu-kung-tiao (諸宮調) — see below.

In Yüan dramas, one of the schemes of tunes in an "act" is:

a A B A B A B A B A B c d

(鄭廷玉, 看錢奴冤家債主), 馮沅君, 古劇說彙, 九 (四). For other examples of different structures, see 蔡瑩, 元劇聯套述例.

[44]　This is apparently based on one of Tu Fu's poems — 觀公孫大娘弟子舞劍器引 — and Chang Hsü's claim that he was inspired by the same dancer.

The single dancer performs a lively military dance, the mute actors stand up and the second dancer, dressed as man, enters and dances the finale with the first dancer.

The conductor recites (a passage of stylized prose in fifty-six words on the two previous themes), *and says,* "The songs and dances having ended, the honoured guests may leave as they please".

Exit the dancers and actors. [45]

The performance consisted of three elements, the military dance, the conductor's recitations on historical episodes and anecdotes, and the dumb shows of which the dance became a part. Here, pure dance and narrative recitation stimulated dramatization to the extent of dumb shows; only the dialogue is lacking to make it fully dramatic.

(c) Poetry and Music in Story-telling

From the days when the Buddhist monks of T'ang dynasty began to attract donations with their "talks on Buddhist books" the interests of entertainment controlled the form of story-telling, therefore it should not be surprising that verse and music soon became part of the early Buddhist talks. The Buddhist monks engaged in such talks were not by any means uniformly religious; a monk of T'ang dynasty

"gathered large crowds with his 'talks' in which, under the name of Buddhism, he recited flagrantly lewd and indecorous matters. Men and women of the street flocked to him, filling the monastery to overflow, called him the Monk Artist and sang songs in imitation of his recitations". [46]

Even musicians found inspiration in the monks' singing:

"In the reign of Ch'ang Ch'ing 長慶 (821-824) monk Wen Hsü 文叙 was famous for his recitation of Buddhist books. He had a beautiful voice and the people found his talks very moving. The musician Huang Mi-Fan 黃米飯 created this tune . . . after the monk's style of singing". [47]

The texts of Buddhist and secular stories of T'ang dynasty discovered at Tun Huang revealed that a style of prose embellished with verse called *pien-wen* (變文 literally "modified style") was then developed for story-telling and since reciting Chinese poetry is nearly singing it and since in T'ang and Sung dynasties poems were prevalently written to be sung, even without the opportunist's activities of the "Monk Artist" singing would have found its way into story-telling before long. Those Chinese novels which are derived from the story-tellers' script all show

---

[45] 史浩, 鄮峯, 眞隱漫錄, 卷四十六.
[46] 趙璘, 因話錄, 卷四, 七款.
[47] 段安節, 樂府雜錄, 文叙子.

extensive use of verse for descriptive and even some narrative passages. [48] When the proportion of verse was high, the shift of interest towards the verse caused a change of name from "talk" (說話) to "talk-with-poems" (詩話, 詞話).

When poems based on stories were sung the performance was also called the *Drum Song* (鼓子詞) [49] of which we have an extant example based on the same story as *Hsi Hsiang Chi* (西廂記). [50] Of musical compositions which were related to narratives, Sung dynasty also produced the *chuan tz'u* 賺詞 (which was really a song cycle), a group of poems sung to tunes of the same key and the *chu-kung-tiao* (諸宮調 literally "melody of mixed keys") longer than the *chuan* or song cycle and consisting of poems sung to tunes of different keys. [51]

The *ch'ang chuan* (唱賺), though lyrical in nature, was sometimes based on "romance and adventures" [52] and were thus related to narratives. Fragmentary texts of the genre are extant. [53] In spite of their lyrical nature they are closely related

---

[48] e.g.五代平話, 金瓶梅詞話 . The customary ways to introduce descriptive passages in verse in Chinese novels are: "How do we know it was so? . . ." (怎見得 . . .) "There is a poem to prove it: . . ." (有詩爲證 . . .) ". . . for which people of later times composed this poem: . . ." (後人有詩曰 . . .).

[49] Probably accompanied by tappings on the drum.

[50] （宋）趙令畤, 侯鯖錄, 卷五, 商調蝶戀花鼓子詞.

[51] In ancient Chinese music, the keys (宮) and modes (調) were distinct. The basic scale, which was similar to the major scale of the European music except that it started with the subdominant of the western tonic (i.e. FGABCDEF'), had seven notes and the seven different octaves starting from each of the notes formed the scale for the seven modes.（宋）蔡西山, 律呂新書, 六十調圖 . A tune to which a poem must conform was of a certain key and mode, and it was not transposed. (Perhaps due to the absolute temperance or inadequate construction of the instruments. The later is, at any rate, the case with *K'un ch'ü*, a style of music which flourished in the Chinese theatre from the sixteenth to the nineteenth century, for which the tunes sung in any one scene are mostly of the same key, because otherwise the flute will have to be changed — Wang Kwang-Ch'i, *Ueber die chinesische klassische Oper* (1934). Ch. 5). In the light of modern knowledge, it is possible that the choice of keys for the particular tunes might have been related to the pronunciation. Vowels have their definite pitch and can be pronounced clearly only in a certain range of notes — see Scholes, *Oxford Companion of Music* (1945), VOICE 8. For this reason the difference between the *chuan* (song cycle) of uniform key and the *chu-kung-tiao* was greater than it may appear to be, for one thing, the *chuan* cannot have been long because the choice of tunes was limited, and for another, the change of key in the *chu-kung-tiao* could have been exploited as an artistic device as modulation is in European music. The Chinese music being without harmony is of course ignorant of the modulation so essential to the structure of western music. Modern Chinese musicians allow the combination of "similar keys" — 王季烈, 集成曲譜, 聲集, 曲談, 二章, 頁九; 吳梅, 顧曲塵談, 一章一節 — meaning probably keys which require little adjustment in the fingering on the flute. Keys have also been connected in China with the moods of the tunes. 芝菴論曲, 八節 (見, 元曲選).

[52] 吳自牧, 夢粱錄, 卷二十, 妓樂.

[53] 王國維, 宋元戲曲史, 四章 (末).

to the Chinese drama because the Chinese dramatic poetry is akin to lyrics. Its developing musical structure was also a step towards the music of the dramas that were to come.

"Originally there was an introduction and a coda, between which two tunes alternated, but later the musical structure was more complicated". [54]

Chu-kung-tiao "was invented in the reigns of Hsi Ning and Yüan Feng (late eleventh century) by K'ung San-Chuan (孔三傳) and all the scholars could recite and sing it". [55] It was a mixture of verse and prose and was partly spoken and partly sung, thus in these respects it was like the Chinese drama, especially when it contained a large amount of dialogue. It consisted of lyrical, narrative and descriptive passages and dialogue and if the narrative and descriptive passages of the extant *chu-kung-tiao* were to be spoken by the characters in the story as they often were in the Chinese dramas, then they would be almost indistinguishable from the dramas. The combination of verse and prose in *chu-kung-tiao* also suggested a flexible and practical scheme for the dramatists. In the *suite (ta ch'ü)* all the movements were in one key, some of them could be omitted (as they were in Sung dynasty) but the order could not be reversed, hence, in so far as the music limits the metrical form of those movements which were sung, it was the most restrictive form for the poet. *Chu- kung-tiao* had no restriction in key (and hence rhyme). The northern dramas of Yüan dynasty followed a compromise musical scheme: the tunes in each "act" must be of the same key but they could be arranged in any order. The change from *chu-kung-tiao* to drama can be studied in the two works on the same subject, *Hsi Hsiang Chi* (西廂記), one a *chu-kung-tiao* and another a drama: the introductory passages remained but the narrative parts were transferred to the *dramatis personae*.

The tendency to dramatize the performance of *chu-kung-tiao* became evident in Ming dynasty:

"*Hsi Hsiang Chi* was performed by one lutist and several dozens of singers sitting together. The lutist played the accompaniment and the singers sang the different parts in turn". [56]

---

[54] 吳自牧, 夢粱錄, 卷二十, 妓樂; 參, 王灼, 碧雞漫志, 卷三, 一段 (石曼卿); 曾慥, 樂府雅詞, 轉踏.

[55] 王灼, 碧雞漫志, 卷二, 三段; 吳自牧, 夢粱錄, 卷二十, 妓樂; 孟元老, 東京夢華錄, 卷五, 京瓦伎藝. There are three works in this genre which are extant:
董解元, 西廂記.
王伯成, 天寶遺事 (散見雍熙樂府等).
無名氏, 劉知遠 (殘本) Kano Naoki (狩野直喜, 1868-1947) recognized in Leningrad Academy among the archaeological finds of a Russian expedition into Mongolia in 1907-8.

[56] (清) 焦循, 劇說, 卷二, 三款, 引, (明) 張元長, 筆談.

55C

Painting of Sung Dynasty Showing Sing-song Girls in a Play

Both actresses wore man's costume, but not stage make-up. Their earrings, bracelets, low neck-line and diminutive man's shoes (to show off their tiny feet) were for the benefit of the potential clients. Thus, for professional reasons, the stage costume was for pretence rather than for disguise. The actress on the right, labelled *mo-ni* type, had a stick (in her belt) probably for hitting the other character in comic situations. The huge flower she wore indicated, by contemporary custom, that she was a star. (See *Wen Wu* 文物 vol. 2, 1980, Pp. 58-62). The drum (of the same type used at present in story-telling) and the clapper on it indicate that the performance was partly narrative.

CHAPTER XXVI

DRAMA AND THEATRE IN YÜAN DYNASTY

In culture, as well as in other aspects of Chinese history, the distinction is often made of the North and the South. The distinction is based partly on meteorological and dietetic differences between the two parts of the country and partly on some ethnic divergence, for the North contains Mongolian and Manchurian blood and the South, admixture of aboriginal tribes in early Chinese history. In the later half of Sung dynasty this division was supplemented by political movements: the northern part was occupied by the Manchurians and later by the Mongolians. Therefore when the Chinese drama emerged at the end of Sung dynasty there were two styles, the northern and the southern dramas. Although differing in technical details and literary style they were similar in their main features, because of their common roots in the literary and theatrical sources of Sung dynasty. The general similarities of the two types and the decline of the southern dramas in Yüan dynasty make it convenient to confine this chapter to the northern type and to discuss the technical differences between the two schools later, in connection with their influence on dramas after Yüan dynasty.

The construction of the northern drama suggests that it was conceived partly as a musical composition and partly as a drama — in the modern sense of the word. A Yüan drama was divided into four *sections* (折 literally "cut") which were not *acts* because they were more musical than dramatic units and they were much shorter than the acts in western dramas. The four sections were usually introduced by and occasionally linked with a short and simple scene called *hsieh-tzu* (楔子 literally "tenon"). [1] During each *section* the locality could change any number of times but as there was no scenery the changes did not involve any pause, especially as they often occurred with the actors on the stage, hence it is unlikely that the audience

---

[1] The word *scene* here means a small unit of dramatic action but does not mean that the locality remains unchanged in it. Northern dramas had the rigid form of the extant plays at the beginning of Yüan dynasty. A jump in the development from the more primitive or experimental forms is believed to have occurred in the age of the earliest dramatists, such as Kuan Han-Ch'ing and Wang Shih-Fu 關漢卿, 王實甫, 參, 王國維, 宋元戲曲史, 九章.

255

noticed any break in the performance such as produced by the drop of the curtain. As far as can be ascertained, the performance was continuous in a drama, in fact, in the dramas printed in Yüan dynasty [2] the division of *sections* was not indicated. Therefore except for musically sensitive (see below) and otherwise attentive spectators, a play in Yüan dynasty was a single continuous unit without any interruptions.

The short length of the drama and the large proportion of arias not essential to the dramatic action made it impossible to cover a plot of any length in a single play, for example, the play *Hsi Hsiang Chi* (西廂記), based on a story of illicit love in the familiar sequence of meeting, intrigue, discovery and separation and having no sub-plot, consisted of a cycle of four dramas (that is, sixteen *sections*), and it was in another drama by a different playwright that the reunion of the hero and the heroine was brought about. In the one-hundred-odd extant plays of this period several stories are treated in cycles of dramas, but the majority of the dramas either have very simple plots or cover only small parts of well known stories.

The style of the dramatic writing was far from being realistic because not only a large proportion of the dialogue was in verse in which neither the diction nor the manner of delivery — singing — approached the usage in actual life, but the dramas contained also many narrative and lyrical passages. [3] For instance, it was customary for an actor who appeared for the first time, especially at the opening of the play, to begin his speech by reciting a poem of four regular verses vaguely moralizing on the play or expressing his private feelings and following it with a series of particulars such as his name, age, profession, family, financial situation, personal plans and other information about himself which the audience should have, usually ending the speech by stating his immediate intention which he put into action forthwith. For characters whose identity and background were clarified by a previous speech, or were otherwise obvious, the self-introducing soliloquy was omitted. As a whole if the dialogue were taken too literally most people represented would appear to have a morbid propensity for talking aloud to themselves and a hyperaesthetic mind for poetic demonstration on the least likely provocation. When one considers the lack of scenery and front curtain and the frequent changes of locality one is led to the conclusion that the audience of Yüan dynasty did not look upon the drama as a reproduction of reality but as a poetical and musical version of it. The four *sections* of a drama were not so much units of the dramatic action as those of the music: in each *section* all the music was in one key. [4] The characters in the plays were given

---

[2] 覆元槧古今雜劇三十種—東京大學刊.

[3] In Yüan dynasty lyrical poems were written in the style of dramatic poetry, called *hsiao-ling-t'ao-shu* 小令套數 and they are indistinguishable from passages in the dramas.

[4] In later times change of key was associated with the change of the mood of the drama — 王季烈, 集成曲譜, 聲集, 曲談, 四章 — this might have been the case with Yüan dramas. (元曲選) 芝菴論曲, 八款.

special licence to conduct themselves as they did for the sake of the particular type of entertainment that resulted. To the audience who knew of no complete dramatization this probably appeared perfectly natural. The drama was poetry and music and acting *based on* a story, not a truthful copy of the happenings in the story, therefore there was no demand for verisimilitude. [5] To men with a dominating love for music the Yüan drama could have appeared to be a solo performance of a singer with supplementary actors, because in a northern drama only one actor sang — though he could be different characters, in "split parts" — all the rest only spoke. [6] When the singing was heavy and the action thin [7] or when the singer was particularly praiseworthy, the performance would partake the character of a dressed recital of operatic arias supported by spoken dialogue and action to give sense to the poetry. Such performances would be extreme cases but they illustrate the importance of music in the Yüan dramas. The extant dramas as a whole show more or less homogeneous treatment of the material with considerable interest in the spoken passages.

The style of acting in Yüan dramas could only be stylized because no naturalistic acting could fit the passages in lyrical and descriptive verse which were sung, nor could it fit even the passages that were, according to directions in the text, declaimed. There were pornographic passages in the dialogue which could never be acted on the stage — for once it was impossible to "suit the action to the word, the word to the action", as Hamlet wanted.

The plots of the Yüan dramas can in most cases be traced to stories popularized by the story-tellers of Sung dynasty and written by poets in ballads, *chuan* (song cycles) and *chu-kung-tiao*. The audience were most likely to know the stories before they saw the plays. [8] The dramas were not classified in Yüan dynasty: only occasionally some dramas were referred to by their distinctive features, such as a comic play or a play of pugilism. The earliest classification was in a book written in Ming

---

(5) In a drama of Ming dynasty there were nine scenes which were entirely in prose, and the author was criticized for being unorthodox: （明）屠陸，曇花記，三，七，十三，三十 齣 等. This shows that the Chinese consider drama as necessarily poetical work.

(6) In the early dramas he might be the singer (or minstrel) of the *chu-kung-tiao*. Actresses did recite *chu-kung-tiao,* see 水滸傳（百回本）五十一回; 馮沅君，古劇說彙，四章，四.

(7) Some of the dramas were almost entirely lyrical passages: 漢宮秋，倩女離魂.

(8) Apparently sometimes dramas were written on contemporary events: — ". . . incensed as an onlooker he put the matter into plays so that it would be better known by the public . . ." 周密，癸辛雜識，別集，上，祖傑. One robber said he would not rob the actors because they might put him in a play and thereby ruin his reputation. 水滸傳（百回本）二十七回. Among the "official copies" of miscellaneous plays was one about Wang Tzu-Kao 王子高六么 whose scandal made contemporary news. 王國維，宋元戲曲史，五章，參，黃雪蓑，青樓集，樊事眞條.

257

dynasty [9] according to which there were twelve types of dramas in Yüan dynasty: 1. on magicians and spirits, 2. on happy recluses, 3. on emperors and ministers, 4. on single-hearted friendship, 5. on filial piety and righteousness, 6. on the evil ways of the wicked, 7. on undeserved suffering, 8. on swordsmen and pugilists, 9. on romance and passion, 10. on separations and reunions, 11. on the fortunes of great beauties, and 12. on gods and daemons. [10] It has been pointed out that the classification does not suffice for even the extant dramas because some of them do not fit any of the twelve types. Nevertheless, it indicates the range of interests in the Yüan dramas, and reveals some characteristics of the psychology of the audience. It is noticeable that the classification was not based on the sentiments of the play, such as the tragic and the comic, but on the subject matter and partly on the type of principal characters. [11] Also some among the twelve types indicate theatrical interests which can scarcely be concurrent with dramatic appeal, such as swordsmanship, feminine beauty, grotesque daemons and the splendour of imperial courts. Even in those dramas in which the plot is an important element, the development is seldom very striking — there is no prominent pattern of conflict, development and resolution. The interest in the admirable (snobbery) and curiosity for the strange (supernatural sensationalism) are evident even in the list of types quoted above. The Chinese dramas came from popular entertainment and the popular taste left its indelible marks on them. Plagiarism and anachronism can be

---

(9) 寧獻王，太和正音譜，雜劇十二科.

(10) A Japanese scholar classified the plays as: 1. historical plays, 2. plays on sorrows and moral lessons, 3. plays on romance, and 4. plays on religious and supernatural subjects. 鹽谷溫，元曲概說（隋樹森譯）. See *ibid.*, 九章 for other classifications. Like the classification in twelve types, this list shows strong elements of pageantry and melodrama. As regards the last type, Buddhist, Taoist and especially Confucianist ethics are no doubt in the dramas. The reason they are not felt to be propaganda is that such ethics is still a part of Chinese life. It is only when religious faith has become an anachronism that its preaching in art becomes embarrassing. Southern dramas were classified as: 1. on loyalty and filial piety, 2. on righteousness, 3. on romance, 4. on adventures, 5. on fame and prosperity, and 6. on gods and fairies.（明）呂天成，曲品，卷下，引.

(11) The subject matter of the plays reflects the uniform moral ideas of the Chinese audience which are perhaps characteristic of the stable social system. For example, a recluse is always supposed to be happy, filial piety is unquestionably meritorious and romance and passion are considered dangerous. To understand Chinese dramas thoroughly requires understanding of the national customs and sentiments — the task is endless. It should not be surprising, however, that the Chinese plays do not fit the European types of dramas, such as tragedy and comedy. The dramas of a nation reflect a people's attitudes towards life. The Greek tragedies and comedies represent two Greek mental attitudes; neither the form of the Greek dramas, nor the dramatic ideals behind them have, even in the European theatre, been accurately revived in later ages. Elizabethan tragedy and comedy are different from those of the Greeks. Chinese dramas do not fall into the same types as Greek or Elizabethan dramas because the Chinese attitude towards life is different. Higgins defined tragedy and comedy as: Tragedy — a loftie kind of poetrie, shewing the rufull end of noble personages, and their

found in practically every drama of this period. [12] There is no pre-occupation with social problems as in the modern European dramas, nor are the insight into human nature and the subtleties of motivation the strong points of the Yüan dramatists. Theirs is an art distinguished by its freshness and spontaneity. [13]

The total number of plays written in Yüan dynasty has been variously estimated between 458 and 1700. [14] Plagiarism and adaptation of text probably made accurate estimation rather difficult.

It is to be remembered that the dramas of Yüan dynasty were written to be played, not to be read; the object of the playwrights was to produce good theatre, not to write good books. One does not do them justice, therefore, by judging them as literature, even though many of them do contain good poetry. It is only as a part of the theatre of Yüan dynasty that they can be seen in the proper perspective. In a history of the Chinese theatre their value does not lie in their literary merits but in the light they throw on the theatrical conditions they represent.

The actual conditions of the theatre in Yüan dynasty are not clearly known. No contemporary drawing or description of the theatre has been discovered, nor are any theatrical records known to have survived. [15] Apart from incidental references, the

---

fal from felicitie; Comedy — a base kind of poetrie which endeth troublesome matters merrilie. (*Nomenclator*, 1584). By these broad definitions the Chinese have both comedies and tragedies. Owing to the popular origin of the Chinese drama, however, the characters are not always "noble personages" in the plays of "rufull ends". The Chinese social organization gives importance to the deeds of the nobility but this bias is more evident in the histories than in the dramas. The tragic hero as the European dramatists understand him and with him tragedy, in the narrow sense of the word, are really lacking in the Chinese dramas. This problem involves moral ideas. In the Confucian system of morality, a "superior man" is resourceful in practical life and accepts the "decrees of heaven" like a philosopher. He cannot, like the tragic hero, bravely serve one single ideal to its bitter end, or struggle with Fate. There cannot be a germ of disaster in his character; he is the very man to whom people look up for examples of ways for averting personal disaster. Suffering, according to the Confucianists, is either natural, like death and sickness, which men should learn to accept with equanimity, or man-made, in the form of bad government and lack of culture, which great men should try to correct and ordinary men should try to evade — in either case the misfortune is not tragic. The Confucianist morality, like the Christian, is a perfectionist's morality, in which all evils can be traced to their sources. Such a morality is incompatible with the true tragic sense.

[12] Plagiarism is still practiced in the Chinese theatre to-day: successful new plays are copied in a matter of days. 齊如山, 京劇之變遷, 頁二九.

[13] Miss Feng Yüan-Chün calls the Yüan dramas simple, puerile, vulgar and absurd 馮沅君, 古劇說彙, 附錄二 but Prof. Wang Kuo-Wei loved them for their naivete. 王國維, 宋元戲曲史, 十二章.

[14] 1700 — 李開先, 張小山樂府序; 585 — 周憲王, 太和正音譜; 458 — 鍾嗣成, 錄鬼簿; 參, 王國維, 宋元戲曲史, 十章; 吉川幸次郎, 元雜劇研究, 序說四.

[15] See, however, frontispiece, 顧學頡, 元人雜劇選（一九五六）a "mural of the reign of T'ai Ting (1324-1328)".

only source of information we now possess is the text of the dramas which fortunately occasionally had theatrical life for their subject. [16]

A painting of Sung dynasty which contains an open-air stage, apparently temporarily erected, shows it to be a platform on strong struts and beams, in front of a small building which was used as dressing room. The stage is railed and covered with a large awning. At its side and near to it is another similar platform, also railed and covered with awning, apparently for ladies among the spectators — men are shown standing in front of the stage. [17] Temporary theatres on open grounds were mentioned in books of Sung dynasty. [18]

> ". . . the streets, for more than a thousand feet, were railed with thorn branches . . . inside, there were 'music booths' for musical performances and dramas . . ." "Below, was erected an open platform (露臺)". [19]

A "Yüan dynasty" stage was discovered in 1932. [20] It is a platform of masonry and is roofed and closed on three sides leaving only the front open. [21]

Theatre appeared to be a flourishing business in Sung and Yüan dynasties: in one street alone there were at one time more than fifty theatres, the biggest holding several thousand people. [22] The theatres were not exclusively for dramatic performances; recitals, minstrelsy, story-telling and other types of entertainment were also performed in them. [23] The exact construction is still obscure, but from contemporary references we learn that it was a substantial permanent building with galleries and a yard for the audience and a stage and dressing rooms for the players.

---

(16) Three plays are particularly valuable in this respect: 藍采和（元明雜劇）; 宦門子弟錯立身（永樂大典戲文）; 杜善夫, 莊家不識勾闌（太平樂府, 卷九).

(17) 宋, 清明上河圖, 見周貽白, 中國戲劇史, 二章五節. The term for theatre in Sung and Yüan dynasty was *kou-lan* 勾闌 which means "railing". According to a book of Ming dynasty "theatre was originally like railing". （明）方以智, 通雅; 周貽白, 中國戲劇史, 頁一一九, 引 meaning perhaps railing to keep out unauthorized spectators.

(18) 周密, 武林舊事, 卷六, 瓦子勾欄; 耐得翁, 都城紀勝, 井市.

(19) 孟元老, 東京夢華錄, 卷六, 元宵. Theatres were also called "booths" 棚 — 梁園棚（藍采和, 第一折, 冲末開場). The name suggests "awning" or "shed", perhaps designating temporary buildings before permanent theatres were built.

(20) 山西萬泉縣, 四望鄉, 見, 周貽白, 中國戲劇史, 頁三〇六.

(21) The side walls are curious, because they spoil visibility. Other theatres (stages) possibly of Sung or Yüan dynasty have also been discovered: 琉璃渠; 陝西朝邑縣西原嶽廟—馮沅君, 古劇說彙, 一章, 一, 註十一; 齎聚賢, 元代演劇的舞臺, 清華月刊, 二卷一期.

(22) 周密, 武林舊事, 卷六, 瓦子勾欄; 孟元老, 東京夢華錄, 卷二, 東角樓街巷.

(23) 孟元老, 東京夢華錄, 卷七, 三月一日開金明池瓊苑.

When a theatre collapsed in Yüan dynasty "more than forty people were killed and the bodies were crushed beyond recognition" [24] and an actor was represented in one of the plays as saying to a man, "If I lock you up in the theatre for ten days, you will be starved to death". [25] Dramas were also presented in "booths in open grounds, and in spite of wind, rain, heat and cold, people crowded to these places". [26]

Playbills, on coloured paper, were posted outside the theatre on the day before the performance in lieu of advertisement [27] and just before the performance, stage properties, especially the weapons, were hung up to attract spectators and a crier was stationed at the gate to bring in customers by telling the people outside the price for admission, the excellence of the plays, the immediate approach of the starting time and the ample space available inside. A drama of Yüan dynasty describes a man from the country seeing the theatre for the first time:

". . . There were green bills on the building and a crowd of people near it. . . . Someone at the gate was crying loud, 'Come, come, before the seats are all taken. The first play is of romance and the second on Liu Shua Huo'. . . . He took two hundred cash from me and let me in. . . . Entering the gate and going up a wooden ramp I saw people in circular tiers sitting there. . . . Above, there was a building like the bell tower and looking down I saw a whirlpool of men. . . . There were women sitting on the stage". [28]

In a play about actors, the head of the company says,

"I am going to play in this theatre. We have posted the coloured bills yesterday — my brothers, you go first to the theatre to get things ready, and I will be coming presently. We players don't live an easy life". "Wang, take the flags, shields, curtains and so on and hang them up for me". [29]

Thus there were no tickets and admission was paid at the gate as in the Elizabethan theatre. It is not known whether the spectators in the yard sat or stood, but as the man described seeing the people "below" like a whirlpool, it might be an indication of standing space in the yard and the mobility of the crowd. The entrance seemed to lead to the gallery and spectators in it appeared to be sitting, because a special place called the "musicians' bench" (樂床) was reserved for the actresses and was mistaken by a man for spectators' seats:

"When I opened the gate of the theatre I saw a man sitting on the

---

(24) 陶宗儀, 輟耕錄, 卷二十四, 勾闌壓.

(25) 藍采和, 第一折, 賺煞.

(26) 孟元老, 東京夢華錄, 卷五, 京瓦伎藝.

(27) 宦門子弟錯立身, 永樂大典戲文三種 (古今小品書籍印行會), 頁五十六; 杜善夫, 莊家不識勾闌, 耍孩兒 (太平樂府, 卷九). They were still used within living memory: 齊如山, 戲班, 六章, 貼戲.

(28) (元) 杜善夫, 莊家不識勾闌, 耍孩兒 (太平樂府, 卷九).

(29) 藍采和, 一折, 正末上引, 天下樂.

'musicians' bench', I said to him, 'Sir, please take a seat in the *gods' loft* (神樓) or the *side booth* (腰棚), these are seats for women in the play'.''[30]

The actresses thus sat somewhere visible to the spectators, probably between acts and in costume, to "throw glances at one spectator and another":

"The actresses sat in a row on the 'musicians' bench', every one of them in tight jacket and close-fitting skirts and wore layers of black gauze on their foreheads, throwing glances at the men in the lofts and booths". [31]

The actors and actresses together with the musicians belonged to the lowest class of the society and although whole families were often in the profession, [32] the women were courtezans as well as actresses. In a play one actress is spoken to in this way:

"You are an actress, if you don't marry me, do you think any respectable man would marry you?" [33]

Of the one hundred and seventeen courtezans in *Ch'ing Lou Chi,* [34] a book about the courtezans of Yüan dynasty, more than half were actresses. [35] Some of the players were stationed permanently in the cities, and apparently there were actors who were quite well-to-do [36] but there were also some on the road performing on temporary stages [37] and acting probably only by permission of the local authorities to whom the actresses sometimes rendered "special services". [38] The average size of the companies is not clearly known. Some passages suggest there were a few dozen[39] but Miss Feng Yüan-Chün believes there were only from ten to thirty players in a company. [40] Some women played men [41] and men and women probably played together. [42] It was the custom for the players to have stage names. [43]

The players could be summoned to private parties and would give recitals not only with musical accompaniment but also with stage property, and sometimes

---

(30) 藍采和, 一折, 天下樂.

(31) 太平樂府, 卷九, (元) 高安道, 疎淡行院哨遍套曲, 七煞.

(32) 宦門子弟錯立身, 永樂大典戲文三種. (古今小品書籍印行會), 頁五六; 參, 藍采和, 一折, 正末上白.

(33) (明) 朱有燉, 桃源景, 一折, 白 also see 無名氏, 耍孩兒, 拘刷行院散套, 十三煞, (太平樂府, 卷九).

(34) 黃雪簑, 青樓集.

(35) A curious fact about the courtezans of Sung and Yüan dynasties is that they played football. 元曲選, 度柳翠, 三折.

(36) 藍采和, 一折, 混江龍.

(37) 水滸傳 (百二十回本), 一百三, 四回.

(38) 參, 宦門子弟錯立身, 永樂大典戲文三種, 頁五十六.

(39) 藍采和, 二折, 尾聲: "百十口火伴".

(40) 馮沅君, 古劇說彙, 二章, 五, 頁四八.

(41) 黃雪簑, 青樓集, 燕山秀.

(42) *Vide* 馮沅君, 古劇說彙, 二章, 四, 頁四六.

(43) 藍采和, 一折, 冲末開場, "樂名".

lingered in restaurants in hope of such temporary engagements. At least sometimes, the audience could select the programme. (44)

Actors were not only famous for their singing, but also for their comic acts, pugilistic skill, acting, etc. (45) They were divided into types according to the character they could impersonate well and each actor or actress apparently played one type only. This practice is favourable to the development of specialized acting which would result not only in types of actors but also in types of characters. Apart from occasional needs for special impersonations, there were four main types, the male character in general *mo* (末), the female character *tan* (旦), the uncouth male character *ching* (淨) and the clown *ch'ou* (丑). (46) The special impersonations most often added were high officials (孤), children (俅) and thieves (孛老). Subdivisions in the four main types were made either according to differences in the characters, such as old women (老旦), young girls (小旦), etc., or according to the players' status, such as second male role (次末), extra player for female roles (外旦), etc. Stage make-up was known at this time, especially for women, but there is no clear evidence that it was ever as heavy as to constitute a mask. The costume was mainly contemporary, probably embellished for theatrical purposes. (47)

Plays were written by societies of writers called *shu-hui* (48) which were also responsible for ballads, song cycles, and other forms of entertainment that required a script. There was apparently among the players some consciousness of the value of the script in a good production:

"If there is a contest-performance with another theatre how are we going to produce something good? We can only put on the powder and do our best. Perhaps we can ask the writers' societies to give us a good script". (49)

It is not clear how the dramatists were paid, but they appeared to be mostly

---

(44) 宦門子弟錯立身, 永樂大典戲文三種, 頁五八; 藍采和, 一折; 黃雪蓑, 青樓集, 小春宴; (太平樂府, 卷九) 無名氏, 耍孩兒, 拘刷行院, 十三煞.

(45) 陶宗儀, 輟耕錄, 卷二十五, 院本名目. Somersaults are often parts of the stage directions — (元曲選) 燕青博魚, 二折, (楊衙內).

(46) The actors of Yüan dynasty are not known to have used masks or "painted faces" like those in the Chinese theatre to-day — masks probably started in Ming dynasty. Yet the type of characters who wear masks now was already distinguished. The division of *ching* type was, therefore, not a matter of wearing masks, but a matter of prominent personal characteristics, like the clown. Pheasant feathers were used in Yüan theatres, but they were not for distinguishing the *ching* type. 虎牢關三戰呂布 (脈望館本), 三折, 迎仙客.

(47) For details see 馮沅君, 古劇說彙, 二章, 十六, 頁六六.

(48) 書會. (元明雜劇) 藍采和, 一折, 油胡蘆; 周密, 武林舊事, 卷六, 諸色伎藝人; (永樂大典戲文) 張協狀元 (開場), (古今小品書籍印行會), 頁十三.

(49) 藍采和, 二折, 梁州.

263

professional people who wrote plays only for their own amusement, for there were merchants, physicians, soldiers and government officials among them. [50] Some of the actors were also playwrights. As success of the plays depended at least partly on good script, drama was not entirely spectacle and the audience were probably generally sensitive to good poetry. [51]

The nearest approach available to a description of the theatre of Yüan dynasty by an eye-witness is probably the following passage from *Shui Hu Chuan* (水滸傳) a novel written in Ming dynasty, but believed to represent the social conditions of late Sung and Yüan dynasty:

"... Lei Heng said, 'I came back a few days ago'. 'While you were away', said Li Hsiao-Erh, 'a new actress called Pai Hsiu-Ying has come to act here; she meant to pay you a visit but you were not at home. She is a pretty girl and can sing well too. At present she is performing in the theatre, in several styles of music and miscellaneous items such as dances, instruments and singing, always drawing a large crowd. Would you like to go and see; she is a good actress really'. As Lei Heng was not particularly occupied he went with Li Hsiao-Erh to the theatre. At the gate there were many playbills with writings in gold and on the flagpole hung various types of stage costume. Entering the theatre he picked the best seat and sat down. There was a comic play on the stage and while he was watching it Li Hsiao-Erh had gone out for a drink. When the play was finished, an old man, in a turban, a dark brown gown and a black girdle came to the stage with a fan in his hand and said, 'I am Pai Yü-Ch'iao of Tung Ching district. Being old I depend now on my daughter's skill in dance and songs. She has been popular all over the country'. As he was speaking there was the sound of a gong and the actress had come on to the stage bowing in all directions, playing the gong with such expert skill that it sounded like peas being poured on it. She stopped the gong and read a poem:

'The young birds cry as the mother bird comes.
The ewe is thin and the young lambs are fat.
For humans it is hard to make a living,
Unlike the wild ducks that fly about without care'.

Lei Heng shouted, 'Bravo', and the girl continued, 'As you have seen on my playbill to-day, this story I am to recite now is of romance ...' and she recited and sang and sang and recited, the whole theatre shouted 'bravo' at her. At a crucial point in the story she was stopped by her father who intercepted the

---

(50) 鍾嗣成, 錄鬼簿.

(51) Dramas were printed in Yüan dynasty — 覆元槧古今雜劇（東京帝國大學刊）— but they appeared to be acting copies because the names of the characters in the drama and the names of the types of actors playing them were used indiscriminately. These dramas, or *libretti,* were sold at that time in book shops. 周密, 武林舊事, 卷六, 小經紀.

recitation with: 'Even though our skill is not worth great riches, it can find favour with understanding audience. The gentlemen have shown their appreciation, let us stop for a while, my child. The next item will be a play . . .' Meanwhile the girl was passing the tray around, saying something about not letting the tray pass untouched and the old man said, 'My child, the gentlemen are all waiting to tip you; you should go round now'. When the girl came to Lei Heng, he reached to his pocket and found he had no money with him, so he said, 'I have forgotten to bring money to-day; I'll tip you tomorrow'. The girl said, 'When the first brew is weak, the second is weaker. You are sitting in the best seat, Sir, would you like to give a first tip?' Lei Heng reddened and said, 'It's not because I wouldn't tip you; I really forgot to bring money'. 'If you were coming to hear me sing, Sir, how could you forget to bring money?' said the girl. 'I wouldn't mind giving you three or five taels, but I forgot to bring some'. The girl answered, 'At the moment I can't see a single cash, Sir, why talk about three or five taels?' At this point the father interrupted them by saying, 'My child, you should have looked and seen if it is a gentleman of the city or a man from the country. Why waste time on him, come let some gentleman give you the first tip'. Lei Heng cried, 'How do you know I am from the country?' and the old man answered, 'If you know what this place is, horns will grow on dogs'. By this time the whole theatre was stirring. Lei Heng, greatly incensed, shouted, 'How dare you insult me?' 'Suppose I do insult a cowherd — what of it?' answered the old man. Someone who knew Lei Heng shouted to the old man, 'You better stop; this is officer Lei', but the old man muttered, 'He looks like an ass to me'. Lei Heng could control himself no longer and from his seat he jumped down to the stage and with fist and foot gave the old man a good beating . . .'' [52]

In the story the actress went to the mayor and had Lei Heng put in jail but asked to have him tied to the gate of the theatre the next day. This led to a quarrel with Lei Heng's mother in which he struck and killed the actress.

From this account one sees how the manners of the actress and her father in the theatre were practically beggarly. It was clear in the book that she had ''connections'' with the mayor's office, hence she was able to bring the humiliation on Lei Heng. [53]

---

[52] 水滸傳（百回本），五十一回.

[53] It is also noteworthy that Lei Heng jumped ''down'' to the stage, indicating probably that he was in the gallery. The actress came ''up'' to the stage 上戲台 in the original, hence it must be a platform stage. cf. directions in Yüan dramas: for entrance, ''come up'' 上; for exit, ''go down'' 下. In palace performances dancers and farce players ''came in'' 入場 and ''went out'' 出場. 孟元老, 東京夢華錄, 卷九, 宰執親上宗室百官入內小壽.

265

CHAPTER XXVII

CHANGES IN THE CHINESE THEATRE
SINCE THE ADVENT OF THE DRAMA

Since the beginning of the Chinese drama at the end of Sung dynasty, there have been no major changes in the Chinese theatre so far as method of staging is concerned. [1] The only changes that have occurred are in the style of dramatic poetry and music. In order to understand the rise and fall of the different styles of Chinese drama, it is necessary to explain first the distinction between popular and classical art in China because the changes in the Chinese drama are closely related to the mutual influence between them.

In a society like the Chinese which consists of a small percentage of the privileged class who have the mental equipment and leisure to enjoy fine arts and a large mass of illiterate people who cannot appreciate the sophisticated part of the Chinese culture, the cultivation of the arts can be expected to be exclusively in the hands of the privileged few. Artistic impulses are nevertheless noticeable in the religious and social activities of the people and under favourable conditions popular art is developed as part of popular entertainment. Popular arts, like ballads and story-telling, are often influenced by the literature and music in aristocratic and court circles and the artists of the privileged class also sometimes get their material from popular sources. In spite of the mutual influence between the two, however, they are persistently kept distinct from each other by the gulf between the life in the two layers of the Chinese society. To the two classes of the Chinese people art has different significance: to the aristocratic part art is mainly an elegant pastime but to the people it is usually part of their social life. In the former deliberate efforts are made to develop the arts and to cultivate the taste but in the latter development is spontaneous and the taste is natural; in the former achievements are carefully preserved in records as part of the Chinese culture, in the latter they are usually lost

---

[1] It is to be remembered that meanwhile the quasi-dramatic forms of entertainment such as puppets, shadow plays, story-telling, etc., went on unchanged.

after the vogue for the particular customs or amusements has died out. Among the leisured class the artistic works are sophisticated but among the people they are naive; the one reach high artistic standards through continuous development and nationwide support, the other often remain crude in sporadic and local movements.

The interaction between the two types of theatrical art throughout the Chinese history may be divided into four periods: (a) from the earliest times to the rise of the drama, (b) the two styles of the early dramas, (c) the innovation of the *K'un* tunes, and (d) the rise of the Peking dramas.

(a) *From the Earliest Times to the Rise of the Drama*

From the earliest times of Chinese culture this distinction can be traced: the *Book of Odes* (詩經), for example, is a mixture of authorized liturgy and popular odes and folk songs. In relation to the beginnings of the theatre one can trace music, dance and impersonation in the state-sponsored and state-controlled ceremonies in the temples of Chou dynasty as well as the unauthorized rituals of the shamans. The musicians and dancers for the temple ceremonies were carefully trained and special officials were appointed to guard the tradition. Music and dance among the people were by no means forbidden, but they were referred to as "folk music" [2] and these unauthorized dancers were defined as "the uncultivated people who could dance well". [3] In the period from Han to Sui dynasty, the lavish spectacles were naturally beyond the means of the common people, but the circus acts and their music [4] enjoyed by the imperial court were accessible to the general public, indeed the fact that the common people did avail themselves of the entertainment was shown by the need to "summon musicians from the four corners of the country" in the reign of emperor Yang-Ti in order to stage a mammoth pageant. [5] Pure entertainment, which started in the courts of late Chou dynasty, was, by the period of North and South, if not earlier, paralleled by similar activities among the people. From then onwards, developments in the Chinese theatre can be traced to both the court and the people and owing to their interaction, it is difficult now, in many cases, to decide the origin of particular advances made in the development of the theatre.

The dramatic dances of T'ang dynasty were of popular origin though they probably attained higher artistic standards only in the artistic atmosphere of the court. [6] In Sung dynasty, with its unprecedented and indeed as yet unequalled, luxuriance of popular entertainment, theatrical development was due to popular rather than court activities. The court theatre, though not as varied in content as the

---

(2) 散樂 literally "scattered music".

(3) 周禮, 春官, 旄人, 夷樂註.

(4) Called "music for miscellaneous entertainment" 雜伎樂.

(5) 隋書, 音樂志, 下.

(6) The *suites* — 大曲 — were also derived from folk music, hence they bore the names of the districts of their origin.

popular, was also exuberant, hence we have now the lists of the more uniform "official copies" as well as the "house copies" of the "miscellaneous plays" of this time. [7]

The court musicians in Sung dynasty must have had considerable influence on the development of the popular entertainment. There was a Music School in the government [8] to train musicians for court functions and special musicians were also available for public functions. [9] The Music School was repeatedly abolished and established — in the reign of Chien Yen 建炎 (1127-1130) it was abolished but it was re-established in the reign of Shao Hsing 紹興 (1131-1162) only to be abolished again at the end of the reign; from the reign of Ch'ien Tao 乾道 (1165-1173) onwards musicians were hired from the people for court functions and in the reign of emperor Li Tsung 理宗 (1225-1265) we hear again of abolishing the Music School and hiring musicians from outside the palace at festivals [10] — the net effect of which must have been the training of musicians in the imperial court to be dispersed among the people.

(b) *The Two Styles of Early Dramas*

Towards the end of Sung dynasty, a popular school of drama was evolved in Chekiang province known at first as *Wenchow dramas* [11] and later as *southern dramas*. [12] At about the same time the *northern dramas* were being developed in the north, then of Chin dynasty (金). [13] The dates for the rise of the southern and northern dramas are not known accurately. According to Ming dynasty writers southern dramas began in the early part of the twelfth century.

"Southern dramas began in emperor Kuang Tsung's reign 光宗 (1190-1194) . . . It is also said that they started in the reign of Hsüan Ho 宣和

---

[7] The effect of dramatic text on the theatre at this time should not be overlooked. Owing to its literary interest and its value for training new actors, it would have been preserved at that time. Thus there was at least one element of the theatre which was recorded and this would contribute to a greater continuity of the tradition.

[8] 教坊

[9] 衙前樂, 宋史, 樂志, 十七.

[10] 錢南揚, 宋金元戲劇考, 燕京學報, 二十期; 宋史, 樂志, 十七.

[11] 溫州雜劇

[12] 南戲

[13] Some idea of the source of local theatres can be seen in their most rudimentary form in *yang-ko* (秧歌) the rural theatre. In its present form it is influenced by the classical theatre and is not an entirely independent development but remnants of folk songs can still be traced in it. Amateur dramatic societies in rural areas in Hopei are formed with a few professional actors and a majority of farmers. The tunes of the songs are known to the audience and though the melodies are poorly fitted to the words the dialogue is made intelligible by repetitions. Accompaniment is by percussion only — gong, drum and castanets. The stories are mostly based on legends with very simple plots, but plays on family affairs are also popular. *Folklore Studies,* Vol. III, i. (Peking) 1944. 趙衞邦, 秧歌, 民俗雜誌, 三期一號.

(1119-1126) but they certainly did not become popular before the capital was moved to the south (1127) . . . The arias were based on the songs written by the scholars of Sung dynasty (詞) and supplemented with folk songs; no consideration was given to keys in the music, hence the scholars took no interest in them''. [14]

"Southern dramas came after the reign of Hsüan Ho 宣和 (1119-1126) about the time when the capital was moved to the south. They were called *Wenchow dramas*. 溫州雜劇 " [15]

"Dramatic composition was first made by the people of Yung Chia (永嘉) . . . Near the end of Sung dynasty it was prevalent in south China but its popularity waned in Yüan dynasty''. [16]

Whether they developed simultaneously or consecutively, and whether they were independent innovations or one was derived from the other are still subjects of conjecture and controversy. [17] At the end of Sung dynasty and the beginning of Yüan dynasty the southern dramas were the more popular, but apparently they did not attract sufficient enlightened patronage to become established as classical theatre, nor, if one may judge by the three extant early dramas of this school, did it appear likely that they would encourage such patronage. [18] The early popularity of the southern school may not be entirely independent of the favourable economic conditions and intellectual atmosphere in that part of the country due to the capital of the South Sung dynasty in Hangchow, nor was its decline unrelated to the fall of Sung dynasty in A.D. 1276 and the choice of Peking by the Mongolian conquerors as the capital of Yüan dynasty.

Those who support the theory of separate origin for the northern and southern dramas are wont to point to the differences between the two schools. These may be most conveniently listed in a table:

Northern Dramas	Southern Dramas
In four *sections* (折)	In any number of scenes (齣)
Music from *suites* (大曲), Taoist music (法曲) and songs of Sung dynasty (詞)	Contains a large proportion of folk music
Only one actor sings	Singing parts unrestricted
Only solos	Singing in unison as well as in solos

[14] （明）徐文長, 南詞敍錄, 首段.
[15] （明）祝允明, 猥談, 八款, 歌曲.
[16] （明）葉子奇, 草木子, 卷四.
[17] The extent of mutual influence is shown by the fact that out of sixty-nine known titles of early southern dramas thirty-seven are duplicated or have equivalents in the northern dramas. 青木正兒, 中國近世戲曲史, 四章（表）.
[18] The popular origin of the southern dramas left its marks in the gross dialogue in some of the dramas of Ming dynasty — Prof. Ch'i Ju-Shan mentioned seven dramas in this category. 齊如山, 京劇之變遷, 頁十九.

Northern Dramas	Southern Dramas
Quicker tempo in the arias	Slow tempo in the arias
Few notes to one word	Many notes to one word
Robust and vigorous music	Effeminate and graceful music
All arias of a *section* in one key	Keys used at random
Accompanied by lutes	Accompanied by flutes and castanets
Some plays have sad endings	All plays end happily
Introduced by a short scene	Introduced by a prologue (家門) [19]

When the Mongols established Yüan dynasty with the capital in Peking conditions for the growth of a classical theatre were shifted to the north, and at the same time the Chinese scholars almost of a sudden directed their energy to writing dramas, hence the rise of a classical theatre in the north. The sudden devotion by the Chinese scholars to a form of writing which was not considered to be orthodox literature and which they believed to have no literary value has been explained in various ways. According to Prof. Wang Kuo-Wei the ultimate cause lies in the low standards of the official examinations in Chin dynasty (金) and the resultant low standard of scholarship which subsisted into Yüan. At the beginning of Yüan dynasty there were no examinations and even after they were re-established many native scholars abstained from them for patriotic reasons. There was, therefore, in Yüan dynasty a large amount of undirected intellectual energy for which an outlet was sooner or later to be found. The Chinese scholars in this period could not, however, apply themselves to research and criticism of past literature as those in Ch'ing dynasty did, because they were not adequately equipped to do so. Consequently their talents found an outlet in popular literature, such as narrative poems and dramas. [20] The sudden devotion of the scholars to dramas has also been attributed to the adoption of dramatic poetry as the subject of the official examinations [21] but this has been shown to be groundless, for one thing this practice was never mentioned in the official history of Yüan dynasty and for another, some of the dramas were written by actors and actors were not allowed to take the examinations.

The high quality of Yüan dramas attracted the interest of the Chinese *literati* to the theatre, an interest which has continued till the present. This body of theatrical audience played an important part in the development of the Chinese drama: the

---

[19] For further musical dissimilarities see 姚燮, 復道人今樂考證, 緣起, 南北曲條. Owing to the difference in the music the northern and southern dramas will sound more widely different than they read. Further evidence of northern influence in the southern dramas lies in the northern tunes in them.

[20] 王國維, 宋元戲曲史, 九章（末段）.

[21] 臧晉叔, 元曲選, 臧序.

literary sophistications in the dramas of Ming dynasty and the rise of a new style of classical theatre after one had become obsolete are, among other things, due to their influence.

Towards the end of Yüan dynasty the literary quality of the southern dramas began to rise and it soon approached that of the northern school so that some of the best southern dramas were included in the private collections of plays. With the advent of Ming dynasty (1368-1643) the centre of the cultural life shifted again to the south — from the beginning of Ming dynasty to 1420 the capital was in Nanking — from then onwards the northern school withered away and the southern dramas became prevalent. (22)

At the beginning of Yüan dynasty, there were only two styles of theatre, one prevalent in Chekiang and one around Peking; they were in effect two local theatres each serving a district, the rest of the country, especially the more remote regions, were, in these early days of the Chinese drama, without theatres. By Ming dynasty, however, several schools of local theatre had already been developed in the south, each distinguished from the rest by dialect, local music and style of singing. (23) These local theatres, either influenced by or derived from the original *southern drama*, must have retained some of its features, but as the history of the local theatres is as yet obscure one cannot be positive on this point. If one may judge by present day practices, the texts of standard dramas were probably freely adapted to local needs.

(c) *The Innovation of the K'un Tunes*

Among the different local theatres the method of staging was, judging by those of to-day, the same and the script was similar, the only differences were then the music and the dialect. If a style of music was found that combined the musical idioms of two or more local styles, it would broaden the circulation of the dramas. This is particularly true in the Chinese theatres because in the arias one does not always hear the words and understand the libretto but one always hears the music. It was probably due to this reason that a musical innovation in the sixteenth century, called *K'un* tunes (崑曲 so called because of its early centre K'un Shan 崑山) gave the classical Chinese theatre a standard form of music which lasted three hundred years.

(It may be noticed that until the rise of *K'un* tunes changes in the Chinese drama were due to the shifting of the cultural centre from the south to the north and back again so that the music of the classical theatre also changed from southern to

---

(22) An expansion of the players' companies probably also occurred at this time: in one play there were sixteen brightly costumed gods —(明) 周憲王, 福祿壽仙官慶會 — and in another animal masquers led a choral dance —(明) 周憲王, 神后山秋獮得騶虞.

(23) At this time theatrical activities in Kiangsu and Chekiang were exuberant, "even people of respectable families played in dramas". (明) 陸容, 菽園雜記, 卷十.

northern music, and so on, but from the rise of *K'un* tunes to the present, the changes in the Chinese drama have been due to musical innovations instead of geographical changes of the cultural centre. This fact is important because it shows the importance of music in the Chinese drama).

Since Chinese dramas as performed are actually operas the preservation of a certain form depends not only on the survival of the text but also on that of the music. The survival of any school of the Chinese theatre depends therefore on the continuity of tradition, that is, on an unbroken line of players' troupes. Of the different elements of the theatre the script survives most easily. The general characteristics of the music can be preserved if there is an adequate system of notation, but the exact style of singing can only be recorded by accurate mechanical reproduction. As to acting and the other details of the actual production, unless there is careful documentation using modern photographic technique, they are doomed to gradual change and eventual extinction.

For lack of adequate musical notation the music of the northern dramas of Yüan dynasty is, for all practical purposes, entirely lost and that of the early southern school, though possibly preserved in scores, cannot now be recovered because the notation is not perfect, being without indication of force and expression or of the detailed value of the notes. [24] For this reason one cannot tell exactly what innovation was involved in the rise of *K'un* tunes.

About the middle of the sixteenth century Wei Liang-Fu 魏良輔 "after studying for ten years in his room" created a style of singing which superseded the "contemporary simple style of singing". [25] It was, for some obscure reason, called "water mill tunes" (水磨調) and it "combined some characteristics of I Yang

---

[24] The survival of the northern tunes after Yüan dynasty was as follows: The northern dramas were for some time popular at the beginning of Ming dynasty (1368-1643) but by the reign of Chia Ching 嘉靖 (1522-1566) they eked out a precarious existence among old court musicians and the singers in the household of a connoisseur gentleman called Ho Yüan-Lang 何元朗 — 何元朗, 四友齋叢說摘抄, 七, 詞曲（新曲苑）; 參, 青木正兒, 中國近世戲曲史, 七章二節; 沈德符, 顧曲雜言, 五款. After the death of this connoisseur the tradition was left in the hands of dwindling devotees among the courtezans in Nanking and the style of singing had probably been changed by then. By the end of the sixteenth century those who could sing northern tunes were dispersing and the rest had abandoned them. Some part of the tradition might have been kept alive in the palace down to late seventeenth century because mention was still being made in that period about court musicians playing northern tunes, though it is not known how truthful they were to the original style. In Ch'ing dynasty dramatists sometimes wrote complete scenes with northern tunes but these were northern tunes only in so far as the notation was concerned, they were sung in the style of *K'un* tunes, and probably *in this form* it still exists in some scores — 周祥生 等, 九宮大成南北宮詞譜; 葉堂, 納書楹曲譜; 王季烈, 集成曲譜 — and indeed some, according to Aoki Masaru, can be found among the existing phonograph records. 青木正兒, 中國近世戲曲史, 七章二節.

[25] 余懷, 寄暢園聞歌記（虞初新志, 卷四）.

273

拷紅

〔桂枝香〕著你行監坐守誰許你

胡行亂走一任你握雨攜雲常

使我提心在手你花言巧語你花

言巧語將沒作有使我出乖露

醜吓哈打打你這賤丫頭不說

出始末根由事教我如何索罷休

Specimen of Chinese Score

The title is the name of the scene from which the aria is taken and the brackets at the beginning contain the name of the tune. The libretto, in large characters, is written with uniform spacing and strings of names of the musical notes (corresponding to "do re mi", etc.) are attached to the words sung to them. Crosses, dots, circles, etc., beside the musical notes indicate different types of beats, for example, the crosses are the accented beats and the distance between two successive crosses is a bar. The key is implied by the name of the tune. Rests and expression marks are not provided for and the value of the notes is not always definite. Some symbols are used for trills, etc. The score is used more as permanent record than as musicians' work sheet and is normally supplemented by the musicians' memory. For details of this type of Chinese musical notation see Wang Kwang-Ch'i, *Ueber die chinesische klassische Oper,* 1934.

(弋陽) and Hai Yen (海鹽) music" both of local theatres in the respective districts. [26] At first it was confined to recitals [27] but later singers in the theatre learned the style also and after Liang Po-Lung 梁伯龍 used it in a play called *Huan Sha-Chi* (浣紗記) the style of singing became well established in the theatre. [28] There were four major styles of music in the sixteenth century:

"At the beginning of the sixteenth century among the local styles of southern music Hai Yen (海鹽) and Yü Yao (餘姚) styles were the most popular, but after the middle of the century the *K'un* tunes created by Wei Liang-Fu and I Yang (弋陽) style were also widely known". [29]

There were some descriptions of the new style:

"*K'un* tunes . . . have a sensual quality above the other styles and can easily make the audience feel intoxicated, especially when sung by the courtezans. It is like *p'iao-ch'ang* (嘌唱) of Sung dynasty, that is, with ripples and eddies added to the old melodies". [30]

Of *p'iao-ch'ang* a writer of Sung dynasty said: "Recently singers add ripples and eddies (泛灩) to the old melodies, called *p'iao-ch'ang* (嘌唱)". [31] It was also said of Wei Liang-Fu that he "could twist the melody like silk". [32] Another description says:

"At this time the southern music was plain and simple. Wei Liang-Fu invented new tunes which, although consistent with the principles of the keys, were different from the old music in an ingenious way. The enunciation according to sounds on the lips or on the teeth was particularly remarkable and the fascination of the music always added to its pathos". [33]

Of enunciation it was said that

". . . the singer's voice should be regulated according to the different intonations and enunciation should be based on the head, the body and the tail of a word". [34]

The *K'un* dramas not only represented a new style of music but, judging by the fact that the acting was always accompanied by music and by the difference in the style of acting between *K'un* dramas and the present local theatres of Kiangsu province, the "new" music most probably influenced the acting at the time of its

---

[26] 朱彝尊, 靜志居詩話, 卷十四, 梁辰魚.
[27] 周貽白, 中國戲劇史, 六章十七節, 引, 沈寵綏, 度曲須知.
[28] 朱彝尊, 靜志居詩話, 卷十四, 梁辰魚.
[29] 徐文長, 南詞敍錄 (十一段); 參, 青木正兒, 中國近世戲曲史, 七章
一節 which contains the geographical distribution of the four styles.
[30] 徐文長, 南詞敍錄 (十一段).
[31] (宋) 程大昌, 演繁露, 卷九, 嘌.
[32] (明) 張大復, 梅花草堂筆談, 見 (新曲苑) 梅花草堂曲談, 十一款.
[33] 余懷, 寄暢園聞歌記 (虞初新志, 卷四).
[34] 沈寵綏, 度曲須知. (周貽白, 中國戲劇史, 六章十七節, 引).

emergence. [35] It also brought about, through scholarly support of the movement, a raise in the social and educational level of the theatrical profession, at least in so far as this style of drama was concerned, and consequently the script was well preserved, a system of musical notation was established [36] and since then scores have been carefully kept, efforts were made to ensure the correspondence between the words and the music and singers were trained in a tradition of clear enunciation.

[37]

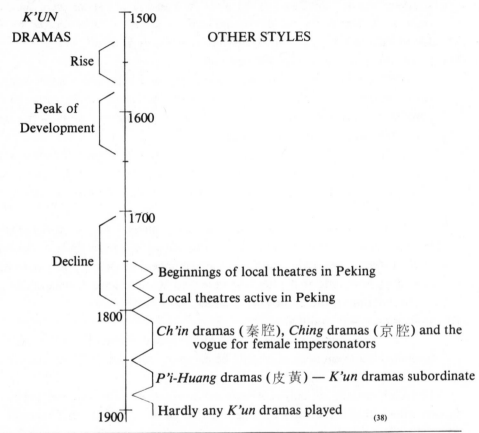

K'UN DRAMAS — OTHER STYLES

- Rise
- Peak of Development
- Decline

1500
1600
1700
1800
1900

Beginnings of local theatres in Peking

Local theatres active in Peking

Ch'in dramas (秦腔), *Ching* dramas (京腔) and the vogue for female impersonators

P'i-Huang dramas (皮黃) — *K'un* dramas subordinate

Hardly any *K'un* dramas played [38]

---

(35) In a collection of dramas of Ming dynasty published in 1835 — 無名氏, 審音鑑古錄 (荊釵記) — there is a scene in which notes on the postures and movements of the actors are printed beside the dialogue. The anonymous editor explained, ''In this scene the postures are complicated and are concerned with the description of scenery; to avoid loss of tradition they are recorded here''. It is however not indicated when the tradition started. For similar versions of other dramas see 北平國劇學會圖書館書目, 上, 二十三.

(36) The earliest score was compiled 1668-1673. 莊親王編, 九宮大成南北詞宮譜. Another important collection was published in the seventeen nineties. 葉堂, 納書楹曲譜, 乾隆末年.

(37) The northern tunes had no correct enunciation, see examples of the northern tunes in 青木正兒, 中國近世戲曲史, 十四章 (四).

(38) 齊如山, 京劇之變遷, 頁十三; 青木正兒, 中國近世戲曲史, 十一章, 引; 十二章, 十三章, 引.

276

(d) *The Rise of the Peking Dramas*

At the beginning of the nineteenth century, however, the *K'un* dramas, after nearly three hundred years of popularity, lost their monopoly of the classical Chinese theatre and towards the last quarter of the century a new style of singing and acting, now known as *Peking dramas* 京戲 (originally called "new dramas" 新戲) replaced them. The transition, which covered more than a century, was in several stages: first, the mixture of other local styles of theatre in a single performance with the *K'un* dramas as the most important part, then the rivalry between the different local styles for ascendancy, with the *K'un* dramas on equal terms with the other schools, then the rise of Peking dramas to eminence against the lingering influence of *K'un* dramas, and finally the complete domination of the Peking dramas.

At the middle of the eighteenth century there were two schools of drama in the imperial court, the classical department (雅部) for *K'un* dramas, and the popular department (花部) for dramas from the local theatres. [39] In *The Red Chamber Dream,* a novel of the eighteenth century, dramatic performances consisted of "*K'un* dramas, *Kao* tunes (高腔), *I Yang* tunes (弋腔) and *P'ing* tunes (平腔)". [40] Towards the end of the century, in Peking, the capital and cultural centre, theatrical taste degenerated into the love for lewd productions and several actors of the *Ch'in* dramas (秦腔) took the opportunity to reap immediate success. [41] From the middle of the eighteenth century various local theatrical companies began to come into the capital, especially *Ch'in* dramas (秦腔) and *Ching* dramas (京腔). *K'un* dramas occupied only a small portion of the repertoire of these local companies. In 1791 at the eightieth birthday of emperor Ch'ien Lung the Hui Company (徽班) entered Peking from Anhwei and this was followed by four others at the beginning of the nineteenth century and with them the *Erh-huang* tunes (二黃腔) entered the capital. The companies also sang *Ch'in* dramas (秦腔) and *Ching* dramas (京腔) and a little of *K'un* dramas. By the middle of the nineteenth century these actors from Anhwei more or less monopolized the theatrical profession in Peking. In 1829 the last company of players for *K'un* dramas in Peking, called Chi Fang Pu (集芳部) disbanded, but *K'un* dramas continued to be occasionally sung by the companies from Anhwei. About the same time companies of players for *K'un* dramas in Soochow also disbanded. At the middle of the nineteenth century *Hsi-p'i* (西皮) and *Erh-huang* (二黃) tunes were combined in the new Peking dramas. [42]

It is to be noticed that between the end of the eighteenth and the middle of the

---

[39] 李斗, 楊州畫舫錄, 卷五; 參, 錢泳, 履園叢話, 藝能篇.

[40] 曹霑 (1724-1764) 紅樓夢, 二十二回, 九十三回.

[41] ·It was a female impersonator of this time, Wei San 魏三, who first used realistic coiffure. (清) 楊懋建, 夢華瑣簿 (一八四三), 二十四款.

[42] 青木正兒, 中國近世戲曲史, 十二章一節.

nineteenth century there was a vacuum in the Chinese theatre and several local schools were competing to take the place of the *K'un* dramas. The local styles were for a time under the influence of an educated and demanding audience, but no new classical theatre was evolved. Some local styles did receive momentary support:

"The melodies of *Kao* tunes (高腔) are simple and easy to learn . . . singers can learn them in a day or two . . . After the decline of *K'un* dramas the players learned *Kao* tunes fast, and as it was easy to produce new tunes in the style and as its old repertoire contained many plays on romance, they were very popular at this time". [43]

This style however soon became out of fashion. There was evidently a search for a satisfactory form of theatre to take the place of the obsolete *K'un* dramas.

The Peking dramas, which at last rose to dominate the Chinese theatre, differed from these local schools in that they were a new style built on materials taken from several local theatres. Perhaps the most important feature of the Peking dramas was the flexibility of their music: whereas in *K'un* dramas the tunes of the arias were specified and performance could not deviate from the score, in Peking dramas only the tempo, the general rhythm and the instrumental bridge passages were fixed, the actual tune was a creation of the singer. This practice put a heavy burden on the players, especially those in the early part of the movement, because they had to be not only resourceful and original musicians but also competent elocutionists and phonologists. At the same time they had the advantage of being freed from the limitations of the individual styles of music and could thereby combine the musical idioms of several local schools. The style of acting, due to the influence of local theatres which invaded Peking, had already deviated from the statuesque and subdued expressions of the *K'un* dramas, and was ready for further changes towards more lively and flexible technique. To raise the new school of drama to a high artistic level from such foundations required great talents. It was due to a succession of talented singer-actors that this new style became established as the classical theatre. [44]

---

[43] 王夢生，梨園佳話，一章，"弋腔爲崑曲皮黃之過渡".

[44] The early singer-actors were in fact the founders of Peking dramas. There were two generations of them who deserve particular mention: the first generation whose career reached its peak about the time of T'ai-p'ing rebellion (eighteen fifties, when Soochow, the home of *K'un* dramas, was destroyed) and the second generation, approximately a quarter of a century later.

The first generation:

程長庚　　余三勝　　張二奎

The second generation:

汪桂芬 老生　　　譚鑫培 老生　　孫菊仙 老生

龔雪圃 老旦　　　黃三 淨　　　劉趕三 丑

楊月樓 文武老生　俞菊生 武生　　陳德霖 正旦

278

The standard of singing and acting, by which the Peking dramas surpassed the other schools of theatre, was and has remained high, but the quality of the script left in the hands of scarcely literate players was low [45] and the music, based on two similar local styles, was limited in its technical resources. [46]

There were attempts in the eighteen seventies and eighties to revive *K'un* dramas in Soochow, but without avail. *K'un* dramas continued in the "classical

---

The rise of the Peking dramas was marked by the importance of the male characters and the craze for the female impersonators subsided.

[45] In Ming and Ch'ing dynasties about one hundred and seventy dramatists and between two and three hundred plays were recorded; — 盧 前, 明清戲曲史, 一章 — these do not include Peking dramas of which there are several hundred.

[46] Some of the theatrical conditions in Peking from the last part of the nineteenth century to the early part of this century can be found in *A Source of Theatrical History for the Last Fifty Years* (五十年來北平戲劇史料, 民二一, 幾禮居戲曲叢書第二種) which contains two lots of theatrical records, from 1883 to 1912 and from 1908 to 1932. For the first period (1883-1912) there were more than twenty-nine companies (it is not known whether the records are complete) each of which had, on the average, one hundred and thirty plays in its repertoire. The distribution of plays in the repertoire of several companies for this period is as follows:

Number of companies	Number of plays	Number of companies	Number of plays
1	256	16	12
2	84	17	13
3	60	18	12
4	41	19	12
5	43	20	8
6	24	21	14
7	24	22	7
8	22	23	7
9	17	24	4
10	23	25	2
11	20	26	1
12	20	27	1
13	22	28	1
14	8	29	1
15	12		

that is, there were 256 plays each of which only one company could play, there were 84 plays each in the repertoire of two companies, etc., and there was one play which all the 29 companies could play. According to the above list, about a third (33.1%) of the productions were plays belonging to the individual companies and no two companies could play the same drama in this group; about half (52%) of the productions belong to one or two or three companies; about two thirds (62.5%) belonged to one to five companies; and about one third (33.1%) could be played by practically every company (24 companies onwards). For the second period no similar list has been prepared but it is known that there were more than 1232 registered actors and actresses.

279

department'' (雅部) in the palace, but unlike the theatre in T'ang and Sung dynasties, the influence of the court on the theatre was then negligible and in any case the "classical department" perished with Ch'ing dynasty in 1911.

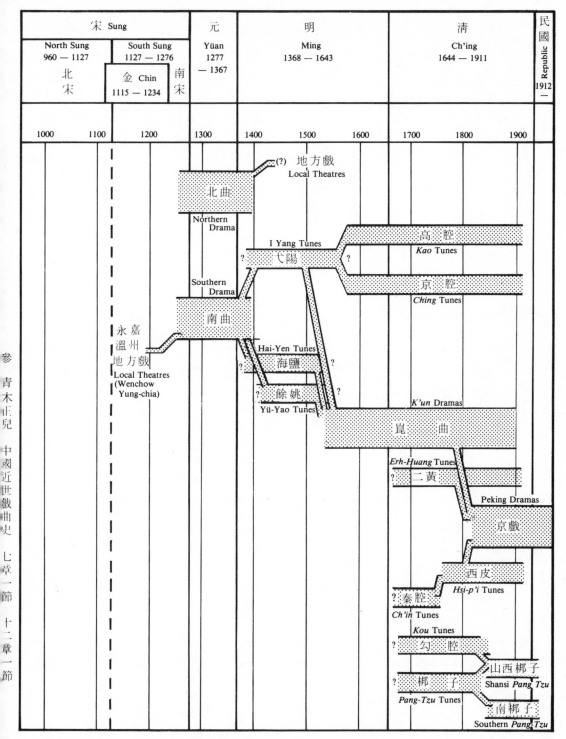

TABLE VI   Schools of Chinese Drama

281

CHAPTER XXVIII

THE DECLINE OF *K'UN* DRAMAS
AND THE FUTURE OF THE CHINESE THEATRE

The gradual decline of *K'un* dramas from the middle of the eighteenth to the middle of the ninteenth century has been differently attributed to several causes: the change of general artistic taste from the refined and subtle to the obvious and exciting in late Ch'ing dynasty [1]; the destruction of Soochow, the home of *K'un* dramas during the T'ai-P'ing rebellion; the influence in Peking of a clique of Anhwei officials who could not understand *K'un* dramas, and others. [2]

It is questionable whether changes in literary styles must be accompanied by changes in music and theatre, especially when, as in late Ch'ing dynasty, literary movements were not particularly connected with the theatre. In any case, to say that the change in style is due to a change in taste is to beg the question. It is true that there was a clique of Anhwei officials in Peking and that with the destruction of Soochow the musicians and players of *K'un* dramas were dispersed and records lost, but these events happened too late to explain the initial stages of the decline, though there is no doubt that they contributed to the final stages. [3]

   "In the middle of Ch'ing dynasty there were a group of Anhwei officials in Peking and for these, for some time, a few Hui dramas were occasionally

---

[1]   Wang Kwang-Ch'i, *Üeber die chinesische klassische Oper* (1934).

[2]   Aoki Masaru gives the following reasons for the decline of *K'un* dramas: 1. craze for the new on the part of the audience, 2. low taste of the audience, and 3. people in Peking could not understand southern music. 青木正兒, 中國近世戲曲史, 十二章二節; 參, 盧冀野, 中國戲劇概論, 十一章.

[3]   Prof. Ch'i Ju-Shan also mentioned that the voice in the style of singing in the *K'un* dramas is too weak and is unsuitable for large theatres. His dating of the decline of *K'un* dramas is: in the reigns of Ch'ien Lung (1736-1796) and Chia Ch'ing (1796-1820) — *K'un* dramas were in supremacy; in the reigns of Hsien Feng (1851-1862) and T'ung Chih (1862-1875) — *K'un* dramas mixed with *P'i-Huang* styles; in the early part of the reign of Kuang Hsü (1875-1909) — there were few *K'un* dramas but they were still played; now (1935) Mei Lan-Fang has more than eighty *K'un* dramas which, for lack of actors to play with him, he cannot produce. 齊如山, 京劇之變遷, 頁十. The dates of T'ai-P'ing rebellion are: 1850-1864.

heard. After the decline of *K'un* dramas and the incapability of I-Yang tunes (弋陽腔) to satisfy the audience, Hui tunes became popular because they were easy to understand and sonorous and pleasing. More people in Peking came to like them and Hui troupes came into the city and took over the classical stage''. [4]

The true reason for the loss of support for *K'un* dramas appears to lie in their inherent characteristics rather than in external pressure. The development of many Chinese arts follows a certain general pattern which can be traced in various schools of poetry and music in the past and is already showing itself in the Peking dramas. A style of art passes through several stages in its development, as follows. In the first stage, we find a few artists with courage and originality using the material from foreign or popular sources to build a style with new powers of expression. They are free from rules of composition and are guided only by their genius. The public accept their works as unorthodox but brilliant achievements and do not worry about the lack of tradition in them. In the second stage, we find the less adventurous and better informed part of the critics being won over and the pedants complaining with nostalgic regrets about the replacement of the old style by the new. At the same time the first generation of great artists has been replaced by a second generation of minor ones, experiments diminish and imitations increase. In the third stage, the founders of the new style have passed from living memory and become legends. New artists, in order to facilitate their learning, resort to rules derived from earlier works. Creative efforts disappear and the art suffers losses in successive imitations without being replenished by new creative achievements. By this time the art is sufficiently old and the public sufficiently wide for systematic criticism to be established, but as the critics have neither direct knowledge nor true understanding of the earliest works they have no idea of the original vitality and freedom, instead, they admire the eclectic and imitative works of later artists, with the result that their aesthetics is based on traditional value which "the great artists of old" are supposed to have cherished and for which no explanation is necessary. From then on, criticism, which should stimulate the development of the art, tends to petrify it, till in the last stage, the true qualities of the earliest works are entirely forgotten and artists impose on themselves more and more complicated and exacting rules. Pride and fastidiousness become standards of value; difficulty is valued for its own sake. The task of criticism then consists of the derivation of further rules from standard works and writing nostalgic panegyrics upon bygone achievements.

Conservatism and the pride in pseudo-aesthetics could sustain the mere form of the art in this way for a considerable length of time, but as the audience becomes more and more expert it also becomes smaller and smaller till at last only those who

---

[4] 王夢生, 梨園佳話, 一章, 徽調之興.

have the taste for complex artificial standards remain devotees, then the time is ripe for another form to emerge which will give genuine artistic pleasure to a new public.

In the actual case, these four stages of development necessarily overlapped, for example, there were creative artists and independently minded critics at all times, but as a whole the more daring artists and critics diminish gradually.

This, it is believed, is what happened to the *K'un* dramas in the three hundred years of their existence.

Some writers traced a trend towards complicated rules of versification in the history of Chinese poetry, culminating in the southern school of dramas:

"In poems of regular verses, the modern style has more restrictions than the ancient, but poems of irregular verses are harder to write than those of regular verses. Dramatic poetry as a whole is harder than lyrical poetry, including those of irregular verses, but in it, the southern style is more difficult than the northern. All this is because the rules of versification became in each step more complicated". [5]

Even the poet and scholar of to-day, Wu Mei, took pride in difficulty for its own sake, and stated paradoxically:

"In writing dramatic poetry one must not be afraid of the difficulty: the more difficult the easier it is to be good". [6]

The increasing complication of the rules of versification is however a fallacy, being based on such periods of each style in which rules were formulated and observed. At the beginnings of each style there were no rules.

In Peking dramas, unorthodox styles were at first looked upon with suspicion, but after the innovators had died, they became legendary figures and their style became the standard of excellence.

"At one time T'an Hsin-P'ei (譚鑫培) was considered to be lesser than Ch'eng Ch'ang-Keng (程長庚) and Yü San-Sheng (余三勝), because of his dexterous ornamentation and shifting of beats. Now T'an's style becomes the standard of good singing". "In the early years of Kuang Hsü's reign (1875-1909) the audience admired a long drawn sonorous note, later they admired the high notes, now (1935) they want ornaments". [7]

Even after the general public had accepted the new style some critics of the old school would still object:

"Nowadays the quick notes on the strings hurts one's ears and the repulsive singing expresses violent emotions and yet everybody thinks it is beautiful, not knowing that when music becomes unrestrained it is a sign that

---

[5] （明）孟子塞, 殘唐再創雜劇（卓人月）小引, 見, 焦循, 劇說, 卷四, 四十七款.

[6] 吳梅, 顧曲塵談, 一章.

[7] 齊如山, 京劇之變遷, 頁六至八.

the people have become vulgar and ungovernable, for the basis of music is the same as that of government''. [8]

The writer goes on to draw a parallel between the music from the late nineteenth century onwards to the wars and revolutions at that time and attributed the close correspondence to the mental state of the people, bemoaning the loss of ''the proper peaceful music''. There were, in the past, similar ideals of ethics in music and similar complaints of moral corruption in new styles of music. [9]

No one can tell as an eye-witness whether the actual performances of early *K'un* dramas were more lively than they are now and whether the appreciation was then more spontaneous than it is at present. One thing is certain: the early dramatists were no mean musicians themselves and knew thoroughly how to match the libretto to the music, but towards the end of Ch'ing dynasty dramatists would write words for arias which could not be sung.

"Before the reign of Ch'ien Lung (1736-1796) there was dramatic poetry and there was drama, but in the reign of Chia Ch'ing (1796-1820) and that of Tao Kuang (1821-1851) there was dramatic poetry but no drama''. [10]

"From the middle of the nineteenth century onwards though dramatists were not lacking most of them had no knowledge of music. They wrote with the belief that 'one can do it without knowing how' .'' [11]

Some Ming dynasty dramas are full of allusions and allegory and are in fact playthings of the poets, not even readable. [12] When the playwrights had lost contact with the theatre their dramas became unsuitable for the stage and the audience could not appreciate the niceties of the singing because singing was not based on the expression of the words but was based on accumulated ''tradition'' the meaning of which was no longer understood. Thus the *K'un* drama became an exotic delicacy. Theatre, unlike poetry, depends for its subsistence on the continual support of a body of audience. If the dramatic taste is such that only a few aesthetes can acquire it after a long initiation, that style of drama is doomed to extinction. When the *K'un* tunes, soon after their creation by the founder, Wei Liang-Fu, spread rapidly

---

[8] 姚華, 曲海一勺, 第二, 原樂, 六款.

[9] cf. Ku Chen's (顧臻) letter to emperor Ch'eng Ti 成帝 (reigned A.D. 326-343). 晉史, 樂志, 下. Ornamentation is probably one of the natural tendencies of musical development, but conservatism in taste is such that at its first appearance the guardians of musical heritage oppose it. In the Greek theatre the simplicity of the music of the Aeschylean period was later replaced by the musical innovations of Timotheus which were distinguished by variety and flexibility but were considered corruptions by contemporary critics. The style was described as like ''the intricate movements of ants in a nest'' but in spite of the ridicule of Aristophanes, it won the day and was used l by Euripides and later dramatists. Haigh, *The Attic Theatre*, 321 *et seq.*

[10] 吳梅, 戲曲概論, 卷下.

[11] 盧冀野, 中國戲劇概論, 十章, 頁二四八.

[12] *Ibid.*

through the southern provinces, the taste for them could not have taken long to acquire. If the appreciation at that time was different from what it is now the style of singing must too have changed: the singers themselves would not know how to sing with genuine expression unless they knew how to appreciate such expression. It is not unreasonable therefore to believe that *K'un* dramas suffered through the codification of critics and artists till at the end of the last century their devotees could boast of little other than sophistication. Therefore they were replaced by the more expressive Peking dramas.

Towards the last years of the popularity of *K'un* dramas the performance was more a recital than a play:

> "When I was in the city (Peking) there were people who loved *K'un* tunes and would bring *Chui Po Ch'iu* (綴白裘 a collection of libretti) to every performance, put it on a desk in front of them and count the beats with their fingers. Everybody respected them as experts". [13]

Similar tendency has been showing itself in the Peking dramas: the audience in Peking are proud of their "listening to the dramas" (聽戲) and deprecates "watching the dramas" (看戲) by the southerners. Yet dramatic music, like dramatic poetry, cannot live long outside the theatre, there is no future in such music. Of the conditions at the beginning of the nineteenth century one writer said:

> "Although the singers of *K'un* tunes are exact in enunciation unless the listener looks at the libretto he cannot understand the words". [14]

The reason for this is twofold: the diction was excessively sophisticated (雅) and there might be musical ornaments.

> "The method of singing a word in a long note can be clarified by the method used by Masters of Ceremonies. When they shout *'pai'* (kneel), the man has to kneel and then bow his head, which takes some time. If the Master of Ceremonies pronounces it as one word, the time is too short, and his voice cannot follow the whole movement as it should do, hence he uses *'pu — ai'* ." [15]

This method can sometimes lead to unintelligibility.

The loss of theatrical qualities — the expressiveness of the delivery and the acting — started very early and became critical only in late Ch'ing dynasty. Of the dramatist T'ang Hsien-Tzu (湯顯祖) of the sixteenth century it was said:

> "He wrote to express his ideas and did not care if the pronunciation of the words broke all the throats in the world". [16]

---

[13] 青木正兒, 中國近世戲曲史, 十二章三節, 引, 梁章鉅, 浪跡續談.
[14] 焦循, 花部農譚, 引言.
[15] 李笠翁, 曲話, 演習第三, 二款.
[16] 王驥德, 曲律, 卷四, 二十二款.

From then onwards, many plays known for the beauty of language have been criticized for the disregard of musical requirements. It is well known that there were no military plays among the *K'un* dramas and that the acting consisted of statuesque postures with one posture for each word in the arias. Spectacular and lively military plays were popular in Ming dynasty, hence they must have been ousted from the *K'un* dramas by the refinement of poetical and musical taste. Acting became lively again in the *P'i-Huang* and *Pang-Tzu* dramas (皮黃, 梆子) and there is greater specialization in the techniques of the male and the female roles (生, 旦) as shown by the finer subdivisions in each of these types. The dullness of some dramatic performances as early as the seventeenth century can be surmised in the following:

"One secret of dramatic writing is to banish sleepiness. Once the audience are overcome by sleepiness even heavenly music and dance by the fairies cannot attract their attention; playing to them becomes like bowing to a mud statue or talking to a moulded idol. I have often told the actors that the best part of a drama is usually at the end; if a spectator has two or three naps, when he wakes up he may feel fresh but having missed some part of the story he cannot understand what he sees. For this reason comic stage business is really the 'waking potion' of the theatre; its importance lies in keeping the audience fresh". [17]

"In the theatrical profession the actors all say that singing is difficult; speaking is easy: in speaking it is only necessary to remember the script well, but in singing one has also to remember the tunes and to remember them thoroughly". [18]

This is opposite to the modern saying "a thousand catties of declamation to four ounces of singing" and indicates the relatively expressionless declamation at the time this was written, hence the author's emphasis on expression in the spoken parts which followed the above passage. On expressionless singing he said:

"Nowadays those who learn to sing first learn the script by heart and then sing it to the tunes; after that the learning is considered complete. As to the explanation of the meaning of the dialogue, not that it is never done but there is no such general practice. Hence an aria can be sung for a day, a year or a lifetime without one's knowing what it says and to whom it is addressed. The mouth sings, the mind doesn't, there is music in the throat but none in the face and the body. This is expressionless singing, like children reciting by rote. Even with correct melody and enunciation, this is still not good singing". [19]

With the decay of the *K'un* dramas, the Chinese theatre lost its last link with the

---

[17] 李笠翁, 曲話, 詞曲第五.
[18] 李笠翁, 曲話, 演習第四.
[19] *Ibid.* 演習第三, 一款.

classical dramas and the traditional method of dramatic writing. [20] In spite of the success of the Peking dramas as theatre, scholars have been looking forward to a new school of literary dramas to continue the history of the Chinese drama. [21] Some looked towards the western-styled naturalistic dramas [22] and others to a new school of opera [23] for a successor. That scholars refuse to take the Peking dramas seriously is because of the lack of literary value in them, for there seems to be a tacit assumption that if a theatre is to have artistic value its script must be good literature. The literary value of the Chinese drama, however, has by no means been uniform throughout its history (although the Chinese drama has perhaps never been as feeble as now) and there was a Chinese theatre before dramas were written at all.

The Chinese have a large reserve of artistic material in the local theatres and it was from this reservoir that the Peking dramas rose in the last century, as the southern dramas did at the beginning of Ming dynasty, to meet the needs of the educated part of the Chinese people. As long as the taste and need for a classical theatre exists, there will always be a classical theatre. It is hardly justified therefore to think that the tradition of the Chinese theatre ceased with the passing of the *K'un* dramas, and it cannot be denied that the Peking dramas have won the support of the most discerning part of the Chinese audience. The high artistic value of the Peking dramas *as performed* is due to the cultivation of theatrical taste among the *literati* in the late nineteenth century: theatre-going had become a cult, and theatregoers were addicts. It is true that readable dramas are no longer being written, but it must be remembered that Chinese dramas were never written simply to be read, but always to be performed, and dramas fit for production are still being written. It is difficult to maintain therefore, either that there is a vacuum in the tradition of the Chinese theatre or that workable dramatic writing has ceased. One can only say that in the change which occurred in the classical theatre in the last century or two the literary standard of the script has fallen to almost the lowest possible level. Only to those interested in the script as reading material does the problem arise: how to raise its literary standard.

As the Chinese drama is a musical as well as a poetical work, the problem of

---

[20] The practice of modifying the text broke the continuity and stability of the tradition but it has the merit of more lively performances. The actors' talent is part of the basis of a dramatic performance and that part is by no means constant — cf. Henry Irving's Shakespearean productions — and the text has to be changed to suit it. Other factors that led to changes in the text are: local dialect, different music, change of taste and the need for shorter dramas occasionally.

[21] Aoki Masaru compared the *K'un* dramas to the tottering Chou dynasty and the Peking dramas to the short-lived Ch'in dynasty and asked where the founder of Han is. 青木正兒, 中國近世戲曲史, 十二章二節.

[22] 盧冀野, 中國戲劇概論, 十二章.

[23] 周貽白, 中國戲劇小史, 八章.

literary quality cannot be isolated from the music and the poetry. Throughout the whole history of the Chinese drama up to the last hundred years, the dramatist was, or was supposed to be, a librettist who wrote libretti to fit existing tunes and a good dramatist must be not only a good poet but also a competent musician and phonologist. It was because play-writing passed into the hands of scholars who were poets but not musicians that the true creative force dried up. The production of readable dramas unfit for the stage flourished but the theatre lost the support of literary men and this was no small element in the decline of the old theatre. In a way, the decline of dramatic writing from Yüan to Ch'ing dynasty was inevitable. Yüan dramatists drew the musical material (which was also the model for the dramatic poetry) from the music of Sung dynasty. This reservoir of music was exhausted in the later dynasties, partly because of changed social conditions which were no longer favourable to the production of popular music and partly because poetry was no longer written to be sung. Later dramatists, therefore, used the old tunes over and over again, and as the original tradition of music became gradually lost, blind observance or total disregard of the partially understood rules set up for the guidance of the poets led to feeble dramatic writing and the whole creative process was diseased, till at last dramatic poetry could no longer be written in the old way. Raising the literary quality of the written dramas will not, therefore, by itself rejuvenate the Chinese theatre.

There is no doubt that a long, and once glorious, tradition of dramatic composition has been lost and is now replaced by improvisation based on limited musical resources, but there is no reason why the tradition cannot be re-built on new foundations. The classical dramas of Yüan dynasty were born when the efforts of scholars, who were equipped with musical and poetical talents, turned to the popular art *as it was*. They wrote dramas which were good primarily for the actual performances and only incidentally good for reading. The Chinese theatre to-day lacks good poetry but its more serious and more deep-rooted defect lies in its crude musical foundation derived from the local theatres. (Its metrical and musical resources are of the simplest kind and its rhyming system — 十三轍 — limits the choice of words in the arias). Good acting and singing can cover, as they have done, feeble and puerile libretti but unsound musical foundation will hamper the development of the music, and without music the Chinese theatre cannot survive. The elementary principles of music such as temperance, scale, key, standard pitch and modes have been studied by the Chinese musicians as early as, if not earlier than, T'ang dynasty and a large amount of literature exists on these subjects. The education of the musicians and singers and the construction of the instruments can certainly be improved without affecting other features of the Peking dramas. The wealth of music in the dramas of Yüan dynasty was not due to individual composers but was inherited from Sung dynasty in the forms of dance music, ballad, Taoist music, foreign tunes and even vendors' cries. (24) If the singers who laid the foundations of the Peking dramas could weld the several schools of local music into a new expressive style, there is no reason why musicians who can now be better educated than they were and can have access through scores and phonograph records to a far greater store of ancient and modern, classical and popular music and to the music of many lands, could not, if they apply themselves to the task, build up a repertoire of tunes for the arias even greater than that of the Yüan dynasty and renew it by fresh additions constantly. The peculiar phonology of the Chinese language makes it necessary either for the dramatist to write dramas to fit the music or for the singers or musicians to compose the music to fit the words. The former is perhaps a healthier practice because when the dramatist has a large number of tunes to choose from his poetic inspiration need not suffer undue fetters (as has been shown in the achievements of the Yüan dramatists), but if he writes without regard to music, the singer, who does not have a large number of alternative pieces of music at his disposal, is unlikely to be able to fit good tunes to the words, and as performed, a good aria on indifferent words is a greater success than a dull aria on beautiful poetry. It is only when lost musical tradition can be replenished and when dramatists are not merely scholars but are writers in close touch with the theatrical needs of the time that healthy development can be maintained; otherwise, dramatic poetry would eventually be written for a set of rules which are no longer explicable and literary virtuosity would be valued for its own sake, as has happened before.

"After the middle of Ming dynasty dramatic writers composed dramas by following the metrical construction of the older works. They vied with each other in the novelty of literary ideas but the connection with music was lost and drama became a matter of writing poetry to be read". (25)

When drama can only be read it atrophies like a biological organ which has lost its function. Above all the lost art of matching music to words and words to music should be salvaged from the rules and traditions by studying the basis of those that are significant and deleting those that are meaningless.

The losses in Peking dramas are already alarming. Between one and two hundred tunes for the percussions of the orchestra were at one time known, but most

---

(24) "In the capital the vendors all have their distinctive cries. People take the melody, make it into tunes and fit them with words".（宋）高承, 事物紀原, 卷九, 吟叫. "People now added music to the cries of the vendors thereby making songs out of them". 吳自牧, 夢梁錄, 卷二, 卷二十, 妓樂. These tunes were used in the dramas of Sung and Yüan dynasties. 王國維, 宋元戲曲史, 八章, "叫聲". Street cries in Paris and London were also used in French and English tunes from the sixteenth century onwards — Scholes, *Oxford Companion to Music*, STREET MUSIC, 2.

(25) 姚燮, 復道人今樂考證, 雜劇院本傳奇之稱, 引, 梁廷枏 (1796-1861).

of these are now lost. [26] There was a tradition that the two gongs should be related in pitch, and that the strings were tuned to the smaller gong, but musicians do not do this now. [27] The style of acting in battle scenes was at one time different for different plays, but it is now mostly the same in all dramas. One actor could still talk about the different styles in 1935. [28] There was a clown called Yü Wu [29] who was specially famous in seven plays, but he did not teach them to any pupils and they are now all lost, [30] and similarly with the skill of Yang San, [31] also a clown. [32] In the reign of Hsien Feng (1851-1862) an actor who played masked characters, called Chang K'uei-Kuan [33] was known for the beauty of his mime of swimming but he too left no pupils. [34] The art of acting in the Chinese theatre is such that creations consist of details instead of principles or methods, hence unless one records them in films they are easily lost. Prof. Ch'i Ju-Shan could remember seeing more than a hundred plays which were in 1935 no longer being played. [35] For new plays that he saw, he mentioned sixteen titles. [36]

The lack of assistance from the educated class is practically complete.

"Many scholars have been interested in the theatre but most of them merely learn from the professionals. These amateurs do not create anything new, they learn something from one good actor and perhaps teach it to others. In my knowledge there are only two amateurs who understand thoroughly the principles of singing and invented many tunes: Sun Ch'un-Shan (孫春山) and Lin Ssu (林四) from whom Ch'en Te-Lin (陳德霖) and Wang Yao-Ch'ing (王瑤卿) respectively learned many melodies. Sun had eight lines in *lento* for a drama [37] which Ch'en Te-Lin remembered but the aria was never put on stage". [38]

There is probably a natural tendency towards stylization in acting in all theatres. In the European theatres we hear that Molière introduced a more natural style of acting and so did Garrick, whose triumphant debut as Richard III was said to be due to his easy and familiar style as compared with the laboured manners of Quin.

---

[26] 王夢生, 梨園佳話, 一章, (末段); 齊如山, 戲班, 二章 "塲面".
[27] 齊如山, 京劇之變遷, 頁十五; 戲劇脚色名詞考, 八章.
[28] 齊如山, 京劇之變遷, 頁十四.
[29] 毓五
[30] *Ibid.* 頁十五
[31] 楊三
[32] *Ibid.* 頁五四
[33] 張奎官
[34] *Ibid.* 頁五一
[35] *Ibid.* 頁三八
[36] *Ibid.* 頁十四
[37] 二本虹霓關
[38] *Ibid.* 頁五

"Garrick's nature displaced Quin's formalism and in precisely the same way did Kean displace Kemble". (*The Tatler* of 1831, quoted in A. M. Nagler, *Sources of Theatrical History,* 453.)

Charles Macklin, the eighteenth century actor famous for his Shylock, was also known for his natural delivery and was not at first well received. [39] These playwrights and actors reaped success by their insight into sincere dramatic expression and their courage to pit it against the stiffened style of their predecessors which the audience had learned to like by sheer habit. These are in fact the conspicuous backward steps in a stream of gradual and unnoticeable stylization. (If there were no gradual stylization one has to conclude that acting was, in primitive theatres, extremely stylized which is impossible because it was then improvised). The problem of the tradition of acting is then to keep the conventions from degenerating into routine and the style from becoming mannerism.

In the history of the European theatre we hear repeatedly of innovators in "natural" styles of acting but rarely of advocates of stylization.

"The tendency of the Kemble style of acting was to emphasize and stress the measure and rhythmic structure of verse. Macready, who aimed at belonging to the 'natural' school of actors, broke away from tradition". (Summers, *The Playhouse of Pepys,* 48.)

"(On Macready) In speaking he paid less attention to the modulation of his tones, and to the rhythmical flow of verse than any other great actor whom we remember". (*The Daily News,* 1851, quoted in Summers, *op. cit.,* 48 f.)

In England, according to Gordon Craig, Kemble, Kean, Macready and Irving were one after another thought to be more "natural". [40] He explains it as difference in kind — different types of artificiality — rather than difference in degree. There may be some difference in kind, but as the word "natural" was repeatedly used some change to freer style seems to be indicated.

In France, the actress Clairon (1726-1803) was said to change from stiff and declamatory style to freer and more natural style in about 1753, on the advice of Marmontel (1723-1799), the dramatist and critic. Dumesnil (1713-1803), rival to Clairon, was also supposed to be more naturalistic than her predecessor. [41] Duclos (1668-1748) was in her time considered stiff and artificial and in her old age she was replaced by the freer methods of the younger generation. Champmesle (1642-1698), from whom Duclos learned her art, favoured the chanting sing-song style and taught it to Desmares (1682-1753) who was replaced by Lecouvreur (1692-1730). Of Dumesnil it was said:

---

[39] For descriptions of the grandiloquent style see Nagler, *op. cit.,* Ch. X.

[40] *On the Art of the Theatre,* 290.

[41] *Vide* Nagler, *op. cit.,* 292 ff.

"Declamation, which, till the time of mademoiselle La Couvreur was a measured recitative, a noted song in a manner, obstructed still farther those outbursts of nature which are represented by a word, by an attitude, by silence, by a cry which escapes in the anguish of grief. These strokes were first made known to us by mademoiselle Dumesnil, when, in *Merope,* with distracted eyes and a broken voice, she, raising her trembling hand, prepared to sacrifice her own son; when Narbas stopped her; when, letting her dagger fall, she was seen to faint away in the arms of her women; when she started from this momentary death with the transports of a mother, and when afterwards, darting forward to Polyfontes and crossing the stage in an instant, she, with tears in her eyes, a face as pale as death, thick sobs and arms extended, cried out, *'Barbare, il est mon fils'* . . . It is but a few years since players have ventured to be what they should be, that is, living pictures; before, they declaimed". (Voltaire, *Appel à toutes les nations: des divers changements arrivés à l'art tragique* (1761), *Works,* London, (1770), XXV).

She seemed to go even further than Clairon, and relied on the inspiration of the moment.

"What acting was ever more perfect than Clairon's? Think over this, study it; and you will find that at the sixth performance of a given part she has every detail of her acting by heart, just as much as every word of her part. . . Now with Dumesnil it is a different matter; she is not like Clairon. She comes on the stage without knowing what she is going to say; half the time she does not know what she is saying: but she has one sublime moment". (Diderot, *Paradoxe sur le comédien,* trans. W. H. Pollock, (1841) 9 ff.)

European critics are also conscious of the deterioration of tradition into meaningless routine:

"I have been shown by a competent and worthy actress how Mrs. Siddons played Lady Macbeth. She would move to the centre of the stage and would begin to make certain movements and certain exclamations which she believed to be a reproduction of what Mrs. Siddons had done. I presume she had received these from some one who had seen Mrs. Siddons. The things which she showed me were utterly worthless in so far as they had no unity, although one action here, another action there, would have some kind of reflected value; and so I began to see the uselessness of this kind of tuition. . ." (G.Craig, *On the Art of the Theatre,* 6.)

"The first generation provides models and later critics reduce to rules what the artistic sense of this generation had found to be expedient. This was only too helpful for mediocrity". (*Oxford Companion to the Theatre,* (1951), 397.)

"Some errors, handed down from age to age,

Plead Custom's force, and still possess the stage . . .

When Falstaff stands detected in a lye,

Why, without meaning, rowls Love's glassy eye?

Why? — there's no cause — at least no cause we know —

It was the Fashion twenty years ago".

(Churchill, *The Rosciad* (1761). *Poems by C. Churchill* (1766), Vol. I. p. 22).

The guardians of a tradition think they are preserving something by keeping the style of acting from changing but what they actually do is make it gradually more stereotyped. Where there is no tradition, actors do not benefit by the great artists before them nor are they hampered by their tradition; each starts from a more or less improvised state near to the spontaneous expressions. In a long tradition like that of the Chinese theatre, however, each generation start their career by learning from the old; repetition stabilizes the form which, by the time the original creators had faded beyond living memory, became hollow mannerisms and was accentuated to make up for the lack of content till at last it became sufficiently empty for the audience to welcome a new and more spontaneous style. If the new style were introduced too early it would have been rejected for lack of tradition but now it appeared refreshing for the richness of its feelings.

Gradual stylization and occasional stereotyping which occurred in the European theatre would have happened too in the Chinese theatre. Chinese conservatism did not allow such changes as Baron and Clairon made in the French theatre; a tradition, for instance, the *K'un* dramas, was upheld at all costs, till it became a set of artificial rules, too devoid of living artistic creation and too rigid for new blood to revive it and had to be entirely replaced.

The problem of preserving the theatrical tradition is essentially the same in China and in Europe and it is: how to keep not only the external form but the spirit of the past achievements and how to free the present generation from the restrictive influence of tradition.

Part IV
The Heritage of the Chinese Theatre

CHAPTER XXIX

THE ORIGINS OF THE CHINESE THEATRE AND DRAMA

Political conservatism, racial temperament and the size of China combine to make changes in the Chinese history in general slower than those in the history of Europe. This is particularly true in the history of the drama: in Europe the Greeks developed it in much less than a century from the revelry connected with Dionysian worship to the highest achievements in dramatic writings, but in China centuries passed between the beginnings of simple impersonation and the rise of the drama. For this reason, the beginning of the Chinese theatre, unlike that of the European theatre, cannot be located with any degree of precision unless one adheres to an exact definition, and according as that definition is general or specific the beginning of the Chinese theatre may be considered as early or late, respectively.

One may begin with the definition of the theatre as *public entertainment by human performers*. This definition would exclude equestrian shows and trained animals but would include singing, instrumental music and acrobatics which are indeed still part of the popular theatre in Europe to-day, for example, the music hall. The beginning of the theatre, thus defined, is the same as that of public entertainment in general because in ancient times entertainment could hardly be provided with mechanical means as in our cinemas and fair grounds to-day and performing animals also came late in history. As such the Chinese theatre may be said to begin with the court jesters of late Chou dynasty. These jesters were personal companions to the dukes and princes they served, as shown by the various references to their witty contributions to ordinary conversation; [1] nevertheless they performed at banquets before the court and its guests, hence they may be said to have provided public entertainment. [2] From late Chou dynasty onwards, the Chinese theatre, thus defined, may be said to have had a generally continuous existence, because the

---

[1] 史記, 滑稽列傳.

[2] Women musicians who were at this time sent from one duke to another as presents (論語, 微子) should probably also be included under the head of early Chinese theatre, but they are not known to have performed in public.

pageants, circus, spectacles and masquers' dances of Han dynasty and the farces and dramatic dances of later times were all performed by human players. [3]

Some people may prefer to define theatre as *public entertainment that involves impersonation and mimicry,* thereby disqualifying recitals, pure dance, acrobatics and conjuring as theatre. By this definition modern ballet is theatre because it usually involves impersonation, puppet plays are theatre even though they are not performed by human actors and pageants are also theatre though they are not dramas. Thus defined the Chinese theatre can be said to begin only in Han dynasty because the court jesters did not, as a rule, impersonate other people and the impersonation in religious ceremonies cannot be considered as theatre because it was not for amusement; it was only in the pageants of Han dynasty that legends and mythological personages were represented in tableaux and short scenes. In this way, the Chinese theatre may be considered to begin among non-dramatic forms of entertainment, such as circus and juggling and the more elaborate dramatic representation of later times, was, even at the height of the Chinese dramatic literature, mixed with the exhibition of physical skills of all sorts because, it may be said, it came from the tableaux and short scenes among circus shows. This suggests that to the Chinese people theatre meant public entertainment in general and that the fact that some form of it involved impersonation, did not appear to them to justify differentiating that form from the rest, hence in Sung dynasty the term *tsa-chü* [4] meant recitations, dances, humorous talks as well as short farces. When *chu-kung-tiao* [5] was recited and sung in the same programme as dramatic performances in Sung and Yüan dynasties the audience probably went to the theatre to enjoy the singing, and the poetry and impersonation could have been considered as an incidental feature, at least by those particularly sensitive to music. Similarly, to those who appreciated the physical skill the military plays could be very similar to pure displays of acrobatics and pugilism which were among the different forms of popular entertainment of that time. This may also explain why in the modern Chinese theatre where dramas are no longer played among acrobatic and juggling exhibitions these elements are absorbed into the style of the dramatic performance.

Theatre may also be defined, as most western people would do, simply as *dramatic performance.* Since the Chinese drama developed slowly through more than a thousand years from simple tableaux representing popular legends in Han dynasty to the lengthy dramas of Ming dynasty, it is impossible to say when the Chinese drama began without specifying clearly what is meant exactly by the word

---

[3] In A.D. 119 emperor Yüan Ti 元帝 abolished the wrestling and circus shows but emperor Ming Ti 明帝 (reigned A.D. 227-239) revived them—王國維, 宋元戲曲史, 一章; 馬端臨, 文獻通考, 卷一四七. This is a short gap in the long periods of the Chinese theatrical history:

[4] 雜劇

[5] 諸宮調

"drama". The Chinese drama may be said to have developed in three stages, with deepening interest in the plot, and "drama" may mean any of the three types of theatrical performance. In the first, from early Han dynasty to Sui dynasty (second century B.C. to the beginning of the seventh century A.D.) simple dramatic scenes were performed among circus acts and in these short scenes there was hardly any plot, rather, the legendary or historical names were tagged to a spectacle or wrestling act to enhance its interest. Circus acts and spectacles, like pure dance, are basically impersonal displays of skill, legendary background adds little to them and the audience could ignore it without missing the essence of the show. In the second stage, from Sui to near the end of Sung dynasty (from the seventh to the thirteenth century), plot or action was essential to the understanding of the farce and the dramatic dances of this period. There was little interest in the story as such, yet, unlike the tableaux of the Han dynasty, the farce and the dramatic dances could not be effective without the audience understanding the story in them. However, the farces and dances in this period were too short to allow any development of the plot: the representation could cover only simple dramatic action without antecedent and subsequent events. Drama, in the ordinary sense of the word, means the representation of a series of developing events from some beginning towards a crisis and ending in the outcome of that crisis. It was only in the third stage of the development of the Chinese drama, from the last part of Sung dynasty till to-day (from the thirteenth century to the present) that drama in this sense existed. At the end of Sung dynasty, partly through the momentum of the expanding and multiplying farces and dramatic dances, partly through the stimulation of puppets and shadow plays, and partly through the musical and metrical innovations in the comedian's songs and the minstrel's recitations of Sung dynasty, the Chinese drama emerged. Even though many dramas in Yüan dynasty were short pieces with simple plots and it was only in Ming dynasty that long stories were represented in full, this stage of the development is distinguished from previous dramatic efforts in that in the plot one event now led to another and that there was some climax, however mild, in each play.

Thus the beginning of the Chinese theatre may be placed in late Chou dynasty (about the sixth century B.C.) or in Han dynasty (about the first century B.C.) and that of the Chinese drama in Sui dynasty (seventh century A.D.) or late Sung dynasty (thirteenth century) according to the particular definitions of theatre and drama chosen. Much controversy would be unnecessary and some apparent contradictions explained if a pedagogical definition of theatre or drama were attached to every statement about their beginnings.

The *origin* of the Chinese theatre has been traced to different elements in the ancient Chinese culture: some scholars found it in the shamans' rituals, some in the ceremonial dances, others in ancient court music and still others in ancient folk dances. [6] The disagreement between the different theories is, however, more apparent than real. The problem would be clarified if in each case a precise meaning is designated to the word "origin". Theatre, however defined, consists of several elements such as impersonation, dance, dramatic action and so forth, and each element may have a separate source. To say that the origin of the Chinese theatre is the ceremonial dance, or the court musicians, is not to make a very significant statement and it would be futile to defend one such statement against another. Instead of comparing categorical statements regarding the origin of the Chinese theatre, it would be more informative to study the actual mode of its development. If the court jesters may be considered as the earliest Chinese actors then the sources of their performance may be said to be the ultimate sources of the Chinese theatre. It may be assumed that the court jesters could not invent something entirely new, something without any connection with the past. They must have derived their dance and song from court music and ceremonial dances, especially as they were themselves musicians by profession and ceremonial dancers were at that time in the charge of officials in the court. The ceremonial dances might in turn be connected with earlier religious ceremonies and folk music. In this sense all the music and dance in ancient times are direct or indirect sources of the Chinese theatre. [7]

According to tradition emperor Ming Huang 明皇 (reigned A.D. 712-756) of T'ang dynasty was the founder of the Chinese theatre, hence he is now deified as its patron god. Emperor Ming Huang was a sensitive music-lover and a proficient musician. He, according to legend, once visited the moon and learned a tune from the goddesses he met there.

"The emperor visited the moon with a magician in A.D. 742 at the Harvest Moon Festival and saw several hundred fairies dancing in a large court yard; he learned the music by heart and taught it to his own musicians in the following day". "The emperor visited the moon and heard some music but when he woke up he could remember only half of it. Yang Ching-Shu 楊敬述 happened to present the emperor with a tune so the emperor made the music he heard into an introduction to Yang's tune, because the style was similar". [8]

"He was versed in music and liked to play the drum and the flute and could compose

---

[6] 盧冀野, 中國戲劇概論, 一章, 頁五, 六; 青木正兒, 中國近世戲曲史, 一章一.

[7] Wit, also an element of the court jester's occupation, may be assumed to have been a part of court life previous to the court jesters although it might not have been consistently exploited for its entertainment value.

[8] Sources quoted in 郭茂倩, 樂府詩集, 卷五十六, 舞曲歌辭, 五. It appears that the legend was based on the unusual but by no means occult phenomenon of composing music in dreams and that the emperor's tune was similar in style to Yang Ching-Shu's because they were both derived from the music of that time.

music with ease". [9] "When his musicians made mistakes he would correct them". [10] He also established a music academy in his Pear Garden and trained three hundred court musicians and hundreds of women attendants in it and called them all "pupils of the Pear Garden" [11] which till to-day is the appellative for the theatrical profession. He composed music on many occasions though none of his works has been preserved [12] and he was the patron of some of the best known court jesters in the Chinese history who distinguished themselves in quick wit and in musicianship. [13]

It is to be remembered however that at the time of this music-loving ruler the Chinese drama was not yet developed. The performances in his Pear Garden were vocal and instrumental recitals, conventional farce [14] and dramatic dances. It is curious that even under such eminent and fervent patronage drama did not develop. As there was no notable advance made towards the drama, he hardly deserved the honour of being its founder; nevertheless his Pear Garden was the first Chinese music academy and he was one of the few Chinese rulers who took personal interest in the cultivation of music and its allied arts. He was certainly the first emperor to consider the theatre as a serious fine art and to attempt to raise its artistic level.

Since, as mentioned before, the development of the Chinese drama from the earliest simple dramatic representations covered many centuries and since the rise of the Chinese drama was related to many influences, the search for the origin of the Chinese drama (as distinguished from that of the Chinese theatre) is not a very rewarding task. It is more interesting to inquire why through more than ten centuries in which impersonation and dialogue were known drama did not develop sooner. The answer is different for different periods. In the earlier pageants and tableaux dramatic interest was choked by the love for spectacles. It is significant that the pageant grew in size till it reached mammoth scale in Sui dynasty but not in the direction of the drama. The farce and the dramatic dances could excite more interest in the plot, but the interest in unfolding events, based on curiosity and suspense, was unknown in China until the growth of fiction in connection with the story-tellers in T'ang dynasty. Even when the drama at last emerged the interest did not lie in the unfolding plot, but lay in the poetry, the music and the acting.

For the immediate predecessor of the Chinese drama, one may point, *for the script,* to *chu-kung-tiao* [15] and, *for the manner of production,* to the farce and dramatic dances of Sung dynasty.

---

[9] （唐）南卓，羯鼓錄，一段.
[10] 新唐書，禮樂志，十二.
[11] *Ibid.*
[12] 南卓，羯鼓錄，一段.
[13] 王國維，優語錄 *passim.*
[14] 參軍戲
[15] 諸宮詞

It was at one time believed that the Chinese drama was not indigenous. This belief was probably due to the apparently sudden rise of dramatic literature with the Mongol rule in Yüan dynasty. [16] That there was foreign influence in the making of Chinese drama, as there was in Chinese music and poetry, can hardly be denied: the circus of Han dynasty, the dramatic dance *Po-T'ou* [17] and some music in the Yüan dramas were all of alien origin. There is however no evidence that the early Chinese dramas were based on foreign models; [18] rather, the various forms of popular entertainment in Sung dynasty suggest strongly that drama was derived from them. The reason for the apparent sudden rise of the drama is twofold: the loss of early dramas and the diversion of literary talents into the theatre in Yüan dynasty. There was a reverse flow of talents in Ming dynasty:

"When our emperors started this present dynasty the whole nation turned to the Confucian teachings and scholars all felt that dramatic writing was below them. Thus old dramas were lost and now no one knows what they were like. There are musicians who can perform in the plays but the old music does not suit modern ears and the southerners do not understand northern tunes so that the audience and the players alike grew less and less every day". [19]

"The native officials deposed in Yüan dynasty directed their energy into dramatic writings out of spite" (because drama was not considered a presentable literature). [20]

---

[16] *Vide* H. A. Giles, *History of Chinese Literature,* Ch. 11.; R. F. Johnston, *The Chinese Drama* (1921), 20.

[17] 撥頭

[18] *Vide* 王國維, 宋元戲曲史, 十六章三節; 青木正兒, 中國近世戲曲史, 二章二節.

[19] （明）何元朗, 四友齋叢說, 見（新曲苑）四友齋曲說, 四款.

[20] 焦循, 劇說, 卷一, 三十六段, 引, 眞珠船; 黃雪簑, 靑樓集, 朱經序
cf. Native scholars in Ch'ing dynasty — also of foreign rule — worked on the textual criticism of ancient books owing to political censor. 魯迅, 中國小說史略, 頁三一四.

CHAPTER XXX

THE TRADITIONAL ATTITUDE AND MANNERS OF THE AUDIENCE

The connection between theatre and religion being slight in China, the Chinese theatre has developed unchecked along hedonistic lines. Indeed at the rise of the drama the pleasure-house was an important centre of theatrical life and its inmates and visitors were some of the first producers and audience, respectively, of the earliest Chinese dramas. Exposition of sociological and moral problems has never been the purpose of the Chinese theatre. [1] In the Chinese theatre of to-day, dramatic appreciation is mixed with eating and drinking and the dramas contain acrobatics and even juggling. It will be shown in the following that these habits of the audience of the Chinese theatre have a long tradition behind them.

Music and dance in the imperial court, even when they reached high artistic level, as in T'ang dynasty, were adjuncts to banquets and celebrations. [2] The dramatic performances at court banquets were often very informal: the actors, who were also court jesters, had licence to jest with the emperor personally. [3] The official programme of a royal banquet in Sung dynasty indicates that dramatic performances were not scheduled to follow the banquet but ran concurrently with it:

> "The emperor ascends the throne; the prime minister offers wine while the oboe, accompanied by the orchestra, plays music for toasts [4]; wine is brought in and the guests take their seats. The emperor lifts the cup; the guests stand behind their seats; music and song. Food is brought in.

---

[1] The European drama of to-day comes from the revival of classical culture in the Renaissance. The original seriousness of purpose in that movement has not yet entirely disappeared in the European theatre.

[2] "Music played at the emperor's meals" was called *shih-chü* 食舉（宋）郭茂倩; 樂府詩集. 卷十三, 燕射歌辭. cf. In Chou dynasty there were "dinner music" 燕樂 — music played at offerings and banquets" —（周禮, 春官, 大宗伯; 春官, 笙師), and "after-dinner music" 雍 —"music played at the end of dinners"—（論語, 八佾; 淮南子, 主術). Recreational music, like the *divertimento*, is also played at meals in Europe.

[3] （唐）南卓, 羯鼓錄, 三段; 王國維, 優語錄 *passim*.

[4] 傾盃, 三臺.

Juggling and acrobatic displays.

The emperor lifts his cup as a sign of invitation; the guests stand behind their seats; music and song.

An actor recites a speech and a poem on the virtues of the emperor and the gratitude of his subjects.

The orchestra plays a *suite*. [5]

The emperor lifts his cup; lute played.

Choral dance by children with a laudatory speech.

Plays (farce and dramatic dances); after which the emperor leaves and there is an interval.

The emperor re-enters, lifts his cup, while reed organ *sheng* [6] is played.

Display of football. [7]

The emperor lifts his cup; zither played. [8]

Choral dance by one hundred and fifty girls, with laudatory speech.

Plays.

The emperor lifts the cup for the last time, the guests stand behind their seats; orchestra plays''. [9]

Not only dramatic appreciation has been mixed with eating and drinking, dramatic performances were often part of a programme including other forms of entertainment. Among the court dances in T'ang dynasty were: ''dancers with goat-heads, nine-headed lions, pole-climbing, juggling, spitting flames, swallowing swords, somersaults and cart-wheels'' and somersaults belonged to the same department as the dramatic dances. [10] At a certain celebration the ''fish and dragon'' shows were so noisy that the angry emperor wanted to stop the celebration but it was suggested to him that a singer could quiet the spectators; this was tried and as the singing started ''the place became as quiet as if there were no spectators there''. [11] Drama was not developed then, but circus and animal masks were already

---

[5] 大曲

[6] 笙

[7] Chinese football originated in T'ang dynasty — 馬端臨, 文獻通考, 樂考, 二十, 蹵 鞠戲 — and was very popular in Sung dynasty; for descriptions see （明）汪雲程, 蹴鞠圖譜.

[8] 箏

[9] 宋史, 樂志, 十七. Other accounts of the state banquets — 周密, 武林舊事, 卷一, 聖節; 孟元老, 東京夢華錄, 卷九, 宰執親王宗室百官入內上壽; 吳自牧, 夢粱錄, 卷三, 宰執親王南班百官入內上壽賜宴 have: music (oboe, lute, flute, xylophone, zither), dances, speeches, plays, juggling, puppets, conjuring, acrobatics and women wrestling.

[10] 段安節, 樂府雜錄, 鼓架部.

[11] *Ibid* "歌"

part of the court music. A programme of entertainment in Sung dynasty performed for the emperor in the open air was as follows:

About a dozen drummers enter. Speech by the leader to the emperor. Flag-throwing.

Lions and leopards (masquers) enter. After a short dance they take their positions on the dancing ground.

Dancer with two flags in his hands performs.

Pole-climbing and tumbling.

More than a hundred brightly dressed soldiers enter. They hold pheasant feathers, shields and wooden swords and amid music arrange themselves in two semi-circles facing each other. Music played, and five to seven couples engage in mock fight.

Fire-cracker. Fireworks display, through which enters a dancer wearing a mask with husks and a wig of loose hair, spitting fire. His face is like a daemon's and he wears black trousers and a blue jacket with short back, both jacket and trousers covered with gold dots. He dances on his bare feet, carrying a large gong, and as he dances he sets off more fireworks.

Fire-cracker. Music played. Enter dancers with faces smeared blue and green, or wearing masks with gold eyes, in silk dresses and covered with leopard's skin. Dance in the manner of chasing spirits, striking the air with the axes, battle-knives and staffs they carry. [12]

Fire-cracker. Enter a dancer in green gown wearing a mask and a long beard, like Chung K'uei (鍾馗), followed by a man playing a small gong. [13]

Two or three thin and tall dancers enter: their bodies and faces are powdered and they wear golden eyes, looking like skeletons. Each has a silk girdle around his waist and each holds a whip. They run about in a ghostly mime.

Fire-cracker. A thick smoke rises; from it appear seven dancers with loose hair and tattooed bodies wearing short blue jackets and silk girdles. One of

[12] cf. the *painted face* of the Chinese theatre to-day.

[13] Chung K'uei is a benign spirit: "Emperor Ming Huang (明皇) of T'ang dynasty was once ill for about a month after an inspection at the military academy. One night he dreamed of two spirits, one big and one small: the smaller spirit, who had a large nose, wore red clothes and was without shoe on one foot, stole the emperor's jade flute and was chased by the bigger spirit, who wore a hat, a blue gown and a pair of leather sandals but whose arms were uncovered. He caught the smaller spirit, cut out the eyes and ate them. The emperor asked the bigger spirit who he was and he answered, 'I am a warrior who did not pass the official contest at the military academy and have devoted myself to chasing away evil spirits'. After this dream the emperor recovered from his illness and was strong again. He summoned his court painter and told him about the dream and wanted the scene to be painted". —(宋) 沈括, 補筆談, 卷二十六;(宋) 高 承, 事物紀原, 卷八.

them has a white flag in his hand and wears a small hat with gold ornaments on it, and the rest wear turbans and hold real knives. Mock fight; followed by the dancers slashing each other's faces and cutting open each other's chests.

Fire-cracker. Thick smoke rises. When it has dispersed one sees a circular cloth screen. Enter several dozens of masquers in strange costume like the statues of daemons and spirits in the temples.

Fire-cracker. Exit masquers. A man with a small gong leads in more than a hundred players with yellow and white powdered faces each holding a wooden sword. The man with the gong shouts orders to the rest and they bow to each other and dance. After their arrangements have been changed a few times they stand in one single line and two by two engage in mock fight. One after another they throw away the sword and throw themselves to the ground with a loud thud.

A man in rustic dress enters and talks for a while; a rustic woman enters and quarrels with the man. They fight with sticks, and at last the man carries the woman away on his back.

Military tattoo.

Two plays acted.

Equestrian shows''. (14)

The farce played by the rustic clowns was probably what was called ''miscellaneous impersonation'' (雜班) in Sung dynasty.

"Modern actors play in the miscellaneous impersonations . . . like physicians, fortune-tellers, courtezans and singers". (15)

"The miscellaneous impersonations (雜扮) which follow the main plays are mostly based on the ignorance of country people when they first see the city and country clowns in comic situations". (16)

At a birthday celebration "there were many forms of entertainment" including "plays, football and *chuan* (唱賺 ballads or song cycles)". (17)

In the dramas of Yüan dynasty (1277-1367) *lu-ch'i* (路歧) in theatrical slang meant actors and actresses, but the term also meant jugglers, acrobats, singers and other itinerant artisans who made their living by entertaining other people. (18) The moralist Wu Lai (吳萊) of the same dynasty complained that the ethical lessons in the dramas were "drowned by the somersaults, strugglings, and spear evolutions"

---

(14) 孟元老, 東京夢華錄, 卷七, 駕登寶津樓諸軍呈百戲.

(15) (宋) 趙彥衛, 雲麓漫鈔 (涉聞梓舊本) 卷十, 五款.

(16) 吳自牧, 夢粱錄, 卷二十, 妓樂; 參, 孟元老, 東京夢華錄, 卷七, 駕登寶津樓諸軍呈百戲.

(17) 周密, 武林舊事, 卷一, 聖節. The football display was by a professional troupe.

(18) 吳自牧, 夢粱錄, 卷二十, 百戲伎藝; 耐得翁, 都城紀勝, 井市; 元明雜劇, 藍采和, 一折, 仙呂點絳唇.

[19] and Marco Polo reported that at the royal banquet there were "comedians, instrumentalists, tumblers, jugglers and a tamed lion". [20] The public theatres in Sung and Yüan dynasties were not entirely for dramatic performances but also housed jugglers and minstrels. [21] In the account of a dramatic performance given in the novel *Shui Hu Chuan* (see Ch. XXVI) [22] the recitation of a story with singing *(chu-kung-tiao)* was to be followed by a play but the programme was interrupted by an argument. Of famous actors one book of Yüan dynasty records: "Wei was good in declamation; Wu in acting and Liu in somersaults". [23] The Chinese have always thought of the theatre as a place of general entertainment: the Chinese words for drama are *hsi* (戲) and *chü* (劇), *hsi* means "to amuse oneself" and *chü,* "to make sport of".

In Ming dynasty, "before the reign of Wan Li 萬曆 (1573-1620) the entertainment at royal banquets consisted of dramas of the northern style, in four sections, between which there were interludes of juggling, flag-manipulations and acrobatics". [24] Since the dramas of Yüan dynasty, both of the northern and of the southern school, were printed in Yüan dynasty without the division into "sections" or scenes, [25] these acrobatic shows were really interruptions — it is to be remembered that there is no front curtain in the Chinese theatre. Another description of performances in the palace in Ming dynasty says,

"... There were more than a hundred items in the performance each involving about a dozen players. The quality of the 'acts' varied widely: some of them were for refined taste, others were crude. As a whole the main object was to present comic situations; in some items in the programme the jokes were told by a speaker, in others they were acted in simple plays, like the farce. The

---

[19] 王圻, 續文獻通考, 卷百十九.

[20] *Travels,* Bk. II. Ch. 14 and 15.

[21] 孟元老, 東京夢華錄, 卷五, 京瓦伎藝, 卷七, 三月一日開金明池瓊林苑. In the fair grounds the variety of the entertainment was even greater, there were: story-telling, humorous talks, shadow plays, ballads, songs, farce, special impersonations, recitation of saints' lives, minstrels, jokes, riddles, conjuring, juggling, puppets, pole-climbing, rope-dancing, wrestling, mock fights, tumbling, skill with staff, weight lifting, football, bow and arrow, trained animals, trained birds and insects, kite-flying, snakes, fireworks, etc. — 周密, 武林舊事, 卷六, 諸色伎藝人. Trained animals included tortoises and frogs. — 陶宗儀, 輟耕錄, 卷二十二, 禽戲. Of riddles there were eight different types. — 耐得翁, 都城紀勝, 瓦舍衆伎; 吳自牧, 夢粱錄, 卷二十, 小說講經史. For descriptions of jugglers and acrobats and conjuring acts see 馬端臨, 文獻通考, 樂考, 二十.

[22] 水滸傳（百回本）, 五十五回.

[23] 陶宗儀, 輟耕錄, 卷二十五, 院本名目.

[24] （明）顧起元, 客座贅語, 卷九, 三十九款, 戲劇.

[25] 永樂大典戲文三種; 覆元槧古今雜劇三十種, 東京帝國大學刊.

311

actors entered each time with a pair of flags, accompanied by the music of gongs and drums. They impersonated such characters as stupid women, swindlers, shop-keepers, ruffians, and so forth. The plays or sketches were mostly about quarrels and the performance was mixed with juggling and other tricks''. (26)

In *Chin P'ing Mei,* a novel of Ming dynasty, dramatic performances mixed with circus acts, choral dances, minstrel's recitations and juggling. (27) In more recent times

"... there used to be theatres in the city (Peking) but they were prohibited in the reign of Chia Ch'ing 嘉慶 (1796-1820). In them one could see juggling, acrobatics, and such like (雜耍) as well as 'fish and dragon', fire-spitting, sword swallowing, story-telling, ballads, etc.''. (28)

In the early part of the reign of Kuan Hsü 光緒 (1875-1909) there was one theatre in Peking which staged these "miscellaneous shows" only. (29) In the local theatres in Chekiang province dramas are still mixed with acrobatic interludes. (30) Acrobatic skill is now occasionally absorbed into the acting and stage-management, for example, in the timing and accurate location of the flames thrown by the property man — in one case it should look as if a cup of wine bursts into flames and a ghost appears from the flames — and in such skills as kicking off a shoe and landing it on the head, or bending backwards, while holding a cup of wine in the mouth, till the head touches the floor. (31)

Probably owing to the existence of story-telling in China, the interest in learning a story does not seem to appeal to the audience of the Chinese theatre. The Chinese did not, in Sung and Yüan dynasties, go to the theatre to learn a story.

"A man who lived next door to a theatre dreamed that he was killed and that his soul was taken to the City God for trial. When he found that his friend also dreamed about it in the same night he was in a bad mood all day. His family tried to persuade him to forget about the dream and go to the theatre to be entertained, but he stayed at home for safety. In the theatre there was a sound of yielding structures and people rushed out of it, but as nothing happened they went back again. At last the building collapsed and he, remembering that his daughter liked to go to the theatre to learn the songs, ran

---

(26) 劉若愚, 明宮史, 木集, 鐘鼓司.
(27) 金瓶梅詞話, 四十九回, 五十八回, 五十九回, 六十四回, 七十六回.
(28) 唐晏, 天咫偶聞 (見, 齊如山, 京劇之變遷, 頁五十); 參, (清) 楊懋建, 夢華瑣簿, 十款.
(29) 齊如山, 京劇之變遷, 頁六十.
(30) 錢南揚, 宋金元戲劇搬演考, 燕京學報, 二十期.
(31) 齊如山, 京劇之變遷, 頁二三.

in to look for her and was crushed to death by the falling timber. His daughter however was safe, because she came out before he went in". [32]

It was remarkable for a girl to be interested in learning the songs rather than in the story. [33] It took four plays in Sung and Yüan dynasty to make a regular programme of a dramatic performance: there were "two main plays" preceded by "an introductory piece" and followed by "miscellaneous impersonations" — the slight interest in the plot is self-evident. [34] The inevitable growth of plot led to the long dramas of Ming and Ch'ing dynasties, often with fifty "scenes" or more, but it is doubtful if they were often performed in full. Here is an account of a dramatic performance in a novel of Ming dynasty:

> "At night there was a dramatic performance by players of Hai Yen district . . . Hsi-Men Ch'ing ordered fifteen tables in the big booth and watched the play with his guests . . . After the play had started for some time . . . (some of the guests wanted to leave) . . . Hsi-Men Ch'ing sent a boy to tell the players to bring the programme to him so that he could pick the more interesting scenes to entertain his guests. In a few moments the leader of the players came and asked the host which part they should play first and Hsi-Men Ch'ing said, 'I don't care; just choose something exciting'. . . The performance went on for a while, but as it was getting very late all the guests stood up and wished to leave. Hsi-Men Ch'ing asked them to take some more wine before they left and saw them to the gate. The players packed their things and left the boxes in the house because they were to perform again in the next day . . . (The next day) Hsi-Men Ch'ing invited the two guests to the booth and offered them wine . . . The players presented the list of plays and the guests selected one play, but after watching it for a while they were impatient to see the end and the drama was not finished . . . The players were told to play the drama given the night before, that is to say, the sections that had not been played". [35]

The classification of Chinese dramas, not according to the predominant sentiment, as tragedy, comedy, farce, etc., but according to the type of technical skill required indicated the centre of interest. Plays are now divided into *military plays* (武戲) — in which acrobatic skill predominates — and *civil plays* (文戲) — in which mime and singing are more important — or into *plays of acting* (做工戲) and *plays of singing* (唱工戲) or, according to the chief roles, as *plays of the young man, plays*

---

[32] 陶宗儀, 輟耕錄, 卷二十四, 勾欄壓.

[33] It is doubtful if even in the recitations of the stories the interest lay much in the unfolding plot. In *The Red Chamber Dream,* a novel of Ch'ing dynasty, the women story-tellers were asked, before they started reciting, what the story was. 曹雪芹, 紅樓夢, 五十四回.

[34] 耐得翁, 都城紀勝, 瓦舍衆伎.

[35] 金瓶梅詞話, 六十三回.

313

of the pretty woman, etc., or, according to the music, as plays in *P'i-Huang* style, *K'un* dramas, *Hui* dramas, etc. [36]

The lack of interest in the plot and the emphasis on the actors' skill led to the performance of several dramatic excerpts in a programme. It is the custom in China that the honoured guests at a private performance have the privilege to order particular plays in the same way as one would order dishes for the dinner in restaurants. In the pilgrimage to a Taoist temple described in *The Red Chamber Dream* the family entertained themselves, after honouring the deities with incense and donations, with a theatrical performance and as a gesture of piety the first three plays were chosen by lot before the gods, afterwards the different members of the family chose other plays. [37] This practice of choosing plays during the performance was known as early as T'ang dynasty [38] and continued in the public theatres of Yüan dynasty. [39] This is of course incompatible with long plays and short excerpts would be more fashionable under such a system. Many plays among the *K'un* dramas are single scenes taken from the dramas of Ming dynasty and are called by the titles of the scenes. [40] Unless the audience know the story, these scenes are usually of scanty emotional content and dramatic interest. A famous collection of dramas compiled in Ch'ing dynasty, *Chui Po Ch'iu,* consists almost entirely of these single scenes. [41] According to Lu Ch'ien, single scenes were occasionally played as early as Yüan dynasty, but began to be fashionable only in the reigns of Cheng Te 正德 (1505-1521) and Chia Ching 嘉靖 (1522-1566), becoming prevalent in the reigns of Shun Chih 順治 (1644-1661) and K'ang Hsi 康熙 (1662-1722). [42] The dramatists of course do not like the audience to see only excerpts. In early Ch'ing dynasty Li Yü wrote:

"When choosing plays for a performance, the eminent people of to-day ask for lists of single scenes instead of complete dramas, because they want to see their favourite excerpts only and do not wish to have to sit through the less interesting parts of the complete dramas. I am of the opinion that single scenes are too short and complete dramas are too long. For new dramas there should

---

[36] cf. "In Chin 金 dynasty (1115-1234) players' troupes were divided into those for military plays, those for civil plays and those for miscellaneous impersonations". （宋）趙彥衞，雲麓漫鈔，卷十，五款:

[37] 曹雪芹，紅樓夢，二十九回.

[38] 崔令欽，教坊記，六段 . "Before the performance the list of tunes was presented to the emperor; only those he ticked were performed".

[39] 馮沅君，古劇說彙，一章四，做場考.

[40] e.g. 春香鬧學，遊園驚夢.

[41] 錢沛思，綴白裘.

[42] 盧前，明清戲曲史，五章，頁七四，七九; 青木正兒，中國近世戲曲史，十三章二節:

be a compromise scheme between the two, in the manner of Yüan dramas, but longer, with perhaps ten or twelve *sections* for the particular need of these busy people'' [43]

The reason why single scenes are too short is given:

"Dramas have to be long if they are to be good, and the performance should not be abridged. In order to express the emotions in a drama and to portray the individual characters involved in the action the drama has to be so long that the evening performance does not finish until day-break. There is not one person in ten who can sit up all night for such performances: most people either must consider their business in the following day or cannot resist the immediate need for sleep and would leave at the middle of the drama so that they miss its best scenes at the end". [44]

He also advocated that:

". . . dramas should be elastic, that is to say, those scenes which could be omitted without damaging the plot should be so labelled in the script and, when necessary, they should be left out, with appropriate narrative passages inserted in the other scenes to make the action explicable". [45]

The reason for the very long theatrical programmes of to-day (about six hours) is partly the attempt to cater for all tastes and partly the need to provide for the Chinese lack of punctuality.

"The theatres of to-day have four parts in their programme: the first part is performed before the majority of the audience arrive and is usually of poor quality. The second part, consisting of three or four excerpts, is better, but the best is the third part, called 'the heavy axle' (壓軸子) in theatrical jargon, and the star actor appears only then. The fourth is a serial production of new dramas based on long stories, each of which takes ten days or more to finish. By the time this part begins the more discerning part of the audience are gone and some actors could go back home to rest. The gentlemen among the audience come at the beginning of the second part to greet their friends; they really watch only the third part of the programme after which they are gone. Only the less educated portion of the audience, curious to know the outcome of the serial production, remains". [46]

The last part is now omitted. There is another reason for long programmes which should be mentioned. It takes some time for the audience to get into the mood

---

[43] 李笠翁, 曲話, 演習第二, 縮長爲短.

[44] *Ibid.*

[45] *Ibid.*

[46] （清）楊懋建, 夢華瑣簿（一八四三）二十款; 參,（清）華胥大夫, 金臺殘淚記（一八·二九）卷三（十三段）.

315

favourable to the appreciation of the best in the drama. One has to be in a theatre for a certain length of time before one can really forget the humdrum daily life and its cares — they fade from one's consciousness very slowly. The bad effect of starting a programme with the best part of it is noticeable in school performances in which this is sometimes tried.

The standard repertoire of the Chinese theatre now consists practically entirely of single scenes. The new plays are invariably long because the audience have to learn their stories in them. There was occasionally some demand for the new plays in the nineteenth century.

"After some years of old plays the theatres would start to produce new plays which became popular for a while but the enthusiasm eventually subsided and old plays were produced again. In the early part of the nineteenth century the emperor often summoned the players into the palace for dramatic performances and in order to compete for this honour the companies all tried to produce new plays. During the T'ai-P'ing rebellion (eighteen fifties) the court was not much interested in entertainment and new plays stopped. Then the war was over, and new plays were again produced to win royal favour, but the Boxer War started (last years of the nineteenth century) and royal interest diminished and new plays again stopped. Then there was the wave of 'returned students' in the government — those who studied in foreign countries and could not understand their own theatre — and new plays became fashionable again". [47]

The dramatic excerpts played in the Chinese theatre are really "virtuosity pieces". In complete dramas many scenes are necessarily without the star actor or else offer little opportunity for his talents. [48]

"Complete plays have no good singing to speak of; their appeal lies only in the plot. The old complete plays are now mostly obsolete but new ones are constantly being produced, each taking several days to finish. Women like this kind of play, but they are not in the true tradition of Peking dramas". [49]

The Chinese audience take the theatre altogether more casually than the western audience. Players in Sung and Yüan dynasties performed in restaurants and private residences, not only in recitals, but in dramas also, and it was customary to bring the properties when they were summoned to these places. [50] The extant drawing of the

---

[47] 齊如山, 京劇之變遷, 頁二八

[48] A Noh performance in the Japanese theatre also consists of several short items but the sequence is a matter of deliberate design to achieve a satisfactory total effect on the audience. E. Fenollosa and E. Pound, *Noh or Accomplishment*. (1916), 9, 14-17; A. Waley, *The Noh Plays of Japan* (1921), 28. This has not been attempted in the Chinese theatre.

[49] 王夢生, 梨園佳話, 二章, 全本戲.

[50] 太平樂府, 卷九, 拘刷行院, 耍孩兒.

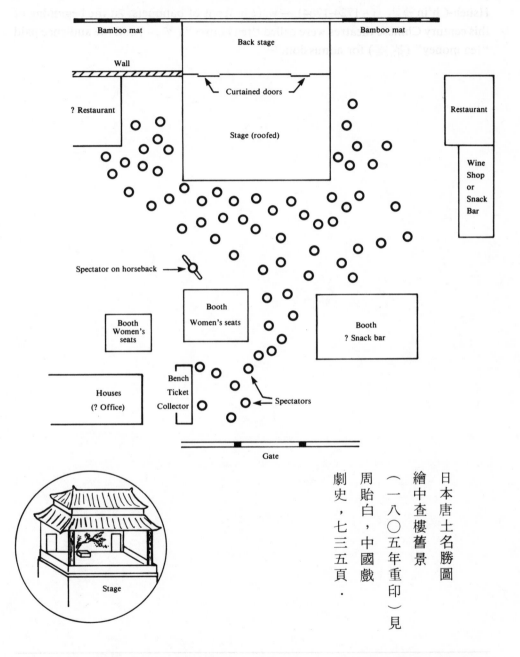

Bamboo mat

Back stage

Wall

Curtained doors

? Restaurant

Stage (roofed)

Restaurant

Wine
Shop
or
Snack
Bar

Bamboo mat

Spectator on horseback

Booth
Women's seats

Booth
Women's
seats

Booth
? Snack bar

Houses
(? Office)

Bench
Ticket
Collector

Spectators

Gate

Stage

日本唐土名勝圖
繪中査樓舊景
（一八〇五年重印）見
周貽白，中國戲
劇史，七三五頁．

Fig. 56 Diagrammatic Representation of an Open-Air Theatre in Peking as Shown in a Japanese Book (Reprinted 1805).

317

open air public theatre of the eighteenth century shows snack bars and one spectator watching the performance on horseback (Fig. 56). Practically all the dramatic performances mentioned in the novel *The Red Chamber Dream* (author Ts'ao Hsüeh-Ch'in 曹雪芹- 1724-1764) — were in front of banquets. At the beginning of this century Chinese theatres were called "tea houses" (茶館) and the audience paid "tea money" (茶錢) for admission. [51]

---

[51] 齊如山, 京劇之變遷, 頁六十; （清）楊懋建, 夢華瑣簿（一八四三） 二至九款.

CHAPTER XXXI

VESTIGES OF NARRATIVE AND LYRICAL ELEMENTS
IN THE CHINESE DRAMA

Non-dramatic elements, such as narrative passages and lyrical poems entered the Chinese drama through two channels: remnants of primitive technique in the farce and passages carried over from the script of the story-tellers, especially in the form of *chu-kung-tiao*.

The ultimate aim of farce is comic effect and plot and dialogue serve to make the comedy explicable. Dramatic illusion is not essential to farce: so long as the story is understood the audience will laugh at the joke. Indeed, elaborate dramatization would be distracting in a farce; the action should lead the audience simply and clearly to the comic situations. For example, the climax of the farce described at the end of Chapter XXIII is the desperate helplessness of the scholar crouching without a stool to imitate a dwarf. The situation arises from the ignorance of the sergeant and volubility of his servant, and these are made clear to the audience in the early part of the farce. There is considerable inconsistency in the play, for instance, the scholar is at first genuinely trying to convince the servant that he is the wanted poet but later he overtly tries to imitate a dwarf and takes the servant into his confidence. This flaw, and others which could easily be located, were apparently ignored both by the playwright and by the audience because they did not lessen the effectiveness of the farce. It can also be noticed that the journey to and from the temple of Confucius is made in a matter of seconds by walking about on the stage and saying, "Coming here; going there". This may be unconvincing but it helps the progress of the action. Again, the self-introduction of the sergeant at the beginning of the play is glaringly undramatic. If, however, the characters were slowly introduced through a naturalistic conversation and the journeys represented more convincingly by exits and re-entrances the audience would have to wait too long for the important part of the farce and by the time the climax was reached in this way, the audience, especially that of the Chinese theatre, might have diverted their minds to other matters. Crude dramatic technique, owing to its economy, was therefore not only admissible but in fact necessary in this type of short farce.

319

It is a standard technique of the Chinese dramatists, from the earliest days of the Chinese drama till the present, that the first character appearing in the play introduces himself in a speech addressed directly to the audience reporting at least his identity and intentions but usually other pertinent information as well. Subsequent entrances by other characters may not require new introductions but when there is a break in the action or when a new thread in the plot is being started, as, for example, the first entrance of the general into the enemy camp or of some unsuspecting party whom fate is to bring into the main stream of the events in the drama, self-introductory speeches are again made. Such speeches are the vestige of the crude dramatic technique in the short farces of Sung dynasty. They can never be considered as naturalistic representation, because they cannot possibly be soliloquies. When making these speeches, the actor should in fact be considered as being temporarily outside the drama, telling the audience what he represents, as if the introductory passage is an explanatory note which some of the characters in the drama are entrusted to deliver. [1]

The main source of the narrative and lyrical elements lies, however, in the story-teller's script with which both the Chinese novel and the Chinese drama are closely connected. For the present purpose the story-teller's script may be divided into four parts, the dialogue, the narrative, the descriptions and the speaker's or author's comments, such as moralizations and psychological observations. By comparing the construction of the Chinese novels, especially those not far removed from the story-teller's script, with that of the early Chinese dramas, one can trace how all the four elements of Chinese story-telling were transferred into the Chinese drama.

When a novel is dramatized part of the *dialogue* can be transposed bodily into the drama, and part of it needs only minor modifications to suit the requirements of dramatic construction, and such transpositions can be found in the two versions of *Hsi Hsiang Chi* (西廂記), the narrative version by Tung Chieh-Yüan (董解元) and the dramatic version by Wang Shih-Fu (王實甫). Even dialogue so transposed is, however, not naturalistic, because in the Chinese story-telling in Sung dynasty part of the dialogue was rhymed or otherwise highly ornamented with rhetorical devices and such dialogue can be found in some Chinese novels like *Chin P'ing Mei*. [2] In later developments, dialogue in the stories was partly in the style of dramatic poetry and was sung, as in *chu-kung-tiao*. Judging by the extant examples, the *chu-*

---

[1] Military officials in modern Chinese dramas cover their face when they declaim or sing the introductory passages. It is said that the covering of the face may be an indication that they speak outside the drama. 齊如山, 中國劇之組織, 一章, 定場白.

[2] 金瓶梅詞話, 參, 馮沅君, 古劇說彙, 五章二節. In that novel it is also stated that the recitation of Buddhist stories was partly sung. In general story-telling in prose was called in Sung dynasty "talks" (說話) and stories with poetical embellishments were called "talks-in-verse" (詩話) or "talks-in-songs" (詞話).

320

kung-tiao of Sung dynasty consisted of a large body of lyrical and descriptive poetry set in the framework of a narrative. The part of the dialogue not in verse was in stylized prose of parallel constructions (駢文). Like the dramatic text of Yüan dynasty there was considerable repetition between the prose and the verse passages and the latter was not essential to the development of the plot. *Chu-kung-tiao* was said to have been "invented by K'ung San-Chuan (孔三傳) about the time of Hsi Ning 熙寧 (1068-1077) and Yüan Feng 元豐 (1079-1085) and to have become very popular among the scholars who all learned to sing it". [3] The large proportion of verse in *chu-kung-tiao* was in turn derived from the fashion of writing lyrical poetry based on a story:

"At the end of Sung dynasty Chao Ling-Chih wrote twelve poems in the style of 'drum songs' (趙令畤, 侯鯖錄, 商調蝶戀花鼓子詞十二首) based on *Hui Chen Chi,* a short story of T'ang dynasty (元稹, 會眞記). They were purely lyrical poems and were not connected by spoken (prose) parts. In the reign of emperor Chang Tsung (1190-1208) of Chin dynasty (金, 章宗) Tung Chieh-Yüan wrote a *chu-kung-tiao* on the same subject (董解元, 西廂搊彈詞) with spoken prose parts interspersed among verse passages. In the performance of the latter one person sings and recites the text and accompanies himself on an instrument". [4]

The innovation of K'ung San-Chuan seemed to be supplying the narrative framework to lyrical poems:

"Chu-kung-tiao was invented by K'ung San-Chuan who put stories in poems for combined singing and recitation".[5]

Theoretically speaking for complete dramatization the *narrative passages* of a story should be entirely changed into action but in practice few dramas, if any, represent all parts of a story, because much of the action can be implied to have taken place or reported to the *dramatis personae* and the audience by messengers. In European dramas an excuse is usually supplied for the messenger's speech so that it can appear natural, but in the Chinese dramas the part of the story not directly represented is told by the prologue or the *dramatis personae* themselves. In one early drama of the southern school the prologue tells the whole story of the drama before action begins, as follows:

Prologue   *(recites a poem summarizing the story and sings a passage inviting the audience to enjoy life generally and this drama in particular; he proceeds to say in his singing that the story has been dramatized before and that he will tell the story by reciting and singing it in the*

---

[3] （宋）王灼, 碧雞漫志, 卷二, 三段.

[4] （清）毛奇齡, 西河詞話, 第三十二款. The "drum song" was also a musically simpler form, being sung in one tune only. 王國維, 宋元戲曲史, 四章二段.

[5] 吳自牧, 夢粱錄, 卷二十, 妓樂.

style of chu-kung-tiao; *this he does, speaking the dialogue in the story as if he represents each character in turn, till he reaches the point when the hero was taken by the bandits).* Was his life in danger? Who can tell by the omens whether he died or lived? Rather than having the story sung to you like this, why not let us act the events in it? Fellows backstage, come let us see an actor enter as the hero in the drama.

(Enter actor dressed as the hero. Exit Prologue).

Actor   Have you heard?

Musicians   Yes.

Actor   Come and send me off.

Musicians   Whom do you want?

Actor   Fellows backstage, play me the introduction. *(Declaims a poem on the enjoyableness of the drama).* I have heard some music just now, I wonder where it came from?

Musicians   That was the introduction.

Actor   Come and accompany me.

Musicians   Coming.

Actor   *(Singing)* Am I like the Doctor Chang?

Musicians   Well enough.

Actor   *(Sings a long lyrical poem).* I am Chang Hsieh . . .[6]

In another southern drama the opening is slightly different:

Prologue   *(recites a poem which summarizes the story and asks the audience to take pleasures while they can; he tells how the ancient stories were searched for a good story for the drama).* Fellows backstage, what are you going to play to-day?

Someone of the company *(tells him the title).*

Prologue   *(sings a poem and recites the story of the drama).*

(Enter the hero of the play). [7]

These examples are from southern dramas of Yüan dynasty or earlier. In Ming dynasty this convention subsisted and the formula for the prologue was: (1) a lyrical poem, (2) the question: "What do we play to-day"? and the answer with the title, (3) the story recited, and (4) another poem. In early Ch'ing dynasty the critic and dramatist Li Yü stipulated:

"At the beginning of the introduction (家門) the prologue should sing a short poem. This poem must not touch the theme of the drama but should be on

---

[6] 永樂大典戲文, 張協狀元 . cf. the *loa* of the early Spanish theatre: a monologue and introduction or short scene before the drama; it fell out of use in the seventeenth century.

[7] 永樂大典戲文, 小孫屠 .

such matters as forgetting one's worries and taking the pretended (drama) as real. The first scene of a drama is like the introduction to an essay: it states the main thoughts of the work in a summary way, then the full representation of the story follows. The prologue who speaks in this introductory scene should hint at the theme at first and then tell the audience the story in greater detail''. ''Talk and writing are the same in principle: at the beginning one should not be too far-fetched, nor be too near the main subject''. [8]

In a play of Ch'ing dynasty, *Peach Blossoms on a Fan* (孔尚任, 桃花扇) the prologue is used with some naturalistic effect, as a bridge between the world of the audience and the world of the drama:

> ''Prologue I am lucky in my old age: this is a peaceful and prosperous period and I have leisure to enjoy myself. Yesterday I saw a new drama, called *Peach Blossoms on a Fan,* which deals with the events in Nanking at the end of Ming dynasty. Although there are in it the grief of separation and the joy of reunion, the subject matter is really about the rise and fall of power and authority, and I know everything in it is true, because I have not only heard about the events but have also seen some of them myself. For this reason, although I am old and useless, I have been asked to act in this play, as a prologue. Thinking about the story, I cannot help cry and laugh and get angry and curse at the same time''.

The prologue, being a convention of the literary drama, has been dropped in the Chinese theatre of to-day, but it shows that the Chinese drama was closely related to and at first carried some of the forms of the story-teller's recitation.

Descriptive passages in Chinese fiction are usually in verse, not only in the story-teller's script but also in novels written to be read. [9] In descriptions of scenery this is probably due to the faith in the greater power of poetry than prose and in erotic passages verse is no doubt also used to veil the indecency. In dramas, these descriptive passages, which are not always essential to the plot, are put into the mouths of some characters who are portrayed as being struck by the beauty of the scenery or awed by the sight of ferocious combats, and so on. [10] The conventional way of introducing these passages in the novel, namely, ''How do we know it was so? . . .''[11] appeared in the dramas of Ming dynasty. [12] In effect some *dramatis*

---

[8] 李笠翁, 曲話, 詞曲第六, 家門.

[9] e.g. 吳承恩, 西遊記.

[10] Even the description of a warrior's appearance was put bodily in the dialogue (元明雜劇, 單鞭奪槊, 四折, "黃鍾醉花陰"下白; "刮地風", "四門子") This suggests hasty adaptation of the story-teller's script.

[11] 怎見得.

[12] 齊如山, 京劇之變遷, 頁二六.

personae were made to speak for the author as in the case of narrative passages. Properly used and in small doses descriptive passages can appear natural in the dialogue, but in the Chinese drama they are often flagrantly undramatic. The style of the poetry is often thoroughly lyrical and taken out of the drama the lines cannot be recognized as dramatic poetry. [13] The proportion of such lines is so high in Yüan dramas that when in some collections [14] the prose passages were left out at the time of publication the part in verse gives no idea now what the plays were about.

It is customary for Chinese story-tellers to insert their own comments into the story. These *commentaries* do not, as a rule, enter the dramas but occasionally some *dramatis personae* make unnaturalistic remarks which bear resemblance to the story-teller's comments as in the poem or couplet at the end of a scene introduced by: "Indeed . . ." [15] Both the story-teller and the dramatist worked with a script which was a combination of prose and verse, narrative and commentary, dialogue and description, passages which were spoken and passages which were sung. The problem of providing an attractive combination of these elements is the same for them. At the beginning of a Chinese story-teller's recitation he chants an introductory poem, like an overture to an opera, during which the audience gradually compose themselves to attentive listening. In this introduction he usually outlines the historical background of the story but he may also add his views on the place of entertainment in a man's life, the high quality of his story, and so on. [16] At the end of the recital he again chants a poem moralizing on the story and some couplets or lines in stylized prose which summarize the legends or history following the events he has just told. As the stories were written not to be read but to be recited, it had to be such that the speaker could sustain the immediate appeal of his recitation for his audience. When one gets tired of reading a novel one can put it aside and continue some other time but the audience of the story-teller cannot ask him to stop the recitation whenever they like. Therefore, unmitigated narration in prose is at a serious disadvantage to a variegated performance with singing, chanting, poems and commentaries. When the drama evolved out of the story-teller's script, this aurally satisfying scheme of mixing various styles of prose

---

[13] Lyrical poems were written in Yüan dynasty in the same style as dramatic poetry — 散套.

[14] e.g. 雍熙樂府, 太平樂府.

[15] "正是" The poems declaimed at the end of a scene — 下場詩 — and those at the end of the whole drama — 散場詩 — are technically different.

[16] Of the three *chu-kung-tiao* extant there are seven introductions (due to alternative introductions given in the text) and the general scheme for them is as follows: (1) the singer's invitation to enjoy the recitation and some moralization usually on the place of pleasures in man's life, (2) either the nature or the summary of the story, (3) name of the author and the high quality of the script, and (4) good performance guaranteed the audience. In *Hsi Hsiang Chi* (董解元, 西廂記) the introduction also includes poems on the four seasons and the background of the story.

and verse became, in part, a model of dramatic writing. [17] Thus a scene in the Chinese drama usually opens with a poem [18] or a couplet [19] spoken by some character in the drama, and similarly at the end of a scene. These poems and couplets are usually only vaguely related to the dramatic theme, they are spoken not because they contribute towards the action but because they are parts of the poetical structure of the scene or drama, analogous to the opening phrases and the coda of a piece of music, setting the emotional keynote of the scene or play.

In the modern European theatre the world of the drama is sharply distinct from that of the audience. In Elizabethan and Restoration theatres the line of demarcation was not as sharp as it is now, because the prologue and epilogue, the latter spoken by one or more of the *dramatis personae*, were not part of the dramatic action and yet they were parts of the dramatic performance. In the Elizabethan theatre the prologue sometimes, as in *Henry V*, appeared several times in the course of the drama. In the Chinese theatre the boundary between the world of the drama and that of the audience is always vague. At private performances, the player who goes around with a list of plays for the audience to choose from changes into theatrical costume — a red gown — at the end of the performance to kowtow and thank the audience on the stage. [20] In *K'un* dramas there was a custom that the major male and female roles in the play bid farewell to the audience, and even in the commercial theatres producing Peking dramas there were at one time two actors dressed as a man and a woman who appeared at the end of each performance. [21] When the actors speak the introductory poem or couplet to the audience they do so, as in the epilogue of Elizabethan dramas, partially as *dramatis personae* and partially as themselves, as *dramatis personae* because they are in costume and partake the action immediately before or afterwards and as actors because these poems are not part of the dramatic dialogue, and are addressed directly to the audience. The couplets printed at the end of Yüan dramas as their titles [22] were, according to Feng Yüan-Chün, spoken by the last actor to leave the stage, who also added, "The drama is now ended". [23] The early Chinese dramas opened and closed in much the same way as the story-tellers' recitation; the only difference was that in the drama the prologue and the last actor to leave the stage, instead of the story-teller, spoke the particular lines. In fact a dramatic performance may be considered

---

[17] cf. the use of singing (poetry) in Yüan dramas: (1) in dramatic dialogue, (2) in lyrical passages, (3) in narratives, and (4) in descriptive passages. 青木正兒, 中國近世戲曲史, 三章一節.

[18] 上場詩, 定場詩.

[19] 上場聯.

[20] 王夢生, 梨園佳話, 四章, 規矩.

[21] *Ibid.*

[22] 題目正名

[23] 馮沅君, 孤本元明雜劇鈔本題記 (民三三), 三節.

as a recitation not by one man but by several players, each speaking a part of the dialogue as well as a part of the introductory, descriptive, lyrical, narrative and moralizing passages.

The survival of non-dramatic elements derived from narrative forms of entertainment has held back full dramatization in the Chinese theatre. To those who take realism as the criterion for good theatre the Chinese drama must appear primitive but if the Chinese drama had become realistic many of its qualities, which the realistic theatre lacks, would have been lost. There appear to be two reasons why dramatization has not been complete: the appreciation of poetry and music and the attitude towards dramatic illusion. Since even in the long stories recited by the story-tellers the interest did not lie in the unfolding plot alone but also in poetry, singing and commentaries, in the drama, which could cover only simple plots, the importance of singing, acting and poetry is proportionately increased. Complete dramatization not only could not augment the poetical and musical elements but would subtract from them, for instance, the poems and couplets at the beginnings and ends of scenes could not exist in naturalistic dramas. Furthermore, the Chinese audience is constantly conscious of the pretence involved in dramatic representation and neither the actors nor the audience make any attempt towards complete dramatic illusion. Complete dramatization can be achieved by slight adjustments in the dialogue as, for example, by disguising an introductory dialogue with padding, but such devices are transparent to all except the simplest tyro. To an audience for whom the drama is always pretence rather than illusion, it matters little whether the dramatization is complete. For this reason there have been in China several forms of quasi-dramatic entertainment.

> "In *lien-hsiang-tz'u* (連廂詞) the musicians of Chin dynasty 金 (1115-1234) imitated those of Liao 遼 (916-1125). There were both singing and acting in this form of entertainment. A singer sat with the musicians — one lutist, one zither-player and one flautist — and three actors who impersonated men and women and acted as the text of the story was sung, for instance, for 'He bowed to Buddha', the man would bow down and for 'She played with a flower', the woman would lift the flower''. [24]

This form of entertainment was popular in Ch'ing dynasty. It differs from the Chinese drama in that it is a semi-dramatic performance based on narrative text whereas the drama is fully dramatic performance based on partially narrative text. A similar form is called *t'an-huang* (灘黃).

> "*T'an-huang* is sung by five players who impersonate man, woman, clown, etc., accompanied by lutes, fiddles and percussion instruments. The script is in dramatic form and is often adapted from existing dramas''. [25]

---

[24] （清）毛奇齡, 西河詞話, 第三十二款.

[25] （清）范祖述, 杭俗遺風, 四十七款.

This type of entertainment is still popular in Chekiang and Kiangsu. The modern script is partially narrative and this may be what the Ch'ing dynasty writer meant by "adaptation". The singers who impersonate the different characters in the story sit in plain clothes among the musicians. In small troupes there are only two singers, one for the hero and one for the heroine, the musicians speaking a line or two in case of need. This is in fact a semi-dramatic performance based on semi-dramatic text. In the "drum songs" (鼓書) in Shantung there are two singers, sometimes they are engaged in dialogue, and sometimes one of them is silent and the other recites the story in narrative form. [26] In China, between narrative recitation and the full-fledged drama, there are many styles of performance; in fact the Chinese drama itself may be considered as one of the intermediate forms. The development towards full dramatization has been gradual, and the manner of performance and the script did not keep pace. In the Chinese drama the script lags behind the *mise-en-scène,* but in *t'an-huang* the manner of performance lags behind the script. The incomplete dramatization in the Chinese theatre accustoms the audience to the lack of dramatic illusion so that even after the advent of the drama the hybrid forms between drama and story-telling continued to exist.

---

[26] 李家瑞, 由說書變成戲劇的痕跡, 中央研究院歷史語言研究所集刊, 七本三分.

CHAPTER XXXII

THE INFLUENCE OF DANCE AND MUSIC IN THE CHINESE THEATRE

Throughout the Chinese history dance has been an important part of the Chinese culture. At first it was related to religion and later, to entertainment.

Primitive dance was a release of physical energy under an emotional state; it relieved the nervous tension and at the same time strengthened the emotional excitement, sometimes towards a dangerous pitch; it was both expression and stimulation. When the primitive shamans danced their charms and spells they were probably intoxicated with religious emotions or perhaps they believed that by working up excitement in themselves they achieved magical efficacy over the daemons. Outside religion dance was also connected in ancient China with recreation and perhaps courtship. [1] In the official religious ceremonies of Chou dynasty, although the dancers were highly trained and the performance conventionalized, dance was still recognized as spontaneous expression of exaltation, the classical definition for dance being:

> "It is sometimes not enough to talk about our feelings, then we wail or sing them. If singing is still not enough, we sigh and groan; when groans and sighs are inadequate, without knowing it, we wave the arms and stamp the feet". [2]

The release of physical energy, as in sport, also has recreational value and can be associated with emotions less profound than religious exaltation. Dances were performed in Chou dynasty in connection with feasting, rejoicing, mourning, military ceremonies, receptions, and celebration, as well as worship. [3] Wild dancing was, however, condemned in the *Book of Rituals* (禮記) and was described in the following terms:

> ". . . the dance nowadays — men and women stooping and stepping

---

[1] 詩經, 陳風.
[2] 禮記, 樂記.
[3] 鄭樵, 通志, 卷四九, 樂府總序, "燕, 吉, 凶, 軍, 賓, 嘉, 祀".

forward, bending and stepping backward, excited by the coarse music and dancing continually in abandon . . .'' [4]

Abandon was not generally approved by the guardians of ancient Chinese culture, but when Tzu Kung reported some wild dancing he saw at a thanksgiving ceremony [5] saying that "the whole city had gone mad" Confucius reassured him that "both tension and relief are parts of a cultured life". [6] The ceremonial dances continued in later dynasties; according to an account of the sixth century A.D.,

"From Chou dynasty till now the dances have not changed although the words sung at the ceremonies have been altered". [7]

Before the latter part of Chou dynasty there was no pure entertainment; dance, which was mostly religious, was at first magic and later, communal expression of religious feelings. The court jesters were the first to dance for entertainment and they were followed by the dancing masquers of Han dynasty. Throughout Han 漢 and Chin 晉 dynasties the dances handed down from Chou dynasty were mixed with those of later origins, both in state entertainment and in the temple ceremonies. [8] Even in early Han dynasty part of the tradition of Chou dynasty had been lost.

"At the beginning of Han dynasty, there was a family of musicians whose ancestors had for generations served as official musicians. They could remember the music and dance but could not explain their principles". [9]

It was in the period of North and South that dance began to be connected with popular entertainment and thereby became part of the Chinese theatre in the form of dramatic dances. (Chapter XXII).

In T'ang dynasty pure dance appeared to be a substantial part of the court theatre. It was so closely connected to music that it was defined as "the expression of music". [10] Dance was then divided into the *supple style* (軟舞) and the *robust style* (健舞) and dance movements were variously described as "startled wild-duck" and "diving swallow". Of special dances, there were the "word dance" (字舞) in which "the dancers bent themselves on the floor to form words, on one occasion, sixteen words in succession", the "flower dance" (花舞) in which "the dancers, dressed in green, grouped together and bent the bodies to form flowers", and the "horse dance" [11] in which "a rider, dressed in silk and holding a whip,

---

[4] 禮記, 樂記.

[5] 八蜡, 參, 禮記, 郊特牲.

[6] 孔子家語 cf. the Bacchanals being cured of their frenzy by the music and the dance — Plato, *Laws,* 790 f. (Jowett (1871), Vol. IV. p.303).

[7] (陳) 智匠, 古今樂錄, 百二十五款.

[8] 馬端臨, 文獻通考, 樂考一至三, 十八, 十九; 晉書, 樂志, 上, 下.

[9] 漢書, 禮樂志; 藝文志 (樂記).

[10] 段安節, 樂府雜錄, 舞工, "舞者樂之容也"

[11] The similarity with the "horse" on the modern Chinese stage is noteworthy.

danced on a stage, with trotting steps in the rhythm of the music". [12] Even elephants and horses danced.

"The foreign chief entertained the Chinese envoy with the elephant dance. When music started a player led in an elephant decorated with gold harness and draped with silk and it moved about in steps to the rhythm of the music". [13]

"Emperor Ming Huang had a hundred horses taught to dance. On his birthday they would perform before Ch'in Chen Lou at his banquets. The horses were divided into two teams, one on the right and one on the left. They were all draped with silk and decorated with gold and pearls. When the special song (of a few dozen stanzas long) was sung the horses, hearing the music, would lift their heads and tails and marched in one direction or another according to the rhythm. There were also scaffolds three stories high with horses, carrying riders, running on them as fast as flying. Another style was to have muscle-men supporting a platform and horses dancing on it". [14]

Pure dances were performed in Sung dynasty by large *corps de ballet*. At a royal birthday celebration

"the conductor, holding his baton, made a speech introducing the children of the *corps de ballet*. There were two-hundred-odd boys, twelve or thirteen years old, arranged in four lines, each with a leader flanked by four attendants. They were all dressed in bright colours, red, green, purple and blue, with a belt at their waist and each holding a flowering branch. Four children in purple, holding a silk banner with these words in gold: [a congratulatory couplet] advanced to the sound of the drums. The music was played and the children, dancing to it, advanced up to the steps of the hall. [The main halls of Chinese buildings are connected with the court yard in front of them by a few steps.] After an introduction by the conductor, the children's leader made a congratulatory speech and the actors all joined in the chorus. The main dance by the whole *corps de ballet* followed and was accompanied by the orchestra and the children's own singing. When it ended, the leader made another speech. A farce was then presented; when it finished the conductor asked for the children to be excused and they retreated in dance steps". [15]

The girls' *corps de ballet* in the same birthday celebration was similar to the above:

"There were more than four hundred girls chosen for their beauty wearing crowns of flowers or buns in the style of fairies . . . The four leaders, holding

---

[12] 段安節, 樂府雜錄（舞工, 註）. Eight styles of dances in the court were listed and described in the official history of this period. 舊唐書, 音樂志, 二.

[13] （唐）劉恂, 嶺表錄異, 卷上, 三十四條.

[14] 新唐書, 禮樂志, 十二. Dancing horses existed before T'ang dynasty — in A.D. 506 — （宋）程大昌, 演繁露, 卷三, 舞馬.

[15] 孟元老, 東京夢華錄, 卷九, 宰執親王宗室百官入內上壽.

batons with silver knobs, were each flanked by four girls carrying flowers and dressed as fairy attendants. The leaders and their attendants danced towards the hall first and the rest followed and arranged themselves in files''.

Then followed the dances with singing and the speeches by the leaders which were as above. [16] The official history of Sung dynasty stated that there were ten types of *choral dances* and that there were regularly seventy-two children in the *corps de ballet*. [17] The costumes for each of the ten types were minutely described. Dances were also connected with stilts, football, conjuring, the ''lion-dance'', spear revolutions, juggling, rope-dancing, pole climbing, somersaults, contortion and jumping through rings of swords. [18] *Choral dances* (舞隊) were by no means confined to royal banquets; a contemporary book mentioned seventy different choral dances in connection with popular entertainment. [19] It was not explained how these popular choral dances were performed but judging by the titles some of them were probably pure dances, as ''New Year's Good Wishes'' (賀豐年) and ''Visit from Tributary States'' (六國朝), others appeared to contain farcical elements as ''Cat Prime Minister'' (貓兒相公), ''The Blind Judge'' (瞎判官), and ''Teaching the Elephant'' (敎象), some might have involved juggling as ''Whipping the Flag'' (撲旗), or acrobatics as ''Stilts'' (踏蹺) and some contained definite dramatic elements as ''Drumming the Pot'' (瓦盆鼓), presumably about the philosopher Chuang-Tzu (莊子) who was reputed to have sung at his wife's death accompanying himself on the pot, [20] and ''Sun Wu-Tzu's Military Lesson for Ladies'' (孫武子敎女兵), no doubt on the demonstration of military discipline on court ladies by Sun Wu-Tzu of the Warring States. [21] Among the seventy titles there are two which were mentioned in other books in Sung dynasty and of which more therefore is known: the ''Three Religions Man'' (三敎人) which originated ''in the poor people who at the end of the year, dressed as women or daemons,

---

[16] *Ibid.*

[17] 宋史, 樂志, 十七.

[18] *Ibid.*

[19] 周密, 武林舊事, 卷二, 舞隊.

[20] 莊子, 至樂.

[21] Sun Wu-Tzu, when asked to demonstrate his skill in military matters by the Prince of Wu to whom he had been recommended, proposed to do so among the court ladies whom he then armed with staffs and divided into two groups each with a leader. After some instructions, he gave the order of attack but the ladies giggled and did not know what to do. He apologized for not having given the instructions clearly, and repeated them and gave the order again. The ladies giggled as before. He declared that the fault lay with the leaders and wanted to execute them, but the Prince intervened and explained that they were his favourites but Sun stated that in his system of military operation when the general was in active command he might ignore the orders from court. After the leaders were put to death the ladies fought with perfect discipline and the emperor was asked to see it, but he said, ''I know your skill already''. 史記, 列傳, 孫武.

carrying torches and beating gongs and drums, asked for tips from door to door'' [22] and *Pao-Lao* (鮑老), a fantastic dance by "a dancer wearing a long wig, a mask with husks, a blue jacket with gold patches cut short at the back and black skirt with gold dots, dancing barefoot carrying a big gong which he swung as he stepped forward and backward''. [23] Several names in this list of *choral dances* also appeared in the list of two hundred and eighty "official copies of miscellaneous plays" (官本雜劇) — see Chapter XXIII — hence, it is very likely that in Sung dynasty farce and choral dances were both called "plays". (雜劇)

Sixty-three names of the dance postures in Sung dynasty have been preserved in a contemporary book. [24] The interpretation of these bare names is difficult and uncertain at best, but Prof. Ch'i Ju-Shan claimed to have traced some similarities with the postures of the modern Chinese actors. [25]

Up to the advent of the Chinese drama, dance had been associated with magic (shamans), worship, social intercourse, recreation [26] and entertainment. It would be strange if dance did not become a part of the Chinese drama. Drama is a form of entertainment in which strong emotions are often represented; to a people who look upon the dance as a means of emotional expression dance should belong to the drama. "When the groans and sighs are insufficient, without knowing it, one would wave the arm and stamp the foot" instead of a definitive explanation of the dance could easily be modified to read like an instruction for actors. At the end of Sung dynasty, when the Chinese drama was being developed, the dance was of course far removed from the spontaneous waving of the arm and stamping of the foot; it had then acquired the rhythm and form of the music which accompanied it, as shown by the dramatic dance *Po-T'ou,* about the son seeking his father's body and *T'a-Yao-*

---

[22] 孟元老, 東京夢華錄, 卷十, 十二月 probably a remnant of the exorcist mentioned in the *Book of Rituals* (周禮, 夏官司馬, 方相氏) — see Ch. XX. The "Three Religions" presumably referred to Confucianism, Taoism and Buddhism, the three religions of China — the beggar was so named in order to widen the collection.

[23] 孟元老, 東京夢華錄, 卷七, 駕登寶津樓諸軍呈百戲. In *Shui Hu Chuan* his dance, described as in a bent position, excited the laughter of the spectators. 水滸傳 (百回本), 三十三回.

[24] 周密, 癸辛雜識, 後集, 四十款 Dance notation is also mentioned in 清朝文獻通考, 卷百七十三.

[25] 齊如山, 國劇身段譜; 二章. ". . . This explanation is based on the meaning of the single words and phrases and some of my readers may think that I have strained my imagination to reach the conclusions. However, a dancer has only two arms and two legs which he can move; hence these interpretations, if not exact, cannot be too far from the original postures".

[26] One of Confucius' pupils was recorded to have said, and been approved by the Master in what he said: ". . . In spring time, when the new spring garments are ready, I like to bathe in the river Ch'i with five or six men and six or seven boys and in the breeze to perform together the Rain Dance (雩), singing on the way back". 論語, 先進. The Rain Dance was "performed in times of drought by eight boys and eight girls, crying as they danced". 公羊傳, 註, 桓公五年 "大雩".

Niang, the lament of the drunkard's wife. [27] Many of the arias in the extant Yüan dramas were sung to the dance tunes of Sung and T'ang dynasties. [28] When an aria was sung to music which had been habitually danced to by a player who was also a trained actor, and who most probably had played in the dramatic dances, the impulse towards making dance movements would be well-nigh irresistible. To the students of theatrical history drama marked a distinct step in the development of the Chinese theatre, but to the audience of late Sung and early Yüan dynasties it was merely an extension of the earlier types of "plays" and was called by the same name, hence it would not appear strange to them if the acting in the early dramas had dance movements. In T'ang dynasty plays were said to be "danced".

"Before the performances the manager of His Majesty's theatre presented him the list of plays, and the emperor ticked those that were to be danced". [29]

It would not be justified, however, to assume that the Yüan dramas were performed entirely in dance movements, because the "miscellaneous plays" of Sung dynasty, of which they were the direct descendants and from which they derived their actors, also contained farces, particularly those of the slap-stick type. Absurdity is the essence of farce and absurdity usually involves exaggeration. Thus the acting in the farces of Sung dynasty was more likely to be exaggerated than realistic. The style of acting in the earliest dramas was therefore most probably a combination of the sophistication of the dance and the over-emphasis of the farce. If one thinks of the rhythmic and pompous struts of the modern Chinese actors and the extravagant tossings of the beard and shakings of the hand, one can visualize how the dance and farce of Sung left their marks in the Chinese theatre.

Dance, as a spectacle, is primarily a display of skill; a dancer's art is based on his technical training and the appreciation of the dance, like that of violin-playing, requires some understanding of the technique. The modern Chinese style of acting is also primarily a matter of technique and training. Not even the most talented amateur can pass as a professional because his lack of proper training shows in all his movements especially those that require acrobatic skill. With only natural charm and a flare for acting an amateur can play in realistic dramas, but without training no one can move a step on the Chinese stage.

Displays of skill, such as juggling, acrobatics, improvisation of verse, and so forth were not in Sung dynasty differentiated from dramatic performances (see Chapter XXIII). Not only in the pleasure houses were all types of entertainment mixed, but at royal banquets too, football display and farce were scheduled in the same

---

[27] Ch. XXII.

[28] 王國維, 宋元戲曲史, 八章. It is to be remembered that dances were in T'ang and Sung dynasties accompanied by singing as well as instrumental music, hence the dance tunes were more suitable for operatic arias than they would seem to be.

[29] 崔令欽, 教坊記, 六段.

programme. When dance, as one form of physical skill, entered the Chinese drama, other types of physical skill, not necessarily of dramatic nature, also became part of the early dramas because the actors were trained in them all. [30] Thus in the Yüan dramas actors were sometimes required by the text to "fall in somersault". [31] The technique of one type of actor [32] in Yüan dynasty consisted of "addresses, declamation, somersault and acting". [33] In dramas of Ming dynasty [34] actors were required to "enter dancing" and to "exit dancing". Some of the dramas, though indifferently plain to read, could be interesting to watch, because the combats, performed by trained pugilists and swordsmen, could be good theatre. [35] Exhibition of skill, sometimes departing from the dramatic content of the play, is still a feature of the military plays of the Chinese theatre.

Dance being primarily an exhibition of skill the interest of the spectators is focused on the dancer's body. The concentration required for the appreciation of good dancing makes stage setting, especially realistic setting, superfluous. The lack of scenery in the Chinese theatre cannot be entirely explained by the lack of realistic painting, because stage machinery attained considerable degree of elaboration as early as the pageants in Han dynasty and transformation scenes were staged in the court spectacles of Sui dynasty. There had been representations of mountain and trees and clouds and thunder (Chapter XXI). The interest in wax works and doll houses was well developed, as in the *water puppets* of Sung dynasty. Such interests however never took root in the Chinese drama. Spectacular staging has on occasions been tried: in the palace of the emperors of Ch'ing dynasty

"... for birthday celebrations there were sixty gods of longevity and these were later augmented to one hundred and twenty. When the Eight Immortals (八仙) came to offer congratulations, innumerable attendants followed them... When Buddha ascended his throne, the various ranks of saints and monks were seated in nine levels, totalling a few thousand men..." [36]

Other spectacles in the same palace theatre included:

---

[30] The term *lu-ch'i* — 路歧 — referred to actors, singers, jugglers, story-tellers, etc., indiscriminately. 馮沅君, 古劇說彙, 一章, 二, 路歧考, 註一.

[31] （元曲選）燕青博魚, 二折, 金盞兒. The particular character was killed just before his exit. This convention is still being observed in the Chinese theatre. 齊如山, 上下場, 頁二三.

[32] 副淨

[33] 陶宗儀, 輟耕錄, 卷二十五, 院本名目.

[34] 金雀記, 四齣; 白兔記, 三齣.

[35] "Like dogs licking hot fat or children watching plays — they love it as much as fear it". （宋）王琪, 雜纂, 卷中 "又愛又怕". The children's fear suggests either vigorous fighting or fantastic masks, but masks, of the type used on the Chinese stage to-day, are not known to have been used in the plays of Sung dynasty.

[36] 趙翼, 簷曝雜記, 卷一, 大戲條.

"Five pagodas rose from the well. . . Five lotus flowers rose from the well opened on the stage and revealed five Buddhas sitting in them. . . A large fish, with several dozens of players in it, appeared and a pump drew water from the well and discharged out of its mouth". [37]

Among the people one patron of the theatre

". . . erected a large stage in the drill grounds [for soldiers] and employed a company of players of about thirty or forty men, all expert in mock fights. For three days and three nights the players displayed their skill in rope-dancing, ladder climbing, somersaults, playing large jars with their feet, jumping through rings, spitting fire, swallowing swords — all of which had nothing to do with the drama. Then there were gods, spirits, daemons, monsters and goblins as well as purgatory scenes of sawing the body, boiling in oil, forrest of spears, icebergs, steel walls and blood pools, which cost tens of thousands of silver taels. The audience were all frightened and under the lamps looked pale. In the scenes of chasing evil spirits and the escape of the souls the audience, more than ten thousand, shouted so loud that the mayor thought pirates had raided the city". [38]

Scenery and front curtain are not entirely unknown:

"The stage suddenly became dark and at the flash of a sword there was a loud bang and the black curtain disappeared. A full moon rose and all around it was covered with translucent clouds of many colours and the trees and fairies of the moon came into view. The whole scene was covered with light scrim inside which were large candles which threw a blue light, as of dawn. The scenery was so wonderful that one forgot it was on a stage". [39]

In a modern production of *The Double Reunion* (奇雙會) it was recorded that the opening scene in heaven started with stage hands holding a curtain about eight feet high and twelve feet wide with bamboo poles on both ends and clouds painted on it. Behind it the stage was set for the scene. When the curtain was removed a god was seen with four spirits bearing "cloud plaques" around him. [40] All these productions have had, however, no influence on the Chinese theatre as a whole, because scenery and spectacle are incompatible with the other elements of the Chinese drama, such as the dance-like acting.

Dance in the Chinese theatre is not an incidental interpolation, but is an integral part of the drama, it is acting itself. Most people are sensitive to the rhythm and the elegance of movements and poses hence acting is always dance, in the broadest sense

---

[37] 曹心泉, 前清內廷演戲回憶錄;'參, 清逸, 內府之沿革, 戲劇叢刊, 二期.
[38] (清) 張岱, 陶菴夢憶, 卷六, 二款, 目蓮戲.
[39] (清) 張岱, 陶菴夢憶, 卷五, 十四款, 劉暉吉女戲.
[40] A. E. Zucker, *The Chinese Theatre* (1925), Ch. 4.

of the word; even in normal life one can distinguish an awkward gait from an attractive one and few people when they are formally dressed walk really naturally. Acting and the quality of dance in it are therefore more prevalent than they may appear to be. The Chinese style of acting differs from the beauty and expressiveness of ordinary movements only in that it has been developed beyond realism and that it partakes the quality of music. Thus dance, acting, music and singing all become interrelated and indissoluble constituents of the Chinese stage and they tend to perpetuate the lack of naturalism in the Chinese theatre. Even the Chinese term for "stage", *wu-t'ai* (舞臺), literally, "dance platform", attests to the Chinese conception of its unrealistic nature. The quality of music enters into every part of the Chinese theatre: singing is musical delivery, poetry is musical language, dance is musical acting, in fact the Chinese dramatic performance is the stage-art become musical.

Music as an independent art, that is, concert music, was unknown in ancient China. Ancient Chinese music was always associated with dance and was in fact considered identical with it, judging by the language used in connection with music and dance. [41] Official musicians were guardians for the tradition of both the music and the dance, and the names for the different styles of music were also those for the dances. [42] In later dynasties although music was sometimes played as accompaniment to singing and sometimes as pure instrumental pieces, the connection with the dance has always been close.

The history of Chinese music is a story of lost traditions and new adoptions: there was hardly any period in the Chinese history when the music was purely indigenous but there were periods in which Chinese music was practically entirely imported. [43] Even in the period of classical Chinese culture — Chou dynasty — there was foreign music in the temple ceremonies. [44] Foreign tributary tribes in Han dynasty offered their music and dances. [45] In the period of North and South, owing to the occupation of northern China by foreign tribes there was an influx of foreign music which in Sui and T'ang dynasties practically replaced native music in the imperial court. Of the ten schools of music under emperor Kao Tsung 高宗

---

[41] 周禮, 春官, 庎人 "掌敎舞散樂". A literal translation would read: ". . . in charge of teaching how to dance secular music".

[42] In ancient civilizations dance and music seemed to develop together. This is certainly the case with Greek music and poetry in which the metrical terms referred originally to movements of the dance, for example, the "foot". A. E. Haigh, *The Attic Theatre,* 311.

[43] 王國維, 宋元戲曲史, 十六章; 馬端臨, 文獻通考, 卷一四八. The reason lies partly in the use of ancient music for religious purposes: the preservation of the musical tradition was in the hands of a few court musicians rather than the people as a whole, hence it was easily lost.

[44] 周禮, 春官, 庎人.

[45] 後漢書, 東夷傳, 一段.

337

(reigned A.D. 627-649) only two were native. [46] In the later half of Sung dynasty the northern part of the country was again under foreign occupation and more foreign music came into the country, especially through popular entertainment. [47] So far as the Chinese drama is concerned the earliest music used was the music of late Sung dynasty [48] but even the music of Yüan dynasty which entered the northern and southern schools of the early dramas was lost. The earliest score was published in 1668 after the *K'un* tunes were in vogue, and the oldest music extant is the now obsolete *K'un* tunes. In them, as in some unknown local theatres possibly, there may be some element of the music of Sung and Yüan dynasties. [49] Although comparison with the instruments of Yüan dynasty shows that there have not been material changes in the types used in the theatre, it is difficult to say to what extent the modern Chinese theatrical music resembles the music of Yüan dynasty. [50]

---

[46] 舊唐書, 音樂志, 二.

[47] Ancient Chinese music being entirely lost, the study of it is now mostly concerned with those aspects which do not depend on the knowledge of the melodies, such as temperament, scale, instruments, general constructions of the compositions, etc.

[48] 王國維, 宋元戲曲史, 八章.

[49] Wang Kwang-Ch'i compared modern gramophone records of *K'un* tunes — of which Odeon Co. made about a hundred and Parlophone Co. also made some — with old scores and found that the intervals are the same but the time value of the notes is sometimes different and that roughly speaking the records and a score published in 1881 —王季烈, 集成曲譜— agree by about ninety percent and that score agrees with the oldest score — 葉廣明, 納書楹曲譜 — in also about ninety percent. See Wang Kwang-Ch'i, *Ueber die chinesische klassische Oper* (1934). This means that owing to the publication of the scores and the stability of *K'un* dramas there has been comparatively little change in the last three hundred years. The history of the Chinese drama is however seven hundred years.

[50] The history of some of the instruments in the Chinese theatre:

Chinese castanets (板)	— mentioned in Sung dynasty ((宋)陳暘, 樂書; (明) 會典).
Small drum (小鼓)	— at least as old as T'ang dynasty (舊唐書, 音樂志) — now called "single-face drum" (單皮鼓).
Hu-ch'in (胡琴)	— came from the northern tribes and used in the palace of Ming dynasty (明史).
"Three strings" (三弦)	— said to originate from Ch'in 秦 dynasty ((清)毛奇齡, 西河詞話). There was a "banjo" (弦裴) in T'ang dynasty (舊唐書, 音樂志).
"Moon lute" (月琴)	— mentioned in T'ang dynasty as being originally made of bronze. (唐書, 元行冲傳)
Flute (笛)	— mentioned in Chou dynasty (周禮).
Sheng (笙)	— mentioned in Chou dynasty (詩經).
Hsiao-na (銷吶)	— similar instruments in T'ang dynasty ("觱篥").
Yun-lo (雲鑼)	— mentioned in the official history of Yüan dynasty.
Cymbals (鈸)	— at least as old as T'ang dynasty, came from the western and southern tribes (通典, 卷一四四).
Hsing (星)	— came from India through the Buddhists.

338

In the style of singing and in the close relationship between singing and speech the Chinese have been consistent from ancient times. Of ancient poetry it was said:

"To modulate one's voice and to pronounce in a long drawn tone are both akin to singing. All ancient poetry was sung hence it was meant to express one's emotions". [51]

A lexicon of Han dynasty defined singing as

"pronouncing with a long drawn voice". [52]

A book of Yüan dynasty on phonology had high opinion of the elocution in the contemporary theatre:

". . . the words should be carefully pronounced according to their intonations as is done in the declamation and singing in southern dramas". [53]

Some of the basic metrical requirements of a poem written for reading are considered to be the same as those for song-words, for example, that the sequence of consonants and that of the "intonations" should not be such that reading or singing requires difficult manipulation of the vocal apparatus. This is why a singer may take the liberty to change the libretto which contains, for instance, too many words with *tz-* (尖音) sounds in succession. [54]

"The spoken part too should sound good. If it twists one's tongue, it hurts the ear; if it is sonorous, the audience will feel refreshed". [55]

There are no codified rules for prose-writing as there are for versification, but the principles are the same. Good Chinese prose makes the reader like to declaim it. Chinese books on dramatic poetry often discuss breathing, phrasing, elocution, rhythm and voice production. [56] According to a book of the thirteenth century:

"*Ch'ang-chuan* (唱賺) should be sung in accurate pitch and clear enunciation . . . the consonants should be distinguished: some are produced by the lips, some by the throat, some by the teeth, some by the tongue, some with closed lips and some with half-closed lips; and each word has a different accent or tone".[57]

齊如山, 中國劇之組織, 八章; 馬端臨, 文獻通考, 樂考, 卷百三十四至百三十九; 通典, 卷百四十四; 清高宗敕撰, 續文獻通考, 卷百一十; (中央音樂學院民族音樂研究所) 中國音樂史參考圖片 (一九五四).

[51] 詩經, 周南關雎序疏, 毛詩註疏, 卷一, "情動於中" 疏.

[52] 說文解字, 繫辭, 卷十六, 欠部, 鍇注, "歌者長引其聲而誦之".

[53] (元) 周德清, 中原音韻, 作詞起例. J. H. Levis believes that Byzantine church music also grew out of reading and he draws analogies between medieval church music and Chinese music. J. H. Levis, *Foundations of Chinese Musical Art* (1936).

[54] 王夢生, 梨園佳話, 一章, 字為唱工之第五步.

[55] 李笠翁, 曲話, 詞曲第四, 一款.

[56] e.g. 芝菴論曲 (元曲選).

[57] 王國維, 宋元戲曲史, 四章, 引, 日本翻元泰定本, 陳元靚, 事林廣記戊集卷二.

Ornaments, and possibly changes of key or mode within a tune, were practiced in Sung dynasty:

> "In *p'iao-ch'ang* (嘌唱) . . . the voice runs on wordless vocalizations and the singer toys with the keys and modes". [58]

Of the southern dramas it was said that there was "little expressiveness in the language but much in the voice. [59] Of singing it was said in the introduction to a collection of Yüan dynasty dramas:

> "A singer should never purse his lips or snap his fingers because these are ugly gestures, nor should he stamp his foot or shake his head to the rhythm of the music or change the accent and force of his voice excessively. These are the manners of vulgar musicians who try to attract attention by flippant and wanton gestures. A good voice is like the cloud floating across the sky, it is free to move in all directions and moves according to its own nature. Listening to good singing one's bad moods melt away and one feels pleased with oneself and comfortable in body and soul. Therefore it is said, 'When the voice permeates one's soul, it feels like sudden coolness in June'." [60]

---

[58] 耐得翁, 都城紀勝, 瓦舍衆伎條 "驅駕虛聲縱弄宮調"; 參, (宋) 沈 義父, 樂府指迷, 二十四款.

[59] 魏良輔, 曲律, 十節, "南曲辭情少聲情多".

[60] 臧晉叔, 元曲選, 元曲論, 末節. It is perhaps always difficult to describe good singing, hence the simile of the cloud. cf. the description of oriental music in the letters of Oswald Sickert in A. Waley, *The Noh Plays of Japan* (1921), Appendix.

CHAPTER XXXIII

THE GENEALOGY OF THE TYPES OF CHARACTERS

The classification of dramatic characters into types, which gives the Chinese theatre a distinctive characteristic, was derived from the early improvised farce in which it was necessary to assign different duties to the players.

Conventionalized farce [1] originated, as mentioned previously (Ch. XXII), from the court jesters' licence to ridicule an official in disgrace as part of his punishment. One of the court jesters would play the guilty official who happened to be of the *ts'an-chün* rank [2] and the other jesters would tease and bully him. A type of slapstick comedy was thus evolved in which the player who originally impersonated the official in disgrace was now the clown, feigning stupidity and being constantly beaten by his assistant, hence he came to be called *ts'an-chün* [3] and his assistant was called *ts'ang-hu,* [4] literally, "blue kite", presumably "because the kite strikes the other birds". [5] At this stage, the classification, not of the characters but of the actors, was necessitated by the improvised nature of the farce, and one of the two actors, the clown, was named after the original part he played, namely, an official of the *ts'an-chün* rank.

As the farce expanded in T'ang and Sung dynasties, the clown, being the most important player, became the head and director of the troupe and the name *ts'an-chün* became a general term for directors, being applied also to the conductors of orchestras and masters of ceremonies. He was also called "the bamboo stick" (竹竿子) after his baton and was mentioned in connection with many state

---

[1] 參軍戲
[2] 參軍
[3] 參軍
[4] 蒼鶻
[5] 陶宗儀, 輟耕錄, 卷二十五, 院本名目.

ceremonies. [6] The manner of his buffoonery may be surmised from the following philosophizing remark of Sung dynasty:

"The wealthy and powerful in this world are like the chief player *ts'an-chün* in the theatre, who would now sit at a desk and roar in anger and threaten the other players with his whip and when the play was over nothing of his authority was left". [7]

The farce then required four or five players and the regular actors were called: the *chief player* (戲頭), the *leader* (引戲), the *gentleman* (assistant to the clown) (副末, 次末), and the *"second official"* (played by the clown) (副淨) with an additional female impersonator or a "high official" when necessary. [8] The duties allotted to them were: "the *chief player* to lay the general plan, the *leader* to give the cues, the *clown* to make a feint and the *gentleman* to complete the joke". [9]

At this time the regular players were named partly according to their duties — the *chief player* and the *leader* — and partly to the type of character they played — the *gentleman* and the *second official* — and the temporary players who played the high officials and the female roles were merely called "impersonators" (裝孤, 裝旦). [10]

After the advent of the drama the larger scope of dramatic representation necessitated the division of the types of characters and, owing to the use of the script which made improvisation obsolete, the actors were no longer classified according

---

[6] 周密, 武林舊事, 卷一, 登門肆赦; 孟元老, 東京夢華錄, 卷九, 宰執親王宗室百官入內上壽. There were apparently two conductors in the court theatre of T'ang dynasty, one stationed "in the hall" and one stationed "below it" (probably in the courtyard). They wore distinctive hats and green gowns with large sleeves and each held a baton decorated with feathers or silk threads. At the beginning of the performance the baton in the hall was lowered into the horizontal position and seeing this, the conductor "below the hall" lowered his baton likewise, then music began. 段安節, 樂府雜錄 (協律郎).

[7] (宋) 洪邁, 容齋隨筆, 卷十四, 五款, 士之處世.

[8] 周密, 武林舊事, 卷四, 乾淳教坊樂部, 雜劇三甲; 陶宗儀, 輟耕錄, 卷二十五, 院本名目.

[9] 吳自牧, 夢粱錄, 卷二十, 妓樂, "主張, 分付, 發喬, 打諢". In one reference — 吳自牧, 夢粱錄, 卷二十 — the *chief player* 戲頭 is called the *gentleman* 末泥. The fact that the *clown* was called the *second official* 次淨, 副淨 and the player to complete the joke was called *second gentlemen* 副末 may be due to the fact that in the farce they played scholars and officials of lower social level, the first scholar was probably played by the *chief player* and the high official, who conducted himself properly, by the extra player 裝孤.

[10] The conjectural etymology of the names of the character-types is a favourite subject for newspaper articles. The older guesses may be found in(明) 寧獻王, 太和正音譜, 詞林須知, 末段 and a succinct statement on the subject in 王國維, 古劇脚色考 *passim*. It suffices here to say that many of the terms were probably colloquialisms and foreign words of late Sung and Yüan dynasties, which may have been further distorted by puns and abbreviations in the hands of illiterate actors.

342

to their duties. The results of these changes can be seen in the extant dramas of Yüan dynasty. [11] The *official* (淨) was no longer the clown but was only partially comic and had acquired since the early days of improvised farce an uncouth and uncanny character [12] and the specialized clown became a new type, *ch'ou* (丑). The female type multiplied into: the *old woman* (老旦), the *principal lady* (正旦), the *minor female role* (大旦), the *girl* (小旦), the *young girl* (旦兒), the *frivolous woman* (色旦), the *ugly woman* (搽旦), the *pretty woman* (花旦) and a few others and the gentleman type was similarly multiplied though not as numerously. The female character-types were also supplemented by the *extra female role* (外旦), the *auxiliary female role* (貼旦) and the *substitute female role* (沖旦). [13]

From Yüan to Ch'ing dynasty, there was no radical change in the types of characters: some minor subdivisions were combined and some new types were established. In the modern Chinese theatre the *official* (淨) has entirely dropped his comic traits and is also called the *painted face* (花臉) owing to the heavy make-up he now wears and, in addition, the warriors, both male (武生) and female (刀馬旦), emerge as new types. [14]

Thus the division of labour in the early Chinese farce, in which each actor was responsible for a definite part *of the action* whatever role he might be playing was carried into the Chinese drama and has now become a *classification of characters* and a scheme of specialization in the actors' training. Of the types in the Chinese theatre of to-day the female impersonator was due to the custom of men playing women and the clown was derived from early farce — both are known in the European theatre, for example, the boy actor of the Elizabethan theatre and the *zanni* in *commedia dell' arte* — the only type peculiar to the Chinese theatre is the *ching* (淨), the uncouth type of male character now called the *painted face* (花臉). He was at first a clown, but in Yüan dynasty his mysteriousness and unreasonableness, which he employed in his early days for sudden comic effect, made him into a new type which is now distinguished by the mask-like make-up he

---

[11] In the Yüan dramas, the main divisions were made according to sex and special histrionic abilities — as the *clown* and the female roles — and the subdivisions were made according to the temperament and age of the character as well as the players' status in the company. The criterion for the classification was therefore by no means simple.

[12] e.g. the warrior-monk in *Hsi Hsiang Chi* 西廂記

[13] *Extra female roles* were probably meant for actors who played women when necessary, as a side line, and "substitute" probably meant that the role might be taken by players who could not normally play the part — or was to be taken by such a player — and was so indicated in the actors' copy of the script which was later put to print.

[14] Military dance was performed in T'ang dynasty by female dancers — 杜甫, 觀公孫 大娘弟子舞劍器行. A version of this dance was performed in theatres in Peking in the early nineteenth century. （清）楊懋建, 夢華瑣簿（一八四三）, 二十四款.

has been wearing since Ming dynasty. [15] Subdivisions within each type which started in Yüan dynasty were evidently a matter of convenient management, because casting depended upon the professional status of the players (for example, "principal-", "second-", "extra-", etc.) as well as their skill and appearance (for example, "old woman", "young girl", "pretty woman", etc.). [16] Once the types were divided, however, the players practised, and were probably trained as they are now, in narrow fields, and the style of acting diversified accordingly. [17]

The classification of character-types produced far-reaching effects in the Chinese theatre through the greater contrast of dramatic characters and the more intensive development of the actor's and singer's art. [18] To divide people into types always involves simplification, because personal characteristics are highly complex and one man can differ from another in many ways and in various degrees. The more or less distinct social classes in China tend to divide people, in real life, into types, so that the Chinese theatre is, in this respect, not entirely unrealistic; nevertheless, some simplification is involved. Most actors can, of course, vary their acting to fit the individual characters portrayed so that the variety of characters is not as meagre as it may appear to be, but the dramatist must indicate which type each of his characters belongs to hence not all shades of personality and temperament are possible. The Chinese audience see humanity in the theatre as consisting of a few striking samples and for the uneducated this must have a profound effect on their general outlook. The audience understand each character in

---

(15) The fact that both the Chinese and the European clown (the latter from Pierrot of the *commedia dell' arte* to the circus clown of to-day) wear heavy white make-up may have a psychological basis. The beginning of the Chinese heavy make-up is not known; the European practice is said to come from the unconscious humour of three French bakers of the early seventeenth century who threw flour at each other. *Oxford Companion to the Theatre*, 135.

(16) The names of the types of characters, rather than the *dramatis personae,* are used in the extant dramas of Yüan dynasty, for example, "Enter principal lady", etc. This shows that the text, as we know it, was based on the players' working copies, because this was the natural way for the players to write their script and they could thus easily tell what types were required in a play.

(17) Specialization is inevitable in stable companies run on the repertory system — in which plays are constantly ready to be presented. Chinese theatres often change the bill every night. In the English stock companies which disappeared at the end of the nineteenth century the actors and actresses were divided into: Leading Man or Tragedian (Hamlet, Macbeth), Old Man (Brabantio), Old Woman (Juliet's nurse), Heavy Father or Heavy Lead (tyrants and villains), Heavy Woman (Lady Macbeth, Emilia in *Othello*), Juvenile Lead (young lover and hero), Juvenile Tragedian (Macduff, Laertes), Low Comedian, Walking Lady (small part), Walking Gentleman, General Utility (all minor roles), Supernumeraries, Leading Singer, Principal Dancer, etc.

(18) In the Chinese theatre of to-day the actor's gait and gestures such as those of the "tab sleeves" are differentiated according to the types of characters. In singing not only the manner of voice production but also the musical figures vary from one type of character to another — e.g. male and female roles never sing exactly the same tune.

the drama at the first look, and expect him to remain true to his type throughout the play. Temperaments and morals tend towards extremes and characters are brought against each other in strong contrast, so that the theme of the Chinese drama is always easy to understand. At the same time, the technique of declamation, dancing and singing becomes highly developed under detail specialization and the general connoisseurship of the audience in these respects is remarkably high.

Character-types in the Chinese theatre are, in a way, similar to the types of singers in the European opera. Operatic singers are divided according to their voice, such as "mezzo-soprano", "castrato", etc., with the result that the *dramatis personae* in operas are also so divided. The infinite varieties of the tone and pitch of the human voice outside the few recognized types of singers are not represented. In the Chinese theatre classification is not only based on the voice but also on the temperament of the character. In the western opera one hears only a few types of voice; in the Chinese theatre one sees only a few types of people.

The female impersonator is a distinctive feature of the Chinese theatre which excludes the exhibition of feminine charm and establishes a style of acting for the female parts which is based not on natural beauty but on training and technique.

In China the practice of men playing women is due, in general, to the attitude towards womanhood and, in particular, to the beginning of the Chinese theatre among the court jesters.

Excessive preventive measures in the contact between the sexes, such as that men and women should not hand things directly to each other except in religious ceremonies [19] and that women should theoretically veil their faces when they go out, [20] gave rise to a heightened erotic sensitivity in men [21] because of which no Chinese women, except those of the lowest social caste, would want to expose themselves to the public eye. Mixed social dancing was probably as old as Chinese history because it was apparently mentioned in the *Book of Odes* [22] but at least in late Chou dynasty it was condemned by the moralists one of whom referred to it as "jesters and dwarfs and men and women were among each other like monkeys, stepping forward and backward in the bent position in a continuous mood of abandon to the depraved music of nowadays". [23] Under such conditions freedom of association was not only indiscreet but actually dangerous and women players performing in public were in fact looked upon with an unwholesome eye.

Women musicians and dancers served in the courts of the princes at the time

---

[19] 禮記, 內則, 孟子, 離婁.
[20] 禮記, 內則.
[21] 參, 禮記, 坊記.
[22] 詩經, 陳風.
[23] 禮記, 樂記.

when court jesters first appeared [24] but they were courtezans rather than actresses. It is not known whether the goddesses in the pageants of Han dynasty were impersonated by men; the fact that they sang and that women acrobats were known at the time suggests they were women players (Ch. XXI). When the debauched emperor at the end of Wei dynasty indulged in his vulgar taste he had to make "young jesters play wanton women". (Ch. XXII). In this particular case actors were chosen to play women probably because they were less modest and restrained. In the later pageants men in large numbers masqueraded as women. Here the object was not to deceive the spectators but to excite their wonder. Like the animal masquers, these female impersonators were to be admired for their felicitous though recognizable disguise. Emperor Hsüan Ti 宣帝 (reigned 579-579) of North Chou dynasty (北周) "collected handsome young men of the city to be dressed as women to sing and dance in his pageants" [25] and emperor Yang Ti's 煬帝 (reigned 605-618) musicians who sang and danced were also "dressed as women wearing jewelry and flowers". [26] Women with "jewelry and flowers" were not wanting — not at any rate in emperor Yang Ti's court, he had boat-loads of them when he sailed on his canal to the south — hence the object of the female impersonation could not have been deception. Women musicians were employed in the court of T'ang dynasty, but in 661 "the empress asked for and was granted the prohibition of women taking part in theatrical performances in any part of the country", [27] showing that women were then invading the Chinese theatre but were considered a disgrace to womankind. Emperor Ming Huang's 明皇 (reigned 712-756) academy for musicians in his Pear Garden was supplemented by the *Mansion of Propitious Spring* (宜春院) which housed a few hundred women musicians and actresses. At this time whole families entered the musical profession and attached themselves to the court, living in special quarters in the capital and often inter-marrying among themselves. [28] The musicians in the academy being connected in family relations, mixed performances at court would not have infringed the social convention of segregation. Outside the imperial court, when, after centuries of the social convention regarding women, an actress was needed in the popular dramatic dance *Stamping and Swaying Woman*, [29] we find that "man dressed as woman" to play *and sing* in it. [30] By the reign of I Tsung 懿宗 (reigned 860-873) three actors were famous for impersonating women, [31]

---

[24] 論語, 微子. For women musicians of later times see 太平御覽, 卷五六八.
[25] 馬端臨, 文獻通考, 樂考二.
[26] 隋書, 音樂志, 下.
[27] 舊唐書, 高宗紀, 顯慶六年.
[28] 崔令欽, 教坊記, 一及八款.
[29] 踏搖娘
[30] 崔令欽, 教坊記, 踏搖娘.
[31] 段安節, 樂府雜錄, 俳優.

and this in spite of the fact that emperor Hsüan Tsung 玄宗 (reigned 712-756) had trained a few hundred women musicians and actresses. [32] Some women players did indeed become famous: "two brothers and the wife of one of them played the conventional farce [33] extremely well, their singing voice reached the clouds" [34] and in the reign of emperor Su Tsung 肅宗 (reigned 756-762) "actresses impersonated officials in green gowns holding bamboo slips". [35] In the period of exuberant growth of farce and dramatic dances in Southern Sung only two women were named among a list of thirty-nine famous players [36] and mixed performance did not appear to be the rule at this time, otherwise the actors of the farce would not need "a player to impersonate the woman (裝旦)". (Ch. XXIII). The performances in the pleasure houses were believably by the girls exclusively. [37] The close connection between the pleasure house and the theatre continued through the rise of the drama and actresses in Yüan dynasty were called "people of the house" [38] and would sit in special seats in the theatre to eye the spectators. (Ch. XXVI). Whole families were in the dual profession of the theatre and the pleasure house, with the former serving probably as advertising campaign. In a drama of that period a man from a respectable family wants to marry an actress and says, "I am a respectable man; I should be good enough to be the son-in-law of people of the house". [39] When touring from one town to another actresses rendered special service to the local magistrate or mayor for his protection. [40] A robber's instruction for his wife in a novel based on the conditions in Yüan dynasty says,

> ". . . The second type of people we must not kill are the itinerant sing-song girls. They travel through counties and provinces to make a living by trying to please their clients and audience, doing what they do not like to do. If we kill them and take their money their companions will eventually know what happens to them and may represent us in their dramas as being mean and thereby ruin our reputation for generations to come". [41]

This throws some light on the hard life of the actresses of that time. Under these

---

[32] Female impersonation was listed as a type of court entertainment in T'ang dynasty and several actors were mentioned as being famous for it. 馬端臨, 文獻通考, 樂考二十 (假婦戲).

[33] 參軍戲

[34] 范攄, 雲溪友議, 卷九, 六款 (稗海全書).

[35] 趙璘, 因話錄, 卷一, 四款.

[36] 周密, 武林舊事, 卷六, 諸色伎藝人, 雜劇.

[37] In Sung dynasty women also performed in "talks on history", "humorous talks", story-telling, riddles, juggling, tumbling, etc. 吳自牧, 夢粱錄, 卷二十, 妓樂, 百戲伎藝, 角觝; 周密, 武林舊事, 卷六, 諸色伎藝人.

[38] 行院

[39] "行院人家". 永樂大典戲文, 宦門子弟錯立身 "麻郎".

[40] 水滸傳 (百回本), 五十一回.

[41] 水滸傳 (百回本), 二十七回.

conditions women, as in the "houses", had sometimes to play men, and several girls of this time were mentioned for their talents "in both male and female roles". [42] The practice of men playing women was likely to have subsisted in Yüan dynasty, especially as the women players were not full-time actresses, therefore it may be said that starting in this period both men and women regularly played male and female roles in the Chinese theatre, sometimes in mixed troupes and sometimes in all women companies. Women players were active also in Ming dynasty: they were mentioned both in connection with dramatic criticism [43] and in dramas on the life of actress-courtezans. [44] At the beginning of Ch'ing dynasty the playwright and critic Li Yü (李漁) taught his all women troupe "to sing the most suggestive songs behind a curtain in order to attract wealthy clients". [45] Women players did not seem to be active in the eighteenth century, not at any rate during the vogue of female impersonators. In recent decades they were not known in Peking until 1914 to 1915 and they created a sensation when they invaded the city. At first they played with men, but the actors, being afraid of their competition, asked the government, through their guild, to prohibit mixed troupes, thinking that women alone could not attract much attention. The women players, however, regrouped themselves and managed to keep a place of their own in the profession. [46] Some actresses are true artists, for instance, Meng Hsiao-Tung (孟小冬), who played male roles, was considered one of the best players of that type, and Hsin Yen-Ch'iu (新艷秋), who played female roles, was ranked next to the best four female impersonators.

To summarize, the earliest Chinese dramas, in the form of simple farce, were played by the court jesters among whom there were no women, hence there were no female roles in the earliest plays. When female roles were required in the expanded theatre of Sung dynasty, men played women because the general nature of the plays — farce or dance — did not require convincing representation. The Chinese attitude towards dramatic illusion made the continued existence of female impersonators in the theatre possible and when women players did sometimes enter the profession they, owing to the social convention, were often courtezans as well. Now after a long tradition of female impersonation the audience prefer men to women in female roles and a special connoisseurship for female impersonation has developed. To the Chinese theatre-goers if a female impersonator is not more feminine-looking than a woman he cannot justify his existence as an artist, though he may justify himself as a stunt. Few women can be superlatively dainty and exquisite, because of the type of

---

[42] （元）黃雪蓑, 靑樓集, 燕山秀, 參, 南春宴, 國玉第. Some of the girls were also famous for playing emperors and some for playing bandits.

[43] 張岱, 陶菴夢憶, 卷五, 十五款（朱楚生條）; 卷二, 五款（朱雲崍）

[44] e.g. 朱有燉, 誠齋樂府.

[45] 青木正兒, 中國近世戲曲史, 十章三節（二）, 引, 娜如山房說尤, 卷下.

[46] 齊如山, 京劇之變遷, 頁四八.

CHAPTER XXXIV

MASKS AND LONG SLEEVES IN CHINESE HISTORY

Masks have been associated with the Chinese theatre from its earliest times but they do not appear to have been a prominent feature of it until Ming dynasty.

The earliest mask on record is the mask of the official exorcist of Chou dynasty (1122-255 B.C.) who wore "bear skin with four gold eyes" [1] believed to be impersonating a benign spirit who had power over the evil ones [2] but the use of masks probably dated further back in Chinese history because grotesque bronze masks of Chou dynasty have been unearthed [3] and these, being flat and hence apparently for decoration or used as ceremonial objects, might have been derived from earlier models which were actually worn on the face. Animal masquers were among the attendants in the imperial court of Han dynasty (206 B.C. — A.D. 220) [4] and a great variety of animal masks were used in the pageants of the same period. [5] A human mask was first mentioned in connection with Yü Liang (庾亮) of Chin 晉 dynasty (A.D. 265-419) "after whose death the musicians of his house made a mask in his likeness and performed a dance to his memory". [6] It appears therefore that although the animal mask was derived from religious practice in ancient times the human mask was an invention of a much later date occasioned perhaps by the desire for a living statue. The mask of Prince Lan-Ling (蘭陵王) of North Ch'i 北齊 dynasty (A.D. 550-577), a warrior with effeminate features who wore it to terrorize his enemies [7] also had a practical purpose, but unlike the dance in memory of Yü Liang of which only the music survived in T'ang dynasty, this mask was the first to enter the Chinese theatre, in the dramatic dance based on the Prince's exploits. [8]

---

[1] 周禮, 夏官司馬.
[2] 陳夢家, 商代的神話與巫術, 燕京學報, 二十期.
[3] Some can be seen in the Art Institute of Chicago.
[4] 漢書, 禮樂志.
[5] 李尤, 平樂觀賦; 張衡, 西京賦.
[6] 隋書, 音樂志, 下, 禮畢.
[7] 舊唐書, 音樂志, 二.
[8] *Ibid.*

Animal masks continued to be used in the dances: in the reign of emperor Wu Ti 武帝 (A.D. 561-578) of North Chou dynasty (北周) the "eighty dancers who, arrayed in a square figure like a city wall, performed a dance in the manner of the barbarians", and wore "wooden animal masks resembling dogs, wigs of threads with gold ornaments and hats made of leopard's skin". [9] In the reign of emperor Yang Ti 煬帝 (A.D. 605-618) there were many masquers among his mammoth spectacles [10] and in the *lion-dance* (師子舞) of T'ang dynasty

> "actors inside the lion-skins imitated the movements of the lions and two other actors with whips played the trainers. There were five lions arranged in their assigned positions and one hundred and forty singers accompanied the dance".
> [11]

In Sung dynasty there were masks which served a practical purpose as when one warrior "wore bronze mask and loose hair when he was fighting rebels" [12] as well as those apparently for decoration only:

> "In the reign of Cheng Ho 政和 (A.D. 1111-1117) for the exorcism of epidemic spirits (大儺) one district sent the emperor one pack of mask(s) and the court, thinking it contained only one, was puzzled by the paucity of the tribute but was amazed to find a set of eight hundred masks of old and young and handsome and ugly faces, each different from the others". [13]

Masks were also extensively used in Sung dynasty in pageants and spectacles. [14] Some dramas of Yüan dynasty were about gods and daemons (see Ch. XXVI), and one would expect the actors playing them to wear masks. [15] In the Chinese theatre of to-day only supernatural characters such as *The Official from Heaven* (天官) wear removable masks. It is not impossible that the detachable mask has never played an important part in the Chinese theatre.

The so-called "masked characters" in the Chinese theatre are in fact actors wearing thick paint which has the same effect as masks, hence the name *painted face* (花臉). Paint cannot be as easily changed as detachable masks therefore it is not as economical and convenient, but the actor can move the muscles of his face and is therefore not deprived of all his capacity for facial expression. Also, detachable masks do not always fit the size of the head and the height of the actor, and their

---

[9] 舊唐書, 音樂志, 二 (首段).

[10] 隋書, 音樂志, 下.

[11] 馬端臨, 文獻通考, 卷百四十五.

[12] 宋史, 卷二百九十, 狄青傳

[13] 陸游, 老學庵筆記, 卷一, 十七款. In Ch'ing dynasty "hundreds of masks, no two of them alike", were used in theatrical performances in the palace. 趙翼, 簷曝雜記, 卷一, 慶典, 大戲 (甌北全集).

[14] 孟元老, 東京夢華錄, 卷七, 駕登寶津樓諸軍呈百戲, 卷十, 除夕.

[15] None however was mentioned in the fifteen plays in which costume and properties are indicated and which have been surveyed by modern scholars (馮沅君, 古劇說彙, 二章, 十六, 十七) perhaps because they happened not to be required in these plays.

absolute immobility makes them look lifeless. [16] On the other hand, paint, as used in the Chinese theatre, does not change the *actual* shape of the actor's face as a detachable mask can; he cannot, for example, have an actually larger nose, and the bright colours and bold patterns, unlike a mask with ordinary features, make the actor, in most cases, lose much of the likeness of a human face, and become devoid of ordinary expressions such as smiles and frowns. Therefore, the *painted face* is not exactly the same as a detachable mask.

Make-up was used in the dramatic dance of T'ang dynasty called *Stamping and Swaying Woman* [17] to imitate the drunkard's red face. [18] It is not known whether the make-up then was heavier than would be consistent with realism. Emperor Chuang Tsung 莊宗 (reigned 923-926) of Later T'ang dynasty 後唐, was said to have "put on powder and ink" to be an actor. [19] In a book of Sung dynasty is an anecdote about a man who, in an act of bravado, "smeared his face with ink and put on a green gown" to perform a weird dance in front of the hall of a high official. [20] In Sung dynasty emperor Hui Tsung 徽宗 (reigned 1101-1125) after seeing the quaint costume of his foreign envoys ordered his dancers "to wear the same dress and put on powder and ink" to imitate their manners in a dance, [21] and at a banquet one official "after putting on a short jacket with small sleeves and smearing his face with blue and red, mixed with the court jesters". [22] In the last instance the make-up seemed to have gone beyond realism.

Heavy and unrealistic make-up must have passed into the dramas of Yüan dynasty with the other elements of the theatre of Sung dynasty. Of an actor it was said that he

". . . wore a black turban with a pen stuck on it. His whole face was covered with lime, and some black strips were drawn on it". [23]

A character in a drama of this period says,

"I am a general but stratagems and warfare I know not; my family do not

---

[16] Theoretically slight modification of the expression is possible by tilting the head (W. T. Benda, *Masks* (1944).) but the change is limited. Quintilian mentioned unsymmetrical masks in the Roman theatre for changing the visible expression by turning one or the other half towards the audience — Bieber, *History of the Greek and Roman Theatre,* 91, Figs. 253 (p. 184), 266 (p. 192).

[17] 踏搖娘 . See Chapter XXII.

[18] 段安節, 樂府雜錄, 鼓架部. According to another reference — 崔令欽, 教坊記 — it was to imitate a rash.

[19] 新五代史, 卷三七, 伶官傳; 王國維, 古劇脚色考, 餘說二.

[20] （宋）李昉等, 太平廣記, 卷四百九十六, 趙存, 引, 溫庭筠, 朝巽子 This case may not however indicate that smearing the face with ink was the theatrical practice of that time because the man might be trying to be conspicuous — he also "deliberately went away slowly after he finished."

[21] 陶宗儀, 輟耕錄, 卷二十五, 院本名目.

[22] 宋史, 卷四七二, 姦臣傳（蔡攸）.

[23] 太平樂府, 卷九, 元, 杜善夫, 莊家不識勾闌, 耍孩兒.

own a flour shop, how is that we two, father and son, are smeared with white powder?'' [24]

Again,

(Prologue)   ''We would readily put on ash and chalk . . .'' [25]

In one drama a courtezan is described as:

''What she puts on her face — here a patch of blue, there a patch of purple, there white, and there black — makes her look like a daemon with a multi-coloured face''. [26]

The last example suggests that daemons wore unrealistic make-up even then.

In the text of the dramas of Ming dynasty (1368-1643), however, painted faces are clearly indicated, for example, ''Enter so-and-so with blue face''. [27] Sometimes the colour of the face is varied, apparently for decorative effect, as shown in the following stage direction:

''One warrior, bearded, with three eyes, dance with spear in first position east.

One warrior, black face, holding staff, dance in first position west.

One warrior, blue face, dance with club in second position east.

One warrior, red face, dance with long sword in second position west.'' [28]

Sometimes clowns also wore unrealistic masks:

''This multi-coloured face suits the comic business''. [29]

It is to be remembered that the *ching* (淨) type was partially comic in Yüan dramas and they wore heavy make-up probably for comic effect. Foreigners, then as now, wore heavy make-up: one stage direction reads,

''. . . powdered face, beard and large nose''. [30]

Of bold patterns it was said,

''The little face is different from the ordinary; it has variegated patterns of powder and ink''. [31]

The influence of the novel was then evident, because the heroes of popular legends who entered the dramas had red or black faces as described in the popular novels. According to Prof. Ch'i Ju-Shan the *painted face* was not much used in Yüan dynasty, but became prevalent in Ming dynasty owing to the vogue of military plays then. There is no doubt that the *ching* type (淨) of character has been expanded since Ming dynasty: many legendary and historical personages who are now played

[24] （元曲選）伍員吹簫，一折，淨白.
[25] 永樂大典戲文，張協狀元（水調歌頭），參，宦門子弟錯立身，（六么令）.
[26] 酷寒亭，二折，正末白.
[27] （六十種曲）曇花記傳奇，十四齣 cf.（六十種曲）蕉帕記，十八齣.
[28] 鄭之珍，目蓮救母，中，二十五折.
[29] （六十種曲）東郭記，十四齣，黃鶯兒.
[30] （六十種曲）紫釵記，三十齣.
[31] （六十種曲）梵香記，四齣，窄地錦檔.

by the *ching* type were then played by the *sheng* type (生), the ordinary male role. [32] Doubling, as between the *ching* type and the *old woman* (老旦), shows that acting and voice were not then as much differentiated as they are now.

Face painting as practised to-day has probably a multiple origin. Chang Hsiao-Hsia believes that it was derived from one or the other of the following:

(1) Accentuated make-up.
(2) Bandits' and robbers' make-up to terrorize their victims or conceal identity.
(3) Gods and spirits in exorcist's rituals.
(4) Warriors' visor.
(5) Imitation of detachable masks. [33]

Used for differentiating the good characters from the bad, it was as old as the shadow plays:

> "In the shadow plays the good characters had normal faces; the bad ones, ugly faces. . ." [34]

On gods and daemons it may be a copy of earlier masks, as Chang Hsiao-Hsia suggests, or it may be direct imitation of their images in the temples, for example, the face of the gods are usually painted gold both in the temples and on the stage and daemons in both places have similarly grotesque appearance. [35] In the latter case the actors are made to look like the statues come to life and the device is, in a sense, realistic. Imitation of statues in the temples and painting masquers' faces white, yellow, blue and green were known in the pageants of Sung dynasty. [36] In a novel of Ming dynasty one of the characters laughed when he saw a strange statue and said,

> ". . . 'The ancient world must have thieves too, for here is represented one with his face smeared with soot, put here for public exhibition', but after going a few steps nearer, he added, 'This is no thief, — I see, this is the temple of Chang Fei' [a warrior of the period of Three Kingdoms] then he began to think within himself, 'If this is the temple of Chang Fei there should be a warrior's helmet on his head . . . but this is an emperor's crown, and with a black face? — yes, this must be the emperor Yü'. [mythical emperor of ancient China known for his success in draining the country]". [37]

---

[32] 齊如山, 戲劇脚色名詞考, 四章, 總論.

[33] 張笑俠, 臉譜大全, 四章.

[34] 吳自牧, 夢梁錄, 卷二十, 百戲伎藝

[35] One explanation for the gold face of Buddha is that in Buddhist books his face is said to "radiate golden light". 齊如山, 臉譜, 頁十一. The face and hands of God were also sometimes painted in gold in medieval dramas: in the transformation scene of Christ in Jean Michel's *Le Passion* (1490) He had *"une face et des mains toute d'or bruny. Et ung gran soleil à rays par derrière"*. and the angels were painted red. *Oxford Companion to the Theatre*, 498.

[36] 孟元老, 東京夢華錄, 卷七, 駕登寶津樓諸軍呈百戲. See Chapter XXX.

[37] (明) 董說, 西遊補, 六回.

355

This shows that ancient emperors and famous warriors were represented as having black faces. For thieves and robbers who in China were known to paint their faces in order to conceal their identity, the practice is also realistic. The most important source, however, is probably the gradual accentuation of make-up. Most of the *masked characters* in the Chinese theatre are neither gods nor robbers, hence their painted faces are purely for theatrical purposes. Records of make-up for different characters were kept in Ming dynasty, and some of them are extant; [38] they look very heavy perhaps because of poor draughtsmanship or that they already represented a late stage of development. Make-up always looks heavy at close quarters, and in copying it from graphic records to the human face, especially for an audience accustomed to unrealistic and striking costume — such as the pheasant feathers, the large beards, the padded warriors, etc. — the make-up could have a natural tendency to become heavier, and a very gradual change through the several centuries of the Chinese theatre would have been sufficient to produce the *painted faces* of to-day. Comparison of records of Ming dynasty and those of to-day for the same *dramatis personae* shows a continual accentuation. It is not yet known however whether the already heavy make-up of Ming dynasty (practically a mask) was derived from realistic make-up of earlier times. Once the practice was established, dramatic characters in new dramas would naturally have *painted faces* like the characters in old dramas. The *painted faces* of to-day also show a tendency towards more striking colours and more complicated patterns. [39]

The basis of stage make-up is the same as that of cosmetics the extreme forms of which also deviate from natural appearance. The courtezans of Yüan dynasty, who had common aims with the actresses, used the beauty spot.

"Courtezans who put a spot of ink on their face are called *hua-tan* (花旦)". [40]

In its milder forms theatrical make-up is neither cosmetics nor disguise, but is necessitated by the size and lighting conditions of the theatre. Here again, the basic nature of the theatre is contrary to naturalism in the narrow sense of the word. In real life the audience seldom look at people under strong lighting and from a distance, which make the face look flat and lose much of its power of expression. Without make-up actors will look unnatural, but with it the distortion in the appearance of the actors under abnormal conditions is compensated for, making the actors' faces approach the audience's *impression* of normal human faces. The Chinese players go one step further: they let their faces look unnatural in the theatre,

---

[38] Cecilia S. L. Zung, *Secrets of the Chinese Drama;* 齊如山, 中國劇之組織, 頁七八.

[39] 齊如山, 中國劇之組織, 頁七八, 七九.

[40] (元) 黃雪蓑, 青樓集, 李定奴條. It may be noticed that *hua-tan* was also a theatrical term for the pretty female roles. A mural of "Yüan" dynasty depicts actors wearing heavy make-up, but not to the extent of modern "masks" — 顧學頡, 元人雜劇選, frontispiece.

but in a dramatically effective way. Stage make-up has been used in the European theatre to make, for example, a young actor look like an old man, in other words to change one type of natural appearance into another; in the Chinese theatre the *painted face* changes the natural appearance into mask. [41]

The "tab-sleeve" (水袖), which plays a very important part in the Chinese style of acting, has a long history. In its present form it is an extension of the normal sleeve in light white silk, more than a foot long and open at the lower seam, reaching the floor when the actor stretches his arm straight downwards. It was added to the stage costume at an unknown date; [42] no ancient Chinese dress had such sleeves. After it was added to the sleeves it must have grown in length, because it is now longer than its purpose — to protect the ends of the normal sleeves — requires. [43]

Long sleeves have been connected with the dance from the earliest days of the Chinese history. The relative proportion of arm and foot movements in the dance is different for different countries and ages. The male dancer in the Spanish *fandango* does not move his arms much but in some Indian dances the feet are hardly used at all and the dances can be performed in the sitting position. [44] Some Roman dances in the time of the early Empire appeared to have prominent arm movements because Ovid (47 B.C.—A.D. 17) advised men with shapely arms not to miss the opportunity of showing them off in the dance. [45] The Chinese word for dance, *wu* 舞 , means arm movement; it is only in the modern term *wu-tao* 舞蹈 that the word for "steps" (*tao* 蹈) is added. Although the ancient definition for dance was "waving the arm and stepping the foot" under excitement [46] there was little mention of foot or leg movements in connection with the ancient dances [47] but the

---

[41] The problem of changing make-up on stage has not often been tackled in the European theatre. It has been suggested that, in scenes of fright or surprise, colour be removed from the face by an oiled glove as the actor puts his hands on his face in the course of the acting — Leman Thomas Rede, *The Road to the Stage* (1827). In the Chinese theatre backstage personnel come on to the stage to help changing costume and make-up.

[42] A mural representing a dramatic performance of "Yüan" dynasty shows no "tab-sleeves" — 顧學頡, 元人雜劇選, frontispiece.

[43] The etymology has often been misunderstood. Literally *shui-hsiu* 水袖 means "water sleeve". Cecilia S. L. Zung *(Secrets of the Chinese Drama)* translated it as "rippling sleeve" and Harold Acton *(Oxford Companion to the Theatre,* CHINA) and A.C. Scott *(World Theatre,* Vol. II, No. 4 (1953), 30-34) as "rippling water sleeve". The word *shui,* "water", actually means that it is the washable part of the sleeve, as in the case of *shui-pan* 水板 — literally "water board" — a kind of notice board with words written directly on it which can be washed and re-used. A special shirt worn under the silk robes in the Chinese theatre to prevent the perspiration from soiling them is called *shui- i* 水衣 or "water shirt" for the same reason. 齊如山, 行頭盔頭, 上, 頁二一.

[44] *Encyclopaedia Britannica,* fourteenth edition, DANCE.

[45] *The Art of Love,* I. 595.

[46] 禮記, 樂記.

[47] cf. terms used in the European ballet: *entrechat, fouetté, pas, pirouette.*

arm movements in the ceremonial dances of Chou dynasty were brought out by such implements as shields, wands fitted with feathers and yak tails. [48] When empty-handed, the dancer "expressed the emotions with his hands and sleeves". [49] The tradition of dancing with long sleeves went even further back into the Chinese history, for the shamans who had been active in the preceding dynasty, Shang (商), were represented by a hieroglyph shaped like a "dancer with two long sleeves". [50] It was specified in Chou dynasty that "the length of the sleeve should be such that when it is folded back the end reaches the elbow". [51] After centuries of the dancer's long sleeves the observation was made in Han dynasty that "long sleeves are good for dancing" [52] a statement which would be inexplicable if applied to most European dance styles. Long sleeves were not only generally good for dancing, but could, like music, excite the desire to dance, as when Li Po wrote,

> ". . . sleeves long, flutes inviting, the arms wanted to wave. Merry with wine, the governor stood up and danced". [53]

Dancing with the sleeves might have originated in the "dance with bare hands" [54] in the ceremonial dances of Chou dynasty, and the large sleeves worn by the Chinese in later ages would tend to perpetuate it. Large sleeves on the dancer have the same effect as long sleeves: with bare arms or close fitting sleeves the spectators can only see the instantaneous movements of the arms at any moment, but the large or long sleeve would sway and float and flutter according to the previous movements of the dancer's arms and hands. Chinese portraits of ancient personages may be idealized and unreliable, but study based on archaeological objects shows that in Han (206 B.C. — A.D. 220) and the Six Dynasties (A.D. 221-588) Chinese dresses had large sleeves. [55] The *Historical Memoirs* by Ssu-Ma Ch'ien also mentioned the fashion of long sleeves:

> "Women nowadays . . . play with their long sleeves and wear pointed shoes". [56]

A children's song in Han dynasty says,

> "If the city people have tall buns, the women around the city do their hair one foot high; if the city people have short eyebrows, the people around the city

[48] 周禮, 春官, 樂師, "干舞, 羽舞, 皇舞, 旄舞."
[49] 周禮, 春官, 樂師, 人舞注.
[50] 許慎, 說文解字, 第五, 上"象人兩褎舞形" The word *hsiu* 褎 means end of sleeve.
[51] 禮記, 深衣.
[52] "長袖善舞" 史記, 范睢蔡澤傳賛.
[53] 李白, 憶昔遊寄譙郡元參軍詩, "袖長管催欲輕舉, 漢東太守醉起舞."
[54] 人舞
[55] Yoshito Harada, Chinese Dress and Personal Ornaments in the Han and Six Dynasties, *The Toyo Bunko Ronsô,* Series A, Vol, XXIII, 1937. 原田淑人, 漢六朝の服飾, 東洋文庫論叢, 第二十三.
[56] 史記, 貨殖列傳 "潁川."

shave off half of theirs; if the city people have large sleeves, the people around the city make theirs with ten yards of material''. [57]

Women's large sleeves in the Six Dynasties are also found on the statuettes of that period. Figurines in the tombs of T'ang dynasty show sleeves extended beyond the hands, and some of them are posed like dancers. [58] Of the many dancing costumes described in the official history of T'ang dynasty several had large sleeves:

> "The *Ch'ing-Shan Dance* (慶善樂) was created by emperor T'ai Tsung 太宗 (reigned 627-649) . . . There were sixty dancers all dressed in purple, and the costume consisted of jacket with large sleeves and skirt to match. The dancers also wore buns of black hair on their heads and leather shoes''. [59]

> "For the *Scarf Dance* (巾 舞) . . . four dancers in green linen dresses with large sleeves danced with the gracefulness of the drifting clouds and the soaring phoenix. They wore silk shoes and had on their heads black buns decorated with gold flowers''. [60]

> "In the reign of Te Tsung 德宗 (reigned 780-805) . . . there were Korean dancers who wore hats of purple silk decorated with feathers, jackets with large sleeves, purple belts, large trousers, red leather shoes and lace of many colours''. [61]

References to the long sleeves in the poems of T'ang and Sung dynasties are numerous. Even in daily wear a man climbing a hill would wave his sleeves, [62] and young women had to roll up their long sleeves in order to stretch forth their hands. [63] On women, they enhanced the beauty of the hands, as in

> ". . . her white wrist raised, her long sleeves flowing''. [64]

and some poets seemed to be particularly sensitive to them and would remember how they half-covered the fan and cushioned the cup. [65] "When the breeze ruffled the sleeves, they made the person wearing them look like a dancer'', [66] and one poet compared the whirling snow flakes to "the sweeping sleeves of dancing court

---

[57] (明) 楊愼，古今風謠，卷上六十一款，城中謠.

[58] 鄭德坤, 沈維鈞, 中國明器，燕京學報專號之一.

[59] 舊唐書, 音樂志, 二.

[60] *Ibid.*

[61] *Ibid.*

[62] 陸游 (1125-1210) 好事近, 登梅仙山絕頂望海 "揮袖上西峯" "Round collar and large sleeves'' were mentioned in the official history of Sung dynasty. 宋史, 輿服志, 五 (襴衫).

[63] 朱敦儒 (twelfth century) 鷓鴣天 "佳人挽袖乞新詞." 劉禹錫 (772-842) 樂天 寄憶舊遊因作報白君以答 "長袂女郎簪翠翹."

[64] 梁簡文帝, 採蓮賦, "素腕舉，紅袖長."

[65] 晏幾道 (eleventh century) 鷓鴣天 "彩袖殷勤捧玉鍾"; 阮郎歸, "綠杯紅 袖趁重陽", 碧牡丹 "翠袖疏紈扇."

[66] 白居易 (772-846) 長恨歌 "風吹仙袂飄飄舉，猶似霓裳羽衣舞."

ladies''. [67] ''In the *Daemons' Dance* of T'ang dynasty the daemons danced with long sleeves''. [68] Describing a dance a poet of early T'ang dynasty said,

"Every note in the music is matched with sleeve movement and the rhythm of the notes paralleled by that of the steps''. [69]

In the poet's imagination sleeves could even cover mountains:

"Emperor T'ai Tsung 太宗 (reigned 627-650) often asked his friends to sing with him. On one occasion the Prince of Ch'ang-Sha sang, 'The country is too small for dancing to and fro'. . . and Li Po (李白) sang, 'If I want the dancer's sleeves to fly freely, I'll let them pass over Wu Sun Mountain, and after I am intoxicated with wine, I like to feel the cool breeze at my sleeves as I come back'.'' [70]

Children also danced with their sleeves.

"The children of the village sang a whole series of songs and went to the festival playing flutes and drums. The singers waved their sleeves in the dance, those who could sing the greatest number of songs were honoured by their companions''. [71]

Dancing puppets had long sleeves too.

"The *Pao-lao* dancer [a fantastic comic dancer] laughed at the flappy sleeves of the dancing puppet, but let the human dancer perform himself, his sleeves are even flappier and longer''. [72]

In the poet Tu Fu's sad reminiscence of a dance he saw in his childhood and whose pupil he met in his old age, he wrote,

". . . the scarlet lips and the embroidered sleeves are now quiet and still''. [73]

---

[67] 姚合 (ninth century) 詠雪詩 "散逐宮娥舞袖廻."

[68] 續文獻通考, 卷百十九, 引, 胡應麟, 少室山房筆叢 "天魔舞袖長."

[69] 謝偃, 觀舞賦 "絃無差袖, 聲必應足."

[70] （宋）劉放, 中山詩話, 第四十四款.

[71] 劉禹錫 (772-842) 集, 竹枝詞序, 見, 全唐詩, 劉禹錫, 十二, 竹枝詞九首.

[72] 陳師道, 后山詩話, 十四款, 楊大年傀儡詩 "鮑老當筵笑郭郎, 笑他舞袖太郎當, 若教鮑老當筵舞, 轉更郎當舞袖長."

[73] 杜甫 (712-770) 觀公孫大娘子弟舞劍器行 "絳唇珠袖兩寂寞". Many other poets in or near T'ang dynasty mentioned the dancer's long sleeves:

（南北朝）徐陵 (507-583) 雜曲 "舞衫廻袖向春風."

（南北朝）皇太子（玉臺新詠, 卷七）北渚 "綠香濺長袖."

咏舞 "袖隨如意風."

率爾成咏 "迎風時引袖."

林下妓 "舞袂寫風枝."

（宋）范成大 (1126-1193) 夜宴曲 "舞娥紫袖如弓彎."

（唐）李白 (701-762) 對酒醉題屈突明府廳 "舞袖爲君開."

（唐）王維 (699-759) 三月三日勤政樓侍宴應制 "舞袖怯春風."

（南北朝）庾肩吾 (c. 520) 詠舞曲應令 "舞袖出芳林."

360

In the official history of Yüan dynasty we find large sleeves again [74] and in Ming dynasty the dancer's sleeves were said to flutter in one of the dramas. [75]

All this goes to show that the movements of the "tab-sleeves" in the Chinese theatre are partially realistic. [76]

The dancer's costume was, at times, long, and that, like the long sleeves, must have had an effect on the style of dancing. [77]

The dancer's feet did not appear to have attracted much attention until they were elevated six feet above the ground in South T'ang 南唐 dynasty (937-975) when emperor Li Hou-Chu [78] "built for his favourite dancer a golden platform in the shape of a lotus flower inlaid with precious stones and festooned with tassels and the dancer, with her feet wrapped in silk, bent herself in the shape of the new moon", [79] and this is believed to have started foot-binding which, like the "tab-sleeve", has had profound influence on the Chinese style of acting. [80]

The Chinese stage costume has been, since the earliest days of dramatic representation, designed for theatrical effect rather than historical accuracy. The costume in the pageants of Han and Sui dynasties was mentioned for its luxury; it is not known how the identity of the various mythical and historical characters was indicated. [81] In the topical farce, the choice of costume was mainly dictated by the need of introducing the characters, such as the poet Li I-Shan and the earth-god (see Chapter XXII), to the audience, hence some historical accuracy may be assumed to

---

（唐）白樂天 **(772-846)** 會昌春連宴即事 "舞袖翻紅炬."
府中夜賞 "舞袖飄颻棹容與."
想東遊五十韻 "舞繁紅袖凝."
和新樓北園偶集 "舞袖飄亂麻."

（唐）李太白 **(701-762)** 醉後贈王歷陽 "舞袖拂雲霄."
邯鄲南亭觀妓 "舞袖拂花枝."
魯中送二從弟赴舉之西京 "舞袖拂秋月."

[74] 元史, 禮樂志, 三, 樂音王隊.

[75] 周憲王, 呂洞賓花月神仙會, 二折, 淨白, 一折, 仙呂點絳唇, "白玉蟾舞袖翩翩."

[76] In the western theatre, the long sleeves of Pagliaccio, Pierrot and Pulcinella, many inches over the hands, might have been used with similar technique. *Vide* P. L. Duchartre, *The Italian Comedy* (trans. R. T. Weaver, 1929), 214, 253, 258.

[77] 庾信 (sixth century A.D.) 看妓, "綠珠歌扇薄, 飛燕舞衫長."

[78] 李後主

[79] 余懷, 婦人鞋襪考.

[80] Foot-binding became prevalent only in Sung dynasty. 陶宗儀, 輟耕錄, 卷十, 纏足. The fashion of small feet was not entirely due to its effect on the gait; the feet were admired for their shape and texture. 韓偓, 香奩集, 咏屧子詩, "六寸膚圓光緻緻."

[81] 張衡, 西京賦; 隋書, 音樂志, 下. See Chapter XXII.

have been attained, but in the conventional farce called *ts'an-chün-hsi* [82] the official in disgrace wore a white gown according to one account and a yellow gown according to another, and in the dramatic dances the drunkard's and the warrior's costumes do not seem to have been uniform either in the different performances described. [83]

In Yüan dynasty the costume, like the stage properties, was part of the special equipment owned by the players, which shows that it was different in style, and perhaps also in richness, from the contemporary dress. A considerable variety is recorded in the dramas of Yüan dynasty recently discovered in Shanghai and it appears to be very similar to the stage costume of to-day. Study of the text of these dramas shows that at that time costume was also chosen to suit the temperament of the particular *dramatis personae*. [84]

---

[82] 參軍戲
[83] 舊唐書, 音樂志, 二; 段安節, 樂府雜錄, 鼓架部. See Chapter XXII.
[84] According to these dramas —(脈望館) 孤本元明雜劇— the variety of the stage costume was as follows:

	Crowns and helmets	Ornaments on the hair	Gowns	Boots and shoes	Belts	Caps	Wigs and beards
For men	46 types	0	47	5	1	6	11
For women	0 types	7	7	1	0	0	

Many of the garments were of periods before Yüan dynasty and the costume was differentiated according to whether the character was old or young, military or civil official, Chinese or foreign, rich or poor, good or bad and of high or low social caste. 馮沅君, 孤本元明雜劇鈔本題記, 頁六至二六.

362

Part V

The Chinese and the European Theatre

CHAPTER XXXV

ON THE COMPARISON OF
THE CHINESE WITH THE EUROPEAN THEATRE

Minor similarities between the Chinese and the European theatre have been mentioned by most western writers on the Chinese theatre and occasionally by writers on European theatre as well. [1] The significance of these similarities is not usually explained by the authors and one is inclined to think that they are to be understood as curious coincidences. Finding similarities between different works of art is considered the proper occupation of the critics, and where similarities exist, influence of one artist on another or common heritage from previous schools is usually stated or implied. Where there is no possible influence of style, as between the Chinese and the European theatre, one can only understand the similarity to be accidental, noteworthy because it is unexpected and strange. [2] Sometimes an author gives one the impression that close similarity covering a considerable area inspired in him the feeling that nothing is really new. It is presumably to exemplify independent statements of universal truth that in Lu Chi-Yeh's *The Chinese Drama,*[3] the dramatic theory of the Chinese dramatist and critic Li Yü [4] is shown to be systematically similar to western theories.

It is human nature to try to understand what is new by looking for an equivalent in what is known. When foreign writers point out European counterparts to some aspects of the Chinese theatre they are probably subconsciously trying to make what is new and strange to them more acceptable. The frequent reference to European theatre and drama by Chinese authors writing in their own language cannot, of course, serve the purpose of elucidation, but is in fact usually connected with a critical point of view towards the Chinese theatre. It is in the discovery of what are

---

[1] See, for example, Tcheng-ki-tong, *Le Théâtre des Chinois* (1886), *Cinquième Partie;* L. C. Arlington, *The Chinese Drama* (1930), xxv, 28, 29; A. E. Zucker, *The Chinese Theatre* (1925), Ch. 9, and A. Nicoll, *Development of the Theatre,* 39, 40.

[2] cf. the "*cothurnus,* masks and *onkos* on the modern Chinese stage", A. Nicoll, *op. cit.,* 40.

[3] 盧冀野, 中國戲劇概論,, 十章, 頁二二三至二三二.

[4] The quotation is from 李漁, 閒情偶寄.

believed to be the shortcomings of the Chinese theatre that most Chinese writers have hitherto found the significance of comparison between the Chinese and the occidental stagecraft.

In the Renaissance of Chinese literature, a movement started in the nineteen twenties aiming at the revaluation of Chinese culture in the light of western knowledge and the introduction of the vernacular as the vehicle of literary expression, Chinese scholars lost considerable confidence in the merits of their traditional culture. A type of snobbery for everything western, usually associated with ignorance in things Chinese, was developed in some universities. To the unreserved admirers of the West difference between some aspect of the Chinese theatre and its European equivalent means the inferiority of the former and similarity is a stamp of value. Not only are the latest western styles looked upon as the highest ideals, but mere mention of things Chinese by western artists is flattering. In *A Brief History of the Chinese Theatre*, published in 1946 the author, after enumerating his suggestions for the improvement of the Chinese theatre, says, "Only then can the modern Chinese drama hope to become like the European opera". The implicit faith in the European opera as a standard is shared by a writer of a complementary foreword to a *Manual of Postures and Gestures in the Chinese Theatre*, published in 1935 who wrote:

> "The Chinese theatre combines singing and dancing in the dramatic performance, like the opera of the western world, except that in the western opera both the music and the dance are recorded in notations".

It is difficult to see whether the writer is confusing the western musical score with the systems of notation proposed for the ballet or he is merely vaguely admiring the western opera. A professor in Peking who was "for many years a student in France, Germany and Switzerland" advocates several lines of reform including separating opera and spoken drama into distinct genres, an approach to the Aristotelian unities, abolishing the female impersonators and the "the stage and auditorium of the Chinese theatre be changed to resemble that of the modern European theatre". Another eminent writer wants to eliminate "useless survivals" such as acrobatics, posturing, masks, the *falsetto* voice and the musical accompaniment. [5] Many other examples of these reformers' views can be given, but it would be tedious. They all seem to be based on the belief that if through independent development the Chinese theatre turns out to be different from the modern European theatre, the Chinese history is to blame.

Similarity with the western theatre and attention by western writers, on the other hand, give some Chinese scholars confidence. One finds in *A History of the Chinese Theatre*, published in 1953, an account of Goethe's introduction of the Chinese shadow play to the Germans in 1774 and 1781, by adapting it to play

---

[5] *Vide* Zucker, *op. cit.*, 117-8.

"Minerva's Birth, Life and Deeds" and "The Judgement of Midas" followed by the observation, "With these events the Chinese shadow play won an imperishable honour in the artistic world . . . if the shadow play has no merits, it would not have had such wide influence". Sometimes the distrust for Chinese theatrical practices is so deep that the encouragement found in the parallelism with western usage can only serve as apologetics. Thus in the comparison between western dramatic theory and the writings of the Chinese critic Li Yü, mentioned above, is quoted the western justification for the lack of scenery on the Shakespearean stage to which the author adds, "We quote the above statement in order to explain as best we can the lack of scenery in the Chinese theatre". He then goes on to speak strongly in favour of scenery.

In spite of the prevalence of the view, at least in China, that the modern European theatre stands as the standard for all theatrical art, in this book no *a priori* assumption is made of the relative value of the Chinese and the European stage. They are to be compared as independent types, each existing in its own right. The similarities between the two traditions of the theatre, of which only isolated instances have been pointed out before, may seem to be mere coincidence but their extensive scope, as will be shown in the following chapters, suggests that they have deeper roots. It is due to the range of common characteristics between the two theatres that the comparative study acquires the significance which justifies the following detailed treatment. The extent of the common characteristics to be shown in the following chapters is due to the fact that in this book the Chinese theatre is not compared with the modern European theatre alone but with its earlier forms as well. The modern European theatre is not to be considered as the culminating point arrived at through a long process of improvements from the more primitive theatres of the past, rather the European theatrical tradition is considered as a continuous movement of which the modern theatre is one phase. Again, no assumption is made of the relative value of the various stages in the changing tradition of the European theatre. The belief that all historical changes have been for the better is based on an overestimation of human wisdom.

Review of European theatre of the past is conducive to the understanding of the Chinese theatre. Apart from the wider appreciation of the nature of theatrical art, the knowledge of theatrical history has a healthy effect on the over-confidence in contemporary theatrical practice. Theatrical audience, perhaps more than the audience of other fine arts, are prone to narrow-mindedness. Owing to the high cost of dramatic productions, actors and directors rely more exclusively than, for example, poets and painters on the financial support of the public and must follow very closely the momentary demands of the audience if they are to avoid unemployment. Dramatic appreciation, just as the appreciation of other arts, is swayed by changing fashions, but the tyranny of fashion is most nearly absolute in the theatre because, unlike poets and musicians, producers cannot afford to cater for a small select group alone nor can they wait for future recognition. Moreover, as theatre is generally looked upon as entertainment, its audience do not consider it necessary, as some music-lovers do, to study the history and theory of the art in order to broaden their appreciation. The lack of variety in theatrical fare conspires with intellectual laziness to discourage the cultivation of aesthetic perspective. Consequently, theatre, like dress, is remarkably uniform at any particular moment although constantly changing with the passage of time. As in dress, obsolete styles are entirely unpresentable, especially if they have been recently superseded. Ancient dramas are sometimes revived, but only in the modern method of staging, not entirely in the original conditions of production. The audience, thus confined to a narrow range of theatrical conventions, are more ready to believe that the form of theatre they know is the only correct form than they would have been if they knew more about theatrical history.

That lack of the historical sense is detrimental to the appreciation of theatres of the past has been pointed out by European writers:

"Critics like William Archer . . . looked on Elizabethan drama as representing a phase in the development of naturalistic drama, a phase in which it is possible to demonstrate that authors of dramatic talent in the modern sense have neglected to rid themselves of naiveties of technique, and inconsistencies of plot and character, because they can rely on the power of language to hide these blemishes from a complaisant audience". "It is true that the naturalistic conception of drama must inevitably lead us astray in evaluating the work of the Elizabethans". [6]

If it is impossible to understand European theatres properly by applying the conception of naturalistic theatre to them, it is even more hopeless to try to appreciate theatres of other countries in the same way.

Unless one sees the history of the theatre as a record of continual progress reaching perfection in the present era, the application of the principles of the naturalistic theatre to the theatres of the past is as difficult to justify as criticism on the modern theatre based on bygone dramatic theories. The logical consequence of narrow views is anarchy of values. In order to appreciate properly the past forms of the theatre it is necessary to accept the different or even contradictory principles governing the various types of theatre: in fact, to know one form of theatre only is a poor way of knowing even that form. True understanding of the theatre begins only when particular principles and standards are abandoned for more general ones, till one attains to the criteria of value which can be applied to all types of theatres. It is in this way that the study of theatrical history helps the understanding of theatres of

---

[6] B. L. Joseph, *Elizabethan Acting,* 114, 115. See also M. C. Bradbrook, *Themes and Conventions of Elizabethan Tragedy,* 2, 3.

other lands, and it is also in this way that the diversities and similarities between the Chinese and the European theatre contribute to the insight into the nature of theatrical art as a whole.

The comparative study of oriental and European theatrical history has an advantage over the study of the European theatre alone in that the complete independence of development can throw some light on the natural evolution of the theatre. The history of the European theatre, in spite of the interruptions by political and religious upheavals, is a more or less continuous development. [7] Though the theatre of classical antiquity disappeared in the Dark Ages, its heritage was reclaimed by the attempts at its revival during the Renaissance. In the last four hundred years European theatre has been divided, roughly speaking, into national schools, but the mutual influence between them overshadows the signs of independent development, and the causes and effects in the history of European theatre are complicated and obscured by reciprocal influence as well as by common heritage. For example, the evolution of the platform stage in Elizabethan public theatres and its effect on the English drama was overwhelmed by the tide of continental theatrical fashions so that its effect on the English theatre soon dwindled to negligible proportions and its influence on English dramaturgy was limited to a relatively short period. Again, the *commedia dell'arte,* after its vigorous growth, was dispersed among several countries in Europe and eventually absorbed by the literary drama. [8] The Chinese drama, on the other hand, is not known to have been affected by foreign influence. Historical generalizations largely hinge on similar sets of cause and effect. Whereas in the history of the European theatre one cannot easily be certain whether like characteristics are due to imitation or to similar independent causes, in the comparison between the Chinese and the European theatre one can be sure, when one finds such similarities, that mutual influence did not cause them. Even apart from causes and effects, common characteristics between the two theatres point to the differentia of the theatre and contribute towards the understanding of its basic nature, and these similarities are all the more remarkable seeing that oriental taste and culture are so different from the European.

Since the independence of the Chinese theatre from external and especially European influence is important to the significance of this comparative study, it will not be out of place to discuss here the theories on possible foreign influences. The theory that the Chinese drama came from the Mongols, which has lost much of its force since the publication of Wang Kuo-Wei's *History of Drama in Sung and Yüan Dynasty,* [9] has been discussed in Ch. XXIX; a more recent theory, that the Chinese

---

[7] cf. the themes of A. Nicoll, *Development of the Theatre,* and J. T. Allen, *Stage Antiquities of the Greeks and Romans and Their Influence.*

[8] W. Smith, *The Commedia dell' Arte,* Chs. V-VII.

[9] 王國維 , 宋元戲曲史.

drama came from India, propounded by Hsü Ti-Shan and Cheng Chen-To [10] will be discussed in the following.

The theory rests, apart from indications that the importation was not impossible, entirely on similarities in theatrical practice and dramatic convention; no mention of the Indian source of the Chinese drama is found in either Chinese or Indian literature. It is stated that as the Indians had dramas as early as Han dynasty (206 B.C. — A.D. 220) and as there were religious and cultural contacts with India in the following dynasties Indian drama could have found its way into China. In theatrical practice the similarity in the worship of stage deities by Chinese and Indian actors is mentioned as support for the theory [11] but in dramatic convention more extensive resemblance is shown, for example: in the Indian drama the dialogue is, as in the Chinese theatre, partly spoken and partly sung; the characters are also divided into types; men also impersonate women; there are prologue and epilogue and the diction varies according to the social status of the *dramatis personae*. [12] It is also stated that Indian dramas are mainly based on national legends and that dreams, letters, pictures, disguises and drunkenness have been used in the development of the plot. Similarity of plots is said to be noticeable and one Indian drama in particular has been analyzed and found to resemble very closely the Chinese drama of Ming dynasty, *The Story of the Lute*. [13] Archaeological finds of Indian dramatic text in Turkistan and the presence of a volume of Indian drama in a Chinese monastery have been mentioned as favourable indications. Prof. Cheng thinks that Indian drama might have reached southern China through travelling merchants at the end of Sung dynasty (A.D. 960-1276) when the southern school of the Chinese drama, which resembles the Indian drama more than the northern school, is known to have developed in Chekiang province.

It may be pointed out that of the Indian drama found in the Chinese monastery it is not known when it was put there. Other purely speculative points need not be commented upon. The similarities in dramatic conventions probably impressed the theorists more than they should do, because a close examination of the Elizabethan theatre will reveal even more extensive resemblance. Disguise and mislaid letters are instruments used by dramatists of many nations and periods and so are the prologue and the epilogue. Many of the common characteristics cited as evidence can be found in European theatres, for instance, the conventional types of characters in

---

[10] 許地山, 梵劇體例及其在漢劇上的點點滴滴, 小說月報, 十七卷號外; 鄭振鐸, 中國文學史, 民二一, 第四十章. See also *Chamber's Encyclopaedia*, CHINESE DRAMA.

[11] See also R. K. Yajnik, *The Indian Theatre, its Origin and Later Developments* (1934), 36.

[12] See also Yajnik, *op. cit.*, 20, 25, 29, 46 and 50.

[13] 琵琶記.

commedia dell' arte, the boy actors in the Elizabethan theatre, the singing in the Greek drama, etc. [14]

Prof. Cheng refers to J. D. Ball's *Things Chinese* for the opinion that Chinese drama resembles Greek drama [15] which was supposedly also the prototype of the Indian drama. [16] The relevant passage in Ball's book is as follows:

> "The Chinese drama sprang up earlier than the time of the caliphate and subsequent ages. The Greek drama was already transplanted and had grown luxuriantly in India. The Mohammedans naturally derived pure ideas from it in their religious shows, and the miracle plays of Europe show how the same principle of dramatic imitation was working there also. So it was in China. The whole idea of the Chinese play is Greek. The mask, the chorus, the music, the colloquy, the scene and the act are Greek. The difference between Chinese plays and those of Terence and Plautus is simply that the Roman dramatists translated a good deal. The Chinese took the idea and worked up the play from their own history and their own social life. The Chinese drama is based on music just as the Greek play was, and the whole conception of the play is foreign, while the details and the language are Chinese. But for the arrival of western musicians in the Sung and Yüan dynasties, blessing the people's ears with more lively and stirring strains than they had ever heard in the old music of China, the modern dramatic music would not have been developed. The spread of education and the love of poetry in the T'ang dynasty constituted a training for dramatic authorship. The Sung dynasty influence in this direction is vouched for by Su Tung-po. After such men had appeared it was easy for the drama and romance to be originated, but it was the increasing inflow of foreign actors and musicians all through the age of the Golden Tartars which gave direction and shape to the new power. Every attempt to explain the Chinese dramas as purely native must therefore fail". [17]

The points about histories of European theatre and Chinese literature do not concern us here; on the Chinese theatre the writer is not always clear, for example, it is difficult to see what he means by "the chorus" in the Chinese theatre, or what *native* conception of the Chinese play he has in mind when he says, ". . . the whole conception of the play is foreign, while the details and the language are Chinese".

---

[14] The Noh plays of Japan also bear close resemblance to the Greek and the Chinese theatre, although they are not known to have been influenced by either, e.g. in the use of masks, the rich costume, singing with simple accompaniment (flute), use of verse, declamation, several plays in a programme, dancing and simple stage properties.

[15] The similarity has apparently also been pointed out by a Bishop Hood of the eighteenth century who "wrote an essay on the Chinese theatre seriously comparing it with the Greek theatre". *Vide* E. Fenollosa and E. Pound, *Noh or Accomplishment* (1916), 101.

[16] Cheng, *op. cit.*

[17] J. D. Ball, *Things Chinese* (1903), 107.

Of the theory of Greek influence on Indian drama modern authorities believe that it does not rest on solid foundations. [18]

A theory that the Chinese theatre is related to the Persian theatre is mentioned in Chou I-Po's *History of the Chinese Theatre* [19] which, if true, may connect the Chinese theatre to the Greek theatre. Against Prof. Wang Kuo-Wei's evidence of the indigenous development of the Chinese drama, however, these theories carry little conviction. If the Chinese can develop their own poetry and painting it seems unnecessary to assume *a priori* that their drama came from other lands. So long as there is no strong evidence to contradict Prof. Wang Kuo-Wei's findings one must think of the Chinese drama as having an independent development.

[18] *Vide Encyclopaedia Britannica* (1952) DRAMA, INDIA: and Yajnik, *op. cit.,* 39; A. B. Keith, *The Sanskrit Drama* (1924), 57-68.

[19] 周貽白, 中國戲劇史, 頁二四九, 二五〇.

CHAPTER XXXVI

THE CHINESE AND THE GREEK THEATRE — I

(Description — Origins — Acting Space — Formal Elements — Emphasis on Skill)

(1)

Before comparing the Chinese theatre with the Greek, it would not be out of place first to describe the Greek theatre briefly.

The Greek theatre differs widely from the theatre as modern people know it in that whereas to us the theatre is always a form of amusement to the ancient Greeks it was never such, instead it was always a part of their religious festivity. We are so used to the idea that theatre is commercialized entertainment, a diversion which lasts two hours or so and which is constantly available to those who can afford the time and the expense that it can hardly be too strongly emphasized that to the Greeks theatrical performances occurred only once or twice a year, in religious celebrations to which everyone was free to go. Both the production and the appreciation of the theatre were then connected with religious sentiments and motives hence the comparatively rare theatrical activities were taken more seriously than the commercial productions of modern times. Perhaps the nearest equivalent we have for the Greek theatre is the performance of oratorios in the church at Christmas and Easter.

The festivals at which dramas were performed were those of the cult of Dionysus, the god of vegetation and wine: in Athens, the *City Dionysia,* in early spring and the *Lenaea,* in mid-winter and in other cities, in similar festivals connected with the god. [1] The total number of days for the festival and the number of plays presented in each day varied from one period to another. [2] In the *City Dionysia,* for example, the festivities lasted five or six days, beginning in a colourful procession of the statue of Dionysus Eleuthereus, which was taken from its temple on the southern side of the Acropolis and paraded through the route in which the

---

[1]   For details see A. W. Pickard-Cambridge, *The Dramatic Festivals of Athens,* Chs. I and II.
[2]   *Ibid.,* 64.

373

statue was supposed to have first entered the city, with escorts, magistrates, priests, sacrificial animals, young virgins, and officials of the festival. There were feasting and merriment, sacrificial ceremonies and dancing. At night the statue was taken by torch light into the theatre, to be present at the dramatic performances in the following days. [3] Several days were given up in each festival to dramatic performances with three or four dramas in each day, starting early in the morning and ending late in the afternoon. Production was organized as a contest between the dramatists who, after their plays had been chosen by the festival officials and financial help from wealthy citizens had been allotted them, took complete charge in the preparation: training the actors and dancers, writing the music, designing the costume, arranging the dances, and so forth. Dramas were written and produced, not for financial gains, but for the honour of winning the competition and they were performed only once, instead of being repeated until financial returns became unprofitable. The audience enjoyed watching the dramas, not as relief from the boredom of everyday life or intellectual luxury and exercise, but as celebration in honour of a god. A few plays were chosen from among a number of newly written ones and months were spent in preparation for a single performance. The wealthy citizens who paid for the expense of the production and the poet who laboured for its success received nothing in return except, when they won a victory, the token prize for the poet and the permanent record of their names, in Athens on a stone monument in the theatre.

The Greeks had three distinct types of dramas: the tragedy, concerned with gods, kings and heroes, not necessarily with unhappy ending, but always involving elevated emotions expressed in dignified diction; the comedy, mostly treating the lives of ordinary people in a humorous or even libellous manner, and the satyr play, the facetious dramatic version of myths and legends. The Greek dramas, unlike modern European dramas, did not tell new stories. The tragedies, for example, were based on national legends which were fairly well known to the whole of the audience. Artistic devices which depend on the knowledge of the plot by the audience, such as dramatic irony, were fully exploited, but effects based on the spectators' ignorance of the outcome, such as those of mystery and detective stories, were impossible in the Greek theatre.

The Greeks held their dramatic performances in huge open-air theatres by daylight. [4] The theatre building consists of three parts: the *orchestra,* a large circular dancing ground, [5] the *auditorium,* a large fan-shaped area of rising tiers of stone seats surrounding the orchestra on a little more than three sides and the *skene,*

---

(3)   A. E. Haigh, *The Attic Theatre,* 6 *et seq.*

(4)   The theatre of Dionysus holds 17,000 people and its last row of seats is 300 feet from the *skene* and 100 feet above the orchestra. Haigh, *The Attic Theatre,* 100, 128.

(5)   Of 64 feet in diameter in the theatre of Dionysus in Athens.

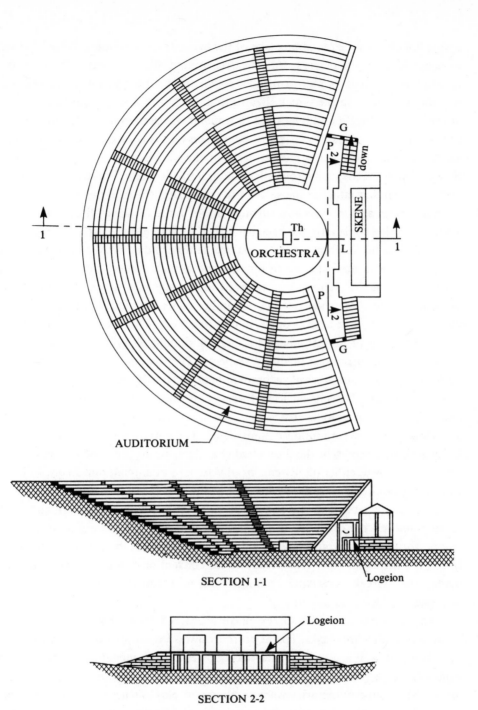

Fig. 57   Typical Greek Theatre

P — Parados   Th — Thymele   L — Logeion   G — Doorway

375

a long building on the remaining side of the orchestra, the facade of which provided a background for the players. [6] In theatres in the Hellenistic period there appeared to be a long and narrow platform called *logium* in the front part of the *skene,* which was the only thing in the Greek theatre that resembled a stage, but the time of its appearance, its height and the extent to which it was used in the different periods of the Greek theatre are still matters of controversy. [7] It is certain, however, that the earliest dramas were performed entirely in the orchestra and even in Hellenistic times only part of the action took place on or near the *skene.* Players could enter and leave the orchestra either at the sides of the orchestra, through the passages between the auditorium and the *skene* or through doors in the facade of the *skene* building. The *skene* being constantly the background of the acting space naturally represented some building in the drama, such as palace, temple and so on. The dramatic action was not always located in front of houses, and in rural scenes, the *skene* was simply ignored. The use of scenery was referred to in ancient writings, but the size and exposure of the *skene* rules out the possibility of realistic stage setting. Properties, when used, must have been brought in and removed in full view of the audience.

The manner of performance of the Greek dramas also differs from that of the modern European dramas in many respects. The dialogue was in verse and was partly spoken without musical accompaniment and partly declaimed and sung to the music of a flute. The partial use of verse and music makes it resemble the light opera, but the conventional structure of the drama and the simplicity of the musical accompaniment have no modern equivalents. The players are of two distinct types, the actors, who represent the individual characters in the play and the chorus, who represent a crowd, either of citizens, or of slaves, or of animals and so on, which one finds in every Greek drama. The number of the dancers in the chorus was fixed for any particular period. The movements of these dancers were highly formalized: they entered and left the orchestra in formations, they chanted or sang lyrics in unison and performed what would now be called figure dances in the course of the drama. In comedy the use of verse and music and the conventions connected with the chorus made the Greek dramatic humour very different from what modern Europeans understand as comedy.

The appearance of the Greek players differed from that of modern actors because they all wore masks. Facial expression was impossible to them. Only two or three actors played in a drama, each taking several parts, including female roles, for women never appeared on the Greek stage, and this was facilitated by the use of masks. Mute supernumeraries were employed to play silent parts and to appear as principal characters when they did not speak. Needless to say, the delivery, under

---

[6]   The old *skene* foundation in the theatre of Dionysus in Athens is 125 by 21 feet. Haigh, *op. cit.,* 113.

[7]   *Vide* A. W. Pickard-Cambridge, *The Theatre of Dionysus in Athens,* for the present knowledge of the evolution of the most important theatre in Greece.

such conditions, could hardly be natural. [8]

(2)

The Chinese and the Greek theatre have certain common characteristics such as dance, music and the use of mask. The similarities are not however due to their connection with primitive religion, the Greek theatre was so connected, the Chinese theatre was not.

The origin of the Greek drama is a difficult subject; many rival theories have been formulated but it is not known for certain which one is the correct theory. The lack of precision in the meaning of "origin" as used by different writers has not contributed towards the clarity of the subject. Various rituals in ancient Greece had mimetic elements and some of them showed, when explained, some pattern similar to that underlying the Greek tragedies. It is not at all clear however whether when the earliest dramatists composed their plays they *knew* they were merely elaborating on the primitive rituals, thereby retaining the basic pattern. For the purpose of this book, it suffices to note that at the time the Greek drama as we know it emerged, it was connected with the Dionysian cult and from then on the Greek theatre bore indelible marks of the Dionysian worship. According to Aristotle *(Poetics,* IV) tragedy came from the leaders of the dithyramb. [9] Dithyramb was a hymn to Dionysus, sung and danced to by a chorus. It is believed that the soloists of the choral lyric engaged in dialogue with the rest of the singers, perhaps in the manner of soloists and chorus in the modern oratorio, and from such dialogue simple drama evolved. We have the authority of Aristotle that at first the plot was short and ludricrous and the language undignified *(Poetics,* IV). Thus the use of verse, the dance, the chorus of dancers, the costume and the mask, all of which belonged to Dionysian worship became parts of the Greek theatre. [10]

In China mimetic elements appeared in the shamans' rituals during the ebullience of shamanism in late Chou dynasty (1122-255 B.C.). Some of the extant

---

[8] For general descriptions of the Greek dramatic performance see A. E. Haigh, *The Attic Theatre* (1907), J. T. Allen, *Stage Antiquities of the Greeks and Romans and Their Influence* (1927) and M. Bieber, *The History of the Greek and Roman Theatre* (1939). Details of the dramatic festivals can be found in A. W. Pickard-Cambridge, *The Dramatic Festivals of Athens* (1953). For photographic views of excavated theatres and reconstructed views of Greek theatres see Bieber, *op. cit.,* Chs. V and IX. Many details of the Greek drama are still matters of controversy. The arguments are however mostly concerned with the dating of various practices, such as the use of *kothurnus,* actors on the *logium,* etc. As the present comparison is made between the Chinese theatre and the Greek theatre as a whole, such problems of dating need not concern us.

[9] For the details of the possible evolution see R. C. Flickinger, *The Greek Theatre and Its Drama,* 1-35.

[10] References for several important theories on the origin of Greek tragedy can be found in Bieber, *History,* p.7 footnote. For Flickinger's emphasis on Aristotle's authority see Flickinger, *op. cit.,* 1-35, and the danger of arguing about the *ultimate* origin, on p.33 *et seq.*

hymns of early shamanism suggest impersonation or even mimicry of the gods, for example:

"The approaching god covers the sun,

His upper garment is of the same colour as the sky and

His skirt is like a bright rainbow". [11]

"The Spirit comes like a cloud". [12]

"The Spirit stops as [the priest] meets and welcomes him".

"In splendour the Spirit descends". [13]

In the original the word for "Spirit", *ling* 靈, suggests that a shaman or shamaness played the god or spirit (see Chapter XX). The flight of imagination in these hymns is not inconsistent with the theory that the change of identity was, as in the Dionysian worship in ancient Greece, [14] under an ecstatic state of mind. The activities of shamans can be found in various periods of the Chinese history; indeed, they can still be found in frontier regions and among the native followers of esoteric cults. [15] Thus Chinese shamanism probably enjoyed a more or less continuous, though no doubt often underground, tradition since prehistoric days. Nevertheless, its rituals are not known to have become progressively more mimetic, nor, at the rise of the Chinese drama, were the rituals related to the theatre.

The reasons why Chinese shamanism, which at one time contained mimetic elements, never developed into dramas as the Greek religious ceremonies did are not far to find. "Greek tragedy was indebted to epic poetry in subject matter, dignity of treatment and of diction and in the development of plot". [16] It is well known that the Chinese have no epic. Drama can be without dignified diction, but it cannot be without plot. If it is to be postulated that every civilized country has a natural tendency towards the formation of epic based on early myths and legends then the

---

(11) "靈之來兮蔽日, 青雲衣兮白霓裳", 楚辭, 九歌, 東君.

(12) "靈之來兮如雲" 湘夫人.

(13) "靈連蜷兮既留" "靈皇皇兮既降", 雲中君.

(14) Bieber, *History,* 15.

(15) In Han dynasty (206 B.C. — A.D. 220) the imperial palace was at one time swamped by shamans and shamanesses whose influence led to "the incident of shamans" in which, among other things, a prince was found guilty of employing bronze and wooden figures, found buried in his mansions, to inflict harm on other members of the royal family. 漢書, 列傳十五, 江充. In the poems of T'ang dynasty (A.D. 618-906) we learn that they were then invited to interpret dreams and officiate libations — 元稹, 聽庾及之彈烏夜啼引, "粧點烏盤邀女巫"; 李商隱, 神絃 "女巫澆酒雲滿空"and they were still noted for their dances — 王維, 魚山神女祠歌, 及涼州郊外游望. In Ch'ing dynasty (1644-1911) shamans'practices were outlawed (清朝文獻通考, 卷一九五) but in an autobiographical novel of the eighteenth century a shamaness was still able to cast spells on members of an aristocratic family (曹雪芹, 紅樓夢, 二十五回). For modern shamans in Inner Mongolia see W. Heissig, *Shamanen und Geisterbeschwörer im Küriye-Banner, Folklore,* Vol. III, i. 1944.

(16) *Poetics,* V; Flickinger, *op. cit.,* 17 footnote.

lack of epic poetry in China has to be explained as being due to the suppression of that natural tendency in the state control of religion in Chou dynasty. What survived in popular religions outside state control would have withered under the anti-religious philosophies of the late Chou dynasty. Through long centuries mimicry was part of theatrical entertainment but there was no drama. It was only after cycles of popular legends had been built up by the story-tellers that drama was developed, and these legends did indeed affect the Chinese drama, as much in the subject matter, as in the *lack* of dignity of treatment and of diction and in the development of the plot, at least in so far as the length of the early dramas allowed.

Even if there were legends connected with shamanism which could serve as the subject matter of passion plays, the intellectual atmosphere of late Chou dynasty was unfavourable to the development of religious dramas. Drama could only grow out of religious rituals after the followers of the religion had outgrown primitive awe and yet maintained interests in the gods, for fear would prevent the ritual from becoming entertainment and lack of interest in the religion would destroy the dramatic fecundity of its rituals. In late Chou dynasty, Chinese religion was separated into two layers, in the temple ceremonies which had lost the quality of magic and become almost a form of mass expression of religious feelings and among the shamans outside the state control, who still communicated with the gods through dance and song. In the temple ceremonies, with which Confucius advised his pupils to "revere the gods and leave them alone", the congregation who had become indifferent towards the gods could not be expected to be interested in their legends, if they had any, and in the unofficial shamanism superstition was still strong enough to prevent adapting the rituals to amuse the spectators.

Another possible source of the drama, the exorcist's rites which by their nature contained miming, was no less frigid in China. *Comos,* which was "negative charm against evil spirits" was at least one important formative element of the Greek comedy, in fact the word "comedy", meaning "revel-song" came from *"comos",* [17] The revel, or *comos,* consisted of singing, dancing, scurrilous jesting against bystanders and ribaldry, and "frequently took the form of a company marching from home to home to the music of a flute-player and rendering a program of singing and dancing at every dwelling". [18] The degeneration of primitive religious rituals into partial entertainment by amateur performers is not unknown in other lands, for example, the mumming play of the British Isles with its staple subject of St. George and a rival knight and the conquest and revival of the latter, is believed to be the remnant of primitive spring rites but is now performed by mummers who go from house to house at Christmas to offer their performance and make collections.

---

[17] *Vide* F. M. Cornford, *The Origin of Attic Comedy* (1914), 20.

[18] Flickinger, *op. cit.,* 38.

(19) The Chinese official exorcist of Chou dynasty, called *Fang-Hsiang-Shih* (20) was probably originally a shaman whose service was enlisted by the court; at any rate, his ritual of exorcism was, in Chou dynasty, performed with serious intent. The custom lasted long after Chou dynasty, both at the court and among the people. The ritual was sometimes accompanied by masquers in elaborate costume and performed with pomp and energy (see Chapter XXII) but in Sung dynasty, among the people, it degenerated into almost pure beggary, in the form of the "three-religions men" (21) who, dressed in fantastic clothes, holding torches and beating gongs, went from house to house at the end of the year for collections. (22) The "three-religions men" entered the earliest Chinese dramas together with other types of characters such as doctors, rustic clowns and so forth probably only to be caricatured, but they are not known to have contributed towards the process of dramatization. The ritual of exorcism, both in the purely religious and in the pseudo-religious forms, has never become as important to the Chinese as the *comos* was to the Greeks, hence even with the advent of the farce, it did not, as the Greek *comos* did with the injection of the Dorian mime, grow into drama. (23)

It was not due to common religious origins, therefore, that dance, music and the use of masks came to be elements of both the Greek and the Chinese theatre. The Chinese use masks in their theatre because of the theatrical effectiveness of the mask — indeed, masks can be found in theatres other than the Chinese and the Greek, for instance, in the Japanese Noh dramas and in the *commedia dell' arte*. Dance became a part of the Chinese theatre because it remained an important part of Chinese life long after primitive religion ceased to have noticeable effect on Chinese culture. The Greek theatre was worship enriched by art; the Chinese theatre was entertainment enriched by art.

(3)

The open acting space in both the Chinese and the Greek theatre, visible from at least three sides, has profound effects not only on the method of staging but also on the nature of the performance. Both the superficial and the deeper similarities between the two theatres can be traced at least partially to this arrangement of the acting space.

The basic problem of theatre design is to provide visibility for a large number of people. The simplest solution to the problem is to raise the level of the performers. This is instinctively adopted by speakers in a crowd and is in fact the basis of the

---

(19) *Vide* E. K. Chambers, *The English Folk-Play* (1933).

(20) 方相氏.

(21) 三教人.

(22) See Ch. XXXII.

(23) Flickinger, *op. cit.,* 47 f.

platform stage, used by mountebanks and other performers of the fair ground. [24] The simplest and most economical platform stage is the open platform: it provides space on three sides for the spectators and leaves one side for the players' entrance and exit. Concealing the two sides of a platform is not only a relatively complicated operation but it also decreases the available space for spectators. The early Chinese theatrical performances in the court of Sung dynasty (A.D. 960-1276) appeared to take place on the floor of the banquet halls like the European court masques, or in the court yard in front of it, and the number of spectators did not seem to be sufficiently great for the problem of theatre design to arise. When commercial theatres were established, they were, by contemporary accounts, essentially similar to the Chinese theatres of to-day, with a platform stage surrounded by spectators.

Visibility may also be secured for an assembly by raising the level of the spectators in proportion to their distance from the performers. This is the scheme adopted in arenas in which the spectacle has to remain on ground level. [25] The fact that in the Greek theatre the spectators instead of the performers were raised may be due to the nature of the Greek dance or to the accidental proximity of the precinct of Dionysus to the southern slope of the Acropolis. It is possible that the patterns of the dithyramb dancers could not be properly seen if the dancers were on a platform but the spectators must see the dancing floor as an area by looking at it from above. Whatever the nature of the dance the southern slope of the Acropolis afforded an ideal space for spectators and a stage was unnecessary. [26] When the slope of the hillside was unavailable or insufficient, wooden stands were provided, and it was the collapse of these wooden seats in 499 B.C. that led to the building of a permanent theatre in Athens. [27] The Greek theatre is therefore essentially a dancing ground surrounded by spectators. The *logium,* probably connected with the orchestra by ramps or steps, became acting space at some unknown date. Most scholars think that in the classical period there was no elevated platform for the actors. [28]

One of the effects of the open acting space is the impracticability of realistic scenery. In order that a dramatic performance may be naturalistic it is not enough that the actors act and speak like ordinary people but they must also be surrounded by objects that one finds in one's daily life. A naturalistic actor on the Chinese stage or the Greek orchestra loses the support of the visual accessories. The modern

---

[24] *Vide* R. Southern, *The Open Stage* (1953); G. R. Kernodle, *From Art to Theatre* (1944); C. W. Hodges, *The Globe Restored* (1953) and M. Bieber, *The History of the Greek and Roman Theatre* (1939), Ch. X.

[25] The raked floor of modern theatres which aims at the *improvement* of sight lines of the stage is another matter. Rising tiers of seats in the arena are for visibility at all, but the raked floor in front of a stage is for comfortable visibility.

[26] For similarly positioned spectators in modern times see Bieber, *History,* Fig. 163 (p. 115).

[27] Haigh, *Theatre,* 83 f; Pickard-Cambridge, *Theatre,* 11-15.

[28] *Vide* Bieber, *History,* 222 ff.

European actors perform behind a hole, but the Chinese and the Greek actors act in front of a wall; the former move inside a "set", the latter stand in open space.

The open acting space affects the psychology of the actors as much as that of the spectators. The actors on the modern European stage are watched from only one direction but those on the Chinese stage and in the Greek orchestra are seen from all directions but one; the former are surrounded by scenery, the latter, by spectators. The Chinese and the Greek actors are literally among the audience, and face them in almost all directions. The modern European stage is carefully contrived to look correct from one direction; the actors and the scenery are parts of a large scale conjuring trick, an illusion, the top and sides of which are carefully concealed, because they do not bear examination. The actors, like the scenery, show one side of themselves to the audience; they can see the audience in the front but they can also see the stage hands and waiting actors in the wings and when necessary can receive silent signs and orders from them. The acting space of the Chinese, the Elizabethan and the Greek theatre has no secret, the actors see the same stage as the audience, and they are completely exposed. The trick of acting on the modern European stage is to look right in one direction like conjuring acts but the open acting space requires that the actors, like statues, should look good from all directions. In the open acting space, the actors, being in the most prominent position possible, tend to address the audience, they act to be watched and speak to be listened to, they are more like orators; on the modern European stage they act to be peeped at and speak to be overheard, like people in pre-arranged conversation in order to deceive unsuspecting eavesdroppers, as is said of the Roman theatre, "our actors talk to each other; the Roman actors declaimed to the audience". [29] The psychological tension and reciprocal response between the audience and the players are more pronounced in the theatres with open acting space, and technical perfection in the fundamentals of the actors' art, such as voice and deportment are more important, because defects are more conspicuous. This is not entirely unrelated to the fact that Chinese and Greek actors are trained as dancers and singers, but the modern European actors are not. The spectators watch an actor in the Greek or the Chinese theatre like an acrobat in the circus ring, instead of a figure in a doll house.

The scenery in the Greek theatre, which was used as early as Aeschylus (525-456 B.C.), was not scenery as we understand it. The size of the orchestra and the audience at the sides made it impracticable to build scenery around the players. Painted boards were fitted only to the wall of the *skene* [30] between the columns behind the orchestra, with the columns as clearly visible to the audience as the painting. [31] The scenery, the use of which is considered as fully established by the

---

[29] Beare, *Roman Stage,* 175.

[30] Haigh, *Theatre,* 186.

[31] Flickinger, *op. cit.,* 235 f.

middle of the fifth century, could be at that time only symbolic because landscape painting was then at its infancy, [32] the illusionistic style of painting familiar to the modern Europeans being then unknown. [33] The background of ancient Greek painting was sketchy to the point of being symbolic — a military tent was suggested by a shield hanging on the wall, a forest by a single tree, the sea shore by a rock and a few shells, the sea by a wavy blue line and a dolphin, a river by a river god holding a vessel and so on — and the same would have satisfied the audience in the theatre. [34] Quick changes of the scenery were provided by the use of *periaktoi* which were triangular prisms with different scenes painted on the three faces, one of which was fitted to the opening provided for it. According to Vitruvius, there was one at each end of the stage, and there was a curious convention that if the change of the scene was a slight one, for instance, from one part of a district to another, only one of the *periaktoi* was turned, and for an entirely new district, both were turned. [35] It is evident that what is called scenery in the Greek theatre resembles very much the "rock and mountain plaque" [36] on the Chinese stage — a small screen painted, in symbolic style, with rocks and mountain peaks put on the stage when the scene is in the wilderness — a device scarcely more realistic than the locality boards occasionally used in the Elizabethan theatre, on which were written the name of the place represented in the scene. "Such devices as the *ekkyklema* and the *periaktoi* would never have been tolerated by them, if their aim had been to produce an illusion by the accurate imitation of real objects". [37]

As the acting space in the Greek theatre could not always look like the scenes represented, sometimes not even remotely so, the problem of indicating the locality to the audience became as much a major problem to the Greek dramatists as it is to the Chinese. For example, the *skene* building could stand for not only a palace or a row of houses, but also as cliff and cave or grove and wooded country. [38] Locality was, as in Chinese dramas, often verbally indicated in the opening speeches of a play as the aged servant says to Orestes at the beginning of Sophocles' *Electra*, "This is ancient Argos for which you longed", or Apollo's words in Euripides' *Alcestis*, "O house of Admetus"! [39] In Old Comedy, where changes of locality were frequent, they were either indicated by dialogue or, where such indication was unnecessary to

---

[32] Haigh, *Theatre*, 182 *et seq.*

[33] J. T. Allen, *Stage Antiquities of the Greeks and Romans* (1927), 102.

[34] *Vide* Pickard-Cambridge, *Theatre*, 123; Flickinger, *op. cit.*, 236; Haigh, *Theatre*, 198.

[35] Haigh, *Theatre*, 197-9; L. B. Campbell, *Scenes and Machines on the English Stage during the Renaissance* (1923), 17.

[36] 石山片

[37] Haigh, *Theatre*, 220.

[38] Pickard-Cambridge, *Theatre*, 68.

[39] For other examples see Flickinger, *op. cit.*, 206; J. T. Allen, *The Greek Theatre of the Fifth Century Before Christ* (1919), 70.

the understanding of the drama, the scenes were unlocated. [40] Clarity in the dramatic action depends however no less on the locality of the entrances and exits than on that of the acting space, in other words, the audience should know not only where the characters are but also where they come from and go to. The *skene* building being the unchanged background of the action, used over and over again, it was inevitable that conventions developed for its use. Thus, of the two *paradoi* — entrances to the orchestra between the auditorium and the *skene* building — the one corresponding to stage left was by convention supposed to lead to the city or harbour and the one on stage right, to distant places by land. [41] This convention originated in the theatre of Dionysus in Athens where the *skene* was apparently at some stage in the development of the Greek drama looked upon not as a stage background but as a real building, a landmark of the city, hence as the west and east *paradoi* in that theatre did really lead to the city and highways respectively, the audience understood the convention, even when the acting space represented other cities, by applying their knowledge of the actual topography. [42] Owing to the prestige and influence of the theatre of Dionysus, the cradle of Greek drama, the convention became adopted in all theatres in Greece. [43] Pollux and Vitruvius also mentioned the convention of the doors on the facade of the *skene,* that the central door was for regal entrances and the side doors were supposed to lead to guest chambers of a palace, [44] but this was more probably a piece of shrewd stage direction than convention. It is interesting to compare the conventions of stage entrances in the Greek and the Chinese theatre: in the former, fixed localities are allotted to them and the convention is simple and easy, in the latter each entrance has a fixed function but no fixed locality, and the convention is more complicated in usage, but more flexible. Imaginative use of the entrances can in both theatres suggest different types of action clearly, for example, simultaneous entrance or exit by both entrances suggests gathering from or dispersal to various places, as in Sophocles' *Ajax,* where the sailors exit by both passages in search of Ajax and after some time enter from opposite sides of the orchestra to say that they have not found him. [45]

Theatres without the front curtain require conventions other than those regulating the use of stage entrances. Motivation for entrances and exit is a problem all dramatists have to solve, but with the front curtain, scenes need not open with entrances and close with exits and the pressure of supplying motivation is somewhat

---

[40]   Flickinger, *op. cit.,* 207; Haigh, *Theatre,* 196.

[41]   Haigh, *Theatre,* 194; for Vitruvius' version of the convention, see Campbell, *op. cit.,* 17.

[42]   Flickinger, *op. cit.,* 233.

[43]   Haigh, *Theatre,* 188 ff.

[44]   Haigh, *Theatre,* 190.

[45]   cf. the "enter severally" on the Elizabethan stage.

mitigated. In the Chinese theatre the problem, in so far as the beginning and end of scenes are concerned, is completely solved by the purely theatric entrances and exits, which do not represent any action in the drama but are merely the players coming into and retreating from the view of the spectators. The Greek theatre did not have this convention and when the action required starting a scene in a tableau, the actors arranged themselves in full view of the spectators. Thus in the *Orestes* of Euripides, before the hero is seen in bed with Electra watching beside him, he must have got in bed in front of all the audience, although according to the text he has been there for five days already. Similarly in Aristophanes' *Clouds,* Strepsiades and his son take their positions to play having lain in front of the house all night. [46] Occasionally, in lieu of the conventional entrance of the Chinese theatre, Greek dramatists could use the *ekkyklema,* a device for wheeling forth, in some unknown manner, a tableau to give the audience a momentary interior view. (This convention is not very different from that of the roving camera eye in modern films, except that instead of the imaginary moving eye, the space is telescoped to provide suitable visibility).

The acting space itself, as in the Chinese theatre, was sometimes telescoped in the imagination when the dramatic action required it. In Aristophanes' *Frogs* the orchestra at one point represents the lake over which Charon ferried Dionysus in a boat (which according to Flickinger was actually a trundle-boat in ancient productions). Charon refuses to ferry the slave Xanthias, so the latter has to walk round the lake (along the edge of the orchestra) while Dionysus and Charon sail across it. At the other shore (opposite side of the orchestra) Dionysus disembarks and calls for Xanthias and, according to the text, catches his faint reply as he comes into sight. After some business, the orchestra is supposed to be a flowery meadow, the change occurring, it may be noted, with the players on it. Dionysus, now actually on the edge of the orchestra directly opposite the *skene,* asks where Pluto lives and is told that he "has come to the very door", after which Dionysus and Xanthias go across the orchestra to knock on a door on the *skene* building. [47] Similarly tombs are sometimes situated near palaces as in Aeschylus' *Libation Bearers* and Euripides' *Helen,* in order to facilitate dramatic construction and they are to be understood in the same way as medieval multiple sets. [48]

Distortion of space is perhaps more drastic on the Chinese stage than in any other theatre, for example, when the actor walks round the stage once to represent a long journey. The contraction of time is almost unavoidable in any drama and on the Chinese stage it may be interpreted as being disguised by the clearing of the stage, because a Chinese drama may be considered as a succession of scenes taken out of a long series of events and put together in the chronological order with the

---

[46] Flickinger, *op. cit.,* 243.

[47] *Vide* Flickinger, *op. cit.,* 88 *et seq.*

[48] Flickinger, *op. cit.,* 248; Allen, *Greek Theatre,* 72 f.

intervals between them omitted. Distortion of time may therefore by said to occur only in the intervals. The Greek drama was performed continuously, hence distortion of time occurred within the action. In Aeschylus' *Agamemnon* the watchman sees the beacon which signals the capture of Troy and, within the course of the play in which no gaps in time are indicated, Agamemnon has finished the sack, traversed the Aegean and appears before the palace. In Euripides' *Suppliants* an Attic army marches from Eleusis to the vicinity of Thebes, a battle is fought there and the news of the victory is brought back to Eleusis, all within thirty-six verses, which "is not for every mile a verse". [49]

For obvious reasons, in the Greek theatre as in the Chinese, only the simplest properties could be employed. At the early stage of its development, the acting space was an open dancing ground with an altar, the *thymele,* at its centre and since this was immovable, it was perforce worked into the action. [50] This altar appeared in many of the later plays, but other properties had to be added, such as tombs, statues, seats, couches, drapes, rugs, screens, shrubbery and so on, and these had to be changed, as the action required, for example, in the scenes preceding and following Orestes' flight from Delphi to Athens in Aeschylus' *Orestes* and *Eumenides.* [51] Properties could only be introduced, removed and changed in full view of the audience as in the Chinese theatre.

Dramatic illusion, as the modern Europeans understand it, was no more the aim of the Greek dramatists than it is of the Chinese. Musical instruments in both theatres take the place of the ingenious machines for modern stage effects: in the Chinese theatre the oboe plays the cries of a baby and in the Greek theatre the flute imitated the nightingale. [52] In both theatres the performance was frankly accepted as pretence and comedians had the licence to joke about the pretence. The *ekkyklema,* a device by which actors could be wheeled out from the *skene* building, was apparently sufficiently unrealistic to be the object of the actors' wit. In Aristophanes' *Acharnians*, Dicaeopolis is at Euripides' house and calls him to come out but the latter answers that he is not at leisure. "Then at least be wheeled out", says the visitor, and Euripides says, "Well, I'll have myself wheeled out", and he is. Again, in *Thesmophoriazusae,* Agathon, not wanting to continue a conversation, orders, "Somebody wheel me in at once". In *Peace,* Trygaeus entreats the man working the crane *(mechane)* to be careful. These blatant references to theatrical devices are funny because the speakers feign simple-mindedness and relapse into down-to-earth realism in the midst of dramatic pretence. They suddenly refuse to play the game and thereby point at the incongruity between the real and the dramatic

---

[49] *Vide* Flickinger, *op. cit.,* 254 f.

[50] M. Bieber, *Die Denkmäler zum Theaterwesen im Altertum* (1920), 10 f.

[51] *Vide* Pickard-Cambridge, *Theatre,* 44 f; J. T. Allen, *Stage Antiquities,* 101.

[52] Pickard-Cambridge, *Festival,* 267.

world. In modern European theatres, such gags would be considered as of very bad taste, because great importance is attached to the maintenance of the dramatic illusion.

(4)

One would perhaps understand the basic nature of the Greek and the Chinese drama better by thinking of them not as reproductions of events but as dance-and-music programmes, as if the oratorio and the masque are combined, with the arias or odes and the dances laid out, like the different parts of a sonata, according to a definite scheme. At the time of Sophocles, the Greek tragedy had the following form:

Prologos — the exposition.

Parodos — entrance song of the chorus.

First *epeisodion* — dramatic scene with dialogue.

First *stasimon* — stationary song of the chorus.

Second *epeisodion*

Second *stasimon*

Etc.

Fifth *stasimon*

Exodos — the recessional song of the chorus. [53]

Even in Comedy, the dramatic presentation was regulated by the conventional sequence of songs and dances as:

Prologos — presentation of the general plot of the play.

Parodos — the entrance song of the chorus.

Agon — the dramatized debate between the principal characters.

Parabasis — the direct address to the audience by the chorus.

Epeisodia — episodes or action of the play.

Stasima — addresses to the audience by the chorus on the conclusions about the play.

Exodus — the exit-song by the chorus. [54]

In all Chinese dramas, even apart from prologue-like opening scenes and introductory soliloquies, the dialogue contains poems and couplets in the middle of the play which cannot be taken as spoken *in the play,* but can only be understood as being addressed directly toward the audience. It may be noticed that in the Greek dramas too the chorus now and then speaks to the audience. In the *parabasis* the chorus wheels round to speak to the audience on the poet's view, the merits of his play, his claims on public acclaim, his opinions on civic questions and the chorus or its leader often also ridicules his rivals in this section of the comedy. [55] Latin

---

[53] Bieber, *History,* 49 f; Flickinger, *op. cit.,* 192.

[54] A. Nicoll, *The Development of the Theatre,* 37 f.

[55] Flickinger, *op. cit.,* 41; Haigh, *Theatre,* 304.

387

dramatists, including Terence, also used the prologue to put the audience in a good mood and prepared them for attentive listening to the play in the same way the prologue [56] in the southern school of Chinese dramas did. [57] It was also customary in the Greek drama for the first actor to appear to introduce himself and then to introduce the actor entering after him by a trick in the dialogue, such as saying, "Here comes so-and-so", or asking him who he is, or addressing him or summoning him by name. [58] Interruptions were apparently tolerated in the Greek theatre in a way unthinkable in modern European dramas. Socrates is said to have encored the first three lines of Euripides' *Orestes*. When a play was bad, it was hissed off before it was finished and the next play started. [59] In Euripides' *Danae*, when the audience heard an eloquent passage in praise of money they hissed it tumultuously and were quieted only when the poet sprang forward and advised them to wait and see what happened to the character who uttered such a sentiment. [60] Chinese plays are not often interrupted by the audience, but the Chinese comedians perhaps make more frequent reference to the pretence involved in drama than the Greek players. In Latin Comedy, however, playwrights became as playful as Chinese comedians, as in Plautus' *Pseudolus* when a character evaded the necessity of explaining the development of the dramatic situation to another by saying, "This play is being performed for the sake of these spectators. They have been here, and are aware of the developments. I'll tell you about them afterwards". [61]

Lack of realism in the Greek theatre, especially in gruesome scenes, is usually thought to be connected with refined sensibility. The taboo on representing murder in the Greek theatre was apparently religious rather than aesthetic: the theatre was sacred precinct and the actors were ministers of the cult, but the practice might well be in accordance with or productive of the finer taste of the audience shown in the text of the extant dramas. [62] Violence and death were represented in the Greek theatre as, for example, the suicide in Sophocles' *Ajax* and the blinded eyes of the king in Sophocles' *Oedipus Rex*, but the unpleasantness of such scenes does not depend so much on the subject matter as on the manner of acting. There are gripping scenes, like the use of force on the daughters of Danaus in Aeschylus' *Suppliants* and the ugly Furies in his *Eumenides*, the latter were said to cause fainting and miscarriage. But modern scholars trust the Greek playwrights of the classical period to keep "action and spectacle and all other aspects of the realism

---

[56] 家門.
[57] Beare, *Roman Stage*, 87.
[58] Flickinger, *op. cit.*, 208.
[59] Haigh, *Theatre*, 344.
[60] Pickard-Cambridge, *Festival*, 282.
[61] *Vide* Flickinger, *op. cit.* 233.
[62] Flickinger, *op. cit.*, 129 *et seq.*

well within bounds". The rule "nothing too much" they observed with scrupulous care. [63] All scenes are permitted on the Chinese stage, but suffering and death are, in the classical theatre, acted with the utmost restraint and usually in symbolic mime. Even the death cries in Aeschylus' *Agamemnon* and Tiresias' description of Polynices' body in Sophocles' *Antigone* would disturb the audience of the Chinese classical theatre.

Tragedy, as the Greek and classical French dramatists understood it, was enjoyed with a certain degree of mental detachment. Both the subject matter and the language were distant from the daily life of the spectators. "The realistic portrayal of ordinary human passions was foreign to the purpose of Greek tragedy", as it is to that of the Chinese theatre. [64]

Like the Chinese theatre the Greek theatre was more theatrical than realistic. On the visual level, this characteristic was shown by the use of mask and colourful costume.

The Greek theatrical mask came from that worn by the revellers in religious festivals which was in turn a remnant of primitive religions preserved perhaps for the fun of dressing up which adults also enjoyed on such occasions or perhaps for the welcome anonymity on the part of respectable citizens who took part in the not always reputable merrymaking. [65] The Chinese theatrical mask is not, it may be remembered, derived from primitive religions. In the multiple origin of the mask in the Chinese theatre of to-day, the influence of accentuated make-up is perhaps the most important. This common theatrical feature in the two theatres was therefore reached through different lines of development. The tendency towards accentuation can however also be traced in the Greek theatre: the theatrical masks with violent expressions of which copies are extant are of late origin and are believed to be due to the depraved taste in the Roman theatre for strength rather than depth of feelings. [66] Indeed how the actors did act in the masks with strong expressions is an interesting technical problem. The fantastic colour patterns on the Chinese masks are symbolic and emotionally expressionless, which accords well with the awe-inspiring inscrutability of the characters wearing them. To play whole scenes in a grinning or weeping mask and to make the mask live must be extremely difficult if not impossible. In fact even with milder but distinctive expressions the impossibility of changing them made them sometimes inconsistent with the reversal of situations in certain dramas so that the dramatists had to find special excuse for the appearance of benumbed sensibility. Thus in Sophocles' *Electra* when the heroine, who had

---

[63]   cf. J. T. Allen, *Stage Antiquities,* 129.

[64]   Haigh, *Theatre,* 277.

[65]   Pickard-Cambridge, *Festival,* 178.

[66]   Pickard-Cambridge, *Festival,* 178 f, and see the many examples of masks in later periods of the Greek theatre in Bieber, *Denkmäler.*

believed her brother dead, unexpectedly held him in her arms, her facial expression could not change from one of sorrow to that of joy and the poet made Orestes ask his sister to continue her lamentations so that their mother would not read her secret in her radiant face, and Electra confirms that old hatred is too ingrained in her for her face to change and her tears are tears of joy. [67] Exaggerated expressions, which are suitable only in short emotional climaxes must make the immobility of the masks an even greater problem. One solution, ingenious but difficult to apply, is, according to Quintilian, to make the two sides of the mask carry different expressions, which are shown alternatively to the audience as the passages in the drama require. [68]

In a long continuous theatrical tradition, masks tend to crystallize into conventional types. The masked characters in the Chinese dramas are divided into types and the actors who play them are divided accordingly, owing to the specialized style of acting. The detailed catalogue of forty-four masks in the *Onomastikon* of Pollux (nine of old and matured men, eleven of youths, seven of slaves and seventeen of women) suggests that the masks mentioned were at least the prominent and most frequently used ones, if not actually conventionalized types. [69] This tendency may be due to the selective survival of what was thought to be the best specimens or it may be due to the consequent convenience in casting and management. In any case, the *dramatis personae* in the Chinese and the late Greek theatre do not consist of all shades and variations of characters but only a few prominent types of humanity. Once thus conventionalized the mask can be used as a means of introducing the characters to the audience. [70]

In the naturalistic drama, which is peopled by ordinary human beings, the need for the mask is hardly felt; it is only in the Chinese and the Greek theatre, where gods and legendary heroes are represented, that the powerful expressiveness of the mask becomes appropriate. For the same reason devils in the medieval dramas were masked. [71]

The use of masks is closely related to that of special footwear and padding. By wearing a mask with a small or a large face an actor can make himself appear taller or shorter than he really is. In the case of the Greek theatrical masks, which were worn over the whole head, the actors must generally tend to look shorter [72] and in order to counteract this illusion, high-soled shoes were used in both the Chinese and

---

[67] *Vide* Flickinger, *op. cit.,* 221 f; Haigh, *Theatre,* 245 f.

[68] *Vide* Bieber, *History,* 182; Pickard-Cambridge, *Festival,* 171.

[69] Nicoll, *Development of the Theatre,* 40 f; Bieber, *History,* 178 f.

[70] Flickinger, *op. cit.,* 212 f; Nicoll, *Development,* 39 f.

[71] *Vide* Nicoll, *Development of the Theatre,* 73; *Masks Mimes and Miracles,* 193.

[72] For example, see Bieber, *Denkmäler,* 113.

the Greek theatre to augment the real height. [73] There can be no doubt that at least in Roman times the *kothurnus* had very thick soles, so much so that actors had to be very careful to avoid stumbling and on one occasion an actor called Aeschines, having fallen, had to be lifted up again by the chorus-trainer. [74] The extreme and dangerous height of the sole [75] was perhaps not entirely a matter of senseless sophistication, but a desperate measure to restore the actors' proportion, for in some pictures even with very thick soles the mask makes the actor look short. [76] In the extreme cases actors on *kothurnus* must have felt and looked like walking on stilts [77] and the usage may appear to be extremely artificial but of the increased dignity in gait and posture due to thick soles there can be little doubt, as the Chinese theatre shows. In fact, in Greek and Roman theatres the height of the sole varied with the social station of the characters. [78] The *onkos,* the extension of the mask above the forehead introduced probably in later times, was also intended to add to the size and impressiveness of the face thereby giving dignity to the general appearance of the actor. The tall headgear of the Chinese actors and the practice of shaving the forehead and the temples of those who wear the "painted face" serve a similar purpose. Padding, which in the Chinese theatre is for the stature of warriors, was also used in the Greek theatre, not only in grotesque extremes, for comic effect, [79] but, at least in later periods, by tragic actors as well. [80]

The costume used in the Greek theatre was a modified version of the ancient Greek dress, with beautiful patterns, but little historical accuracy. [81] "Historical accuracy and archaeological minuteness in the mounting of a play were matters of complete indifference to the Greeks". [82] That these characteristics are similar to

---

[73] *Vide* Bieber, *Denkmäler,* Tafel 55-58. The use of *kothurnus,* the high-soled shoe, in early Greek theatre has been questioned by K. K. Smith in *The Use of the High-Soled Shoe or Buskin in Greek Tragedy of the Fifth and Fourth Centuries B.C.* (Harvard Studies in Classical Philology, Vol. XVI, 1905). It is believed that no thick-soled shoes were used in the classical period and that they were used only in the Imperial times and then only two to three inches thick. Tafel 55 in Bieber, *Denkmäler* and Fig. 24 (p. 202) in O. Navarre, *Le Théâtre grec* (1925) show thick soles of a proportion near to that used in the modern Chinese theatre though of apparently different construction. The gradual thickening of the sole can be traced in Navarre's book by comparing pictures of early Greek actors with the murals in Pompeii.

[74] Haigh, *Theatre,* 249.

[75] See Tafel 58, Bieber, *Denkmäler.*

[76] *Vide* Tafel 56, Bieber, *Denkmäler.*

[77] *Vide* Haigh, *Theatre,* p. 249, Fig. 19.

[78] Haigh, *Theatre,* 248.

[79] Haigh, *Theatre,* 259 ff.

[80] *Ibid.* 254.

[81] Haigh, *Theatre,* 250 f; Bieber, *History,* Figs. 62 and 63 on pp. 52-3; Pickard-Cambridge, *Festival,* 212 f, and Figs. 28 and 165.

[82] Haigh, *Theatre,* 238.

those of the Chinese theatrical costume is not coincidence, but is rather due to the freedom from the conditions imposed by realism and the desire to use the costume to the greatest theatrical advantage. With the mask and the special costume, characters in the Greek drama could not look like any ordinary human beings known to the Greek audience; they were, like the characters in Chinese dramas, a separate race of gods and heroes. Special costume was a means of introducing particular gods to the audience and in the New Comedy, special accessories were also used to indicate particular types of characters. [83] If one considers the comparative rarity of books in ancient China and ancient Greece, and the lack of the means of popular education to which we are so accustomed, such as magazines, newspapers, radio and so forth it is not difficult to realize that Greek and Chinese dramas had immense influence on the mind of the people, especially in their visual conception of their gods and heroes. When Greek children learned the epic poems and when Chinese children listened to the story-tellers the images of the characters that passed through their minds must have been those they learned from their respective theatres. [84] The vase painters of Greece at the end of the fifth century and in most of the fourth century adopted the theatrical dress for the gods and royalty as well as priests and priestesses, and the illustrations in Chinese novels and popular prints illustrating national legends are similarly derived from the theatre. [85] The Greek actors amused Lucian with their "cavernous mouths" and "chest- and stomach-paddings" as well as the "huge boots" with which they could hardly walk in safety. [86] At one time, when a country audience in Spain saw a Greek play for the first time they were alarmed at the wide mouth of the mask, the long strides of the actor, his huge figure and his unearthly dress, and when he lifted his voice to declaim his lines, there was a general panic and all fled out of the theatre. [87] According to Arlington, a foreign visitor usually leaves the Chinese theatre "under the impression that it never fell to his lot before to have been in such a pandemonium of unearthly sounds and grotesque sights". [88] Such observations should be significant to the enthusiasts who want to revive the Greek dramas as they were produced in ancient times. It is highly doubtful if the modern audience can appreciate and understand, for example, the conventionalized costume in the New Comedy, by which the audience could tell the type of character at a glance [89] nor are they likely to accept the chorus of the Old

---

[83] Allen, *Stage Antiquities*, 141; Nicoll, *Development of the Theatre*, 38 f.

[84] cf. Haigh, *Theatre*, 4.

[85] *Vide* Nicoll, *Development of the Theatre*, Fig. 20 (p. 40) which is a popular print of a Chinese theatrical scene, and Pickard-Cambridge, *Festival*, 219.

[86] Haigh, *Theatre*, 254.

[87] Haigh, *Theatre*, 254.

[88] Arlington, *The Chinese Drama*, 3.

[89] Allen, *Stage Antiquities*, 141.

Comedy which represents, in fantastic costume, not only ants, wasps, birds, frogs, fish and snakes, but also ships, clouds, dreams, cities, seasons, islands and laws. [90]

(5)

As previously explained the emphasis on the histrionic and musical skill in the Chinese actor is closely related to the compressed construction of the Chinese plays. Instead of the representation of the developing events in a story the Chinese play usually covers only a short episode at the crucial point of the plot. In the Greek tragedies the dramatists treated the story in a similar way, not so much because the audience appreciated histrionic skill as because the continuous presence of the chorus made such construction necessary.

The characteristic of Greek dramatic construction has been explained thus:

> The ancient playwrights "set the audience, as it were, at the post where the race is to be concluded; and, saving them the tedious expectation of seeing the poet set out and ride the beginning of the course, they suffer you not to behold him, till he is in sight of the goal, and just upon you". [91]

In other words the action is restricted to the culmination only, the whole play corresponding to the fifth act of most modern plays. [92] However, in order to understand what the culmination is about the audience must either have had the information contained in the missing first four acts or be told of it at the beginning of the play. It may be noticed that both the Chinese and the Greek plays were based on popular legends so that the audience had at least partial knowledge of the stories of the plays. Antiphanes laid stress on the advantage possessed by tragedy, as against comedy, in being able to count on a general knowledge of its themes. Although Aristotle (*Poetics,* IX) stated that even the well known stories were familiar to only a few, it is clear from the passages preceding this statement that in tragedy legendary themes were the rule rather than the exception, therefore in most cases the audience must have some knowledge of the plot. [93] Most of the stories of the Chinese plays, ancient and modern, have been repeated so often in popular novels, by story-tellers and in different dramas on the same legends that the Chinese audience cannot help being familiar with them. Nevertheless, in most Chinese and Greek dramas, the story was told either by a formal prologue, as in Euripides and in the southern school of Chinese dramas, or by the opening speech at the beginning of the play, partly perhaps because the dramatists tried to cater for the ignorant portion of the audience to which Aristotle referred and partly because it usually required the knowledge of the details of the plot to understand the drama

---

[90] *Vide* Haigh, *Theatre,* 297 ff; Bieber, *Denkmäler,* 128.

[91] Dryden, *Dramatic Essays,* Everyman's Library Ed., 12 f.

[92] *Vide* Flickinger, *op. cit.,* 265.

[93] Pickard-Cambridge, *Festival,* 284.

393

thoroughly and both Chinese and Greek dramatists took liberty with existing legends. In Euripides the exact position the drama occupied in the legend was further defined by the *epiphany* spoken by a deity at the end of the play relating the ensuing events, thereby giving the drama a more precise emotional significance by setting it against the future as well as the past. [94]

The Chinese and the Greek audience did not go to the theatre to learn a story; even for those who did not know the plot and could enjoy the story as such, the interest would be exhausted after the prologue or the opening scene. Curiosity for the outcome of the plot could not be relied upon to hold the Chinese and Greek audience in the theatre. If they were curious of the outcome Dryden would have been right in thinking that as soon as the Athenians heard that the play was on Oedipus they knew all that was to follow — his murder of his father, his marriage to his mother, and all the rest — and "sat with a kind of yawning expectation till he was to come with his eyes pulled out, and speak a hundred or two verses in a tragic tone in complaint of his misfortune". [95] The artistic function of well-known stories in Greek tragedies has been explained:

> "But why does the prologue let out the secret of what is coming? Why does it spoil the excitement beforehand? Because, we must answer, there is no secret, and the poet does not aim at that sort of excitement . . . But the enjoyment which the poet aims at is not the enjoyment of reading a detective story for the first time; it is that of reading *Hamlet* or *Paradise Lost* for the second, or fifth, or tenth". [96]

Indeed, the sense of fatality in the Greek tragedies would have been lost if the audience knew only as much as the characters in the drama were supposed to know. With his omniscience,

> "the spectator, beholding the dramatic characters' fruitless toil and plotting, baseless exultation, and needless despondency seems to be admitted behind the scenes of this world's tragedy, and to view the spectacle through the great dramatists' eyes, learning that men must be content with little, humble ever, distrustful of fortune and fearful of the powers above".[97]

The full knowledge of the story on the part of the audience is the requisite condition of dramatic irony. This type of dramatic construction is not fashionable in the European theatre of to-day, but some modern critics and writers, perhaps under classical influence, have been sympathetic with it:

> "I rather think it would not exceed my powers to rouse the very strongest interests in the spectator even if I resolved to make a work when the

---

[94] *Vide* Flickinger, *op. cit.*, 258.

[95] *Vide* F. L. Lucas, *Tragedy* (1935), 85 f.

[96] G. Murray, *Euripides and His Age*, 206.

[97] Flickinger, *op. cit.*, 317.

denouement was revealed in the first scene''. [98]

It may be the gossipy character of modern European dramas that causes their audience to look forward habitually to new stories rather than new significance of old stories. Goethe said,

> "If I were to begin my artistic life again, I should never deal with a new story. I should always invest the old stories with new and vital meanings". [99]

Nietzsche differentiated between the interest in the story as such and that in the delicate emotions in it:

> "If the same *motif* is not treated in a hundred ways by different authors, the audience never get beyond their interest in the subject matter, but if they become thoroughly familiar with the theme through many different versions and no longer find in it the charm of curiosity and emotional agitation, then they will begin to understand and enjoy the various shades in the new treatments". [100]

The word "drama", which comes from Greek had, when it was first used, a different meaning from what we are accustomed to now. It was not so much whole stories that the dramatists presented to the audience as the most interesting moments of the stories, not so much the flow and movement as the situation and its meaning. According to Nietzsche,

> "It is unfortunate for the aesthetes that the word drama got to be translated into 'action' . . . even by philologists who ought to know better. What ancient drama had in view was *grand pathetic scenes* — it even excluded action, or placed it *before* the piece or *behind* the scenes. According to the usage of the Dorian language, where the word originated, it meant 'event', 'history' — both in the hieratic sense. The oldest drama represented local legends, 'sacred history', upon which the foundation of the cult rested — thus it was not 'action' but fatality". [101]

In some Greek dramas, action, as modern Europeans understand it, was reduced to the bare minimum, and the dramatic crisis was reached not by development of plot but by dialogue, as in Aeschylus' *Suppliants*. Similar structure can be found in many modern Chinese plays, for example, *The Son's Lesson* [102] which revolves around the emotional deadlock between a well-meaning stepmother and a young and thoughtless child, and *The Clandestine Visit* [103] which deals with the escape and

---

[98] Lessing, *Hamburgische Dramaturgie*, H. Zimmern, *Selected Prose Works of G. E. Lessing* (1900), 377.

[99] Quoted in Flickinger, *op. cit.*, 125.

[100] *Vide* Nietzsche, *Human All-Too-Human*, I. (Ed. Oscar Levy), 172.

[101] *Vide* Nietzsche, *The Case of Wagner* (Ed. Oscar Levy), 26. His italics.

[102] 三娘教子.

[103] 四郎探母.

brief visit of a captive to his mother and his voluntary return to captivity.

The narrow compass of the action in early Greek tragedies might be due to the inevitable simplicity at the early stage of the development of the drama, but the continuation of compressed action in the Greek theatre was certainly related to the inertia of the chorus. The chorus was the heritage of the religious origin of the Greek drama, it was not a theatrical tool of the dramatists' choice, but an element which they had to work into their plays, and the attempt was by no means always successful. [104] Whether the play required a crowd or not the chorus had to be in the orchestra throughout the play and they had to sing odes at intervals. Their entrances were not always perfectly motivated and sometimes not at all, and their presence and customary singing occasionally embarrassed the dramatists. [105] The chorus, derived from the dithyramb, the predecessor of the Greek drama, became a convention in the Greek theatre which should never be judged from the naturalistic point of view. John Dennis, for example, was not really fair in his supposed dramatization of a Spanish invasion, *à la grecque:*

> "Suppose, then, that an express gives notice to Queen Elizabeth of the landing of the Spaniards upon our coast, and of great number of subjects revolting and running in to them. The Queen, upon the reception of this news, falls a lamenting her condition . . . But then, Sir, suppose as soon as the Queen has left lamenting, the ladies about her, in their ruffs and farthingalls, fell a dancing a *Saraband* to a doleful ditty. Do you think, Sir, that . . . it would have been possible to have beheld it without laughing . . .?" [106]

The parody shows how less natural the dancing and singing by the chorus would look than the mere reading of Greek plays would suggest. If the chorus was preserved in the Greek theatre even at the risk of incongruities, it can hardly be surprising that the dramatists had to adjust the locality and time limits of their plays to suit its continual presence. The entrances and exits of the chorus were conventionalized, they could not be easily manoeuvred in and out of the acting space and with the chorus constantly in the orchestra it was difficult, by any convention, to indicate clearly changes of place and lapses of time. It is true that in the choral ode the passage of time could be accelerated so that it corresponds roughly to the convention of the curtain drop in the modern theatre, [107] yet with the audience

---

(104) *Vide* Flickinger, *op. cit.,* 140.

(105) For the influence of the chorus on the Greek drama see Flickinger, *op. cit.,* 133-161. The embarrassment occasionally caused by the chorus was ingeniously disguised by the dramatists, for example, in Sophocles' *Philoctetes,* Neoptolemus suggests that Philoctetes be given an opportunity to sleep, and then the chorus sings an invocation to slumber, which being sung to be heard by the whole theatre, would actually waken anyone from the heaviest sleep. For other examples see *ibid.,* 153 f.

(106) John Dennis, *The Impartial Critick* (1693), quoted in Flickinger, *op. cit.,* 152.

(107) Flickinger, *op. cit.,* 252.

seeing the chorus all the time, this acceleration could not be carried too far, hence the Greek drama was generally confined to a period of twenty-four hours. [108] Thus the Greek dramatists had to choose the most poignant portion of the plot and build a drama on it.

---

[108] For more detailed discussion on this point see Flickinger, *op. cit.,* Ch. VI.

CHAPTER XXXVII

THE CHINESE AND THE GREEK THEATRE — II

*(Actors' Training — The Dance — The Music — Festival Atmosphere —
The Differences)*

(6)

Emphasis is laid in the Chinese and the Greek theatre on the technical skill of the poets and the players. The Greek drama, with its poetical form derived from the lyrics, contained, like the Chinese drama, a strong lyrical element. [1] The Chinese and the Greek dramatists had to be able to write dialogue in verse and with a good understanding of music, they were in fact librettists who wrote with real poetical intent. Portions of Greek and Chinese dramas can be admired as poetry, apart from their connection with the plot. Sophocles is said to have recited a portion of *Oedipus Coloneus* at a trial in which he was accused by his son and to have moved the jury with it. [2] In some editions of Chinese plays of the Yüan dynasty, only the portions in verse were printed and these were apparently meant to be enjoyed as pure poetry, because without the prose parts one can have no idea what the dramas were about.

Great importance was attached, by the Greek players and audience alike, to the voice. The vastness of the Greek theatre which ruled out naturalistic delivery made the strength of the voice a desirable asset and the poetry made the artistic sensibility of the speaker specially valuable. [3] According to Cicero, Greek tragic actors spent years training their voice and this was far from being wasted effort because the "refined and scrupulous ear" of the Athenians was rather unsparing: if an actor should spoil the metre in the slightest degree, by making a mistake about a quantity or by dropping or inserting a syllable, there would be a storm of disapproval from the audience. [4] That the Greek and Chinese actors needed professional vocal

---

[1] Bieber, *History,* 4.

[2] Haigh, *The Tragic Drama of the Greeks* (1896), 133.

[3] *Vide* Haigh, *Theatre,* 272-3.

[4] *Ibid.,* 274-6.

training till their skill was far above the reach of amateurish efforts is understandable when it is remembered that actors had to play female roles of various ages and that they not only had to speak but also to chant and sing. [5] Beauty of tone was much valued and actors trained the voice by fasting, diet control and vocal exercises. [6] Plato would expel "the actors with their beautiful voices" from his ideal state. [7] Vocal skill was extolled to such an extent that vulgar actors injected exhibitions of pure skill into their performances, such as the sound of the seas and animal cries, in order to startle and impress the populace. [8] Judging by Aristotle's praise of the tragic actor Theodorus that unlike other actors, he seemed to speak with his own voice, the actors' speaking voice must have been in general unnatural. [9] Being without such highly trained voice, the supernumeraries in the Greek theatre, like those in the Chinese, could not speak even a few words but must remain entirely mute. In the Greek theatre the mute actors often played important characters temporarily and there were scenes in which silence on their part was unnatural in the dramatic situation and yet the dramatists had no choice but to disguise the awkwardness as best they could, for example, in Euripides' *Orestes* when the hero threatens to kill Hermione, Menelaus, who is trying to deter Orestes, turns to Pylades, who is to be played by a mute, and asks, "Do you, also, share in this murder, Pylades?" and Orestes has to save the situation by saying, "His silence gives consent, my word will suffice". [10]

The "scrupulous ears" of the ancient Athenians also made them sensitive to the acoustic qualities of their theatre. Modern observations on the good acoustic quality of Greek theatres made in excavated sites do not prove much, because it is a well known fact that theatres react very differently to sound when they are full of people. Charles de Brosses who was at an actual performance in an open air Roman theatre in Verona was surprised to find that though it seated thirty thousand people, those in the last row could hear the actors clearly. [11] According to Aristotle when the orchestra of some theatre was strewn with chaff, the chorus was not heard so well [12] and Vitruvius mentioned the practice of suspending hollow vessels of bronze, of different tones, in niches in various parts of the auditorium in order to add resonance to the actors' voice. [13]

---

[5] *Ibid.*, 272.

[6] Pickard-Cambridge, *Festival,* 166 and 168: Haigh, *Theatre,* 274.

[7] Haigh, *Theatre,* 274.

[8] Haigh, *Theatre,* 274.

[9] *Ibid.*, 274.

[10] See Flickinger, *op. cit.*, Ch. III for full discussion of the effect of the paucity of actors on the Greek drama.

[11] de Brosses, *Letters,* trans. R. S. Gower (1897), 14.

[12] *Vide* Haigh, *Theatre,* 107

[13] *Ibid.*, 174. The Japanese have also used jars suspended in different positions under their stage for the

In the naturalistic style of acting amateurish efforts are passable. In a theatre as large as a Greek theatre, if the players acted in a naturalistic way, the audience, except a small portion near the orchestra, could not see what they were doing. [14] Even in the earliest times of the Greek theatre, the chorus, if not the actors, were highly trained. The dramatist then trained them himself. The length of the period of training is not known, but that it was more than rehearsals can be judged by the fact that wealthy citizens were appointed to bear the expenses, that sometimes the chorus were lodged with the choregus and that professional trainers were employed. [15] By the beginning of the third century B.C. actors and musicians connected with the theatre were organized into guilds, [16] like the Chinese actors' guild of to-day, and unlike the naturalistic theatre amateurs did not seem to be able to intrude. The high technical accomplishment of the Greek actors was due to their extremely small number: [17] the Greek theatre started with one actor only and even in its best dramas only two or three of them were employed. It was the practice to keep them busy throughout the drama by split parts and double roles, that is, instead of one actor playing one character in the drama, a role might be played in different scenes of the drama by different actors and the actors changed or even interchanged their parts as required. [18] The two or three actors, supplemented by a few mutes, could thus be made to act a play with more speaking parts than actors, for, roughly speaking, the dramatist had only to keep the number of the speaking parts in any scene below the number of actors. In the Greek theatre this was so ingeniously disguised that one does not readily suspect the practice when reading a Greek tragedy. [19] Similar conditions existed in the early Chinese theatre, for example, in the northern dramas of Yüan dynasty, there was only one singer and double role was an established practice. [20] Occasionally one other player sang also, perhaps because like the addition of the second actor in the Greek drama, the meagre supply of actors gradually grew. It is one of the amazing facts in the history of drama that some of the best plays in China and in Europe were written under what the modern dramatists would consider as crippling conditions. [21] An early Greek drama or a northern drama in Yüan dynasty, as produced, probably had the quality of a solo

---

same purpose — see Fenollosa, E. and Pound, E., *Noh, A Study of the Classical Stage of Japan* (1916), 58.

[14] cf. Bieber, *History,* 152.

[15] Haigh, *Theatre,* 60 ff; Pickard-Cambridge, *Festival,* 85 *et seq.*

[16] Pickard-Cambridge, *Festival,* 286 ff.

[17] Bieber, *History,* 151.

[18] *Vide* Pickard-Cambridge, *Festival,* 139 and 142.

[19] For details, see Flickinger, *op. cit.,* Ch. III, *passim.*

[20] 王國維, 宋元戲曲史, 十一章.

[21] Some scholars believe that the small number of actors in the Greek drama had an advantage in that it has the tendency to make the dialogue clearer. Haigh, *Theatre,* 226.

performance supported by assistant players. The chief player in the Greek theatre, the protagonist, was like a star; he not only played the most important part but also spoke the important lines of other parts. [22] Unlike the modern dramas, the average quality of the performance was not lowered by the mediocre actors in minor roles. Men playing female parts, a practice common to the Chinese and the Greek theatre and due to the same moral convention, [23] in itself required special skill, but the Greek actor had also sometimes to play both male and female parts in the same drama. That there was at least occasional success of actors in female roles is shown by the fact that the actor Theodorus was famous for female parts. Specialized skill was so highly developed that another actor, Nicostratus, was famous as messenger. [24] From the fifth to the third century B.C. tragic and comic actors were separate and extremely few actors could play as both. [25] It was partly due to the specialization in histrionic skill that caused the Chinese actors to be classified according to the types of characters they played. [26] The meaning of the word "acting" has changed greatly since the time of ancient Greece: it was then a transformation but now it is more exhibition. At any rate, the modern European actor has lost the ability to change sex, though most actors can still change their age. [27]

The precise manner of Greek acting cannot, by the nature of things, be known. It must have been influenced by the poetical and musical character of the dialogue, the use of mask and the size of the theatre. The vastness of the theatre would tend to make acting stylized for the sheer need of visibility and the use of masks must have had some effect on the actors who wore them, [28] besides making naturalistic acting incongruous with it. [29] The use of masks deprived all the actors of facial expressions, they had to compensate for that loss with gesture and voice. Aristotle even defined the science of acting as being "concerned with the voice and the mode of adapting it to the expressions of the different passions". [30] Various postures of the Greek actors, which show remarkable control of the body, can be seen from contemporary vase paintings of theatrical scenes, for example, the actor practising

---

[22] Pickard-Cambridge, *Festival,* 96 and 131.

[23] Bieber, *History,* 15.

[24] Flickinger, *op. cit.,* 191.

[25] *Vide* J. B. O'Connor, *Chapters in the History of Actors and Acting in Ancient Greece* (1908), Ch. II.

[26] See Ch. XXXIII.

[27] It has been said that the practice of female impersonation was responsible for the lack of feminine tenderness in Greek heroines — Flickinger, *op. cit.,* 189. It is not certain however that that was not due to the requirements of tragic heroism and the Greek conception of legendary womanhood.

[28] W. T. Benda, *Masks,* 57.

[29] One can safely say that owing to the great difference in the size of theatre, the Chinese style of acting is correspondingly different from the Greek.

[30] Haigh, *Theatre,* 273.

standing on one foot in preparation for a satyr play on the Naples crater in Abb. 97, M. Bieber, *Die Denkmäler zum Theaterwesen im Altertum* (1920) and the satyrs in action on another crater in Abb. 98 of the same book. [31] These pictures give us some idea of how delightful it must have been for the Greek audience to *watch* the actors.

(7)

All theatres were closely connected with the dance in the early stage of their development: the Greek drama originated in the dithyramb, the hymn in honour of Dionysus, which was sung and danced to; [32] the Chinese drama was preceded by dramatic dances and the Japanese Noh play, which, so far as it is known, had an independent development, was derived from several types of dances. [33] To primitive people dance is a means of direct emotional expression and as such belongs naturally to the drama; it is only in advanced civilizations where it has become either a performance of expert skill for professional exhibitions or a conventionalized social activity of slight and narrow emotional content, that it becomes divorced from the drama, as, for example, in present day Europe. Dance accompanied all religious and social activities of primitive people, they prayed, threatened, rejoiced, celebrated, mourned, bragged with dance; it was with them more spontaneous and improvised than it is now with us. In both ancient Greece and ancient China dance was very much a part of everyday life: in Greece a man could dance in public without losing his dignity [34] and in China even Confucius approved of a suggestion for carefree enjoyment which consisted of bathing with friends in a river and dancing, on the way back, the *yü*, [35] a dance of supplication for rain, just for the fun of dancing. [36] Plato understood dancing to be regulated and ordered motion which is instinctive in man and believed that it should be developed in conformity with the moral and artistic sense of educated men, [37] and in the *Book of Music* [38] written by "later disciples of Confucius" [39] dance is defined as the spontaneous movements under emotions too great to be adequately expressed by singing and ejaculations and in the

---

[31] See also *ibid.,* Abb. 104, the Pandora crater in London and the theatrical poses in the Andromeda bowl in Berlin on p. 103, *ibid.*

[32] Pickard-Cambridge, *Festival,* 78.

[33] Arthur Waley, *The Noh Plays of Japan* (1921), 17 ff.

[34] Haigh, *Theatre,* 311 f.

[35] 雩.

[36] 論語, 先進.

[37] *Laws,* quoted in Pickard-Cambridge, *Festival,* 251.

[38] 樂記.

[39] 漢書, 藝文志, 樂記注.

ancient *Book of Divination* one reads, ". . . to make music and dance in order to satisfy one's spirit". [40] The strength of religious feelings was probably the reason why incantation and dance were used in working magic, and the effect of dance on the mental state of the dancers, sometimes reaching ecstatic and hysterical levels — as can still be seen in China — must have convinced the followers of such cults of the efficacy of the dance. That dangerous passions could be excited by dancing is difficult for us moderns to realize, but such must have been the case, judging by the emphasis in both Chinese and Greek writers on the need of putting the dance to worthwhile educational purpose. In Chou dynasty (1122-255 B.C.) children of aristocratic families began learning poetry, music and dance when they were thirteen [41] and ancient emperors were said to "cultivate virtue with music and dance". [42] Perhaps it was the common point of view of educationists that made Plato and the Confucianists classify the dance in the identical manner: the military and the peaceful dances. [43]

The incorporation of dance in the Greek drama can be better understood if one remembers that at the time drama was developed, dance was almost synonymous with stylish acting. [44] Aristotle considered dancing to be postures and gestures with rhythm [45] which would include all that are nowadays called ballet and mime. Emphatic gesticulations, without any movement of the foot, as in choral odes of a thoughtful and meditative cast, were also called dance. [46] The text of the great tragedies shows that the chorus expressed strong emotions, such as joy, horror, grief, etc., by emphatic gestures of the hand. [47] The audience in the Greek theatre had themselves the experience of direct emotional expressions in the dance, hence as used in the drama it was a language familiar to them. The restriction of the dance in modern European life to narrow artistic and social functions has all but deprived the actors of the use and the audience of the appreciation of the dramatic expressions in the dance.

The Chinese drama is not as closely connected with primitive dancing as the Greek, in fact the quotations from Chinese sources on the nature of dancing mentioned above were written many centuries before the rise of the Chinese drama. They are nevertheless pertinent to the dance in the Chinese theatre because although

---

[40] 易, 繫辭, 下, 十二, "鼓之舞之以盡神".
[41] 禮記, 內則, 五十二節.
[42] 易, 上經, 十六, 坤下震上, 豫 "先王以作樂崇德".
[43] *Vide Laws* vii, and the sections on music in the various Chinese dynastic histories, for example, 舊唐書, 音樂志, 一.
[44] Pickard-Cambridge, *Festival*, 251 f; Haigh, *Theatre*, 312.
[45] *Poetics*, 1.
[46] A. E. Haigh, *The Tragic Drama of the Greeks* (1896), 358; Pickard-Cambridge, *Festival*, 253.
[47] Pickard-Cambridge, *Festival*, 254.

the expressive dances to which they refer were lost in later dynasties, yet, being contained in the canon of the national religion these views on the nature and function of the dance served as the basis of all subsequent thinking on the subject. Unknown to their original writers, the theory of emotional expression for ritual dances became the principles of later dramatic art.

> "When singing is insufficient to express one's feelings, sighs follow, and if sighing is still inadequate, without knowing it one waves one's arm and steps with one's foot". [48]

Here dancing is understood by the ancient Chinese to be the involuntary supplement to vocal expressions under emotional stress. Plato's conception of the dance was even more embracing, for, according to him it originated in the instinctive tendency of mankind to accompany speech and song with explanatory movements of the body. [49] With such a broad conception of the dance, the coordination between the movements of the body and the speech or song naturally became important. Damon, the musical adviser of Plato, quoted Athenaeus as saying that dancing should not become independent of the words, nor should words be left without the assistance of appropriate dancing, [50] and Plutarch thought that the combination of poetry and dancing, or words and gestures, produced a perfect imitation [51] the gestures being intimately associated with the words from moment to moment. [52] This last remark on the coordination of movement to words "from moment to moment" corresponds closely to the customary description of the stylish acting in *K'un* dramas [53] namely, "a movement to each word". [54] It was perhaps due to this close connection between dancing and poetry that Plutarch thought dancing might be defined as "poetry without words". [55] The close connection is also shown by the fact that technical terms in metrical phraseology referred originally to the movements of the dance, for instance, the smallest division of a verse was called a "foot" and a two-feet unit was a "basis" or "stepping". [56] The metrical construction of tragedy was affected by the dance, for according to Aristotle the early use of the trochaic tetrameter in it was due to the suitability of that meter for dancing. [57] Western scholars are certainly aware of the mutually strengthened

---

[48] 禮記, 樂記 (末段).

[49] *Vide* Haigh, *Theatre,* 312.

[50] *Vide* Pickard-Cambridge, *Festival,* 252.

[51] *Symposiaca* quoted in Haigh, *Theatre,* 313.

[52] Pickard-Cambridge, *op. cit.,* 254.

[53] 崑曲.

[54] 有言必動. It is not impossible that Plutarch, writing at the end of the first century A.D. was referring to the later developments in the Greek theatre which, like the *K'un* dramas, had suffered from the excess of word to word gesticulation, as pointed out by Haigh — *The Attic Theatre,* 314.

[55] *Vide* Haigh, *Theatre,* 313.

[56] Haigh, *Theatre,* 311.

[57] *Poetics,* IV.

artistic effects in a theatre with music and dance which the modern European drama has lost. According to Haigh, in the Greek theatre "the music, the poetry and the dancing were blended together into one harmonious whole each part gaining an advantage by its combination with the other two". [58]

Next to the face, the hands, by virtue of the delicate control over them, are perhaps the most expressive parts of the human body. [59] It appears that the Greek and Roman dancers exploited the expressions of the hands quite as much as modern Asian dancers, for example, those of India and Burma. A dancer in the employ of Aeschylus was said "to depict events with his hands in the most skillful manner" and another celebrated dancer was described as being able "to speak with his hands". [60] Thorough exploitation led to systemization in the Greek as in the Chinese theatre. Plutarch divided dancing into three parts, Movements, Postures and Indications. There appeared to be standard postures for Apollo, Pan and other well known characters, and the Indications, in which the dancers did not depict any passion or object, were standard manners of pointing at heaven or earth or by-standers. [61] A similar degree of standardization has been reached in the modern Chinese theatre where, according to Prof. Ch'i Ju-Shan's *Manual on the Postures and Movements in the Chinese Drama,* [62] there are fifty-three standard manners of pointing with the hand, of which fourteen are different ways of pointing at oneself. As Haigh said of the Greek tragedy, in the Chinese theatre "the art of dancing was reduced to a regular system and the various attitudes and postures were taught in a methodical manner". [63]

Apart from the element of dancing in Greek acting, the formal movements of the chorus in the Greek drama which could hardly represent any dramatic action, can only be considered as pure dancing. Although the number of the chorus members varied with the type of drama and was different in different periods, the dancers were, except on rare occasions, drawn up in formations of military regularity, both on their first entrance and during the progress of the play. For example, the chorus in the dramas of Sophocles and Euripides consisted of fifteen dancers and they entered the orchestra either in three columns side by side with five dancers in each or in five columns with three in each. The rectangular formation, three abreast and five deep or vice versa, was kept throughout the play even when they moved about; no attempt was made to imitate the fluctuating movement and haphazard grouping of the crowds as in those introduced into modern operas and

---

[58] Haigh, *Theatre,* 311.

[59] cf. the lessons of gestures for Elizabethan orators quoted in B. L. Joseph, *Elizabethan Acting* (1951), which consisted almost entirely of the deportment of the hands.

[60] *Vide* Haigh, *Theatre,* 312.

[61] *Vide* Haigh, *Theatre,* 313.

[62] 齊如山, 國劇身段譜, 三章二節.

[63] *Vide* Haigh, *Theatre,* 317.

dramas. In most cases, they entered the orchestra at the conclusion of the *prologos* or introductory scene in the drama, marching in accurate formation, sometimes accompanied by the entrance-song called *parodos* which they chanted, sometimes silently, and they made their exit in a similar manner. [64] Similar formal movements can be found in the Chinese theatre in the many standard entrances, exits, evolutions and parades of armies, emperors and their courts, officials and their attendants and heads of families and their servants.

Consistent with the formal movements and groupings, the acting of the chorus was conventional. At the end of *Persae,* for example, when the Persian Elders follow Xerxes to the palace, they fall into a new posture at each fresh exclamation of grief, first beating their breasts, then plucking their beards, then rending their garments, then tearing their hair and in this way the chorus made their exit from the orchestra. [65] Sometimes the Greek players went even further than the Chinese in conventions and dropped all pretence of representing dramatic action, the chorus accompanying descriptive passages spoken by the actors with dumb show and mimetic dance, as was done in the *Clouds* when Strepsiades described his quarrel with Pheidippides. The audience was obviously appreciative of such performance, for Telestes, a dancer employed by Aeschylus, was said to "dance the *Seven against Thebes*" so well as to bring the various events of the descriptive speeches in the play before the very eyes of the spectators. [66]

The modern European audience, if they could watch the real performance of a Greek drama, would not think it was entirely drama as they understood drama to be. They would either consider it as a hybrid production with the formal movements of the chorus as incongruous adjuncts to the dramatic action sustained by the actors or take the entire performance as homogeneous ballet. To them the flute-player who marched at the head of the chorus in and out of the orchestra and who, with other flautists and harpists when required, remained in the orchestra throughout the drama must be as distracting as the musicians on the Chinese stage, [67] and the flute-player in the Roman theatre, who would accompany the actors on the raised stage, stepping up now to one now to another to serve them in turn, must look as absurd as the tea-drinking of Chinese actors during the performance. [68] To the Greeks and the Chinese, who were not brought up in the tradition of naturalism, the problem whether the performance was drama or dance naturally could not arise. The acting space in the Greek and the Chinese theatre was also a dancing ground, in fact, lines were marked in the orchestra in the Greek theatre to assist the evolution of the

---

[64] For details of the disposition of the chorus see Pickard-Cambridge, *Festival,* Ch. V and 247 ff; Haigh, *Theatre,* 288-319.

[65] *Vide* Aeschylus, *Persae.*

[66] *Vide* Haigh, *Theatre,* 317.

[67] *Vide* Haigh, *Theatre,* 271.

[68] *Vide* W. Beare, *The Roman Stage,* 175.

choral dances, [69] and nothing could be more natural on the dancing ground than the presence of musicians. The Greek actors, like the Chinese, were in fact dancers, hence the early poet-actors, Thespis and Phrynichus were called "dancers". [70]

In primitive civilizations dance changed the mental state of the dancers. In a similar way, in the drama, dance and music work on the mind of the audience. The effects of the dance-drama are partly sensuous. In the exploitation of these effects the Chinese and the Greek theatre differ from the modern European drama.

(8)

The use of music in both the Greek and the Chinese theatre may be said to be due to the fact that people of primitive civilizations are more conscious than we moderns of the power of music. Both Greek and Chinese ancient writers were deeply concerned with the moral effects of different types of music and made it one of the most important subjects in their educational systems. In Confucian books, the term *li-yüeh,* "ritual and music" [71] means culture and in Chou dynasty music was one of the six subjects of elementary education. [72] Music from the different parts of China had, it was thought, different moral effects and the music of the country of Cheng [73] was the well known scapegoat of Confucianists' criticisms. [74] In a candid manner, a duke asked a disciple of Confucius why it was that he, the duke, found no pleasure in the more edifying classical music but was stirred by the then modern styles and he had it explained to him how the classical music, though dull, had beneficial effects but the new music and new dance corrupted the mind. [75] Plato likewise took music seriously in the educational system of his Ideal State and wanted to exclude certain modes, such as the Ionian and the Lydian, because they had, to him, unhealthy influence upon character [76] and Aristotle held similar views. [77]

To modern music-lovers, who recognize only the artistic value of music, the ethical significance these ancient writers gave to modes and melodies is difficult to understand. We recognize the effect of music on our moods but do not believe it has any further psychological importance. The whole of the *Book of Music* [78] was

---

[69] Haigh, *Theatre,* 107.

[70] Haigh, *Drama,* 356.

[71] 禮樂.

[72] "六藝", 周禮, 地官, 保氏.

[73] 鄭聲.

[74] *Vide* 論語, 衞靈公 and the commentaries on the *Book of Odes* 詩經, 鄭風, 鄘風.

[75] 禮記, 樂記 "魏文侯問於子夏".

[76] *Republic,* iii.

[77] *Vide* Pickard-Cambridge, *Festival,* 264 ff.

[78] 禮記, 樂記.

essentially an explanation of the dual significance of music, first as the expression of men's feelings and thus a truthful index of their sentiments and also as a medium for expression and transmission of mass psychology, with incalculable effects on the mind of the people as a whole. In ancient Greece the Ionian music was believed to be at first severe and sober but the degeneracy of the nation later changed its mood. [79] The subtle relationship between music and man's emotional life it not perhaps entirely unrecognized to-day, as in the explanation of musical characteristics by the *zeitgeist* and the tinge of moral disapproval of vulgar music. The ancient views on the musical art, not entirely incomprehensible even to the modern mind, may be considered as the theoretical basis of the use of music in the Greek and the Chinese theatre, the former, because they were contemporary with the best period of the Greek theatre and the latter, because of the prestige of the Confucian canon in China. Against such theoretical background music in the drama could not be understood as serving a decorative function, to provide a variation in the sensuous interest of the performance, nor as occasional reinforcement of dramatic effect, but was an integral part of dramatic expression, on the same level as verse in the dialogue and gestures in the acting.

The Greek and the Chinese theatrical music have no counterpart in modern European theatres: the musical effects were closely knit into the artistic design of the drama and yet in both theatres the immense resources of the symphony orchestra were unknown. In the Greek theatre a flute-player or harpist normally accompanied the singing and the dancing, the instruments — a simple clarinet or lyre — playing the same tune as the song, with occasional bridge passages, called *diaulia*, [80] and in the Chinese theatre, apart from the percussion instruments for marking the rhythm, the accompaniment consists virtually of a fiddle alone, also played in unison with the aria. The tone colours and the multifarious musical effects which the symphony orchestra can provide were absent in the Greek and the Chinese theatre. However, it need not be assumed that strong dramatic effects cannot be achieved with simple instruments, it is all a matter of habit and sensibility; in the Noh plays of Japan, for example, the orchestra is also of the simplest kind but we have the testimony of a European scholar that the nerves of the audience are in the hands of the drummers who by a sudden *accelerando* can create an atmosphere of almost unendurable tension. [81] It would be tedious to quote the parallel remarks on the Chinese drama and the serious attention Greek critics paid to their accompanist. [82]

The main function of music in the Greek theatre, as in the Chinese, was lyrical expression and the vocal music was in both far more important than the

---

[79] Haigh, *Theatre*, 321.

[80] Haigh, *Theatre*, 320-1; Pickard-Cambridge, *Festival*, 164.

[81] A. Waley, *The Noh Plays of Japan* (1921), 29.

[82] *Vide* Pickard-Cambridge, *Festival*, 266; Haigh, *Theatre*, 321 f.

instrumental. [83] This principle led to the almost identical classification of modes of delivery in the two theatres: the dialogue was partly sung, partly spoken and partly declaimed or chanted, the last being called *nien* [84] in Chinese and *parakataloge* in Greek. [85] The Greek *parakataloge,* also translated as "recitative", was accompanied by the flute, and was sometimes referred to as speaking and sometimes as singing, showing that it must have lain somewhere between the two. [86] As in the Chinese drama, singing replaced speech in those scenes of the Greek drama where emotions were deeply aroused and found their fittest expression in music, and the declamation and *parakataloge* was used as a transition from speech to song. [87] In other words, the range of vocal expression was increased in the drama beyond that of ordinary speech by the addition of musical qualities in various degrees. The part of the dialogue that was spoken in the Greek drama was written in iambic trimeter, which was akin to prose, and the recitative was in tetrameter. [88]

The close connection between music and lyrical expression in the Greek and the Chinese theatre might also be due to the peculiarities of speech inflexion in both languages: in Chinese, intonation is the key to correct pronunciation and in Greek, according to some scholars, the pronunciation had a quasi-melodic quality. It has been pointed out that the Greek terms of pronunciation were musical terms, which suggests that Greek words, as spoken, had musical or "tonal" accents rather than stress accents, as in English. The rise and fall of pitch in ordinary spoken English are definitely noticeable and are different in different social classes and districts; and they are also noticeable in other European languages. In ancient Greek, apart from the natural speech inflexions, the musical accent might be more pronounced and might also depend on the collocation of the words and the degree of emphasis which it had in a particular context. [89] The musical quality of speech was certainly closely studied by the scholars in ancient Greece: Aristoxenus, a pupil of Aristotle, said in his *Harmonics* that in speech the pitch of the voice moved continuously whereas in singing it moved in intervals, in other words, the voice had no definite pitch in speech, but it had in singing. [90] According to the rhetorician Dionysus of

---

[83] Haigh, *Theatre,* 319; Pickard-Cambridge, *Festival,* 265. Why did primitive actors sing the dialogue? Singing may be due to the effort to make dialogue audible to a large audience — in prolonging the vocalization, as in street cries (vendors), and porters' cries of names of destinations at railway stations. The pitch of the voice is changed in these cries perhaps because that attracts attention, or because it facilitates the crying.

[84] 唸.

[85] Haigh, *Theatre,* 268 f.

[86] Pickard-Cambridge, *Festival,* 155-6.

[87] Haigh, *Theatre,* 268-9.

[88] For details see Pickard-Cambridge, *Festival,* 153 ff; Haigh, *Theatre,* 266-271.

[89] *Vide* D. B. Monro, *The Modes of Ancient Greek Music* (1894), 113-126.

[90] *Ibid.,* 115.

Halicarnassus speech covered about a fifth in interval and in the song, the melody might not correspond to the natural pitch of the words as spoken. [91] Exactly how and to what extent the Greek musicians made the scansion of the words correspond to the musical phrasing and the melody to the speech inflexion is not at present known; but such correspondence was at least achieved at some time as some of the extant fragments of Greek music show. [92] There can be little doubt however that music was considered entirely subordinate to poetry. Plutarch thought the words were the main attraction, and music was mere seasoning and Pratinas declared that the Muse had made Poetry the mistress and that the flute was but the servant of poetry. [93] Plato complained about the various signs of separation of poetry and music, such as putting unmusical language into verse, making melody and rhythm without words, and using the lyre and the flute without the voice. He did not seem to believe in music as a language by itself, for he thought the words were necessary in order that we could know what the music meant. [94] Apparently Greek poems, like ancient Chinese poems down to Sung dynasty, were mainly written to be sung, not to be read and for poetry, speaking it was not always distinguished from singing it because even in Roman times Horace still talked of "speaking a song" and Ovid claimed that his elegiacs were "sung all over Rome". [95] It is impossible in Chinese music to use the same tune for several poems, and this, though possible in Greek music, was not, it is believed, well liked. [96] In ancient Greece, fitting melodies to poems was probably not a matter of arithmetic either. [97]

It is natural that before the song disintegrated into its two elements (poems written to be read and melodies played as tunes) great emphasis was placed on the distinctness of the words as sung. In modern operas, clarity of enunciation is more a theoretical than an actual merit of the singers and the music, especially in part-singing, and translation of texts are often sufficient to make the words indistinguishable without any technical incompetence on the part of the singers and composers. In the Chinese as in the Greek theatre it is of vital importance that the words should be clearly heard. [98] In the Chinese theatre though the story can still be understood if the words in the arias are not clearly heard because the passages that

---

[91] *Ibid.*, 116.

[92] *Vide* Pickard-Cambridge, *Festival,* 266; Monro, *op. cit.,* 116.

[93] Haigh, *Theatre,* 319, 320.

[94] Monro, *op. cit.,* 119 f.

[95] W. Beare, *The Roman Stage,* 216 ff.

[96] Monro, *op. cit.,* 119 f.

[97] Close connection between melody and speech inflexion has also been experimented upon in modern times in what is called *Sprechgesang,* or *Sprechstimme,* of which Schoenberg's *Pierrot Lunaire* is an example.

[98] cf. the phonetic shifts under emotional stress which, faithfully reproduced, make naturalistic actors unintelligible.

are sung are mostly lyrics not instrumental in the development of the plot, yet much of the beauty of the singing will then be lost. In the Greek theatre, as the audience heard a great part of the dialogue from the singers, if they missed the words, they could not have heard much of the drama. [99] In the time of Euripides, an elaborate and florid type of music was introduced into the dramas, and it was thought that the consequent lack of precision in enunciation and the obscurity of the words were some of the causes of the rapid decline of Greek drama in the fourth century. [100] As compared with the Greek and the Chinese singers modern European musicians may be said to treat the voice as one of the instruments. [101]

The similarities between the Chinese and the Greek theatrical music not only cover the dramatic function of music but also extend to some aspects of its structure. Music in the early Chinese theatre was, like Greek music, modal in nature. The physical basis of musical modes lies in the difference of the scales used, a difference not in the relative pitch, which is a matter of keys, but in the size of the intervals between one note and the next in the scale, and the result of using different modes is the variety of flavour or shade of feeling as, for example, between the major and minor scale in modern European music. The existence of different modes in the Chinese music of T'ang and Sung dynasties and in ancient Greek music was probably due to the blending of hitherto isolated regional cultures, hence in both cases, most of the names for the modes were derived from names of districts and tribes. To those who can appreciate modal music the difference in the shade of feeling between the modes can hardly be missed, thus the Dorian mode was majestic and dignified; the Mixolydian, pathetic; the early Ionic mode, severe and sober and the Phrygian, passionate and enthusiastic, [102] and probably owing to lack of knowledge in acoustics, the same ambiguity between mode and key can be found in both Chinese and Greek writings.

The existence of modal music both in China and in Greece is not, as may be thought to be, a curious coincidence. In order to understand the reason why, it should first be explained that there is no such thing as an ideal musical scale, all scales, in so far as they have served as bases for some style of music are of equal authority. [103] When different peoples developed their music independently, it was natural that they had different modes, it would be curious coincidence indeed if they

---

[99] Pickard-Cambridge, *Festival,* 265; Haigh, *Theatre,* 319.

[100] Pickard-Cambridge, *Festival,* 266.

[101] Monro, *op. cit.,* 125.

[102] Haigh, *Theatre,* 321; Pickard-Cambridge, *Festival,* 263; Monro, *op. cit.,* 13 *et seq.* cf. Euripides, "Sir, unless you were very stupid and insensible, you could not laugh while I sing in the grave Mixolydian mode". — Plutarch, *De Audiendo, Plutarch's Miscellanies and Essays,* Ed. W. W. Goodwin, I. 458 — *vide* （元曲選）芝庵論曲，八款 for similar statements.

[103] P. A. Scholes, *The Oxford Companion to Music* (1945), SCALE 3. cf. how linguistics has shown that the parts of speech of Indo-European languages are not the norm.

all happened to use the same scale. Indian classical music, for example, is still modal. It was only in the last five hundred years and only in Europe that combination of notes in harmony imposed a preference on the different scales with respect to facility of writing music with harmony, which restricted European music to two modes only. It is due to the lack of knowledge of harmony that the ancient Greeks and the Chinese of T'ang and Sung dynasties could retain their musical modes and could remain sensitive not only to change of keys but also to change of modes [104] and it was for the same reason that the accompaniment in both theatres never grew beyond the simplest kind. [105]

(9)

In spite of the commercial nature of the Chinese theatre from its earliest days and the independence of its origin upon religion, dramatic performances have become part of many religious festivals and the majority of theatrical events in China are those that take place in village festivities. In the villages and small towns, in which the greater part of the Chinese population is distributed, there is no commercial theatre and dramatic performances, as in ancient Athens, can only be seen a few times in the year. In China festivities connected with popular religion are more a matter of custom than a matter of faith, hence, like Christmas in the western world, they concern every one in the community, not just a cult or coterie. It is difficult to live in China and not be involved in some of the religious or pseudo-religious events: the villages have their local earth-gods, [106] the cities have their guardian gods, [107] the trade guilds have their patron gods and there are many mountain-gods, river-gods belonging to particular districts as well as the more or less universal thunder-god, god of wealth, god of war and canonized saints and warriors. Festivals in honour of these gods, often celebrated as their birthdays, are general holidays for the districts concerned. Shops are closed and farms deserted, the people, one and all, put on their best clothes and enjoy themselves, even servants and apprentices are relieved from their duties in so far as the necessities of the celebrations allow. Large numbers of people crowd into the open air theatre in the village square or in front of the temple, which accommodates thousands, the greater part of the auditorium being standing room. Around the theatre temporary booths are set up to sell food and drink and itinerant salesmen bring their toys, trinkets, candies, artificial flowers, fireworks and so on. Special pastry articles are made for

---

[104] Monro, *op. cit.*, 125.

[105] The occasional chords in Greek music (Monro, *op. cit.*, 121 f.) and in the Chinese *ch'in* — 琴 — a kind of zither, can hardly be called harmony in the modern sense of the word, which is the technique of combining not only chords with notes but also one chord with another.

[106] 土地.

[107] 城隍.

the occasion, tree branches, and tinselled charms decorate house-doors and candles are lit, incense is burnt and offerings are placed in front of ancestral shrines. The atmosphere of universal hospitality pervades the place, bare acquaintances are warmly invited to the dinners, everywhere there is the smell of wine and tea and the sound of fire-crackers and the distant music from the theatre. The village suddenly becomes a crowded place, the population having been greatly augmented by the guests of the inhabitants and people from other villages who come for the free-for-all theatrical performance financed by the celebrating village. Quarrels and other signs of ill will, with or without excuse, are considered particularly offensive on this day.

Similarly the dramatic festivals in ancient Greece were not only religious but communal and civic celebrations. Women, courtezans, children, slaves, visitors as well as priests and city officials thronged the theatre to watch the dramas, and even prisoners were released so that they could share the festivities. Business was abandoned, the law-courts were closed, distraints for debt were forbidden during the festival. [108] The whole city kept holiday and gave themselves up to pleasures, and personal violence in the theatre was regarded as a crime against religion. The audience wore crowns in honour of Dionysus by the express command of the oracle. [109]

In ancient Greek theatres, as the performance lasted all day and it was difficult to get out from the crowd before the end of the performance, food was brought into the theatre and consumed, as Aristotle tells us, when the acting was bad, and perhaps not only then. Philochorus, half a century after Aristotle, tells how the Athenian spectators before him used to come to the theatre wearing garlands on their heads and keep themselves refreshed throughout the performances with wine and with dried fruits and confectionery, which might also be used to pelt the actors whom they did not like. [110] The Greek theatre, with its backless stone seats, and lengthy performances, could not be very much more comfortable than the space for standing spectators in Chinese village theatres. But discomfort no more damped the enthusiasm of the Greek audience than it does the Chinese. Pleasure and disapproval were freely shown, the latter with hisses and groans and the former with shouts and clapping of hands. The Athenians also made noise with their sandals by kicking against the stone seats when they disliked the actors and country audiences threw figs, olives and stones at bad actors. [111] Plato complained of their noisiness, which, considering the presence of children, slaves and women would seem inevitable, and beadles were planted in the theatre to keep order. [112] Despite the

[108] Haigh, *Theatre,* 1; Pickard-Cambridge, *Festival,* 269.

[109] Haigh, *Theatre,* 1, 342, 343.

[110] Pickard-Cambridge, *Festival,* 279.

[111] Haigh, *Theatre,* 344.

[112] Pickard-Cambridge, *Festival,* 279 ff.

boisterousness, the Greek audience seemed generally appreciative. Aeschylus was once nearly killed in the theatre because he was supposed to have revealed part of the mysteries in his tragedy and was only saved by flying for refuge to the altar of Dionysus in the orchestra, and Euripides caused a great uproar with his sceptical line, "Zeus, whoever Zeus be, for I know not save by report". [113] They burst into tears for the performance of skilled actors and understood dramatic suspense, as when they dreaded lest the old man who was to arrest Merope's blow, when she was about to murder her son, should not arrive in time. [114]

Whereas in Europe, religious ceremonies gave rise to drama, in China, a reverse development occasionally takes place. Connections between modern Chinese theatre and popular religion can be traced in the *festival plays* [115] based on legends related to the festivals and performed in commercial theatres only at the particular seasons. Perhaps the most popular of these are *Love on the Celestial River* [116] on the story of the two fairy lovers who are permitted to meet each other only on the seventh night of the seventh lunar month on the Silver River (The Milky Way) and *Story of the White Snake Lady* [117] on the adventures of White Snake Lady, connected with the Dragon Boat Festival in early June. [118] The genre is, according to Prof. Ch'i Ju-Shan, of recent origin, starting in the imperial palace of the Ch'ing dynasty and becoming extremely popular there only in the reign of Ch'ien Lung 乾隆 (1736-1796) in which period a great many of such plays were written. [119]

The religious connection of these *festival plays* is, however, mere excuse for topical entertainment, the dramatic performance has no religious significance otherwise. The critic Wang Meng-Sheng recorded a case of a well-known drama turned into a ritual of exorcism:

"In my youth I saw in Szechwan province performances of what amounts to a serial play based on the story of *The Rescue of Mu-Lien's Mother* [120] starting with the birth of the heroine, which was followed by her life as a young girl, then her coming of age, then discussion of marriage, etc., complete with small details of family affairs. It took more than ten days for the play to reach her wedding and on this day an actor was dressed as a bride in exactly the same way as the local custom prescribed and, sitting in the bridal carriage, he was paraded around the town with music and attendants, the bridegroom and

---

[113] Haigh, *Theatre,* 346.

[114] Pickard-Cambridge, *Festival,* 281.

[115] 應節戲.

[116] 天河配.

[117] 白蛇傳.

[118] See Ch. XIII.

[119] 齊如山, 京劇之變遷, 頁十三.

[120] 目蓮救母.

relatives, all in proper costume, following on horseback or in carriages, and the people in the streets watched them as they would a real wedding procession, also observing the customs and manners appropriate for such occasions. The bride was then taken to the theatre where a mock marriage ceremony was performed on the stage. The play continued with the birth of her child and her life at home, cooking, sewing and reading Buddhist scriptures and becoming in her later years a vegetarian just as a woman in that district would do. Later when the son died she abandoned religious practices and her soul was taken by a daemon into purgatory. At this point in the play, however, she was taken to parade through the town by the same route covered by her wedding procession and daemons struck her with three-pronged spears, the actor who played her being protected by a thick straw padding underneath the costume. The whole drama took about a month to complete and was supposed to have the effect of exorcizing evil spirits. Although there was singing and acting in the drama, the audience took part in much of the action, such as the feasts for the birth of babies, wedding parties and the service at her death: in these scenes the audience mixed with the actors and could not be distinguished from them''. [121]
In the original book, this was mentioned in connection with the Chinese imitations of the naturalistic drama. Indeed it is perhaps the most realistic drama ever performed and should compare favourably with any play N. P. Okhlopkov (1900-1967) produced in his Realistic Theatre (closed in 1938) in which the audience was often drawn into the action. As is hereby shown, realism in drama can be pushed to the extreme only when the performance is allowed to turn into a ritual and the audience into the congregation who partake in the ceremony. [122] It is not known whether for the play in Sung dynasty the same performance was then repeated for fifteen days or, as some scholars think, extraneous matters were added to make a long play lasting half a month. [123] Judging by the shortness of early Chinese plays, the former seems to be the more probable, in which case the modern performance recorded by Wang Meng-Sheng must be counted as one of the longest plays ever performed. [124]

---

[121] 王夢生, 梨園佳話, 四章, "新戲".

[122] The psychology of adopting the particular drama as a ritual of exorcism is also interesting, the purgatory scenes and the eventual rescue of the soul of the heroine by her son may be related to the idea of sacrifice. Plays based on the same story have been popular in China since the earliest days of the Chinese theatre, perhaps owing to the possibility of spectacle in the purgatory scenes. In Sung dynasty it was "acted for fifteen days with increasing audience towards the end". 孟元老, 東京夢華錄, 卷八, 中元節.

[123] 周貽白, 中國戲曲論叢 (一九五二), 頁六.

[124] cf. a Passion performed in 1547 in Valenciennes, which lasted twenty-five days. — H. d'Outreman, *Histoire de la ville et comté de Valenciennes* (1639), quoted in A. M. Nagler, *Sources of Theatrical History* (1952), 47.

In spite of similarities, the Chinese theatre differs from the Greek theatre in several ways.

Whereas in the Chinese theatre realism is altogether lacking, in the Greek theatre there was at least some tendency towards verisimilitude in dramatic representation. From the beginnings of the Greek drama, the playwrights tried to fit the action to the actual *locale* of the acting space, thus, in Aeschylus' early plays, *Suppliants* and *Prometheus,* the scenes were laid in open spaces, probably because the *skene* was then not yet built or too small and far from the orchestra to be considered as background for the action, but later, with the *skene* as background, the action of the tragedies mostly took place in front of some building. [125] Used in this way the *skene* was the most realistic set in any theatre, because unlike the temporary scenery on the modern European stage, it was a real permanent building, standing in the open air and serving the usual purpose of a house. The actors opened and closed and went through real doors and stood on the real roof. In Aeschylus' *Agamemnon,* for example, real horses and chariot could be drawn into the orchestra and the audience would approach very closely the crowd that watched the return of a king. In spite of the lack of artificial lighting, some realistic effect might have been sought when the time in the play was synchronized with the time of the performance, as in *Iphigenia in Aulis* which opens at dawn. [126] For spectacular effects, the Greek theatre had *ekkyklema, mechane* and other mechanical devices [127] which though they could hardly be more than conventions, as they must have fallen far behind what modern European audience understand as spectacle, yet did represent efforts in the direction of realism. In particular features, as the thunder machine, the Greeks might have nearly attained modern perfection. [128] In contrast, the Chinese theatre has no set whatsoever, but only a perfectly flexible acting space on a simple platform, without any mechanical devices, not even a trap door.

The Greek theatre is unique in having a chorus and with this feature it differs from all other theatres, including the Chinese. The chorus was not a product of dramatic evolution, rather it was the non-dramatic soil from which, with the successive addition of one actor after another, the Greek drama came into being. [129] A Greek tragedy consists of dramatic dialogue built upon and supported by the groundwork of lyrical odes; it may be compared to a plant shown together with the pot it grows in. The large body of dancers, even though the number was reduced to twelve from

---

[125] Bieber, *History,* 107 f; Flickinger, *op. cit.,* 226. About two thirds of the extant tragedies have action in front of a palace or temple — Pickard-Cambridge, *Theatre,* 122.

[126] *Vide* Nicoll, *Development of the Theatre,* 21.

[127] Haigh, *Theatre,* 202 et seq.

[128] *Ibid.,* 218.

[129] Haigh, *Theatre,* 222 et seq.

the original fifty, was at best a clumsy element for the dramatists to manipulate. The task of joining them smoothly to the action, and of motivating their conduct, including the traditional singing and dancing at regular intervals was almost an impossible one. [130] The wonders the Greek poets did with the chorus need not be enumerated here. Owing to its basically non-dramatic nature, it is not surprising that from the earliest times of the Greek theatre the element gradually dwindled out of existence. In the earliest Greek dramas extant — (Aeschylus: 525-456) — the choral odes occupy three fifths of the total text; in Sophocles (496-406) it varies from a quarter to a seventh and by the time of Euripides' *Orestes* (Euripides: 480-406) it is about a ninth of the text. [131] At the time of Aristotle, the practice of disconnecting the chorus from the action and making them into musical interludes had become universal. [132] While it lasted, it was used for several dramatic purposes, with beautiful effects, and since then no theatre has quite achieved that special quality due to the chorus. Some of the purposes are, however, occasionally served in other theatres without the chorus. For example, the doctor and the gentlewoman in Lady Macbeth's sleep-walking scene and the fisherman in the drama of Ch'ing dynasty *Peach Blossoms on a Fan,* [133] are commentators who though in the play are in fact also spectators, as the Greek chorus sometimes are. [134] The Chinese drama, for different reasons, also contains a large proportion of lyrical poetry and when part of the drama is sung or declaimed, the audience have the opportunity, as the Greek audience had during the choral odes, to savour the emotional and poetic significance of the drama. When the choral passages were actually seen and heard in the theatre it must have a similar relaxing effect on the audience as it has on the reader. In them the emotions of the audience are given a rest and their nerves are soothed with lyrical poetry and dancing and music before they are further drawn into the emotional response towards the drama. This effect can also be achieved by alternating the more serious scenes of a drama with the comic scenes, as is done in parts of the long Chinese drama *The Story of the Lute.* [135] Sometimes the Greek chorus represent people not closely connected with the action in the drama, as when they play servants or sympathetic witnesses, for example, in *Iphigenia among the Taurians* and Aeschylus' *Libation-Bearers* in both of which they are concerned with the issues but are not directly involved in them. Thus they occupy an emotional position midway between the audience and the characters in the dramas, and, as if by

---

[130] *Vide* Flickinger, *op. cit.,* Ch. II. *passim.*

[131] Haigh, *Theatre,* 285.

[132] Haigh, *Theatre,* 287; *Poetics,* 18.

[133] 孔尙任 , 桃花扇.

[134] For the equivalents of other functions of the chorus in later European dramas see F. L. Lucas, *Tragedy* (1928), 64-72.

[135] 高則誠 , 琵琶記.

example, teach the audience to respond to the drama. Similar effect is achieved in the modern Chinese play of palace intrigue *The Crooked Bridge,* [136] in which a chorus of masked earth-gods, looking exactly the same, line the stage behind and to the sides of the actors. They are, by convention, invisible to the people in the drama and they accompany most of the action, standing silently behind the actors, sometimes miming among themselves to indicate concern over the fortunes of the characters and occasionally intervene through supernatural means to avert the dangers and alleviate the sufferings of the hero and heroine, but they remain outside the main action. Nevertheless, it was only in the Greek theatre that the chorus could be fully and constantly exploited. It was a convention which the Greek audience accepted because it was the original form of their religious ceremony of which the drama later became a part. If under those conditions the chorus was continually losing ground in the theatre, the survival of choruses revived in other times and other lands must be rather doubtful.

A sharp contrast between the Chinese and the Greek theatre lies in the social status of the players. No country has ever esteemed the actors as much as the ancient Greeks did nor any people despised them more than the Chinese did and, to a certain extent, still do. The early Greek dramatic performances were on the semi-professional basis; it was not until the third century before Christ that the players and musicians were organized into guilds. [137] The Greek actors were treated not as a theatrical profession but as officials of the Dionysian cult, exempt from conscription and free to travel in times of war; [138] they were more respected than the ordinary citizen. The Chinese actors were deprived of civil rights and looked upon in the same way as prostitutes, which the early actresses certainly were, and almost as beggars, whom they often resembled in their way of earning a living. The fact that both Greek and Chinese players sometimes assisted in or successfully accomplished diplomatic missions does not imply any degree of social equality between them. [139] The Greek actors were so trusted probably because they were free to travel in times of war and perhaps they, being religious officials, were trusted to maintain neutrality in politics. The court jester Shih[140] of late Chou dynasty once served as a diplomat in a court intrigue and explained to the princess who gave him the mission that, he being a jester, could "speak no offence". [141] Yet later, when he was probably used as a political tool, he was executed by Confucius on the spot and it was said that "his head and legs were taken out by different doors". [142] In recent

---

[136] 九曲橋.
[137] Bieber, *History,* 158.
[138] Haigh, *Theatre,* 278 ff.
[139] *Vide* Pickard-Cambridge, *Festival,* 287.
[140] 優施.
[141] "言無郵" 國語, 晉語, 第八.
[142] 穀梁傳, 定公十年.

times, a discharged high official, who had been reported dead in order to evade further prosecution, wrote a play and asked the famous actor Ch'en Te-Lin [143] to act in it in the palace in the hope that royal attention could be attracted to the author and a pardon negotiated. The actor, perhaps wisely, declined to help. [144] It may be due to their quick eloquence and supposed neutrality that Chinese actors sometimes assisted in indirect political negotiations but the main reason for such temporary missions lay in their low social status which made them in the eyes of their social superiors incapable of giving offence.

There is perhaps something in the unsteady livelihood of the theatrical profession which tends to corrupt the actors; even of the Greek actors Aristotle asked why they were generally depraved [145] and he suggested that it was because they spent most of their time making a living leaving none for self-cultivation and they lived in habitual intemperance. [146] The rapid alternation between luxury and poverty could have been another reason. [147] In later times, they were said to be whipped and to be wandering about in beggary and starvation. [148]

---

[143] 陳德霖.

[144] 齊如山, 京劇之變遷, 頁二五.

[145] *Problems*, XXX. 10.

[146] Pickard-Cambridge, *Festival*, 287.

[147] Haigh, *Theatre*, 282.

[148] According to Lucian (c. A.D. 160), see Pickard-Cambridge, *Festival*, 315.

CHAPTER XXXVIII

THE CHINESE THEATRE AND THE *COMMEDIA DELL' ARTE*

(Description—Popular Taste—Conventions—Improvisation—Types of Characters
—Evolution—Theatre vs Drama)

(1)

The *commedia dell' arte,* which originated in Italy and was prevalent in Europe from the sixteenth to the beginning of the eighteenth century, was distinguished by the improvisation and professional skill of its players, the farcical content of the dramas and the prominent types of characters. The distinction of the *commedia dell' arte* from other forms of Italian drama cannot, however, be absolute; its form never achieved complete independence. Its content was mainly farcical, but it was also connected with neo-classical plays and in the later part of its history, with the sentimental plots of the Spanish theatre; its players were mainly professional, but it was also cultivated by academic amateurs; it was improvised, but its actors kept memoranda of speeches and jokes; its characters were mainly, but not invariably, the prominent types called "masks"; and though it was essentially a popular theatre, it was patronized by the courts of all the larger countries in Europe — indeed, but for the aristocratic patronage it might not have achieved the artistic standards it did. [1] "Since these exceptions do not occur simultaneously, the *commedia dell' arte* may be said to exist by virtue of a quorum of its characteristics". [2] It differed from other types of theatre not in the physical conditions of the stage — for it was equally at home on the simple platform stage and on the stage with scenery — but in the method of production and the quality of the performance. The nearest approach to the script was the scenario, an outline of the plot which was explained to the actors before the performance, the details of the dialogue and the action being left to improvisation. The smooth progress of the performance depended on the players' familiarity with each other's technique and

---

[1]   W. Smith, *The Commedia dell' arte* (1912), Ch. III.

[2]   K. M. Lea, *Italian Popular Comedy* (1934), 3.

421

the repetition of stock situations in different plays and monotony was avoided by ingenious shuffling and renovation through minor changes. The dialogue and stage business were, therefore, the creation of the players who were advised to read good authors to form a style for the laments, addresses, dialogues, conceits and soliloquies for various occasions. As it was safer to improvise stage business and dialogue which had little or no bearing on the development of the plot, a large portion of the *commedia dell' arte* was side-play, or *lazzi,* which, being irrelevant to the main narrative, would probably appear to the modern audience as the most striking feature of that theatre, if they could see an authentic performance. The side-play appealed to the audience not by its ancillary function in the drama, but by its immediate comic effect and the display of virtuosity. (3)

Owing to the limited variety of the plots the characters consisted of four classes according to their functions in the plays: parents, lovers, servants and miscellaneous caricatures. It is in the nature of the *commedia dell' arte* that all the characters were exaggerated examples of humanity each with his special mixture of idiosyncrasies. The repeated appearance of particular mixtures of personal characteristics in different plays was the basis of the "masks" which stood between a type and an individual. In so far as the personality of a "mask" remained the same it was like an individual, but in so far as it appeared in different plays unconnected with each other, it was a type. The name of a "mask" was sometimes a proper name, as Franceschina, and sometimes a generic name, as Capitano.

Some of the "masks" may be briefly described as follows. One of the "masks" for parents was Pantalone, a Venetian by dialect and a *Magnifico* by dress, given to reprimands, tirades and long-winded advice, relaxing into absurdities in discussions of love and feasting. Also as a parent was the Bolognese lawyer, Graziano, the Doctor, who was also amorous and gullible but grosser than Pantalone, and given to "saying everything the wrong way round". The lovers, usually the lost or erring children of Pantalone and Graziano, were hardly characters in their own right; the parts were exaggerated, but apart from their predominant romantic inclination they behaved as the situations of the love intrigue required, their attraction consisting mainly in their eloquence and natural charm. Often used as the rival in love was the Capitano, either Spanish or Greek, a braggart soldier, known as much for his ridiculous lies as for his cowardice. Of the servants, or *zanni,* there were many "masks" of which Arlecchino and Pulcinella are now the best known owing to their partial survival till to-day. They belonged to two sub-types, the astute and witty servant and the awkward booby, respectively. The former planned disguises and false messages, arranged the love affairs of his masters and squeezed money from the old lecher; and the latter pretended "not understanding anything that was said to him" so as to

---

(3) In seventeenth century Germany *Haupt- und Staatsaktionen* plays were also based on improvised dialogue.

give "rise to delightful equivocations, ridiculous mistakes and other clownish tricks". Parallel to the man-servants, there were "masks" for the serving maids who were in the confidence of their mistresses and advised on and executed their love affairs. [4]

From the characters the dramatic contents of the *commedia dell' arte* can readily be visualized. Gosson, who had written "a cast of Italian deuises, called, The Comedie of Captaine Mario" stated that "the grounde worke of Commedies, is loue, cosenedge, flatterie, bawderie, slye conueighance of whoredome; The persons, cookes, queanes, knaues, baudes, parasites, courtezannes, lecherous olde men, amorous yong men". [5]

The *commedia dell' arte* was a type of theatre which, like the modern Chinese theatre, rose out of the popular theatre and bore prominent marks of popular taste. In both types of theatre the form had hardened before aristocratic patronage and literary interests could change it. [6] The *commedia dell' arte,* like the Chinese theatre of to-day, had no literary value and could not be properly judged by literary standards. [7]

Literature is not for the many and can hardly be depended upon to draw a crowd. In the development of a style of drama, when the audience of the popular entertainment becomes more select literary merits can be expected to be introduced but in some cases the taste for and the technique of histrionic skill can be so highly developed that the contents of the plays remain at the popular level. In the *commedia dell' arte* the whole technique of production and acting was based on the farcical nature of the plays and in the Chinese theatre the major media of dramatic expression have been vocal and gesticulatory acting, hence in the former serious drama would destroy the style of acting and in the latter literary merits are felt to be unnecessary. It is in these types of theatre that "the player's function is one thing, and the poet's another". [8] When the *commedia dell' arte* disappeared, therefore, little was left of it: the script, the most durable part of the theatre. was of the least importance in it. As in the modern Chinese theatre many actors in Italy must have carried part of their art to their graves, for, like dancers and singers, a great actor is for the most part inimitable and his art is the most fragile part of the theatre.

If and when literary merits did enter the popular theatre, as in the dramas of

---

[4] For other types see Lea, *op. cit.,* Ch. II; Nicoll, *Mask, Mimes and Miracles,* Ch. IV.

[5] Stephen Gosson, *Playes Confuted in fiue Actions, vide* Chambers, *Elizabethan Stage,* IV, 214, 215.

[6] Aristocratic patronage is believed to be an influence in the rise of the *commedia dell' arte.* W. Smith, *The Commedia dell' arte,* 19 f.

[7] Theatre had sometimes literary and sometimes histrionic merits: in the Greek theatre, the actors became so important in the fourth century before Christ that by then no dramas of literary value were written. Haigh, *The Attic Theatre,* 229.

[8] Basilio Locatelli, Preface to his first collection on scenarii, Lea, *op. cit.,* 136.

Yüan dynasty, they were not the literary merits admired by the scholars, but those cherished by people of unsophisticated taste. Zucker referred to the "extremely crude technique . . . the poor motivation . . . the paucity of invention . . . and numerous absurdities" in the Chinese theatre. [9] Professor Wang Kuo-Wei, himself an admirer of the dramas of Yüan dynasty, wrote:

> "The dramatists of Yüan dynasty were not, in general, among people of learning and position and when they wrote the plays they had no intention of making themselves known to posterity, rather, they wrote to amuse themselves and to please the theatregoers. They did not care whether the plot was crude or not, they did not try to veil the vulgarity of their mind or the absurdities in their dramatic characters. The plays were the spontaneous products of the age, and probably the most spontaneous works in the whole of Chinese literature. . . The merits of Yüan dramas do not lie in their structure or themes but in their language . . . in the vividness of the lyrical, descriptive and narrative verse". [10]

"Malgré l'incroyable, il y règne de l'intérêt, et, malgré la foule des événements, tout est de la clarté la plus lumineuse", Voltaire once said. Only in a generous mood can one say this of Chinese dramas.

Farce, by its nature, is subject neither to morals nor to dramatic craftsmanship. The audience become, for the time being, morally insensitive and ready to accept the grossest improbabilities. The motivation in the *commedia dell' arte* was uniformly crude: old fathers always want to marry their inevitably beautiful daughters to rich and ugly friends and young wives are always furnished with old and inconsiderate husbands so that they have good excuse to take lovers. [11] Complications of family affairs are deftly nullified by the recognition of lost children or the magician's supernatural power or the physician's ability to revive dead bodies, all of which work simply and swiftly, without any need for preparations in the plot. Disguise is symbolic and speedily accomplished; it is transparent to the audience but it deceives the characters in the play. [12] The story as such is a poor story but it is only a means to an end, the stage business is all. Names of the plays were soon forgotten but the names of famous players were remembered. Like the modern Chinese theatre, *commedia dell' arte* was the actor's art not the dramatist's. It was the practice to change the names of the characters and modify minor episodes and give the same play as a new one. [13]

In popular art vulgarity invariably leads to grossness. Respectable women

---

[9] A. E. Zucker, *The Chinese Theatre,* Ch. II.
[10] 王國維, 宋元戲曲史, 十二章.
[11] Lea, *op. cit.,* 195 ff.
[12] Lea, *op. cit.,* 329.
[13] Lea, *op. cit.,* 319.

scarcely went to see the *commedia dell' arte*. [14] Garzoni says of the actors that,

> "They are less civil than donkeys in their action, no better than pimps and ruffians in their gestures, equal to prostitutes in their immodesty of speech. Knavery and lewdness inspire all their motions". [15]

In the plays indecent jests and obscene gestures were so common and so crude that Lea believes "many of them are perhaps best left in obscurity". [16] Contemporary engravings show scenes with hardly discreet stage business. [17]

Like the Chinese players, the actors and actresses of the *commedia dell' arte* were practically social outcasts. Both the church and the civil authorities looked on them as corruptive agents of public morals. The laws "forbade their entrance into decent houses, relegating them to dark corners of the city where they lurked with thieves and prostitutes". [18] In spite of the whitewashing in W. Smith's *Italian Actors of the Renaissance,* immorality was evidently rife among actors and actresses who were considered as *mignons* and prostitutes. [19] Hard living conditions could not but have their effect on morality but social conditions also encouraged their depravity. Florinda Andreini was extolled because "she was one of the few great beauties who could come into Duke Vincenzo's court without being drawn into his harem". [20] The morals of the actresses and their patrons in the eighteenth century in Italy can be studied in some detail in the *Memoirs* of Count Gozzi who was the script-writer of Sacchi's company and had an open liaison with the leading actress Teodora Ricci. [21] The players' character did not seem to be particularly attractive; Gozzi, who associated closely with them for many years, thought they were greedy, ambitious, and without feelings. [22] Some of them were illiterate.

(2)

The "mimetic instinct", the desire to act for an audience, may be said to

---

[14] Lea, *op. cit.,* 315; *The Memoirs of Count Carlo Gozzi,* trans. by J. A. Symonds (1890), i, 42, 71; Smith, *The Commedia dell' arte,* 204.

[15] Garzoni, *Piazza Universale,* quoted in Symonds, *op. cit.,* i, 75.

[16] Lea, *op. cit.,* 68.

[17] *Vide* P. L. Duchartre, *The Italian Comedy* (trans. R. T. Weaver) Ills. between pp. 56-57 and on pp. 187 and 281.

[18] Symonds, *op. cit.,* i, 70.

[19] Duchartre, *op. cit.,* 74.

[20] Smith, *Italian Actors,* 133.

[21] In spite of his self-righteousness Gozzi, owing to the different moral outlook of his times, left us considerable details of the relationship. The actress was married; the relationship between Gozzi, her husband and her other "admirers", together with the reaction of Mme Ricci to his eventual withdrawal of his "protection" can be followed in considerable detail.

[22] Symonds, *op. cit.,* ii, 137 *et seq.*

consist of two parts, the desire to imitate and the desire to display. The audience watch the mimetic performance both to wonder at the nearly convincing mimicry and to enjoy the skill and virtuosity. In most styles of theatre the display of skill is absorbed into the mimicry and the actor's virtuosity is directed entirely towards dramatic ends, but in the Chinese theatre and the *commedia dell' arte* the actor's skill has a place of its own apart from the drama, hence the overt acrobatics in the military plays of the former and the *lazzi,* or comic by-play, of the latter. Popular entertainment, with which the Chinese theatre and the *commedia dell' arte* are closely connected in the historical as well as in the artistic sense, cannot be operated in the same way as the modern commercialized theatre. In modern theatres the audience, having paid for the admission, would sit through dull moments in the hope that the performance would become more exciting later but the entertainment offered to the crowd of the fairground has to be continuously striking in order to keep the crowd from straying and to arrest the steps of the passers-by, often in competition with other attractions. In the former it is the total effect of the drama that the audience take with them and judge the performance by, but in the latter it is the immediate effect from one moment to another that is important, because that is what determines the size of the audience. "The few go to the theatre to consider, to cry, to conjecture; the many go to be amused", [23] and the crowd which popular entertainment caters for pay only after they have sampled satisfaction and stop to watch only because they have been impressed or amused. To reap quick results, the actors surprise the audience with stunts and feats, with clowning and practical jokes — the ludicrous, the difficult and the grotesque required much less time to appreciate than, for example, the sentimental and the mysterious — thus acrobatics and broad farce become stable elements of the Chinese theatre and the *commedia dell' arte*. Farce and accentuated stage business probably belong to all primitive theatres, for example, they were in the conventional farce of T'ang and Sung dynasties [24] and the *phlyakes* in Hellenistic times [25] and are usually discarded after drama is developed, but in the *commedia dell' arte* they had become so firmly rooted in the style of production that other influences introduced in the later stage of its development could not oust them, and in spite of its high artistic quality due to aristocratic patronage, it bore, like the Chinese theatre, the marks of its low birth throughout its history.

The connection between the beginning of the Chinese drama and the popular entertainment of Sung dynasty and the popular origin of the modern Chinese theatre have been discussed in Chapters XXIV and XXVII. The popular nature of the

---

[23] K. M. Lea, *The Italian Popular Comedy,* 185.

[24] 參軍戲.

[25] See Ch. XXII and M. Bieber, *History of the Greek and Roman Theatre,* Ch. X.

commedia dell' arte is best illustrated by quoting from Garzoni's *Piazza Universale* (1585):

"In one corner you will see our gallant Fortunato spinning yarns with Fritata, entertaining the crowd every evening from four till six with stories, fables, dialogues, mimicking, extempore songs, squabbling, making up, dying with laughter, quarrelling again, throwing themselves against the bench, arguing, and at last handing round the hat to try how many 'gazette' they can raise by their most refined and elegant prattle. In another corner Burattino, yelling as if the executioner were flogging him, with his porter's sack over his shoulders and a rogue's cap on his brows shouts to the audience at the top of his voice. The people come nearer, the common folk shoving, the gentlemen making their way to the front, and he has hardly delivered a ridiculous entertaining prologue but he begins some queer story of his master who would break the arms, choke out the breath, and rob the world of as many of the auditors who have made a ring about him . . . There is a Gratiano blathering, and a Florentine near by; in another corner Gradella makes a fool of the Milanese lover and leaves him among the jars and boxes on the piazza at the mercy of his enemies. When this adventure is over Gradella sets up a screeching song, or pretends to be a blind man and holding a puppy instead of a theorbo he begins the invention of the "balle di Macalepo' that lasts two hours, to the disgust of the audience who disperse jeering at the stupid charlatan who stands firm on three whole gazettes and two soldi in small change, protesting to heaven and earth that he would never want to shut up shop except when the audience leaves him without so much as a 'Good Evening' . . . Cieco da Forli is there with his rhymes and his extempore patter . . . Nor does Zan della Vigna fail to put in an appearance to divert the mob with all kinds of juggling. Catullo with his lyre, and the Mantuan dressed like a 'Zani', face the crowds and quite quietly put up the bench, adjust the bagpipes, and present themselves in a kitchen comedy in which Zani makes jealousy between Pedrolina and her mistress . . ."
(26)

The *commedia dell' arte* might not have descended directly from the mountebanks and jugglers of the sixteenth century (27) but some flow of personnel must have occurred to produce the evident similarity in technique. In the early Chinese theatre in Sung dynasty, theatre was considered as one type of a large variety of popular entertainment. Garzoni's catalogue of the types of popular entertainment in

---

(26) Quoted in Lea, *op. cit.,* 59 f. For accounts of tumbling girls, performing dogs and goats, etc., from the same source — Garzoni — see Symonds, *op. cit.,* i, 76-80. For similar accounts by English travellers in Italy see Lea, *op. cit.,* 343-7. For pictorial representations see *Enciclopedia dello Spettacolo,* Vol. III. Tav. LXXV, A. G. Bragaglia, *Pulcinella,* 28.

(27) cf. Smith, *The Commedia dell' arte,* 28 f.

Italy [28] also includes riddling couplets, jests, maxims, singing, instrumental music, extempore speeches, mock fights, quarrels, story-telling, snake charmers, dog trainers, gymnastics, acrobatics, conjuring, fisticuffs, indecencies, mock death and lament, mock pick-pocketing and mock preaching on current morals. [29] The boisterousness of the audience can be expected: in Pisa it was necessary to forbid the flinging of lemons, oranges, apples, turnips and other disagreeable substances. [30]

The extreme form of the exhibition of skill in the *commedia dell' arte* lay perhaps in the *cantarina* and *ballerina,* who sang, played instruments and danced but contributed nothing to the action, their only connection with the drama being occasionally singing the story. [31] Actors were also accomplished acrobats: they could turn a somersault, walk on their hands or do the "split". Acrobatic skill was naturally very serviceable in the practical jokes and some players were known for their special skill: a Scaramouche could, at eighty-four box his fellow-actor's ear with his foot and an actor called Vindentini could turn a somersault with a glass of water in his hand. [32] The Chinese actor Yang Hsiao-Lou, [33] famous in military roles, could, even in his old age, leap, turn in the air and land himself in a chair several yards away.

Acrobatics is to the actor's physical dexterity as ventriloquism is to his vocal abilities; both are beyond the capabilities of an ordinary person and both are seldom required in acting. Yet, in the complete control of the body the actor is similar to the acrobat and in the modification of his natural voice for dramatic purposes he is something of a ventriloquist. The extent to which acrobatics is needed in a theatre depends on the type of dramas: modern European dramatists avoid scenes which require any gymnastic skill for proper presentation and when occasionally such scenes are unavoidable, as in revivals of Shakespeare, the audience make allowance for the sketchy acting. In the Chinese theatre and the *commedia dell' arte* the subjects of the dramas are such that the actors' physical skills have ample opportunity to be shown. The demanding gymnastic training given to the Chinese players is not only to make them into acrobats but also to improve the control of their bodies which is conspicuous in their gait and posture. The appreciation of acrobatic skill, however, brings into the theatre pseudo-dramatic and non-dramatic elements for the sole purpose of acrobatic display. It seems to be a difficult task to

[28] In *La Piazza Universale,* 1585.

[29] Smith, *The Commedia dell' arte,* 30-66. cf. the types of popular entertainment in Sung dynasty mentioned in Ch. XXIII.

[30] Lea, *op. cit.,* 315.

[31] M. Sand, *The History of the Harlequinade* (1915), 28; Duchartre, *The Italian Comedy,* 268; Nicoll, *Development of the Theatre,* 107.

[32] Duchartre, *op. cit.,* 36.

[33] 楊小樓.

keep art uncontaminated by the preoccupation of technique: ventriloquism was exploited in the Greek theatre [34] and the interest in the *cadenza* in classical European music is scarcely musical. It is the appreciation of technique too that lies behind the practice of *encore*. Though it has now become in concerts the request for extra value of the audience's money, it was at one time used in the theatre to show genuine appreciation. Fine poetic passages were repeated in the Greek theatre at the request of the audience [35] and operatic arias also used to be encored. In such cases, when a new effect is achieved, the connoisseurs would miss the exact manner of execution and would like to be given a second chance. Without the appreciation of pure technique the repetitions of similar comic stage business in the *commedia dell' arte* and those of the battles and combats in the Chinese theatre, would not have been tolerable. In particular types of drama, acrobatics, being geared to the action, can become almost an art. The "acrobatic clown" [36] of the Chinese stage, like the *zanni* in the *commedia dell' arte,* expresses his comic character with his whole body, just as the Chinese stage warrior does his prowess and heroism. Acrobatics becomes a means of achieving some dramatic purpose, instead of an end in itself with emphasis on difficulty and danger, as in the circus. Critics of the Chinese theatre have been intolerant of the acrobatics, but the fact that virtuosity sometimes deviates from the purpose it serves is not a sound objection to cultivating virtuosity.

"*Lazzi*" means antics, gambols, tricks or comic turns. In their simplest form they are merely appropriate gestures, such as *lazzi* of joy, of recognition, of kissing the hand and so on, but they can also be dumb show and by-play, as in the *lazzi* of hiding in the corner and talking in sleep, or pieces of buffoonery, as getting rid of poison supposedly swallowed and drawing up and down the stage after each other in chairs in their efforts to provoke or escape a confidence. There are sometimes riddles, quibbles and anecdotes, as in agonizing the lover by protracting his bad news with sobs and verbiage or betraying all his master's secrets by elaborate pretence of keeping secrets, or escaping an execution by requesting to remove the clothes first and play a trick on the executioner in a struggle with a tight garment, or playing the peace-maker and hurrying to and fro across the stage misinterpreting one party to another. [37] In the *lazzi,* as in the *cadenza,* the performer is given freedom to display virtuosity without being hampered by the progress of the plot or the musical composition. [38]

When a *lazzo* becomes episodic it is called "*burla*" or "*intermedio*". For example, the *burla* of the false arm was described by Locatelli as follows:

---

[34] Haigh, *The Attic Theatre,* 274.

[35] Haigh, *op. cit.,* 344.

[36] 武丑.

[37] *Vide* Lea, *op. cit.,* 66-70.

[38] cf. Symonds, *op. cit.,* i, 63.

"The thief comes down the street pretending that he wants to buy Zanni's cloak and remarking aside that he will play him a trick. Zanni points out the beauties of the cloak, but refuses to let him handle it until the thief gives him the false arm to hold while he examines the garment and inquires the price. After talking a little the thief makes off, leaving Zanni with the false arm in the middle of his antics of admiring the cloak. Presently he realizes the hoax and goes in pursuit". [39]

Burle may become sub-plot or they may be mere padding. [40]

The comedians of the Chinese theatre are not allowed to introduce a large amount of comic stage business into the dramas, but when a comedian takes the leading role in a play [41] much of the action consists in the display of his skill.

Farce, by its nature, can never be wholly naturalistic. "We care for neither character nor motives, but are content to be amused by whatever absurdity may be trumped up", nor do we ask for probability in the ways in which the characters trick and cheat each other, "all that we want is to see them doing it again, to watch them fight on the merest excuse and to run into their own booby traps". [42] It has to be comprehensible though not necessarily credible. Theatricality usually goes with it. Masked characters mixed with unmasked ones in *commedia dell' arte*, contemporary dress on the women mixed with the purely conventional costume on Harlequin and Pulcinella. In appearance some of the characters were a separate race who existed only on the stage, but the women were all real, indeed their charm and attractiveness conformed to the contemporary ideals. As in the Chinese *K'un* dramas, clowns spoke different dialects. [43] These mixtures alone constituted convention, but conventional stage actions similar to those on the Chinese stage were also used, for example, a lantern to indicate night time. [44] Spectacles of naval battles, sieges, tournaments and other spectacles such as Heaven and Hell were also sometimes added [45] and were not apparently thought to be incongruous. Sumptuous properties were used [46] and yet curtains stood for walls and actors held them back in order to eavesdrop. [47]

In its departure from naturalism, the *commedia dell' arte* was like the Chinese theatre but in its lack of serious emotional content, it was different. Its interest was

---

[39] Lea, *op. cit.*, 186.

[40] *Vide* Lea, *op. cit.*, 186-190.

[41] Such plays are called "comedians' plays". 丑戲 .

[42] Lea, *op. cit.*, 185.

[43] Symonds, *op. cit.*, i, 35.

[44] Lea, *op. cit.*, 329.

[45] Lea, *op. cit.*, 197, 327, 331.

[46] *Ibid.*, 327 ff.

[47] *Ibid.*, 328.

confined to a narrow range, from facetiousness to wit; it was not intended to stir deep feelings.

(3)

Lack of realism opened the way to the use of masks: some of the characters in the *commedia dell' arte,* like those in the modern Chinese theatre, wore them. The masks of the *commedia dell' arte* were of two kinds, the vizard and the grotesque mask. The vizard, which was used at that time for festivity or anonymity, was realistic rather than theatrical [48] but the grotesque mask, often with a fantastic nose, was an artificial device. [49] The masks were made of leather, hence the moulding could change the shape of the face, and the effects of colour did not seem to have been exploited. [50] The Chinese theatrical mask is the reverse: bright colour patterns are painted on the actor's face. In the case of vizards, the face was only partly covered and though expressions with the eyes were hardly possible, those of the mouth could still be seen. Unlike the masks in the Greek theatre, however, those of the *commedia dell' arte* did not show violent expressions, rather, they were of that neutral mysteriousness adaptable to the emotions of the moment according to the expressions of the actor's body movements. [51]

The characters of the *commedia dell' arte* also addressed the audience directly. [52] The necessity to keep the audience of the fair ground from straying away increased the usefulness of direct relationship between the players and the audience.

In the *commedia dell' arte* men could play women and women, men. When Lord Herbert of Cherbury saw the Italian players in Paris in 1608, what struck him most was "women playing boys". [53] This was done sometimes in the disguise, which was transparent to the audience, in order to complicate the plot, as in *Twelfth Night,* [54] and sometimes for the advertisement value in preliminary parades.

> "No sooner have they made their entrance than the drum beats to let all the world know that the players are arrived. The first lady of the troupe, decked out like a man, with a sword in her right hand, goes round, inviting the folk to a comedy or tragedy or pastoral in the precincts of Pellegrino". [55]

Men played female roles sometimes for comic effect, as when Harlequin or Scaramouche played a nurse or young courtezan or pregnant woman or lady of quality, [56] but the part of the maid-servant Francesquina was taken by a man and

---

[48] *Vide* Duchartre, *op. cit.,* 258, 263, 300.

[49] *Vide ibid.,* 33, 44, 54, 236, 176; Symonds, *op. cit.,* ii, opp. p. 256.

[50] Duchartre, *op. cit.,* 49.

[51] cf. Duchartre, *op. cit.,* 42.

[52] Sand, *op. cit.,* 28; Duchartre, *op. cit.,* 150, monologue of despair by Harlequin.

[53] *Vide* Lea, *op. cit.* 179.

[54] *Ibid.,* 180.

[55] Garzoni, *Piazza Universale,* quoted in Symonds, *op. cit.,* i, 73 f.

[56] Duchartre, *op. cit.,* 38.

apparently played with serious intent. [57] The practice did not seem to have been as successful as in the Chinese theatre, because according to Niccolo Barbieri,

"These young men do not know how to dress themselves in the attire of the other sex, and they must therefore dress at home with the aid of their wives or some feather-brained maid with whom they make free and lively . . . These lads pass openly through the city, chatting and romping together, and often they arrive at the theatre so completely dishevelled that their friends or teachers must needs comb their hair again, refurbish their paint, and rearrange their finery". [58]

It is not surprising that female roles were mainly played by women considering how the attraction of the actresses lay mainly in their natural beauty and charm. [59] The women in the plays wore contemporary fashions with very low neck-lines.[60]

The *commedia dell' arte* was frankly a mixed exhibition of acrobatics, horse-play and women. The drama was overtly a pretence; dramatic illusion as the modern European audience understand it was entirely absent; the world of the drama and that of the audience were hardly distinct. Goethe mentioned to Eckermann that a favourite trick of a Neapolitan Pulcinella he saw was pretending to forget he was in the play until he was reminded that he was acting. [61] Here a player could step from one world into the other and back again because the transition was not violent. In the naturalistic theatre the audience may take Pulcinella seriously, and even if they do not, the "gag" will be felt to be in bad taste.

(4)

That the clowns should "speak no more than is set down for them" referred to the quantity rather than the precision of the dialogue because the objection was that "in the mean time some necessary question of the play" was being suspended. The clown's technique is necessarily the technique of improvisation because he, more than any other actor, is in close contact with the audience whom he often addresses directly, and he must, like a clever conversationalist, be constantly aware of the response in every moment. Comic effect depends on the occasion and the instantaneous mood of the audience and on the split-second timing of the nuance in voice and gesture, it survives precariously on the psychological atmosphere of the moment and can perish in the slightest mishap. Not only will a written comic speech not be funny to the reader but a gramophone record of a comic speech often produces little effect. Good clowns, like good speakers, consciously and

---

[57] Lea, *op. cit.* 504.

[58] Quoted in Duchartre, *op. cit.,* 266.

[59] cf. Duchartre, *op. cit.,* 264.

[60] *Vide* Symonds, *op. cit.,* i, Ills. opp. pp. 24 and 48; Duchartre, *op. cit.,* 89, 151.

[61] *Vide* Smith, *The Commedia dell' arte,* 204 f.

unconsciously adjust their performance to suit the moods of the audience. [62] The atmosphere of gaiety in a theatre has to be induced and maintained so that the sudden impact of small absurdities can trigger the mechanism of laughter. The slightest hesitations kill the joke and put the audience out of ease. The smoothness and liveliness required in sustained farce can hardly be achieved outside professional improvisation, hence the method of the *commedia dell' arte* and of the clown in the Chinese theatre. All speeches in the *commedia dell' arte* are of adjustable length. [63] In the Chinese dramas of Ming dynasty the clown's parts are indicated but not written out, hence they must have been improvised. In the modern Chinese theatre the script contains the clown's speeches, but the comedians indulge in improvised departures for better results. [64]

Change in theatrical conditions and difference of histrionic talents perennially threaten the purity of dramatic texts: in the fourth century before Christ when acting was well developed in the Greek theatre, standard texts had to be deposited in the state archives and deviations in performances fined [65] and in England, where no such precautions were taken, liberty was taken with Shakespeare's plays from Davenant onwards: Nahum Tate had a *King Lear* without the Fool and with the marriage of Cordelia and Edgar, Davenant had a *Romeo and Juliet* with happy ending and Colley Cibber put his own lines and lines from *Henry IV, Henry VI* and *Richard II* into his *Richard III*. The corruption of dramas of high literary value for decadent taste will be deplored by book lovers, but the corrosive effect of individual histrionic talents always exists and changes made for fluency in the performance, at least in scripts not of the highest literary merits, will not be an offence to theatre-lovers. In this respect the *commedia dell' arte* lies at the opposite extrem. of literary dramas: its dialogue was entirely fluid and the chief player, who was also the manager, could change even the scenario to suit the talents of the company [66] and

---

[62] It is said that in the Japanese Noh plays the actors watch the mood of the audience and, when it shows signs of unhealthy extremes, try to counteract it by changing the style of acting in order to produce a harmonious psychological effect. (See Arthur Waley, *The Noh Plays of Japan* (1921), Introduction, p.44). This is probably the only theatre in which such an adjustment is consciously made and the only theatre in which it is made in serious dramas.

[63] Lea, *op. cit.,* 23.

[64] 齊如山, 京劇之變遷, 頁二一. Some Chinese players have extraordinary ability to improvise. The famous actor T'an Hsin-P'ei (譚鑫培) was at one time late at a palace performance and missed some of the words in the text because he did not have sufficient time to smoke his opium before he played. The Empress Dowager, being a connoisseur, noticed the ommissions and ordered him to be whipped but commuted the punishment, after supplication of the actor and his manager, to one of playing an old woman in a farce, for which he was not trained T'an, however, gave a delightful performance by improvisation, and was doubly tipped for it. 王夢生, 梨園佳話, 三章, 譚鑫培.

[65] Bieber, *History of the Greek and Roman Theatre,* 158.

[66] Symonds, *op. cit.,* i, 59 *et seq.*

the Chinese dramas lie between the two extremes, for throughout the history of the Chinese drama the plays were continually being modified and re-written to meet contemporary needs.

(5)

The comparative study of the evolution of character-types in the *commedia dell' arte* and the Chinese theatre is interesting owing to the light it throws on the tendency of primitive theatres to produce them.

First, some explanation on the exact nature of the "masks" in the *commedia dell' arte* will not be out of place. A "mask" is a stock character recurring in the plays of the *commedia dell' arte* who is identified, apart from his name and costume, by the particular set of psychological and histrionic characteristics. He differs from a character in a modern European drama in that he appears in plays unconnected with each other carrying his name, his costume and his personality essentially unchanged through them all and that he can sometimes play different types of dramatic characters such as the nurse, the bawd, the midwife and so on. [67] To illustrate, suppose the practice were adopted in Shakespeare's plays, then the Nerrisa of *Merchant of Venice* could enter *Othello* and take the place of Emilia without change of name or character and she could play Celia in *As You Like It* in the same manner. It is to be remembered that the *commedia dell' arte* are played practically entirely by the "masks", and that the *dramatis personae* have no names other than the names of the "masks", as when one says, "Pantalone plays the father, Harlequin plays his servant, Pulcinella plays the thief", etc. Every play therefore is essentially about the same people. Except for the fact that other companies also have Pantalones and Harlequins, the names are almost the stage names of the particular players and one can visualize the situation by imagining a troupe of players, each with a strong speciality which he shows in every role he plays in the different plays: the *dramatis personae* change nominally but the players and their characteristics remain the same. Similar situations exist in the films where the range of acting for the stars is usually narrow and the names of the *dramatis personae* dwindle to negligible importance beside those of the stars, so that one would say, "Gary Cooper is the sheriff, Judy Holliday is his daughter", etc., without knowing the names of the sheriff and the daughter. Owing to the standardization of the *dramatis personae* in the *commedia dell' arte*, the "masks" are types of dramatic characters and owing to the specialization of the actors playing them, they are also types of players.

In the earliest Chinese conventional farce there were two players called *ts'an-chün*, [68] who was the clown, and *ts'ang-hu*, [69] who was the assistant. They adopted

---

[67] Lea, *op. cit.*, 227.

[68] 參軍.

[69] 蒼鶻.

434

in different farces the identity of various *dramatis personae* whose names were usually of no importance, for the audience saw them and recognized them as *ts'an-chün* and *ts'ang-hu*. In these early farces there was hardly any problem of characterization and whatever the clown and the assistant played, the latter, by the then convention, struck the former in the slapstick action. Later, in Sung dynasty, the conventional farce expanded and required four regular players and one or two occasional additions, and the four players were called *mo-ni,* [70] *yin-hsi,* [71] *fu-ching* [72] and *fu-mo* [73] each with a separate function in the performance, as, one to lay the general plan, another to feign stupidity, and so forth. At this stage the types of players were still more prominent than the roles they took in the plays. [74]

The exact manner of evolution of the "masks" in the *commedia dell' arte* was lost in the unrecorded history of popular entertainment. In the early Chinese theatre, however, we find the slow emergence of similar types, first in the clown and his assistant and then in the four or five players required in the more elaborate farces. The need for differentiation of function even when there were only two players was obviously due to the improvisation, which could hardly work without an arranged division of labour. In the earliest stage of the popular theatre in China there was hardly any dramatic representation involved: although according to later accounts the clown, *ts'an-chün,* was originally an official in disgrace whom the court jesters had licence to tease and bully, yet when the conventional farce was established the original identity was forgotten and the performance was essentially a spectacle of one man molesting another who deserved ill treatment. There were then two types of players, but hardly two types of characters. As the farce grew in scope, more players were added and they too, in order to work together smoothly in improvisations, had assigned functions. Farce is mainly built upon absurdities and requires caricatures for its *dramatis personae,* hence the players were all prominent types, and division of labour became differentiation of types.

The survival of the stock characters in the *commedia dell' arte* has been attributed to a few possible reasons:

> "Whether their survival was due to their functional importance, or to the talent of their earliest impersonators, or to the fickleness of popularity, it is now impossible to judge". [75]

Whatever co-existing reasons there were, the functional importance must be counted as one of the reasons, because the types could survive without the talents of their

---

[70] 末泥.

[71] 引戲.

[72] 副淨.

[73] 副末.

[74] See Chs. XXII, XXIII and XXXIII.

[75] Lea, *op. cit.*, 231.

early impersonators but smooth performances based on impersonation would be impossible without a division of function. The stock characters fell into four groups: parents, servants, lovers and minor local types [76] because they were the types required by the kind of plot — family disorder, love, intrigue and knavery.

So far, the Chinese players and the organization of their farce were very much like the *commedia dell' arte* — the players of farce were like the "masks" both as types of players and as types of characters and they carried their characteristics unchanged into every farce. In the Yüan dynasty, however, as the number of types multiplied the nature of their differentiation changed, the types no longer had constant characteristics but had to adapt themselves to the individual needs of the dramas. The old types were inadequate because the content of the dramas had widened beyond the simple farcical action. Dramatic performance was no longer improvised and division of labour was necessitated by specialized training and easy management rather than by the mechanics of improvisation. In this light, the *commedia dell' arte* was like the conventional farce of Sung dynasty grown several times bigger without changing the method of production. There must have been an influence which entered the Chinese theatre at the end of Sung dynasty without which the Chinese theatre might well have developed towards something very much like the *commedia dell' arte*. It would be interesting, in relation to the general tendencies in primitive theatres, to locate this influence and this will be done in the following.

So long as a theatre is at the farcical stage exaggeration in the characters is inevitable and so long as the performance is improvised division of labour is necessary, and these two characteristics — improvisation and caricature — cause the differentiation of the players' functions in the performance to merge into the difference in the psychological characteristics of the *dramatis personae*. Theoretically the scope of the performance can be increased to the equivalent of full-length dramas without changing this nature of the performance, and this happened in the *commedia dell' arte*. It was not the limiting size that stopped the development of the Chinese theatre in this direction but the limitation of farce in its subject matter and emotional interest. Towards the end of Sung dynasty, the influence of the story-tellers entered the Chinese theatre and dramas of varied emotional appeal followed the collection and dissemination of legends by the story-tellers. The conventional farce was a performance by different types of clowns, but the new dramas required more than clowns and more than clownish technique to play. Thus the fixed characteristics of the farce-players had to be abandoned for the numerous individual traits of the new *dramatis personae* and this was now possible because the advent of the script made division of labour no longer necessary. Thus, by Yüan dynasty, the basic similarity of the early Chinese theatre with the *commedia dell'*

---

[76] Lea, *op. cit.*, 17.

arte had disappeared. In Italy in the sixteenth century literary influence on the public theatre was comparatively slight, and when present was confined mainly to that of Latin comedies which the farcical technique of the *commedia dell' arte* could easily digest, and thus we see, as it were, an overgrown version of the Sung dynasty farce in Renaissance Italy.

Since Yüan dynasty, the classification of Chinese dramatic characters has become a matter of theatrical management and education rather than of dramatic construction, a matter of specialized skill rather than of exaggerated characteristics. [77] The types of characters in the Chinese theatre now cover a wide range of personalities even though they lack fine shadings, wider at any rate than those of the *commedia dell' arte*. On the other hand, the "masks" in the *commedia dell' arte* are stock characters, "they are not people but personages". Just as a legendary hero is the sum total of innumerable versions of his biography, and is continually being modified so long as the legend is active, so a "mask" is defined by the complete collection of individual presentations. Throughout the history of the *commedia dell' arte* new variants of the old "masks" were continually added to the tradition by the inventiveness of the actors and actresses. [78] "The mask of Pantalone is the abstract of the behaviour of innumerable Pantalones: anything that a Pantalone did or said is a potential, anything that he continued to do or say is an actual, formative influence towards the development of the mask". [79] What he did on a certain occasion tells us what he might do in the future. His history shows his habits, and his habits constitute his tradition. He and his fellow stock characters became so real as personages that in the seventeenth century they mixed regularly with *dramatis personae* of the comedies, tragedies and pastorals of the Italian theatre. [80]

The development of prominent types of characters is inevitable in a continuous tradition of farce or farcical element in a theatre. Neither the naturalistic vagueness of personal characteristics nor the balanced normality of human psychology is compatible with the absurd extremities required by the purpose of farce. A pedant or braggart, for example, is not farcical if the pedantry or bragging is kept within probable limits; there may then be comedy, but not farce. Exaggeration does not admit of delicate shading; the figures are drawn in bold outline and glaring colours, as in cartoons and puppets. Once a creation is successful he can be used again, the audience will stay to see his new antics for his past reputation and the lack of psychological development and analysis does not worry the audience of a farce. In the Elizabethan jig, stock characters like the miserly old man, the wanton young woman, the soldier and so on were nearly formed, [81] and in the dramas of that

---

[77] cf. the boy actors of the Elizabethan theatre as a type.

[78] Duchartre, *op. cit.,* Chs. XII — XXII.

[79] Lea, *op. cit.,* 17.

[80] *Ibid.,* 18.

[81] *Vide* Lawrence, *Pre-Restoration Stage Studies,* 90.

period interest in psychology made the dramatic characters infinitely variable but the farcical element still produced the clown, who played himself in all dramas. Stock characters were also a characteristic of the Roman *atellanae,* [82] and of the Old Comedy. [83]

The same lack of interest in psychology allows the stock situations in the farce. [84] The possible types of dramatic situations are very limited [85] but their repetition in dramas is not noticeable owing to the varied emotions involved. In the farce, it is action that counts, not feelings, and similar situations become stock situations through the stock characters who play in them.

Another tendency towards the formation of stock characters lies in the repetition of minor characters whose function in the drama requires only simple characteristics, a tendency noticeable in the dramas of Yüan and Ming dynasties. The maid-servant in the Chinese dramas is usually a necessary tool in love-intrigues but apart from low cunning and temporary loyalty to the heroine her function requires no further characterization. It became a custom for the dramatists to give her the name of Mei-Hsiang, [86] probably because the unimportance of the role was not felt to justify the invention of names, till she became a stock character. The lackeys of the villain were also simply obsequious cowards and were, like gaolers, called by customary names. [87] In the modern Chinese theatre the secondary villains [88] who have neither enough authority to be Machiavels nor enough stupidity to make their wickedness ludicrous, and the comic female roles [89] who usually play bawds or gossips when the part is unimportant, also come very near to a "mask" in the *commedia dell' arte.*

(6)

The fact that the modern Chinese theatre and the *commedia dell' arte,* both good theatre without literary value, came into being when literary dramas were not lacking warrants close study because it can elucidate the relation between theatre and literature. In China, towards the end of the eighteenth century, the style of theatre in which literary values were respected, the *K'un* dramas, was gradually losing its popularity, surviving mainly on such artificial interests as technique of

---

[82] Lea, *op. cit.,* 226.

[83] F. M. Cornford, *The Origin of Attic Comedy,* Ch. VIII.

[84] cf. C. R. Baskervill, *The Elizabethan Jig,* Chs. VII — IX.

[85] According to Gozzi there are only thirty-six types of tragic situations — see G. Polti, *The Thirty-six Dramatic Situations,* trans. Lucille Ray (1916).

[86] 梅香.

[87] e.g. 柳隆卿, 胡子轉, 張千, 宋萬.

[88] 二花臉.

[89] 搽旦.

elocution and literary *finesse*. A need for genuine histrionic art was evidently felt, because along with the classical *K'un* dramas which lingered for a dwindling coterie, several local and comparatively primitive styles of theatre were introduced into the capital and cultural centre, Peking, and this in spite of the difference in dialect. In the latter half of the nineteenth century the modern Chinese theatre, derived from these local styles, displaced the local theatres in Peking as well as the classical *K'un* dramas. This happened because an expressive and flexible style of acting and singing had been established, mainly through the genius of a few actors, who must be considered as it founders. [90] At least in this stage of the history of the Chinese theatre — the decline of *K'un* dramas and the rise of Peking dramas — literary interests were not sufficient to satisfy the native need for an expressive style of theatre and they alone could not sustain the life of a traditional theatre. The public had at that time to choose between the respect for literary values which was associated with an arid style of production and a lively histrionic art based on vulgar script and, as it turned out, in the theatre, the votes of the theatregoers overpowered those of the book-lovers. The *K'un* dramas became obsolete not because they had lost their literary merits which were in fact well preserved in the guarded script, but because they had lost the tradition of acting which made them satisfying in the early part of their history and which it was difficult to preserve against the gradual deterioration of several centuries. In Italy at the time of the Renaissance the theatrical needs of the people re-asserted themselves after the inactivity of the Middle Ages and efforts were made to revive the ancient theatre. Some of these efforts, such as the Florentine attempt to reconstruct the performance of Greek dramas, led eventually to new styles of European theatre such as the opera, but the cultivation of a new taste was too slow and too much limited to academic circles for the needs of the general public. The sacred plays were restricted both in their subject matter and in their function and the spectacles indulged in at the courts were beyond the means of the people. [91] The *commedia erudita,* based on classical models, fostered literary values, but was not suitable script for the popular theatre because the acting tradition, as in the case of *K'un* dramas, had long been lost in the Middle Ages, so that it could only be read. In the Greek theatre literary and theatrical values were combined but the imitation of Greek and Roman dramas in the Renaissance amounted only to a crippled resurrection. Under these circumstances the popular need for a theatre found its outlet in the *commedia dell' arte:* when that need could not absorb the service of existing dramatic scripts which had literary value, it found its own way. [92]

---

[90] See Ch. XXVII and Ch. XXVIII.

[91] cf. Symonds, *op. cit.,* i, 26.

[92] Even in the Middle Ages there was popular comedy in Italy alongside the church dramas. Lea, *op. cit.,* 228.

The origin of the *commedia dell' arte* has been variously traced to the European mime, the Roman farce called the *atellanae* and to the creation of particular actors in the sixteenth century. The tradition of the mime was said to have returned to Italy through the westward migration of the players after the fall of the Eastern Empire in 1453 and support for this theory was claimed in the similarities of characteristics. Analogies have also been traced between *atellanae* and the *commedia dell' arte* but the silence of the Middle Ages makes it difficult to follow the lineage. Since common characteristics in popular farce can be found in theatres as far apart as the Sung dynasty farce and the *commedia dell' arte,* the analogies between the European mimes, the *atellanae* and the *commedia dell' arte* point rather to certain natural tendencies in popular theatres than to historical connection. The rise of the *commedia dell' arte* may perhaps be best understood as the expression of the theatrical needs of the people released in the new freedom of the Renaissance and the innovation both by the collective efforts of innumerable players and the outstanding achievements of some actors [93] all drawing on the material available at the time such as the plots from the *commedia erudita,* the tumbler's tricks, the mountebank's speeches, the improvisation in the rustic farce, [94] the local types of characters in popular farce and the comic potentialities of the dialects. [95] Thus for a while in the history of European theatre the theatre was, as it is in present day China, divorced from literature: at one extreme Terence and Plautus were recited without any acting [96] and at the other the *commedia dell' arte* developed and subsisted without the written drama.

The survival of the modern Chinese theatre is based on the tradition of acting which is being kept alive by the training guilds. It is impossible to foretell when and in what manner this tradition will die out, but the facts about the end of the *commedia dell' arte,* which also subsisted on histrionic tradition alone, must be significant to those who are concerned with the survival of the Chinese theatre, especially in connection with the effects of certain proposed reforms. The decline of the *commedia dell' arte* in the eighteenth century was the combined result of several influences: the loss of solidarity and long cooperation among the players which were necessitated by the hard conditions of its earlier days but were threatened by easier circumstances, the rivalry of literary dramas which by then had found a style of acting, the introduction of literary elements into it to form a hybrid style thus sapping the vigour of improvisation and, perhaps, also the fickleness of public taste. Some scholars believe that the scenic luxury of the French theatre in the eighteenth

---

[93] Lea, *op. cit.,* 233 ff.

[94] Symonds, *op. cit.,* i, 33.

[95] For a fuller discussion on the origin of the *commedia dell' arte* see Lea, *op. cit.,* Ch. IV.

[96] Symonds, *op. cit.,* i. 26.

century contributed to its fall. [97] Stage setting could not augment the appeal of the *commedia dell' arte* which lay in the verbal and physical wit, and this was why it was equally at home on the temporary platform in the market place and the gorgeous stage in the princely palace. [98] The scenery of the Renaissance and later was more spectacular than illusionary, otherwise it would not have been congruous with the many unrealistic elements in the *commedia dell' arte* and yet its effect was hardly healthy. It appears that the *commedia dell' arte,* like the Elizabethan and the Chinese dramas, belonged to the open stage and would be out of its natural elements elsewhere. For a theatre like the *commedia dell' arte* and the Chinese theatre, once the tradition declines it is rapidly lost because there is no permanent script to prolong its decay and once it is lost, there is no text to encourage its revival.

In the Chinese "new culture drama", or *wen-ming-hsi,* [99] in vogue in the early part of this century, a theatrical experiment was made on improvised dramas: the style of acting was derived from the naturalistic theatre which Chinese dramatists copied from western models and the plots were partly invented and partly taken from contemporary journalism. It died almost as soon as it was born. [100] It had neither the intellectual interests of the western naturalistic theatre nor the studied art of acting of the traditional Chinese theatre and was probably the only test ever conducted on the survival of the realistic theatre stripped of such interests in it as may be realized by reading the dramas, such as formulation of social problems, and re-valuation of current morality.

(7)

The modern Chinese theatre and the *commedia dell' arte,* through their lack of literary merits, exemplify the distinction between theatrical and literary values. The distinction is, on the one hand, essential to the proper evaluation of the two types of theatre and, on the other, clarifies certain problems in dramatic criticism.

Owing to the customary association of theatre and drama with each other, many critics and most laymen believe that they are synonymous. The indiscriminate use of the two words does not often cause serious ambiguity because the context usually shows which is meant, but the confusion between theatrical and dramatic value encouraged by such usage is bound to cause difficulties in theory and indeed, as the symptom of such difficulties the problem arises in dramatic criticism whether reference to theatrical conditions and the conventions arising therefrom is a proper task of a critic. Some writers think it is, on the ground that all dramas are written to be performed in some theatre, but others think it is not, because they claim that the

---

[97] Lea, *op. cit.,* 336.

[98] *Ibid.,* 309 f.

[99] 文明戲.

[100] See Ch. I.

value of the drama is independent of its connections with the theatre. At one extreme is Diderot's idea that the essential part of a play was not created by the poet at all, but by the actor, and at the other extreme, Spingarn believes that "for aesthetic criticism the theatre simply does not exist". [101]

It seems that much controversy will become unnecessary if the distinction is made between theatre and drama. Commentaries on dramatic performances in the daily newspapers as well as criticisms of dramas published by book companies are both called *dramatic criticism* even though the two are entirely different, the one being opinions of an event and the other, book reviews.

Although in the European history theatre and drama emerged simultaneously in the sixth century before Christ in ancient Greece, there is no reason to believe they must always be connected with each other. In China, for example, theatre and drama developed in different times: stage machinery and stage effects existed more than a thousand years before the rise of the drama. The masques and spectacles of the European courts in the sixteenth and the seventeenth centuries and the revue theatre of to-day are further examples of theatre without drama.

As the word "drama" may mean either the printed book or the performance based on it, it will help to clarify one's thinking if one distinguishes between the drama-as-performed which is one kind of *theatre* and drama-as-read which is *literature*. The former is a show and the latter is a form of writing. The term "dramatic art" which may mean either the literary or the theatrical art or some undefined combination of the two is best avoided altogether. The experience of watching a dramatic performance in a theatre and that of reading a drama alone are different in nature and the psychology involved in the appreciation in each case is not the same. In the theatre, one is subjected to a sequence of combined visual and aural impressions in the company of a crowd but when reading a book of drama, one is alone and the words produce their effect through the images they conjure in one's mind. In the theatre one is aware of the reactions of the fellow spectators — except in some modern European theatres in which this is difficult — and the actors play to the whole assembly, but reading is normally a solitary pleasure, one communes with the author through his writing. In the theatre the artistic, emotional as well as sensuous effects are immediate, one cannot stop to savour them even if one wishes to, but when reading one can stop and ponder or brood over what one has read.

The link between the theatre — the crowd watching and listening to the players

---

[101] It lies beyond the purpose of this book to trace this "historic controversy among dramatic critics" through the ages. For the statement of the problem see, for example, R. C. Flickinger, *The Greek Theatre and Its Drama*, xi-xv and for a brief historical survey see J. E. Spingarn, "Dramatic Criticism and the Theatre" in his *Creative Criticism* (1917). See also K. M. Lea, *The Italian Popular Comedy,* 339-342.

— and the drama — the book which one reads like any other work of literature — is the *script*. The script is often, but not always, a necessary equipment of the theatre: the link is incidental, not essential. Some dramas are written to be read only, and are not meant to be nor can be staged, they are in fact novels or poems in dialogue form; and some theatrical performances do not require a script, for example, the modern ballet and the *commedia dell' arte*. Milton's *Samson Agonistes* and Shelley's *Prometheus Unbound* are examples of dramas without stage potentialities. In England in the nineteenth century poetic drama was divorced from the stage and Browning, Keats, Scott, Coleridge, Wordsworth, Tennyson, Arnold and Swinburne had all tried their hands at the genre. In ancient Rome, Seneca's plays were almost certainly written to be read only and are now called Closet Drama. The Chinese call the same type Desk Drama [102] as distinguished from Stage Drama. [103] Thus the script is neither a necessary, nor when it is used, a sufficient part of the theatre and the written drama can have no potentiality of being a script and can thus be entirely unconnected with the theatre. The value of the script, as part of the theatrical equipment, depends alone on whether *with the other components of the theatre* a good performance can be produced from it.

If the script also makes interesting reading it serves a purpose for which it is not originally intended. Similarly, music-lovers may wish to listen to ballet music as a concert suite or operatic arias as songs. If they find them enjoyable outside their original functions and contexts, the pleasures are happy by-products for which the music was not designed.

Much disagreement could be avoided if, when a book of drama is said to be good or bad, the point of view were specified. It may be good as a script, capable of a moving performance and this is the producer's point of view, or it may be good as literature, capable of inspiring its readers, and this is the reader's point of view. Some books of drama may be good or bad from both points of view and some may be good from one and bad from the other; there is no *a priori* reason why good theatre must be based on good literature or a readable script must be capable of a beautiful performance. No one assumes that a good film must be based on a readable script. Movie scripts are not, it is true, generally considered reading material hence it appears strange to think of their literary value, but theoretically the relation between drama and theatre is the same.

In studying the dramas of bygone ages, modern scholars often adopt a point of view which neither the dramatists nor the contemporary theatregoers could have realized or understood. Of the various aspects of the theatres of the past the script alone could survive in its entirety: the method of staging, the style of delivery, the

---

(102) 案頭曲.
(103) 場上曲.

costume and make-up and so on which were, like the script, essential elements of the theatre at that time, are usually obliterated by time and can only be very imperfectly reconstructed. Perhaps the difficulty of full reconstruction and the more or less perfect state of the script discourage the interest in a theatre of the past as a whole and encourage the interest in the script as reading material, as a book among other books that came down to us from that age. The fact that the script differs from other books because it was not written to be read is often forgotten in the discussion on its significance and value. It is idle to condemn the book-lover's interest in dramas of the past: so long as reading books of drama gives some people pleasure the activity is artistically justified. It is only when the book-lover presumes to judge the drama, which was originally a script, by reading alone and to propose their way of understanding as the only sensible way of understanding that the distinction between the reader and the theatre audience requires emphasis.

The book-lover's way of thinking is manifested in the view, implied in some writings on theatrical history, that the high levels of literary accomplishment in dramas coincided with the peaks of theatrical development. When the field of vision is narrowed to cover one aspect of the theatre, namely the script, and one way of using it, namely reading it, it is not surprising that its literary value is taken to be the measuring rod of the theatre. The decline of poetry in the theatre, for example, is sometimes mourned for as if the whole theatrical art went with poetry. It was due to this point of view that critics of to-day had low opinions of the *commedia dell' arte* [104] even though people of taste and discernment were at that time fascinated by it. One may believe that the Roman pantomime was highly enjoyable as theatre. [105] Some music taken from the theatre makes good concert pieces, yet there is no reason to assume that the artistic standard of theatrical music is a reliable measure of the value of the contemporary theatre as a whole. To mistake music or literature for the whole of theatre is equally to mistake the part for the whole. Both in ancient Greece and in modern England periods of great dramatic literature were followed by periods of great acting: after the Elizabethan dramatists we find the great actors and actresses of the eighteenth century and after the great Greek tragedians of the fifth century we find the period of great acting in the fourth century. "In Athens, the fourth century was the period when acting was brought to the greatest perfection. To such an extent had the importance of the actor's profession increased, that in Aristotle's time a play depended more for its success upon the skill of the actor than upon the genius of the poet". [106] Mrs. Siddons and Garrick thrilled their audience in plays which are now obscure to us; we may read better plays than their audience but we must envy the theatregoers of that age. Whether the satisfaction of the

---

[104] Lea, *op. cit.,* 225.

[105] *Vide* Lucian, *Works,* H. W. Fowler and F. G. Fowler, Vol. II, 238 *et seq.,* "Of Pantomime".

[106] Haigh, *The Attic Theatre,* 229.

English audience in the eighteenth century was not greater than those of the seventeenth and whether the Greeks in the fourth century did not enjoy the theatre more than those in the fifth century may have to remain an open question forever, but the pleasure one derives from great actors in mediocre plays and the boredom of watching bad actors in masterpieces of literature are common experiences to all regular playgoers. There are reasons for believing that the Elizabethan theatre and the Chinese theatre of Yüan dynasty were institutions of high artistic standard but the fact that they were can neither be considered as the cause nor cited as the evidence of high literary value of the contemporary script, nor *vice versa*. That no dramas of outstanding literary value were produced in times when the theatre was atrophied is due to the lack of incentive and inspiration, not to the identity of theatrical and literary values. It is at least theoretically possible for writers to produce in such periods readable closet dramas, or novels in dialogue form.

When we survey whole periods of theatrical history the slender connection between dramatic literature and theatre becomes evident. Even in the best periods — best, from the literary pont of view — only a very small percentage of the scripts survived on their literary merits. In the Elizabethan period, probably two to three thousand plays were produced of which about a quarter have survived and a very small portion of the survivals is worth reading. [107] If we judge the value of the original performances by the literary value of the scripts we are forced to the impossible conclusion that the Elizabethan theatre was composed mainly of artistic failures except for a few plays. This was the golden period of English drama and one of the most productive periods in the literary sense. In a similar period in China, the Yüan dynasty, plagiarism in all degrees, among other things, makes it difficult to estimate the proportional survival of the dramas, but there can be little doubt that at least four times the extant plays perished. [108] In other periods the rate of producing literature from the theatre, both in China and elsewhere, is much smaller, yet all or most of the plays written were staged and some of the now lesser known plays were contemporary successes in the theatre. Even with overwhelming literary merits, the literary value of the drama does not coincide with its success as script: some of Shakespeare's best plays might have been acted "not above once". [109] If we get the impression from reading Elizabethan plays that the plays in the Elizabethan theatres were mostly by Shakespeare, Marlowe and Jonson with a sprinkling of Messinger, Greene and Beaumont, our sense of proportion is entirely wrong. The Elizabethans did not concentrate on the performances of Shakespeare's plays as we do in reading them, not because they were less sensitive than we are to poetry but because they were more responsive to their theatre. The fact that *Oedipus Rex,* one of the greatest

---

[107] Lea, *op. cit.,* 341.

[108] See Ch. XXVI.

[109] W. Poel, *Shakespeare in the Theatre,* 46.

plays ever written, did not win the prize [110] need not surprise us: we evaluate the play by reading it but the judges did not read it, they only saw a performance based on it. Even to-day, the connection between dramatic literature and theatre is slight: there are more shows worth seeing than scripts worth reading and the script that makes good reading material is not necessarily connected with a good show. In the modern Chinese theatre the best dramas from the literary point of view are those written by Professor Ch'i Ju-Shan [111] and by Wang Hsiao-Nung [112] but they are far from being the most popular plays because without Mei Lan-Fang [113] to play in the former and Wang to play in his own plays the occasional performances of these by other actors are not even pleasurable. The percentage of good books among the scripts used in the theatre is so small in most periods that the production of dramatic literature from the theatre appears, in a broad survey, almost an accidental process. Many dramatists were forgotten by posterity because they could not claim literary merits for their works, but that does not mean they were not artists contributing to the art of the theatre. Their fame was ephemeral because theatre was and still is a fragile art. They were soon forgotten not because they did not create, or rather join in the creation, but because what they partook in creating was perishable. Therefore, if a dramatist wants his work to survive long he should write for readers rather than for producers. Dramatists must choose between serving contemporary theatrical needs for immediate gains or the literary aims for lasting fame, they either try to be good script-writers or good poets. They may, like some of the Greek and Elizabethan dramatists, succeed in both, but the double achievement is coincidental not automatic. There were prosperous script-writers in the past who are entirely forgotten now.

Nowadays, dramatists strive after literary fame, but there were times when they were just script-writers, and they were apprehensive of the misapplication of their product.

"Comedies are writ to be spoken, not read: Remember the life of these things consists in action".

(Marston, *Parasitaster or the Fawne* (1606), Preface).

"I would faine leave the paper; onely one thing afflicts mee, to thinke that scenes inuented, meerely to be spoken, should be inforcively published to be read . . . but I shal intreat . . . that the vnhandsome shape which this trifle in reading presents, may bee pardoned, for the pleasure it once afforded you, when it was presented with the soule of lively action".

(Marston, *The Malcontent* (1604), Preface).

---

[110] Haigh, *op. cit.*, 35.
[111] 齊如山.
[112] 汪笑儂.
[113] 梅蘭芳.

To the practising script-writer the distinction between a good script and a drama good for reading must appear self-evident. The Chinese dramatist Li Yü said,

> "Hitherto those who write the spoken part in dramas write as if to be read, without considering whether when spoken on the stage the words would sound right. I have often read such passages and think they are clear enough, but when I hear them spoken on the stage they no longer sound lucid". [114]

The effect of the lines delivered on the stage is so different from that of reading them that in extreme cases, in which the readers' understanding of the poetry exceeds the capabilities of histrionic talents, it is impossible to stage the dramas to the satisfaction of the readers. Shakespeare's dialogue was effective script, but it was effective in a way very different from the readers' appreciation of his poetry. Raleigh thought that,

> "The truth is that his best things are not effective on the stage. These packed utterances are glimpses merely of the hurry of unspoken thought; they come and are gone; they cannot be delivered emphatically, nor fully understood in the pause that separates them from the next sentence; and when they are understood, the reader feels no desire to applaud; he is seized by them, his thoughts are set a-working, and he is glad to be free from the importunacy of spectacle and action".   (Walter Raleigh, *Shakespeare* (1907), 146).

Just as the church music written by some classical composers is too powerful for worship and is fit only for the concert hall, Shakespeare is sometimes too great for the theatre and can only be fully understood when read, hence Charles Lamb's protest that *King Lear* cannot and should not be staged. [115] Some passages in Shakespeare are more poetry than drama. [116] Craig analyzed Macbeth's speech about the phantom dagger to show that we can never have the same experience in reading as in watching Shakespeare. [117] When lines are spoken on the stage the audience receive the impression of a scurry of emotions, they cannot pause to parse them and dispute the exact sense as Shakespearean scholars do tirelessly but they get the right impression of the state of mind of the speaker. [118] In Shakespeare there is the irresistible temptation to read him purely as poetry. Thus Bradley preferred a glimpse into Shakespeare's mind to mingling with the crowd at the Globe, [119] and Hazlitt observed that "some of his obscure contemporaries have the advantage over Shakespeare himself in so much as we have never seen their work represented on the stage", that is to say, the lesser Elizabethan dramatists are easier to understand

---

[114] 李漁 , 曲話, 詞曲第四, 詞別繁減.

[115] C. Lamb, On the Tragedies of Shakespeare, in *The Dramatic Essays of Charles Lamb* (1891).

[116] K. M. Lea, *op. cit.*, 340.

[117] Craig, *On the Art of the Theatre*, 117 f, 143.

[118] *Vide* Granville-Barker, *Prefaces*, I, 12.

[119] *Oxford Lectures on Poetry*, 361.

because we know them only by reading. [120] In this "advantage" we reach the curious position that the best way to understand drama is not to see it. The paradox is solved if we remember that Hazlitt was thinking as a book-lover about some dramatic script which had outgrown its original purpose — a special point of view under special conditions. The same attitude makes one conscious of "defects" in Shakespeare which are unnoticeable in the theatre, for example, only when the plays are read many times over and carefully studied do questions arise on the double time in *Othello*, the age of Hamlet and the geography of Bohemia; in the theatre no one will notice the inconsistencies. Literary critics may point out the recurring imagery and the developed metaphor of the plays and they are no doubt interesting to the readers of Shakespeare, but the audience at the Globe, and indeed hasty readers too, could not appreciate them at all. On the other hand, the plays, as they appear to the readers, are full of gaps, for whatever in the original performance did not involve talking the script does not record. [121] All pageants, dumb shows, masques, fencing matches, horseplay, wrestling, banquets, and battles are lost to the readers. The appeal of *Midsummer Night's Dream* and *Tempest* would be extremely different if we could watch them in the original settings and style of production. In short, even though in Shakespeare there are very strong reasons to look upon the plays as literature rather than as script, yet, as in the case of all dramatists, the Shakespeare of the readers is very different from the Shakespeare of his spectators. The beauties and "defects" the readers can see are alike unnoticeable to the spectators and the spectacles enjoyed by the audience at the Globe can never be reconstructed to the readers of to-day. One gets a distorted perspective of the theatre of a certain period by reading the extant dramas alone not only because the dramas represent a minute residuum of the scripts used then but also because the scripts themselves are inadequate for conveying a picture of the contemporary theatre. The masque is a case in point: although the script contains descriptions of the costume and scenery, the impression obtained in reading it cannot compare with that of actually seeing the dancing and hearing the singing and watching the scenic transformations which are the main content of the masque. "The glory of all these solemnities", as Jonson said, "had perished like a blaze and gone out in the beholders' eyes". [122]

We deceive ourselves to think that it is possible to revive theatres of the past. We do not know what the Greek dramas looked like and sounded like, we only know the words. The producers of the past worked with a whole set of theatrical apparatus: the theatre building with the stage, the actors with their training in the particular

---

[120] *Elizabethan Literature*, Lecture III.

[121] cf. Lea, *op. cit.*, 341 f.

[122] Jonson, Preface to *Hymenaei*. See also Chambers, *The Elizabethan Stage*, I, 195 *et seq.* for the splendour of the court masque.

style of acting, the musicians and stage hands, the costume, the property man and the make-up man and sometimes the dancers as well. Among all these he also used the script. The script survived through printing and copying, but the theatre building, apart from drawings and specifications, could not survive structural decay, and the rest of the producer's apparatus existed only in the tradition and died with the actors and other theatrical personnel. The only tool those who try to revive past theatres can now possess is the script, all the rest they can know only indirectly and usually very imperfectly. Even if it is possible to reconstruct the theatre building and to stage the drama accurate to every detail there is still the audience missing, the audience with the particular type of taste. [123] The modern European audience can no more appreciate Shakespeare or Sophocles produced in the original manner than they can foreign theatres — they would only be confused and irritated. [124] Unless there is an unbroken tradition, theatres of the past are lost for good; we can gather some knowledge about them through the script and other records but we can never have the actual experience of them. In the attempts to revive past theatres, even the limited information available on the theatres cannot always be advisedly applied because the modern audience are unable to appreciate a style of production too distant from the style of to-day. The result is too often a modified modern production based on out-of-date script. The style of delivery may be incongruous with the language of the script, the acting incongruous with the dialogue, the clowns, the dance, the formal entrances, the prologue may be entirely omitted, and the omissions would be the more conspicuous and disturbing if the integrity of the text is insisted upon. If from the pleasure one derives from such revivals is deducted that due to the prestige of the dramatists and that of hearing poetical passages, the remainder, which is what theatre alone can provide, is often very small. Artistic sensibility involves the sense of the fitness of things, and this sense is often outraged in these revivals.

In medieval times the problems of using dramatic scripts for which the theatrical tradition had been lost was solved in a way more naive and less pretentious than in modern revivals. Terence was recited by a speaker or reader and *mimi ioculatores* acted it in pantomime. It was even assumed that that was the original way of production. [125] Even in the time of Quintilian and Pliny, when the ancient theatrical tradition had declined, the tragic poet read the drama to the audience. [126] In the eighteenth and the nineteenth centuries English actors took great liberty with Shakespeare's text in order to fit it to the current style of production and dramatic

---

[123] cf. A. H. Thorndike, *Shakespeare's Theatre* (1916), 403; G. F. Reynolds, *The Staging of Elizabethan Plays at the Red Bull Theatre 1605-1625* (1940), 190.

[124] Reynolds, *Modern Philology,* Vol. 3, 97.

[125] Nicoll, *Mask, Mimes and Miracles,* 152 *et seq.*

[126] Gibbon, *Decline and Fall of the Roman Empire,* Ch. XXXI, Games and Spectacles, note.

taste. They probably succeeded better in pleasing the audience than do modern Shakespearean producers.

The book-lover's over-estimation of the importance of the script is coupled with his under-estimation of that of acting.

> ". . . and what doth a Player else, but onely say that without book, which we may read within Book?" [127]

Jonson had slightly more faith in acting:

> "A dramatick exhibition is a book recited with concomitants that encrease or diminish its effect". (Preface to *Shakespeare* (1765), Ed. Malone (1790), Vol. I, 18).

A similar idea lies behind the following:

> ". . . because in a novel comment is possible, it does not impoverish the feelings to reduce the language of the characters to that of ordinary speech. Their feelings can still be defined by descriptions so that they are seen to be delicate and not coarse, precise and not vague. Whereas the drama, where the dialogue has to define as well as to present the feeling, if the language of real life is adopted for the characters, has no other means of defining their feeling — for action cannot define but only present them". [128]

The restrictive nature of colloquial dialogue need not be discussed here. In the above passage it is assumed that as in the drama it is impossible to insert the playwright's description of the characters' feelings, the characters have to accomplish in their dialogue something equivalent to the description. The expressiveness of voice and gesture seems to be entirely ignored.

The power of good delivery is in fact much greater than Jonson suggested. John Bulwer (*Chironomia,* 1644) related that Queen Elizabeth, impressed at one time by a sermon preached in her presence, asked for the text in order to read it, but on reading it found that it was "one of the best sermons she ever heard, and the worst she ever read". [129] Gordon Craig found the same thing with circus clowns:

> "I have taken the trouble now and then hurriedly to write down the conversation between the clowns in a circus, and to a great extent it resembles the conversations in Molière, in essentials the method is practically the same, but when recorded the result is anything but funny". [130]

This was what Marston foresaw when he said, ". . . that the vnhandsome shape which this trifle in reading presents, may bee pardoned, for the pleasure it once afforded you, when it was presented with the soule of lively action" [131] and

---

[127] Sir Richard Baker, *Theatrum Triumphans* (1670), 43.

[128] M. C. Bradbrook, *Themes and Conventions of Elizabethan Tragedy* (1935), 43.

[129] *Vide* B. L. Joseph, *Elizabethan Acting* (1951), 143. For the histrionic talents of the preachers at that time see *ibid., passim.*

[130] E. G. Craig, *The Theatre Advancing* (1921), 25.

[131] Preface to Marston, *Malcontent,* 1604.

"remember the life of these things consists in action". [132] The experience of Queen Elizabeth and Gordon Craig seems to show that action contains "the life of these things" and is not merely able to "encrease or diminish" the effect.

"Action is eloquence, and the eyes of the ignorant
More learned than the ears". (*Coriolanus,* III, ii.)

In the rapid sequence of impressions one gets in the theatre, not only the ignorant are more susceptible to the effects of action.

"Edmund Kean, as Hamlet, after concluding his words to Ophelia 'To a nunnery, go!' and departing abruptly out of sight of the audience, used to come on the stage again, and approach slowly the amazed Ophelia still remaining in the centre; take her hand gently, and, after gazing steadily and earnestly in her face for a few seconds, and with a marked expression of tenderness on his own countenance, appeared to be choked in his efforts to say something, smothered her hand with passionate kisses, and rushed wildly and finally from her presence". (New Variorum *Hamlet,* Vol. II, 251).

Hazlitt called this "the finest commentary that was ever made on Shakespeare". [133] "It is only the pantomime part of tragedy . . . which is sure to tell, and tell completely on the stage". [134] When Mrs. Siddons as Lady Macbeth noticed the daggers and snatched them from Macbeth, her "Give ME the daggers", caused "a general start" among those sitting near Boaden in the crowded theatre. [135] Examples of electrifying moments of great acting can be multiplied endlessly. It is significant that in the examples quoted above, Mrs. Siddons' line is not particularly poetical and Kean's "finest commentary on Shakespeare" lies entirely outside the text. If great actors can put into what they "say without book" something that we do not conceive of when we "read within book" it should hardly be surprising that they can give a script that does not make good reading a rich and moving performance, as Queen Elizabeth's preacher did with his "worst sermon she ever read". Just as the book-lover's conception of a dramatic character, say Hamlet, consists of his own and his commentators' interpretation of the Prince, to the theatregoer Hamlet is what the actors he likes have portrayed. From the point of view of the actor a good script is one which makes it easy for him to enrich the performance with expressive acting.

Acting is not only interpretive but also, at least potentially, creative. In its extreme development, as in pantomime, it is completely dissociated from speech and could, by itself, constitute a theatrical programme. It was said of the Roman pantomime that "every gesture had its significance; and therein lay his chief

---

[132] Preface to Marston, *The Fawne,* 1606.

[133] *View of the English Stage,* Mr. Kean's Hamlet.

[134] *Ibid.,* Mr. Kean's Richard II.

[135] James Boaden, *Memoirs of Mrs. Siddons* (1827), 259.

excellence". A foreigner, "seeing five masks laid ready — that being the number of parts in the piece — and only one pantomime, asked who were going to play the other parts. He was informed that the whole piece would be performed by a single actor. 'Your humble servant, sir', cried our foreigner to the artist, 'I observe that you have but one body: it had escaped me, that you possessed several souls'." "I know not", said Lucian, "what truth there may be in Plato's analysis of the soul into the three elements of spirit, appetite and reason: but each of the three is admirably illustrated by the pantomime; he shows us the angry man, he shows us the lover, and he shows us every passion under the control of reason". [136] A pantomime actor must know music, understand rhythm, and human character and passions, he must also know the painter's and the sculptor's art. [137] Enthusiasm for pantomime among the people of Antioch was such that "each individual was all eyes and ears for the performance; not a word, not a gesture escaped them". [138] Here, in spite of the lack of literary value in the Roman theatre, we have a highly developed histrionic art for which there is probably no modern counterpart. In the Chinese court theatre of T'ang dynasty there were no dramas, because Chinese drama was not yet developed, and yet expert and famous musicians and actors were recorded in contemporary books. [139] In the play *L'Opera de Campagne* (1691) the dialogue breaks off at the fourth scene and a note says that though the scene is "one of the most delightful in the whole comedy, it is one of those which cannot be expressed in print and has no value when written down" and the reason is that in it "Arlequin recounts in dumb show all he has seen" — another example of dramatic expression outside literary means. [140]

Acting, the player's art, lies outside the domain of the dramatist and cannot be a part of his script. Dramatists in the past were satisfied with general indications of action in the stage directions, but in some modern plays not only are the individual tempers of the *dramatis personae* carefully explained and their movements specified, but vocal acting, as stammering and ejaculations, are included in the text with the help of elaborate punctuation. Some modern dramatists seem to be doubtful of the actors' ability to interpret their plays correctly, and the result is that some plays read more like descriptions of the performance than the script. If the actors are so unimaginative that they need detailed stage directions it is doubtful whether the directions would help. The piece of Kean's stage business in *Hamlet* mentioned above, for example, if it becomes a stage direction, cannot be followed to advantage

---

[136] From works of Lucian (c. A.D. 125-180) trans. H. W. Fowler and F. G. Fowler (1905), II, 249 ff, Of Pantomime.

[137] *Ibid.*

[138] *Ibid.*

[139] 段安節, 樂府雜錄; 崔令欽, 教坊記.

[140] From *Le Théâtre Italien* by Gherardi quoted in Nicoll, *Development of the Theatre*, 113.

by every actor, because each actor, to act with sincerity, must follow his own conception of the character and the emotional situation. In the improvised Italian comedies, or *commedia dell' arte,* the delivery and movements must have achieved a fluency rare in modern dramas in which actors have to speak lines written by some one other than themselves.

Theatrical value is sometimes associated with literary value, but it is by no means coincident with or even dependent on literature. The confusion of the two standards is due to the preoccupation with certain types of theatre and can be dispelled by a broader view. Improvised comedies, on the one hand, and plays produced from dramas with elaborate stage directions, on the other, are two extreme types of the theatre. In the former the distinction between theatrical and literary value is clear but in the latter they are practically combined. When theatre is deprived of music, dance, rich costume and style in acting and delivery it approaches play-reading. The voice and gestures of the speakers follow the suggestions in the text and are generally adjusted to the tone of the dialogue in the same way as a reader of novels would imagine the characters to speak. Outside the script little is required for the production, some scenery and costume are employed but if they are strictly realistic they add little to the meaning of the script. Those who know no other type of theatre easily imagine that the object of the theatre is to present the author's ideas and that the values of theatrical art are exclusively literary in nature. It is then appropriate to write criticisms for the performance in the same way as one writes book reviews. (141)

---

(141) Conversely it is possible for experienced producers reading the script of, say, a musical comedy, to see in their mind's eye the dances and hear the music. If they comment on the script, what they say will apply to the performance, because they can see the theatrical values of the performance by the script alone. In such cases dramatic criticism will have a double meaning, but this is more or less hypothetical.

CHAPTER XXXIX

THE CHINESE AND THE ELIZABETHAN THEATRE — I [1]

(Introduction — Description — The Open Stage — Lack of Realism — Lack of Scenery)

(1)

The extent to which the physical conditions of the theatre influence the style of production and the dramatic construction is a problem which interests both theorists of the theatre and students of dramatic literature. That dramatic writings are affected by the physical conditions of the stage can be seen in Roman comedies, or at any rate, in what is extant of Menander, Plautus and Terence, in which the action is always in front of two houses facing a street. The effects of the Elizabethan theatre on the plays of Shakespeare and his contemporaries are more extensive and subtle than those of the conventional setting of the Roman comedies [2] hence the painstaking work done by Shakespearean scholars on even the small details of the construction of the Elizabethan theatre. [3]

Theoretically, one way of studying these effects is to choose two similarly constructed theatres and analyze the similarities in the dramas written for them. It is not easy, however, to get conclusive results in this manner by comparing European theatres with each other, because it is not easy then to determine whether a similar

---

[1] Throughout this chapter and the next two chapters, the term "Elizabethan theatre" means, unless otherwise specified, the public theatre in Elizabethan England — to be precise, from the beginning of Elizabeth's reign, 1558, to the closing of the theatres in 1648. There were at that time also court theatre and private theatre in England, but these were influenced by continental stage practices and were not purely English and the comparison between them and the Chinese theatre would be more complicated and less interesting.

[2] See for example, M. C. Bradbrook, *Elizabethan Stage Conditions* (1932), G. F. Reynolds, *The Staging of Elizabethan Plays at the Red Bull Theatre* (1940) and W. J. Lawrence, "The Evolution and Influence of the Elizabethan Playhouse" in *The Elizabethan Playhouse and Other Studies* (1912).

[3] See for example, W. J. Lawrence, *The Elizabethan Playhouse and Other Studies* (1912), *Second series* (1913), Reynolds, *op. cit.* and J. C. Adams, *The Globe Playhouse Its Design and Equipment* (1942).

feature in the dramas is due to common influence by the stage conditions or to direct influence between the dramatists or common source in earlier dramas. The history of the European theatre since the Renaissance is like the record of an orchard in which cross graftings have been continuously made since its earliest days and in which it is now very difficult to tell the shape of the original fruits. For example, the early French theatre was influenced by the multiple stage of medieval times, the Italian opera affected the staging of all European dramas in the seventeenth century and later and the pure English pedigree in the Elizabethan theatre was terminated by the strong continental influence in the Restoration theatre. [4] The Chinese and the Elizabethan theatre in reference to each other provide a rare opportunity for studying the significance of the platform stage because the construction of the theatre building is almost identical but the development of the two theatres is completely independent. [5] If now similar features are found in their method of staging and dramatic conventions, one can with more confidence consider them to be due to parallel physical conditions, especially if the similarities are extensive and inter-related.

The *mise-en-scène* of Elizabethan plays is of particular interest to Shakespearean scholars and much valuable work has been done in this field. Owing to the lack of direct information, however, many details of Elizabethan staging are still matters of controversy and conjecture. Rival theories can often claim equal consistency with available data, such as the text and contemporary descriptions of the stage, and in such cases it is difficult to choose one theory in preference to another. It is here that the study of the Chinese theatre might help the Shakespearean scholars. When the choice between alternative theories is a matter of opinion, it is often more illuminating to study the theorists than their evidence, because the views of the theorists cannot but be influenced by their past experience. In fact, the main theories for the method of staging Elizabethan plays are based on the principles of other European theatres; thus, Brodmeier's alternation theory was based on the Restoration theatre, Reynolds' simultaneous setting, on medieval multiple setting and Chambers' successive staging, although not bearing clear resemblance to any European theatre, had partial precedents in the unlocalized and undivided acting space of the moralities and interludes and the convention of

---

[4] cf. W. Poel, "Some Notes on Shakespeare's Stage and Plays", *Bulletin of the John Rylands Library*, Vol. 3, No. 1, 216.

[5] Elizabethan dramatists had some vague ideas of China's vastness and exaggerated notions of some oddities of the imperial court, but there is no evidence that they knew of the Chinese theatre — see R. R. Cawley, *The Voyagers and Elizabethan Drama* (1938), 208-232. The Chinese drama was developed several centuries before the Elizabethan age, therefore, even if the Chinese knew the Elizabethan drama in the sixteenth or seventeenth century, the knowledge would have had no influence on the shaping of the Chinese drama.

changing locality by clearing the acting space of all actors in Greek theatres. [6] Early theorists did not make great progress because they could not see the Shakespearean stage to be very different from the stage they knew, for example, Malone believed there was a front curtain in the Elizabethan theatre. [7] Modern Shakespearean scholars cannot watch the original performance of Elizabethan plays, but they can study a very similar stage in action in the Chinese theatre, and can draw inferences about Shakespearean staging. [8] For example, about the Elizabethan stage doors William Archer [9] thought that "it is really a darkening of counsel to cling to a pair of doors flatly facing the audience. That they cannot have been in common use we know from the very frequent occasions on which two men or bodies of men enter simultaneously from opposite directions and squarely encounter each other in the middle of the stage. To do this on the De Witt stage, the one party would have to make a right wheel and the other a left — an impossibly ineffective manoeuvre". The manoeuvre described happens to be exactly a style of double entrance of two armies on the Chinese stage the effectiveness of which is obvious to those who see it and indeed lies mainly in the "wheeling around". It bears the picturesque name of "Twin Dragons Emerging". [10] The stage doors on the Elizabethan stage might have been oblique, as Archer thought they should be, for some other reason, but certainly not for the impossibility of effective simultaneous entrance of two armies. It may be argued that the Elizabethan style of staging was probably different from that of the Chinese and what is effective to the Chinese audience might not have been so to the Elizabethans, but this is merely begging the question, the exact "manoeuvre" being unknown there is no saying that it might not have been even more effective than the "Twin Dragons Emerging". A Chinese reader of writings on the Elizabethan theatre cannot help wondering now and again whether the European writers would take the same views they did if they had seen the Chinese theatre. It is difficult for him to escape the feeling that with full knowledge of the Chinese theatre western scholars would make different interpretations of the Elizabethan dramatic text in so far as stage property and stage construction are concerned and that extensive experimental revival, if that is possible, would have led them toward the same conclusions as the

---

[6] *Vide* J. T. Allen, *The Greek Theatre of the Fifth Century Before Christ* (1920), 74 f; V. E. Albright, *The Shakespearian Stage* (1909), Ch. II.; C. Brodmeier, *Die Shakespeare-Bühne nach den alten Bühnen-Anweisungen* (1904); G. F. Reynolds, Some Principles of Elizabethan Staging, *Modern Philology,* April 1905 and June 1905; E. K. Chambers, *The Elizabethan Stage* (1923), Chs. XX and XXI, especially p. 50 n.

[7] W. Archer, The Elizabethan Stage, *The Quarterly Review,* Vol. 208. No. 415, p. 445.

[8] Wm. Poel proposed to study the Hindu drama because it was thought to bear some resemblance to English drama — see W. Poel, Hindu Drama on the English Stage, *The Asiatic Quarterly Review,* N. S., Vol. 1 (1913), 319-331.

[9] *Quarterly Review,* CCXLI (1924).

[10] "二龍出水" — see Fig. 40, Ch. XIV.

knowledge of the Chinese theatre. The use of mime in lieu of property and setting, for example, is unknown in the modern European theatre and perhaps for this reason it is by no means a favourite interpretation of the Elizabethan dramatic text. In *Romeo and Juliet* II. i, Romeo enters, speaks two lines and then leaps a wall. Benvolio enters with Mercutio and says he saw Romeo leap a wall. At this time Romeo is out of sight to Mercutio, who calls on him to appear. The problem here is: how does Romeo jump the wall? Bradbrook finds it difficult to conceive of this scene without the real wall. [11] In the same play, IV. i, Paris is talking with Friar Laurence in the latter's cell and the friar can see Juliet coming, which suggests that Juliet is on the stage before she meets Paris and the friar, and she has to go through a door into the cell, because afterwards she says, "O! shut the door". In an earlier scene at the cell, when the nurse comes to see the friar after Romeo has killed Tybalt, the stage direction in the *First Folio* reads *"Enter Nurse and knockes"*, that is, she knocks at the door while she is on stage. [12] William Poel thought that the nurse comes first to the edge of the stage and knocks her crutch on the floor standing behind the gallants on the stage who serve as a wall and a door. [13] It is true that Elizabethan players on the early inn-yard stage had to push through the audience in order to enter the acting space, [14] but such a conventional door depends rather precariously on the correct supply of gallants. Chambers suggested a conventional door both sides of which are visible to the audience [15] but unless the door is transparent it must interfere with the view for some of the most expensive seats at the sides of the stage. [16] In such cases, of which there are many, where neither the text nor contemporary documents help to decide whether there was a real door or wall or whether pantomime took the place of setting, opinion, one way or the other, depends on mental habits. Whatever the door was, it could not be difficult for the producer to arrange or for the audience to appreciate, otherwise the playwright would have made adjustments in the text to avoid it. The reluctance to assume an imaginary door, which is certainly easy to arrange, is probably due to the doubt whether the audience would accept it. The Chinese theatre shows that once the convention is established, the audience accept it with perfect ease. It is not here suggested that pantomime *was* used to a large extent in the Elizabethan theatre in lieu of stage property and stage setting, rather, the question is raised whether

---

[11] Bradbrook, *Stage Conditions,* 39; also Chambers, *Eliz. Stage,* III, 98.

[12] For comparison of the stage directions in the different editions see Chambers, *Eliz. Stage,* III, 51 n. For a similar scene in *Captain Thomas Stukeley* see Chambers, *Eliz. Stage,* III, 84.

[13] *Vide* R. Speaight, *William Poel and the Elizabethan Revival* (1954), 86.

[14] J. Q. Adams, *Shakespearean Playhouses* (1917), Ch. 1, p.2.

[15] Chambers, *Eliz. Stage,* III, 84 ff.

[16] J. C. Adams, *The Globe Playhouse* (1942), 70-81. Other cases for such a door are in *Alchemist,* III. v, *Henry VIII,* V. ii and iii, see Chambers, *Eliz. Stage,* III, 123.

modern European scholars would not have thought so in otherwise difficult problems of staging if they had been familiar with the Chinese theatre. At least one western writer found it easier to understand the Elizabethan stage after knowing the Chinese theatre and he asked, "If human nature can endure this convention in Peking, with the above-mentioned tiger, why should we assume that three hundred years ago people felt as we do now, and based on this the novel theory that stages were darkened then?" [17] He also pointed out that at the beginning of this century European scholars assumed that the Elizabethan stage had something like the front curtain as well as other features of the naturalistic stage simply because they could not imagine it otherwise, [18] but he betrayed his own provincialism by saying that the audience in Peking "endure" conventions, for if stage conventions are "endured", there is strong reason to believe, as Prof. Stephenson did, that "the ingenious Elizabethans" could easily "invent such a method of staging" so as to make them unnecessary. [19]

(2)

The sudden rise of the popular theatre in England in the later part of the sixteenth century is spectacular both in its scope and in its literary value. What had been occasional crude entertainment in the form of moralities and interludes became dramas of high literary standard, constantly available to the public in the then new commercial theatres. Among the social conditions which favoured this rapid development perhaps the most important are the decay of feudalism and the growth of cities, because with the former the servants of the noble households who supplied merriment on festive occasions in amateur capacity had to travel and make a living by offering dramatic entertainment to the general public, thus forming a supply of players, and with the latter, large reserves of potential audience became concentrated. [20] Performances took place at first in inn-yards on temporary stages, but as the audience grew in size special buildings were erected for the purpose of producing plays. (The first theatre was built by Burbage in 1576). The Elizabethan playhouse bore resemblance partly to the inn-yard and partly to the bull- and bear-baiting rings, which were also for the specific purpose of commercialized entertainment. The general shape of the theatre, round or octagonal, and the spectators' seats arranged around a "yard" which was not roofed were features of

---

[17] A. E. Zucker, *The Chinese Theatre* (1925), 216.

[18] Zucker, *op. cit.,* 214-219. See also Chambers, *Eliz. Stage,* III, 78 note 4, for references on this "curtain".

[19] Zucker, *op. cit.,* 215.

[20] *Vide* W. Raleigh, *Shakespeare* (1907), 97 f. cf. the dispersal of court musicians and actors in Sung dynasty — see Ch. XXVII.

Fig. 58   The Elizabethan Playhouse

St — "The study", rear stage
Ch — "chamber", upper stage
P   — pillar
SD — stage door
C   — curtain
W   — window

NOTE: The size of The Globe has been found to be:
   84 ft. between opposite outside walls.
   34 ft. high (to the eaves line).
   54 ft. across the interior yard.
   The stage: 4 to 5 ft. high, 29 ft. deep and 43 ft. wide at the back.
(J. C. Adams, *The Globe Playhouse,* 3, 39, 90 and 98).
For pictorial representations and reconstructions
   of the Elizabethan theatre, see:
J. Q. Adams, *Shakespearean Playhouse* (1917)
J. C. Adams, *The Globe Playhouse* (1942)
C. W. Hodges, *The Globe Restored* (1953)
R. Watkins, *On Producing Shakespeare* (1950)

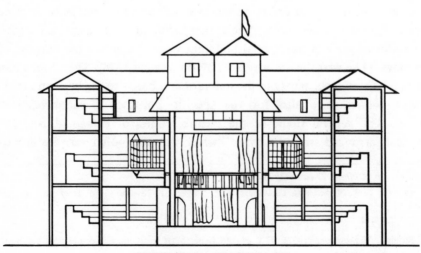

SECTION FACING STAGE

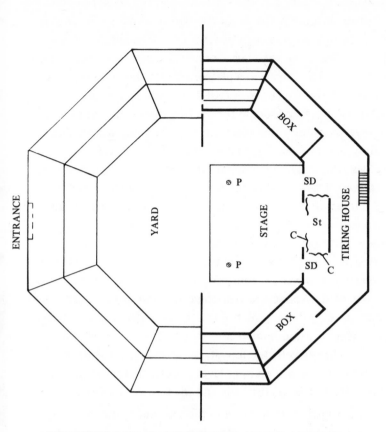

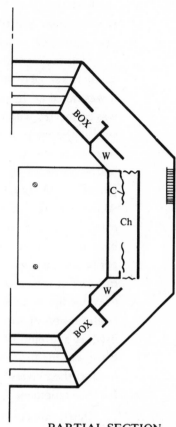

TOP VIEW AND HALF SECTION AT STAGE LEVEL

**PARTIAL SECTION
AT SECOND LEVEL**

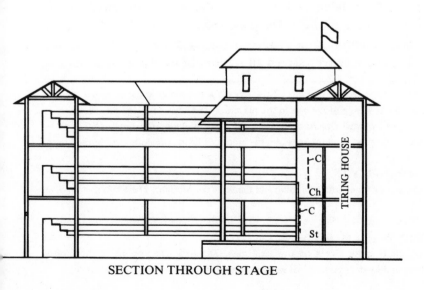

SECTION THROUGH STAGE

461

the bear rings and the galleries and the standing room around the stage resembled the balconies and the yard of an inn. Apart from the two or three galleries, one above another, in which spectators sat on rough benches or stools, and the "yard" in which the "groundlings" stood close together around the stage, spectators also sat on the stage on hired stools.[21] The stage was a platform protruding into the yard, it was railed at the perimeter, partly covered by a roof supported by two pillars and was connected with the players' dressing room at the back by two doors one on each side at the back of the stage. Although this platform was the main acting space, there were several subsidiary parts of the stage adjacent to and connected with the platform. Below the stage was the *cellar* which might represent Hell and from which ghosts would cry (as in *Hamlet,* I. v.) and spirits would appear through trap doors. Above the stage was the *hut* which could represent Heaven and from which gods often descended on a throne lowered through an opening in the ceiling. [22] At the back of the stage, between the stage doors, was the *rear stage* which might be a permanent or a temporary structure. [23] It was used for indoor scenes or the interior of tomb or cave and a tableau or scene could be arranged in it and "discovered" by drawing the curtain in front of it. Above the rear stage was the *upper stage,* the continuation of the second storey gallery, which might house the musicians or be used as a stretch of battlement or a monument and so on. The space behind the stage was the *tiring house,* on three levels; the lowest, on stage level, was probably used as the players' dressing room, and the upper levels, probably for storage and for the equipment for stage effects such as the bells and the thunder machine. [24]

Performances, weather permitting, took place in the afternoon, the only stage lighting being daylight, so that some plays failed because of darkness in late afternoons. [25] When there was a performance, a flag with the trade mark of the theatre flew on top of the building and just before the play started three trumpet blasts were sounded from the roof. [26] The play, lasting two or three hours, was often followed by a jig, a short dramatic dance, of puerile or bawdy character, sung to popular tunes. The audience represented all sections of the Elizabethan society,

---

[21] These spectators naturally spoiled the visibility of the action for the people in the yard, but the seats on the stage were a regular source of income to the players — see Reynolds, *Red Bull,* 8.

[22] W. J. Lawrence — *The Physical Conditions of the Elizabethan Public Playhouse* (1927), 98 — thought that thunder, lightning, cannon, bells and the crane for lifting the gods were housed in the hut.

[23] *Vide* Reynolds, *Red Bull,* Ch. VII.

[24] For variations in the shape of the theatre building and the stage see Albright, *The Shakesperian Stage* (1909), 78.

[25] *Vide* Chambers, *Eliz. Stage,* II, 543. A similar case in the Chinese theatre is mentioned in 齊如山, 京劇之變遷, 頁五七 — see Ch. XV.

[26] For similar trumpet blasts in the Greek theatre see Haigh, *The Attic Theatre,* 69. In the Chinese village theatre a long and loud "overture" of gongs and drums announces the performance.

from illiterates to courtiers. Those who paid the minimum charge for general admission stood in the yard, others who could afford more could sit in the galleries but the best seats were those in the two lower galleries which were near the stage and those on the stage itself. The spectators ate, drank, played cards, read and talked in the theatre and were, as compared with modern European audiences, uninhibited in their expressions of approval or dislike.

There were no painted scenery and front curtain on the Elizabethan stage, and properties were kept to the bare minimum. [27] The dialogue, mainly in blank verse, was spoken but incidental songs and dances were added and music was played for royal entrances, marches, banquets, dumb shows and so on. The costume was rich and colourful, but lacked historical accuracy, contemporary dress, sometimes with slight additions, being used for all places and all periods. Bouts of most realistic fencing and fisticuffs were part of the drama. Female characters, as in the Chinese theatre, were played by actors.

(3)

The similarity between the construction of the Chinese and the Elizabethan theatre is due to the similar models from which their shapes were derived. The Elizabethan theatre is the inn-yard theatre; the Chinese, the tea-house theatre. A description of the theatres in Peking in 1810 shows remarkable parallels to the Elizabethan theatre:

"The theatres in Peking, called 'tea houses', [28] give two kinds of performance, the public and the private. At the former the general public is admitted by paying a fee to the theatre and at the latter, which is financed by private funds, only invited guests are admitted. Performance takes place in the afternoon. Inside the theatre the stage is at one end of the building, with space around it for spectators. Opposite the stage is the main hall and above the hall, as well as on both sides of the building, there is a gallery. At private performances the honoured guests sit in front of the stage, but at public performances that space is occupied by the riff-raff and is called 'down the well' by the gentlemen in the gallery. Admission to the main floor is by seats, but in the gallery it is by tea tables and the space near the stage is called 'gentlemen's seats'. [29] There are two stage doors, the one on stage right is the 'entrance door' and that on the left is the 'exit door'. Gallery seats near the exit door are the most expensive and are mostly reserved by the gallants. At private performances the right side of the gallery is screened for the ladies. Those in the gallery usually like dramas of romance and intrigue and those downstairs,

---

[27] Lawrence, *Physical Conditions,* 40-41.
[28] 茶園
[29] 官座

463

combats, crime and violence, hence the programme usually consists of both". [30]

The Chinese theatre is like the Elizabethan playhouse because the Chinese tea house is like the English inn-yard. [31] Similarly, the early Spanish theatre called *corral* (yard) had almost the same construction and origin as the Elizabethan theatre. De Witt's drawing of the stage in The Swan [32] is exactly like a Chinese stage, except for the real stage doors — instead of door openings only — and the spectators over the stage. The arrangement of the audience in the galleries, in the yard and on the stage is identical with both the Chinese temple theatre and the tea-house theatre, the fact that in the tea-house theatre all spectators on the main floor have seats and that spectators always stand on the Chinese stage are of minor importance. Pictorial reconstructions of the Elizabethan theatre often look strikingly like a Chinese theatre. [33] In spite of the adjuncts to the Elizabethan platform stage for which there are no Chinese counterparts, the stages of the two theatres are also very similar, because among the various parts of the Elizabethan stage the platform is by far the most important acting space.

The most important characteristic of the platform stage is not its appearance but its position in relation to the spectators. When the platform stage is reconstructed inside the proscenium arch, as has been tried in some revivals of Elizabethan dramas, the appearance of the stage is reproduced, but it does not give the illusion of a different theatre, rather it appears to be a modern play *about* the Shakespearean theatre. [34] The distinctive quality of the open stage lies in the prominence of its floor plan which makes it look three-dimensional and enables the audience to see the action in the round. On its advantage over the picture-frame stage it has been said:

> "The indistinct muddle of the picture-stage, with everybody getting in
> everybody else's way and a general uncertainty among the audience as to who is
> who and which side is which, makes many a finale a sad anti-climax". [35]

In other words, the picture-stage is often like a chess board to a child looking at it on the level of the table top. The upstage and downstage positions always differ in their

---

[30] 周貽白，中國戲劇史，頁七三六，引，包世臣，都劇賦序；參，（清代燕都梨園史料）金臺殘淚記，卷三，十一款；夢華瑣簿，二至九款，十八款．

[31] *Vide* Lawrence, *Pre-Restoration Stage Studies,* Ch. 1. The Inn-Yard Playing Places: Their Influence and Characteristics.

[32] See, for example, Reynolds, *Red Bull,* Frontispiece.

[33] See, for example, C. W. Hodges, *The Globe Restored,* 59, 89, 170-6; and Zucker, *The Chinese Theatre,* pp, 198-9, where the photograph of a Chinese theatre is compared with a reconstructed view of Fortune.

[34] *Vide* R. Speaight, *William Poel and the Elizabethan Revival,* p. 97 and Ill. opp. p. 192.

[35] Watkins, *On Producing Shakespeare,* 183 f.

importance, that is, in their quality to attract and hold the attention of the audience and this is because unless the upstage position is raised above the stage floor, distance, poor sight lines (for the side seats), and interference by people downstage, all conspire to make an actor less readily visible. [36] On a picture-stage, with its sides concealed from view this difference can be so great that the usefulness of the stage is more or less reduced to a thin layer of the acting space near the footlights. It is not surprising that in some modern movements in the theatre, such as that of Georg Fuchs in the Munich Art Theatre, a shallow stage was used to make actors look like figures on a bas-relief. [37]

On the open stage, on the other hand, the acting was directed peripherally to the audience. If the actors played towards one direction only, as in the modern European theatre, it would be difficult to reconcile that with the fact that in both the Elizabethan and the Chinese theatre some of the most expensive seats were situated at the sides of the stage. [38]

On a stage which is visible from three sides any scenery or built set has to be confined to the back of the stage and properties used downstage have to be low and small, for obvious reasons. It is doubtful that painted scenery was used in the Elizabethan theatre [39] but large properties such as trees, tents, river banks (built set), thrones, tables and beds were certainly freely employed and these were moved on to and from the stage in full view of the audience except in some cases when they could be covered by the curtains of the rear stage. [40] Change of scenery and property seems somehow more convincing when it is carried out unseen, as in the modern European theatre; the audience of to-day have some of the child-like faith in conjurers and would object to the shamefaced visible shifting of property in the Elizabethan and Chinese theatre. In addition to the lack of canvas work, therefore, the movement of the property makes the open stage look unnaturalistic even if it is fully furnished with properties.

Drama is essentially pretence: we pretend that the actors are the characters in the drama and the stage is the scene of action. On the open stage this fundamental nature of drama is brought home more strongly to the audience because of the discrepancy between the appearance of the stage and the scene it represents. It would be a misconception to think that the Elizabethans and the Chinese looked forward to the same kind of dramatic illusion as the audience of the naturalistic theatre do and that the paucity of stage setting in their theatres shows their greater credulity. The

---

[36] cf. *ibid.,* 131 *et seq.*

[37] *Vide* S. Cheney, *The New Movement in the Theatre* (1914), 144.

[38] cf. R. Southern, *The Open Stage, passim.,* and *vide* Lawrence, *Elizabethan Playhouse, First series,* 38.

[39] *Vide* Lawrence, *Physical Conditions,* 40-41.

[40] *Vide* Reynolds, *Red Bull, passim.*

dramatists were fully aware of the fact that the stage did not look like the scenes it represented:

"But pardon, gentles all,
The flat unraised spirits that hath dar'd
On this unworthy scaffold to bring forth
So great an object: can this cockpit hold
The vasty fields of France? or may we cram
Within this wooden O the very casques
That did affright the air at Agincourt?
O, pardon! since a crooked figure may
Attest in little place a million;
And let us, ciphers to this great accompt,
On your imaginary forces work.
Suppose within the girdle of these walls
Are now confin'd two mighty monarchies,
Whose high upreared and abutting fronts
The perilous narrow ocean parts asunder:"

(Chorus, *Henry V,* I)

Far from the presumption that the stage can *look* like the scenes, it is here offered merely as a *symbol,* like the "crooked figure" that "may attest a million" and all that the symbol can do is to touch off the "imaginary forces". The audience is shown how their imagination should work:

"Piece out our imperfection with your thoughts
Into a thousand parts divide one man,
And make imaginary puissance;
Think when we talk of horses that you see them
Printing their proud hoofs i' the receiving earth". [41]

The Chorus in *Pericles* III. i. makes a similar plea:

"In your imagination hold
This stage the ship, . . ."

In extreme cases the stage can be as much as the whole world:

"Would your apprehensions helpe poore art,
Into three parts deuiding this our stage,
They all at once shall take their leaues of you.
Thinke this England, this Spaine, this Persia".

(Spoken by Fame, the Presenter, in Rowley's *The Travels of the Three English Brothers).*

Then *"Enter three seuerall waies the three Brothers",* and *"Fame giues to each a prospective glasse, they seme to see one another".*

---

[41] *Ibid.*

The Elizabethans and the Chinese have the benefit of being able to "piece out the imperfections" of the stage with their thoughts and, when necessary, "into a thousand parts to divide one man". All art appeals to us through imagination, not through empirical knowledge. Imagination has the speed of thought and is unfettered by the laws of space and time. In reading a poem or a novel one's thoughts fly from one person or place to another and the sequence of images may be quicker or slower than they would have been in actual life, simultaneous events may appear consecutively in the mind, consecutive events may be mixed together and the sequence of images may be the reverse of what it would be in reality. It is taken for granted that experience may be telescoped and jumbled up in art. From this point of view there is nothing strange in the rapid succession of widely different scenes in the Elizabethan and Chinese dramas.

"Then let your fancies deeme upon a stage,

One man a thousand, and one houre an age".

(John Kirke, *The Seven Champions of Christendom,* III. Chorus).

The awareness on the part of the Elizabethan audience that drama is pretence can hardly be doubted, if even the dramatists pointed it out in this manner. Shakespearean critics have realized this before now:

"The truth is that the spectators are always in their senses, and know from the first act to the last, that the stage is only a stage and that the players are only players. They come to hear a certain number of lines recited with just gesture and elegant modulation. The lines relate to some action and an action must be in some place; but the different actions that complete a story may be in places very remote from each other; and where is the absurdity of allowing that space to represent first *Athens,* and then *Sicily* which was always known to be neither *Sicily* nor *Athens,* but a modern theatre"? [42]

That the stage was considered as a stage only was also verified by the contemporary comment in Jasper Mayne's poem on Jonson *(Jonsonus Virbius,* 1638).

"The stage was still a stage, two entrances

Were not two parts o' the world, disjoin'd by sea". [43]

Absurdity results only when the spectators cease to be "in their senses". Even in the most thoroughly naturalistic theatre, however, no spectator really forgets the pretence involved in the drama, although the diligence and earnestness of the scenic

---

[42] Samuel Johnson, Preface to *Shakespeare* (1765), I, xxvii. cf. Cervantes, *Rufian dichoso,* Act II.

"To the auditor it matters

Little that I in a moment

Pass from Germany to Guinea,

Though from off this stage I move not.

Human thought, indeed is nimble". — see H. A. Rennert, *The Spanish Stage* (1909), 95.

[43] Quoted by Reynolds, *Modern Philology,* Vol. II, No. 4, p. 602.

designers make one think that nothing is left undone to help the audience do so. Modern European audiences also accept the multiple identity of the stage in the course of a drama; the only difference between them and the Chinese or Elizabethan audience is that they demand close imitation of the scene represented and the concealment of the changings. The psychology of the audience towards the drama may vary between two extremes: they may take the drama as a performance with skill and beauty, or they may take it almost as a real sight, as when one looks through the neighbour's window — almost, because although the audience temporarily push their knowledge that the drama is pretence out of their consciousness they can call it into play when their voluntary make-believe tends to excite inappropriate action. The curious fact is that for those who can suffer delusion in the theatre scenery is unnecessary.

"At the border of Kiangsu and Chekiang province merchants of the district assembled once in every year to pay homage to the local gods with, among other things, dramatic performances. On one occasion when the actors were playing the historical episode of the traitor Ch'in Kuei [44] murdering the loyal general Yüeh Fei [45] and his son, a man jumped on to the stage and stabbed and killed the actor playing the traitor. When asked at court why he killed the actor, the man answered that he did not know anyone among the actors but stirred by the hatred for the traitor he, for a moment, felt he was willing to die with him and did not manage to distinguish the false from the real".

Nearly as dangerous and quite as complete was the delusion described in the following:

"In Ming dynasty in the county of Wu-hsien [46] was a wood-chopper of large and robust build who, though illiterate, liked to hear stories old and new and could discuss history with some intelligence. One day when he was watching the drama called *Pure Loyalty* he jumped up to the stage and beat the actor playing the traitor till the victim almost bled to death. People tried to pull him away but he cried, 'Traitors like this deserve to die, what are we waiting for'? 'But this is a play', said the others, 'he is not the real traitor'. 'I know he is not', answered the man, 'if he were, I would have used my hatchet forthwith'."

This sometimes happened to people not expected to get excited:

"Chou Liao-Chou [47] once struck an actor playing the traitor in the drama *Pure Loyalty* at a welcoming party given in his honour in Hangchow. The guests present were surprised and all were anxious to know whether the actor had

---

[44] 秦檜
[45] 岳飛
[46] 吳縣
[47] 周蓼洲

offended him in some way. In the next morning he explained to a friend that for a moment he could not contain his anger''. [48]

A parallel case in seventeenth century England is recorded in Edmund Gayton's *Festivous Notes upon Don Quixote* (1654):

"Our *Don* is not so much transported with *Belanis* his Blowes as a passionate Butcher of our Nation was, who being at the Play, called *the Greeks and Trojans,* and seeing *Hector* overpowered by *Mirmydons,* got upon the Stage, and with his good Batoone tooke the true *Trojans* part so stoutly, that he routed the *Greeks,* and rayled upon them loudly for a company of cowardly slaves to assault one man with so much odds. He strooke moreover such an especiall acquaintance with *Hector,* that for a long time *Hector* could not obtaine leave of him to be kill'd, that the Play might go on; and the cudgelled *Mirmydons* durst not enter againe, till *Hector,* having prevailed upon his unexpected second, return'd him over the Stage againe into the yard from whence he came''. [49]

If scenery is unnecessary for creating delusion in the pathological, one is inclined to think that it is neither necessary for illusion in the sensitive, and the aim of the naturalistic theatre could be achieved without it, provided the imagination of the audience is trained. Similarly, if to sane minds no amount of scenery is sufficient to produce delusion, one is inclined to believe that for people with blunted imagination no amount of it can produce illusion. In this light things like Belasco's real restaurant built on the stage and productions of realistic drama on the "actual" *locale* appear as desperate attempts to save the hopeless. At the opposite extreme, there are people in whom illusion could be produced without either stage or actors:

"There was once a wealthy orphan who was fond of shadow plays and was encouraged by his idle companions to indulge in them. Whenever he saw the famous warrior Kuan Kung [50] about to be beheaded, he would cry and ask the players to delay the execution for another day''. [51]

Whether the Elizabethan and the Chinese audience indulged in the dramatic illusion of the modern European theatre cannot, therefore, be determined by the amount of scenery used. If they did experience illusion, it could not, at any rate, be of the type known to the audience of to-day, with its strong visual component. In studying theatres of the past it is important to keep constantly in mind the fact that the audience had no experience of illusionary scenery. It is misleading, for example, to think of the descriptive passages, the mime and the stage effects of the

---

[48] 焦循，劇說，卷六，引，極齋雜錄; 蓴鄉贅筆; 顧彩髯樵傳.
[49] Quoted in Reynolds, *Red Bull,* 10.
[50] 關公
[51]（宋）張耒，明道雜誌，第五十款.

Elizabethan and Chinese theatres as *substitutes* for scenery. [52] As the audience did not expect to see realistic scenery they could not have missed it and there was nothing lacking for which a substitute was required. To the Chinese, descriptive passages and mime, like the lyrical poetry and the dance, are parts of the drama, and when they see the naturalistic drama, instead of being satisfied with scenery which they never missed, they are disappointed by the lack of poetry and mime. [53] To the Elizabethans "the actors were not set against a background, real or imaginary; the audience did not visualize a setting for them". [54]

(4)

Theatre always has a dual nature: the performance and the illusion. It is actually a performance in the real world of the audience, but for the sake of the illusion it is taken to be the unreal world of the drama. The stage is both a raised platform and the scene in the drama, the players are both actors earning a living and characters in the play and the dialogue is both poetry written by a dramatist and the conversation of the *dramatis personae.* In other words, everything in the theatre has a *theatric* aspect as well as a *dramatic* aspect.

Dramatic illusion consists of ignoring the theatric aspects of a dramatic performance. The modern audience tries to exclude the awareness of the theatric aspects from the consciousness. This is accomplished, more than anything else, by the sustained consistency of the dramatic aspects: that is why the occasional falling of a flat or glimpse of the stage personnel is so religiously avoided. The Elizabethan and the Chinese dramatists, however, made references to the theatric aspects freely, which would be bad jokes if the audience cherished dramatic illusion in the same way as the modern European audience do. It is difficult to escape the conclusion, therefore, that the Elizabethans and the Chinese, often, if not always, looked upon the stage merely as a raised platform for a skilled performance, and that there was no effort made to dispel the awareness of the theatric features.

Whereas in modern revivals of Shakespeare the actors usually do their best to make the dialogue sound natural and conceal the fact that it is in verse, the dramatist pointed boldly to the fact that it *was* blank verse, as in *As You Like It,* IV. i.

Orlando Good day and happiness, dear Rosalind!

Jaques Nay then, God be wi' you, an you speak in blank verse.

In *Henry VIII,* V. iv. at the end of a scene suggesting a street crowd the Porter,

---

[52] cf. Reynolds, *Red Bull,* 166.

[53] This was the experience of a foreigner in China who appreciated the Chinese theatre; see J. F. Allen, *The Chinese Theatre Handbook,* 46.

[54] Bradbrook, *Themes and Conventions of Elizabethan Tragedy* (1935), 8.

trying to clear a path for the procession shouts to the people gathered about the stage door:

"You i' the camlet, get up o' the rail:

I'll pick you o'er the pales else". (55)

It is difficult to believe that the whole scene was for building up an illusion only to be wantonly destroyed at the very end. Again, in Middleton's *Black Book* (1604):

Lucifer	And now that I have vaulted so high
	Above the stage rails of this earthen globe
	I must turn actor and join companies,
	To share my comic sleek-ey'd villainies.

not only stage rails but the actors' companies too are spoken of. In the Chinese theatre mention of the stage sometimes comes at the end of a descriptive passage and would cancel out all dramatic illusion which the description might have helped to build, if we considered it as substitute for scenery. In *The Strange Retribution* (56) the potter, newly rich by his plunder, is showing his house to his former friend the sandal-maker. As they walk round and round the stage, the former points out the beauties of the porch, the terrace, the garden and so forth and each time the latter answers, "Ay, this is the porch", "This is the garden", and so on till at the end of the tour the potter asks, "Now, what do you think of this house you see?" and is answered, "I don't see anything, except a stage". The effect must be similar to that in *Henry VIII*, V. iv. just quoted, where after a whole scene suggestive of the street, the Porter gives away the fact that they are only crowding on the stage. In *The Hector of Germany* (1615). V. v.:

Enter Frenchman and Englishman druncke.

Frenchman	Players, by this light players: O I love a play with all my heart.
Englishman	Begin, begin, we are set *(sit on the Railes)*.

the dialogue reduces the world of the drama to that of the audience. Sometimes the two worlds are allowed to mix, as in Beaumont, *Knight of the Burning Pestle,* where a Citizen climbs up from the yard and interrupts the Prologue,

"Hold your peace, goodman Boy"!

and amid the bickering which follows, Citizen's Wife also wants to come up,

"Husband! shall I come up, husband?"

and he replies,

"Ay cony — Ralph, help your mistress this way, —

Pray gentlemen, make her a little room. — I pray you,

sir, lend me your hand to help up my wife. I thank you,

sir, — so". (57)

---

(55) The front and sides of the stage were paled — Lawrence, *Elizabethan Playhouse, First series,* 18.

(56) 奇寃報

(57) cf. Bradbrook, *Themes and Conventions,* 120 f.

Sometimes the dialogue merely points to the architectural features of the stage, as in Chapman, *Caesar and Pompey,* V.i.

Pompey	We are now like
	The two poles propping heaven, on which heaven moves,
	And they are fixed and quiet.

referring to the pillars and ceiling on the stage. Although the pillars do not in this instance stand for any property in the drama, if the audience did indulge in dramatic illusion the effect of the passage would be the same as if a modern actor mentions the battens and spotlights on the stage. The stage trap is mentioned in Middleton, *Women Beware Women,* V. i.

Guardiano	. . . look you, Sir,
	This is the trap-door to 't.
Ward	I know't of old, uncle, since the last triumph; here rose up a Devil with one eye, I remember, with a company of fire-works at's tail.
Guardiano	Prithee leave squibbing now, mark me, and fail not;
	But when thou hear'st me give a stamp, down with't:
	The villian's caught then.

Stamping was the cue for those working the trap in the cellar. [58]

It is only when the stage is looked upon as a stage that its theatric features can enter the action *as theatric features,* for example, in *The Faithful Shepherdess,* V.i.:

Clorin	Soon again he ease shall find
	If I can but still his mind:
	This Curtain thus I do display
	To keep the piercing air away.

as if a modern actor would say, "Turn off that flood lantern so that my friend can sleep". In the Chinese theatre this type of remark is only made for comic effect by clowns but Elizabethan convention apparently allowed even a serious character to do so.

The attitude of the audience was perhaps occasionally that represented by the Prologus in *Every Man in His Humour* (1616):

Prologus	Or, with three rustie swords,
	And helpe of some few foot-and-halfe foote words,
	Fight ouer *Yorke,* and *Lancasters* long iarres:
	And in the tyring-house bring wounds, to scarres.

The Chinese attitude towards the play as a play shows itself in a rather extreme form in a drama called *The Loyal Brother* [59] in which two actors both play double

---

[58] Adams, *Globe Playhouse,* 116.

[59]（ 明 ）（ 六十種曲 ）沈璟, 義俠記, 十九齣.

roles and the first roles they play die in the earlier part of the play, and when in their second roles they meet each other in the later part of the play a clown tells the audience jokingly of the parts they have been playing. Apparently the audience are to enjoy the ridiculous impossibility of a "dead" man coming to life to play another part. [60] Doubling was extensively, and split parts sometimes, used in Elizabethan dramas. [61] Without make-up and in a small theatre, the actors in double roles must have been easily recognizable, indeed there are reasons to believe that when the female parts were doubled there was serious danger of misunderstanding, owing to the prevalent disguise-theme. [62] Money collectors were also used as supernumeraries, [63] and they too must have been recognizable. As in the early Chinese theatre, the need for doubling was due to limited personnel. [64]

Shakespeare can create illusion by these very allusions to theatric aspects of the drama, as in *Twelfth Night*, III, iv, where Signor Fabian, commenting on Malvolio's appearance, says:

"If this were played upon a stage now, I could condemn it as an improbable fiction".

turning a real piece of improbable fiction to advantage. Likewise, Cleopatra becomes real when she says, after she has resolved to kill herself:

". . . I shall see
Some squeaking Cleopatra boy my greatness
I' the posture of a whore". (*Antony and Cleopatra*, V. ii).

Again, in *Love's Labour's Lost*, V. ii:

Biron	Our wooing doth not end like an old play;
	Jack hath not Jill: these ladies' courtesy
	Might well have made our sport a comedy.
King	Come, sir, it wants a twelvemonth and a day,
	And then 'twill end.
Biron	That's too long for a play.

By imitating the attitude of the audience towards the play the actors make themselves appear to belong to the real world of the audience and the unreal world of the drama to appear one level further removed. In a naturalistic play, this type of trick should theoretically still work, but the mere mention of drama as pretence may

---

[60] cf. "Let's retire to the dressing room and wait", spoken by the clown — *Ibid.*

[61] Lawrence, *Pre-Restoration Stage Studies*, Ch. III. The Practice of Doubling and Its Influence on Early Dramaturgy.

[62] *Ibid.*, 43 and 59.

[63] Lawrence, *Elizabethan Playhouse, Second series*, 99.

[64] Between 1494 and 1552 the King's Men increased from four to eight; in the mid-sixteenth century companies were about ten to twelve men strong — A. Harbage, *Shakespeare and the Rival Traditions* (1952), 9.

spoil the precariously maintained dramatic illusion of the modern European audience.

Topical allusions which would tend to destroy dramatic illusion were also used by Shakespeare. Not only does the Gravedigger in *Hamlet* (V. i) refer to a tavern near to the Globe:

"Go, get thee to Vaughan; fetch me a stoup of liquor". [65]

but Hamlet himself gives a lenghty discussion (II. ii) on the children players, "little eyases", who rivalled the adult companies in Shakespeare's time and gave them some concern. [66] During the conversation, Hamlet is even told that the children invaded the Globe as well as other theatres, and it is only with an abrupt transition that the Prince gets back to the subject of his uncle,

"It is not very strange; for my uncle . . ."

The incongruity of these allusions can only be fully realized when we hear a modern Hamlet talk about the latest innovations of Hollywood and their commercial significance and the Gravedigger sends his assistant to buy cold drink from Soho.

Not only in gags and interpolated passages but also in the most serious scenes the dramatist referred to theatric features. Hamlet sees the Ghost with Marcellus and Horatio in Act I and at the end of the Act Hamlet asks his companions to swear secrecy. The Ghost, now unseen, cries, "Swear" from *"Beneath"*, that is, under the stage. Hamlet tries to appear light-hearted and answers the Ghost in several jocular remarks and says to the others,

"Come on, — you hear the fellow in the cellarage, —

Consent to swear".

the "cellarage" being the space under the stage. It is understandable that Coleridge, living in a different theatrical tradition, thought this passage indefensible, [67] because in mentioning a part of the stage by name Hamlet is, in effect, joking with the audience, who can appreciate the joke, but the dialogue is directed to Marcellus and Horatio, in the play, who, if they were to understand it, would also have to consider the play as a play and the stage as a wooden platform, instead of the battlements in Elsinore. It is as if the audience were so used to the idea of the drama as a pretence that they even expected the characters in the play to feel the same way.

Some passages of *Antonio and Mellida,* Act V are similar in principle to the jokes of the Chinese actors playing double roles mentioned above. When Alberto makes his exit with,

"Farewell, dear friends: expect no more of me

Thus ends my part in this lover's comedy"

he is speaking as a player not as Alberto. The characters in the same play discussed

---

[65] See New Variorum *Hamlet.*

[66] *Vide* Chambers, *Eliz. Stage,* I, 378 ff.

[67] *Vide* New Variorum *Hamlet.*

their parts in the induction, and in the course of the play when the lovers meet each other in the marsh they greet each other in Italian, and when they have left the stage Mellida's page apologizes for this to the audience. "There was", according to Bradbrook, "no question of the characters stepping out of the picture, because they were never in it". [68]

There is nevertheless a slight difference between the Elizabethan and the Chinese attitude towards the lack of realism. The Chinese always accept it as a matter of course whereas the Elizabethans accepted it sometimes with an apology:

> "Our stage so lamely can express a Sea,
>
> That we are forst by *Chorus* to discourse
>
> What should have beene in action".

>> (Heywood, *The Fair Maid of the West,* Chorus).

It is not only when the dramatist resorts to narrative that he becomes apologetic, he uses the same tone in the first chorus in *Henry V.* Nor does the need for apology appear to originate from the inadequacy of the stage setting, because the open stage is hardly adequate to represent any scene realistically, in or out of doors. It was apparently only when unusually vast dimensions and long distances were involved, with which the audience was not familiar, that extra encouragement for imagination was thought to be necessary.

> "Thus with imagin'd wing our swift scene flies
>
> In motion of no less celerity
>
> Than that of thought . . .
>
> . . . .
>
> Work, work your thoughts, and therein see a siege,
>
> Behold the ordenance on their carriages,
>
> With fatal mouths gaping on girded Harfleur".

>> (*Henry V,* III. Chorus).

The earnestness contrasts with the playfulness of the Chinese players. Owing to the use of large properties on the stage, the Elizabethans were probably used to slightly more scenic effects than the Chinese and the more extensive scenery in the court and private theatres of the time could not but have some influence on the public taste. The Chinese, on the other hand, are used to a dance-like style of acting which is compatible only with the minimum of stage setting — to them the representation of a story, especially the visual component of it, is always a means to an end.

(5)

Lack of scenery and the range of scenes in the drama have reciprocal effects on each other. In theatres with elaborate scenery the dramatist's choice of scenes is

---

[68] Bradbrook, *Themes and Conventions,* 116.

limited by what the stage carpenter can do to meet the current demands for realism, but in theatres without scenery the audience demand little, hence the dramatist can employ scenes for which it would be difficult to design good scenery. [69] Thus in the Elizabethan and the Chinese dramas the scenes are many and short, and many of them located out of doors, as wilderness, battlefield, on board ship and so forth.

Variety of scenes in turn affects the range of the acting. In dramas of domestic scenes the type of acting is restricted to what people do in their everyday life, such as sitting, talking and lighting cigarettes. If a long tradition of such dramas is established the actors, in the end, will not know how to fight a mortal combat, or struggle in a storm-striken ship or march in a royal procession so that even some of the visual pleasures in real life are impossible on the stage.

The types of scenes in Elizabethan dramas are, roughly speaking, the following: the unlocated scene, wilderness with or without cave or hut, battlefield with or without tents, garden, street or market place, hall and chamber. [70] In the Chinese dramas the range of scenes is practically unlimited, but those most usually employed are: the hall, the chamber, the court room, the drill ground, land journey, river and boat, battlefield and prison; and of the less frequently used scenes may be mentioned: mountain pass, scenes in the clouds, purgatory scenes and dungeons. The difference between the wide range of scenes in the Elizabethan and Chinese theatre on the one hand and the limited variety of locality in the Greek tragedies on the other, is due to the *skene* building in the Greek theatre which is a real building and serves as a genuine stage set. The facade of the tiring house of the Elizabethan theatre is not substantial enough to tie down the variety of scenes to one or a few types: the rear and upper stage are not structures that can be found in ordinary houses, hence they are widely adaptable. [71] As a rule the fewer visual adjuncts to the stage, permanent or temporary, the greater the variety of scenes. [72] If the rear stage was a temporary structure, [73] as it appeared to be in some theatres, the Elizabethan stage had no permanent background on the stage level, like the Chinese stage, and in any case, the Elizabethan stage is as perfectly flexible as a bare platform.

The open stage has a twofold effect on the continuity of the action; it makes continuous performance, as in the Elizabethan and Chinese theatres, not only desirable but also necessary. It is well known that the act and scene divisions in Shakespeare were added by later editors, and that there was nothing in the original

---

[69] cf. the increase of scenes when a stage play is adapted into a film. For the effect of stage scenery on dramatic construction see Lawrence, *Elizabethan Playhouse, Second series,* 151 *et seq.*

[70] Chambers, *Eliz. Stage,* III, Ch. XX.

[71] Chambers, *Eliz. Stage,* III, 134.

[72] cf. Reynolds, *Red Bull,* 189.

[73] *Vide ibid.,* Ch. VII.

text to indicate pauses between different sections of the drama. [74] The dramatic action was broken by dumb shows, pageants, music, chorus and so forth but the performance is generally believed to have been continuous. [75] Continuity was necessary because the psychological effect of the drop curtain was lacking and because pauses, if inserted between scenes, would be too numerous for sound theatrical production. The drop curtain is a signal from the stage manager to the audience to take their minds off the play and to expect an inevitable interval, and audiences trained to the practice accept the pause with equanimity. When action stops in a Chinese theatre, however, the audience is left facing an empty stage in the constant state of expectancy, and when pauses are necessary, for instance, for the change of costume of the hero, they have to be kept extremely short, or else a meaningless scene is inserted (as in *The Intoxicated Royal Concubine* [76] when the two eunuchs compete with each other in the kinds of flowers they can fetch). Even different plays run straight one into another in the Chinese theatre. Judging by the Chinese practice, the pauses, if any, in the Elizabethan theatre were likely to be very short.

As literature a modern play may be compared with an Elizabethan one without reference to the act-divisions but as theatre the pauses between acts and scenes make the modern European drama differ radically from an Elizabethan drama. Theatrical effects, like the effect of a piece of music or circus performance, depend on good timing; good theatre is very much a matter of pace and rhythm. A four- or five-act modern play consists of as many units of visual-and-aural experience connected together by the story. In the intervals the audience, to pass the time, engage themselves in activities remote from dramatic appreciation, and the flow of sensuous and emotional impressions is broken. In a continuous performance of a large number of scenes, on the other hand, there is the cinematographic effect — the visual and emotional content of the drama forming a *context,* the effect of one moment depending on those of the preceding moments in what is called *"montage"* in films. Imaginative reading will reveal these effects in many passages in Shakespeare, for example, the scenes preceding and following the battles in *King Lear* and the sequence in *The Merchant of Venice* of Portia rounding up business in Venice and the moonlit garden scene with Lorenzo and Jessica at Belmont. (It would be inaccurate, therefore, to think of the Chinese and the Elizabethan stage as makeshift. The platform stage, in spite of its simplicity, is perfectly well suited to the type of drama performed on it). Editors of Shakespeare sometimes cut the play into acts right through some continuous action, as at the end of Act III in *Twelfth Night,* where there was no change of locality and the action should be continuous with the

---

[74] For contrary views see Lawrence, *Speeding Up Shakespeare,* Ch. 1.

[75] Chambers, *Eliz. Stage,* III, 124-5.

[76] 貴妃醉酒

beginning of Act IV. [77] Even when the locality does change, continuous action is maintained by special conventions, as in *Romeo and Juliet* I. iv-v, where the masquers "march about the Stage, and Servingmen come forth with their napkins" thus completing a journey and witnessing the end of a dinner within a few seconds. [78] In the mind of the modern reader the change of locality is associated with change of scenery and the pause, therefore the play may appear to be divided into scenes, but the Elizabethan audience watching the rapid flow of action could not be always aware of the locality. [79] In fact, even the dramatist sometimes seemed to forget the locality, as in the scene in *Othello* IV. i, where Bianca can enter freely and yet Othello discusses the most confidential matters with Iago.

---

[77] *Vide* W. Poel, *Bulletin of John Rylands Library,* Vol. 3, No. 1, p. 227.

[78] *Vide* R. Watkins, *On Producing Shakespeare* (1950), 104 for other examples.

[79] *Vide* Granville-Barker, *Prefaces,* I, 10 f.

CHAPTER XL

THE CHINESE AND THE ELIZABETHAN THEATRE — II

(Location of Scenes — Stage Conventions — Narrative Elements — Costume — Popular Taste — Boy Actors)

(6)

Scenery is a visual supplement which aids the imagination to accept the dramatic pretence but it also serves to define locality. The open stage can be without the visual effects of scenery but cannot always dispense with the definition of locality. The problem of location is particularly important in the Elizabethan and Chinese theatres owing to the large number of scenes in the dramas and the consequent need to inform the audience frequently of the locality represented. [1]

Locality can be defined in many ways other than by scenery, such as: by the characters appearing in the scene, as gaolers or inn-keepers; by the action, as battles; by previous dialogue, as in expressed intention to visit a place; by simultaneous dialogue, as in soliloquies spoken in hiding; by mime, as a thief entering a house or a fugitive swimming in water; by property, as the bed; and by the title of the play, as in some "one-act" Chinese plays. In the Elizabethan theatre occasionally the presenter gives a detailed guide for the locality of the scenes. [2]

Both the Elizabethan and the Chinese playwright have to employ these means of scene-location. There is however some difference in emphasis and frequency. In the Chinese theatre location is usually defined by action and mime and, if these are not sufficient, dialogue is employed; in the Elizabethan theatre mime alone was rarely, if at all, used for the purpose, but the stage properties, which were more extensively used than in the Chinese theatre, usually specified the locality for the audience. Here we see the effect of the different styles of acting and properties: the

---

[1] For the possible use of painted backcloth in Elizabethan theatres see Chambers, *Eliz. Stage,* III, 129 and 133.

[2] *Vide* Chambers, *Eliz. Stage,* III. 128 f.

479

Chinese actors can perform highly specialized pantomime and the Chinese properties are symbolic rather than realistic, for example, the "wind flags" and the significance of different arrangements of the table and chairs. [3] It is sometimes desirable to define the locality of the scene before the players appear and this was done in the Elizabethan theatre, apart from previous dialogue, by the presenter or chorus [4] but in the Chinese theatre this is done by singing, usually *ad libitum*, [5] off stage before the entrance.

Apart from the method of scene-location, there is a deeper difference between the Elizabethan and the Chinese theatre in the habitual precision in the latter as regards location and the occasional vagueness in the former, and this in spite of the Elizabethan concessions to realism and the thorough conventionalism of the Chinese stage. All dramatists have to give a clear and coherent account of a story in the framework of stage representation and the sequence of scenes to be represented is a perennial problem to them. Minor Elizabethan dramatists did not always handle dramatic construction with dexterity: sometimes beds are brought out of doors under lame excuse, apparently to avoid more complicated and tedious construction of the text. [6] Occasionally banquets are brought on in a desert, as in *King Leir,* Sc. 24 and *The Blind Beggar of Alexandria,* Sc. 3. The ambiguity of locality in *Othello* IV. i. and III. iv. has been mentioned and it may be explained as a choice of ambiguity in preference to awkward staging. The preference was perhaps justified because the Elizabethan audience, accustomed to the lack of definite location in the moralities and interludes, were not fully aware of the exact locality of every scene. In the text of Shakespeare, the indications of scene-location were added by later editors [7] and their vagueness is sometimes all too apparent. Even in court productions, where the locality board was used and, under Italian influence, some form of simultaneous setting was provided, the locality was still partially left to the imagination of the audience. [8] Some modern scholars take the view that

> "We shall no longer try to give a geographical locality to scenes which Shakespeare was not at pains to define". [9]

The ambiguity in scene-location is different from the deliberately undefined locality; one is vague, the other is neutral. The inevitable scenery of the modern European theatre conceals the fact that in many scenes there is no need to define the

---

[3] See Chapter IV.

[4] Chambers, *Eliz. Stage,* III. 128.

[5] 倒板

[6] For examples see Albright, *The Shakesperian Stage,* 146.

[7] W. Archer, *The Quarterly Review,* Vol. 208. No. 415. p. 447.

[8] Chambers, *Eliz. Stage,* III, 31 f, 41, 43 f.

[9] R. Watkins, *On Producing Shakespeare,* 25.

locality because it neither clarifies the action nor enhances the dramatic interest, for example, scenes in which a message is told or a soliloquy spoken, in fact many highly dramatic scenes such as departures, reconciliations, reunions, remonstrance, supplication and so on lose nothing in emotional significance for being unlocated, so long as the audience imagine them to be in the appropriate privacy. On the open stage it is easier to see what scenes do and what scenes do not require localization. In the Chinese theatre, unlocalized scenes are few, but certainly present, for example, when a character speaks the self-introducing solilioquy and then proceeds to carry out the intentions he expresses, he is on the unlocalized stage until he becomes involved in the subsequent action. In the Elizabethan theatre, scenes in the comedies, which gain nothing by definite location, are usually vaguely laid in a town, for instance, in *The Comedy of Errors.* [10] Unlocalized scenes are the heritage of the interludes and moralities which preceded the Elizabethan dramas and the farce which preceded the Chinese. Take, for example, the farce of Sung dynasty in which a player satirized the greed and corruption of a governor by appearing at a palace performance in the guise of an earth-god [11] of a certain province and explained that even he had become the property of the governor. In this case the locality is understood to be the palace itself, the locality of the action coincides with that of the performance and there is no need to define it. In another farce, in which the actor, exploiting the then current plagiarism, played the poet Li I-Shan in tatters complaining that he had been relentlessly robbed, exact locality is irrelevant to the farcical effects. [12] In the moralities and interludes of sixteenth century England, with their abstract characters such as Grammar, Logic, Rhetoric, Geometry, Music and Astronomy (cf. Marston's *Histriomastix)* definite locality is superfluous if not inappropriate — the stage is to be considered purely as an acting space and scene-location has no meaning. In the farce and semi-moralities, with the admixture of some real personages, the locality was vaguely understood to be in England or London, and as drama of entirely real persons was developed, locality became more accurately defined. [13]

The application of modern mental habits to the study of Elizabethan theatre is hardly the best way to understand it. The perennial search for locality by modern readers of Shakespeare is due to the perennial scenery in the modern European theatre. To the Elizabethans a well written and well acted scene is beautiful wherever it is supposed to be. It is in the unlocalized scenes that W. Poel's sweeping statement is true:

---

[10] *Vide* Bradbrook, *Themes and Conventions,* 7. cf. Greek comedy which is vaguely located in Athens — Flickinger, *The Greek Theatre and Its Drama,* 206 f.

[11] 土地

[12] See Chapter XXII.

[13] Chambers, *Eliz. Stage,* III, 21-22, 24 f.

"There was only one locality recognized and that one was the platform, which projected to the centre of the auditorium where the story was recited". [14] According to Thorndike, in Shakespeare, definitely localized scenes were a minority, the scenes were mostly unlocalized or vaguely localized. [15]

In the unlocalized scenes the theatric aspect of the stage becomes prominent. This is particularly noticeable when the upper stage is used as unlocalized acting space. In the text the stage direction reads *"Above"*, and to the audience the actors in the upper stage are also merely "above", for example, in *Richard III,* III. vii. [16] Players upstage can become prominent in several ways, such as raising their level, flanking them with two rows of people stretching downstage, and facing the other players towards them. Unlocalized upper stage can only be understood as putting some players at a higher level and is in fact a matter of stage grouping. The Chinese players achieve the same effect by chairs and tables, as in scenes where a deity or spirit stands on a higher level at the back of the stage watching the action. [17]

As the Elizabethan and the Chinese drama require frequent changes of locality and as the changes are not aided by scenery, the chief problem of stagecraft is: how to indicate such changes to the audience. [18] As a rule, in both Chinese and Elizabethan theatres the change is indicated by the evacuation of the stage of all players [19] but occasionally the stage can represent two or more places successively with the players remaining on it. In the latter case a journey is always involved. The simplest case of this is exemplified in *Romeo and Juliet* I. iv.-v. in which Romeo and his companions go to Capulet's house and the stage is first the streets of Verona then the hall in Capulet's house. [20] Strictly speaking, the locality changes twice in all journey scenes: once from the starting place to the road and then from the road to the destination, the last locality being indicated at the correct moment by such devices as the opening of the curtain of the rear stage in the Elizabethan theatre and the coming forward of the host or enemy, as the case may be, in the Chinese theatre. [21] The Chinese stage can represent a room in an upper storey after the mime of mounting the stair; the actor does not leave the stage but he walks in a special way for a short distance. In a similar manner, in Marston's *Sophonisba,* Act IV, the characters go from a bedroom to a wood and back without leaving the stage. When the stage represents the battlefield, as it often does in the Elizabethan and the

---

[14] W. Poel, *Shakespeare in the Theatre,* 43.

[15] Thorndike, *Shakespeare's Theatre,* 102 *et seq.*

[16] *Vide* Reynolds, *Red Bull,* 105 f; Lawrence, *Elizabethan Playhouse, First series,* 7.

[17] e.g. in the modern play *The Strange Retribution* 奇冤報.

[18] cf. R. C. Rhodes, *The Stagery of Shakespeare* (1922), 76.

[19] Chambers, *Eliz. Stage,* III. 102, 121, Chapter XXI. *passim.*

[20] For other examples see Reynolds. Some Principles of Elizabethan Staging, Pt. II. *Modern Philology,* Vol. III. pp. 75-6; Chambers, *Eliz. Stage,* III. 99 f.

[21] *Vide* Reynolds, *Red Bull,* 103.

Chinese theatre, it has sometimes to be divided into two parts for the two opposing camps, as in *Richard III,* V. iii, and in such scenes, as the second army enters, half of the stage changes its locality to become its camp, even though the other army remains on the stage all the time. [22]

In all other cases, change of locality is accompanied by entrance and exit, hence the convention governing them is the key to the *mise-en-scène* of the theatre.[23]These conventions affect the dialogue and the dramatic construction to a greater extent than is obvious at first sight.

The Chinese convention of stage entrances is extremely simple: there are only two doorways at the back of the stage, and the one on stage right is the entrance and the other, the exit. When all players have left the stage *through the stage exit* and some players enter by the stage entrance the locality of the stage has to be re-defined. There is usually, but not always, a change of locality in such a manoeuvre, for example, the same scene may be occupied successively by two different groups of characters who do not meet each other. If a player leaves by the entrance door he must return by the same door and it is understood that he returns to the same scene, and similarly if after his exit he re-enters by the exit door the locality remains unchanged and he must leave again by the same door — these are not repeated, but merely hesitant entrances and exits.

The Elizabethan convention is similar but not identical. Change of locality is also indicated by the evacuation and re-occupation of the stage, [24] but there the analogy ends, for there are more than two entrances to the Elizabethan stage and their uses, in so far as entrances and exits are concerned, are undifferentiated. Rhodes [25] mentions Poel's theory of the use of the two stage doors, one for entrances and one for exits, "a statement which he reiterated", but the theory cannot be true because multiple entry was often used, as, for example, in the opening tableau of Marston's *Sophonisba,* and in *Richard III,* III. vii, *"Enter Richard and Buckingham at severall Doores".* A modified form of the theory is proposed by Watkins:

> "The fact that one character or group of characters has gone out of one door means that the next-comer will enter by the other — to avoid the appearance of their having met each other". [26]

---

[22] *Vide* Reynolds, *Modern Philology,* Vol. 3. p. 77.

[23] cf. 齊如山，上下場 ; Anna Spitzbarth, *Untersuchungen zur Spieltechnik der Griechischen Tragödie* (1946), VIII. *Die Formen des Auf- und Abtretens;* Mary Johnston, *Exits and Entrances in Roman Comedy* (1933); K. Rees, The Significance of the Paradoi in the Greek Theatre, *The Amer. Journ. Phil.* XXXII. 1911.

[24] Reynolds, Two Conventions of the Elizabethan Stage, *Mod. Phil.* XVII. (1919).

[25] Rhodes, *Stagery of Shakespeare,* 93.

[26] Watkins, *On Producing Shakespeare,* 73.

The theory is put forward on the ground of its simplicity and its contribution to the clarity of dramatic action. But for the entrance from the rear stage, which is often necessary in the Elizabethan drama, the convention is almost identical with the Chinese stage practice. The theory may be true, but not owing to its simplicity, because multiple entrance, for the use of which no doubt can be entertained, [27] makes the proposed convention more complicated than it looks. Thus, it is supposed that in *Hamlet* V. i. Hamlet and Horatio enter by one door and the funeral procession, to suggest coming from a different place, enters by another. According to the "simple" rule, the Gravediggers must enter by a third door and the royal couple and Laertes in the previous scene leave perhaps by a fourth. [28] Multiple entrances being extensively used in Elizabethan dramas it is doubtful whether the consequent constant rotation of the use of the stage doors would contribute towards clarity, or is possible in successive multiple entries. [29] Separate entrance and exit were probably only used when two consecutive scenes of different locality were manned by the same characters as in *Hamlet* I. iv.-v. where in order to gain privacy, the Ghost lures Hamlet to follow him; exeunt Ghost and Hamlet; Marcellus and Horatio follow, but lose them; then the Ghost and Hamlet enter by another door and the stage becomes a different part of the battlement. [30] Again, in *Second Maidens Tragedy, "Exit"* the Tyrant from a court room scene (1.1719) and five lines later *"Enter the Tirant agen at a farder dore, which opened, bringes hym to the Toombe"*. [31] Indeed the Elizabethan stage could not have the simple two-doors convention of the Chinese theatre because it had several other avenues of access than the stage doors: from the rear stage, from the cellar through the trap door, from above through the ceiling, jumping or climbing down from the upper stage and, occasionally, coming up from the yard. If a simple and easy convention had been adopted in the Elizabethan theatre the problems of Elizabethan staging would not have been the object of so much labour and controversy. [32]

The use of the stage doors was not however *ad hoc*; some rules must have

---

[27] Chambers, *Eliz. Stage,* III. 73.

[28] *Vide* Watkins, *op.cit.,* 73.

[29] The "simple" convention becomes complicated in this case because the differentiated *function* of the stage doors — for entrance and exit — is confused with differentiated *locality*. If we follow the former convention — of differentiated function — Horatio and Hamlet should enter by the same door as the funeral procession, as the scene would be played on the Chinese stage. Or, if we follow the latter convention — of differentiated locality — they should enter by a separate door to denote coming from a different place. When the two are mixed complication results, because the place of an entrance may be the same as that of the previous exit.

[30] *Vide* Lawrence, *Pre-Restoration Stage Studies,* 109-110.

[31] Other examples in Chambers, *Eliz. Stage,* III. 126 n; Reynolds, Some Principles of Elizabethan Staging, Pt. II., *Mod. Phil.* Vol. III. pp. 75-76.

[32] *Vide* Reynolds, *Red Bull,* 115-30.

governed it.

"And first obserue your doors of entrance, and your exit; not much unlike the players at the theatres; keeping your decorums, even in fantasticality. As for example: if you prove to be a northern gentleman, I would wish you to pass through the north door, more often especially than any of the other; and so, according to your countries, take note of your entrances". [33]
The convention was probably one of occasional differentiated locality.

The difference between the Elizabethan and the Chinese stage doors begins in their construction. The Elizabethan stage doors are large, about eight or nine feet high, and of sturdy make, because not only soldiers with colours, pikes, scaling ladders, and cressets on poles but also conquerors standing upright in chariots can go through them. [34] There are two leaves which swing into the tiring house and they are fitted with knockers, locks and wicket doors, the knockers sometimes on both the stage side and the other side. [35] The wicket door is used by the prompter but sometimes by actors as well, for instance, when two characters talk with each other across the closed door, [36] thus the space beyond the stage doors is sometimes used as acting space as in the Chinese theatre. There are also door posts, which sometimes serve dramatic purposes. [37] The rear stage may also have a door and window at the back. [38]

The origin of the Elizabethan stage doors is not definitely known; Lawrence thinks it might have come from the doors at the end of banquet halls, [39] and, probably through Italian influence, they became connected with the scene-location in the Elizabethan drama. [40] Throughout the Elizabethan period and in fact even as late as 1639 the playwright conveyed essential information to the audience by inscriptions, such as "I am a Prodigall" written on the breast of a prodigal (in *A Tricke to Cheat the Divell,* acted 1639) and the inscribed bannerets in the procession in Beaumont and Fletcher's *Four Plays in One.* [41] Now, on the Roman stage definite stable locality was allocated to the stage entrances so that as a rule a character who left the stage by a particular door must return by the same door [42] and on the "Terence stage" of Renaissance Europe problems of locality were solved

---

[33] T. Dekker, *The Gull's Hornbook,* Ch. iv. 2nd para.

[34] J. C. Adams, *The Globe Playhouse,* 149; Chambers, *Eliz. Stage,* III. 75.

[35] Adams, *The Globe Playhouse,* 150-3; Reynolds, *Red Bull,* 115 *et seq.*

[36] Adams, *The Globe Playhouse,* 155 f.

[37] *Ibid.,* 163-6.

[38] *Ibid.,* 177-203.

[39] Lawrence, *Elizabethan Playhouse, First series,* 6.

[40] *Ibid.,* 44.

[41] *Ibid.,* 54.

[42] In other words the convention of the stage doors was one of differentiated locality — see Beare, *The Roman Stage,* 173.

by labelled openings at the back of the stage. [43] Similar labels are known to have been used on the Elizabethan stage. [44] Occasionally the locality board might have been held by the prologue or some player. [45] Even when it was on the door, it was understood to designate either the locality of the place the characters came from or went to when they passed through it, or, in a vague way, also the locality of the stage after the characters had made their entrance through that door.

It can be noticed that whereas on the Chinese stage the locality of the acting space is defined by action or dialogue thereby determining that of the entrance and exit door, in the Elizabethan theatre when locality boards were used the process was the reverse: the locality of the acting space followed that of the doors. When locality boards were not used, the Elizabethan dramatists located their scenes in much the same way as the Chinese except for the more frequent use of realistic properties. [46] Theoretically, there are three localities on the open stage which require definition, where the characters come from (entrance), where they go to (exit), and where they are (acting space), but in practice, in most scenes, it is necessary to define only one of them because the locality of the others may then become self-evident or it may be immaterial. On the Chinese stage, the locality of the exit can be defined by the action, but the audience cannot easily be informed of the locality of the entrance — though it can sometimes be done, as in *P'ing Kuei's Return* [47] which begins with off stage singing, "With my horse I leave the border of Hsi Liang". As the locality board was not prevalently used in the Elizabethan public theatres, Elizabethan scene-location as a rule started with the acting space. [48]

Before analyzing the use of the stage doors in the Elizabethan and the Chinese theatre, a distinction may first be made between the stage-entrances and doors represented on the stage. The stage entrance is an opening through which the actors approach or leave the stage, it is a theatric feature which need not be connected with the action, and the door represented in the drama is part of the setting, belonging to the dramatic action, and may be real as in modern European theatres, or imaginary, as in Chinese theatres. In the Chinese theatre, the two are physically distinct, the entrances are openings on the back wall of the stage, never representing any door and the doors in the drama are always imaginary and exist only through the actors' miming. Some difficulties in the reconstruction of the Elizabethan method of

---

[43] Nicoll, *Development of the Theatre,* 83.

[44] Lawrence, *Elizabethan Playhouse, First series,* Ch. III; Chambers, *Eliz. Stage,* III. 122, 126, 137, 154; W. W. Greg, *Dramatic Documents* (1931), xi; Thorndike, *Shakespeare's Theatre,* 132; Reynolds, *Mod. Phil.* Vol. II. No. 4, p. 600 *et seq.*

[45] W. Poel, *Bulletin of the John Rylands Library,* Vol. 3. No. 1, p. 220.

[46] Bradbrook, *Themes and Conventions,* 10 f.

[47] 武家坡

[48] Lawrence, *Elizabethan Playhouse, First series,* 14, 65.

staging would not have occurred if the Elizabethan players had not combined the stage entrances with the doors in the drama and made the stage doors on the tiring house facade serve both purposes. When the scene is unlocated or when the stage doors have no geographical locations, the doorways are stage entrances and the doors, with their locks and knockers, have to be ignored. With the use of the more realistic stage properties on the Elizabethan stage, the stage doors sometimes also serve as part of the stage setting of the interior or facade of houses. In this capacity they form part of the scene instead of being features of the theatre building. The Elizabethans apparently found no difficulty in now ignoring the door fixtures [49] now accepting them as part of the scene, but when they are taken as scenic doors in *two consecutive* scenes difficult problems in staging can arise, for example, when the first scene is indoors and the second outdoors with the stage side of the doors representing successively the two sides of the house doors. Such a case can be found in *Arden of Feversham,* Act III, in which the stage represents the inside of a house in one scene and the outside in the next. [50] Here the dramatist is faced with a problem unknown to Chinese and modern European playwrights, namely, to signal to the audience the changed significance of the stage door. Apparently the only means at his disposal is the dialogue. The difficulty is increased when a large piece of property remains on the stage throughout the scenes, as in *II Iron Age.* Here a scene begins with the Trojans outside the city congratulating themselves on the departure of the Greeks and finding the horse they left behind. They leave the stage. The Greeks from the fleet enter and hide in ambush — this scene being still outside the city. *"Enter Synon with a torch aboue"* and Ulysses says, "Now with a soft march enter at this breach" and the stage direction reads *"They march softly in at one doore and presently in at another".* Then the Greeks "leape from out the Horse . . ." The scene of course changes from the outside to the inside of the city at Ulysses' order but the audience are supposed to see one side of the doors as the Trojans go into the city and another as the Greeks enter the city, and the horse is supposed to have been moved from one scene to another. [51] The change is indicated in a roundabout way: when the Greeks enter and hide in ambush they are probably passing over the stage, leaving the stage empty; at *"They march softly in at one doore"* they enter again and where they stand the stage still represents ground outside the city, and at *"and presently in at another"* they must have left the stage momentarily and enter again by another door, then the stage represents ground inside the city. Throughout this scene, the stage doors sometimes serve as city gate and sometimes as stage entrances (for example, from the fleet) and their significance changes with kaleidoscopic rapidity.

---

[49] Chambers, *Eliz. Stage,* III. 75 — door as theatrical feature.

[50] For details see Reynolds, *Red Bull,* 115 f.

[51] Reynolds, *Red Bull,* 113 f.

The stage doors, opening into the tiring house, do not satisfy all the requirements of scenic doors because in some scenes both the ground inside and that outside the door have to be visible to the audience. Thus in *The Golden Age* there is a scene in which Jupiter sneaks into the tower in which Danae is held. First *"Enter Iupiter like a Pedler, the Clowne his man, with packs at their backes"*. They are outside the tower. Later, *"He rings the bell. Enter the 4 Beldams"* one of them saying, "To the gate, to the gate, and know who 'tis ere you open". After some dialogue one of the women invites Jupiter into the Porter's lodge and a little later one of them says, "Shut the gate for feare the King come, and if he ring clap the Pedlers into some of yon old rotten corners". [52] Here, not only are two parties both on the stage supposed to be on the opposite sides of the gate but the gate is actually closed after one party has entered it. It is not known how this was represented on the Elizabethan stage. In the neo-classical tradition, semi-interior scenes are understood to be located in front of the house where domestic discussions can take place, and Chambers cited many examples of similar scenes, called "threshold scenes", in the Elizabethan dramas, where the scene is supposed to be the porch or lobby. [53] The convention apparently arises from the need to represent either the outside and the inside of the door simultaneously or a continuous scene starting out-of-doors leading to action indoors. In both cases, unless the porch is considered "indoors" an imaginary gate or door is implied, as on the Chinese stage, although the Elizabethans probably did not open and close it in mime. In *Taming of a Shrew*, Induction 1, *"Enter a Tapster, beating out of his doores Slie Droonken"* suggests that the stage is partly indoors and partly outdoors. Similar interpretation is suggested by *Soliman and Perseda,* Sc. vii. (a Senator's) "What make you lingering here about my doores?" and *Humorous Day's Mirth,* Sc. v. (Moren's) "Thrust this ass out of the doors", and in the same scene, "Well, come in, sweet bird". The assumption of the porch dispenses with the opening and closing of the imaginary door or gate, but occasionally this might not be avoidable, as in *Knack to Know an Honest Man,* Sc. ix (Lelio's) "Heaue me the doores from of the hinges straight", and Sc. xv. (Lelio's) "my door doth ope". The modern reluctance to assume that there was a convention which permitted invisible doors like those of the Chinese theatre is perhaps influenced by the consideration that the Elizabethans were used to the real scenic doors in the stage doors. The Chinese have no difficulties with their scenic doors because they are entirely imaginary and are understood to disappear automatically when all the players have left the stage and the scene has to be relocated. By the use of mime characters on the stage are understood to be on either one or the other side of a door. Entering a city is an action often represented and this is done by the symbolic city gate being held by stage hands near the exit door (stage

---

(52) *Vide* Reynolds, *Red Bull,* 126.

(53) *Vide* Chambers, *Eliz. Stage,* III, 59-65.

left), the army walking through it disappearing into the backstage, and re-entering by the entrance door, then the scene becomes inside the city.

It has been found that at least in some Elizabethan public theatres the rear stage was a temporary and removable structure. [54] Then, when the rear stage is not used, the Elizabethan stage is, on the stage level, identical with the Chinese stage. Yet the use of the stage doors is fundamentally different on the two stages: first, whereas the Chinese stage doors had separate functions, the Elizabethan stage doors represent different localities and second, in the Chinese theatre stage entrance and scenic doors are distinct but in the Elizabethan they are often the same. The separate functions of the Chinese stage doors result in a simple convention, but the differentiated locality of the Elizabethan stage doors allows multiple entry from different places. [55] On the Chinese stage, double entry can only be made when one party is coming from afar (for example, an approaching army) and the other party having just been on the stage now reappears from the exit door (for example, a stationary army coming out from their camp). The Chinese convention also makes all entrances and exits purely theatric; they become formalized and are in fact the opening and closing sequence of a dance, with the quality of the introduction and coda in music.

The permanent fixtures on the tiring house facade are sometimes scenic features and sometimes parts of the theatre building, and when they are unwanted in the stage setting, they have to be ignored. The rear stage, for example, was sometimes called "chamber" or "study", that is, a room in the drama, and sometimes "cabinet" or "closet", a stage fixture. [56] The real doors can sometimes be used to heighten dramatic effects, as in the electrifying knockings in the murder scene in *Macbeth*. The Elizabethan stage is a mixture of neutral acting space and permanent scenic fixtures, the Elizabethan theatre is a mixture of imagination and spectacle, of convention and realism, and, it may not be far-fetched to say, the dramas are mixtures of poetry and sensationalism.

(7)

The wide variety of scenes in the Elizabethan and Chinese dramas makes it impossible to build realistic setting and to stage realistic action, for example, in battles, in journeys and in shipwrecks. The platform stage is made to represent what only the best equipped film studio of to-day can reproduce with any degree of

---

[54] Reynolds, *Red Bull*, Ch. VII.

[55] cf. *Cymbeline*, V. ii, where, like the Chinese stage armies, the opposing forces at first share the stage supposedly without seeing each other — see Reynolds, *Mod. Phil*. Vol. II, No. 4, p. 600.

[56] Reynolds, *Red Bull*, 135.

similitude. As the stage and the action usually cannot look like what they represent, they are, as the chorus in *Henry V* stated, only symbols, not reproductions, and as symbols, their meanings have to be learned. The tacit agreement between the producer and the audience on the correspondence between symbols and their meanings constitutes stage conventions. The need for conventions is the same in the Elizabethan and the Chinese theatre — indeed it is the same for all open stages — but the details differ, because as a whole the Elizabethan playwrights had more properties at their command than their Chinese counterparts. The conventions of entrances and exits and of the locality of scenes have been dealt with; some other conventions will be discussed in the following.

Modern playwrights avoid journeying scenes because they cannot be easily staged in a realistic way, but the Elizabethan and Chinese dramatists, who have less facilities to stage them, employ them freely, because their audience look upon the stage more as a stage than modern Europeans do. The manner of representation is the same in the two theatres, namely, by "marching about the stage" as the stage direction indicates when Romeo and his friends go to Juliet's home. [57] The Elizabethan audience must have the same type of imagination as the audience of the moving picture, in which the camera's eye follows the travelling people and the same screen represents successively different parts of the journey till they reach the destination, because in a journeying scene the stage represents, in effect, such a "moving" locality. In the Chinese theatre the shift from the normal stationary scene to the "moving" scene is sometimes indicated by the travellers saying aloud,

> "Walking and walking,
> Turning this way — round that corner". [58]

The actual amount of walking done is very small on the Chinese stage, usually one small circle, occasionally two, and this gross discrepancy between the real and stage journey is frankly stated by the travellers who sometimes recite during the journey:

> "Three or five steps from my door
> Presently — this must be his house". [59]

Similar degree of abbreviation was achieved in Greene's *Pinner of Wakefield,* IV, iii, where in a single line of the text, the characters move from one end of the town to the other. [60] Scenes in which travellers walk around the stage and then the host at their destination enters to meet them are very common in the Chinese theatre. In *2 If You Know Not Me,* too, troops start from Tilbury, and *"As they march about*

---

[57] *Romeo and Juliet,* I. iv. v.

[58] "行行走走，轉灣抹角" This formula is used particularly often in dramas of Ming dynasty.

[59] "出門三五步，咫尺是他家".

[60] Hodges, *Globe Restored,* 67.

the stage, Sir Francis Drake and Sir Martin Furbisher meet them''.

The convention is sometimes disguised in the Elizabethan dramas. When Romeo hears of Juliet's death, he decides to go to Verona and orders horses, then,

> "Well, Juliet, I will lie with thee to-night,
> Let's see for means: O mischief! thou art swift
> To enter in the thoughts of desperate men.
> I do remember an apothecary,
> And hereabouts he dwells, which late I noted". (38)

A vivid description of the shop follows, and then in lines 55-57:

> "As I remember, this should be the house:
> Being holiday, this beggar's shop is shut.
> What, ho! apothecary!"
>
> *Enter apothecary*

Romeo is on the stage all the time but moves from the vicinity of the shop to its front between "hereabouts he dwells" and "this should be the house", the description of the shop taking up the time for the journey. There is no shop visible on the stage during the journey, therefore the apothecary has to have a holiday and poetry has to fill the function of scenery.

Sometimes two stationary scenes may be linked by a journeying scene without any breaks and in such cases the properties in the first stationary scene are substituted by those of the second while the journey lasts. There is no special name for this convention in the Chinese theatre, but in the Elizabethan theatre, when the journey is implied, modern scholars call it a "split" scene, and a possible example is in *1 If You Know Not Me*. [61] The first stationary scene shows Queen Mary and her court and in this scene a commission is dispatched to visit Elizabeth. In the second stationary scene, the stage direction reads, *"Enter Elizabeth, in her bed",* meaning, probably, that she is discovered in bed in the rear stage. There are some thirty-five lines in which the throne in the first scene may be substituted by the bed in the second, and a journey is understood to have taken place even though the players remain on the stage. [62] For such scenes, one of the formulae spoken by journeying characters on the Chinese stage is apposite:

> "The stage is a small place, but
> One turn is ten thousand miles". [63]

The apparent unreasonableness of the compression is entirely a matter of mental habit.

> "We are accustomed still to the convention of dramatic time by which we

---

[61] *Vide* Reynolds, *Red Bull,* 59 n.

[62] For examples of foreshortened space both in stationary and in journeying scenes see Chambers, *Eliz. Stage,* III, 99 f.

[63] "戲台方寸地，一轉萬里山"

allow two hours to pass in ten minutes, or, in the act interval, twenty years in a quarter of an hour. We have lost the very similar convention of dramatic distance, if one may coin a new term, which, no more illogically or unreasonably, allowed two feet to represent as many miles and annihilated space as the other does time". [64]

It is for the convention both of time and of place that the chorus in *Henry V, I.* pleads:

> "For 'tis your thoughts that now must deck our kings,
> Carry them here and there, jumping o'er times,
> Turning the accomplishments of many years
> Into an hour-glass: . . ."

With the battle scenes arises the problem of horses on the stage. To serve realism requires circus facilities and even then it is doubtful whether the Chinese actors can sing as well on horseback as standing on the stage. As the Chinese and the Elizabethans do not demand realism the problem becomes one of providing a workable substitute.

Modern scholars are inclined to the view that no real horses appeared on the Elizabethan stage. [65] Horses however are sometimes indicated in the text, as in *Richard II (Thomas of Woodstock), III. ii, "Enter a spruce Courtier a horse-backe"*. Barrett Wendell [66] thinks that wickerwork hobby horses were used and they were tied to the actors' waists with false legs dangling from the saddles, the real legs being hid by long skirts. "Monstrous as such a proceeding seems, it might still occur in serious tragedy on the Chinese stage, and the Chinese stage is very like the Elizabethan". [67]

Hobby horses are not used on the Chinese stage now, but they were used in Yüan (1277-1367) and Ming (1368-1643) dynasties. "Bamboo horse" is mentioned in two dramas printed in Yüan dynasty [68] and in another drama of Yüan [69] mounting and dismounting as well as descent from carriage are indicated. In a play of Ming dynasty [70] the stage directions read, *". . . calls for a horse . . . the property brought in . . . rides on bamboo horse . . . exit . . . on bamboo horse"*. The famous drama of Ming dynasty, *P'i P'a Chi* 琵琶記（十齣）mentions the horse extensively, as

---

[64] Reynolds, *Mod. Phil.* Vol. 3, p. 79.

[65] *Vide* Lawrence, *Pre-Restoration Stage Studies,* 270-5; Reynolds, *Red Bull,* 87.

[66] *William Shakespeare* (1902), 308.

[67] For similar opinion by Chambers, see *Eliz. Stage,* III, 75 n; see also W. J. Lawrence, Horses on the Elizabethan Stage, *Times Literary Supplement,* 5 June, 1919.

[68] 元槧三十種：蕭何追韓信"尾"；霍光鬼諫"賺煞尾"，參，李太白貶夜郎，"衮綉球"．

[69] 隔江鬪智，二折，諸葛亮白，四折，趙雲白．

[70] （宣德憲藩本）朱有燉，曲江池，三折 Another edition （雜劇十段錦）mentions "horse" only.

"falls from a horse" and "rides a horse". [71] It is not known exactly how these scenes were acted but on the modern Chinese stage the whip is always used to denote that the horse, though invisible, is supposed to be on the stage.

Perhaps owing to the relative docility of the ass, the animal is used occasionally on the Chinese stage, as in the farce *The Visit and Row of the In-Laws* [72] and real asses were also used in the Elizabethan theatre as in *Soliman and Perseda,* I. iv, *"Piston getteth vp on his Asse, and rideth with him to the doore".* [73] At the end of the seventeenth century actors could speak the epilogue on it. [74] Disguised actors were also probably used in English theatres, as they are in the Chinese, but they, unlike the Chinese actors, were not just for appearance, for they carried riders. [75] It was not until 1668 at the Theatre Royal that real horses appeared. [76]

In the *Rape of Lucrece,* Tullia is described as driving her chariot across her father's body, but this Reynolds believes to be merely a "rhetorical flourish". [77] Horses appear to be sometimes inconsistently avoided by Elizabethan dramatists. In *Sir Thomas Wyatt,* Guilford and Jane are directed to ride to the Tower but the stage direction reads, *"A dead march, and passe round the stage".* [78] In *Macbeth,* III. i, Banquo goes riding with his son:

Macbeth   Ride you this afternoon?
Banquo   Ay, my good lord.

and in III. iii, the murder scene, we read,

Third Murderer   Hark, I hear horses.

and three lines later,

First Murderer   His horses go about.

Just as the horses are about to appear, however, they are explained away:

Third Murderer   . . . but he does usually,
                    So all men do, from hence to the palace gate
                    Make it their walk.

Conspicuous omissions of the horses can also be found in *Doctor Faustus,* Sc. II. and *Cymbeline,* IV. i. [79] If there were real horses on the stage the chorus in *Henry*

---

(71) （參，元明雜劇，單鞭奪槊，三折）.

(72) 探親相罵

(73) *Vide* T. S. Graves, The Ass as Actor, *South Atlantic Quarterly,* Vol. VX. 1916, pp. 175-82.

(74) See Lawrence, *Elizabethan Playhouse, First series,* Ill, facing p. 169.

(75) Henslowe's inventory of the properties belonging to the Admiral's Men in 1598 includes one lion, two lion's heads, a lion s skin, a bear's skin, a bear's head and a black dog. Lawrence, *Those Nut-Cracking Elizabethans,* II. For the problem of animals on the Elizabethan Stage see *ibid.,* Ch. II.

(76) *Vide* Lawrence, *Pre-Restoration Stage Studies,* 276.

(77) Reynolds, *Red Bull,* 87.

(78) *Ibid.,* 87.

(79) For other examples see Lawrence, *Pre-Restoration Stage Studies,* 275; Reynolds, *Red Bull,* 87.

V, I., would not have asked the audience to

"Think when we talk of horses that you see them

Printing their proud hoofs i' the receiving earth".

In battle scenes, for example, *1 Henry VI,* III. iii, and *King Lear,* V. i. horses are entirely omitted. Whether or not the Elizabethan audience understood that part of the armies were on horseback it is difficult to say. On the Chinese stage, fighting warriors, though understood to be on horseback, do not carry the whips. Occasionally the English stage-horse came very near to the Chinese: in *Look About You,* at the beginning, is the direction *"Enter Robert Hood, a young nobleman, a servant with him with riding wands in their hands, as if they have been new-lighted".* Hood tells his servant, "Go walk the horses, wait me on the hill", and later he cries, "Holla, there — my horse", just before his exit. [80]

The Chinese convention of the stage horse, like other Chinese stage conventions, is versatile: an actor can be shown not only riding a horse, but also mounting and dismounting it, leading it and tying and untying it. The Elizabethans appear to prefer adjustments in the text to avoid horses, and when this is not successful, to ignore them altogether, as in *Macbeth,* I. iii, in which when Macbeth and Banquo meet the Witches they must be on horseback, so must Ross and Angus be when they enter, and yet no horses are mentioned. To the Chinese, the representation has to be theoretically correct, though the horse need not be actually seen; they can imagine a horse when they see a whip but they cannot imagine a warrior without a horse.

In theatres without scenery the audience must imagine what they do not see as well as ignore what they do see. The Elizabethans, like the Chinese, had to ignore many objects which were on the stage with the actors, such as the gallants, unwanted properties, musicians, stage hands and unwanted stage fixtures. The rear stage, for example, had to be ignored when the stage represented the open space, and the gallants, though their dress was not very unlike the actors', must be excluded from the attention. According to some scholars, stage furniture and built sets used in the previous scene or required in the following one could, by convention, be left on the stage. [81] "This convention allowed the presence upon the stage of a property or furnishing which was incongruous to the scene in progress, and which, during that scene, was thought of as absent, though standing in plain sight. This incongruity took two forms: either the close juxtaposition upon the stage of two properties which in reality should have been a much greater distance apart or the presence of a property in a scene where it could never naturally have been, as a tree, for example, in the midst of a room scene". [82] Reynolds' theory is mainly supported by analysis

---

[80] Lawrence, *Those Nut-Cracking Elizabethans,* 23.

[81] Reynolds, Trees on the Stage of Shakespeare, *Mod. Phil.* Vol. V, 153-168.

[82] Reynolds, Some Principles of Elizabethan Staging, *Mod. Phil.* Vol. 3, p. 69.

of the text, but the practicability of the convention is shown on the Chinese stage, the rear part of which is always a temporary storeroom for the property man.

On the open stage, all property has to be brought in and removed in full view of the audience and stage hands as well as actors appear on the stage. The Chinese property man is an important member of the company: he has to possess thorough knowledge and accurate memory of all the plays in the repertoire and he must not make even momentary mistakes if the performance is to progress smoothly. The Elizabethan stage hands were probably under the direction of the prompter and thus correspond to the assistants of the Chinese property man. They wore the blue coats of serving men, a dress surviving with little modification in the Christ's Hospital, and bore the badge of their master in silver, since they were officially the servants of noble households. [83] The work of the Chinese property man was partly done in the Elizabethan theatre by the characters in the drama. For example, in banquet-scenes, the chairs, table and food were brought in by the servants in the drama, [84] occasionally even by prominent characters, [85] and curtains were sometimes drawn by important personages. [86] The stage hands had to be constantly busy on the Elizabethan stage because furniture was brought in a few moments before it was used and removed immediately after it had served its purpose, as on the Chinese stage. The reason for this is the same in the two theatres: space is required for action. [87] Archer believed that convention permitted the stage hands to remove inanimate objects but not dead bodies [88] but it seems unlikely that there was such a general convention. There is no indication that the dead bodies on the Elizabethan stage, like those on the Chinese, stood up and walked away. At the end of *Hamlet,* the bodies are borne away by the soldiers, but, for *Romeo and Juliet* and *Othello,* the last stage direction is simply *"Exeunt"* and if, the play being over, the dead do not walk away they must be carried away by the stage hands, because those in the drama have already left the scene. In the middle of a play bodies appear also to be removed by stage hands, as in Banquo's murder scene (*Macbeth,* III. iii.) where the last line is

> *First Murderer*   Well, let's away, and say how much is done. [89]

The Chinese method was in fact suggested for the English stage: in *The Rehearsal,* over a stage strewn with corpses Smith asks Bayes, "How shall all these dead men go off? — for I see none alive to help 'em", and Bayes replies, "Go off, why, as they

[83]   W. Poel, *Bulletin of the John Rylands Library,* Vol. 3, No. 1, p. 222.

[84]   Albright, *Shakesperian Stage,* 137-40.

[85]   Chambers, *Eliz. Stage,* III, 112-3.

[86]   Lawrence, *Physical Conditions,* 49.

[87]   *Vide,* Lawrence, *Those Nut-Cracking Elizabethans,* 118.

[88]   W. Archer, *The Quarterly Review,* Vol. 208, No. 415, p. 45.

[89]   On the removal of dead bodies on the English stage see Lawrence, *Those Nut-Cracking Elizabethans,* Ch. VI. Bearers of the Dead.

came on; upon their legs: how should they go off? Why do you think the people here don't know they are not dead?" [90] At least on one occasion the Chinese method was, by force of circumstances, used: Mrs. Hamilton, a popular actress in the mid-eighteenth century, was in *Tamerlane* and died in a chair as Arpasia; the stage hands found it difficult to remove the chair, on account of her size and weight; and she, irritated by the audience's laughter, ordered them to stop their struggles, stood up, curtsied and walked off the stage. [91]

There are reasons to believe that the stage hands were called "stage keepers" in Elizabethan times and that they wore terrible masks besides their blue uniform and remained on the stage throughout the performance serving several more functions than property and curtain movements. [92] The "stage keeper" was also a cleaner, for he swept the stage and "gathered broken apples"; and the beadle, for he kept order, especially between the gallants on the stage and the groundlings and bound cut-purses to the post on the stage; and the waiter, serving the gallants on the stage with pipe and tobacco; and the supernumerary, serving as a guard or a soldier in battle scenes. The uniform distinguished him from the actors and showed his presence to potential trouble-makers but the function of the false face is not as clear. Hotson believes that it "reduced them to suitable impersonality and terrified the trouble-makers" — for, as he points out, town whippers also wore terrible masks [93] — but, if it were terrifying its powerful theatrical appeal would have made it very distracting to the audience. The dark clothes of the Chinese property man are considered sufficient to reduce him to inconspicuousness, but the Japanese stage hands also "cover their faces with a black veil". [94]

Musicians formed an indispensable part of the Elizabethan theatre and were in service at every performance. When they played for processions, funerals, dumb shows and scenes which required soft music or "hellish" music, they were out of sight, being in the "music room" somewhere behind and over the stage. [95] Sometimes they played on the stage, as a dance band, and then they acted as the musicians in the drama and were given a few lines, [96] as, for example, in *Romeo and Juliet,* IV. v, and *Othello,* III. i. This practice, which lasted until the early years of the eighteenth century, [97] is, in a way, more realistic than the modern practice of accompanying incidental songs with the orchestra in the pit, thus having the singer in the world of the drama and his accompanists in the world of the audience, yet, as

---

[90] Lawrence, *op. cit.,* 78 f.

[91] Bellamy, *Apology,* quoted in Lawrence, *op. cit.,* 82.

[92] L. Hotson, False Faces on Shakespeare's Stage. *Times Literary Supplement,* 16 May, 1952.

[93] *Ibid.*

[94] 齊如山, 戲劇脚色名詞考, 八章, 頁三一.

[95] Lawrence, *Physical Conditions,* 85 f; Lawrence, *Elizabethan Playhouse, Second series,* 90 ff.

[96] Lawrence, *Elizabethan Playhouse, Second series,* 159.

[97] Lawrence, *Elizabethan Playhouse, Second series,* 160.

with the stage hands playing guards and soldiers, the musicians, wearing no make-up (which was unknown in the Elizabethan theatre), must be plainly recognizable to the audience. Like the lutanists who came on to the stage to accompany dramatic singers [98] the musicians in dancing scenes were probably considered by the audience as a theatric rather than dramatic feature. [99]

Night scenes on the Elizabethan stage, as on the Chinese, were indicated by dialogue and gestures as well as candles and lamps. [100] Acting in a supposedly dark scene appears to be very similar to that on the Chinese stage: a stage direction in *II The Iron Age* reads,

> *"Pyrhus, Diomed and the rest, leape from out the Horse, and, as if groping in the darke, meete with Agamemnon and the rest".*

Again, in Haughton's *Englishmen for My Money,* two characters, supposed to be groping in the dark, bump into the poles on the stage one after another and presently declare them to be maypoles. [101] Dreams were dumb shows in the Elizabethan theatre, [102] but in the Chinese theatre they are indicated by the dreamer who remains in the scene and starts and finishes a dream in a conventionalized sleeping position, and those in the dream cannot be dumb because the emotional significance of the dream usually requires them to do some singing.

The pillars on the Elizabethan stage are quite as versatile as the table on the Chinese stage. The pillar could be a tree, an obstruction for hiding, notice post, road-side cross, gates of a bridge or unidentified post for binding rogues. [103] They are sometimes worked into the stage business, as in *Englishmen for My Money,* Sc. vii-ix,

> "Watt be dis Post? . . . This Post; why tis the May-pole on Iuie-bridge going to Westminster . . . Soft, heere's an other: Oh now I know in deede where I am; wee are now at the fardest end of Shoredich, for this is the May-pole".

Jumps into water were also represented on the Elizabethan stage, as: *Locrine,* IV. v, *"Fling himselfe into the riuer",* and *Weakest Goeth to the Wall,* I. i, *"The Dutches of Burgundie . . . leaps into a Riuer, leauing the child vpon the banke".* [104] These scenes must be very similar to equivalent scenes on the Chinese stage because on a platform stage, the possible manners of staging them are extremely limited, being some sort of symbolic jump into an invisible river.

Two armies can march each on a half of the Chinese stage and supposedly

---

[98] Lawrence, *Physical Conditions,* 84.

[99] In the early Spanish theatre, the guitar-player was also on the stage — see Thorndike, *Shakespeare's Theatre,* 78, 93.

[100] Lawrence, *Pre-Restoration Stage Studies,* 128 f; Reynolds, *Red Bull,* 166.

[101] *Vide* Hodges, *Globe Restored,* 30. See below.

[102] Lawrence, *Elizabethan Playhouse, Second series,* 167.

[103] Reynolds, *Mod. Phil,* Vol. V, p. 160; J. C. Adams, *The Globe Playhouse,* 112.

[104] *Vide* Chambers, *Eliz. Stage,* III. 51.

not see each other, and something very similar can be found on the Elizabethan stage. In *Richard III,* V. iii, two armies, each with a tent, are on the stage and there is no contact and in *Cymbeline,* V. ii, two armies march in by separate doors, *"They march over and go out"*, and *"Then enter again in skirmish"*.

The general scheme for battles in the Elizabethan and the Chinese theatre consists of the parade of the armies, single combats and the march of the victorious side. Considering the importance of single combats in ancient warfare, this scheme is not altogether unrealistic, though the size of the armies has naturally to be symbolic only. [105] The parade may be considered as the journey-scene of the armies approaching each other and serves to show the audience that a war is imminent. In the single combat the stage is to be understood as a small portion of the battlefield, hence no other forces are in sight. The fighting in the Elizabethan theatre involved real fencing skill. [106] Large scale fighting was avoided on the Elizabethan stage and merely suggested by off stage noises, but is represented on the Chinese stage in a group display of acrobatics. [107] The apologetic chorus in *Henry V,* IV., admits:

> "We shall much disgrace
> With four or five most vile and ragged foils,
> Right ill disposed in brawl ridiculous
> The name of Agincourt. Yet sit and see:
> Minding true things by what their mockeries be".

The appearance of a riot on the Elizabethan stage may be surmised from an old stage direction. [108]

> *"Enter all the factions of noblemen, peasants and citizens fighting. The ruder sort drive in the rest, and cry: 'A sacke! A sacke! Havocke, havocke! Burne the lawiers bookes! Tear the silks out of the shops!' In that confusion, the scholler escaping from among them, they all go out, and leave him upon the stage"*.

Apart from any real havoc and confusion, there is here also commentary and report. Except in battles and processions, crowds are not shown on the Chinese stage.

Elizabethan and Chinese stage conventions also include complete symbolism which the uninitiated can never, without help, understand. A scene in the Chinese drama may show a man asleep, leaning on a desk, two boys make a "scissor cross" downstage (simultaneously crossing the stage in opposite directions) and the man wakes up. This means a sudden enlightenment or release from an evil spell and the two boys are "the two pages of Wen-Ch'ang", the god of literature. [109] In *The Platt*

---

[105] *Vide* Chambers, *Eliz. Stage,* III. 52-54.

[106] Watkins, *On Producing Shakespeare,* 83-97.

[107] See, for example, *Julius Caesar,* V; *Macbeth,* V. vi. vii; *King Lear,* V. i-iii.

[108] Quoted in W. Poel, *Bulletin of John Rylands Library,* Vol. 3, No. 1, p. 222.

[109] 文昌二童

of the Secound Parte of the Seven Deadlie Sinns, we find *"Henry speakes and Lidgate, Lechery passeth over the stag",* in *2 Henry IV, "Enter Rumour, painted full of tongues"* and in *Cambyses, "Shame with a black trumpet".* [110]

(8)

In the modern European theatre the world of the drama is kept rigorously distinct and separate from that of the audience. When the curtain is raised, the audience suddenly confronts this separate world in which the characters talk to each other but never to the audience and behave as if the audience does not exist. In the Chinese and the Elizabethan theatre, however, the prologue introduces the audience formally to the play and the characters in the drama now and then address the audience directly. The prologue is a player but does not belong to the drama; he speaks from the stage and is a part of the show, yet he converses with the audience. He is in fact a link between the two worlds.

It was the tradition of the southern dramas, a tradition upheld on the Chinese stage until the middle of Ch'ing dynasty, for the prologue [111] to address the audience in much the same way as a speaker nowadays would introduce his talk, in other words, he tries to put the audience in a sympathetic and receptive mood and he tells the name of the play and other relevant information which may arouse interest and assist appreciation. [112]

Although there is no fixed formula for the Elizabethan prologue, its aim and matter are not very dissimilar to the Chinese type. Thus,

> "Our Comedy or Interlude, which we intend to play
>
> Is named Royster Doyster, indeed,
>
> Which against the vainglorious doth inveigh,
>
> Whose humour the roysting continually doth feed".
>
> (Ralph Roister Doister, c.1551).

Instead of telling the audience the name of the play he might also hold the title board in his hand. [113] In *Wily Beguiled,* the prologue, like his brother in the dramas of Ming dynasty, asks a player the name of the play and is told, "Sir you may look vpon the Title". He complains that it is *"Spectrum* once again", and then the title board is changed to the right one. [114] Sometimes the prologue moves directly into the drama:

Lucifer   And now that I have vaulted up so high

Above the stage rails of this earthen Globe

---

[110] C. W. Hodges, *Globe Restored,* 77 f, 183.

[111] 家門

[112] See Ch. XXXI. Direct address was also used in early Spanish dramas — see Shoemaker, *The Multiple Stage in Spain During the Fifteenth and Sixteenth Centuries* (1935), 6.

[113] Lawrence, *Elizabethan Playhouse, First series,* Ch. III.

[114] cf. Ch. XXXI; *vide* Chambers, *Eliz. Stage,* III, 126 n.

<blockquote>
I must turn actor and join companies
. . . ."
</blockquote>

(Middleton, The Black Booke, 1604).

The prologue in the Chinese theatre was probably derived from the introduction with which the story-teller addressed his audience before he recited the tale, especially when story-telling took the semi-poetic form called chu-kung-tiao [115] in Sung dynasty, a form similar in several ways to the early Chinese dramas. The Elizabethan prologue, who represented the poet, had his ancestors in the chorus of the neo-classical tragedy, the presenter of dumb shows and the "exposytour" in the miracles and moralities. [116] It had a lasting effect on the Elizabethan drama, for Jonson and Marston were still using it at the beginning of the seventeenth century. [117]

The function of the prologue, however, is not confined to his capacity as the mouthpiece of the poet or manager in which he plays the host to the audience; he is also responsible for acquainting the audience with the background of the story so that they are not puzzled by the earlier part of the play. The latter function is that of the narrator as, for example, in Romeo and Juliet and Troilus and Cressida. In the Chinese theatre of to-day, this function is divided among the characters who introduce themselves in a narrative at their first entrance, for the information of the audience, and while they are delivering these soliloquies, they may be considered as playing the chorus temporarily. This device was used also in miracle plays, in which the personages "would convey information directly to the audience, not only of their circumstances, but of their feelings, motives and intentions", [118] but in the Elizabethan dramas, it is disguised into dialogue, for example, in Hamlet, I. i, Marcellus, after seeing the Ghost with Horatio, asks,

<blockquote>
"Good now, sit down, and tell me, he that knows,
Why this same strict and most observant watch
So nightly toils the subject of the land;
. . . ."
</blockquote>

It is a long question (ten lines), containing much information of the conditions in Denmark, and Horatio's is an even longer answer (twenty-eight lines), giving more information on the background of the play. Similar expository soliloquies can be found in Richard III, I.i. (by Gloucester) and King Lear, I. ii. (by Edmund). Sometimes the disguise is rather thin, as in As You Like It, I. i, where Orlando ostensibly complains to a servant about his plight but is in fact telling the audience

---

[115] 諸宮調

[116] Chambers, Eliz. Stage, II, 547. In some Elizabethan dramas there are more than one presenter: in The Old Wives' Tale there are four, in James IV, three — see Chambers, Eliz. Stage. III, 48, 92.

[117] Chambers, Eliz. Stage. II, 547 n.

[118] Bradbrook, Stage Conditions, 87.

about himself and his family troubles. In this scene, after a quarrel with Oliver, he and the servant retreat and Oliver is left to question Charles about the news at court.

Charles   There's no news at the court, sir, but the old news: that is, the old duke is banished by his younger brother the new duke; . . .

Charles reports "the old news" in great detail, taking care also to add that the "young brother" is "the new duke". Oliver, who is apparently not up-to-date with old news, asks whether the old duke's daughter was banished with him or not and other details of the background.

Disguised introductions can become embarrassingly obvious, as Sheridan showed in *The Critic,* II. ii.:

Sir Walter Raleigh   Philip, you know, is proud Iberia's king.
Sir Christ. Hatton   He is . . .
Sir Walter Raleigh   You also know —
Dangle   Mr. Puff, if Sir Christopher knows all this why does Sir Walter go on telling him?

Often, in the middle of a play, the audience should be told of the moods and designs of some of the characters. In the Chinese theatre the information is given to the audience in the candid self-introductions, but in Elizabethan dramas it is disguised in soliloquies. Arnold distinguishes between "verbal soliloquy", which is talking aloud to oneself and "mental soliloquy", which is silent thoughts made audible [119] and Joseph adds "direct address", which is spoken specifically for the audience. [120] Except convincing "verbal soliloquy", all monologue should, in fact, be considered as a theatric rather than dramatic feature — it is more like the prologue's speech than part of the dramatic action. If we take soliloquies as representation of true happenings, the speakers must appear boastful or morbid. [121] Thus in *King Lear,* III. vi, Edgar speaks his moralizing thoughts, in *Othello,* at the end of Act. I, Iago reveals his estimation of Othello and his dastardly intentions, in *King Lear,* I. ii. (195), Edmund speaks truthfully about his own character and in *As You Like It,* I. i, towards the end of the scene, Oliver tells the audience about his feelings and his intentions towards his brother — all in an unrealistic manner.

Sometimes characters introduce each other by telling the audience what they think of each other. In *Antony and Cleopatra,* I. i,

Philo   Look where they come.
               Take but good note, and you shall see in him
               The triple pillar of the world transform'd
               Into a strumpet's fool: behold and see.

and similarly in *Othello,* III. iii, before Iago says, "Look where he comes", he has

---

[119] M. L. Arnold, *The Soliloquies of Shakespeare* (1911).

[120] B. L. Joseph, *Elizabethan Acting* (1951), 117.

[121] Bradbrook, *Stage Conditions,* 89.

made an analysis of the situation at hand. In the two preceding examples, Philo is talking to a companion and Iago is talking to himself, but the object is the same: the audience learns valuable information from the speakers. Sometimes soliloquies are addressed more openly to the audience, as in *King Lear,* III. ii. (79), where, at the end of the scene, the Fool says, "I'll speak a prophecy ere I go": and the fifteen lines that follow are in the nature of a tag, having nothing to do with the action, and in the opening comic speech of Launce in *Two Gentlemen of Verona,* II. iii, in which the clown says, "Nay, I'll show you the manner of it", speaking to the audience. In *Henry VI, Pt. III,* II. v, the King delivers a long speech on his weariness and day dreams audibly about the attractions of pastoral life, then towards the end:

> "And to conclude, the shepherd's homely curds,
> His cold thin drink out of his leather bottle,
> Etc., etc."

This conclusion in the style of a sermon or lecture is followed by *"Enter a Son that hath killed his Father with the dead body",* and *"Enter a Father that hath killed his Son, with the body in his arms",* both speaking long lamentations, which cannot conceivably be parts of the action but can only be considered as lecture demonstrations.

The Elizabethans even allowed dramatic dialogue and direct address to the audience to mix, as in Nicholas Udall's *Ralph Roister Doister,* where Mathew Merygreeke first enters and tells the audience about himself and Rafe Royster, then the latter joins him on the stage:

R. Royster	Come, death, when thou wilt! I am weary of my life!
M. Mery	I told you, I, we should wowe another wife!
R. Royster	Why did God make me suche a goodly person?
M. Mery	He is in, by the weke. We shall haue sport anon.
R. Royster	And where is my trustie friende, Mathew Merygreeke?
M. Mery	I wyll make as I sawe him not. He doth me seeke.
R. Royster	I haue hym espyed, me thinketh, yond is hee.
	Hough, Mathew Merygreeke, my friend! a worde with thee!
M. Mery	I wyll not heare him, but make as I had haste.
	(Pretending to go)
	Farewell, all my good friendes! the tyme away dothe waste;
	And the tide, they say, tarieth for no man.

(Actus I, scæna ii).

Characters in Elizabethan dramas often report their own deaths. Of the better known tragic heroes and heroines, we have:

Romeo	Thus with a kiss I die.	*(Romeo and Juliet,* V. iii.)
Juliet	O happy dagger	
	This is thy sheath; there rest, and let me die.	

(Romeo and Juliet, V. iii.)

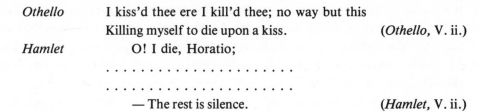

Othello	I kiss'd thee ere I kill'd thee; no way but this	
	Killing myself to die upon a kiss.	(*Othello*, V. ii.)
Hamlet	O! I die, Horatio;	
	. . . .	
	. . . .	
	— The rest is silence.	(*Hamlet,* V. ii.)

As compared with these, Cleopatra's end, where the poison prevents her from finishing her sentence, and that of King Lear, who does not know it is coming, are much more realistic. These last-breath speeches are in fact a formal way of the characters taking their leave of the audience, especially necessary when the latter might otherwise be left in doubt whether the character has really died.[122]

When a character leaves a scene, it is the custom in both Chinese and Elizabethan dramas for him to speak a couplet, and this is what Othello does as he dies. The appropriateness of the convention which is discernible in reading and evident in the actual performances of the Chinese drama where it is complemented by appropriate acting, points to a psychological basis of the convention in connection with the sense of finality. In a sermon, climactic effect is achieved by succinct summarizing expressions at the end and part of that effect is found in the closing couplets as spoken or sung by Chinese players, in which the rhyme and the balanced musical phrases help to enhance the appeal. It cannot of course be understood as part of the dramatic dialogue; it is directed to the audience whose attention is thereby drawn to the exit of the character. Stronger effect can be achieved by distributing consecutive couplets among the characters all about to leave the stage, and in the Chinese theatre they line up downstage in a manner that reminds one of opera singers in a quartet. This may be the mode of delivery in Greene's *Tu Quoque or The City Gallant,* where a rhymed tag of sixteen lines is distributed among eight people with two for each. [123] As in the epilogue, here the actors, not the characters they play, speak.

"The king's a beggar, now the play is done":
as the King says in the epilogue of *All's Well That Ends Well.* In Restoration dramas tags occurred not only at the end of acts and scenes but in the middle of scenes as well. [124] In short, the Chinese, Elizabethan and Restoration conceptions of the dramatic illusion permit the oratorical use of the dialogue. [125]

Narrative prologue is a remnant of primitive technique, and it is normally changed into dialogue as dramatic technique develops. [126] In the Chinese dramas of

---

[122] cf. Bethel, *Shakespeare and the Popular Dramatic Tradition*, 82.

[123] Lawrence, *Elizabethan Playhouse, Second series,* 181.

[124] Lawrence, *Elizabethan Playhouse, Second series,* 183-4.

[125] cf. Reynolds, *Red Bull,* 165.

[126] Bradbrook, *Themes and Conventions,* 44.

the northern school an introductory scene called *hsieh-tzu* [127] supplied the audience with the information on the background. In the Elizabethan theatre, at the earliest stage of development, the presenter was an undisguised mouthpiece of the author and sometimes even pretended to be the author himself and he introduced the characters and expounded the moral. [128] Later, the introduction became a play to introduce a play, called *induction,* as in *The Taming of the Shrew.* The induction stands between the world of the drama and that of the audience making the drama one step further removed from the real world. Sometimes characters in the induction mix with those in the play, as in *James IV,* where Bohun is in the induction but his sons are in the play. [129] This can only occur when the two worlds are not sharply divided, as drama and the world of the audience never are in the minds of the Elizabethans and the Chinese. Jonson, for example, made "conscious appeals to the artificiality of the play by showing the actors as their real selves. The boys, even the book-keeper, come on and discuss the play, their parts and the audience". [130] In early Elizabethan dramas morality characters, who exist only in the world of intellectual abstractions, mix with real characters, as Chastity and Lust, with Mrs. Saunders and Browne. [131] In Robert Yarington's *Two Lamentable Tragedies,* the characters in the induction, Truth, Falsehood and Homicide, enter periodically to comment on the action. [132]

Whereas mixing the characters belonging to two separate worlds has the effect of blurring their line of demarcation, the play within a play can make the audience feel that the induction belongs to their world. In the earlier version of *The Taming of the Shrew,* when the Duke, in the course of the action, orders two of the characters to be taken to prison, Sly wakes up at the word from his drunken sleep, and protests, "I say we'll have no sending to prison". In vain the Lords remind him that this is but a play, acted in jest. [133] The mind of the audience shows a reluctance to accept the complicated triple world: the real world, the induction and the play, and tends to simplify them into two only. Here, to avoid the same mistake as Sly's, the audience are tempted to merge the world of the induction with that of his own, thereby making the Duke and Lords appear real. It is probably to guard against the same tendency that dramatists take pains to distinguish clearly the play within a play by inflated diction and gesture, as in *Hamlet.* The same psychological trick as Sly's drunken remark is used in *Antony and Cleopatra,* V. ii,

---

(127) 楔子

(128) cf. the *loa* in the Spanish drama, which summarizes the story and comments on the play and the poet. Rennert, *The Spanish Stage,* 279.

(129) cf. Bradbrook, *Themes and Conventions,* 45.

(130) *Ibid.,* 45.

(131) *Vide ibid.,* 27.

(132) For a similar arrangement in *The Looking Glass,* see Chambers, *Eliz. Stage,* III, 92.

(133) *Vide* Raleigh, *Shakespeare,* 111.

Cleopatra   . . . and I shall see
        Some squeaking Cleopatra boy my greatness
        I' the posture of a whore.
spoken by a very "Cleopatra boy".

If the audience can be fully aware of the unreality of the induction, the play becomes twice removed from reality, an effect achieved by Chinese novelists whose custom it is to encase the novel in a shell of "induction" which opens and concludes the story, making it seem like a myth or fairy tale. [134] Or else the unreality of the induction can spread back into the world of the audience so that "all the world's a stage". Spoken on a bare stage, which is obviously unreal as a scene in the drama, this statement gains special poignancy. When Macbeth says,

        "Life's but a walking shadow, a poor player
        That struts and frets his hour upon the stage
        And then is heard no more".   (*Macbeth,* V. v.)

he catches the momentary vision of the unreality of this life which is brought on him by extreme grief, but as he refers to a player, the audience tend to think of the play he speaks about as unreal and his world to be indentical with the world of the audience. In *Tempest,* the effect is more systematically exploited:

Prospero   These our actors
        As I foretold you, were all spirits and
        Are melted into air, into thin air.   (*Tempest,* IV. i.)

"On the actual stage, the masque is executed by players, pretending to be spirits, pretending to be real actors, pretending to be supposed goddesses and rustics". [135] One loses count, and in mental laziness wants to think everything is unreal, hence the force of what immediately follows:

        And, like the baseless fabric of this vision,
        The cloud-capp'd towers, the gorgeous palaces,
        The solemn temples, the great globe itself,
        Yea, all which it inherit, shall dissolve
        And, like this insubstantial pageant faded,
        Leave not a rack behind. We are such stuff
        As dreams are made on, and our little life
        Is rounded with a sleep.

Strictly speaking, even if we take Prospero's words for it, all that is insubstantial is *his* world, with its towers, palaces and temples, but as he, himself in the play, points out the unreality of the masque, to which the audience agree, and then declares *his*

---

[134] In *The Red Chamber Dream* — 曹霑, 紅樓夢 — the "induction" shows two archetypes of man as seen in Chinese aristocratic society, but the author ingeniously merged the induction into the story.

[135] Tillyard, *Shakespeare's Last Plays,* 80.

world unreal nonetheless, the audience fall under the illusion that he is talking of *their* world.

(9)

In the Chinese and the Elizabethan theatre, not only the locality of the scenes, the "dramatic time" and part of the action are conventional but the costume, the plot and the characterization are conventional as well.

That costume design is governed by the principle of historical accuracy and geographical correctness is a peculiarity of the naturalistic theatre; everywhere else stage costume design is aimed at splendour and beauty. The main characteristics of the Elizabethan stage costume, like that of the Chinese theatre, are richness and beauty, with some symbolism when required.

It is difficult to compare the cost of Elizabethan stage costume with modern equivalents because the value of money in Elizabethan society is difficult to assess. [136] Of clearer significance is the fact that the total cost of the costume is about the same as that of the theatre building. [137] The richness by itself is impressive, but it is all the more striking if one reminds oneself of the paucity of the stage settings and the great change in the relative emphasis on the various elements of dramatic production that has occurred since then.

Elizabethan actors wore contemporary fashion with symbolic touches to indicate different nationalities. [138] Cleopatra's "Cut my lace, Charmian" (*Antony and Cleopatra,* I. iii.) shows that she wore Elizabethan stays, and Cassius wore a doublet. [139] There must have been some distinctive costume for the Greeks and Turks, for in *Hoffman* the lovers are disguised as Greeks, and in *A Very Woman,* IV. i, a Turkish costume is required. In the Chinese theatre, the costume remains "the same for different historical periods and for different seasons of the year" but varies according "to age and nationality of the characters". [140] It appears that in both theatres there is geographical differentiation in the costume because it serves to make the action clear and there is no historical accuracy because it does not serve a similar purpose.

There was in the Elizabethan theatre "a robe to go invisible in" [141] which Prospero needs in *Tempest,* III. i, and Faustus, in the Papal Court. Some special costume, of unknown appearance, had special significance to the audience, as the

---

[136] "A cloak might cost 19 pounds" — Bradbrook, *Themes and Conventions,* 14.

[137] Lawrence, *Pre-Restoration Stage Studies,* 252.

[138] S. L. Bethell, *Shakespeare and the Popular Dramatic Tradition* (1944), 46; Thorndike, *Shakespeare's Theatre,* 397.

[139] Bradbrook, *Themes and Conventions,* 15.

[140] 齊如山, 中國劇之組織, 頁四三.

[141] *Henslowe's Diary,* Ed. W. W. Greg, 123.

506

"suit of glass" worn by Peele's *Edward III* and "his parasite's costume" which "Sarpego puts on" in *The Gentleman Usher,* II. ii. [142]

Colours had special meanings to the Elizabethans and the Chinese, indeed they still have to us, and costume designers naturally exploited them. [143] A singularly modern use of stage decor existed in the black drapery on the Elizabethan stage for tragedies. [144] Black was also used for fiendish characters, mourning and funerals and white for the innocent and pure, such as angels, good spirits and brides. [145] The convention governing colours was not apparently clear-cut, because Thorndike states that green was for foresters and white for shepherds. [146] Extensive lists have been compiled for the colour symbolism of the Elizabethans but it is not known how closely the costume designers of the Elizabethan theatre followed such systems. [147]

The contrasted colours of the costume enrich the visual pleasures in the Chinese and Elizabethan theatres. Theories have been formulated for the emotional and suggestive effects of colours in the Chinese theatre. [148] The psychological response to colour, as to music, is almost instinctive — it is not surprising that the significance of colour in theatrical costume was not confined to the Chinese and the English stage but was also noticeable in the Roman theatre. [149]

Stage disguise can never, of course, be realistic because it has to be "successful" to the characters in the play and yet transparent to the audience; if it is successful to the audience too, they cannot understand the plot. It was the Elizabethan practice to change only the garments in stage disguises and the same is true for the Chinese stage, and sometimes, as in the Chinese theatre, disguise was carried out on the stage. [150]

Colour symbolism in stage costume was probably derived from morality plays

---

[142] *Vide* Bradbrook, *Themes and Conventions,* 15.

[143] *Vide* D. C. Allen, "Symbolic Colour in the Literature of the English Renaissance", *Philological Quarterly,* XV (1936).

[144] Chambers, *Eliz. Stage,* III, 79-80; Adams, *The Globe Playhouse,* 145.

[145] Bradbrook, *Themes and Conventions,* 16.

[146] Thorndike, *Shakespeare's Theatre,* 390.

[147] *Vide* Cecile de Banke, *Shakespearean Stage Production Then and Now* (1953), 152-161. With real enthusiam for sartorial details the author listed twenty-eight Elizabethan fabrics together with their contemporary uses and their modern equivalents, twenty-nine simple colours known to the Elizabethans and the particular symbolism of each of them, such as "desire", "love", "lost love", "deceptive love", "young love", etc., and twenty-six colour- and fabric-combinations "used by court and nobility". The historical evidence for the detailed colour symbolism is not clearly explained, but the colour combinations are based on "Elizabethan portraits, diaries and household accounts". Notes on colour symbolism are also to be found in M. C. Linthicum, *Costume in the Drama of Shakespeare and his Contemporaries* (1936), 13-23.

[148] 澹雲, 國劇之印象作用, 戲劇叢刊, 第三期.

[149] Bieber, *History of the Greek and Roman Theatre,* 320 f.

[150] Bradbrook, *op. cit.,* 17.

in which white and black were used for good and bad characters respectively [151] and the Stuart masques, with their predominant symbolism, had naturally a large share of that influence. [152] The richness of costume and its anachronism were also found in the medieval pageants, where the exhibition of rich costume was one of the main attractions, and the impetus to lavish expenditure due to the rivalry between the different guilds responsible for the various sections of the pageant cannot be ignored. The Elizabethan audience, used to rich stage costume in the miracles before public theatres were established, naturally demanded the same in the dramas.

The difference between the Elizabethan and the Chinese stage costume lies in the use of contemporary dresses in the former, which must have reduced the psychological distance between the world of the drama and the world of the audience. The dramatic function of the costume is, however, the same:

"The Romans had also gay clothing and every man's apparel was applicable to his part and person. The old man in white, the rich men in purple, the parasite disguisedly, the young men in gorgeous colours, there wanted no device nor good judgment of the comedy, whence I suppose our players both drew their plays and forms of garments". [153]

"Costume was something more than idly decorative; it was a note of rank, profession, or trade, and so helped to tell the story". [154]

Make-up, which is used extensively and exaggeratedly in the Chinese theatre, does not seem to have been used in the Elizabethan theatre, even though the women at that time used cosmetics — sometimes not with the best judgment, as Hamlet's reference to painting "an inch thick" shows. Philip Stubbes (*Anatomy of Abuses,* 1583) condemned separately boy-actors for being "trained up in filthy speeches, unnatural and unseemly gestures" and "the women of England, many of them, who use to colour their faces with oils, liquors, unguents and waters made to that end". In heavy disguise, make-up might have been used, as in Celia's suggestion (*As You Like It,* I. iv.) to counterfeit a peasant's complexion with "a kind of umber" to "smirch her face". The purpose of make-up, when required, was served by friction:

"Present not your selfe on the Stage (especially at a new play) vntill the quaking prologue hath (by rubbing) got cullor into his cheekes, and is ready to giue the trumpets their Cue that hees vpon point to enter". [155]

Masks were used only on rare occasions [156] and mainly in the form of vizards

---

[151] Bradbrook, *op. cit.,* 16 f.

[152] A. Nicoll, *Stuart Masques and the Renaissance Stage,* 156 f.

[153] Thomas Lodge, *Defence of Plays,* quoted in Bradbrook, *Themes and Conventions,* 15.

[154] Raleigh, *Shakespeare,* 120.

[155] T. Dekker, *The Gull's Hornbook* (1609), How a Gallant should behaue himself in a Playhouse — see Chambers, *Eliz. Stage,* IV, 367.

[156] Thorndike, *Shakespeare's Theatre,* 371.

which were required by the action. It is used in this capacity in *The Hector of Germany*. [157] It must have been generally ugly, because even Mercutio says,

"Give me a case to put my visage in:
A visor for a visor! what care I,
What curious eye doth quote deformities?"

(*Romeo and Juliet*, I. iii.)

In *The Longer Thou Livest The More Fool Thou Art* (c.1559) God's Judgment has "a terrible visure" and Confusion "an ill fauoured visure", and in *All For Money* (between 1558 and 1577) Damnation, Judas, and Dives have vizards. Reference was also made in contemporary books to "an ill-favoured vizar, such as I have seen in stage plays, when they dance Machachinas". [158]   In Fletcher's *Night Walker,* one passage reads,

"We must disguise, to fright these reverend watches . . .
Here's a devil's face". [159]

These masks are however part of the drama; they are dramatic rather than theatrical masks. The masks Macbeth's murderers wear may be theatric:

"What are these faces?"   (*Macbeth,* IV. ii.)

and the black mask Death wears should be considered as theatrical. [160] In Middleton's *Masque of the Inner Temple,* there is a direction for three Good Days in white costume, three Bad Days in black, and three Indifferent Days in striped clothes and streaked faces. [161] The Indifferent Days seem to wear what is identical to the Chinese "painted faces".

A note of theatricality is also to be found in the footwear and headgear of the Elizabethan actors, which are not dissimilar to those in the Chinese theatre. The players wore what were called "pumps", which were made of leather, slashed, pinked and heeled, with roses on them, [162] hence Hamlet's

"Would not this, sir, and a forest of feathers, if the rest of
my fortunes turn Turk with me, with two Provincial roses on my
razed shoes, get me a fellowship in a cry of players,
sir?"   (*Hamlet,* III. ii.)

The female impersonators sometimes wore chopines, a fashion imported from

---

[157] Reynolds, *Red Bull,* 174.

[158] Chambers, *Eliz. Stage,* I, 371 n. Vizards were often used in masques in which there was a custom for the dancers to unmask themselves at the end of the performance — *Ibid.,* I, 151, 162, 196; III, 241, 280 — and were probably also used in *Parnassus* — *Ibid.,* IV, 38.

[159] John Lilly's Camilda calls the masquing vizard of Philautus "so ill a face" — Hotson, *Times Literary Supplement,* 16 May, 1952.

[160] Hotson, *op. cit.*

[161] *Vide* Bradbrook, *Themes and Conventions,* 16.

[162] de Banke, *op. cit.,* 181.

Venice, with soles five or six inches thick. [163] Hamlet greets the boy player with

"Your ladyship is nearer heaven than when I saw you last, by the altitude of a chopine". (*Hamlet,* II. ii.)

As "a forest of feathers" suggests, feathers were much used on garment and headgear. [164]

(10)

Costume is not the only thing that is anachronistic on the Elizabethan and the Chinese stage. Brutus and the conspirators hear the clock strike in *Julius Caesar,* II. i. and Macbeth speaks of "cannons overcharged with double-cracks". (*Macbeth,* I. ii.). Less conspicuous is the Porter's knowledge of the ways of Jesuit equivocators (*Macbeth,* II. iii.) of which Professor Schüking thought "one might as well to-day interrupt the performance by reading the latest edition of the evening papers to the audience". [165] Theoretically speaking, topical allusions are as incongruous as anachronisms, but the suspicion of inadvertence makes the latter appear as a fault.

It is yet an open question whether pointing out anachronisms in dramas constitutes a criticism, especially in Elizabethan and Chinese theatres in which illusionary effect is mild and consequently anachronism less noticeable. If anachronism is considered to be a fault, logical consistency requires that historical and geographical accuracy be observed in language, diction, pronunciation and manners. For the audience who have accepted the convention which permits anachronisms, they are not merely tolerated, they simply pass unnoticed, as the incorrect language of stage foreigners and wrong diction of historical plays are now unquestioned. Dramas are not exhibition-pageants of an anthropological museum; appreciation of dramas requires not only imagination but also the suspension of fastidious demands on precision.

Elizabethan and Chinese theatres both rose out of popular entertainment and were influenced by popular taste and mentality, and the concessions to tradition, though incongruous in the later dramas of mature literary stature, were retained by force of convention. Simple understanding requires exaggeration of characteristics in the *dramatis personae* which led, in the Chinese theatre, to the development of the various types of characters each with its accentuated psychology to be played only with special skill in acting. Types of characters did develop in the Elizabethan theatre, although they, except the boy actors and the clowns, did not require specialized technique and were not therefore labelled as those in the Chinese theatre

---

[163] de Banke, *op. cit.,* 181; M. C. Linthicum, *Costume in the Drama of Shakespeare and his Contemporaries,* 248-250, plate facing 250 — it appears to be very similar to the type of Manchurian ladies' shoes worn on the Chinese stage.

[164] de Banke, *op. cit.,* Pt. III, Ch. II; see also Hodges, *Globe Restored,* Ills. on pp. 79, 151, 152 and 165.

[165] L. L. Schüking, *Character Problems in Shakespeare's Plays,* 24.

are. [166] There were the bluff soldier, the cheated tool villian, the pathetic child, the lustful tyrant and so forth. [167] The differentiation was considered necessary for play-writing, for according to Whetstone's precept:

> "To work a comeddie kindly, grave old man should instruct, young men should shew imperfections of youth, strumpets should be lascivious, Boyes unhappe and clowns should speak disorderlye". [168]

different types should be allotted different kinds of action. Richard Edwardes too thought that

> "the greatest Skyll is this, rightly to touche
> All thynges to the quicke: & eke to frame eche person so,
> That by his common talke, you may his nature rightly knowe:
> A Royster ought not preache, that were to straunge to heare,
> But as from vertue he doth swerve, so ought his woordes appeare:
> The olde man is sober, the young man rashe, the Lover triumphyng in ioyes,
> The Matron grave, the Harlot wilde & full of wanton toyes".
>
> (*Damon and Pithias* (1571), Prologue).

> "There was no blurring or running together of these sharply divided classes. Age and youth were kept so rigidly distinct that the young are nearly all adolescent and the old quite senile". [169]

This applies exactly to the Chinese drama. (See Chapter V).

> "Characters could neither interact upon each other, nor develop, for the type was sharply defined and could not be modified". [170]

The shortness of the modern Chinese dramas makes gradual interaction and development virtually impossible. In both Chinese and Elizabethan dramas, psychological states are usually extreme and clear-cut and changes are abrupt and complete, for example, unalloyed malice, love at first sight, complete repentance and sudden reconciliation. The more realistic complexities and vagueness of the mind and the undistinguished mediocrity of ordinary personalities are unknown.

That European tragedy deals with kings and princes and comedy with the common people is a heritage from the classical theatre and it persisted till the end of the eighteenth century. [171] The social structure encouraged the view that only the nobility live elevated emotional lives and have grand feelings, the common people being capable, so far as drama is concerned, only of unbalanced emotions and grotesque personalities. Similar importance is invested in people of high social

---

(166) *Vide* Bradbrook, *Themes and Conventions,* 56-61.

(167) *Vide* Lea, *Italian Popular Comedy,* 390 f.

(168) Bradbrook, *Themes and Conventions,* 56.

(169) Bradbrook, *Themes and Conventions,* 57.

(170) Bradbrook, *Themes and Conventions,* 61.

(171) Bradbrook, *Themes and Conventions,* 55. For similar conception in Corneille see Bradbrook, *Stage Conditions,* 100.

positions in the Chinese drama, but, perhaps owing to the popular origin of the theatre, many Chinese heroes and heroines are common people.

Miss Feng Yüan-Chün accused the dramatists of Yüan dynasty of "simplicity, puerility, vulgarity and absurdity". [172] The objection applies equally well to many Elizabethan dramas, especially the earlier and the minor works.

Even in Shakespeare grossness is frequent and often found in the conversation between a lady and man. In *The Taming of the Shrew* (II. i.) Petruchio, talking with Kate, exploits the remark that she is waspish; Portia, in the last scene in *Merchant of Venice,* is outspoken about her intentions with the "doctor" and this in front of friends and servants; Hamlet asks Rosencrantz why he laughs at "man delights me not" (*Hamlet,* II. ii.) and jests with Ophelia when she says, "You are keen, my lord". (III. ii.); Emilia misunderstands Desdemona's "By this heavenly light" (*Othello,* IV. iii.); Cleopatra discussed "good will" in "play" with an eunuch (*Antony and Cleopatra,* II. v.) and Helena discussed with Parolles how to "barricade virginity against men" (*All's Well That Ends Well,* I. i.). In Shakespeare alone, a complete list of examples will run into a book. [173] The allusions to obscenities in Shakespeare are mainly in *double entendre,* but minor dramatists are more frank. In Field's *Amends for Ladies,* Lord Feesimple describes a wedding as he peers through a window:

> "Look look! the parson joins the doctor's hand and hers: now the doctor kisses her, by this light! (*Omnes whoop*). Now goes his gown off. Heyday! he has red breeches on. Zounds! the physician is got o' th' top of her: belike it is the mother she has. Hark! the bed creaks".

Many similar passages, including references to sexual perversions of various kinds, can be cited. [174] No survey has been made of the Chinese equivalents; a few plays of this kind have been mentioned by Professor Ch'i Ju-Shan. [175]

Grossness, like vulgarity, is a matter of mental habit; its force lies in unfamiliarity. The type of information that is considered suitable or elegant to be disclosed in public and the degree of frankness with which this may be done vary with the social class, the country and the historical period. As a whole, the Elizabethan and the Yüan dramatists were allowed more licence than modern playwrights are, hence their plays appear bawdy to us. Suggestive and openly obscene passages were, however, obviously a part of the theatrical convention and when the audience expected them habitually, they could not feel the psychological impact we imagine they did. Whereas in the modern readers the censure has

---

[172] 馮沅君, 古劇說彙, 附錄二, 頁三七七, "簡單, 幼稚, 俚俗, 荒唐".

[173] *Vide* W. R. Davies, *Shakespeare's Boy Actors* (1939), Ch. V.

[174] *Vide* A. Harbage, *Shakespeare and the Rival Traditions* (1952), Pt. II, Chs. III and IV.

[175] 齊如山, 京劇之變遷, 頁十九.

produced a state of mind with which the response to erotic literature is so certain one way or the other that its artistic aspect is obscured, to those brought up on freer conventions of speech the sensational appeal is dulled by repetition and the facetious or romantic aspect becomes prominent. [176] The charge of vulgarity or of grossness can only be a relative one, because the embarrassment we feel for the manners and language in Elizabethan and Yüan dynasty dramas their original audience did not feel. In the Elizabethan dramas bawdy passages are often out of character with the speaker; they were inserted because they were expected by the audience and they had to be spoken by someone. [177] Even when erotic passages were worked into the romantic scenes, lack of censure removed the sense of trangressed conscience and the fascination of wrongdoing.

The erotic elements in old Chinese dramas are due to the fact that the Chinese theatre has suffered little official censure. At the beginning of Ming dynasty (1368-1643) it was only forbidden to represent emperors in the plays; it was towards the end of Ch'ing dynasty (1644-1911) that obscene plays were banned. (See Chapter VIII). In Elizabethan England, the court fostered the freedom of the theatre against the opposition by the Puritans. [178]

In the actual performance of Elizabethan and Chinese dramas absurdities abound: the invisible Prospero, the "non-existent" property man, the journeying scenes and so forth, but even in the text, besides anachronisms, the credulity of the reader is called for, for example, the sea coast of Bohemia in *The Winter's Tale,* the double time-keeping in *Othello* and the inconsistent age of Hamlet. If these pass unnoticed, there are still the unbelievable situations such as the efficacy of Juliet's sleeping potion, the successful disguises in *As You Like It,* the indistinguishable substitutes and the sudden success in official examinations after a brief period of preparation in the Chinese plays, the remarkable preservation of youthful appearance in many heroines in both theatres, the freedom taken with recorded facts in historical plays, and many others. Sheer repetition makes them credible and once the legends are established their probability is not to be questioned. Everything must serve the end of building dramatic situations, as Raleigh says, "If Cordelia had been perfectly tender and tactful, there would have been no play" [179] and as the Chinese saying goes: "Without coincidences — no story". [180] It is the custom of Chinese

---

[176] cf. Harbage, *op. cit.,* 298.

[177] cf. Bradbrook, *Themes and Conventions,* 118.

[178] The court, perhaps for their superfluous leisure, has patronized the theatre in both Elizabethan England and nineteenth century China. In the former, the Queen's Men performed under the excuse of rehearsing for court performances (Adams, *Shakespearean Playhouses,* 8) and in the latter, lazy actors evaded engagements under the same excuse — 齊如山，戲班，六章 "回戲".

[179] Raleigh, *Shakespeare,* 135.

[180] "無巧不成書"

critics to suggest, after pointing out improbabilities, "Let us lend it a credulous ear". [181] Dramatic construction and characterization can attain and have attained consummate ingenuity and meticulous consistency, but ingenuity and verisimilitude as such have no artistic value, not, at any rate, by the standards of the Elizabethan and Chinese dramas.

> "For the effect of genius is not to convince the audience but rather to transport them out of themselves. . . The object of poetry is to enthral".
> (Longinus, *On the Sublime,* I. 4).

The improbabilities are not, of course, put in the dramas for their own sake; they serve the purpose of carrying a message:

> "It seems to me that we should be tolerant when poets are too childlike. . . But for infantilism in critics I do not see a word of defence or apology possible to be spoken. . . When they are so little developed, so shut up in their own view-point, that they do not know the difference between receiving a communication and making up a fairy-story. . ." (M. Eastman, *The Literary Mind* (1931), 121).

Improbability is inevitably introduced into dramas through the compression, simplification and accentuation necessary to create contrast and conflict; dramatic plots and motivations, if carefully analyzed, all show improbabilities. [182] Drama is not social document; it is not even psychological document. [183] It is doubtful whether it is possible to analyze the motives of dramatic characters as we do our own and those of people we know well, because dramas are not full biographies and the characters must lack the fullness and complexities of real people. They are not copies of real people, and the dramas are not case histories for the psychiatrist. In drama, not only time and space, but also situation and psychology are fictitious. Documentary drama is impossible because one cannot find "a slice of life" dramatically significant; real events are too slow and scattered to form the terse artistic pattern that dramatic writing requires. The dramatists create quick developments and concentrate on those sections at which events are brought to an issue.

> "Realistic narrative, characterization and speech starve the drama, because it is already too concentrated a form to accept the limitation of the novel in addition: it must be more selective, and selection is only possible through a convention". [184]

Puerility and vulgarity are the characteristics of probably all popular art before it comes under the influence of literary sophistication. It is at this stage — before sophistication — that spontaneity, sincerity and the charm of naivety predominate.

---

[181] "姑妄聽之"

[182] E. E. Stoll, *Art and Artifice in Shakespeare* (1934), xv, 2.

[183] *Ibid.,* 167.

[184] Bradbrook, *Themes and Conventions,* 43.

Popular taste did not demand the classic model of dramatic construction in *exposition — conflict — resolution.*

> "The constructive importance of acts and scenes seems almost to have been unobserved; almost every scene began with an entrance and ended, not with a situation, but with an exit, binding the whole play into one connected story; while in many cases the plot was not dramatic, but rather a history, a novel, or a romance told in dialogue. *Tamberlaine* is such a play; so are most of Shakespeare's historical plays. They begin at the beginning, and they tell the whole story with all its details. It is useless to attempt to fit them into the dramatic strait-jacket of exposition, climax and resolution. What is obviously true of these plays is probably true of many others. One may be permitted to question whether it ever occurred to most of the dramatists that there was such a thing as dramatic construction in the sense in which we understand it; and to doubt if there is much advantage, except a possible pedagogic one, in striving to make their plays comply with this modern theory. Rather, theirs was a narrative art, and their subjects were often narrative subjects. They dealt with these subjects as a novelist does, giving the smaller points as well as the greater. Often the plays lack any dominating conflict, but are rather a series of dramatic situations clustered about some single figure". [185]

This shows how futile it is to try to find the modern idea of dramatic construction in Chinese dramas.

> "The commonest complaint against the Elizabethan drama is that the action is illogical, or overcrowded. . . The first and most essential thing to be realized is that consecutive or causal succession of events is not of the first importance". [186]

This was the stage in the history of the English drama when the taste of the audience still carried the influence of moralities, interludes, street pageants, bear-baiting, fencing matches and ballad singers, [187] and in the Chinese drama of Yüan dynasty, when dramas were performed in brothels and fair grounds and competed for patronage with conjurors, story-tellers, puppets, jugglers, riddle games and fireworks. Later,

> ". . . in Ford and Shirley there is a coarsening of the feeling (which is accompanied, inevitably, by a coarsening of the poetic fibre) together with an increased dexterity in the manipulation of the emotional effects of narrative and character". [188]

Similarly in Ming dynasty, characterization and plot improved and vulgarity and

---

[185] Reynolds, *Mod. Phil.,* Vol. 3, p. 93.

[186] Bradbrook, *Themes and Conventions,* 31.

[187] cf. W. Poel, *Bulletin of John Rylands Library,* Vol. 3, p. 215 f.

[188] Bradbrook, *op. cit.,* 240.

puerility were eliminated, but vitality and true feelings also disappeared from the Chinese drama.

(11)

Actors playing female roles is a practice common to the Elizabethan and the Chinese theatre and one which gives rise in both to a style of histrionic art and mode of appreciation free from the influence of the players' personal charms. In both cases, the practice is due to the social convention but in the Elizabethan theatre the training of school boys in elocution would have made it easier for some private theatres to employ them than to train actresses and their choir boys in medieval dramas provided a precedent. [189] In England, however, the tradition of the female impersonation was short: after women invaded the stage in the later part of the seventeenth century the boy actors rapidly became outmoded: but in China, both men and women still play female roles to-day. In this respect the Spanish theatre resembles the Chinese, for in the sixteenth century actresses played women first but boys played them later [190] and in the seventeenth century the bigger troupes employed women, but the smaller ones still used boys. [191]

Chinese actors in female roles use *falsetto* voice both for speaking and for singing and, thanks to the exiguous growth of beard among the Chinese people, female impersonators can remain on stage as long as actors who play male roles, and many did not retire until after "at every smile the powder flies down from the face". The Elizabethan boy actors appear to use a more natural tone. The boy's voice breaks at about twelve but with training treble voice in singing can be preserved until sixteen and in speaking until twenty. [192] Female parts were however played even by men past middle age. [193] When an early actress appeared as Desdemona in *The Moor of Venice* on 8 December 1660, the prologue said:

> "Our women are defective, and so siz'd
> You'd think they were some of the Guard disguiz'd
> For (to speak truth) men act, that are between
> Forty and fifty, wenches of fifteen;
> With bone so large, and nerve so imcomplyant,
> When you call Desdemona, enter Giant". [194]

With training, a man can acquire a soft and high tenor voice which it is difficult to distinguish from a woman's [195] and it is probably in this voice that men "between

[189] W. R. Davies, *Shakespeare's Boy Actors* (1939), 3.

[190] Rennert, *The Spanish Stage*, 19.

[191] Augustin de Rojas Villandrando, *Viage entrentenido*, quoted in A. M. Nagler, *Sources of Theatrical History*, 57.

[192] Davies, *op. cit.*, 35.

[193] Thorndike, *Shakespeare's Theatre*, 373.

[194] *A Royal Arbor of Loyal Poesie* (1664), quoted in Davies, *op. cit.*, 19.

[195] Davies, *op. cit.*, 36.

forty and fifty" could play young women.

So far as appearance is concerned, the success of the boy actors cannot be doubted. Pepys, referring to Kynaston in Fletcher's *Loyal Subject,* said, "He made the loveliest lady that ever I saw in my life". [196] Of the same female impersonator it was said that,

> "it has since been disputable among the judicious whether any woman that succeeded him so sensibly touched the audience as he". [197]

Kynaston happened to be an actor in the Restoration period who was famous enough to leave his name in diaries and other historical sources. At this time the boy actors were on the decline. It can hardly be doubted that in their heyday, in the early part of the seventeenth century, their skill was commendable. To this one may compare some foreigners' impressions of the Chinese female impersonators:

> "It is not as though the roles were merely acceptably well done: they are acted with consummate art. The young women impersonated by young men are full of feminine grace and seduction". [198]

> "Every finger of the female impersonator must contribute to the effect of fragile femininity. A genius for doing the right thing in the right way, supreme theatrical instinct, is the final test. 'She whose movements are disciplined, she who is a living harmony, a lyric in flesh and blood', wrote Sarcey of Sarah Bernhardt. Alter the pronoun, and these words apply to Mei Lan-fang". [199]

The effect of the boy actors on the personality of Shakespeare's heroines has been studied. [200] If there was such effect, the boy actors, in spite of their expert ability to simulate the appearance of women, must have had limitation in the portrayal of their feelings. It would be difficult to trace the effect of the female impersonators in the Chinese dramas.

The fact that English boy actors of the seventeenth century compared favourably in appearance with the most beautiful women and that Chinese female impersonators are usually indistinguishable from actresses can justify the practice but does not prove its advantage. To say that successful female impersonation represents the triumph of art over nature is to appreciate difficulty for its own sake. The real advantage of boy actors lies in the fact that with them there is little danger of turning art into exhibition. Few women would not prefer being admired as women to being admired as artists; theirs is the vanity of natural attributes, not acquired skill. The temptation for actresses to parade rather than to act is all the greater because whereas art requires long cultivation, beauty requires only a little

---

[196] *Vide* Thorndike, *Shakespeare's Theatre,* 372.

[197] John Downes, *Roscius Anglicanus* (1708), Mr. Kynaston.

[198] B. S. Allen, *Chinese Theatre Handbook* (1925), 23.

[199] *The Oxford Companion to the Theatre* (1951), CHINA (Harold Acton).

[200] *Vide* Davies, *op. cit.,* Chs. II and III.

artificial aid. Theatregoers, unlike poetry- and art-lovers, are not as a whole distinguished by their preoccupation with true artistic appreciation; they look for entertainment and readily accept the excitement for feminine beauty as praiseworthy theatrical fare.

Actresses invaded the English stage about the time when scenery became permanent practice in public theatres, that is, shortly after the middle of the seventeenth century. [201] A famous actress, Mrs. Bracegirdle (1663-1748), who was in about the second generation of English actresses, was much admired in a manner shown by contemporary panegyrics:

"For it will be no extravagant thing to say, scarce an Audience saw her, that were less than half of them Lovers, without a suspected Favourite among them".

and yet,

"She had no greater Claim to Beauty, than what the most desirable *Brunette* might pretend to. But her Youth, and lively Aspect, threw out such a Glow of Health, and Cheerfulness, that, on the Stage, few Spectators that were not past it, could behold her without Desire".

The attractiveness of her person was not the only reason for the admiration:

"Mrs. *Bracegirdle* was not but just blooming to her Maturity; her Reputation, as an Actress, gradually rising with that of her Person; never any Woman was in such general Favour of her Spectators, which, to the last Scene of her Dramatick Life, she maintain'd, by not being unguarded in her private Character. This Discretion contributed, not a little, to make her the *Cara,* the Darling of the theatre". "An tho' she might be said to have been the Universal Passion, and under the highest Temptation; her Constancy in resisting them, served but to increase the number of her Admirers".

The effect of her career on dramatic writing and dramatic appreciation was explained:

"She inspired the best Authors to write for her, and two of them, when they gave her a Lover, in a Play, seem'd palpably to plead their own Passions, and make their private Court to her, in fictitious Characters. In all the chief Parts she acted, the Desirable was so prominent, that no Judge could be cold enough to consider, from which other particular Excellence, She became delightful". [202]

Her merits were catalogued in detail:

"She was of a lovely Height, with dark-brown Hair and Eyebrows, black sparkling Eyes, and a fresh blushy Complexion, and, whenever she exerted

---

[201] In 1661 Pepys mentioned he first saw an actress. Lawrence, *Elizabethan Playhouse, Second series,* 137.

[202] The above passages are from Cibber, *An Apology for the Life of Mr. Colley Cibber* (1740), 141 f.

herself, had an involuntary Flushing in her Breast, Neck and Face, having continually a chearful Aspect, and a fine Set of even white Teeth . . . she was finely shap'd and had very handsome Legs and Feet; and her Gait, or Walk, was free, manlike, and modest, when in Breeches". [203]

The last remark gives some hint of the reason for the attraction of women in breeches. The significant silence over her histrionic abilities points to the fact that she appealed, not to any artistic sense, but to the instinct of the male part of the audience, and she knew how to capitalize on her assets through the intricacies of the psychology of sex. It would be a mistake to think that all actresses of the seventeenth century English stage had as unalloyed an appeal as Mrs. Bracegirdle, yet, judging by the fact that they always wore contemporary fashion on the stage no matter what the period of the play was and that no plain actress became well known for skill in acting, one can safely surmise that the audience then was mainly concerned with natural charms and could not "be cold enough to consider, from which other Excellence" an actress became delightful. The social conditions in Restoration times were particularly favourable for this kind of relationship between the actresses and the audience: there were only two theatres in London and many of the audience knew the actors and actresses personally. [204]

Delightful as pretty actresses may be, they do not serve the interests of art. According to Sir Walter Raleigh,

"Poetry, like religion, is outraged when it is made a platform for the exhibition of their own talent and passion by those who are its ministers. With the disappearance of the boy players the poetic drama died in England, and it has had no second life". [205]

What is true of the poetry in the English drama is also true of the histrionic art in the Chinese theatre. Chinese connoisseurs prefer female impersonators to actresses because by their standards the beauty of a female role is different from the natural beauty of a woman; the former is the artificially intensified version of femininity which can be marred by natural manners. The difference is that between a dancer's pose and a natural carriage or between a singer's trained voice and a sweet natural voice. The Chinese style of acting has developed to such a stage that a soldier cannot play himself as well as an actor can play a soldier, nor can a fisherman, nor a scholar, nor a woman. A good Chinese female impersonator is to a beautiful woman as a good portrait in oil is to a photograph.

That actors are better stage-females than women themselves sounds paradoxical to modern European ears because most of them are brought up in the tradition of

---

[203] A. Aston, *A Brief Supplement to Colley Cibber, Esq. His Lives of the Late Famous Actors and Actresses* (1748), 81 f.

[204] Nicoll, *Development of the Theatre,* 169.

[205] W. Raleigh, *Shakespeare* (1901), 120.

519

naturalism and naturalistic plays "affect the mind and the nerves precisely as they are affected by events in real life". [206] "The modern playwright uses his technical resources to work directly on the nerves, and produce a state of bodily excitement". [207] Of the actresses' part in this excitement, Purdom declared bluntly: "The exhibition of girls and women on our stage is a main part of its attraction". [208] But excitement is incompatible with the appreciation of poetry and true histrionic art. Neither poetry, or great acting, which is akin to great dancing, produces bodily excitement. The appreciation of great art requires heightened critical faculties available only with concentration of mind in the most serene mood; agitation and abandon make one dull just as intoxication destroys the delicate palate. Exhibition of feminine charm and passionate love-making produce immediate and strong emotional stirrings among the audience with which the tragic and comic situations of the dramatist's intention have to compete. [209] Audiences then idolize their favourite actresses and do their best to see in the lives of the idols the romance and sometimes, the attractive licentiousness, which life does not give to the average theatregoer. [210] The Elizabethan and the Chinese theatre, however, do not aim at producing momentary excitement and personal admiration. For Shakespeare, and indeed also for the best of the Chinese theatre, "an alert and critically detached audience is implied and an attitude to tragedy very different from that to which we are accustomed". [211] It was evidently with detachment that Goethe once watched a female impersonator in Italy and left us a lucid summary of the pleasure such players always give:

> "We Germans remember how the parts of old men were represented to the point of deception by an able young man, and how that actor afforded us a double pleasure. In the same way, we experience a double charm from the fact that these people are not women, but play the part of women. We see a youth who has studied the idiosyncrasies of the female sex in their character and behaviour; he has learned to know them, and reproduces them as artist; he plays not himself, but a third, and, in truth, a foreign nature. We come to understand the female sex so much the better because someone has observed and meditated on their ways, and not the process itself, but the result of the process, is presented to us". [212]

In other words, the object of the female impersonation is not imitation but creation;

---

[206] Bethell, *Shakespeare and the Popular Dramatic Tradition*, 70.

[207] Bradbrook, *Stage Conditions*, 125.

[208] C. B. Purdom, *Producing Shakespeare* (1950), 130.

[209] cf. Granville-Barker, *Prefaces*, I, 15.

[210] cf. Davies, *op. cit.*, 181-2.

[211] Bethell, *Shakespeare and the Popular Dramatic Tradition*, 39.

[212] *Goethe's Travels in Italy*, trans. C. Nisbeth (1883), 569 f.

what we see is not the natural woman but an actor's study of the woman. After the general remarks quoted above Goethe continued with the description of the role as played by the actor which could have been written for the heroine in the modern Chinese play *The Amour of the Dragon and the Phoenix* [213] about the advances made by an *incognito* emperor to a dauntless waitress:

"The public could not refuse giving universal applause to the *Locandiera* of Goldoni. The young man who took the part of hostess of an inn expressed as happily as possible the different shades of such a character — the composed coldness of a maiden who looks after her business, who is polite, friendly, and obliging to everyone, but neither loves nor wishes to be loved, still less will give ear to the passionate suits of her distinguished guests; the secret tender coquetries by which she contrives to captivate anew her male guests; her offended pride when one of them meets her in a harsh, unfriendly way; the many dainty blandishments by which she allures him, and, finally, her triumph in having got the better of him also". [214]

The by-ways of human nature are such, however, that detachment is not easily maintained even with full knowledge of the player's sex:

"People consoled themselves by the reflection that this time at least it was not true; people clapped their hands in merry spirits to the young man, rejoicing that he knew so well the dangerous qualities of the loved sex, and that by a happy imitation of their behaviour he revenged us, as it were, on the fair ones for all the ills of that kind we had suffered at their hands". [215]

This is hardly in conformity with the detachment that Goethe preached for dramatic appreciation but one can believe that it was true of the Italian audience he saw. Similar psychology is at any rate not unknown in the Chinese theatre, of which the penetrating Lu Hsün [216] said, "The best part about men playing women is that the male part of the audience see the men as women and the female part know that they are after all really men; in either case one sees them as the opposite sex". Shakespeare exploited the apparent dual sexuality of the boy actor in the epilogue in *As You Like It,* spoken by Rosalind, and addressed to both men and women. Kynaston dazzled Pepys by appearing both in male and in female roles and excelling in both:

"Kinaston, the boy, had the good turn to appear in three shapes: first, as a poor woman in ordinary clothes, to please Morose; then in fine clothes, as a gallant, and in them was clearly the prettiest woman in the whole house, and

---

[213] 遊龍戲鳳
[214] *Ibid.*
[215] *Ibid.*
[216] 魯迅

lastly, as a man; and then likewise did appear the handsomest man in the house''. (217)

It is not difficult to see that the innocent feat was a highly dangerous pleasure for those, men and women, who either were naturally inclined or could learn to appreciate the erotic appeals of their own sex. The rides ladies of quality took with Kynaston in Hyde Park after the play, with him in costume, (218) might have been innocent but the association of some Chinese women with players are not as open.

Sexual admiration for the boy actors cannot do as much harm to artistic appreciation as that for actresses, because homosexuals are a minority, but that boy actors provide opportunity for such admiration on a commercial scale can hardly be denied and is evidenced by the fact that both the Elizabethan and the Chinese theatre are connected with charges of homosexual vice.

"Then, these goodly pageants being done euery mate sorts to his mate, euery one brings another homeward of their way verye freendly, and in their secret conclaues (couertly) they play the Sodomites, or worse''. (Philip Stubbes, *Anatomy of Abuses,* 1583, see Chambers, *Eliz. Stage,* IV, 223 f.).

"Yea witness . . . M. *Stubs,* his Anatomy of Abuses, p. 105 where he affirmes, *that Players and Play-haunters in the secret conclaves play the Sodomites:* together with *some moderne examples of such, who have been desperately enamored with Players Boyes thus clad in woman's apparell, so farre as to solicite them by words, by Letters, even actually to abuse them''.*
(William Prynne, *Histriomastix,* 1633, p. 211 f).

These are the exaggerated attacks by the Puritans who criticized the Elizabethan theatre with all vehemence and under all possible excuses, but similar observation was made by the theatrical profession itself:

"When boys play'd women's parts, you'd think the Stage,
Was innocent in that untempting Age.
No: for your amorous Fathers then, like you,
Amongst those Boys had Play-house Misses too''. (219)

Thomas Dekker advised the gallant that "by sitting on the stage, you may (with small cost) purchase the deere acquaintance of the boyes''. (220) For similar reasons the gallery seats near the exit stage door in the Chinese theatre were at one time the most expensive and were mostly reserved by the gallants. (221)

---

(217) *Diary,* 7 January, 1661.

(218) Colley Cibber's *Apology* (1746), Ch. V.

(219) Epilogue to *The Parsons Wedding,* printed in *Covent Garden Drollery,* 1672. *Vide* Summers, *The Playhouse of Pepys,* 292.

(220) T. Dekker, *The Gull's Hornbook* (1609), *vide* Chambers, *Eliz. Stage,* IV, 367.

(221) See Ch. II.

Allusions to homosexuality in Elizabethan plays are few, but by no means non- existent, [222] for example,

 Hamlet Why did you laugh then, when I said, "man delights not me?"
(Hamlet, II. ii.).

In the Restoration theatre one finds more allusions in the plays as well as more details about the behaviour of the players and their patrons, thanks to the stimulating effect on gossip by scandal in high society. Kynaston was notoriously homosexual and his intrigues with the Duke of Buckingham were subjects of contemporary satires. [223] James Nokes, who also played women, had the same reputation. [224] In recent times in China, high society and low were similarly connected with the players, but as the public attitude towards homosexual liaison was hardly different from that involving women, gossip was not the only vehicle for preserving information: the admirers of the boy players themselves left a large mass of mediocre verse which now forms the rubbish through which students of the Chinese theatrical history have to dig for useful information. [225]

---

[222] *Vide* A. Harbage, *Shakespeare and the Rival Traditions* (1952), 211-214.

[223] Summers, *The Playhouse of Pepys*, 295.

[224] Summers, *op. cit.*, 331, 293-296.

[225] The association of famous female impersonators with gossip both in seventeenth century England and in modern China raises the questions whether imitating female manners in early youth does not divert the normal development of sexual psychology into abnormal channels and whether those who are born homosexuals are more propitious for female roles. If the early training of the boy actors does affect their minds, in societies where homosexuals cannot easily follow their inclinations, the Puritans' cries in Elizabethan times had more serious significance than the unreserved objection to theatre made them appear to be. On the other hand, if female impersonation merely provides opportunities for natural homosexuals to exercise their inborn traits, only for those who look upon homosexuality with greater horror than heterosexual irregularities will the practice of female impersonation mar its artistic appreciation, because the admiration of actresses is no less dangerous and is more prevalent. The homosexuality among Chinese actors can hardly be independent of the strictly isolated life and hard apprenticeship, the economic pressure, and their living close together through puberty. Those among the audience who admire female impersonators for reasons other than art will always find boys more attractive than women, but without a corresponding inclination on the part of actors, such patrons can hardly be more than silent admirers.

CHAPTER XLI

THE CHINESE AND THE ELIZABETHAN THEATRE — III

(The Style of Acting — Sensuous Elements — The Audience —
Aberrations of Taste — Differences — On Conventions)

(12)

"The effects of the poetic imagination are wrought largely by suggestion, and the bare stage, by sparing the audience a hundred irrelevant distractions, helped poetry to do its work". [1]

Apart from poetic imagination, the most immediate effect of the bare stage on the drama is perhaps that on the style of acting.

Acting can suffer from excessive accessories. When the stage is complete with correct architectural details and furnishings, acting will tend to become natural movements which are hardly expressive in the artistic sense of the word. Without the knick-knacks that surround us in our daily life the actor, in order to make himself understood, is forced to fall back on the resources of gesticulatory expression the full potential of which is far from being realized in practical life. Depriving the actor of speech, as in dumb shows, has the same effect: the hands and eyes can do much of what the tongue is not allowed to do.

The Chinese style of acting is what is now called ballet; in fact, the whole performance of the Chinese drama is dramatic dance, accompanied throughout by music and far removed from naturalism. The exact nature of the acting in the Elizabethan theatre can perhaps never be known, but the general characteristics can be surmised from contemporary references to it.

In the preface of an unprinted play it is stated:

"The other parts of action is in ye gesture, wch must be various, as required; as in a sorrowful parte, ye head must hang downe; in a proud, ye head

---

[1] Raleigh, *Shakespeare*, 120.

must bee lofty; in an amorous, closed eies, hanging downe lookes, and crossed armes; in a hastie, fumeing and scratching ye head, etc". [2]

The text of Shakespeare contains some references to contemporary style of walking on the stage:

> "And, like a strutting player, whose conceit
> Lies in his hamstring and does think it rich
> To hear the wooden dialogue and sound
> 'Twixt his stretched footing and the scaffoldage —"
>
> (*Troilus and Cressida,* I.iii.)

Macbeth also remembers the player's strut,

> "a poor player
> That struts and frets his hour upon the stage".
>
> (*Macbeth,* V.v.)

One of the characters in Chapman's *A Humorous Day's Mirth* (I.i.) speaks of

"a king in an old fashioned play, having his wife, his council, his children and his fool about him, to whom he will sit and point very learnedly, as followeth,

> 'My council grave, and you, my noble peers,
> My tender wife, and you, my children dear,
> And thou, my fool'.

thus will I sit as it were and point out all my humorous acquaintance".

Strong emotions were expressed emphatically; for grief, by lying on the floor:

> *Romeo* . . . then mightst thou tear thy hair,
> And fall upon the ground, as I do now,
> Taking the measure of an unmade grave.

and later when Nurse asks where Romeo is,

> *Friar Laurance* There on the ground . . . (*Romeo and Juliet,* III.iii.)

and for joy, by cutting capers, as in *Charlemagne,* when Ganelon the Senecal man pretends that he is not disturbed by the news of his banishment. [3] Facial expressions were by no means subdued:

"Your courtier theoric is he that hath arrived at his furthest and doth now know the court by speculation rather than practice, this is his face: a fastidious and oblique face, that looks as it went with a vice and were screwed thus".

> (*Cynthia's Revels,* II.ii.)

---

[2] Quoted in C. B. Purdom, *Producing Shakespeare,* 123.

[3] *Vide* Bradbrook, *Themes and Conventions,* 22.

and in *The Return from Parnassus,* IV.iii.:

>"I was once at a Comedie in Cambridge, and there I saw a parasite make faces and mouths of all sorts on this fashion".

Hamlet shouts to the player

>"Pox, leave thy damnable faces and begin".   (*Hamlet,* III.ii.)

and Lady Macbeth asks Macbeth when he sees Banquo's ghost

>"Why do you make such faces?"   (*Macbeth,* III.iv.)

According to Lodge, the ghost that "cried so miserably: Hamlet, Revenge", was like an oyster wife, which hints at the long drawn voice. [4]

The accentuated style of acting may be due to the tradition established in the miracle plays before the Elizabethan dramas. [5] Popular theatre requires exaggeration in order to impress the dull wit of the common people. The open stage, however, must have been instrumental in preserving the tradition, for it is a natural show place, more suitable for display of skill and style than for realistic imitation. [6]

Apart from stylization in action, the Elizabethans and the Chinese had in real life what would seem to us artificial manners, especially in the upper classes, [7] hence to imitate their daily manners the actors had to be pompous. Each age probably has its own mannerisms and future historians, when they see us in films, will perhaps think our manners affected just as we do our fathers'. In any case, decorum in Elizabethan England and nineteenth century China concerned both the tone of speech and the bodily movements, and to be decorous one has to be trained. In Elizabethan times, "the ordinary commoner was not 'exercised in speaking'; it was therefore as a result of their professionally acquired facility that the players drew upon themselves, until well into the eighteenth century, the complaint that they continued to act outside the theatre, to wear splendid clothes, to talk and swagger with the air of noblemen". [8] Women are at all times more affected in their manners than men, hence along with "God hath given you one face, and you make yourselves another" Hamlet complains "you jig, you ample and you lisp", [9] and Stephen Gosson (*Playes Confuted in Fiue Actions,* p. 197.) found objection in the boy players putting on "the attyre, the gesture" of a woman. [10] Whereas the Elizabethans objected to the players aping their social superiors, Arlington, referring to the Chinese stage struts, complained of the original:

>"All actors, more especially the leading actors, must walk in a measured

---

[4]   *Vide* Bradbrook, *Themes and Conventions,* 24.

[5]   Bradbrook, *op. cit.,* 21.

[6]   cf. the classical drama in Japan, called *Noh* 能 ,which means "exhibition of talent".

[7]   B. L. Joseph, *Elizabethan Acting* (1951), 93 *infra;* Arlington, *The Chinese Drama,* 70 n.

[8]   Joseph, *op. cit.,* 93. See also Chambers, *Eliz. Stage,* IV. 204, quoting Stephen Gosson, *The School of Abuse,* p. 39.

[9]   *Hamlet,* III. i.

[10]   *Vide* Chambers, *Eliz. Stage,* IV. 217.

step or strut, called *fang-pu,* and showing, as they lift their feet, the sole of each boot, which is thick-soled and whitened, called *liang-hsueh-ti-erh* (亮靴底兒) 'exposing the soles of the boots': just as we often see the old style official strut along like a turkey cock, as it is considered by them *infra dig* to walk as an ordinary man would. This peacock strut is seldom seen nowadays, except on the stage: however, there are still a few mandarins left who practice it. When it disappears entirely, and we see an official driving his own motor-car, we shall know that the millennium — in China — has come at last!''. [11]

The Elizabethan and the Chinese stage versions of contemporary upper-class manners were not naturalistic but stylized. The fact that the semi-professional child players, who owing to their age could never have looked realistic, nevertheless caused real concern to the adult companies [12] shows that the audience did not value realism as much as skill. The Elizabethan players, like the Chinese, went through a hard apprenticeship at an early age and were trained in tumbling, dancing and singing. [13] The apprentices would "abide with and serve" their masters [14] which means that their lives, like those of the Chinese student-actors, were strictly controlled. The period of training of Elizabethan actors was seven years or more [15] but they played on the stage long before the period of apprenticeship was complete. [16]

All gesticulatory expression cultivated on the professional level tends to become dance. A repertoire of technique is built up from which the trained player can draw to modify and apply. Hence the Chinese drama should rather be said to be danced than to be acted. Orators in sixteenth century England cultivated their gestures in this way and their performance was called "dance", as in Cornelius Agrippa, *Of the Vanity and Uncertainty of Arts and Sciences* (1575), chapter on the subject, "Of Rhetorisme, or of the Rhetoricall Daunsing":

"There was moreouer the *Rhetoricall* daunsing, not vnlike that of the stage players, but not so vehemente, whiche *Socrates, Plato, Cicero, Quintilian,* and very many of the *Stoickes* thought very profitable, and necessary for an Oratour: so that it were done with a certayne apt gesture of the bodie, and a setled framing of the countenaunce, and body: and also with the stedfastnesse of the eyes, with the grauity of the countenaunce, with the sounde of the voice applied to euery worde and sentence, with an effectuall mouing of the body to such things, as are expressed, but without greate sturring of the bodie. Yet this

---

[11] L. C. Arlington, *The Chinese Drama* (1930), 70 n.

[12] Thorndike, *Shakespeare's Theatre,* 20 f; *Hamlet,* II. ii.

[13] Davies, *Shakespeare's Boy Actors,* 4.

[14] Henslowe's *Diary* shows he bought a boy John Brystow for eight pounds — Baldwin, *The Organization and Personnel of the Shakespearean Company,* 36.

[15] Baldwin, *The Organization and Personnel of the Shakespearean Company,* 33 f.

[16] Chambers, *William Shakespeare,* II. 82 f.

daunsing or Histrionicall Rhetoricke in the ende began to be lefte of all
Oratours . . . and at this presente it is altogyther laid aside: onely it is obserued
of some staged Friers (albeit in times paste stage players were banished out of
the Churche, and denied the holy Sacrament of Communion) of which some we
see at this day to crie out of the pulpit to the people with maruelous strayning of
the voyce, with a diuers fashioned countenaunce, with a rolling and wanton eie,
with casting abroade of the armes, with daunsing feete, with inflamed reines,
and with diuers mouings, reuolutions, turnings aboute, vpward lookes,
leapings, gesturing with all his body, as that which bicause of the vuconstancie
of the minde is enforced to turne with it''. [17]

In Vives, *On the Causes of the Corruption of the Arts* (1531), it is taken for granted
that declamatory voice is trained by singing teachers: "if its nature is being
investigated, it is the task of the philosopher; if the method of training it, of the
singing teacher". [18] Rhetorical delivery, consisting of modulation of voice and the
extensive use of simultaneous gestures, was a regular part of the school education in
Renaissance England and was used by players, lawyers, preachers and other public
speakers of the time. [19] John Bulwer published his *Chirologia* and *Chironomia* in
1644, giving details of rhetorical delivery, including the use of gestures, which he
called "manuall rhetoric". [20] It is to be remembered that the children players in the
private theatres in Elizabethan London were trained in schools and in the public
theatres the audience could hardly be satisfied with naturalism when they were used
to the formalized gestures in their preachers and lawyers. [21] When Hamlet says,
"Nor do not saw the air too much with your hand, thus", he is speaking not against
rhetoric, but its excess. [22]

It is understandably difficult to maintain a statuesque pose on a stage shared by
spectators but the habitual lack of naturalistic immobility probably augmented the
difficulty. A contemporary complaint reads:

> "Actors, you rogues, come away, cleanse your throats, blow your noses,
> and wipe your mouths ere you enter that you may have no occasion to spit or
> cough when you are non-plus. And this I bar, over and besides, that none of
> you stroke your beards to make action, play with your cod-piece points or stand
> fumbling on your buttons when you know not how to bestow yourself; serve
> God, and act cleanly". [23]

---

[17] *Vide* Joseph, *op. cit.,* 5 f.

[18] *Vide* Joseph, *op. cit.,* 35.

[19] Joseph, *op. cit.,* Ch. 1.

[20] See Joseph, *op. cit., passim.* for quotations and illustrations of hand gestures from Bulwer's books.

[21] cf. Bradbrook, *Stage Conditions,* 109.

[22] *Hamlet,* III. ii.

[23] Nashe, *Summer's Last Will and Testament,* Prologue.

The use of blank verse in Elizabethan dramas precludes naturalistic delivery. Poetic drama is not written to be spoken as colloquial conversation, as some modern revivals of Shakespeare show only too well. Prosodical and rhetorical devices in Elizabethan dramas are for certain *oral* effects: [24] the stress and cadence and rhyme and rhythm have their dramatic purposes, hence to speak the lines as if they are colloquial speech is to defeat those purposes. Modern *readers* still accept poetry as proper language for dramas, to them the rhetoric and the verse still appear "natural", but to the modern theatre audience, when the lines are spoken with flourish, the linguistic devices appear artificial, and sometimes actors try to disguise them, thereby destroying their beauty. Parts of the dialogue in Shakespeare's early plays are written as sonnets, for example, when Romeo meets Juliet:

Romeo If I profane with my unworthiest hand
     This holy shrine, the gentle sin is this;
     My lips, two blushing pilgrims, ready stand
     To smooth that rough touch with a tender kiss.

Juliet   Good pilgrim, you do wrong your hand too much,
     Which mannerly devotion shows in this;
     For saints have hands that pilgrim's hands do touch,
     And palm to palm is holy palmer's kiss.

Romeo Have not saints lips, and holy palmers too?

Juliet   Ay, pilgrim, lips that they must use in prayer.

Romeo O! then, dear saint, let lips do what hands do;
     They pray, grant thou, lest faith turn to despair.

Juliet   Saints do not move, though grant for prayers' sake.

Romeo Then move not, while my prayers' effect I take.

                   (*Romeo and Juliet,* I.v.) [25]

The overt use of the poetic devices makes this part of the dialogue sound like an operatic duet. Content, diction, meter and rhyme all cry out against translating it into conversation in prose.

Again, take the dialogue in *As You Like It,* V.ii, which is at one point about as repetitive as a *rondo:*

Silvius It is to be all made of sighs and tears;
     And so am I for Phebe.

Phebe   And I for Ganymede.

Orlando And I for Rosalind.

Rosalind And I for no woman.

Silvius It is to all made of faith and service;
     And so am I for Phebe.

---

[24] *Vide* Joseph, *op. cit.,* Ch. VI.

[25] For discussion of the oral effects of this passage see Joseph, *op. cit.,* 128 f.

Phebe	And I for Ganymede.
Orlando	And I for Rosalind.
Rosalind	And I for no woman.
	(Etc., etc.)

This goes on till Rosalind puts an end to it,

> "Pray you, no more of this: 'tis like the howling of Irish wolves against the moon".

but no sooner has she stopped it in others than she is at it herself:

"[To Silvius] I will help you, if I can:

[To Phebe]   I would love you, if I could.
               To-morrow meet me all together.

[To Phebe]   I will marry you, if ever I marry woman,
               and I'll be married to-morrow:

[To Orlando] I will satisfy you, if ever I satisfied man,
               and you shall be married to-morrow:

[To Silvius] I will content you, if what pleases you contents you,
               and you shall be married to-morrow.

[To Orlando] As you love Rosalind, meet:

[To Silvius] As you love Phebe, meet:
               And as I love no woman, I'll meet.
               So fare you well: I have left you commands.

Silvius	I'll not fail, if I live.
Phebe	Nor I.
Orlando	Nor I.

As in Handel's oratorio, repetitions pile on repetitions; one can.hear the "howling" in "And a - a - y for Ganymede". "And a - a - y for Rosalind". However painfully artificial and even comical it may look on paper, it can be quite serious and can sound attractive on the stage. The modern Chinese play *The Lotus Lamp*, [26] the action of which consists mainly of a couple separately questioning the two sons about an accident at school in which one of them killed a schoolmate, contains symmetrical and repetitive dialogue several times the length of that in *As You Like It,* V.ii, and yet it does not sound tedious. It is only when such dialogue is transplanted into the naturalistic tradition that it has to be reduced to burlesque, as was done by Terence Gray when Act IV, Scene v of *Romeo and Juliet,* which is normally cut in modern revivals, was produced in The Festival Theatre at Cambridge, a theatre "to attack the realistic tradition of acting and production". [27]

---

[26] 寶蓮燈

[27] Bethell, *Shakespeare and the Popular Dramatic Tradition* (1944), 134 f.

The reply to the critics on that occasion was the quotation from the scene:

> *Nurse*   O woe! O woeful, woeful, woeful day!
> Most lamentable day, most woeful day,
> That ever, ever I did yet behold!
> O day! O day! O day! O hateful day!
> Never was seen so black a day as this:
> O woeful day, O woeful day!

and other passages of similar import, though in different tones, spoken by the other mourners. The quotation was as much a confession of ignorance of the original manner of production as a defence for interpreting it as burlesque. A tacit assumption appeared to have been made that Shakespearean acting must be either serious in the way modern European audience know it, or burlesque, and the passages were cited to show that the scene was not the former.

It has, in fact, been stated as a general conclusion that realistic speech starves the drama. [28] A reproduction of colloquial speech precludes any delicate and precise use of words [29] and the most efficient use of vocal modulations, and this has been done till in most modern European dramas the only interest lies in the consistency of plot and characterization. The Elizabethan and the Yüan dramatists were, on the other hand, in love with their languages, the former, owing to the Renaissance and the latter, to the release from the conventions of classical Chinese literature. The linguistic resources of the Elizabethan and, potentially, even the modern Chinese dramas are wider and richer than colloquial speech. Prose is used occasionally in both schools of drama, but the main medium is verse, including couplets, lyrics and songs. [30]

When diction and syntax differ from the colloquial so must the tone and rhythm. Apparently Hamlet wants his players to speak as in poetry-reading, "trippingly on the tongue". [31] The style of delivery has changed so much since Elizabethan times that "the two and a half hours in which a play in Shakespeare's time was often acted would not be possible to-day, even without delays for acts and scenes, with the method of elocution now in vogue". [32] It is believed that Elizabethan actors could speak, on the average, twenty lines in a minute. [33] In spite of the speed, the range of tone and force appears to be considerable and the exercise was recommended for reasons of health. [34]

---

[28] Bradbrook, *Themes and Conventions,* 43.

[29] Bradbrook, *Stage Conditions,* 126.

[30] Bradbrook, *Themes and Conventions,* 97.

[31] *Hamlet,* III. ii.

[32] Poel, *Shakespeare in the Theatre,* 59.

[33] Adams, *Globe Playhouse,* 190.

[34] *Vide* Joseph, *op. cit.,* 35.

"And if thereto bee vsed a cleare and lowde reading of bigge tuned soundes by stops and certayne Pauses, as our comicall felowes now do, that measure rhetoricke by their peuish Rhythmes, it wil bring exceeding much good to the breast and Muscles". [35]

The similarity between the Elizabethan actors and orators does not mean that lines were merely recited on the stage, because oractors then, unlike orators now, made a special study of gestures to suit their words. [36] The contemporary idea of theatrical appreciation can be seen in Sir Richard Baker, *Theatrum Triumphans* (1670):

"For, it is not the scurrility, and ribaldry, that gives the contentment . . . but it is the *Ingeniousness* of the Speech, when it is fitted to the Person; and the *Gracefulness* of the *Action,* when it is fitted to the Speech; and therefore a Play *read,* hath not half the pleasure of a Play *Acted:* for though it have the pleasure of *ingenious Speeches;* yet it wants the pleasure of *Graceful action;* and we may well acknowledg, the *Gracefulness of action,* is the greatest pleasure of a *Play;* seeing it is the greatest pleasure of (the Art of pleasure) *Rhetorick:* in which we may be bold to say; there never had been so good Oratours, if there had not first been Players: seeing the best Oratours that ever were, account it no shame, to have learned the gracefulness of their Action, even from Players: *Demosthenes* from *Satyrus; and Cicero* from *Roscius".* [37]

About a century later, people could still think of going to the theatre "to hear a certain number of lines recited with just gesture and elegant modulation". (Samuel Johnson, Preface to *Shakespeare,* 1765).

The psychological aim of Elizabethan acting was not to stir the emotions. Nowadays actors imitate the part but do not *act* in the Elizabethan and Chinese sense of the word, except in farce. They are now concerned with putting as much life into the part as possible instead of making *themselves* articulate and expressive. Shakespeare, if not the other Elizabethan dramatists, did not aim at exploiting the feelings of the audience; he ignored many opportunities for touching scenes, for example, Hamlet's first interview with Ophelia, which is merely given in report. [38] "The speeches were spoken with passion, but it was not a passion which attempted to reproduce that which an actual person in such a situation would feel". [39] Elizabethan acting preserved the "balance between the respective claims of literature, emotion and mime". [40]

---

[35] *The Touchstone of Complexions* (1581).

[36] Joseph, *op. cit.,* Ch. 1.

[37] *Vide* Joseph, *op. cit.,* 141.

[38] cf. Bradbrook, *Stage Conditions,* 118.

[39] *Ibid.,* 119.

[40] Joseph, *op. cit.,* 75.

It is scarcely necessary to say that the wide range of vocal and gesticulatory expressions in the Elizabethan theatre, their mutually complementary functions, their departure from naturalism, their foundation in specialized technique and training and their aim, not of stirring feelings, but of revealing beauty — all these are also the characteristics of the Chinese theatre. [41]

(13)

The Elizabethan and Chinese audiences did not look forward to beauty of voice and gesture alone. Sensuous pleasures, which have now left the European drama and are served by other forms of theatre such as ballet, opera and revue, were in the Elizabethan and Chinese theatres mostly absorbed into the drama, which was the only form of theatre. The Elizabethan dramatist might have to work into his play some songs and dances, swordplay and battles, some arresting costume or spectacular property, a part for some actor with special talents, fine lines for discerning gentlemen and jests for the gulls, topical allusions and, almost always, bawdry and clowning. Juggling, tumbling, wrestling and fencing had sometimes to be incorporated in the action. [42] Of the types of spectacles, Chambers named battles, trials, funerals, banquets, weddings, rustic merrymaking, and dumb shows (for dreams and magicians' conjuring). [43] Some plays, like *Histriomastix* and *Jack Drum's Entertainment,* are medleys. [44] "Even in its supreme achievement, the plays of Shakespeare, the English drama betrays its experimentation, its lack of determined standards, and its confusion of artistic ideals with the demands of the populace". [45] "Besides poetry, the resources that lay to Shakespeare's hand were costume, gesture, dramatic grouping of the actors, procession, music, dancing and all kinds of bodily activity". [46] Singing and dance have become means of dramatic expression in the Chinese theatre, like declamation and music, and battle scenes, acrobatics, clowning and gags are too the regular adjuncts to the Chinese drama — by no means essential to the action but expected nevertheless by the audience. [47]

---

[41] The danger of mistaking the excitation of surface emotions for aesthetic experience exists everywhere, including the Chinese theatre. One Chinese theatrical anecdote reads: ". . . he played in *The Orphan of Chao* but the audience showed no emotion. After he came back from the stage he slapped himself till his cheeks were both red and, hugging the doll as the orphan, rehearsed in front of the dressing mirror, crying for a while and declaiming for a while. Some days later, he played the same role and the audience sobbed by the hundreds". 李開先, 詞謔（顏容）. 見, 周貽白, 中國戲劇史, 頁四六二.

[42] Raleigh, *Shakespeare,* 101-2.

[43] Chambers, *Eliz. Stage,* I. 185. See also L. B. Wright, Vaudeville Dancing and Acrobatics in Elizabethan Plays, *Englische Studien,* lxiii, 1928.

[44] *Vide* Bradbrook, *Themes and Conventions,* 35.

[45] Thorndike, *Shakespeare's Theatre,* 329.

[46] Raleigh, *Shakespeare,* 120.

[47] For gags in Shakespeare's text see Chambers, *William Shakespeare,* I. 154, 157, 285, 391.

Elizabethan actors had to be gymnasts, in order to execute leaps from walls and into traps, [48] and fly upon a wire. [49] The standard of swordsmanship required was high, because the audience was critical as well as appreciative; there is a stage direction in *The Devil's Law Case,* V.ii, for continuing a duel "a good length". [50] For fencing there is, for example, the last act of *Hamlet*; for daggers or rapiers, *Romeo and Juliet,* III.i.; for swordplay, the last act of *Macbeth*; for wrestling, *As You Like It,* I.ii.; and for slapstick comedy, *The Comedy of Errors*. It is difficult to find any dramatic purpose for the comic scene after Juliet's funeral (*Romeo and Juliet,* IV.v.) or that in *Othello,* III.iv, with Desdemona as the clown's assistant, or that at the beginning of Act III in the same play — they are in the plays to please some section of the audience.

Acrobatics was never far from the Elizabethan theatre:

". . . there is no tumbler
Runs through his hoop with more dexterity
Than I about this business".

(Fletcher's *The Noble Gentleman,* Act II.)

In 1583, on New Year's Day, Simon's men had to perform *matachins,* a series of intricate sword-dances in which combats were imitated, [51] and masks were probably used. [52] It must have resembled the Chinese stage fight which is also a dance to a certain degree. In Gosson's *Playes Confuted in Fiue Actions* (1582), it is maintained that the devil entices the eyes in the playhouse by sending in "garish apparell, masques, vaulting, tumbling, dauncing of gigges, galiardes, moriscoes, hobby-horses, shewing of judgeling castes — nothing forgot that might serve to set out the matter with pompe, or ravish the beholders with variety of pleasure". [53] Theatres were not entirely for dramatic performances: The Curtain, The Rose, The Swan, The Bull Inn and The Bel Savage Inn were sometimes used for fencing matches, and The Cross Keys Inn was once used for a performing horse. [54] Real horses might have been introduced into the masque; [55] and in any case, bears were used in *Mucedorus* and *Winter's Tale* (III.iii.). [56] Dances and speeches entertained the audience between acts [57] and puppet shows, imported from Italy, were worked into masques.

---

[48] Bradbrook, *Themes and Conventions,* 23.

[49] Chambers, *Eliz. Stage,* III. 77.

[50] Bradbrook, *Themes and Conventions,* 23.

[51] Lawrence, *Old Theatre Days and Ways,* 68.

[52] Chambers, *Eliz. Stage,* I. 371 n.

[53] *Vide* Lawrence, *Elizabethan Playhouse, First series,* 3.

[54] Chambers, *Eliz. Stage,* II. 380, 382, 383, 402, 414.

[55] Chambers, *Eliz. Stage,* III. 279.

[56] Chambers, *Eliz. Stage,* IV. 35. For the view that the bears might not have been real see Lawrence, *Those Nut-Cracking Elizabethans,* 25 ff.

[57] Chambers, *Eliz. Stage,* II. 557.

[58] Tarlton improvised poems after the plays on subjects chosen by the audience. [59] In *The Rich Cabinet of Rare Gems* (1616), the essential accomplishments of a good player are specified as "dancing, activity, music, song, elocution, ability of body, memory, vigilancy, skill of weapon, pregnancy of wit and such like", which also suggests the need to improvise in Elizabethan dramas. [60] Suppleness and control of the body were achieved by training boy actors in tumbling and fencing. [61]

The variety of extra-dramatic business indicates that reading Elizabethan dramas, as with Chinese dramas, yields a very poor idea of the actual performance. The visual effects of processions, pageants, battles and tableaux are entirely missing in the text.

Pageant accompanied the entry of kings and princes as well as on other occasions and the group movements can have such a complicated pattern as to become almost a dance, as in *Every Man out of His Humour*, III.i.:

> "*Orange and Clove: Puntavolo and Carlo: Fastidioso, Deliro and Matalente: Sogliano. They walk up and down and salute as they meet in the walk. They shift: Fastidioso mixes with Puntavolo: Carlo with Sogliano: Deliro and Matalente: Clove and Orange: four couple*".

The reception of the Greek generals for Cressida in *Troilus and Cressida,* IV.v, with its succession of couplets distributed between the various characters present, must have been acted like a dance. Dance or masque was overtly incorporated into *As You Like It, Love's Labour's Lost, Romeo and Juliet* and *The Tempest*. Many comedies ended in a terminal dance. [62]

Solo dance merely suffers on a picture-frame stage; figure dance is lost on it. The open stage, on which the floor plan is prominent, exposes awkward groupings and reveals elegant movements. [63] When the pattern of the movements is exploited, as in the pantomime, ceremonies and dumb shows in the Elizabethan theatre, it becomes figure dance. [64] Even for small groups, the position of the actors on the stage has an effect on their style of acting.

> "Its true indeede, honest *Dick,* but the slaues are somewhat proud, and besides, tis a good sporte in a part, to see them neuer speake in their walke, but at the end of the stage, iust as though in walking with a fellow we should neuer

---

[58] Chambers, *Eliz. Stage,* I. 281, III. 373, 382. There were separate puppet shows: *The Actors Remonstrance or Complaint,* in W. C. Hazlitt, *The English Drama and Stage* (1869), 262.

[59] Chambers, *Eliz. Stage,* II. 553, cf. improvised verse as a type of popular entertainment in Sung dynasty — see Ch. XXIV.

[60] Lawrence, *Old Theatre Days and Ways,* 68; See W. C. Hazlitt ed., *The English Drama and Stage under the Tudor and Stuart Princes 1543-1664* (1869), 228-230.

[61] Davies, *Boy Actors,* 33 f.

[62] Lawrence, *Elizabethan Playhouse, Second series,* 184.

[63] cf. Southern, *The Open Stage,* 20.

[64] cf. Reynolds, *Red Bull,* 176.

speake but at a stile, a gate, or a ditch, where a man can go no further".

(The Return from Parnassus, IV.iii.)

Here explanation is attempted for what it purely a theatrical gesture: actors taking the vantage points downstage before speaking. [65]

The opening parades of the opposing armies in the Elizabethan battle scenes, with the flags and weapons, must have had some dance quality, as on the Chinese stage to-day. It was usual to swear in some very ceremonious and theatrical manner; in *Hoffman* the Revengers circle round one of the group who kneels in the middle. [66] Even in static grouping, advantage is taken of the floor plan of the open stage. Dumb shows with their mute miming and accompanying music, as in Hamlet's players, have no equivalent in the modern European drama, their parallels can only be found in some scenes in operas in which music forms a commentary on the action and some scenes in the films. A funeral procession in *A Chaste Maid in Cheapside,* IV.v. is as follows:

> *"Enter at one door, recorders dolefully playing, the coffin of Touchwood Junior . . . at the other door the coffin of Moll . . . While all the company seem to weep and moan there is a sad song in the music room".*

The use of the sad song gives the whole scene a symbolic quality. Music also accompanied meditations, ceremonies, love scenes and tableaux; [67] it cannot be part of the action and must therefore be considered as background music. Sometimes the stage setting for meditation-scenes is symbolic as well, with perhaps a death's head, a book and a candle on a table. [68] One can see in the Chinese theatre how a solemn scene like this on the open stage can transform the whole theatre into a temple in the mind of the audience. In *The Devil's Law Case,* Romelio, having been presented with his own coffin in the manner of the *Duchess of Malfi,* recites a long meditation on death with a friar kneeling on one side, the bellman and his mother telling her beads on the other. [69] Ghosts and Furies performed weird and sinister dances, especially in Chapman's plays. [70] The witches' incantations in *Macbeth,* I.i. and I.iii. suggest dancing.

> "The weird sisters, hand in hand,
> Posters of the sea and land,
> Thus do go about, about:
> Thrice to thine, and thrice to mine.
> And thrice again, to make up nine,
> Peace! the charm's wound up".

---

[65] cf. the manner of entrance on the Chinese stage.

[66] Bradbrook, *Themes and Conventions,* 26.

[67] Bradbrook, *op. cit.,* 19. cf. modern films.

[68] Bradbrook, *op. cit.,* 28.

[69] Bradbrook, *op. cit.,* 28.

[70] For examples see Bradbrook, *op. cit.,* 26 n.

and in Act IV, scene i. of the same play, one of the witches recites,

"Round about the cauldron go".

and after each has spoken her part, they all join in the refrain:

"Double, double toil and trouble;

Fire burn and cauldron bubble".

Patterned movements, when associated with the action, "affected the quality of the feeling" in it, [71] and this can certainly be said of the Chinese drama. Dumb shows and tableaux are not exactly parts of the action, but are in fact symbolic scenes — symbolic scenes are rare in the Chinese theatre, but not entirely non-existent, for example, the dance of the "Avenging God" [72] in *The Story of the Black Pot*. [73]

Spectacles in the Elizabethan dramas are due to the love of the audience for them. "If tragedy and comedy had not succeeded in absorbing spectacle, they would have been overwhelmed by it. . . . Elizabethan drama is abundantly spectacular, and often enough the spectacle is irrelevant or excessive, but as a rule it is, formally at least, within the plot". [74] To the European audience of the Renaissance it might not matter as much as it does to us whether spectacle was formerly in the action or not; to them it was important that there should be spectacle. [75]

The demands on the technical skills of the Elizabethan and the Chinese actors are heavy but their social status is low and their livelihood precarious. Apprenticeship in both cases is about seven years, and in the Elizabethan theatre, the first three or four years are spent in assisting the prompter, such as placing chairs and producing stage effects. [76] Under such conditions it would be surprising if some players do not live in easy morals; it is only human nature to seek relief from anxiety and hardship. "Doubtless, there is a certain instability of temperament which the life of the theatre, with its ups and downs of fortune, its unreal sentiments and its artificially stimulated emotions, is well calculated to encourage". [77] It is no coincidence, therefore, that both Elizabethan and Chinese actors were considered to belong to the same social class as rogues and vagabonds. [78]

(14)

The importance of the audience as an influence on the quality of the theatre is due ultimately to the financial responsibilities of the producer. No dramatist or

---

[71] Bradbrook, *Themes and Conventions*, 27.

[72] 判官

[73] 烏盆記 — see Ch. XII.

[74] Chambers, *Eliz. Stage*, I. 185.

[75] cf. spectacle unconnected with the drama in the Italian theatre of the sixteenth century.

[76] Baldwin, *The Organization and Personnel of the Shakespearean Company*, 33, 293.

[77] Chambers, *Eliz. Stage*, I. 351.

[78] Chambers, *Eliz. Stage*, IV. 324, 337.

producer can dictate the type of performance he offers to the audience. Theoretically he can change their taste slowly by gradual modifications or risk losses in a brief period of possibly quick conversion, but actually the high cost of production gives the audience practically complete control of the type and quality of the play. For this reason, the extent of the similarity between the Elizabethan and the Chinese audience is a significant part of the comparative study of the theatres.

The exuberance of theatrical activity in the London of Elizabethan times is very similar to that in the late Sung and Yüan dynasties in China. [79] Weekly attendance at the then London theatres has been variously estimated as 30,000 among a population of 100,000 [80] and thirteen percent (20,800) of a population of 160,000. [81] In the latter half of the Elizabethan reign, there were in London fourteen theatres and twenty companies of players, and five hundred actors in this period are known by name. [82] It is to be remembered that the quality of enthusiasm among the audience of the past is different from that of to-day. In England of the sixteenth century and China of Yüan dynasty (1277-1367) there was no newspaper and radio, few people had books and still less in large numbers, most people could not read and Elizabethan London had few facilities for public amusements. Theatre was to the illiterate not only entertainment but also education [83] and had the fascination of knowledge without effort: to many of them theatre provided all that they learned about psychology, foreign lands, history and the effective use of their language.

The similar social conditions made even the methods of advertisement nearly identical. In both theatres playbills were posted in conspicuous places in the city and on the outside of the theatre. [84] Before the beginning of the play the Elizabethan manager flew a flag and three trumpet blasts announced the beginning of a play, but in the theatres of Yüan dynasty, costumes and weapons were hung out to indicate that a performance was at hand. [85] Announcement of the next performance after the epilogue is not known to have been used in China. [86] The Elizabethan practice of collection at strategic moments of the performance in inn-yards [87] and payment at the door [88] were both used in the early Chinese theatre. [89]

---

[79] See Ch. XXVI.

[80] Thorndike, *Shakespeare's Theatre*, 407.

[81] A. Harbage, *Shakespeare's Audience* (1941), 41.

[82] Hodges, *Globe Restored*, 15 f.

[83] cf. Thorndike, *Shakespeare's Theatre*, 412.

[84] Chambers, *Eliz. Stage*, II. 547.

[85] Lawrence, *Physical Conditions*, 96.

[86] Playbills were however posted in China a day before the performance — 馮沅君, 古劇說彙, 一章四節; 參, 齊如山, 戲班, 頁六十九.

[87] Adams, *Shakespearean Playhouses*, Ch. 1.

[88] Lawrence, *Elizabethan Playhouse, Second series,* Ch. IV. Early Systems of Admission.

[89] See Ch. XXVI.

The basic difference between the Elizabethan and the Chinese theatre on the one hand and the modern European theatre on the other may be said to be the unreserved hedonistic nature of the former. Theatre was to the Elizabethans and still is to the Chinese a place for unrestrained pleasures; there is no air of intellectualism and moralism in it. [90] Whereas in the modern European theatre dramatic appreciation is the only permissible activity for the audience, the Elizabethan and the Chinese audience also engaged themselves in eating, drinking, smoking and other pleasurable activities. [91] Taphouses, adjoined to the Elizabethan theatres and owned by the theatre proprietors, sold eatables and drinks; even in the private theatres, wine and beer were served. [92] The audience had to come early in order to get good seats, because the only way to reserve them was by actual occupation, and pamphlets were read and cards played in order to mitigate the tedium of waiting. [93] Light women were regularly among the audience and they and their fresh acquaintances naturally did not confine themselves to dramatic appreciation. [94] In Yüan dynasty, the connection between the Chinese theatre and the pleasure house could hardly be closer. To-day that connection no longer exists, but the Chinese theatre is still considered as a place of mixed pleasures.

The ability of the Elizabethan audience to stand continuous performance for two or three hours and of the Chinese audience, for five hours or more, is doubtlessly due to their freedom to refresh themselves during the progress of the plays. In the Chinese theatre one can practically order a whole meal and in the Elizabethan, one could buy beer, ale, fruit, bread, and sweetmeats. [95] Tobacco was served to the seated spectators:

> "The Tobacco-man, that used to walk up and downe, selling for a penny-
> pipe, that which was not worth twelve-pence an horse-load; . . ." [96]

The lack of intervals may also be related to the generally relaxed attitude of the audience: the performance was not aimed at producing emotional agitation.

A happy picture of the crowd in the Elizabethan theatre is left us in *The Roaring Girl,* I.i.:

> Nay, when you look into my galleries,
> How bravely they're trimmed up, you all shall swear
> You're highly pleas'd to see what's set down there:
> Stories of men and women, mix'd together,

---

[90] The last statement applies only partially to the Elizabethan private theatres.

[91] *Vide* Lawrence, *Those Nut-Cracking Elizabethans* (1935), Ch. I.

[92] Lawrence, *Pre-Restoration Stage Studies,* 25 f.

[93] Chambers, *Eliz. Stage,* II. 548 f; Lawrence, *Elizabethan Playhouse, First series,* 13.

[94] Chambers, *Eliz. Stage,* II. 548 f.

[95] Chambers, *Eliz. Stage,* II. 548 f; Reynolds, *Red Bull,* 9.

[96] *The Actors Remonstrance or Complaint,* in W. C. Hazlitt, *The English Drama and Stage* (1869), 264, 265.

Fair ones with foul, like sunshine in wet weather;
Within one square a thousand heads are laid,

Then the yard:

      . . . then, sir, below,
The very floor, as't were, waves to and fro,
And, like a floating island, seems to move
Upon a sea bound in with shores above. [97]

In a very similar theatre, a Yüan dramatist saw the spectators "sat in circling rows" and moved like a "human whirlpool" in the yard. [98] In the yard of the Elizabethan theatre, "the penny patrons were so glewed together in crowdes . . . that when they came foorth, their faces lookt as if they had been per boylde". [99] The liveliness of the Elizabethan spectators is shown as through the eyes of a Puritan critic:

> "You shall see such heauing, and shoouing, suche ytching and shouldring, too sitte by women; Such care for their garments, that they bee not trode on: Such eyes to their lappes, that no chippes light in them: Such pillowes to their backes, that they take no hurte: Such masking in their eares, I know not what: Such giuing them Pippins to passe the time: Suche playing at foote Saunt without Cardes: Such ticking, such toying, such smiling, such winking . . . that it is a right comedie, . . ." [100]

Owing to the lack of scenery in the Elizabethan and the Chinese theatre, spectators sitting on the stage were tolerated even though they must have spoiled the view for some of the audience. In the Chinese theatre the custom survives to-day, but as the custom only allows spectators standing at the back of the stage, the inconvenience they cause is small. The objection to the audience on the Elizabethan stage was not so much for the obstruction they caused as for their deliberate efforts at distracting the audience. Dekker's satirical advice to the gallant to sit on the stage begins as follows:

> "For do but cast vp a reckoning, what large cummings in are pursd vp by sitting on the Stage. First a conspicuous *Eminence* is gotten; by which meanes the best and most essenciall parts of a Gallant (good cloathes, a proportionable legge, white hand, the Persian lock, and a tolerable beard) are perfectly reuealed". [101]

These gallants could "haue a good stoole for sixpence", and at least the obnoxious among them would, while the Prologue was about to begin, "creepe from behind the Arras, with [their] *Tripos* or three-footed stoole in one hand, and a teston

---

[97] Quoted in Adams, *Shakespearean Playhouses*, 279.

[98] "孿孿坐"，"人漩渦"，太平樂府, 卷九, 莊家不識勾闌.

[99] Dekker, *Seuen Deadly Sinnes of London* (1606), quoted in Harbage, *Shakespeare's Audience*, 19.

[100] Gosson, *Schoole of Abuse* (1579) — see Chambers, *Eliz. Stage*, IV. 203.

[101] T. Dekker, *The Gull's Hornbook* — see Chambers, *Eliz. Stage*, IV. 366.

mounted betweene a forefinger and a thumbe in the other". Stage keepers served them with tobacco and pipe, [102] and late comers spread their bodies on the stage, probably because the supply of stools had been exhausted. [103] One gathers from Dekker's jibes that they often made themselves objectionable by movements and noise calculated to attract attention and thereby created disturbance:

> "It shall crowne you with rich commendation to laugh alowd in the middest of the most serious and saddest scene of the terriblest Tragedy: and to let that clapper (your tongue) be tost so high that all the house may ring of it . . ."

> ". . . neither are you to be hunted from thence though the Scar-crows in the yard, hoot at you, hisse at you, spit at you, yea throw durt euen in your teeth: tis most Gentlemanlike patience to endure all this, and to laugh at the silly Animals: but if the *Rabble* with a full throat, crie away with the foole, you were worse then a mad-man to tarry by it: for the Gentleman and the foole should neuer sit on the Stage together". [104]

It is remarkable how Elizabethan spectators could distinguish between players and gallants on the stage, they being dressed similarly and the latter were by no means immobile. It might be due to this difficulty that theatrical etiquette did not allow players to sit among the "gentlemen" on the stage. [105] The Elizabethan audience were used to the mixing of spectators with players, because the early interludes were played in the middle of a hall, where the spectators made room for the performance and surrounded the actors throughout the play. [106] The players then regularly addressed the spectators directly: in the induction of *Fulgens and Lucres,* two actors playing spectators say one to another:

> "I thought verely by your apparel,
>
> That ye had bene a player". [107]

According to Stephen Gosson,

> "In the playhouses at London, it is the fashion of youthes to go first into the yarde, and to carry theire eye through euery gallery, then like vnto the rauens where they spye the carion thither they flye, and presse as nere to ye fairest as they can". [108]

---

[102] Hotson, *Times Literary Supplement,* 16 May, 1952.

[103] W. Poel, *Bulletin of John Rylands Library,* Vol. 3, No. 1, p. 222 f.

[104] *Vide* Chambers, *Eliz. Stage,* IV. 367.

[105] *Vide The Malcontent,* Induction; also Rhodes, *Stagery of Shakespeare,* 92.

[106] The practice of sitting on the stage might not, however, be simultaneous with the appearance of the public theatres: Burbage's Theatre was built in 1576, but the earliest spectators known to be "over the stage" (in rooms at the back of the stage, overlooking it) were in 1592, and on the stage, in 1596. *Vide* Chambers, *Eliz. Stage,* II. 535.

[107] *Vide* Chambers, *Eliz. Stage,* III. 23-24.

[108] Stephen Gosson, *Playes Confuted in fiue Actions,* see Chambers, *Eliz. Stage,* IV, 218.

The more daring among the light women were apparently undaunted by the lack of privacy:

"Whosoeuer shal visit the chappel of Satan, I meane the Theatre, shal finde there no want of yong ruffins, nor lacke of harlots, vtterlie past al shame: who presse to the fore-frunt of the scaffoldes, to the end to showe their impudencie, and to be an obiect to al mens eies. Yea, such is their open shameles behauior, as euerie man maie perceaue by their wanton gestures, wherevnto they are giuen; yea, they seeme there to be like brothels of the stewes. For often without respect of the place, and company which behold them, they commit that filthines openlie, which is horrible to be done in secret; as if whatsoeuer they did, were warranted". (109)

The "filthiness" of which the Puritans complained was probably what Dekker referred to when he said of Satan that

"You may take him . . . in the afternoones, in the twopenny roomes of a Play-House, like a Puny, seated Cheeke by Iowle with a Punke". (110)

Things went further in the semi-privacy of the "rooms":

"No, those boxes, by the iniquity of custome, conspiracy of waiting-women and Gentlemen-Ushers, that there sweat together, and the couetousnes of Sharers, are contemptibly thrust into the reare, and much new Satten is there dambd by being smothred to death in darknesse". (111)

Lawrence feared the worst for this passage (112) believing that the "lord's room" was then "a licentious rendezvous for the lower middle classes", which elicited "But my dear Sir!" from Harbage. (113)

The advantage taken of the theatre by the prostitutes was common knowledge and the theatrical profession defended themselves by saying,

". . . though some have taxed our Houses unjustly for being the receptacles of Harlots, the exchanges where they meet and make their bargaines with their franck chapmen of the Country and City, yet we may justly excuse our selves of either knowledge or consent in these lewd practices, we having no propheticke soules to know womens honesty by instinct, nor commission to examine them". (114)

A promise is then made on behalf of the players that in the future they will cease to

---

(109) *Second and Third Blast of Retrait from Plaies and Theaters* (1580), quoted in Harbage, *Shakespeare's Audience*, 98; and Chambers, *Eliz. Stage*, IV. 208 f.

(110) Dekker. *News from Hell* (1600), see Adams, *The Globe Playhouse*, 66.

(111) Dekker, *The Gull's Hornbook* — Chambers, *Eliz. Stage*, IV. 366.

(112) Lawrence, *Elizabethan Playhouse, First series*, 30-31.

(113) Harbage, *Shakespeare's Audience*, 99.

(114) *The Actors Remonstrance or Complaint* (1643) quoted in W. C. Hazlitt, *English Drama and Stage*, 261 f.

admit into their "sixpenny rooms those unwholesome enticing harlots that sit there merely to be taken up by apprentices and lawyers' clerks". [115] A foreigner of the Venetian embassy gave us a description of a courtezan at close range:

"Scarcely was I seated ere a very elegant dame, but in a mask, came and placed herself beside me . . . She asked me for my address both in French and English; and, on my turning a deaf ear, she determined to honour me by showing me some fine diamonds on her fingers, repeatedly taking off no fewer than three gloves, which were worn one over the other . . . This lady's bodice was of yellow satin richly embroidered, her petticoat of gold tissue with stripes, her robe of red velvet with a raised pile, lined with yellow muslin with broad stripes of pure gold. She wore an apron of point lace of various patterns; her head tire was highly perfumed, and the collar of white satin beneath the delicately-wrought ruff struck me as extremely pretty". [116]

It is not unlikely that the popularity of the Elizabethan theatre was partly due to the new opportunity to meet women there. Thomas Nashe thought it was advantageous for the young gallant to

"embolden his blushing face by courting faire women on the sodaine, and looke into all Estates by conuersing with them in publike places". [117]

The Chinese theatre in Yüan dynasty and the Elizabethan theatre were, in atmosphere, more like modern music halls and night clubs than modern theatres. The physical proximity of the Elizabethan theatres in London to the "stews" on the south side of the Thames also accounted for the activities of light women among the audience. Bankside, where the theatres were mostly concentrated, was also an area for gambling parlours and bull-rings. [118]

(15)

The taste of the Elizabethan audience for erotic matter has left its mark on the text of the dramas. Apart from bawdry, which is comic in nature, the erotic theme was often treated seriously, as in Juliet's expectant speech when she is waiting for Romeo after their marriage (*Romeo and Juliet*, III.ii.) and similar speeches spoken by Troilus (*Troilus and Cressida*, III.ii.) and Falstaff (*Merry Wives of Windsor*, V.v.). In Field's *Amends for Ladies*, Act IV, scene i, Lady Bright and Bold, disguised as a maid, is shown half-dressed and retiring to bed and in the following

---

[115] Lawrence, *Elizabethan Playhouse, First series*, 37.

[116] *Diaries and Despatches of the Venetian Embassy at the Court of King James I in the Years 1617, 1618. Quarterly Review*, CII, p. 416.

[117] *Pierce Penilesse, His Supplication to the Divell*, 1592 — Harbage, *op. cit.*, 98.

[118] Adams, *Shakespearean Playhouses*, Ch. VII., for contemporary maps see *ibid., passim.*

scene a description is given of the moves in a narrowly averted rape. [119] Sometimes seduction scenes are veiled in symbolic dumb shows and music, as in *A Warning for Fair Women,* Act II.,

> *"Next comes Lust before Browne, leading Mistress Sanders covered with a black veil, Chastity, all in white, pulling her back softly by the arm. Then Drury, thrusting away Chastity, Roger following. They march about, and then sit to the table. The Furies fill wine. Lust drinks to Browne, he to Mistress Sanders; she pledgeth him. Lust embraceth her; she thrusteth Chastity from her; Chastity wrings her hands and departs".*

and in Marston's *Sophonisba,* where while a "treble viol and bass lute play softly within the canopy" Syphax says,

> "O, you dear founts of pleasure, blood and beauty,
>
> Raise active Venus with fruition
>
> Of such provoking sweetness — Hark, she comes!"

then, with "short song to soft music above" "enter Erictho in the shape of Sophonisba, her face veiled, and hasteth within the canopy" followed by Syphax. [120] In Kyd's *Spanish Tragedy* (II.iv.) action is indicated in the dialogue:

Bel.	If I be Venus, thou must needs be Mars;
	And where Mars reigneth, there must needs be wars.
Hor.	Then thus begin our wars: put forth thy hand,
	That it may combat with my ruder hand.
Bel.	Set forth thy foot to try the push of mine.
Hor.	But first my looks shall combat against thine.
Bel.	Then ward thyself: I dart this kiss at thee.
Hor.	Thus I retort the dart thou threw'st at me.
Bel.	Nay, then to gain the glory of the field,
	My twining arms shall yoke and make thee yield.
Hor.	Nay, then my arms are large and strong withal:
	Thus elms by vines are compass'd, till they fall.
Bel.	O, let me go, for in my troubled eyes
	Now may'st thou read that life in passion dies.
Hor.	O, stay a while, and I will die with thee;
	So shalt thou yield, and yet have conquer'd me.

---

[119] Even perversions are openly spoken of, as when Syphax is thinking of various rapes:

"I'll tack thy head

To the low earth, whilst strength of two black knaves

Thy limbs all wide shall strain".

(Marston, *Sophonisba,* III. i.) For other cases of sexual perversion see A. Harbage, *Shakespeare and the Rival Traditions* (1952), 210 ff.

[120] For other examples of similar scenes see Harbage, *Shakespeare and the Rival Traditions,* 204. cf. E. Partridge, *Shakespeare's Bawdy* (1948), 3-56.

Amorous action is also indicated in stage directions, as in Jonson's *The Devil Is an Ass* (II.ii.) where Wittipol and Mistress Fitzdottrel make love through the windows of their houses — in the 1632 edition, the author tells us in the margin of the action as produced in Blackfriars:

"acted at two windo's, as out of two contiguous buildings"

and as the encounter progresses Wittipol

"grows more familiar in his Courtship, playes with her paps, kisseth her hands, etc". [121]

Nudity does not seem to have been exploited in the Elizabethan theatre, although "naked" men dancing in nets were mentioned by the Puritan critics. [122]

However robust the sensibility of the audience, human nature is such that erotic matter is usually presented in public under veil. According to Castelvetro *(Poetics of Aristotle,* 1571):

". . . it is to be noted that [indecencies] do not make us laugh when they are set openly before the eyes of the body or of the mind in the presence of others; rather they overcome us with shame . . . Then the aforesaid things make us laugh when they are presented . . . under a veil, by means of which we are able to give the appearance of laughing not at the indecency but at something else". [123]

The Chinese dramatist and critic Li Yü stipulated that indecencies should only be presented either in *double entendre* or half finished sentences. [124] Occasionally however a Chinese clown shocks the audience into laughter by being unexpectedly outspoken. This can be effective only when it is rare, otherwise it becomes tedious. In such cases the audience are not "overcome with shame" probably because there is in the clown an element of childlike defiance and a fool's disregard for propriety; one can detect an element of satire for the sophistication involved in fig-leaves. It is not in the subject matter that the Elizabethan and the Chinese dramatists differ from modern European playwrights, but in the frankness with which the subject is treated. The degree of licence is entirely a matter of custom and habit, it is doubtful that it can be considered as a reliable measure of the morality of the age. Modern customs allow considerable eroticism in public, as shown in spectacles other than the drama, but it is not thought to be a proper element of the drama, because the audience of modern European dramas are no longer a pleasure-loving crowd.

The Elizabethan theatrical taste can be better understood against the background of the other types of contemporary public entertainment which were sometimes offered in the theatres and with which pseudo-dramatic performances

---

[121] *Vide* Hodges, *Globe Restored,* 63.

[122] Chambers, *Eliz. Stage,* IV. 200.

[123] Quoted in Harbage, *Shakespeare and the Rival Traditions,* 219.

[124] 李笠翁, 曲話, 曲詞第五, 戒淫褻.

were sometimes mixed. Next to drama, bull- and bear-baiting were the most popular forms of entertainment in Elizabethan times and the shape of the theatre building was in fact partly influenced by that of the bull-baiting rings. A mixed performance at Southwark on the twenty-fourth of August 1584 was recorded by Lupold von Wedel:

"There is a round building three stories high, in which are kept about a hundred large English dogs, with separate wooden kennels for each of them. These dogs were made to fight singly with three bears, the second bear being larger than the first and the third larger than the second. After this a horse was brought in and chased by the dogs, and at last a bull, who defended himself bravely. The next was that a number of men and women came forward from a separate compartment, dancing, conversing and fighting with each other: also a man who threw some white bread among the crowd, that scrambled for it. Right over the middle of the place a rose was fixed, this rose being set on fire by a rocket: suddenly lots of apples and pears fell out of it down upon the people standing below. Whilst the people were scrambling for the apples, some rockets were made to fall down upon them out of the rose, which caused a great fright but amused the spectators. After this, rockets and other fireworks came flying out of all corners, and that was the end of the play". [125]

Details of bull-baiting are given in an account of the visit of Frederick, Duke of Württemberg, on the first of September 1592:

"His Highness was shown in London the English dogs, of which there were about 120, all kept in the same enclosure, but each in a separate kennel. In order to gratify his Highness, and at his desire, two bears and a bull were baited; at such times you can perceive the breed and mettle of the dogs, for although they receive serious injuries from the bears, are caught by the horns of the bull, and tossed into the air so as frequently to fall down again upon the horns, they do not give in, so that one is obliged to pull them back by their tails, and force open their jaws. Four dogs at once were set on the bull; they, however, could not gain any advantage over him, for he so artfully contrived to ward off their attacks that they could not well get at him; on the contrary, the bull served them very scurvily by striking and butting at them". [126]

Another type of spectacle was recorded by a secretary to the Duke of Najera, who visited Henry VIII in 1544.

"Into the same place they brought a pony with an ape fastened on its back, and to see the animal kicking amongst the dogs, with the screams of the ape,

[125] Chambers, *Eliz. Stage,* II. 455.
[126] W. B. Rye, *England as Seen by Foreigners in the Days of Elizabeth and James the First* (1865) — Chambers, *Eliz. Stage,* II. 455.

beholding the curs hanging from the ears and neck of the pony, is very laughable''. [127]

Yet another type, similar to bear-baiting, was mentioned by Dekker:

"At length a blind bear was tied to the stake, and instead of baiting him with dogs, a company of creatures that had the shapes of men and faces of Christians (being either colliers, carters, or watermen) took the office of beadles upon them, and whipped Monsieur Hunkes till the blood ran down his old shoulders''. [128]

It was of bear-baiting that Macbeth speaks:

"They have tied me to a stake; I cannot fly,
But bear-like I must fight the course''. (*Macbeth*, V.vii.)

Hope Theatre had a removable stage so that it could be easily converted into an animal-baiting ring, which occurred regularly once in a fortnight, and Ben Jonson mentioned that the place stank. [129] The first English theatre, called The Theatre, built in 1576 by Burbage, was erected also for such shows as fencing, tumbling and rope-dancing, [130] and there was also fencing in The Swan. [131] Acrobats were imported from Italy [132] but there were tumblers among native players [133] and tumbling and vaulting, called "activities", were presented at court [134] as well as in Germany by travelling English players. [135] Sometimes vaulting performances involved a horse. [136] "Activities" were also part of the performance in the public theatres [137] and acrobatics was probably worked into *The Labours of Hercules*. [138] In Elizabethan times, tumblers, dancers and players were considered to be the same type of people. [139]

Different observers of a theatre will take note of different aspects of it; what is to one insignificant may seem important to another. The Europeans can only see the Chinese theatre with alien eyes, to them all that differs from their theatre is

---

[127] Chambers, *Eliz. Stage*, II. 454.

[128] Dekker, *Work for Armourers* (1609) — see Chambers, *Eliz. Stage*, II. 457.

[129] Adams, *Shakespearean Playhouses*, 330.

[130] Thorndike, *Shakespeare's Theatre*, 44, 56.

[131] Chambers, *Eliz. Stage*, II. 395, 413.

[132] Lawrence, *Old Theatre Days and Ways*, Ch. V. Elizabethan Acrobats; Chambers, *Eliz. Stage*, II. 261-3, IV. 154.

[133] Chambers, *Eliz. Stage*, II. 99, 101.

[134] Chambers, *Eliz. Stage*, II. 110, 111, 118 f, 136, 176; IV. 101 ff, 156; Chambers, *William Shakespeare*, II. 305, 306.

[135] Chambers, *Eliz. Stage*, II. 272, 273.

[136] Chambers, *Eliz. Stage*, II. 529 n.

[137] Chambers, *William Shakespeare*, I. 32, 33-35, 37-39.

[138] Chambers, *Eliz. Stage*, II. 550.

[139] Chambers, *Eliz. Stage*, IV. 205, 206, 273, 279.

noteworthy. The unfamiliar is recorded as curiosity and ignored as an element of the theatrical art. It is no doubt difficult for them to realize that to the Chinese all that pertains to their theatre are matters of course. Similarly in the Elizabethan theatre the modern students of theatrical history may be tempted to consider all differences with the theatre of to-day as "abnormal" although to the Elizabethans nothing about their theatre would seem strange. The uninformed student of poetry is as much mistaken in thinking that the Elizabethan theatre was a dedicated institution for poetical composition as the contemporary Puritans were in seeing it as the "chapel of Satan"; different mental positions distort the view differently. In order to understand the Elizabethan and the Chinese theatre as the Elizabethans and the Chinese of Yüan dynasty did, it is important to remember that the theatre was in both cases still near to the fair ground, both in fact and in spirit. The same crowd in Elizabethan London went to see bear-baiting and to the theatres near the "rings", just as the same Chinese crowd in Yüan dynasty went to see the jugglers, puppet players, story-tellers, pugilists' matches and conjurers as to watch the plays, and the Chinese theatre was then also used for other types of entertainment. It is only against such a psychological background that one can understand the attitude of the Elizabethans and the Chinese towards the theatre. The relative importance of intellectual and sensuous interests is so different in the modern European theatre that some emphasis on this point appears justified.

One can picture the atmosphere of an Elizabethan or Chinese playhouse by thinking of a large crowd in the mood for excitement. The audience in the Elizabethan theatre was literally a crowd: the capacity of Fortune, for example, is estimated to be between two and three thousand, [140] and that of a Chinese temple theatre is generally above seven thousand. [141] Such a large crowd is inevitably a mixed one. [142]

> "For, as we see at all the play-house doores,
> When ended is the play, the dance, and song,
> A thousand Townesmen, gentlemen, and whores,
> Porters and serving-men together throng". [143]

The taste of the audience is naturally far from being homogeneous. It is said of the Chinese theatre of the nineteenth century that

> "Those in the gallery usually like dramas on romance and intrigue, and

---

[140] For the capacity of Elizabethan theatres see Harbage, *Shakepeare's Audience,* Ch. II.

[141] It is difficult to generalize on the capacity of Chinese theatres — the type and size varying so much. The standing room of the temple theatres makes them capacious even with moderate size, for example, a yard 100 ft. by 100 ft. will accommodate 7,000 standing spectators allowing 10 in. by 20 in. for each of them.

[142] For the composition of the Elizabethan audience see Harbage, *Shakespeare's Audience,* Ch. III.

[143] Sir John Davies, "In Cosmun" Epigram No. 17, quoted in Harbage, *op. cit.,* 84.

those downstairs, combats, crime and violence, hence the programme usually consists of both". [144]

The Chinese producer can offer both types of drama because the programme normally consists of several plays, but the Elizabethan players had to incorporate fencing and battle-scenes in their tragedies. Exactly the same problem was formulated by Lovelace in 1649:

"His *Schollars* school'd, sayd if he had been wise

He should have wove in one two comedies.

The first for th' gallery, in which the throne

To their amazement should descend alone,

The rosin-lightning flash and monster spire

Squibs, and words hotter than his fire.

Th' other for the gentlemen o' th' pit

Like to themselves all spirit, fancy, wit". [145]

From this mixture, the Puritans were, in principle, missing.

"For such playes are made to sport, and delight the auditorie, which consisting most of young gallants, and Protestants (for no true Puritanes will endure to bee present at playes) . . ." [146]

The effect of their absence cannot of course be ignored.

"The absence of this body of sober middle-class opinion was of incalculable importance: the average Elizabethan dramatist was not over-scrupulous how he obtained his effects, and his opportunities for introducing gross and licentious matter were increased as the restraints of solid burgess disapproval were removed, and the encouragement of a dissolute raffish element was given fuller scope". [147]

Since then the "sober middle-class opinion" must have produced its effect on the British theatre (otherwise Bennett would not have been able to notice its absence in the Elizabethan theatre). There being no Puritanical element in Chinese society, the hedonism of the theatre continued until some years ago a new brand of Puritanism stifled more than theatrical enjoyment.

The predominant manners of the crowd in the Elizabethan theatre were, by modern standards, bad; rowdiness if not riotousness may be believed to be characteristic. [148] Their expressions of approval and of disapproval were alike unrestrained:

". . . in the Theaters they generally take vp a wonderfull laughter, and

---

[144] 包世臣, 都劇賦序, 見, 周貽白, 中國戲劇史, 頁七三六.

[145] Epilogue to his lost play *The Scholars* (1649), quoted in Lawrence, *Pre-Restoration Stage Studies* (1927), 315.

[146] Ecclesiastical document in manuscript, quoted in Harbage, *Shakespeare's Audience*, 71.

[147] H. S. Bennett, *Shakespeare's Audience* (1944), p. 3 — Reprint from *The Proceedings of the British Academy*, Vol. XXX.

[148] *Vide* Harbage, *Shakespeare's Audience*, 92-116.

shout altogether with one voyce, when they see some notable cosenedge practised''. [149]

For unfortunate poets,

> ''As they stand gaping to recieue their merrit,
> Instead of plaudits, their chiefest blisses,
> Let their desarts be crowned with mewes and hisses''. [150]

Mewes and hisses [151] were also used on the spectators on the stage when they made a nuisance of themselves:

> ''But on the very Rushes where the Commedy is to daunce, yea and vnder the state of *Cambises* himselfe must our fethered *Estridge,* like a peece of Ordnance be planted valiantly (because impudently) beating downe the mewes and hisses of the opposed rascality''. [152]

The audience also shouted at the players, as Jonson's ''caprichious gallants'' who

> ''haue taken such a habit of dislike in all things, that they will approue nothing, be it neuer so conceited or elaborate, but sit disperst, making faces, and spitting, wagging their vpright eares, and cry filthy, filthy''. [153]

Applause was by hand clapping and cries:

> ''Player is much out of countenance, if foolles doe not laugh at them, boyes clappe their hands, pesants ope their throates, and the rude raskal rabble cry excellent, excellent''. [154]

No applause is sincere if the audience is not free to hiss. The free and immediate response of the Chinese and the Elizabethan audience must have an effect on the performance — the appreciative audience making the good performance better and the bad one worse. [155] In the modern theatre, the actors act by themselves and the

---

(149) Gosson, *Playes Confuted in fiue Actions* (1582), see Chambers, *Eliz. Stage,* IV. 213 ff.

(150) John Day, *Isle of Gulls* (1606), IV. iv.

(151) On hissing in the English theatre, especially in Elizabethan times, see Lawrence, *Old Theatre Days and Ways,* Ch. X. Getting the Bird.

(152) Dekker, *The Gull's Hornbook,* see Chambers, *Eliz. Stage,* IV. 366.

(153) Jonson, *The Case is Altered,* II. vii. quoted in Harbage, *Shakespeare's Audience,* 109.

(154) T. G., *The Rich Cabinet Furnished with Varietie of Descriptions* (1616), in W. C. Hazlitt, ed., *The English Drama and Stage under the Tudor and Stuart Princes 1543-1664* (1869), 228-230.

(155) The ancient Greeks also shouted and hissed freely at their players and figs, olives and stone were used for pelting unpopular actors. (Haigh, *The Attic Theatre,* 344). The manners in the Spanish theatre in the Renaissance period were similar to the Elizabethans'. (Rennert, *The Spanish Stage,* 116 f). The Chinese actors in Peking are accustomed to genuine appreciation and cannot act well in front of Philistines. When the famous T'an Hsin-P'ei (譚鑫培) was engaged to play in Shanghai, he was welcomed by the city with unprecedented lavish advertisements in the streets and the best of personal services and attention, but was disgusted after a few performances with the ignorant applause of the audience. Being tied to a contract, he continued to act, but deliberately sang with wrong pronunciation and missed the beats in the music, out of spite. A man in the gallery waited for his mistake and shouted a sarcastic ''bravo'' but the audience, being admirers of T'an, threw the expert in the gallery out of the theatre and gave him a sound beating. 王夢生, 梨園佳話, 三章, "譚鑫培".

spectators watch by themselves. "We sit in decorous rows, scrupulously ignoring our neighbors, applauding generously and in cautious unison whatever is tolerable and well meant, suffering in docile silence whatever is feeble, dull or foolish". [156] The Elizabethans and the Chinese, on the other hand, enjoyed their theatre with gusto: there was more traffic among the audience themselves, theatre-going was then literally an *activity*.

(16)

There are of course differences in certain areas between the Chinese and the Elizabethan theatre. The modern Chinese theatre differs from the Elizabethan theatre in greater emphasis on histrionic and musical accomplishments and in more thorough conventionalism.

The Chinese theatre of to-day is not so much the dramatist's art as the player's. It is difficult to ascertain to what extent acting and singing were valued in the Chinese theatre of Yüan dynasty: the fact that some players were known for their specialized roles does not indicate with exactitude the relative importance of actors and dramatists. Dramas of high literary quality were however written at that time and there were indications that the text had a great influence on the success of the play. [157] To-day the Chinese dramas have no literary value at all; the artistic value of the Chinese theatre lies now entirely in its highly developed histrionic technique. The same plays are performed over and over again and the audience know the text of the famous plays almost by heart, but they still go to watch them because the interest of the plays lies mainly in what the players build on the text, not in the text itself.

In the Elizabethan theatre the audience were much more interested in the text. A new play was performed only for a few days [158] and, though it might be repeated later, it became out of date in a year or two [159] and revivals were the exception rather than the rule. [160] New plays could be depended upon to draw the crowd because the audience were accustomed to emotional as well as visual sensationalism. Beaumont and Fletcher as well as Jonson could excite the curiosity of the audience by keeping them in the dark. [161] Apart from the histories and some Greek legends, the story of the plays was unknown to the audience, hence irony and other literary delicacies in Shakespeare's and other dramatists' work could not have been noticed

---

[156] Harbage, *op. cit.,* 92.

[157] See Ch. XXVI.

[158] Raleigh, *Shakespeare,* 107; Lawrence, *Those Nut-Cracking Elizabethans,* 176.

[159] Thorndike, *Shakespeare's Theatre,* 262.

[160] *Vide* Chambers, *Eliz. Stage,* III. 104, also II. 148. A new play might be repeated within a week but as a rule one performance a week was the limit, and after a play had been performed for a few weeks, the intervals between its appearances increased rapidly.

[161] Harbage, *Shakespeare's Audience,* Chs. V and VI.

by the contemporary audience, not at any rate at first hearing. [162] Elizabethans are not known to have made repeated visits habitually to the same plays, hence the Shakespeare which the modern readers know by intensive study is very different from what his audience heard spoken once in the theatre. When Juliet says,

> "O! think'st thou we shall ever meet again?"

and Romeo answers,

> "I doubt it not; . . ."

the audience, unlike the reader, cannot know that they will meet again, but in a tomb. Juliet's

> "O God! I have an ill-divining soul:
> Methinks I see thee, now thou art so low,
> As one dead in the bottom of a tomb:"

and

> "Be fickle, fortune;
> For then, I hope, thou wilt not keep him long,
> But send him back".

(Romeo and Juliet, III.v.)

cannot have any particular significance to those who do not know the end of the story. There are not many instances in which the dialogue of an Elizabethan play gains emotional overtones through knowledge of subsequent events; the Elizabethan dramatists did not particularly exploit dramatic irony. Characters in Elizabethan plays become more interesting to the audience gradually in the progress of the plays; but the characters in Chinese dramas are mostly well known to the audience.

In spite of the conventions in the Elizabethan theatre there were partial efforts towards realism. The back wall of the Chinese stage is always a theatric feature instead of part of the scene, it is often covered with tapestry for the decoration of the stage and lined with spectators, never with scenery or setting. The rear and upper stage of the Elizabethan theatre, however, are in fact a permanent "built set"; they are concealed with curtains when not in use but become solid scenery whenever required. Although this facade of the tiring house cannot be changed like movable scenery, yet its ability to hold actors and its reasonable resemblance to what it represents give the Elizabethan stage a realistic quality which the Chinese stage lacks. The use of singing in the Elizabethan theatre not as a style of delivery but as incidental embellishment must have further influence on the naturalism in the acting.

The main acting space of the Chinese and the Elizabethan stage is a simple platform, but the Elizabethan stage has also auxiliary acting space on four levels,

---

[162] cf. A. C. Sprague, *Shakespeare and the Audience* (1935), 145 f.

extending both above and below the platform. Beneath the main stage, and connected with it through traps, is the *cellar,* which can represent hell, wine cellar, underground cave, dungeon, prison or ship compartments below deck. [163] The *rear stage,* or inner stage, on the platform level, may stand for shop, throne room, bed chamber, hermit's cell, chapel, cave, law court, tomb vault or tent. [164] Above this is the *upper stage,* which represents city wall, balcony, tower, fort, prison or the seating space for the audience watching a play in the play, [165] and on the two sides of the upper stage are windowed side-balconies which represent the facade of the second storey of houses when the stage represents the street. [166] The third floor of the tiring house is also open to the main stage and can become part of the scene as tower or the elevated positions on board ship. [167] The partial ceiling of the stage is the "heaven" which can open to let through the "throne" carrying the deities, on its descent or ascent. [168] The Elizabethan stage doors, unlike Chinese stage doors, have real knockers, locks and wicket doors. [169] The stage trap is another feature of the Elizabethan theatre which is lacking on the Chinese stage. There are at least five traps on the Elizabethan stage [170] and the largest one, probably about eight feet by four feet, can carry several actors or large sets, and most of them can raise or lower their load at various speeds, with music to disguise the noise. [171]

Curtains on the Elizabethan stage are theatric features only in such scenes where the rear stage, which they cover, is to be ignored, then they are the same as the tapestry at the back of the Chinese stage. For indoors scenes, they are dramatic features, being part of the scenes, as when Polonius and the King hide behind them to spy on Hamlet and Ophelia and when Polonius is killed behind them in the closet scene. [172] They are realistic because tapestry was often used in Elizabethan houses

---

[163] Adams, *The Globe Playhouse,* 126 f; Watkins, *On Producing Shakespeare,* 52.

[164] *Vide* Adams, *op. cit.,* 173 *et seq.*

[165] Adams, *op. cit.,* 241-297; Albright, *Shakesperian Stage,* 63.

[166] Adams, *op. cit.,* 256-275.

[167] Adams, *op. cit.,* 298-308.

[168] Adams, *op. cit.,* 367-369, 376-378. The only multiple-level stages in China are those in the imperial palaces in Peking which were used for spectacular plays on royal birthdays. They were built as three platforms one on top of the other, on which hundreds of players, dressed as gods and fairies, could give the emperor their birthday good wishes. The visibility of the upper two levels are, for obvious reasons, poor except from a particular position which is probably why the construction has never been used in commercial or temple theatres. For reproduction of the multiple-stage see 周貽白, 中國戲劇史, 頁六九五, 六九六.

[169] Adams, *op. cit.,* 153-161; Lawrence, *Physical Conditions,* 20 f.

[170] *Vide* Lawrence, *Pre-Restoration Stage Studies,* Ch. VII. Stage Traps in the Early English Theatre.

[171] For the capacity and method of working of Elizabethan stage traps see J. C. Adams, *The Globe Playhouse,* 113-123, 209-217, 219-228.

[172] *Hamlet,* III. i. iv.

for decoration. [173] When used for discovering scenes and tableaux they are again theatric features [174] and then they are used like the front curtain, one of the chief instruments of the naturalistic stage, thus introducing an element of naturalism into the Elizabethan theatre. [175]

Large properties are, in their function, akin to built sets. Properties and built sets are often imaginary and at best symbolic on the Chinese stage but on the Elizabethan they are generally realistic and occasionally imaginary. There are real beds, coffins, hearses, chairs of state, carriages for deities, trees, tents, shop counters, altars, racks, scaffolds, fences, walls, tombs and Hell mouths, [176] and properties having the same decorative function as costumes, such as weapons, are, as in the Chinese theatre, real and well made. [177] Properties which are often used such as lanterns, tables, chairs, pens, swords and so on seem to be the same in both theatres, but the real chains, images of gods, wall portraits, rich cradles, feather beds, distaffs and spindles and "a goat led in" on the Elizabethan stage would certainly be symbolic on the Chinese. [178]

Whereas all stage effects in the Chinese theatre are imitations by musical instruments they, and the off stage noises, were all realistic in the Elizabethan theatre. [179] The bells in *Macbeth* and *Othello* were stored in the turret above the stage and the cannon was installed on the top of the theatre for special effects. On one occasion, namely a performance of *Henry VIII* on 29th June, 1613, the cannon caused the fire that burnt down the first Globe theatre. [180] The Chinese stage deities enter and leave just like other characters, but the Elizabethan stage gods really came down from "heaven". [181] The devils could spit fire and fireworks were extensively used in scenes with devils. [182] For lightning, rosin was blown through the candle flame [183] and thunder was, according to Jonson, "roll'd bullet" and "tempestuous drum". [184] Rain was probably imaginary [185] but flames were imitated by fireworks [186] and Jove's thunderbolt was a squib running slantingly on a

---

[173] Chambers, *Eliz. Stage,* III. 80 f.

[174] cf. Chambers, *Eliz. Stage,* III. 81.

[175] cf. Rhodes, *The Stagery of Shakespeare,* 97.

[176] Reynolds, *Red Bull,* Ch. IV; Chambers, *Eliz. Stage,* III. 52-59.

[177] Reynolds, *op. cit.,* 85-87.

[178] See Reynolds, *op. cit.,* 85-87 for a list of about fifty small properties used in the Red Bull.

[179] Lawrence, *Pre-Restoration Stage Studies,* Ch. IX. Illusion of Sounds in the Elizabethan Theatre; Reynolds, *Red Bull,* Ch. VIII. Elizabethan Stage Effects.

[180] Adams, *Globe Playhouse,* 27.

[181] Reynolds, *Red Bull,* 106.

[182] Lawrence, *Pre-Restoration Stage Studies,* Ch. XI. Characteristics of Platform Stage Spectacle.

[183] Lawrence, *op. cit.,* 263, 315; Lawrence, *Elizabethan Playhouse, Second series,* 19.

[184] Reynolds, *Red Bull,* 171.

[185] Reynolds, *op. cit.,* 170.

[186] *Ibid.,* Ch. VIII.

taut wire. [187] The blazing star appears to have been a favourite spectacle [188] but as it could hardly have been realistic it was probably more in the nature of a convention. [189] The primitive yet enthusiastic efforts to produce spectacle were described by Jonson:

> . . . as other playes should be.
>
> Where neither *Chorus* wafts you ore the seas:
>
> Nor creaking throne comes downe, the boyes to please;
>
> Nor nimble squibbe is seene, to make afear'd
>
> The gentlewomen; nor roll'd bullet heard
>
> To say, it thunders; nor tempestuous drumme
>
> Rumbles, to tell you when the storme doth come;
>
> (Prologue, *Every Man In His Humour*)

When the throne descended, music was played, partly for dramatic effect, and partly to hide the creaking. [190] John Melton, in his *Astrologaster* (1620), stated that when "a man goe to the Fortune in Golden Lane to see the tragedie of *Doctor Faustus* he might see shaggehayr'd devills runne roaring over the stage with squibs in their mouths, while drummers make thunder in the tyring-house, and the twelve-penny hirelings make artificial lightning in their heavens". [191] In the plays produced in the Red Bull, it was not uncommon to see *"Enter a Fury all fire-workes"*, *"Medea with strange fiery-workes"* and *"fire-workes all ouer the house"*. In *The Brazen Age,* one stage direction reads,

> *"Enter Hercules from a rocke aboue, tearing down trees. . . All the Princes breake downe the trees, and make a fire, in which Hercules placeth himselfe. . . Iupiter aboue strikes him with a thunder-bolt, his body sinkes, and from the heauens discends a hand in a cloud that from the place where Hercules was burnt, brings vp a starre, and fixed it in the firmament".*

There is *"A hand from out a cloud, threatneth a burning sword"* in *Looking Glass for London and England;* there are *"Three sunnes appeare in the aire"* in *2 Contention of York and Lancaster;* and *"With a sudden thunderclap the sky is on fire and the blazing star appears"* in *Captain Thomas Stukeley.* [192] In *The Golden Age,* V. *"Pluto drawes hell: the Fates put upon him a burning Roabe, and present him with a Mace, and burning crowne";* in *The Silver Age,* II. *"Iupiter appeares in his glory under a Raine-bow";* in the same play, IV. *"Thunder, lightnings, Iupiter descends in his maiesty, his Thunderbolt burning. . . As he toucheth the bed it fires, and all flyes up",* and V. *"Enter Pluto with a club of fire, a burning crowne,*

---

[187] Lawrence, *Physical Conditions,* 98.

[188] Lawrence, *Pre-Restoration Stage Studies,* 261; Chambers, *Eliz. Stage,* III. 76 n.

[189] Bradbrook, *Themes and Conventions,* 17 f; Chambers, *Eliz. Stage,* III. 77.

[190] Lawrence, *Pre-Restoration Stage Studies,* 315; Adams, *The Globe Playhouse,* 365.

[191] *Vide* Lawrence, *Elizabethan Playhouse, Second series,* 18.

[192] Chambers, *Eliz. Stage,* III. 76.

Prosperpine, the Judges, the Fates, and a guard of Divels, all with burning weapons''. [193] In the court plays, there is a burning rock (with real flames) in *The Knight in the Burning Rock;* a "monster", with man inside it, in *Perseus and Andromeda;* [194] hounds' heads in *The History of the Cenofalles;* and tourney and barriers in *Paris and Vienna,* with players on hobby horses. [195] Fireworks were also used in *England's Joy.* [196] Machines of various kinds were used at court for spectacular effects. [197]

The efforts might not be entirely successful:

> "With that a little rosin flasheth forth,
> Like smoke out of a tobacco pipe, or a boys squib".
>
> *(Warning for Fair Women,* Induction)

but the intention was there. [198] In contrast with the above mentioned Elizabethan stage practice, the Chinese stage deities sometimes have symbolic rosin flames thrown in front of them by the property man, the traveller caught in a storm puts his sleeve over his head while the drum rolls for the thunder, and lightning and thunder appear, when necessary, in human form, as when striking the wicked characters dead.

The Chinese may share the love for the spectacular with the Elizabethans as the rosin powder used on the Chinese stage shows, but as regards gruesome sights they are very different from the Englishmen of the sixteenth century. All gruesome objects are veiled by symbolism on the Chinese stage, but in the Elizabethan playhouse it was customary to use an animal bladder, liver, heart, lungs or sponge to imitate bleeding from a wound. [199] Among the properties used at the Red Bull, were severed heads made to individual likeness, coffins, bowls of blood, limbs, a bleeding heart with a knife stuck in it, an aborted infant, a crown of thorns, four men standing in their torments (one of them a kettle of brimstone), a handful of snakes and a severed bull's head. [200] Even in Shakespeare, Gloucester's eyes are put out on the stage. In Peele's *The Battle of Alcazar,* mutilation was acted with real blood and the internal organs of an animal. [201] In the early seventeenth century, decapitation scenes came into vogue and dummy heads, which bled, were used. [202] Well made

---

[193] *Vide* Chambers, *Eliz. Stage,* III. 110 n.

[194] cf. the Chinese "dragon".

[195] Chambers, *Eliz. Stage,* I, 232; IV. 501.

[196] Chambers, *Eliz. Stage,* III. 501.

[197] Chambers, *Eliz. Stage,* I, 233 f; III. 241, 376, 378-9.

[198] For other examples of spectacles on the Elizabethan stage see Lawrence, *Pre-Restoration Stage Studies,* Ch. XI; Reynolds, *Red Bull,* 171-2; Chambers, *Eliz. Stage,* III. 109-110.

[199] Reynolds, *Red Bull,* 40-41.

[200] *Ibid.,* 85-87.

[201] *Vide* Lawrence, *Pre-Restoration Stage Studies,* 236 f.

[202] Lawrence, *op. cit.,* 246 f; Hodges, *Globe Restored,* 75.

dummy bodies were also used for mutilation of a corpse, a jump to death, a fall onto pikes and a hanging corpse. [203] Realism in these scenes was carried out to great detail: in *The Spanish Tragedy,* Act III, the letter was supposed to be written in blood, and the letter used was written in red ink, presumably in order to satisfy the gallants on the stage who could see it closely. [204] Many scenes in the Elizabethan theatre must have been on the same level as Madame Tussaud's. [205] Realism of this kind sometimes involved dangerous action, apparently for the thrill of circus acts. On 16 November, 1586, an accident occurred to the Admiral's Men which was related in a letter by Philip Gawdy to his father:

> "My L. Admyrall his men and players having a devyse in ther playe to tye one of their fellowes to a poste and so to shoote him to deathe, having borrowed their callyvers one of the players handes swerved his peece being charged with bullett missed the fellowe he aymed at and killed a chyld, and a woman great with chyld forthwith, and hurt an other man in the head very soore". [206]

In the theatre there is always the temptation to inject realism at the crucial moment in order to heighten the dramatic effect, such as the bladder under the wound or tears in an actor's voice. These devices stir superficial emotions which the undiscriminating may take to be genuine merit. The area and the extent of realistic touches appear to be entirely a matter of fashion and mental habit. The Elizabethans were accustomed to bloody sights through the bear-baiting rings which stood near the theatres and "the licensed fury of the crowd around gallows or pillory". [207] Firewords and puppets were part of the Bear Garden entertainment. [208] The conjuring in *Faustus* and *The Witch of Edmonton,* if produced with the plays to-day, would be felt to be intrusions, but the Elizabethans would hardly have thought so. [209]

The reason for the realistic aspects of the Elizabethan theatre may be partly found in the shortness of its history. Primitive theatres, in spite of their lack of facilities, are most in need of realism, because the more realistic a theatre is, the easier it can be understood by the untutored audience and the Elizabethan public theatres were popular theatres. Stage convention, the alternative way of understanding dramas, is a language; its usefulness depends on its currency which

---

[203] Lawrence, *Speeding Up Shakespeare,* 130 f; Bradbrook, *Themes and Conventions,* 18.

[204] Lawrence, *Pre-Restoration Stage Studies,* 224.

[205] Bradbrook, *Themes and Conventions,* 19. For other examples of scenes of hanging, torture, beheading and bleeding see Lawrence, *Pre-Restoration Stage Studies,* Ch. X. Elizabethan Stage Realism.

[206] Quoted in Chambers, *Eliz. Stage,* II, 135.

[207] H. S. Bennett, *Shakespeare's Audience* (1944), 8.

[208] Lawrence, *Pre-Restoration Stage Studies,* 255.

[209] *Vide* L. B. Wright, Juggling Tricks and Conjuring on the English Stage before 1642, *Mod. Phil,* xxiv. 1927.

can only be established by long tradition. Theatres of short duration or rapidly changing fashions cannot but be more or less realistic, there being no time for conventions to develop or stabilize. The Elizabethan theatre, as compared with the modern Chinese theatre, had a very short history: from the building of Burbage's Theatre in 1576 to the closing of the theatres in the sixteen forties there was little more than half a century and within that period there was little constancy of style and tradition. [210] In the total seventy-odd years of the Elizabethan theatre, staging must of necessity be tentative at first and stable tradition could only have established in the later part of the period, if it was established. [211] There was in fact no rigid convention, [212] the same plays might be staged differently according to available facilities. [213] "Not by one principle, but by a jumble of principles was it ruled". [214] It is the fact that "in the Elizabethan drama there is no firm principle of what is to be postulated as a convention and what is not" that Eliot thinks is "fundamentally objectionable". [215] "Having accepted a certain distance from reality" the Elizabethan dramatists "did not stick to it": [216] in spite of the realistic details, the basic method of staging lacks realism. [217] Thus the stage doors could be knocked and locked, but sometimes doors must have been imaginary, as in Greene's *Tu Quoque,* where a stage direction reads, *"Enter and knockes".* [218] Shipwrecked sailors were actually wet and the company's ledger was used as records of state [219] and yet night scenes were acted in bright daylight and "chorus wafted" the audience "over the seas". The general rule appears to be: "Everything that could be shown was shown, and what could not be shown was conveyed imaginatively". [220] It is obvious from the dramatic text that many scenes can be at best partially represented, such as forest, tomb, battlements, cave, alcove, riverbank, rock, city wall, prison, ship, bridge, clouds, Hell, garden, shop and so forth, [221] and in such cases the Elizabethan stage is a curious mixture of scenery and imagination. In Heywood's *Rape of Lucrece,* V. iii, a bridge and the riverbank have to be imagined and Horatius is supposed to fall into the Tiber and swim in it, and he is conveniently out of sight:

---

[210] cf. Granville-Barker, *Prefaces,* I. 4.

[211] *Vide* Thorndike, *Shakespeare's Theatre,* 95.

[212] Reynolds, *Mod. Phil.* Vol. 2, p. 581.

[213] Reynolds, *Red Bull,* 187 f.

[214] Lawrence, *Pre-Restoration Stage Studies,* 199.

[215] T. S. Eliot, Four Elizabethan Dramatists (in *Selected Essays,* 1917-32).

[216] Reynolds, *Red Bull,* 193.

[217] *Ibid.,* 189.

[218] *Vide* Reynolds, *Red Bull,* 47.

[219] Bradbrook, *Themes and Conventions,* 19.

[220] Lawrence, *Pre-Restoration Stage Studies,* 199; Reynolds, *Red Bull, passim.*

[221] Reynolds, *Red Bull,* Ch. V.

"Lo! he swims armed as he is,
Whilst all the army have discharged their arrows,
Of which the shield upon his back is full".[222]

The exact position of the city gate is still controversial but the city wall must be some adaptation of the tiring-house facade, with partially realistic results, [223] because the defenders can appear on the walls and parley with the besieging army, they can descend and open the gate, they can shoot and be shot at from below. [224]

The earliest Chinese dramas of late Sung dynasty were preceded by the farce and dramatic dances which, being commercialized and continually performed, must have established certain stage conventions which the later writers of longer dramas would find conveniently available. The "bamboo horse" might well be a piece of realism necessitated by the more complicated action, but it was subsequently displaced by convention. Influences other than the lack of stable conventions on Elizabethan stage realism cannot, however, be ignored. The Elizabethan theatre was preceded by the medieval dramas and could not be entirely free from the medieval tradition. Theatre was not commercialized in medieval times: performances took place only at festivals a few times a year, hence realism, as much as the lack of facilities allowed, was necessary to make the plays intelligible. Multiple setting was the medieval method of locating the scenes: large sets, representing various localities such as Heaven, Garden of Eden, Jerusalem and so on were arranged all at once in the market place and the space in front of them could be any one of the localities symbolized by the sets. [225] Before the Elizabethan public theatres were built, interludes were performed in the inn-yards and at such performances the gallery behind the temporary stage is believed to have been pressed into dramatic service hence it was retained in the public theatres built specially for the production of plays and became the upper stage. [226] Together with the rear stage, which might be the remnant of a curtained space behind the stage in the inn-yard, they formed the ever present adjunct to the platform. The facade of the tiring house was called upon to represent a great many different settings and served as various kinds of background and when not required it was ignored. [227] In its service as auxiliary acting space, in its continual presence and in its capacity to be ignored, it is the same as the medieval settings, the only difference is the flexible identity. The Elizabethan stage may therefore be thought of as a compressed version of the medieval stage, with features

[222] For other scenes with seashore and riverbank see Chambers, *Eliz. Stage*, III, 107. The trap probably stood for the water.

[223] Lawrence, *Physical Conditions*, 60 f; Chambers, *Eliz. Stage*, III, 54, 96.

[224] cf. the extensive use of the city wall in *1 Henry VI*.

[225] Chambers, *Medieval Stage*, II, 83 ff, 136.

[226] Lawrence, *Elizabethan Playhouse, Second series*, 26.

[227] Chambers, *Eliz. Stage*, III, 50 *et seq.*

of the inn-yard which had been pressed into service as settings. [228]

The music in the Chinese theatre, through its influence on the style of acting and delivery, should be counted as an important factor in the lack of realism. In the private theatres of Elizabethan London, the theatrical elements that appealed to popular taste, including spectacle, were omitted and music was augmented — there were no more tumbling, squibs, devils, ballets, bawdry, fights and clowns. [229] The types of music played were: overture concert (which lasted as long as one hour), the inter-act music, the prelude to acts, the concluding flourish of the play, the incidental music, music accompanying dumb shows and music for "atmosphere" such as "doleful dumps", "infernal music", "soft music" and so on. [230] The use of music to adjust the mood of the audience to that of the coming scenes and to mark the end of the play is similar to the opera, but as such the music has no effect on the style of acting. In the public theatres music was also used to accompany ceremonies, to charm and control the insane, to accompany dumb shows, tableaux and love scenes, [231] to accompany songs, to herald the approach of important persons (e.g royal tucket) and to complement funeral and infernal scenes. [232] It can be noticed that music that accompanies action can either be part of the action, such as the royal tucket, the funeral music and songs, which are realistic; or serve to accentuate the emotions in the scene, as in love scenes, and infernal scenes, where the music is not realistic. The former can have no effect on the acting, as far as realism is concerned, and the latter tends to change acting towards mime and dance. The latter type was as much a part of the public as of the private theatres, but its influence appears to be insufficient to keep the English stage from becoming more and more realistic. Even in Elizabethan times scenery was used in the private theatres and windows were shuttered for night scenes. [233] The groundlings in the public theatres had their own leanings towards realism: in 1611 a real garlic seller was employed in a jig at Fortune in order that the audience could enjoy the actual idiosyncrasies of the type. [234] When the theatres opened again in the Restoration period, scenery and actresses soon entered the English theatre and the platform stage of the Elizabethan times left hardly any lasting influence.

(17)

Convention, on which all dramatic performances on the open stage must be

---

[228] *Vide* Adams, *Globe Playhouse,* 170, 241.

[229] J. Isaacs, *Production and Stage Management at Blackfriars Theatre* (1933), 6; Chambers, *Eliz. Stage,* III, 130-131.

[230] Isaacs, *op. cit.,* 12-13.

[231] Bradbrook, *Themes and Conventions,* 19.

[232] Lawrence, *Elizabethan Playhouse, First series,* 78; Reynolds, *Red Bull,* 168-9.

[233] Lawrence, *Elizabethan Playhouse, Second series,* 8 f.

[234] Lawrence, *Pre-Restoration Stage Studies,* 98.

based, may be defined as the part of the disparity between the stage and the scene it represents which the audience agrees to overlook and succeeds in forgetting. According to the various reasons for the disparity between the real and the fictitious, conventions may be divided into five types as follows:

1. By the very nature of theatre, drama cannot be the same as the real world, for instance, the presence of a large body of audience is unrealistic, especially in theatres with an open stage where the audience at one side of the stage can see at once the actors on it and the audience on the other side of it. It is impossible to eliminate this unrealistic feature of the theatre without reducing drama to something else, such as parade, ritual, contest, festive dance or worship. Similarly, the level of the actor's voice, the language of stage foreigners and the lighting of night scenes cannot but be unrealistic, otherwise the audience cannot see or hear or understand the drama properly and the purpose of the performance is defeated. These discrepancies even the most fastidious audience know to be unavoidable and all theatregoers have agreed so implicitly to ignore them that to point them out as conventions appears odd.

2. Real events move so slowly and in such a shapeless manner that if they are represented in full they will be unbearably boring. Drama requires satisfying pattern and rhythm; dramatic events must have coherence, unity and direction. To this end the events of a story are selected and compressed before they become a drama and additional devices such as prologue, introductory dialogue, aside and soliloquy have to be employed in order that the audience get all the information required to understand the drama. The special devices may be evaded or disguised, for example, asides disguised as talking to oneself, but the selection of a few scenes out of a series of events and the accelerated development of the plot must remain as conventions.

3. It is sometimes impossible and often difficult to reproduce faithfully real sights and sounds on the stage. Not only are such scenes as the sea, the open field, a fire or a storm difficult to represent, but even in interior scenes the set cannot easily be perfect — one can always recognize it as scenery. Theoretically it is possible to build at least some sets which are indistinguishable from the real scene, but owing to the cost involved this is not often accomplished and the less the scenery, the more the conventions.

4. The object of theatre is not representation alone; it can also include spectacle, emotional appeal, artistic expression, sensuous pleasure and so on and for these purposes music, dance, mask, poetry, costume and singing, which are all unrealistic, may be introduced. To accept them as part of the drama as, for example, the background music in the films and singing in the opera, involves convention. These features cannot be easily disguised and when they are abolished for the sake of realism, the artistic aims they serve are sacrificed. [235]

5. Sometimes unrealistic elements are left in a school of drama by its predecessor, such as the chorus in the Greek theatre and the acrobatics in the Chinese theatre. It also constitutes a convention to accept them as part of the drama.

The implications of the convention of changed locality was discussed by Farquhar (1678-1707) as follows:

> "As for example, here is a new play; the house is throng'd, the prologue's spoken, and the curtain drawn represents you the scene of Grand Cairo. Whereabouts are you now, sir? Were you not the very minute before in the pit in the English playhouse talking to a wench, and now, *presto pass,* you are spirited away to the banks of the river Nile. Surely, sir, this is a most intolerable improbability; yet this you must allow me, or else you destroy the very constitution of representation. Then, in the second act, with a flourish of fiddles, I change the scene to Astrachan. *O, this is intolerable!* Look 'ee, sir, 'tis not a jot more intolerable than the other; for you'll find that 'tis much about the same distance between Egypt and Astrachan, as it is between Drury Lane and Grand Cairo; and if you please to let your fancy take post, it will perform the journey in the same moment of time, without any disturbance in the world to your person". (*A Discourse upon Comedy,* last but two para.)

Dryden, for his improvements on Shakespeare's *Troilus and Cressida,* had

> "no leaping from Troy to the Grecian tents, and thence back again in the same act; but a due proportion of time allow'd for every motion". (*Works,* (1725), Vol. V, p. 16, Preface to *Troilus and Cressida,* 2nd para.)

That changes of locality are tolerable in proportion to the shortness of the distance involved and that slow changes are allowable but quick ones are not seem to be based on the same kind of logic as "the wickedness of stealing chicken every day, and the innocence of doing so once in a while". [236] The fallacy of seeing degrees of credulity in dramatic convention stems from thinking of drama as a copy rather than as a pretence, of its aim as deception rather than amusement. Absurdity is felt only when one applies the empirical knowledge derived from reality to the play, but the players do not observe the laws of space and time;

> "they do but jest".

---

[235] cf. the use of stage lighting in modern European theatres. When Henry Irving introduced stage lighting for general effects instead of only for particular scenes, such as moonlight, the critics thought the transgression of naturalism outrageous. *Oxford Companion to the Theatre* (1951), p. 468.

[236] See *Mencius.*

CHAPTER XLII

HISTORIES OF THE CHINESE AND THE EUROPEAN THEATRE — I

(Introduction — Fools and Jesters — Court Pageants — Differentiation within the European Theatre)

(1)

Western writers on the Chinese theatre have hitherto approached the subject from the point of view of naturalism. Although comparisons between the Chinese theatre of to-day and European theatres of the past have occasionally been made, yet as a whole the Chinese theatre is seen against the principles of the naturalistic theatre as a background, with the result that striking differences between the two theatres are given undue emphasis and artistic standards outside naturalism are overlooked. Most of the western writers on the Chinese theatre betray the traveller's pre-occupation with the unfamiliar. Considering the newness of theatrical history as an academic subject, this should not be surprising: Dörpfeld's *Das griechische Theater* was published only in 1896, Brodmeier's *Die Shakespeare-Bühne nach den alten Bühnen-Anweisungen* only in 1904, Mantzius' *History of Theatrical Art in Ancient and Modern Times* in 1903-9, and Wang Kuo-Wei's *History of Drama in Sung and Yüan Dynasties* in 1911. [1] Before scholarly findings become common knowledge most theatregoers naturally have no other ideas except those applicable to the current theatrical style.

Apart from the danger of assuming that naturalism constitutes the highest principle of the theatre, which some naive playgoers imply, to limit the comparison to modern European theatres is to lose historical perspective on the problem. Both the Chinese and the European theatre have been constantly changing, and in the latter the changes have been drastic. The theatre of to-day is but a momentary stage between the theatre of the past and that of the future. In spite of the vast

---

[1] 王國維，宋元戲曲史.

565

difference between the Chinese and the European theatre of to-day they must have a common basis, because theatre, like poetry and music, is subject to certain universal aesthetic principles. In fact, it is this common basis that makes comparative studies significant. The meaning behind the similarities and differences between the Chinese and the European theatre becomes obscured only when the view is narrowed to the present.

The difference in social and cultural conditions of Europe and Asia makes it highly improbable that the theatres of the two continents developed along the same direction and at the same speed, hence, even though they may, as a whole, share many common characteristics, in any particular period they are more likely than not to differ from each other. If, for example, a European visited China in the Yüan dynasty (1277-1367) he would find the then Chinese theatre very different from the miracle plays he knew: he would perhaps be surprised at the commercialization of the theatre, for in Europe dramas were then confined to religious subjects and performed only on holidays; he would find it strange that Chinese dramas should cover such widely different subjects and were performed on a small stage, instead of in the cathedral or at the market place, that the dialogue should be partly sung instead of being entirely spoken and that other performances such as recitation of stories were mixed with the dramas. [2] If, however, a Spaniard or an Englishman visited China in the sixteenth century he would find the Chinese stage and method of staging very much the same as in his native theatre. In recent decades, the European theatre has again become very different from the Chinese. Comparisons based on simultaneous momentary developments will, therefore, lead to unreliable conclusions; only by surveying the histories of both theatres as a whole can one get a stable and significant view.

The comparative uniformity of the national schools of theatre in Europe in modern times may give rise to the illusion of the universal validity of their standards. The uniformity is however due to mutual influence and common heritage, and the standards carry only the weight of one tradition. It is particularly misleading to set the Chinese theatre against naturalism which represents only one period in one line of development. General conclusions pertaining to the evolution of the theatre can only be drawn from the study of the theatres of all the different countries, especially those which developed independently of each other, by treating their differences, not as deviations from an arbitrarily chosen set of standards, but as disagreement among standards of equal validity. Such a study is beyond the scope of this book, but comparison between the Chinese and European theatres should throw more light on the development of world theatre than the study of each alone.

---

[2] Marco Polo was in China during the Yüan dynasty but unfortunately in his *Travels* little is said about the Chinese theatre.

566

Before a theory of evolution can be formulated for the theatre, certain questions in the comparative history have to be settled first. For example, it will be significant to find out whether the possible types of theatres developed by the different races are limited in number so that the types of theatre of one country will be the same as those of another provided they both have had a long history, or whether the types are infinitely varied and there can be no similarity except by coincidence. If the types developed by different races are similar, it will be important to determine whether they occurred in a definite sequence in all countries so that one can call the earliest type "primitive theatre" and the latest "modern theatre" not only in the factual but also in the theoretical sense. Perhaps of equal importance is the question then whether in this uniform sequence of types each type is a stage through which every changing theatre must pass or whether in different countries development follows a general direction but not through identical steps. Some of the most fundamental ideas which serve as intruments in historical and aesthetic thinking such as the idea of progress — the universal direction of development — and the idea of the essential theatre — the lowest common denominator of all theatres — can only be defined in a comparative study. The European theatre shows certain general tendencies, such as from the open stage to scenery, from dancing to realistic acting, from poetry to prose, from music to speech, from mask to make-up and from legend to contemporary problems, but they may not be the tendencies of the theatres of other races, and if they are not it is futile to use them as general criteria for classifying types of theatre as "primitive" or "advanced". Although the Chinese and the European theatres are only two independent lines of theatrical evolution, their comparative study may yield decisive answers to the questions mentioned above, for example, if in their histories the Chinese and the European theatre show the same tendency towards, say, journalistic subject matter, it is still doubtful whether that tendency is a universal one, but, if they do not show that same tendency, then one may conclude that there is no such general trend in the world theatre. [3] Only when these problems are solved will the comparison of the Chinese with the naturalistic theatre acquire significance.

In the foregoing chapters the modern Chinese theatre has been compared with three types of European theatre, each for a particular reason — with the Greek theatre for the survival of elements of primitive ritual, with the *commedia dell' arte* for the complete dissociation from literature and with the Elizabethan theatre for the conventions of the platform stage — now comparison is extended to other types

---

[3] Comparative history of world theatre can solve some problems which would interest the cultural anthropologist, such as whether theatre and drama emerge at a definite stage of civilization and in a fixed manner, and whether and to what extent social conditions determine the form of the theatre after it has evolved. These questions cannot be adequately answered here, but some relevant data can be found in this study.

of the Chinese and the European theatre. This can be conveniently done by considering first the theatres before commercialization and then those after it.

(2)

Art as an independent activity unconnected with religion and social life came late in history. Theatre, for example, had, until modern times, always been a part of some festivity. In ancient times religion and social convention meant more to the people than they do now, and the lives of ancient people were regulated by them to a much greater extent. Ancient Greece is a case in point and medieval Europe is another. In Roman times theatre was purely for amusement but holidays were the excuse for the theatrical and allied performances which were at least nominally for celebrations. [4] Some elements of the Roman theatre, such as the *atellanae*, appeared to come from rustic farce and must have originally been a part of the peasants' social life. [5] When classical theatre was revived in the Renaissance the form was reinstated but the function was lost; theatre was taken out of its social context and literary drama became a plaything of the dilettanti. It was in the court and among the people that masques, interludes, farces, and other quasi-dramatic activities of the fair ground, the banqueting hall, and the village square, had some social function. [6] Since then, except for the little religious pageantry which still survives in Italy, and some propaganda plays, theatre has become pure entertainment with little religious and social significance. [7]

In China, the early rudimentary theatrical activities were connected with court life, first in the form of jesters and masquers and then also in pageants and spectacles. Then in Sung dynasty popular entertainment in numerous forms was developed, partly in parallel with court entertainment and partly independently, and it was among these popular shows and under the impetus of the lengthening farce that the Chinese drama was born. Although other forms of the popular entertainment of Sung dynasty have suffered decline and extinction, the drama has had a continuous tradition. Generally speaking the Chinese theatre has been for amusement only — though owing to its entertainment value it has also been attached to religious and other celebrations.

---

[4] Beare, *The Roman Stage,* 154 f.

[5] Beare, *op. cit.,* 129.

[6] Chambers believes that the migration of the drama from the church to the market place and thence to the banqueting hall was an important step in the development of the interlude, which shows the close relation between social function and the development of the theatre. Chambers, *Medieval Stage,* II. 180 f.

[7] In early Elizabethan times prayers for the Queen or lord were worked into interludes to be spoken at the end of them, but the practice did not last long. Chambers, *Eliz. Stage,* I. 190, 245; II. 550; IV. 20.

When theatre becomes popular entertainment commercialization sets in, players are no longer court jesters or followers of a religion, theatre becomes a distinct profession, and is freed from the conditions imposed on it by its religious and social functions so that it tends to develop along hedonistic lines. Theatrical performances occurred only when occasions required them, now they can be given at any time; the players were at one time amateurs, now they are professionals. Specialized personnel and the need to earn a living from day to day give the commercialized theatre more continuous and intensive cultivation which was denied it when it was connected with religion. Such being the effect of commercialization on the development of the theatre, its timing in a theatrical history relative to the rise of the drama is an important factor governing the characteristics of the drama. Whereas in Europe drama was developed from religious activities long before the commercialization of the theatre, in China it was evolved only after theatre had become pure entertainment, hence the connection between religion and the Chinese drama has been slight and the Chinese theatre has been more thoroughly hedonistic. In Europe religion once fostered drama but the two have become estranged; in China drama was raised in the fairground and became attached to religious ceremonies afterwards. There has been nothing in the Chinese theatre similar in function to the religious or quasi-religious plays of ancient Greece and medieval Europe, rather, the background for the rise of the Chinese drama was more like the medley of popular entertainment in ancient Rome. Nor has there been a situation in the Chinese history analogous to that of the Renaissance when classical culture was unearthed and appreciated under social conditions very different from those which gave that culture its life. The modern Chinese theatre is connected through unbroken tradition with the popular theatre of Sung dynasty (960-1276) and its development has always been a matter of natural growth, but the European theatre since the Renaissance stems from a revival of ancient dramatic text for which the theatrical conditions were not, at the time of the revival, fully understood, and from reconstructions of the classical dramatic performance based on imperfect knowledge. These historical facts have important bearings on the difference between the Chinese and the European theatre of to-day.

In Europe, drama rose at least twice from the ritual — in the Dionysian cult in Athens and in the Christian liturgy of the medieval church — but in China court jesters instead of priests were instrumental in the development of the theatre. Chinese primitive ritual and European court jesters did, nevertheless, show theatrical potentialities.

The mimetic elements in the ritual of early Chinese shamans [8] and ancestral

---

[8] Bk. II. Ch. 50 of Marco Polo's *Travels* (Ed. M. Komroff, 1942) appears to be a description of shamans' ritual: dance, hymns, male and female "sorcerers", libations of blood, liquor and water, incense and "possession" by spirits who talked inside the possessed are mentioned. Shamans

569

worship exhibited a stronger tendency towards dramatization than was obvious in the Greek dithyramb [9] which was probably more like the ceremonial dances in Chou dynasty. Some of the ceremonial dances and music, performed by professional musicians and trained dancers, must have attained a certain degree of artistic excellence, because Confucius, for one, found it deeply moving [10] but there was no sign of dramatization: whatever made the dithyramb become dramatic was missing. Perhaps due to lack of legend or to the sterile anti-religious philosophies of late Chou dynasty no drama was developed from shamanism. Modern Chinese dramas based on myths and legends of popular religion and performed at religious festivals are not of the same order as Greek dramas and medieval mysteries, because the ritualistic quality is totally lacking.

Of court jesters in Europe there were, as early as Hellenistic times, "laughter makers" in the courts of Philip and Alexander. In the households of wealthy Romans were *moriones* and *scurrae,* human monstrosities including fools, kept to amuse the masters. The conventional witty fool emerged in medieval times and acquired a somewhat uniform appearance: the shaved head, the motley dress with bells, the tight breeches, the asses' ears, the coxcomb, and the short staff with the head and the bladder (for sham castigation). In the Renaissance period, every country in Europe had its court jesters and they lingered on until the nineteenth century. [11]

Fools amused their masters with their natural or assumed subnormal intelligence. Real mental deficiency was often associated with physical deformity, [12] hence both in China and in Europe court jesters, some of them dwarfs, were relieved of social responsibilities. A pygmy called Danga (a tribal name) was kept by Dadkeri-Assi, a Pharaoh of the Fifth Dynasty. [13] Dwarfs were sometimes kept in European courts for amusement, and some of them were immortalized by the brush of Velasquez. Dwarfs were annually drafted from a certain district for the imperial court of T'ang dynasty (618-906), and one governor of that district made himself famous by instigating the abolishment of the practice. [14] There were probably women jesters in the court of Han dynasty [15] and the ancient Romans as well as the

---

apparently had specialized skills of some kind — perhaps in hypnotism, or dance, or mimicry — because Confucius once quoted a saying: Those who do not persevere cannot become physicians or shamans. 論語, 子路.

[9] See Ch. XX.

[10] "I did not expect music could be so beautiful". 論語, 述而.

[11] E. Welsford, *The Fool His Social and Literary History* (1935), 186 *supra.*

[12] Welsford, *The Fool,* 55 *et seq.*

[13] Welsford, *op. cit.,* 56.

[14] 新唐書, 列傳百十九, 陽城傳.

[15] See Ch. XXI.

Frenchmen of the seventeenth century also had female fools. [16] Among the dwarfs in the royal household of Queen Elizabeth was a woman called Mrs. Thomasin. [17]

The European court jesters from medieval times onwards and the Chinese court jesters from their earliest days, entertained their masters and guests with their wit, and occasionally served them with good sense. "The fool knows the truth because he is a social outcast, and spectators see most of the game". [18] Junker Peter, fool of Herzog Wolfgang Wilhelm zu Neuberg, had to drink the health of certain spiritual dignitaries and pretended a pain in the stomach, saying that it was not strange that such people should disagree in the stomach, considering that they caused such unrest in the churches. [19]

In so far as the jesters' performances were directed towards some audience they contained the germ of the theatre. Triboulet, court fool of Louis XII and Francis I, had talents for mimicry, music and dance. [20] Fools in seventeenth century France had talents for *ex tempore* verse. [21] One is tempted to indulge in the speculation that if the European drama had not developed in religion it would have been developed by the court fools. Fools outside the court, such as village fools and primitive stage buffoons, might have contributed towards the development of the primitive rustic farce in Europe, but like most things related to primitive theatres, their contributions were unrecorded.

In Europe revellers in medieval festivities sometimes assumed the identity of fools, as in the Feast of Fools. [22] Players of farce called themselves fools in fifteenth century France. [23] With their innate theatricality fools entered the European drama and became clowns, "the intermediacy between the stage and the auditorium". [24] They stood apart from the rest of the characters and always played themselves, for example, the clowns in the Elizabethan dramas and *Hanswurst*, the German stage jester of the seventeenth and eighteenth centuries. Court jesters as dramatic characters were exploited by European dramatists, as in *As You Like It* and *King Lear*, and one court jester, Will Somers, Henry VIII's fool, became the hero of Nashe's *Will Summers Last Will and Testament*. [25] *Hanswurst* was banished from

---

[16] Welsford, *op. cit.*, 60, 153. A well known female fool of the French court was Mathurine; for other female fools see J. Dorian, *History of Court Fools* (1858), 62 ff.

[17] Chambers, *Eliz. Stage*, I. 48.

[18] Welsford, *The Fool*, 319.

[19] Welsford, *op. cit.*, 140.

[20] *Ibid.*, 147.

[21] *Ibid.*, 154 f.

[22] Welsford, *op. cit.*, Ch. IX; Chambers, *Med. Stage*, Chs. XIII and XIV.

[23] Welsford, *op. cit.*, 207 ff.

[24] Welsford, *op. cit.*, xii.

[25] *Vide* O. M. Busby, *Studies in the Development of the Fool in the Elizabethan Drama* (1923), Ch. 1. The Origins of the English Stage Fool.

the German stage by Gottsched (1700-66) and the clowns of other European dramas shared his fate. With their disappearance the world of the drama became more sharply divided from that of the audience. The difference in the psychology of the European and the Chinese audience is in no small degree due to the survival of the clown in the Chinese theatre.

(3)

Apart from jesters, theatrical activities also entered court life as the embellishment of its social life, such as pageant, masque and spectacles.

The splendour and dignity of court ceremonies give court life a certain degree of theatricality. [26] Reverence and solemnity first dictate good manners, then good manners are emphasized till they become conventional and lose contact with genuine feelings. From the atmosphere of make-believe it is a short step to the consciously histrionic, and the overt pretence, which precludes hypocrisy, facilitates the change. Life involves a great deal of acting at all social levels: we try to make good impressions on other people, we follow the conventions of social intercourse, we carry out customary ceremonies of introduction, greetings and departure mechanically and we behave differently in different company even though we may be in the same mood. Only in the artificiality and idleness of the court, however, does social convention breed pageantry.

A Chinese court pageant of Southern Dynasties (A.D. 420-588) is described in a poem of that period preserved in an anthology of Sung dynasty (A.D. 960-1276):

> An old foreigner came from a western country to offer his best wishes to the emperor. "His home is the whole universe, his acquaintances include the [legendary] Three Ancient Kings. In the West he visited the Primordial Vapours, in the East he crossed the Bottomless Sea, in the South he sailed in the Infinite Ocean and in the North he reached the Land's End. The fairies are his friends, the ancient heroes are his companions, gods invited him as their honoured guest and goddesses served him with celestial wine. His age is as great as the Southern Mountains, his heart, as pure as diamond. With blue eyes and white hair, large eye-brows and prominent nose, he not only can act tirelessly in plays but also can drink endless toasts to his host. Flute-players lead him in the front, attendants follow him in the rear . . ." [His address] "Your Majesty has banished Confusion from this country and planted Peace in it; your glory reaches the four corners of the earth, all the peoples rejoice in your benevolence. Therefore your humble visitor has driven his own chariot to come to your capital in order to see your wonderful palace and especially this your

---

[26] Civic ceremonies too have their theatrical aspects — see A. S. Venezky, *Pageantry on the Shakespearean Stage* (1951), Chs. I and II.

magnificent hall. These my followers are unworthy of your attention but they are humble in heart and obedient in spirit, perhaps Your Majesty will graciously forgive their presence''. ''The sound of song and flutes rose in the hall up to the sky; to the beats of the drums they danced according to the rhythm. The old foreigner had in his pocket a wonderful song to present to the emperor; however, as he was about to sing it he, being old, forgot the words, and only wished His Majesty a Happy and Long Life''. [27]

In Renaissance England, ''the Tudor kings and queens came and went about their public affairs in a constant atmosphere of make-believe, with a sibyl lurking in every court-yard and gateway, and a satyr in the boscage of every park, to turn the ceremonies of welcome and farewell, without which sovereigns must not move, by the arts of song and dance and mimetic dialogue, to favour and to prettiness''. [28] Speeches and songs similar in purport to the above-mentioned were common in European court pageantry; one, which was ''written by Thomas Watson and sung in six parts at Elvetham by the Graces and Hours to greet the Queen'' (Elizabeth), is as follows:

With fragrant flowers we strew the way,
And make this our chiefe holliday:
For though this clime were blest of yore
Yet was it never proud before,
    O beauteous Quene of second Troy,
    Accept of our unfained joy.
Now th'ayre is sweeter than sweet balme,
And Satyrs daunce about the palme:
Now earth, with verdure newly dight
Gives perfect singe of her delight.
    O beauteous Quene of second Troy,
    Accept of our unfained joy.
Now birds record new harmonie
And trees doe whistle melodie;
Now everie thing that nature breeds
Doth clad itselfe in pleasant weeds.
    O beauteous Quene of second Troy,
    Accept of our unfained joy. [29]

Ceremonies of welcome and farewell were regularly conducted by nymphs and

---

[27] 郭茂倩, 樂府詩集, 卷五十一, 清商曲辭, 八, 上雲樂, 周捨 (或范雲), 老胡文康.

[28] Chambers, *Eliz. Stage,* I. 107.

[29] John Nichols, *The Progresses and Public Processions of Queen Elizabeth* (1823), quoted in Venezky, *op. cit.,* 79.

fairies and sibyls and allegorical figures in the summer "progress" when the Queen (Elizabeth) visited the noblemen's estates for hunting and "change of air". [30] In Ch'ing dynasty (1644-1911) emperors were greeted on their birthdays by "hundreds of actors" dressed as Buddhas, saints and other immortals. [31] Plans for the celebration of King James' entry to London called for actors attired as the Genius of the City of London accompanied by St. George and St. Andrew, [32] which shows that at least some of the ceremonies were professional work. It was customary in Elizabethan England to write masques and plays specially for social occasions like weddings and to insert speeches appropriate to the occasions. [33]

In Italy dramatic elements were sometimes worked into banquets. Vasari described one in which the guests first met Ceres who asked the company to follow her into hell in pursuit of her daughter Proserpine and then went through a huge serpent's mouth into a dark room in which they heard Ceres inquiring of Cerberus if her daughter had been there and Pluto refusing to give up Proserpine. In another room they were invited to Pluto's wedding feast, served almost in total darkness on black-draped tables, by a hideous devil holding a fork. The dishes were all of horrid animals and dead men's bones, made of sugar, with delicacies hidden underneath. After the banquet, scenes of hellish punishments with rumblings, cries and wailings were acted in semi-darkness. [34] (What extraordinary ideas for the promotion of appetite!)

Another court event to which theatrical elements were added was the tournament. In sixteenth century England mock combat was of three types: the tilt, with spears on horseback; the tourney, with swords on horseback and the foot-tourney, with swords on foot. The contest was conducted in a mimetic form, with the opponents assuming the identity of "strange knights" or allegorical characters such as "children of Desire" or Biblical characters, such as Adam and Eve. The contestants were accompanied by charioteers and Amazons and other characters necessary for the mimetic introduction to the tournament. Parts of the performance such as the trumpeter, the shields and emblems, the challenging speech and its answer, were remnants of ancient custom but the assumed identity of the contestants and the scenic adjuncts were additions to satisfy the desire for spectacle. Temples of Vesta rose out of the earth, songs were sung by Vestal Virgins, a triumphal car was

---

[30] *Vide* Chambers, *Eliz. Stage,* I. Ch. IV. The sovereign's amusement on such occasions consisted of hunting, watching water pageants, listening to welcome speeches, fireworks, animal baiting, acrobatic displays, plays, masques, dialogues and feasting — see Chambers, *Eliz. Stage,* I. 123 ff. Country dancing, concerts, football and presentation of gifts were also sometimes included — *Eliz. Stage,* III. 312.

[31] See Ch. XXXII.

[32] Venezky, *op. cit.,* 78.

[33] Lawrence, *Pre-Restoration Stage Studies,* 138 f.

[34] Vasari, *Lives,* quoted in Nicoll, *Stuart Masques and the Renaissance Stage,* 30.

drawn out with Fate in it, and eagles came out of a tower, which concealed musicians within. [35]

Sham tournaments with theatrical embellishments were called *Barriers*. Quasi-theatrical performances which grew around other types of social activities bore other names, for example, if the nucleus of the performance was a speech of welcome, it was called *Entertainment,* and if a dance, *Masque.* [36] Pageantry was also worked into archery shows. [37]

These examples of social activity embellished with theatrical elements are, in a sense, the reverse of naturalism: whereas naturalism creates the illusion that the stage is as real as the world of the audience, pageantry of the type just described makes the world of the audience appear unreal. Actors playing mythical and allegorical characters mix and converse with the audience making the real merge with the illusionary.

These efforts were, however, as Thorndike said of the medieval theatre, "essentially amateur and remain subject to occasion and circumstances, without attaining self-support, independence or the power of free development". [38] Of greater stability in form were the masques and court spectacles which, unlike pageants, were less subject to occasion and might be indulged in almost at any time.

Masque was a mixture of spectacle and social dance in which the performers and spectators were indistinguishable. Its nearest modern equivalent is the costume ball, but it was more complicated and on a more lavish scale. Apart from the dance of the audience in masquerade, there were also scenery, stage machinery and sumptuous costumes, singing and music, dialogue between mythological and allegorical figures and grotesque dances by professional dancers. [39] The costume ball satisfies at once the desire to see and the desire to show off. The Elizabethan masque was originally a dance in masquerade [40] and, as in modern carnival balls, special displays of dancing or clowning were sometimes added. It was only under court conditions, however, that lavish exhibition of moving scenery and other stage machinery was possible. [41] It was not theatre grafted to the social dance, but rather theatre grown out of its elaborations, [42] for the performers were mainly the guests who were people of rank and distinction, the professional players being hired only to assist in some of the dances. [43]

---

[35] For details see Chambers, *Eliz. Stage,* I. 139-148; III. 212.

[36] H. A. Evans, *English Masques* (1897), xii.

[37] Chambers, *Eliz. Stage,* I. 139.

[38] Thorndike, *Shakespeare's Theatre,* 13.

[39] Thorndike, *Shakespeare's Theatre,* 176 *et seq.*

[40] Evans, *op. cit.,* xiv. f.

[41] *Ibid.,* xvi. f.

[42] Nicholl, *Stuart Masques and the Renaissance Stage,* 29; Chambers, *Eliz. Stage,* I. 213.

[43] Evans, *op. cit.,* lii.

The masque normally begins with an introductory scene which varies from a speech by a presenter making a mock explanation of how the mythical characters represented by the masquers come to the place, to a whole scene involving several characters with action which leads to the entrance of the masquers. The arrival of the masquers, eight or twelve or sixteen in number, is designed to surprise and dazzle the spectators; they issue, at the proper moment, from "a great concave shell" or "a glorious bower", or they descend from the heavens on a cloud. Then the entrance dance and the main dance follow, which are figure dances carefully rehearsed beforehand and performed by the masquers alone. After this the audience join the masquers in the more lively dances, called the Revels, such as galliards and corantos and the masque closes with the "going-out-dance" of the masquers. [44] Masquers could, as in the "word dances" of T'ang dynasty, [45] form letters. [46] Costume was sometimes borrowed or hired, as in the Chinese court spectacles. [47] A sixteenth century English masque may be quoted here as an example:

Devices to be shewed before the Queenes Majestie, by waye of maskinge, at Nottingham castell, after the metinge of the

Quene of Scotts. [in 1562.]

The Firste Night

Firste a pryson to be made in the haule, the name whereof is Extreme Oblyvion, and the Kepers name thereof, Argus, otherwise called Circumspection: then a maske of Ladyes to come in after this sorte.

Firste Pallas, rydinge upon an unycorne, havinge in her hande a Standarde, in which is to be paynted ij Ladyes hands, knitt one faste within thother, and over th' ands written in letters of golde, Fides.

Then ij Ladyes rydinge together, th' one uppon a golden Lyon, with a · crowne of gold on his heade: th' other uppon a redd Lyon, with the like crowne of Gold; signifyinge ij Vertues, that is to saye, the Ladye on the golden Lyone is to be called Prudentia, and the Ladye on the redd Lyon Temperantia.

After this to followe vj or viij Ladyes maskers, bringinge in, captive, Discorde, and False Reporte, with ropes of gold about there necks. When theis have marched about the haule, then Pallas to declare before the Quenes Majestie in verse, that the goddes, understandinge the noble meteinge of those ij quenes, hathe willed her to declare unto them, that those ij vertues, Prudentia

---

[44] Evans, op. cit., xxxiv. f. Masques can be more complicated than what is described above: there may be two sets of dancers, called the double masque, and the main masque may also be preceded by an ante-masque, which is designed as a foil and in contrast to it, as Hell before Heaven, Chaos before Peace.

[45] See Ch. XXXII.

[46] Chambers, Eliz. Stage, I. 199.

[47] See Ch. XXI; Chambers, Eliz. Stage, I. 212.

and Temperantia, *have made greate and longe sute unto Jupiter, that it wold please hym to gyve unto them False Reporte and Discorde, to be punished as they thinke good; and that those Ladyes have nowe in there presence determyned to committ them faste bounde into th' afforesayde pryson of Extreme Oblyvion, there to be kepte by th' afforesayde gaylor Argus, otherwise Circumspection, for ever; unto whome* Prudentia *shall delyver a locke whereuppon shalbe wrytten* In Eternum. *Then* Temperantia *shall likewise delyver unto Argus a key whose name shalbe* Nunquam, *signifyinge, that when False Report and Discorde are committed to the pryson of Extreme Oblyvion and locked there everlastinglie, he should put in the key to lett them out* Nunquam: *and when he hathe so done, then the trompetts to blowe, and th' inglishe Ladies to take the nobilite of the straungers, and dance.* (48)

Masques were also popular in French and Italian courts. In them the world of the audience merged with that of the drama, and performers and spectators were undifferentiated. (49) Torch-bearers and musicians, who were not part of the drama, mixed with the dancers, (50) wearing costume which harmonized with that of the masquers. (51) They were not felt to be incongruous because the performance was a dance, of which dramatic illusion was not the aim, and they were necessary accessories.

In China, choral dances performed by children in special costume accompanied by songs and embellished with speeches addressed to the sovereign were part of the court entertainment in Sung dynasty. (52) Like the European court masque these dances were the theatrical embellishment of court life, but they did not, as far as is known, contain dramatic dialogue, nor did the audience join in the dance. (53) In modern times the congratulatory pieces in the Chinese theatre have definite social functions and cannot be counted as pure entertainment, (54) but they differ from court masques in that they do not originate from social life, rather, they are theatre adapted to meet the needs of the occasion. (55)

Symbolism, which is still an instrument in the Chinese theatre to help the telling of the story, was used extensively in the court masque. The characters could represent Countries, Continents, Time, Seasons, Virtue, Truth, Eternity, Naval

---

(48) From Evans, *op. cit.*, xxiii. Continuation of the same theme was designed for the second and third nights. For other descriptions of English masques see Chambers, *Eliz. Stage,* I. Chs. V and VI.

(49) cf. Nicoll, *Stuart Masques and the Renaissance Stage,* 213.

(50) Chambers, *Eliz. Stage,* I. 149.

(51) Chambers, *Eliz. Stage,* I. 195.

(52) See Chs. XXV and XXXII.

(53) Social dance in which men and women mixed was not known in China except in Chou dynasty.

(54) See Ch. XIII.

(55) In Elizabethan times plays were also performed, as in China, at the annual feast of guilds. Chambers, *Eliz. Stage,* I. 221.

Victory, Hope, Sleep, Silence, Melancholy, Invention, Reason, Poetry, History, Architecture, and so on. [56] The possibilities appear limitless and a whole language could be built on the codified symbolism. Jonson called them "court Hieroglyphicks". [57] Part of the pleasure of the masque lies in guessing the visual riddle, for the costume gives some hint of the identity of the abstract characters. [58] Compared with such extremes, the symbolism in the European moralities and the modern Chinese theatre is very mild.

Another point of similarity with the Chinese theatre lies in the emphasis on the beauty of the costume, which, being freed from naturalism by mythology and allegory, became an art and had to be designed rather than merely tailored. [59]

More purely theatrical in nature than the masque are the European court spectacles in which the spectators do not join in the performance. The aim of lavish spectacles is to arouse wonder and amazement, hence they do not stand repetition. For this reason and for the prohibitive cost, they lack a long continuous tradition. Their form is, therefore, influenced by two conditions, the practically unlimited financial support, and the reliance on native imagination of the producers — neither the skill of the producers nor the taste of the audience is enriched by continual development and long tradition. Owing to these limiting factors the Chinese and European court spectacles, though widely different in time and developed independently, are remarkably similar to each other. Here is a description of the spectacle presented by Bernardo Buontalenti in Florence in 1589:

"First came a musical interlude in which an allegorical figure seated on a slowly descending cloud against a starry background 'sang a most exquisite song'. Then came a wondrous scene of cloud and sky, the clouds passing through the air and disappearing behind a magnificent temple. In this *intermedio* appeared no less than forty-four musicians. When the time for the second *intermedio* arrived 'the setting changed again and showed a prospect all of mountains, rocks and fountains'. Amid these slowly rose a mountain representing Parnassus on which were seated eighteen nymphs chanting a lyric. Suddenly the set divided and two dark caverns were revealed, and from these issued twelve musicians. In the third *intermedio* was another cavern in a dark wood whence came thirty-six musicians and four ballet dancers: this was 'a very fine musical ballet, a lovely and magnificent intermedio'. During its course appeared a fearsome Dragon, which was finally put to death by Apollo, who descended from the skies. Soon the time came for the fourth *intermedio*. Once more the prospect changed, and there 'passed through the air' a deity 'in a

---

(56) Nicoll, *Stuart Masque and the Renaissance Stage,* 37 and Ch. VI.

(57) Jonson, *Poems,* An Expostulation with Inigo Jones.

(58) Nicholl, *op. cit.,* 155 f.

(59) *Ibid.,* Ch. VII.

golden chariot' drawn by two dragons. In a cloud were seen diverse spirits, and below a Hell, with Lucifer, 'a terrible monster', and other 'infernal furies' working at Vulcan's smithy and singing 'lovely, but dismal, madrigals'. The fifth *intermedio* presented a most realistic sea with vessels riding the waves. Amid these waves was shown a shell bearing Amphitrite accompanied by dolphins and Tritons. As these sang their songs a ship with twenty men aboard came on stage: it 'sailed across and tacked with such skill as seemed incredible to the onlookers'. The watchman in the crow's-nest sang a madrigal while a dolphin danced below — this, according to contemporaries, was a stupendous show. Finally came the sixth and last entertainment, with an enormous 'Paradise', full of clouds, Jove in the middle surrounded by his fellow-deities. Fifty musicians were concealed in these clouds, and forty others came on the stage below. 'The grandeur of the spectacle', declared one eye-witness, 'cannot be told; he who did not actually see it must fail to credit its wonders'." [60]

In the spectacles which formed the intermission of the English masque the favourite scenes were cities with receding rows of houses, mountains, rocks, seas, clouds, temples, castles, groves, fountains and ships; the mountains rose from below, the clouds moved and opened and the rocks cracked to let out masquers. [61]

Among the spectacles of Han (206 B.C. — A.D. 220) and Sui dynasties (A.D. 589-617) we also find "rumbling thunder", "tall mountains", "range of hills with trees, grass and fairy fruits", "dancing animal masquers", "fairy sitting on a bird", "goddess singing on a cloud", "huge fish and dragon" and scenic transformations such as moving clouds and sudden disappearance or entrance of masquers. [62] Palace ground was sometimes flooded in Han dynasty for water pageants, as in Spain, where in 1570 a large pool was built in Madrid for mock naval battles in the festivities at the entrance of Phillip II's second wife into the city. [63] In Roman times, naval battles staged in flooded theatres, called *Naumachia,* involved real killing. [64] Water pageants, less bloody in nature, were also staged in Elizabethan England. [65]

Both in China and in Europe, the court played an important part in the development of the theatre: its leisure created the demand for entertainment and its wealth supplied the means. [66] The immense expense made it impossible to reproduce the same type of entertainment in commercial theatres, and the special social

---

[60] Nicoll, *Stuart Masques and the Renaissance Stage,* 62 f.

[61] Nicoll, *op. cit.,* Ch. III.

[62] See Ch. XXI.

[63] W. H. Shoemaker, *The Multiple Stage in Spain During the Fifteenth and Sixteenth Centuries,* 112.

[64] See S. Cheney, *The Theatre* (1952), Ill. p. 101.

[65] Venezky, *Pageantry on the Shakespearean Stage,* Pl. VIII. facing p. 160; Chambers, *Eliz. Stage,* I. 123; 138 f.

[66] The cost of a single spectacle was on the order of £21,000, which is equivalent to £200,000 today — see Nicoll, *Stuart Masques and the Renaissance Stage,* 29.

requirements of the court had no parallel among the people. Although dramatic themes entered into court spectacles and became their bases, yet the emphasis was as a whole on lighthearted amusement and true dramatic interest could not grow in them. This is why in spite of the apparent tendency in the spectacles of Han dynasty and later, Chinese drama did not develop among them, and in England, although court masques attained high poetical standards, as dramas their merits are slight. Theatre which grew out of court life was a place for organized flattery and extravagant toys, hence both in China and in Europe there were the complimentary speeches, the bearing of gifts, the scenic display, the lavish costume, the music, the dancing, the acrobatics, the fireworks and the contests. [67]

Nevertheless, the court had influence on commercial theatre — both in its rise and in its form. The scenery of the European theatre, for example, was mainly derived from court theatre in which it was first used: the popular theatres, such as the *commedia dell' arte* and the Elizabethan theatre, were originally without it. The elements of dance and parade, which court spectacles contained, also entered into the Elizabethan and the Chinese theatre. [68] The Chinese drama came from the people, but not without indirect influence from the court: the rise of the Chinese drama nearly coincided with the decline of the native government and the establishment of foreign rule — a fact which led some scholars to think that the drama came from the foreigners, but actually it was not the foreigners who brought the drama but the repeated dispersal of the native court musicians [69] in the decaying Sung dynasty and their activities among the people which gave an additional stimulus to the rise of the drama. [70] Similar conditions can be found in the history of Elizabethan England where, owing to the decay of feudalism, the players and musicians of noble households, instead of entertaining their masters occasionally, had to travel and provide popular entertainment continually in order to make a living. [71] The first English players were dancers and jesters and their performances were farces, or interludes, these being the types easiest to produce and to appreciate. [72] Court patronage and the efforts of the university men who turned dramatists later raised the artistic standard of the Elizabethan drama high above the reach of the groundlings who first fostered its growth. [73] In a similar way, the fall of Sung dynasty supplied the Chinese theatre with a class of unemployed writers who diverted their talents into the dramas of Yüan dynasty. [74]

---

[67] Chambers, *Eliz. Stage,* I. 123 f.
[68] Chambers, *Eliz. Stage,* I. 186 f.
[69] 教坊
[70] See Ch. XXVII.
[71] Raleigh, *Shakespeare,* 97-99.
[72] *Ibid.,* 100.
[73] *Ibid.,* 103.
[74] See Ch. XXVII.

At the beginning the Chinese and the European drama had the same general characteristics: both in the Greek and in the Yüan theatre poetry, music and dance were means of dramatic expression, dramas were based on legends and drama was a performance with skill and beauty rather than a convincing reproduction of real life. The Chinese drama has remained essentially the same but the European drama has changed beyond recognition. The word "theatre", which came from the Greeks, meant originally "a place to see" and the word "drama", also originally Greek, meant "a thing done". [75] Aristotle counted Spectacle, Verse and Music as three of the six parts of Tragedy. (*Poetics*, vi.). Drama therefore began with action and spectacle, and in its earliest stages the performance was more important than the script, the play of the body predominated the play of the mind. The word "audience", meaning "those who listen", is derived from Latin and represents a later phase of theatrical development: the first theatregoers were spectators rather than audience. The modern European drama, however, has lost music, dance and poetry. Dialogue has become the most important if not the only important part of the drama and action has given place to the presentation of ideas. What was "a thing done" becomes "a thing spoken", which often might as well be "a thing read", because in the theatre there is now much less "to see". Discussion of intellectual problems is sometimes the whole purpose of the play and the actors, who were once dancers, now move almost apologetically through their parts, being reduced to the mouthpieces of different bodies of opinions. Theatre becomes a schoolroom and the stage a pulpit, for adult education sugared with entertainment. Dramatists no longer work on the senses but juggle with people's ideas, and the members of the audience no longer come to see and to be amazed, they come now to ponder over stage dialects, to analyse their own minds and to exercise their intellects. Plays like Bernard Shaw's *Back to Methuselah,* a "metabiological pentateuch", are in fact philosophical dialogues, like those of Plato, and can hardly be more remote from drama as action and spectacle.

The fundamental difference between the histories of the Chinese and the European drama is the relative stability of the former and the drift of the latter away from spectacle; the Chinese drama is still a show, the European drama is scarcely such. The cause of this drift may be traced to the disintegration of the means of dramatic expression. Even in the later part of the history of Greek theatre the disintegration had started: the dramatic function of the chorus had by then dwindled to nil and dance interludes entirely unconnected with the plot took their place. The dancers who were in earlier times characters in the play, and their dances which were one of the means of dramatic expression had become divorced from the drama. In Roman times the tradition of Greek theatrical music and Greek acting was lost and

---

[75] R. C. Flickinger, *The Greek Theatre and Its Drama,* 6, 8, 17, 60.

performances consisted of solo declamation of passages taken from the tragedies. [76] Of the many elements which went to make up a performance of the Greek drama the Romans only knew the building and the script, and to imitate the dramatic writings of the Greeks became the toy of the *literati,* till plays, like Seneca's, could only be read but could not be staged. The art of acting became divorced from drama and was developed separately in the pantomime, the mime and the dances. [77] The Greek dramatists and players held the secret of cementing together the various means of dramatic expression but that secret was lost, and without it the Greek theatre could not, even in Roman times, be revived. The text was eventually also ignored in the Roman theatre, and nothing of the Greek theatre was left, except the building. The tradition of the Greek theatre was not cut short, it petered out of existence.

In the Roman theatre the mimetic instinct started anew towards the drama, as in the *atellanae* and the mime, which came from the people and owed little, if anything, to the Greek theatre. However, the preoccupation of the Roman holiday crowd in vulgar pleasures, if nothing else, prevented their growth into literary dramas and in any case, the church soon put an end to any possible development. In the Middle Ages, European drama had a second birth through religion and grew from the mimetic element latent in the Christian liturgy to the mysteries and miracles staged for the instruction of the congregation. [78] As compared with the Greek theatre, however, the church drama suffered several disadvantages. First, the Christian religion, unlike the Dionysian, is always suspicious of abandoned enjoyment, for which the Chinese and the Greek theatre was developed; [79] secondly, the Christian legends form a vast reservoir of dramatic subject matter so that dramatists need not, as in the Greek theatre, choose subjects outside the cult, and within the canon, dogma fetters the imagination by discouraging excessive deviations from the scripture. The Dionysian cult had no Bible and Greek legends were elastic. [80] The stories of the Bible were written for reading not for acting, hence in the church drama we find the narrative form of writing forcibly used as basis for theatrical production. The frequent shift from one locality to another, common to most narrative writing, determined the multiple staging of the church dramas — the simultaneous representation of all the localities covered in the drama, such as Heaven, Hell, Garden of Eden, Jerusalem and so on, in various parts of the church or market place — and the long narratives gave rise to the cyclic form of the drama, which progressed from one episode to another without their being directed towards a climax, except in so far as the original narrative contained any climactic

---

[76] Bieber, *The History of the Greek and Roman Theatre,* 324 f, 401; Beare, *The Roman Stage,* 19.

[77] Bieber, *op. cit.,* 301 f, 415. cf. modern European ballet.

[78] Chambers, *Medieval Stage,* 3 *et seq.*

[79] cf. Aristophanes' *Frogs* in which Dionysus is a coward and a fool, beaten in front of the audience.

[80] *Vide* Flickinger, *The Greek Theatre and Its Drama,* 123.

construction. [81] The Greek drama started with a festive dance and grew in the free treatment of popular legends but the medieval church drama started with an unsuitable script and was stuck with it. [82]

However, neither the ecclesiastical drama nor its offshoot the moralities had any important influence on the European drama of to-day. Continuous tradition in the European drama can be traced backwards only as far as the Renaissance. The beginning of the modern European drama in the Renaissance was not due to natural evolution but due to artificial cultivation. Unlike Greek and medieval church drama, there was no evolution of drama from mimetic ritual, instead, ancient dramas were unearthed, studied and imitated. Even in the Elizabethan theatre and in the *commedia dell' arte,* both of which came from the popular theatre, the influence of classical model was noticeable, the former through the university wits and the latter through the *commedia erudita.* All that the scholars of the Renaissance could recover of the classical theatre were, however, the script and the architecture of the theatre building based on Vitruvius. Of the other elements of the Greek and Roman theatre, it appears that what they did not know they did not miss, and *commedia erudita,* written on classical models, were acted without the other theatrical apparati which made up the original spectacle. A French edition of Terence, published in 1552, shows actors who are not speaking sitting at the back of the stage, and in 1561 J. C. Scaliger had noted that the plays as acted in France had the peculiar convention that those who were silent were understood to be off the stage. [83] The artificiality of such revivals becomes conspicuous when we compare the *commedia erudita,* which is almost pure literature, with the *commedia dell' arte,* which has no literary value but appeals to the audience through its lively acting. Meanwhile, amid the new growth of the visual arts and music theatre developed under its own momentum. Recitation of literary drama could not last long, some means had to be found to give the text a lively performance and invention must make up the deficiency left by ignorance. It was in the efforts of a group of Florentine art-lovers — noblemen, poets and musicians — called *camerata,* to revive the Greek dramatic performance at the end of the sixteenth century that the European opera was born. The gaps in the knowledge of the Greek theatre were then, as they could only be, filled with contemporary notions: instead of a single flute or harp there was an orchestra and instead of solos and chorus in unison, part singing was introduced. The result was, at that time, neither one thing nor another, and was called "opera", which meant "works". In the earliest "works" the music only served to heighten the

---

[81] Chambers, *Medieval Stage,* 125, 130.

[82] *Vide* Chambers, *Medieval Stage,* II. 3 n for a theory that the gospel narratives of the Passion in St. Mark and St. Matthew were based upon a dramatic version. (J. M. Robertson, The Gospel Mystery-Play, *The Reformer,* N.S. iii, 1901). This theory Chambers rejected.

[83] Nicoll, *Development of the Theatre,* 116.

effects of the words, but later on the magnificent development of European music in the polyphonic school of musical composition loaded the opera with more and more beautiful music. Spectacular scenery, which became a main part of its attraction after its commercialization in the middle of the seventeenth century, also continued to develop in the opera, till literary and histrionic merits had alike vanished from it, and in the eighteenth century the Neapolitan opera was either "spectacle for the eye" or "concert in costume". If one considers the musical intricacies of an opera by Wagner or Richard Strauss and the grandeur of Wagner's scenery and compares them with the austerity of the Greek theatre one can hardly imagine two theatres more unlike to each other.

Another form of modern European theatre, the ballet, probably had its ultimate roots in primitive ritual, but was first developed in the French court in the middle of the seventeenth century in the contemporary vogue of mimetic balls. The English court masque, probably derived from religious ceremony, [84] was imitated in Italian and French courts, and in the latter, especially owing to the personal enthusiasm of Louis XIV. [85] It developed under the collaboration of Molière and Lully into *ballet de cour* or *ballet à entrées*. which was a mixture of drama, dance and music. [86] Since then the dramatic content of the ballet has been meagre and has probably never reached even its level in the *ballet de cour,* but in the technical aspects of the dance several innovators had made ballet into the highly specialized style of dancing it is to-day. By convention ballet dancers do not speak or sing, and indeed they cannot, owing to the vigorous movements. Without dialogue the dramatic theme is either absent as in pure ballets, or confined to the simplest plots as in the ballets of puerile sentimentality.

In spite of the serious intent of the Renaissance scholars the Greek dramatic performance was far from being revived. Although for some time Italian and French dramatists drew on Greek themes and most of the great European dramatists were directly or indirectly influenced by the Greek dramas, yet the characteristics of the Greek theatre can scarcely be found in the modern European theatre. Poetry was in the sixteenth and seventeenth centuries a regular means of dramatic expression but by the nineteenth century English poetic dramas were written to be read only. Instead of bringing back the spectacle in the Greek theatre, the Renaissance started several forms of theatre, each with one highly developed element and each almost affiliated to the art that element represents: opera which is music, ballet which is dance and drama which is literature. The Greek dramatic performance was, as it were, broken up and each fragment has had a new life. The native mimetic instinct has, since the Renaissance, made fresh starts in generating a form of drama with

---

[84] Chambers, *Eliz. Stage,* I. 150.

[85] The modern ballet may be said to begin in *L'Académie Nationale de la Danse,* founded in 1661.

[86] A. L. Haskell, *Ballet* (1938), 17 ff.

song and dance, as in the Elizabethan jig which had some influence on the English ballad opera, and in the German *Singspiel,* [87] but they did not grow into any notable form. The Chinese drama, on the other hand, has remained intact from what corresponds to medieval times till to-day, with these elements still bound up in one dramatic purpose. According to some observers,

"Because the constituents of the Chinese drama are entirely subordinated to a single artistic intention the result is a higher standard of finish than anything to be seen in western theatres". [88]

The extreme development of one element of the theatre has an unhealthy effect on the other elements. Music is so eloquent in the opera that the singers cease to act, in fact they are not trained in acting and most of them are bad actors. The literary value of the libretto is not sufficient to make them worth reading and when sung the dialogue is only theoretically discernible even in the solos, and in the choruses and quartets in which different characters sometimes sing different words, the general drift of the emotion is all that can be gathered from the music. It is indeed difficult to imagine how a style of acting could be devised to suit the sumptuous music of western operas: realism lacks rhythm and gracefulness and dancing is usually too simple. In the ballet, the music is not as dramatically significant as in the opera and yet elaborate dances are required to do justice to the music. In some of Wagner's operas music has acquired such power that instead of an aid to dramatic expression it has become a commentary on the drama. The intellectual content too suffered in the seventeenth and early eighteenth centuries, and as Lord Chesterfield said, "People who go to the opera should leave their minds at home". Gluck and Wagner were two of the reformers who tried to make opera stand on its own feet as drama rather than as music, but to-day opera is still predominantly a musician's rather than a dramatist's art, and can be enjoyed by listening to gramophone records alone. In the ballet, the *dramatis personae* are all dumb; when they want to say something they gesticulate anxiously. Opera singers cannot normally act, but they can still move about; the ballet dancers cannot make a sound. The theorists of modern ballet assure us that technique is merely a means to dramatic expression, an ideal attained perhaps in isolated moments, but it is doubtful whether without the display of skill the audience would enjoy any ballet for the dramatic expression it offers. The lack of real dramatic interest in the ballet continued from its earliest days till now, and is due to the limitation of the type rather than the defect of any particular school or period. When Noverre tried to curb the worship of technical virtuosity and advocated dramatic expression as the main purpose of ballet [89] he had, in practice, to supplement the performance with long written explanations.

---

[87] C. R. Baskerville, *The Elizabethan Jig* (1929), 161.

[88] L. C. Arlington and H. Acton, *Famous Chinese Plays* (1937), xiii.

[89] *Lettres sur la danse et les ballets* (1760).

CHAPTER XLIII

HISTORIES OF THE CHINESE AND THE EUROPEAN THEATRE — II

(Stage—Scenery—Front Curtain—Spectators on Stage—Costume—Style of Acting
—Tags—Men Playing Women)

(5)

With the dissociation of dance and music from the drama and the addition of scenery to it, the European drama began, from the sixteenth century onwards, to diverge from the general characteristics which the Greek and the Chinese drama shared. Yet in the four hundred years of modern European theatre it is only since the last decade of the nineteenth century that naturalism has become the prevalent style of production and the stage deprived of all theatricality; up to the early part of the nineteenth century the European drama had many of the characteristics which now make the Chinese drama stand in such strong contrast to naturalism. The ideal of naturalism: to make the response of the audience approach that of witnessing real events: is served by certain means of production such as the box set, the picture stage and the realistic dialogue. It will be shown that these methods were not used in the European theatre until very recently and that as a whole the European theatre since the Renaissance is marked by convention and theatricality.

The location of the theatre determines the construction of the acting space and through it, the nature of the performance. In the various types of European theatre of the past the stage was very different from the picture-stage of to-day. The Greek theatre is the hillside theatre; the medieval, the cathedral theatre; the Elizabethan, the inn-yard theatre and the modern Chinese theatre, the tea-house theatre; and the acting space in them varied accordingly. [1] When a performance of some sort takes place before any but the smallest audience it is common sense to raise the level of the performers to improve visibility, hence the platform stage is the most universal of all

---

[1] Convenient collections of pictorial records of European theatres can be found in S. Cheney, *Stage Decoration* (1928), Part II. and *Theatre Arts Prints* (Theatre Arts, Inc.) (1929).

stages: not only the Chinese, but the Japanese, the Indians, the Elizabethans and the *phlyakes* all used the platform stage. [2] The Spanish *corral* theatre, located in the yard formed by surrounding houses, [3] had a stage similar to that of the Chinese and the Elizabethan theatre. [4] The Greek and the medieval church theatre are, however, exceptions. In the case of the Greek theatre, the drama was a part of the ritual of the Dionysian cult, but as Greek temples were shrines which were too small to hold a congregation, the worshippers gathered in the vicinity of the Temple of Dionysus on the southern side of the Acropolis in Athens which happened to have a slope, thereby providing a suitable place for the spectators watching the dancers. [5] The stage, which had now become a major and complicated portion of the European theatre building, was non-existent in the earliest European theatre: for about thirty years in early fifth century there was not even a background to the acting space, and there was, according to some scholars, no stage at all until the beginning of the Christian era, at the end of the history of Greek drama, which means that for a period longer than the time between Shakespeare and the present there was a theatre without a stage. [6] The medieval drama which, like the Greek drama, grew out of ritual, was housed in the church which was a spacious edifice large enough to hold a congregation as well as the "sets" representing the localities required in the miracles and mysteries. [7]

Of the various theatres of antiquity it was the Greek theatre which, owing to its classical prestige, exerted an influence on the architecture of the subsequent European playhouses. In spite of the rising tiers of spectators which allowed the action to take place in the orchestra [8] the Greek theatre had, in its later days, a narrow platform behind the orchestra which was used as acting space. In Roman times this platform was slightly deepened and the orchestra, owing to the decreasing

---

[2]   For the worldwide significance of the platform stage see Bieber, *History of the Greek and Roman Theatre,* 300, quoting E. Bethe, *Prolegomena zur Geschichte des Theaters in Altertum* (1920); also R. Southern, *The Open Stage, passim.* For the open stage in different parts of Europe in the Renaissance see H. H. Borcherdt, *Das europäische Theater im Mittelalter und der Renaissance* (1935), 135, 136, 181.

[3]   *Vide* S. Cheney, *The Theatre,* 252.

[4]   Rennert, *The Spanish Stage,* Ch. V and p. 65.

[5]   The slope of the auditorium of the Dionysian theatre as it stands was artificially increased, but there was originally a natural slope. See J. T. Allen, *The Greek Theatre of the Fifth Century before Christ* (1919), 23; and Flickinger, *The Greek Theatre and Its Drama,* p. 344, Fig. 81.

[6]   Flickinger, *The Greek Theatre and Its Drama,* 60, 65. See however T. B. L. Webster, *Greek Theatre Production,* 21.

[7]   Some form of platform stage was also used when the dramas were produced outside the church — Nicoll, *Development of the Theatre,* p. 70, Fig. 59; S. Cheney, *Stage Decoration,* Pls. 14 and 15; G. Cohen, *Le Théâtre en France au Moyen Âge,* II. Pls. LIX and LX.

[8]   See Ch. XXXVI (1).

importance of the chorus who danced there, was curtailed and sometimes used to provide seating for the audience. [9] At this time the Dark Ages intervened and free development of the theatre ceased.

When cultural life came back to Europe in the Renaissance, the heritage of stage construction was complicated by other types of theatre and there were five types of stage. [10]

1. The simple platform stage — from the popular theatre.
2. The stage with the permanent facade at the back, as in Palladio's Teatro Olimpico — from the Roman stage.
3. The formal designs of scenes due to Serlio, one for comedy, one for tragedy and one for satyr play — from Vitruvius' idea of the Roman stage. [11]
4. The simultaneous setting of Hotel de Bourgogne — from the medieval drama. [12]
5. The elaborate devices for the shifting of scenery — a Renaissance product. [13]

Of the five types it was the last, the only one with potentialities of naturalistic staging, which was destined to have practically exclusive influence on the modern European theatre and the construction of the European theatre was since that time modified to fit the needs of housing and shifting the scenery. Among the people, theatre developed without the aid of scenery, as in the Elizabethan and the early Spanish theatre, but at court scenery was among the expensive toys, such as costume and machines, which the nobility could well afford [14] and the taste of the court eventually prevailed. The methods of staging were at first tentative and several types were simultaneously used. The multiple setting which was used in Spain and lingered in the Hôtel de Bourgogne in Paris into the seventeenth century was eventually discarded because as it was developed for the ecclesiastical drama it could not be readily adapted for the changing dramatic content in the Renaissance dramas and the relatively static background of the Roman stage was incompatible with the love for the newly discovered art of spectacular scenery. [15] The simple platform stage was for a while used in Spain and England, but had to be deleted for the scenery, leaving, in the English theatre, only a slight mark in the form of the apron stage which lasted till within living memory. On the continent the influence of the simple

---

[9] Bieber, *History of the Greek and Roman Theatre*, 256; Nicoll, *Development of the Theatre*, 51.

[10] Nicoll, *Development of the Theatre*, 118.

[11] L. B. Campbell, *Scenes and Machines on the English Stage During the Renaissance* (1923), 36-38.

[12] K. Macgowan and W. Melnitz, *The Living Theatre* (1955), 198.

[13] For pictorial views of these types see R. Southern, *Changeable Scenery*, 26-27.

[14] Thorndike, *Shakespeare's Theatre*, 4 f.

[15] W. H. Shoemaker, *The Multiple Stage in Spain During the Fifteenth and Sixteenth Centuries* (1935).

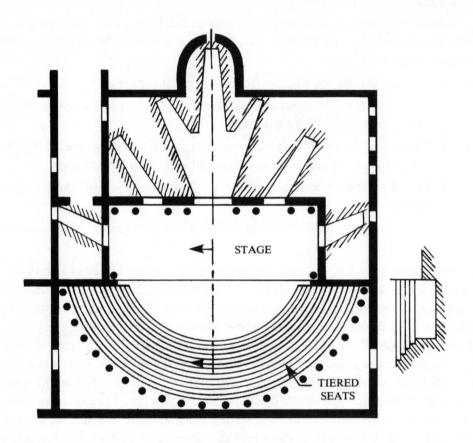

Fig. 59
TEATRO OLIMPICO
VICENZA, 1585
by Palladio and Scamozzi
(No change of scenery)

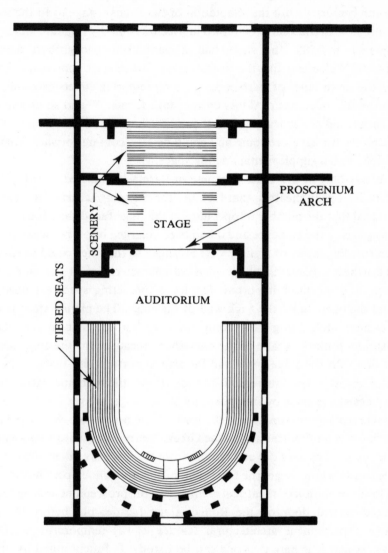

Fig. 60
**TEATRO FARNESE
IN PARMA, 1618**
"Father of Modern European Theatres"

platform stage is not noticeable [16] instead, the picture stage developed the machine play of the seventeenth century and the naturalistic theatre of Antoine.

Perspective painting was introduced into the theatre at the beginning of the sixteenth century [17] but the adaptation of the Roman stage to fit the scenery was a slow process. In the Teatro Olimpico in Vicenza, built by Palladio and Scamozzi and completed in 1585, the stage had a permanent background decorated with architectural elements like the Roman stage, the nearest approach to scenery there being the seven lanes of false perspective representing streets extending backwards from the five openings or doors on the stage facade [18] and so arranged that each audience could see at least one of them. [19] Characters in the drama could hide at these places for eavesdropping and could be seen coming forward from them, thus they constituted supplementary acting space. [20]

It was only in the Teatro Farnese in Parma, completed in 1618, the father of modern European theatres, that facilities for changing scenery was provided. It can be noticed that the number of openings on the stage facade had been reduced to one opening facing the audience and it had been enlarged into a proscenium arch behind which receding layers of scenery were arranged so that they could be easily changed. [21] This theatre contains all the physical characteristics of the modern European theatre; and the most important feature is the acting space extended backwards behind the opening on the back wall of the stage. The picture stage framed by the proscenium arch being now complete it is natural that in the next step the auditorium took the shape of the horseshoe, because now the angle formed by the sight line with the stage front had become important and seats at the side of the auditorium were for this reason inferior. If we allow compensation for the poor sight lines at the sides by the proximity to the stage, we get the contour of equally desirable seats approximately in the form of the horseshoe. Where the angle of the sight line was unimportant, as in the Greek theatre, the auditorium was fan-shaped; and if the seats at the sides and remote from the stage are taken away from the fan-shaped auditorium we get the floor plan of the horseshoe opera house.

In the evolution of theatrical architecture the proscenium arch appears to be the enlarged central door on the Roman stage facade, but before the proscenium became a permanent architectural feature it was temporarily erected in court spectacles and it is here that one can best study its function and its origin. In the early pageants there was the triumphal arch which served as an ornamented frame.

---

[16] Nicoll, *Development of the Theatre,* 145.

[17] *Ibid.,* 86.

[18] *Vide ibid.,* p. 92, Fig. 86.

[19] Theoretically the perspective looks right only from one position in the theatre.

[20] *Vide* J. T. Allen, *Stage Antiquities* (1927), Ch. XI; Duchartre, *The Italian Comedy,* 60 f.

[21] For earlier and temporary proscenium arches see G. R. Kernodle, *From Art to Theatre* (1947), 79, 196.

Sabbatini (c. 1574-1654), the Italian scenic designer, used the front wings to mask the rest of the sets. The form of these front wings was "an artificial festoon of leaves and fruit" or "a piece of cloth simulating brocade sprinkled with gold, in hanging folds and golden tassels". [22] The true function of the proscenium arch was then, and still is, to cover the outer edges of the canvas pieces: in the seventeenth century sometimes only two vertical front wings were used for the purpose, thus forming an incomplete arch. [23] The audience looking through the proscenium opening is allowed to see only one part of the scenery which is so arranged that the rough sides, which would reveal signs of carpentry and thereby destroy the illusion, cannot be seen, just as the receding perspective pieces behind the doors of the Roman type stage facade (like those in the Teatro Olimpico) were partially concealed. As the conjurer hides the more telling parts of his instruments with cunning disguise, so the early scenic designers had a pleasant way of masking the unpresentable. What is now a simple hole on the end wall of the theatre was a highly ornamented *part of the scenery,* with children, leaves, flowers, emblems and so forth. [24] The arch and the scenery are now separate, one is an architectural feature and the other a life size doll-house, but at the beginning they were both integral parts of a lavish decoration, in fact, the arch was then called "ornaments". [25]

The proscenium opening is now the sharp boundary between the world of the drama and the world of the audience but when scenery was at first used the two worlds were joined by the intermediate proscenium arch, carefully designed and made with its sham drapery, painted figures and the arms of the prince or title of the masque. [26] Even on the permanent stage with proscenium arch, some theatres of the seventeenth century had three proscenium arches, one facing the audience and two set at an angle at the sides of the stage, each with scenery behind it, but separated from each other by pillars and drapery. [27] The acting space in these cases was surrounded by architectural elements as well as scenery, as in the case of the Teatro Olimpico, though the architectural elements had decreased in proportion as compared with the Roman stage. Since the proscenium arch was looked at as a rich picture frame, the stage, with its scenery, must have been decorative rather than illusionary. The stage became a peep show only recently.

(6)

So far as the method of staging is concerned, the distinctive characteristics of the naturalistic theatre are: the use of scenery for illusion, the segregation of actors

---

[22] Nicoll, *Stuart Masques and the Renaissance Stage,* 44.

[23] *Ibid.,* 44, 45 (Fig. 9), 46 (Fig. 10).

[24] *Ibid.,* 47.

[25] *Ibid.,* 47.

[26] *Ibid.,* 46 f.

[27] *Vide* Nicoll, *Development of the Theatre,* p. 139, Fig. 158.

and audience and the abolishment of neutral acting space — space without scenery and property. To achieve these objectives the boundary between stage and auditorium, conventionally represented by the row of footlights, is jealously guarded from trespassing in either direction: acting space is confined within the set and changes of scenery are carried out unseen. Since the sixteenth century all the instruments required for naturalistic staging — the proscenium arch, the curtain, the receding stage and the scenery — have been available but, curious as it may seem from the point of view of naturalism, they were not used for the purpose of creating illusion until the late nineteenth century.

Scenery in the European theatre is nominally as old as the Greek drama, but before the Renaissance it could hardly be more than symbolic. European theatres before the sixteenth century were practically all out-of-doors, and realistic scenery was a physical impossibility. Even when the church was used as theatre the dispersion of the action to different parts of the church limited setting to simple properties. The Greeks did not know how to paint realistic pictures and when the symbolic paintings were inserted between the columns behind the acting space the background of the actors remained essentially unchanged. [28] It was only when, in the Renaissance, the European stage moved indoors to the palaces of the nobility and the principles of perspective painting were discovered that it was possible to build scenery as modern Europeans understand it. Vitruvius' work on classical architecture, which contains detail designs of Greco-Roman theatres, was discovered in 1414 and was widely circulated in the early part of the sixteenth century. Based on Vitruvius' ideas on scenery, Serlio (1475-1554) conceived of three different types of scenic background, one for tragedy, one for comedy and one for satyr play. [29] Serlio's scenery remained unchanged for each type of drama and the first changeable scenery was that designed by Bernardo Buontalenti (1536-1608) for the *intermezzi* in the celebration of Grand Duke Ferdinand I's marriage in Florence in 1589.

Stage machinery on a large scale was employed at first to illustrate the supernatural aspects of the Christian religion. Vasari [30] tells of a representation of the Annunciation designed by Filippo Brunelleschi (1377-1446) in the church of S. Felice in Florence about 1400, in which there was a "nosegay" of cherubim suspended in the copper dome in the roof of the church which stood for heaven and an angel descended in a copper globe amid music, singing and incense. Later in the fifteenth century this type of spectacle became more elaborate and included such devices as moving clouds (which concealed the ropes and pulleys) and a mountain

---

[28] See Ch. XXXVI (3).

[29] *Vide* L. B. Campbell, *Scenes and Machines During the Renaissance,* 36-38.

[30] *Lives* (1850) London, I. 457 ff. Filippo Brunelleschi.

with Christ and angels on it, which moved bodily into "heaven". [31]

In the sixteenth and seventeenth centuries scenery and stage machinery underwent vigorous development under aristocratic patronage because it was a novel plaything and sufficiently expensive and capable of innovations to become the object of rivalry between the princely courts. Patrons tried to enlist the services of the best machinists and scenic designers to compete with each other in the splendour and novelty of their theatrical entertainment. Magnificence in production became a matter of personal prestige. With the large financial support possible in the small number of productions per year stage scenery became conjuring on a gigantic scale, to inspire wonder and admiration. Perspective which was at first used in the modest scenes of Serlio and in the receding layers of scenery behind the doors of Roman stage facade to create the illusion of lanes of buildings stretching into great distances, had now a more flexible use in a wider scope. Opera further stimulated the development of stage spectacle and permanent theatres with stable stocks of scenery were built, first by the court for private use and then by the public, the first public theatre of this type being the San Cassiano in Venice, in 1638.

The interest in the scenery at this time was not however in the illusion which it could help to create. It was not the verisimilitude but the unexpectedness of the representation that was valued; the aim was not convincing scenes but amazing sights, and what the audience appreciated was not imitation but imagination. The receding lanes of buildings, for example, had no dramatic function at all but care was taken that everyone in the audience could look down at least one lane. Perspective was then a new visual experience not to be missed. In tragedy or comedy it was considered proper to use a fixed background but in pastoral dramas and *intermedii* changes and displays of scenery were fashionable. [32] It may be noticed that scenic changes instead of being dictated by the requirements of the plot were matters of convention and varied inversely with the amount of dramatic interest. The best scenery was not the most lifelike but the most surprising; interior and quiet scenes were unworthy subjects, whole towns should rise and vanish and rivers overflow and dry up. Some idea of the wonders then presented in the theatre can be obtained through Richard Lascelles, in his *Italian Voyage* (1670):

"I have seen upon the stage Rivers swelling and Boats rowing upon them; waters overflowing their banks and stage, man flying in the air, Serpents crawling upon the stage, Houses falling on the suddain, Temples and *Boscos* appearing, whole towns, known towns, starting up on a sudden with men walking in the streets, the Sun appearing and chasing away darkness, sugar

---

[31] Conjuring of a less theatrical type was used by Tibetan lamas for religious instruction — see Marco Polo, *Travels,* Ed. M. Komroff (1942), Bk. I. Ch. 31, p. 64., Bk. I. Ch. 61, pp. 108, 109 n.

[32] W. Smith, *Italian Actors of the Renaissance* (1930), 88.

plums fall upon the spectators' heads like Hail, Rubans flash in the ladies' faces like lightning, with a thousand like representations''.

The water was sometimes real, for the auditorium of the Teatro Farnese in Parma was flooded in 1628 to stage Neptune's entrance with marine monsters and islands, and drained again at a signal during the performance. [33]

In the seventeenth century the vogue of stage machinery spread across Europe and as extraordinary scenes required extraordinary dramatic content the "machine play" was developed to provide the suitable opportunities to the scenic designer. In the eighteenth century the machine play became gradually out of fashion but the taste for scenic display did not appear to have abated and satisfaction was provided both inside and outside the theatre. At the end of the eighteenth century de Loutherbourg, once Garrick's scenic designer, gave an exhibition called "Eidophusikon" consisting of scenes of storm, fire, volcanoes and clouds. Scenic design was then considered a branch of painting, a kind of three dimensional painting: Loutherbourg was elected to the Royal Academy in 1781. In the nineteenth century the fascination of scenery became part of the appeal of the melodrama which not only had its characteristic artistry of sentimental effects but also relied on sensational scenes such as burning and toppling castles, exploding ships, crashing trains and horse-racing. Outside the theatre the love for scenic splendour found outlet in Albert Smith's (1816-60) profitable one man entertainment which was in fact travelogue with scenic illustration, spiced with stories and songs — one was for a journey across India, one was called "The Ascent of Mont Blanc" and one described travels in China. In the early part of the century pure scenic display took the name of *diorama* and was shown in Drury Lane Theatre in London: a long strip of canvas was slowly wound across the stage presenting such subjects as Niagara Falls and a journey through Egypt. [34]

Judging by the *type* of scenes alone one can realize that down to the nineteenth century scenery was not valued or used for its illusion; indeed the lack of convincing lifelike quality was the very thing criticized by the playwrights of the naturalistic school at the end of the nineteenth century. Scenery was partly overt display of ingenuity, and partly stage decoration. [35] In a production of the garden scene in *Romeo and Juliet* in the eighteenth century there was a moon in the scenery but a chandelier also hung in front of Juliet's balcony. [36]

The realistic set was introduced in the middle of the nineteenth century, before the rise of the cult of naturalism, by Madame Vestris who was also the first to use the

---

[33] Scenic transformations of this kind were known in the third century A.D. in Roman arenas, *vide* Gibbon, *Decline and Fall of the Roman Empire,* Ch. XII.

[34] R. Speaight, *Juvenile Drama,* 29.

[35] cf. the use of scenery in Chinese shadow plays.

[36] *Vide* Nicoll, *Development of the Theatre,* p. 176, Fig. 209.

box set with ceiling as early as 1841, if not earlier. She with her husband Charles Mathews and their librettist J. R. Planché were responsible for many an extravaganza, farce and burlesque in the Olympic and Lyceum theatres in London in the early part of the nineteenth century and realistic sets were another attraction in her spectacles. It was not until after Antoine founded the *Théâtre Libre* in Paris in 1887 that manifestos were issued and naturalism became a creed; then the supply of real properties and lifelike stage sets became connected with dramatic theory. Since then the authentic stage set has sometimes replaced the merely imitative: in Belasco's (1859-1931) production of *The Governor's Lady* in 1912 an exact replica of Child's restaurant was built on the stage, and other attempts at putting dramatic action in actual surroundings have also been made. Scenery, which had been for showing the audience what they normally did not see, was now for showing what they saw every day.

The modern European stage started in the sixteenth century with a simple platform having an ornamented background (as in the Teatro Olimpico) but since the seventeenth century it has been a complicated machine with structures and mechanisms above and below the platform to enrich the visual side of the drama with innumerable scenic exhibitions. The part of the theatre building behind the curtain is usually larger in volume than the auditorium. With the grid, the fly floor, the cellar, the traps, the sloat cut and other complicated mechanisms the stage is not merely a place for acting but an enormous box of tricks.[37] A court theatre in Paris, distinguished for the spectacles produced in it, was indeed called *Salle des Machines*. This magic box which grew out of the love for counterfeit sights that surpass the expectation in scope or in splendour and which has been mainly used to amaze the audience, was recently adopted for producing scenes as nearly indistinguishable as possible from the actual *locale*. As the standard of verisimilitude is raised the types of scenes become limited and are now mostly interiors. [38]

In China, the interest in stage machinery showed itself at one time but it did not last long enough to meet the rise of the drama, hence its effect on the drama cannot be traced in the Chinese theatrical history. In modern Europe so few theatres are without scenery that its effect on the European dramas cannot be easily seen either, because there are few dramas written for the bare stage with which one can make comparisons. The rigour of the improvised acting in the *commedia dell' arte* is believed to have been sapped by scenery in the eighteenth century [39] and the gradual

---

[37] See S. Cheney, *Stage Decoration* (1928), Pl. 39, p. 61.

[38] Reaction, however, has already set in since the beginning of this century. Appia and Craig, who had wide influence on the modern European theatre, advocated stage setting and lighting not as a pictorial background, but as abstract architectural environment to suit and to strengthen the moods of the drama.

decline of poetic drama in England coincided with the increasing importation of continental scenic devices in the eighteenth century. Scenery, except what is purely decorative, must necessarily tend to oust unrealistic elements from the drama because they are incongruous with the realistic background and the naturalistic style of acting; rhetoric in the dialogue and refinement in the delivery must suffer. Ben Jonson, as can be expected from his differences with Inigo Jones, thought that "things which are objected to sense . . . are but momentary and merely taking". [40] Flecknoe, who could speak from direct experience of the transition from simple platform stage to stage with scenery, looked on the Elizabethan theatre with nostalgia.

> "Now for the difference betwixt our Theatres and those of former times; they were but plain and simple, with no other Scenes nor Decorations of the stage, but onely old Tapestry, and the Stage strew'd with Rushes, with their Habits accordingly, whereas ours now for cost and ornament are arriv'd to the height of Magnificence; but that which makes our Stage the better, makes our Playes the worse perhaps, they striving now to make them more for sight then hearing". [41]

His was the rare chance of observing within his life time the changes in the actual performance after the introduction of scenery and against his views it is difficult to think of the Elizabethan and Chinese stage as crude and defective. The Elizabethan stage is well suited to the purposes of the Elizabethan drama and to those with some knowledge of the Elizabethan method of staging it is only too clearly visible how Elizabethan plays suffer on the modern stage. [42]

(7)

The function of the front curtain in the European theatre of to-day is a complex one. The most obvious reason for it is the necessity to conceal the changes of scenery — by a curious convention the audience can overlook the physical impossibility of the same stage being different localities successively if the supposed change occurs unseen, but not otherwise. The front curtain also makes it possible to begin and end scenes with the actors on the stage thereby dispensing with the formal entrance and exit in which they present themselves to and take their leave of the audience. With it the dramatist can also take advantage of the surprise caused by suddenly disclosed scenes and in conjunction with the interval, curtain drop also indicates the

---

[39] K. M. Lea, *Italian Popular Comedy* (1934), 336.

[40] Preface to *Hymenaei*.

[41] Richard Flecknoe, *A Short Discourse of the English Stage* (1664), in J. E. Spingarn, *Critical Essays of the Seventeenth Century* (1908), Vol. II. 95.

[42] cf. Drinkwater, *Shakespeare, (Great Lives)*, 87.

accelerated passage of time in the drama. Perhaps less conspicuous than any of the functions mentioned above is that of the barrier between the stage and the auditorium. As shutter to the magic box which the stage has become it guards the secrets and enhances the mystery of the stage: proscenium arch, footlights, and the change of floor level define the line of demarcation, but the curtain is a physical obstruction like the door in a door-opening. This function of the curtain becomes noticeable when it is lowered between scenes having the same scenery and with no actors on the stage at the end of the scenes. In the modern European theatre the stage not in action and left in full view of the audience is instinctively avoided. The illusion attached to the pretended locality of the stage is active by virtue of the players on it; when the play is not in progress, a stage, however completely disguised, is a stage only, therefore it must not be seen by the audience. Among these different functions of the front curtain of to-day, only that of sudden disclosure was exploited in the European theatre before the later half of the nineteenth century.

Curtain of one form or another has been used on the European stage almost, but not quite, as long as scenery. The fact that some of the plays of Euripides and Sophocles start with an assembled body of characters has led scholars like Dörpfeld and Reisch to think that there was a front curtain in the Greek theatre — another instance of the limited value of the script as evidence for the method of staging. [43] The first stage curtain in Europe was in the Roman theatre and was first mentioned by Cicero in the first century before Christ as rising (to conceal) at the end of a mime but Donatus said it was introduced in A.D. 133. [44] It was also mentioned by Ovid, Phaedrus, Virgil and Horace. The curtain, called *aulaeum,* which was raised to conceal and dropped to reveal the stage, has been thought to be a low screen, owing to the difficulty of reconstructing the method of its working on a wide stage without overhead supports, [45] and if it was a low screen it could only cover part of the stage, or at least so it would appear to the audience in the higher seats in the tiered auditorium. Another curtain, called *siparium,* was mentioned by Donatus, Apuleius and Seneca and was probably a smaller curtain which opened by being folded up. [46] The use of the curtain in spite of the difficulty of working it on the Roman stage points to the pressing demand for it to heighten the effect of sudden display. Scenery was said to have been introduced in 99 B.C. and it would have made the front curtain specially desirable. [47]

In the Renaissance the *aulaeum* was revived and Ariosto (*Orlando Furioso,* 1515) speaks of it falling to reveal brilliant lamps, triumphal arches, towers, statues

---

[43]   *Vide* W. J. Lawrence, *Elizabethan Playhouse and Other Studies, First series,* 111.

[44]   *Vide* Beare, *The Roman Stage,* 256-266; Lawrence, *op. cit.,* 113 f.

[45]   Lawrence, *op. cit.,* 113; Beare, *op. cit.,* 266.

[46]   Beare, *op. cit.,* 262 f.

[47]   Beare, *op. cit.,* 260 f.

and pictures. [48] In 1519 at the performance of Ariosto's *I Suppositi,* a curtain of this kind designed by Rafael was used, and the same construction was still used in Italy at the beginning of the seventeenth century. The example was followed in the court theatres in England: Ben Jonson's *Masque of Blackness* given at Whitehall in 1605 contains the instruction, *"First for the scene was drawn a landtschap consisting of small woods, and here and there a void place filled with huntings; which falling, an artificial sea was seen to shoot forth as if it flowed to the land".* [49] Court spectacles of this period being what they were, the curtain was, as can be expected, used for the advantage of sudden disclosure. Vasari, who superintended the performance in 1565 of *La Cofanaria* in Florence, described a gorgeous *aulaeum* which fell to reveal "to the gaze of the astounded audience a view of Paradise, with angels seated on the clouds and indulging in vocal and instrumental harmony". [50] In 1607, in a masque by Marston presented at Castle Ashby,

> "Suddenly, upon this songe, the cornets were winded, and the travers that was drawn before the Masquers sanke downe. The whole shewe presently appeereth, which presented itself in this figure: the whole body of it seemed to be the syde of a steepely assending wood, on the top of which, in a fayre oak, sat a golden eagle, under whose wings satt in eight severall thrones the eight Masquers". [51]

Even in tragedy the curtain was used for surprise: an eye-witness of a performance of *Oedipus Rex* in Teatro Olimpico in 1585 reported that,

> "there was sound of trumpets and drums, and four squibs exploded. In a twinkling of an eye the curtain fell before the stage. I can hardly express in words, nor can it be imagined, how great the joy was, and the infinite pleasure felt by spectators when they, after a moment of stunned surprise, watched the prologue and when the sound of harmonized voices and divers instruments could be heard from a distance behind the scenic facade". [52]

In Nicola Sabbatini's *Pratica di fabricar Scene e Machine ne' Teatri* (1638) a curtain is described but the use of it for changing scenes is not recommended, instead, it is suggested that trumpets or drums or some intentional disturbance at the back of the auditorium be used to distract the audience. [53] The curtain that rose to discover superseded the *aulaeum* in the later part of the seventeenth century both in Italian and in English court masques and the curtain was now "suddenly drawne up" or

---

[48] Lawrence, *op. cit.,* 114; J. T. Allen, *Stage Antiquities,* 164.

[49] *Vide* Lawrence, *op. cit.,* 115 f.

[50] Lawrence, *op. cit.,* 116.

[51] Lawrence, *op. cit.,* 117 f; Thorndike, *Shakespeare's Theatre,* 182 f.

[52] Letter by Filippo Pigafetta, quoted in Nagler, *Sources of Theatrical History,* 85 f.

[53] Nicoll, *Development of the Theatre,* 103.

"flew up on the sudden" [54] and since then the front curtain has been raised directly upward either by rolling or by folding in valances, or up and to the sides by folding in loops.

Change of scenery in court spectacles was not utilitarian and abrupt, but deliberate and slow; the scenes were not shifted, they were transformed; it was not conjuring but magic. Clouds moved apart and thrones appeared in heaven from behind, castles turned into mounds, rocks opened to let out dancers, scenes were moved away to reveal further scenes or revolved to show different masquers in different surroundings and all this done with suitable music. If the movements were concealed, half of the designer's efforts would be wasted. [55] When unpresentable scene-shifting had to be done, the curtain was divided into two parts, the upper and lower or the right and left and manipulated separately, so that one part of the scene could be shown while another part was being prepared. [56] The curtain was like a magician's cloth, but was so richly decorated and carefully designed to fit the theme that together with the proscenium arch it was almost part of the scenery.

Before the court theatres of the Renaissance dramatic action in the European theatre was spread over a large area. The early Greek players performed in the orchestra, the Roman stage was very wide and the medieval drama had scattered action. A curtain then could only cover either the whole acting space partially, as with the Roman *aulaeum,* or part of it completely, as in the wagons of the medieval pageant-drama and the curtained portions on the Elizabethan and early French and Spanish stages. [57] Even in early court masques the sets were scattered in different parts of the hall. With the proscenium arch, however, scenery became concentrated behind it and total concealment was then possible. [58] Yet after the proscenium arch and the curtain had become permanent features of commercial theatres they were not used to conceal scene-shifting. [59] In the Restoration theatre the front curtain rose at the end of the prologue, which was spoken in front of it, and remained out of sight until after the epilogue was spoken when it fell to mark the end of the performance. During the play the end of an act was marked by an empty stage, and within the act change of scene was carried out not only in full view of the audience but often with the actors remaining on the stage. [60] Scenery could be partially changed: the backcloth could be changed and the wings remained. [61] When the locality of the scene changed with the scenery, the actors, though remaining on the

---

[54] Lawrence, *op. cit.,* 118 f.

[55] Nicoll, *Stuart Masques and the Renaissance Stage,* 39-44.

[56] Chambers, *Eliz. Stage,* I. 181 f.

[57] Thorndike, *Shakespeare's Theatre,* 11, 98.

[58] Chambers, *Eliz. Stage,* I. 181 f.

[59] R. Southern, *Changeable Scenery* (1952), Ch. I. *passim.*

[60] Lawrence, *Elizabethan Playhouse, First series,* 170 f.

[61] R. Southern, *Changeable Scenery,* 155.

stage, were understood to have moved from one place to another. The convention had the advantage of continuous action and flexibility of location, because actors could go upstage and two flats could shut them off and they would have automatically made their exit, and those remaining in front of the newly moved flats would be in a new scene. [62] The flats could also be pulled open and actors emerging from behind were understood to be coming out of a door, [63] and doors on the scene were supposed to be shut by closing the flats. Only after the middle of the eighteenth century was the Act-Drop, a cloth bearing decorative picture and different from the front curtain, lowered between the acts to cover the stage during the intervals. [64] In the nineteenth century scenes continued to be shifted in view of the audience and Dickens (1812-70) gives us a description of it:

> "We behold, with throbbing bosoms, the heroine in the grasp of a proud and ruthless baron: her virtue and her life alike in danger; drawing forth her dagger to preserve the one at the cost of the other; and as our expectations are wrought up to the highest pitch, a whistle is heard: and we are straightway transported to the great hall of the castle: where a grey-headed seneschal sings a funny chorus with a funnier body of vassals, who are free of all sorts of places from church vaults to palaces, and roam about in company, carolling perpetually". *(Oliver Twist, Ch. 17.)*

The whistle was the prompter's signal to shift scenery. [65] The satire here, it may be noticed, is on melodrama, not on the visible shifting of scenery. In 1880 when Henry Irving revived *The Corsican Brothers* he introduced a crimson velvet curtain, distinct from the Act-Drop, to hide scene-shifting [66] which took thirty-eight seconds. [67] In the nineteenth century for successive scenes with built sets, which could not be changed quickly, a "carpenter's scene", played in front of a curtain, was inserted to provide time. [68] Since then the waits between the acts have become longer and longer, the "old, quick fire, continuous, varied shows of the Stuarts and the Georgians" have passed away, [69] and the workings of the European stage have become a secret seen only by those who operate it.

(8)

The type of dramatic illusion cherished by the modern European theatregoers requires the isolation of the actors: intrusion of spectator or stage hand into a

---

[62] Nicoll, *Development of the Theatre*, 167; Lawrence, *Elizabethan Playhouse, Second series,* 178 f.

[63] Albright, *Shakespearian Stage,* 100 f.

[64] R. Southern, *Changeable Scenery,* 170.

[65] Lawrence, *Old Theatre Days and Ways,* 37 f; R. Southern, *Changeable Scenery,* 136.

[66] *Vide* Nicoll, *Development of the Theatre,* 190.

[67] R. Southern, *Changeable Scenery,* 24.

[68] Southern, *op. cit.,* 23, 267.

[69] *Ibid.,* 24.

dramatic scene in action is considered a calamity. Yet, the proscenium arch and front curtain notwithstanding, the European actors were surrounded by spectators and mixed with stage hands until recent times.

In medieval dramas, both in the church and in the market place, the spectators mixed intimately with the players, and in the popular theatre of the sixteenth and seventeenth centuries the spectators surrounded and sat on the platform stage. [70] Even in the court theatres of that time scenery was not confined to the space behind the proscenium arch [71] and the stage was connected with the auditorium by steps and ramps [72] so that dancers could come down to the main floor to perform ballets with the spectators surrounding them. [73] It was not until the advent of the opera that the audience and the actors became separated by the impassable orchestra. In the Elizabethan theatre the gulls sitting on the stage to show off their fineries could not be closer to the players, for some of them even pressed near to the "state" or throne seat. [74]

From Restoration times onwards the proscenium arch became established as a permanent feature in the English theatre, yet it did not prevent the admixture of audience with actors. The proscenium arch which at the present coincides approximately with the front edge of the stage and which confines scenery and action to the space behind it, was, in the seventeenth and eighteenth centuries, half way up the stage, that is to say, the stage was then divided into two parts: upstage behind the proscenium arch where scenery was concentrated it was narrower and downstage in front of the proscenium arch where there was no scenery the floor plan of the stage extended forward and opened like a bell mouth to the stage front. The part in front of the proscenium arch, called the forestage or the apron stage, was the main acting space, being nearer to the auditorium, and was flanked on the sides by stage doors and boxes on the stage level and by boxes and galleries above it. [75] In other words, the auditorium floor stopped at the stage front but the boxes at the sides of the theatre extended further on the sides of the forestage till it met the proscenium and, in the opposite direction, the scenery stopped at the proscenium arch but the stage extended beyond it between the boxes on its sides. The main acting space was bounded in the front by the auditorium, at the sides by the boxes and at the back by the proscenium arch and curtain or scenery beyond. This forestage was

---

[70] Nicoll, *Development of the Theatre,* p. 114, Fig. 128.

[71] *Vide* S. Cheney, *Stage Decoration,* Pl. 27, showing sets on the main floor in a spectacle in 1581.

[72] Cheney, *Stage Decoration,* Pl. 28; Nicoll, *Development of the Theatre,* 87-89.

[73] *Vide* Macgowan, *The Living Stage,* 96; G. Craig, *Books and Theatres* (1925), Plate on p.40; also P. Sonrel, *Traité de Scénographie* (1943), Pl. XIII showing scenery on the main floor.

[74] Reynolds, *Red Bull,* 64.

[75] *Vide Lawrence, Elizabethan Playhouse, First series,* 157-191, Proscenium Doors: an Elizabethan Heritage; for pictorial views see Nicoll, *Development of the Theatre,* Figs. 202 (p.172), 203 and 204 (p.173), 242 (p.186), 243 (p.187) and 245 (p.189).

603

by no means a shallow strip of space: in 1778 Drury Lane theatre had no less than twelve boxes on the two sides of the stage in four vertical rows. [76] and a print for the theatre in 1808 shows that in the two vertical rows nearer the footlights there were eight boxes, two on the stage level and six above it, and further upstage there were two proscenium doors set at an angle above which were four boxes two on each side. [77] Other theatres in London such as Covent Garden, Haymarket, Royalty and King Lynn had similar arrangements [78] and so did theatres in Paris. [79] This arrangement of the English stage lasted well into the nineteenth century: in Haymarket theatre the apron stage was curtailed in 1843 [80] and the last of proscenium doors, according to Lawrence, subsisted in the Adelphi theatre in Liverpool until the beginning of this century. [81] It may be noticed that the forestage had its own entrances in the proscenium doors in front of the proscenium arch so that actors normally made their entrances and exits not in and out of the set but through doors which were parts of the theatre-building. [82] These entrances and exits must have been formal rather than realistic, because actually the actors were seen walking on and off the *stage* not the scene, but somehow they were understood to enter and leave the locality represented by the scenery situated some distance behind them. While Lawrence believes that there were only two proscenium doors [83] Richard Southern thinks there were in some theatres as many as six, three on each side and that they were used in highly conventionalized ways, for example, an actor going out of one door and coming back from another represented going through the same door from one room into another, and though the scenery remained the same the locality of the stage was understood to have changed. [84] The balconies or boxes above the proscenium doors, though in front of the proscenium arch, were also used for acting space like the upper stage of the Elizabethan theatre. [85] The scenery could not have been considered to be of vital importance because the audience in the stage boxes, which were some of the most expensive seats and by no means a negligible part of the audience in number, could only get an imperfect view of it, and that only by

---

[76] Lawrence, *op. cit.,* 179; see also model of Wren's Playhouse in Southern, *Changeable Scenery,* Ill. facing p.176.
[77] Nicoll, *Development of the Theatre,* 187.
[78] *Vide* R. Southern, *The Open Stage,* 28 f.
[79] S. Cheney, *Stage Decoration,* Pl. 33.
[80] Nicoll, *op. cit.,* 187.
[81] Lawrence, *Elizabethan Playhouse, First series,* 189.
[82] Nicoll, *Development of the Theatre,* 168; Lawrence, *Elizabethan Playhouse, First series,* 161 and 171 f where it is explained that only eavesdroppers "entered at the back", that is, from the set.
[83] Lawrence, *Elizabethan Playhouse, First series,* 164 f.
[84] *Vide Oxford Companion to the Theatre,* 635. For the highly conventionalized use of the proscenium doors in the seventeenth century, including such conventions as knocking on the sword for knocking at the door, see Southern, *Changeable Scenery,* 127-130, 133-135.
[85] Lawrence, *Elizabethan Playhouse, First series,* 172.

stretching their necks, their boxes being half facing the auditorium. Portions of plays were performed with the curtain down, as in Sheridan's *The Critic,* written for production in Drury Lane theatre in 1799. [86]

Spectators not only sat in the stage boxes, "they also occupied benches running on the sides of the stage from the orchestra half way to the back scenes and railed in with heavy balustrades or draped enclosures" as shown by Hogarth's painting of *The Beggar's Opera.* [87] Attempts were made in the seventeenth century to stop the practice, but without success. [88] The merit of the seats on the stage and in the stage boxes appears to be the opportunity to be seen by the audience, because they were not the most convenient places to watch the performance: witness "ladies of fashion in London, thirty years ago, sitting at the very backs of the performers" — the poorest place to see, but the best place to be seen. [89] This is more remarkable than the spectators at the back of the Chinese stage, because the English stage had scenery and the players wore contemporary clothes so that it would not be as easy as in the Chinese theatre to distinguish who were in the play and who were not. [90] The amount of spectators on the stage is astonishing:

"But, my kind reader, suppose an audience behind the curtain up to the clouds, with persons of a menial cast on the ground, beaux and no beaux crowding the only entrance, what a play it must have been whenever Romeo was breaking open the supposed tomb, which was no more than a screen on those nights set up, and Mrs. Cibber prostrating herself on an old couch, covered with black cloth, as the tomb of the Capulets, with at least (on a great benefit night) two hundred persons behind her, which formed the back ground, as an unfrequented hallowed place of *chapless* skulls, which was to convey the idea of where the heads of all her buried ancestors were packed".

The distribution of this large body of spectators was as follows:

"The stage spectators were not content with piling on raised seats, till their heads reached the theatrical cloudings; which seats were closed in with dirty worn out scenery, to inclose the painted round from the first wing, the main *entrance* being up steps from the middle of the *back scene,* but when that amphitheatre was filled, there would be a group of ill-dressed lads and persons sitting on the stage in front, three or four rows deep, otherwise those who sat behind could not have seen, and a riot would have ensued: So in fact a performer on a popular night could not step his foot with safety, least he either should thereby hurt or offend, or be thrown down amongst scores of idle tipsey apprentices".

---

[86] Lawrence, *op. cit.,* 176 f.

[87] Lawrence, *Elizabethan Playhouse, First series,* 178.

[88] Lawrence, *Old Theatre Days and Ways,* 229.

[89] This and the following quotations are from Tate Wilkinson, *Memoirs* (1790), IV. 108-116.

[90] See Hogarth's painting in Nagler, *Sources of Theatrical History,* 378.

Despite the scenery, the stage must have been then looked upon as a platform for declamation, otherwise it is difficult to understand how a crowd of two hundred on it could have been tolerated. Things had gone to such extremes that the players suffered interference from the spectators:

"The first time Holland acted Hamlet it was for his own benefit, when the stage was in the situation here described. On seeing the Ghost he was much frightened, and felt the sensation and terror usual on that thrilling occasion, and his hat flew a-la-mode off his head. An inoffensive woman in red cloak, (a friend of Holland's) hearing Hamlet complain the air bit shrewdly, and was very cold, with infinite composure crossed the stage, took up the hat, and with the greatest care placed it fast on Hamlet's head, who on the occasion was as much alarmed in *reality* as he had just then been feigning. But the audience burst out into such incessant peals of laughter, that the Ghost moved off without any ceremony, and Hamlet, scorning to be outdone in courtesy, immediately followed with roars of applause: The poor woman stood astonished, which increased the roar, etc. It was some time before the laughter subsided; and they could not resist a repetition (that merry tragedy night) on the reappearance of the Ghost and Hamlet".

The inconvenience was not confined to such accidents, for

"Mr. Quin, aged sixty-five, with the heavy dress of Falstaff, (notwithstanding the impatience of the audience to see their old acquaintance) was several minutes before he could pass through the numbers that wedged and hemmed him in, he was so cruelly encompassed around".

Even allowing for the lack of stage illusion on the part of the spectators, it is still amazing that the seats on the stage were fashionable: not only were those near the "clouds" dirty and uncomfortable, but

"the stage, which was not thirty years ago near so wide as at present, also the stage doors, (which must be well remembered), and the stage boxes, before which there were false canvas, inclosed fronts on each side of two or three seats, on to the lamps, for ladies of distinction, which rendered it next to impossible for those ladies in the stage boxes to see at all; but still it was the fashion, and therefore a course charming and delightful. — And whenever a Don Choleric in the *Fop's Fortune,* or Sir Amorous Vainwit, in *Woman's a Riddle,* or Charles in *The Busy Body,* tried to find out secrets or plot an escape from a balcony, they always bowed and thrust themselves into the boxes over the stage door amidst the company, who were greatly disturbed, and obliged to give up their seats".

The reason why seats on the stage were tolerated was supplied by Wilkinson himself:

"Yet strange as it would now seem and insufferable, yet certain it is that I have seen occasionally many plays acted with great applause to such mummery, as to general appearance and conception: A strange proof, and the strongest I think that can be given, how far a mind may be led by attention, custom, and a willingness to be pleased without the least aid of probability: its chief and sole object certainly tended only to create laughter and disgust".

Against the occasional inconvenience of the players and the audience, the vanity of fashionable spectators and the avarice of the manager conspired to perpetuate and aggravate the custom. Eventually, however, the ridiculous extreme was reached:

"To the disgrace of common apprehension we have often seen likewise in our theatres two audiences, one on the stage, and another before the curtain; more especially at the actors' benefits, when a large amphitheatre has covered almost the whole stage; and the battle of Bosworth Field has been fought in less space than that which is commonly allotted to a cock-match". (Thomas Davies, *Memoirs of the Life of David Garrick* (1808), I. 375.)

In 1762 Garrick banished the spectators from the stage, but not without first enlarging the auditorium so that the income was not reduced. However, spectators still sat on the sides of the stage on occasion in the early nineteenth century. [91]

The practice which started in England at least as early as 1596 was first noticed in France in 1649 when it was already well established. Voltaire and his admirers blamed the failure of some of his plays on the presence of spectators: on the cold reception of *Sémiramis* (1748) it was said that,

"The stage was confined by a crowd of spectators, some placed on seats raised one above another, others standing at the bottom of the stage, and along the side scenes; so that the affrighted Sémiramis, and the shade of Ninus coming from his tomb, were obliged to penetrate through a thick row of *petits maîtres*. This impropriety threw ridicule on the gravity of the theatrical action". [92]

Considering Tate Wilkinson's testimony of theatrical successes in spite of the spectators on the stage, Marmontel's grudge against them was not entirely fair. The truth is, in *Sémiramis* Voltaire introduced scenic effects: Ninus' ghost rises out of the tomb to flashes of lightning and peals of thunder: and the spectators spoiled the scene. An eighteenth century print of Hotel de Bourgogne shows the body of spectators at the two sides of the theatre continued through the proscenium arch into the stage so that the actors were between the spectators and if the curtain fell it would cut some spectators off from the auditorium. [93] In 1759 Voltaire succeeded in getting the spectators on the stage banished from the Comédie Française — after a generous patron paid for the loss involved — and other French theatres followed the

---

[91] Rhodes, *Stagery of Shakespeare*, 92.

[92] Marmontel, *Memoirs* (1805), 394.

[93] *Vide* T. W. Stevens, *The Theatre from Athens to Broadway* (1938), 141.

example. [94] Considering the scenic wonders of Garrick's designer Loutherbourg it is not difficult to see that it was the machines that drove the spectators from the stage.

Besides spectators stage hands also shared the European stage with the players. As scenery was not shifted behind closed curtains until late nineteenth century, tables and chairs and other properties had to be moved in full view of the audience. [95] A type of stage hand peculiar to the European stage was the candle-snuffer whose expert handling in the eighteenth century was generally rewarded with a round of applause, [96] and whose neglect of the lights excited the gods to cries of "Snuffers! snuffers!" [97] They began in the private theatres in the early seventeenth century and remained on the English stage until the introduction of gas lighting; but they were not confined to England, French theatres also had them in the eighteenth century. [98] In Foote's comedy *The Orators* one of the characters was a candle-snuffer. The real candle-snuffer served at various times as a fighting lion in an Italian opera and a mourner at Juliet's funeral.[99] Musicians came on to the stage in the Restoration period until at least the opening years of the eighteenth century, and they often joined in the action. [100] Stage hands were, as in the Chinese theatre, taken for granted; when there was dissatisfaction it was for their untidy appearance, not for their presence.

"We cannot forbear noticing and commending an improvement in one particular hitherto unknown to the Belfast Theatre; two boys in livery are in constant attendance to bring on and remove chairs, tables and other articles necessary in a change of scene. They are a genteel appendage seen in the London and Dublin theatres, and since there must be persons to execute the office (for we know of no other means than the hands of servants) it is pleasing to see these well dressed boys, in lieu of perhaps a ragged little being without shoes or stockings, whom we formerly have seen obtrude himself for the purpose". [101]

Stage hands for the removal of furniture were sometimes applauded; [102] and this in spite of the fact that they were heard as well as seen. [103] It was not until the latter

---

[94] Nagler, *Sources of Theatrical History,* 324.

[95] Lawrence, *Old Theatre Days and Ways,* 130; Southern, *Changeable Scenery,* 262; Lawrence, *Those Nut-Cracking Elizabethans,* Ch. IX. Bygone Stage Furniture and its Removers.

[96] Lawrence, *Elizabethan Playhouse, Second series,* 16.

[97] Lawrence, *Old Theatre Days and Ways,* 130.

[98] *Ibid.,* 132.

[99] *Ibid.,* 134 f.

[100] Lawrence, *Elizabethan Playhouse, Second series,* 160 f.

[101] *The Belfast Newsletter,* December 24, 1813, quoted in Lawrence, *Pre-Restoration Stage Studies,* 303.

[102] Lawrence, *Those Nut-Cracking Elizabethans,* 124.

[103] *Ibid.,* 127.

half of the nineteenth century that furniture began to be manoeuvred through traps. [104]

As on the Chinese stage, means were provided on the English stage to prevent soiling the costume, both in Elizabethan times and after.

> "You might haue writ in the margent of your play-booke, Let there be a fewe rushes laide in the place where Backwinter shall tumble, for feare of raying his Cloathes: or set downe, Enter Backwinter, with his boy bringing a brush after him, to take off the dust if need require. But you will ne'er haue my wardrobe wit while you liue". [105]

The playfulness of the Elizabethan dramatists also allowed the rushes to represent green grass when dramatic action required. [106] In the eighteenth century stage hands rushed the "tragic carpet" for the hero to collapse or die upon. [107] This piece of stage equipment seems to be less serviceable than the Chinese cushions, for in 1773:

> "The first night that Murphy's *Grecian Daughter* was performed in Dublin, Mahon played Dionysius, the tyrant. It was the ridiculous custom at that time, when the principal character was to die, for two men to walk on with a carpet and spread it on the stage for the hero to fall on and die in comfort. Dionysius was stabbed and had to expire. Mahon fell upon the carpet and began his dying speech. Possessed with inspiration from the Tragic Muse, he grinned and frothed, and threw his eyes around and about, and grasped the carpet with both hands, and writhed and twisted, speaking all the time, by which means, before his speech was half finished, he had wrapped himself so tightly up in this tragic table-cloth of Melpomene, that nothing could be seen of him but the tip of his nose, red with fury". [108]

To prevent disorder among the spectators on the stage, military guards were posted in the eighteenth century on each side of the proscenium. As the action took place mainly in front of the proscenium arch the guards could see the performance and this sometimes caused unfortunate interruptions in dramatic appreciation. A story of Drury Lane was told by Steele in the nineteenth issue of *The Guardian:*

> "It was a cause of great sorrow and melancholy to me some nights ago at a play to see a crowd in the habits of the gentry of England stupid to the noblest sentiment we have. The circumstance happened in the scene of distress betwixt Piery and Anna Bullen in Banks' popular tragedy of *Virtue Betrayed.* One of the sentinels who stood on the stage, to prevent disorders which the most

---

[104] *Ibid.*, 128. Note that the curtain was not used for change of scenes.

[105] Nashe, *Summers Last Will and Testament* (1592), *vide* J. C. Adams, *The Globe Playhouse*, 102-8.

[106] Adams, *Globe Playhouse*, 106 f.

[107] *Vide* Lawrence, *Those Nut-Cracking Elizabethans*, Ch. VIII. The Evolution of the Tragic Carpet. cf. the cushions on the Chinese stage.

[108] John O'Keeffe, *Recollections*, quoted in Lawrence, *Those Nut-Cracking Elizabethans*, 111.

unmanly race of young men that ever was seen in any age frequently raised in public assemblies, upon Piery's beseeching to be heard, burst into tears, upon which the greater part of the audience fell into a loud and ignorant laughter which others, who were touched with the liberal compassion in the poor fellow, could hardly suppress by their clapping. But the man, without the least confusion or shame on his countenance for what had happened, wiped away the tears, and was still intent upon the play. The distress still rising, the soldier was so much moved that he was obliged to turn his face from the audience, to their no small merriment. Piery had the gallantry to take no notice of his honest heart, and, as I am told, gave him a crown to help him in his affliction. It is certain this poor fellow, in his humble condition, had such a lively compassion as a soul unwedded to the world; were it otherwise, gay lights and dresses, with appearance of people of fashion and wealth, to which his fortune could not be familiar, would have taken up all his attention and admiration''. [109]

In a performance of Rich's pantomime *Orpheus and Eurydice* in Covent Garden in 1740, an eye-witness reported how the mechanical serpent, "of enormous size and covered all over with gold and green scales and with red spots, his eyes shining like fire, wriggling about the stage with head upraised and making an awful hissing noise" frightened one of the two grenadiers of the guard, who dropped his musket and drew his sword in preparation and how "the spectators laughed again and again". [110]

Towards the end of the eighteenth century the guard was abolished and when needed was posted out of sight in the wings, but in the nineteenth century it became the custom to post guards of honour in front of the royal box, a practice which lasted to Queen Victoria's days. [111]

The ability to ignore incongruous people on the stage appears to be a matter of custom. In the Japanese theatre, *Ningyo-shibai,* two-thirds life-size puppets are manipulated directly by hand — not through strings and rods — in front of scenery. The puppets are most expressive but the men who play them are fully visible. Concealment of incongruous persons on the stage varied among different countries in Europe:

"An English tourist who paid a visit to the Teatro Politeama in Genoa one night in 1890, when the opera of *La Gioconda* was in the bill, was astonished to find that there was no prompter's box, and that the *suggitore* sat in his place without any attempt at concealment, and with his score leaning against the footlights". [112]

---

[109] Quoted in Lawrence, *Old Theatre Days and Ways,* 230-1.

[110] Letter by César de Saussure, quoted in Lawrence, *op. cit.,* 232.

[111] See Ills. facing pp. 236 and 240, Lawrence, *Old Theatre Days and Ways.*

[112] Lawrence, *Old Theatre Days and Ways,* 30.

By what has been shown of the use of scenery and front curtain and the custom of spectators and stage hands on the stage, it appears that one would be mistaken to think that all drama aims at creating illusion and that the simple *mise-en-scène* of early theatres delayed the progress towards naturalism by its lack of visual accessories, rather, it seems that the conception of drama as performance with skill and beauty and stage as a raised platform for acting resisted the influence of the visual adjuncts for about three hundred years. If the aim of drama is, by its nature, to create illusion, it is difficult to explain why theatre was not immediately naturalistic after scenery made realistic representation possible.

(9)

Drama, like sculpture, has the dual nature of imitation and art. The rival requirements of being lifelike and being beautiful are not always compatible with each other and the style of the works varies according to the relative emphasis placed on them. The importance of exact imitation attached to the European drama since the last part of the nineteenth century requires not only the realistic scenery and the isolation of the acting space but also the use of real properties and correct costume and a style of acting and delivery which approaches the everyday behaviour and speech of the audience. These, however, were by no means the characteristics of the European theatre before the advent of naturalism.

Stage property is now usually considered as a necessity rather than an embellishment, and its design is merely a matter of choosing between exact copies and recognizably lifelike substitutes. Large properties like furniture have, however, important effects on the appearance of the stage and, in extreme quantities, on the style of acting. Stage furniture in the European theatres is now usually overshadowed by the scenery but on the bare platform stage its composition is suggestive of the type of scene represented and can be, if not expressive, at least eloquent. The arrangement of simple stage furniture has probably never been systematically cultivated as an art either in the West or in China, but according to Gordon Craig, on Molière's stage the chairs and tables, few in number, constituted effective stage setting. [113] This tradition, he said, is now lost. For those who want to exploit the powerful effects of simple stage setting the Chinese platform stage should make interesting study.

Theatrical costume throughout the histories of the European and Chinese theatres is so uniformly unrealistic that historical accuracy appears as the exception rather than the rule. [114] The leader of savage dancers, and children in improvised dramas, put on something different from what they normally wear, because it

---

[113] G. Craig, *Scene*, 15.

[114] Special costumes are also used in the Japanese Noh Plays: "Chinese do not wear Chinese clothes". Toyoichiro Nogami, *Japanese Noh Plays* (1934), "Masks and Costumes".

reinforces their sense of changed identity and attracts the attention of the audience. Even to-day circus performers, stage clowns, music-hall artists, exotic dancers in night clubs and ballet dancers still have purely theatrical costumes, designed for beauty or comic effect and without counterpart in the real world, and so did the players in the *commedia dell' arte,* the English pantomime and the singers in the opera. On the Greek and the Roman stage, costume was either beautified versions or grotesque exaggerations of the contemporary dress [115] and in the medieval pageants and the Elizabethan theatre it was deliberately rich and gorgeous. [116] In the court spectacles of Renaissance Europe, mythological and allegorical characters provided the golden opportunity for creative costume design: the designer enjoyed practically absolute freedom and unlimited financial support and his success formed a major part of the total pleasure which the performance could give. What is now tailoring with informed antiquarianism was then a real art. [117] Even servants in the European dramas, like those on the Chinese stage to-day, were dressed in rich clothes:

> "I aim, first of all, at dressing the actors as richly as possible, yet with proportionate variations, for sumptuous costumes seem to me to add much to the beauty of comedies and more so of tragedies. I should not hesitate to dress a servant in velvet or coloured satin provided that his master's costume had sufficient embroidery and gold ornament to make a proper distinction between the garments". [118]

In the European dramas of the seventeenth and eighteenth centuries all characters wore contemporary dress except foreigners for whom some touches of foreign dress were added, such as the Roman breastplate and kilt and the oriental turban, and actresses, then as now, lost no chance to display their charms. [119] Clairon (1723-1803), writing her advice to actresses, said:

> "Our actresses, it seems to me, no longer fear costumes which reveal and outline; they dress like statues of antiquity in a way which taxes their shapes, doubtless through love of nature and of truth".

After advocating simplicity of dress she added,

> "Fillets, flowers, pearls, veils and coloured stones, were the *only* ornaments with which women were acquainted before the establishment of trade with the Indies, and the conquest of the New World". [120]

---

[115] Roman low comedians blackened their faces with soot or wore papyrus masks. M. Sand, *History of the Harlequinade* (1915), I. 11.

[116] In the medieval theatre, colour of the costume was sometimes used for symbolism — see the stage direction in *The Castle of Perseverance* quoted in Nicoll, *Development of the Theatre,* 76.

[117] For unrealistic costume in other forms of European theatre see T. Komisarjevsky, *The Costume of the Theatre* (1931), *passim.*

[118] Leone Hebreo de' Sommi, *Dialoghi in materia de rappresentazioni sceniche* (c.1550), quoted in Nicoll, *Development of the Theatre,* 211 f.

[119] See Nagler, *Sources of Theatrical History,* Ills. on pp. 306-7.

[120] *Mémoires de Mlle. Clairon,* quoted in Nagler, *Sources of Theatrical History,* 302. Italics mine.

Of make-up she asked,

> "Is it possible that an actress, whose countenance is enamelled with paint, and, consequently incapable of any motion, can give expression to the passions of rage, terror, despair, love or anger?" [121]

which shows extremely heavy make-up in her time. [122] Diderot complained that "ostentation spoils everything" and called the actresses "all those powdered, becurled, tricked-out dolls". [123] When Clairon appeared in Voltaire's *L'Orphelin de la Chine* (1755) she wore pseudo-Chinese costume "with bare arms and without paniers" and was hailed for her courage in fidelity to historical accuracy, [124] for it was considered a daring innovation; but the costume was designed by Joseph Vernet, whom Voltaire had asked to design something neither too Chinese nor too French, lest the audience laugh at it. [125] In the late eighteenth century the French designer Louis René Boquet brought wide paniers into fashion and Quin in England actually played Coriolanus in a ballet-skirt of Boquet's style which Garrick afterwards abolished in his "realistic" reform. Garrick himself played Macbeth in the scarlet of the King's livery and, according to Komisarjevsky, [126] when he played the part of an ancient Greek in 1758 he "wore the costume of a Venetian gondolier, on the ground that the majority of Venetian gondoliers at that time were of Greek origin", and Garrick was considered a realist. The actresses wore whatever, according to contemporary taste, made them beautiful [127] and there were Electras, who survived in prints, who had the high headdress of the seventeen-seventies. Mrs. Bellamy (1727-88) boasted of possessing "a superb suit of clothes that had belonged to the Princess of Wales" and said,

> "This was made into a dress for me to play the Character of Cleopatra, and as the ground of it was silver tissue, my mother thought that by turning the body of it in, it would be a no unbecoming addition to my waiste, which was remarkably small".

The dress was sent to the theatre for "sewing on a number of diamonds" and then,

> "Mrs. Furnival (who owed me a grudge, on account of my eclipsing her, as the more favourable reception I met with from the public, gave her room to conclude I did; and likewise for the stir which had been made last season about

---

(121) *Mémoires,* quoted in Nagler, *op. cit.,* 303.

(122) In the Opéra in Paris masks were worn by the dancers in the earlier part of the eighteenth century and were abolished by Pierre Gardel (?-1776) who thus started a tradition of wider range of pantomime with bare-faced dancers — *Oxford Companion to the Theatre,* GARDEL.

(123) F. C. Green, *Diderot's Writings on the Theatre* (1936), "De la poésie dramatique" 190 f.

(124) *Vide* Diderot, *op. cit.,* 191.

(125) *Vide* Nagler, *Sources of Theatrical History,* 301.

(126) *Costume of the Theatre,* 130.

(127) Komisarjevsky, *The Costume of the Theatre,* 130. This happened, it is believed, even in the Greek theatre — T. B. L. Webster, *Greek Theatre Production* (1956), 167.

the character of Constance) accidentally passed by the door of my dressing room in the way to her own, as it stood open. Seeing my rich dress thus lying exposed, and observing no person by to prevent her, she stepped in and carried off the Queen of Egypt's paraphernalia, to adorn herself in the character of Octavia, the Roman matron, which she was to perform''. [128]

When actresses are concerned with remarkably small waists, it is hardly surprising that the same dress can be worn by English, Roman and Egyptian royalty.

The first attempt towards correct details on the English stage was made by Kemble in his production of *King John* in 1823, with the assistance of J. R. Planché and "a number of learned enthusiasts". [129] Soon revivals of Shakespeare's plays were billed as dressed in correct, authentic garments and "authorities" were quoted in the advertisements. This principle of production was applied by Kean even to *The Winter's Tale* which he produced in 1856 and it did not prevent his noticing that the "reference made to the Delphic oracle, Christian burial, an Emperor of Russia, and an Italian painter of the sixteenth century" constituted chronological contradiction, but they did not stop him from changing Bohemia to Bithynia, because the metre was not thereby affected and consistency was achieved with the period he had chosen for the play — classical Greek. "Pyrrhic dance" and the "festival of Dionysia" were reproduced and Shakespeare's text adapted to suit — all this done with the advice of "eminent professors", lecturers on ancient music, and qualified architects one of whom was acknowledged for the "vegetation peculiar to Bithynia adopted from his private drawings, taken on the spot". [130] Mrs. Kean, playing Hermione, wore a perfectly correct Greek costume, but she wore it over a crinoline. Even in the later half of the nineteenth century, Mrs. Bancroft (1839-1921) played Peg Woffington in what she thought to be, but really was not, eighteenth century costume. [131] Towards the end of the century the subject matter of European drama changed to the problems of modern life and historical accuracy in costume took on a new meaning.

The movement of historically accurate productions in the mid-nineteenth century was not so much a service to realism — for the majority of the audience could hardly tell the difference — as an appeal to curiosity; it was not fastidiousness and historical knowledge on the part of the audience that prompted it but their susceptibility to presumed authority, especially in the exotic. As Voltaire shrewdly saw, authenticity would only make them laugh, so they were given spectacle instead of instruction. The difficulty Kean encountered in *The Winter's Tale* reveals the disparity between theatricality and erudition.

---

[128] *An Apology for the Life of George Anne Bellamy*, I. 130-136.

[129] Nicoll, *Development of the Theatre*, 191.

[130] *Vide* Nicoll, *Development of the Theatre*, 191-3.

[131] cf. Komisarjevsky, *Costume of the Theatre*, Ch. IX.

In human vanity one finds the wisdom of instinct: many productions in historical costume show only too well how much beauty in dress can be lost on players who do not know how to wear it — for to wear a garment is not merely to put it on, only by constant practice and study can anyone *carry* it well. Historical accuracy in the European stage costume had a formidable enemy in the vanity of the actresses. Among human beings it is the female of the species that displays colours, and it would be too much to expect actresses to shed their instinct when they are on the stage, where they can do it best. Even to-day, in spite of the "correctness" of stage costume dresses that "reveal and outline" are noticeable. [132] Contemporary fashion on actresses is probably the most important factor in bringing personal admiration and real emotional excitement into dramatic appreciation. Nevertheless, throughout the history of the European drama details of the costume are often chosen purely for theatrical effect, as the *cothurnus* of the Greco-Roman actors, the devil's mask in the medieval drama, [133] the Fool's cap in the moralities, Harlequin's dress in *commedia dell' arte,* the chopine and the rose on the Elizabethan stage shoes, the tall plumes on Roman and oriental characters in the eighteenth century [134] and the thick-soled shoes for the male characters in the Restoration theatre. [135]

(10)

The style of acting is an elusive thing: without seeing it one cannot get a very accurate idea by reading the accounts of eye-witnesses. In every period there are actors and actresses who act "naturally", but moving pictures of twenty years ago look hopelessly stylized now, even though they looked perfectly natural then. Descriptions of famous actors and actresses from the seventeenth century onwards are voluminous but most of them are useless for the present purpose: determining the degree of naturalism in the contemporary acting; hence evidence one way or the other has to be sought elsewhere.

Of Garrick it was said that,

"It gives one a sense of freedom and well-being to observe the strength and certainty of his movements, and what complete command he has over the muscles of his body". [136]

and of Betterton,

"In the just Delivery of Poetical Numbers, particularly where the Sentiments are pathetick, it is scarce credible upon how minute an Article of Sound depends

---

(132) *Vide* Komisarjevsky, *Costume of the Theatre*, Ch. VIII.

(133) Nicoll, *Development of the Theatre*, Fig. 63 (p.73).

(134) *Ibid.*, Figs. 216-9 (p.179), Figs. 235-9 (p.183).

(135) Summers, *The Playhouse of Pepys*, 47.

(136) *Vide* M. L. Mare and W. H. Quarrell, *Lichtenberg's Visits to England as Described in His Letters and Diaries* (1938), 6 f.

their greatest Beauty or Inaffection. The Voice of a Singer is not more strictly ty'd to Time and Tune, than that of an Actor in theatrical Elocution: The least Syllable too long or too slightly dwelt upon in a Period depreciates it to nothing; which very Syllable if rightly touch'd shall, like the heightening Stroke of Light from a Master's pencil, give Life and Spirit to the whole''. [137]

Of the English actors of the eighteenth century general reference was made to

". . . the good old Manner of singing and quavering out their tragic Notes''. [138] Likewise, the actor's faults which Hamlet found were hardly those to be found in the tradition of naturalism, for they were: to "mouth" a speech; to saw the air too much with the hand; to tear a passion to tatters, to very rags, to split the ears of the groundlings; to out-herod Herod; and to strut and bellow. The case was not for hypothetical players but players that he had "seen play, and heard others praise, and that highly". (*Hamlet,* III. ii). It is the impossibility of applying these remarks to naturalistic acting that makes them instructive.

In the later half of the eighteenth century the ideal for theatrical art in Germany was expressiveness with beauty, an ideal which Goethe tried to attain in the Weimar court theatre when it was in his charge. A well known manual at the time, J. J. Engel's *Ideen zu einer Mimik* (1785), contains detailed instructions for gestures and postures which are both expressive and elegant. The illustrations show that Engel's idea of good acting is, by present day European standards, highly rhetorical. The work was translated into Italian, French and English, the last by Henry Siddons, son of the great Sarah Siddons. [139]

Interesting comparisons can be made between the illustrations in Engel's manual and those in Cecilia S. L. Zung's *Secrets of the Chinese Drama:* they are equally stylized in the two books but in the former they are more emotionally expressive and in the latter, more graceful.

The history of the proscenium doors on the English stage reveals some aspects of the style of acting. In 1782 they were replaced with stage boxes in Covent Garden, and discontent ensued.

"I well remember the effect of its additional boxes in the situation of the old stage doors, and that these essential things in the new structure were behind the curtain. The actors seemed to feel embarrassed by the more extended area of the stage. There was no springing off with the established glance at the pit and projected right arm. The actor was obliged to edge away in his retreat towards the far distant wings with somewhat of the tedium, but not all the awkwardness, which is observed in the exits at the Italian Opera''. [140]

[137] Cibber, *Apology,* Ch. V.

[138] Benjamin Victor, *The History of the Theatres* (1761), II. 164.

[139] H. Siddons, *Practical Illustrations of rhetorical Gestures and Action adapted to the English Drama from a work on the Subject by M. Engel,* London, 1812.

[140] Boaden, *Memoirs of Mrs. Siddons* (1827), Ch. VIII.

The proscenium doors, situated in front of the curtain and the scenery, were architectural elements of the theatre, hence the exit referred to above was not so much dramatic action as formal retreat, that is why "springing off with projected right arm" was appropriate. The doors stood for whatever passage the action required; a contemporary wit asked:

> "What stationary absurdity can vie with that ligneous barricade which, decorated with frappant and tintinnabulant appendages, now serves as the entrance of the lowly cottage, and now as the exit of a lady's chamber: at one time insinuating plastic harlequin into a butcher's shop, and at another yawning as a floodgate, to precipitate the Cyprians of St. Giles's into the embraces of Macbeth".

When Drury Lane was rebuilt in 1812 after the fire, the absence of the proscenium doors had unforeseen effects on the efficiency of the actors.

> "The children of Thespis are general in their censures of the architect in having placed the locality of exit at such a distance from the oily radiators which now dazzle the eyes of him who addresses you. I am, cries the Queen of Terrors, robbed of my fair proportions. When the King-killing thane hints to the breathless auditory the murders he means to perpetrate in the castle of Macduff 'ere my purpose cool', so vast is the interval he has to travel before he can escape from the stage, that his purpose has even time to freeze. Your condition, cries the Muse of Smiles, is hard, but it is cygnet's down in comparison with mine. The peerless peer of capers and congees has laid it down as a rule, that the best good things uttered by the morning visitor should conduct him rapidly to the doorway, last impression vying in durability with first. But when on this boarded elongation it falls to my lot to say a good thing, to ejaculate, 'keep moving', or to chaunt 'hic hoc horum genitivo', many are the moments that must elapse ere I can hide myself from public vision in the recesses of O.P. or P.S." [141]

Before the fire the proscenium doors in this theatre were removed and restored at least once, and after its rebuilding in 1812 they were again restored within a year or two [142] — an instance of the close connection between stage doors and the style of acting. Soon, however, they became used only for taking bows and were called "call doors".

In the seventeenth and eighteenth centuries the scenery on the English stage was in effect a three-dimensional backdrop, "dim and distant", [143] because the main

---

[141] "P.S." is Prompt Side (stage left), "O.P." is Opposite Prompt. The above two quotations are from Lawrence, *Elizabethan Playhouse, First series,* 185, where the source is not indicated — it is probably from *The Drama; or Theatrical Pocket Magazine.*

[142] Lawrence, *op. cit.,* 179-186.

[143] Lawrence, *Those Nut-Cracking Elizabethans,* 78.

acting space was the forestage in the front, flanked by spectators in boxes and on the stage. The boundary line of the set which is now at the front edge of the stage was then half way upstage, and the transition of the open acting space and the set consisted of decorative compositions, of drapery, with folds, swags, fringes, cords and tassels painted on canvas, called proscenium wings, like similar decorations on the proscenium arches of earlier court spectacles. The actors were seen in the round, as on a platform stage. The effect of the enveloping scenery on the style of acting was not yet operative: actors would tend to act towards and speak to the audience rather than act among themselves and talk to each other. In the late eighteenth century, de Loutherbourg, Garrick's scenic designer, introduced border battens behind the proscenium arch thereby forcing the actors to remain among the scenery for the advantage of better illumination. They were not, however, ready to keep themselves there: in the rebuilt Drury Lane after 1812 the proscenium arch was replaced by a gilded picture frame and actors were forbidden to step beyond it, yet direct address to the audience would not be curbed and the actors all grumbled. William Dowton (1765-1851), famous as Falstaff, cried, "Don't tell me of frames and pictures! if I can't be heard by the audience in the frame, I'll walk out of it". When a similar adjustment was made at the Queen's Theatre, Manchester, in 1846, a local journal protested that it was "an outrage upon the best principle of theatrical usage". [144] But the development towards the modern stage went on, "the forestage shrank . . . the scenery came nearer and embraced the man". [145]

(11)

Formal exits were then, as they are on the Chinese stage at the present, associated with moralizing tags. Actors before retreating from the sight of the audience took their leave, outside the impersonation, by speaking something arresting to make a final impression and to beg applause. [146] At the end of the play there was the epilogue in which an actor representing the company bade the audience farewell and sometimes the principal players made a joint effort, as Mottley's tragedy *Antiochus* (produced in 1721) indicates:

>"*Epilogue. The Curtain falling, Mrs. Seymour comes forward with Mr. Quin and Mr. Egleton.*
>
>*Mrs. Seymour*   What now! Pray hold, there's something more to say.
>   There ought to be an Epilogue to th' Play.
>   Are you to speak it, Sir, or Mr. Quin?
>   The Company expects you should begin:
>   They look as if they long'd to be dismiss'd,
>   At least I do, I'm sure, to be undress'd.

---

[144] *Vide* Lawrence, *op. cit.*, 184.

[145] R. Southern, *The Open Stage*, 51 f.

[146] *Vide* A. N. Wiley, *Rare Prologues and Epilogues 1642-1700* (1940).

618

The epilogue is usually addressed to the audience, as those of *All's Well that Ends Well* and *As You Like It,* but sometimes it takes the form of an epigrammatic summing up of the moral of the play:

> "Ah, the same love that tempts us into sin,
>
> If it be true love, works out its redemption;
>
> And he who seeks repentance for the past,
>
> Should woo the Angel Virtue in the future".
>
> *(The Lady of Lyons,* 1838)

For simultaneous exit on the Chinese stage lines are distributed among several actors and parallel cases are found in Greene's *Tu Quoque; or the City Gallant* (sixteen lines among eight speakers, a couplet each) and *The Adventures Five Hours* (1662). [147] The end of an act and of a scene involves finality of lesser order and tags or rhymed lines, generally shorter than the epilogue, were spoken, such as,

> "Heaven has no rage, like love to hatred turned.
>
> Nor hell a fury, like a woman scorned".
>
> (Congreve, *The Mourning Bride,* Act III)

As there was no curtain fall at the end of acts and scenes, these tags were particularly appropriate for indicating a break in the action. [148] However, rhymed tags were sometimes also given to exits in the middle of the scene, as in Chinese dramas. [149]

One famous epilogue on the English stage achieved its calculated comic effect by ignoring realism entirely. In Dryden's *Tyrannick Love; or, The Royal Martyr,* a tragedy produced at the Theatre Royal, 1669, the epilogue was "spoken by Mrs. Ellen (played by Nell Gwyn), when she was to be carried off dead by the Bearers". Suddenly she jumped up, gave one of the men a box on the ear and said,

> "Hold, are you mad? You damn'd confounded Dog,
>
> I am to rise, and speak the Epilogue".

Downstage she addressed the audience:

> "I come, kind Gentlemen, strange News to tell ye,
>
> I am the Ghost of poor departed Nelly".

and ended with:

> "Here Nelly lies, who, tho' she liv'd a Slattern,
>
> Yet dy'd a Princess acting in St. Cath'rin".

She retired to where the *cercueil* was awaiting her, reclined gracefully thereon, and was borne away. [150] At this time players could still make fun of the dramatic illusion.

Tags lasted till after the middle of the nineteenth century [151] and in the early

---

[147] *Vide* Lawrence, *Elizabethan Playhouse, Second series,* 178-188.

[148] Summers, *Restoration Theatre,* 153 f.

[149] Lawrence, *Elizabethan Playhouse, Second series,* 184.

[150] Summers, *Restoration Theatre,* 183; Lawrence, *Elizabethan Playhouse, Second series,* 179.

[151] Lawrence, *Elizabethan Playhouse, Second series,* 180.

part of that century it appeared that the convention of directly addressing the audience allowed the actors, in emergency, to interrupt the performance to talk to them. *The British Stage and Literary Cabinet* reported the following event in Drury Lane on 21 January, 1820:

> "Mr. Pope, who played Iago, being deservedly hissed, came forward and addressed the audience saying that during a service of five and thirty years, he had never neglected his duty, and that although he might now be deemed unfit to perform many of the characters he had formerly sustained with credit, he could assure the audience that he did not appear in them from choice. His circumstances, he was sorry to say, did not admit of him quitting the stage. He then shed a few tears and proceeded with the part". [152]

And Iago of all characters.

(12)

Men playing women and women playing men involve a technique of acting far removed from the theory of living the part and a mode of appreciation different from the excitement over real people and real events. Real skill is required and sex appeal is distinct from art. In the ancient and medieval European theatres only the Romans indulged in the natural appreciation of actresses: [153] the women in the medieval dramas were played by men: but since the end of the seventeenth century female roles in European dramas have been normally, though not invariably, played by actresses. The admiration of the actresses is a distinct type of dramatic appreciation. Of Clairon it was said that she had

> "eyes full of fire and which breathed voluptuousness . . . she had beautiful teeth, her bosom was well moulded . . . Looking at her, one experienced a pleasure which the other senses were anxious to share". [154]

and of the theatre of the present day,

> "One of the greatest attractions is the sex-appeal element of the productions, presented, of course, in the guise of 'sweet' peroxided blondes with unquestionably virginal faces, but in the most ingenious, disturbing, and quite unexpected déshabillés". [155]

Male roles are however often played by women and in these "breeches parts", as they are called, the actresses have a special charm.

Men play female as well as male parts, sometimes for comic effects, as they did in the Roman *atellanae,* judging by such titles as "Maccus Virgo", and "Maccus

---

[152] Quoted in *The Listener* Vol. LIII, No. 1371, June 9, 1955.

[153] Gibbon, *Decline and Fall of the Roman Empire,* Ch. XL. Birth and vices of the Empress Theodora.

[154] T. Komisarjevsky, *Costume of the Theatre,* 125.

[155] *Ibid.,* 165.

Miles" [156] and in the *commedia dell' arte,* as when Harlequin played the nurse. [157] In these cases they were overtly in disguise and were readily recognizable as men, otherwise the comic effect would be lost. The female parts in the medieval plays were played by priests. [158] The ugly women in the English pantomime, called "the Dame", such as Cinderella's sisters, are still played by men. Men played women in early Italian plays but they were replaced by women early in the sixteenth century. [159] Occasional female impersonation lingered on: men played women in a play in 1542 and Leone de Sommi in his *Dialoghi in materia di rappresentazioni sceniche* (written between 1567-90), gave directions for men playing serving maids. [160]

In the eighteenth century "the decency of the church only allowed handsome youths to play the part of actresses in Rome". It was said that "dressed in female attire, these boys looked like veritable women". [161] The pressure of necessity did not, however, last long enough to create a tradition. Edward Kynaston (c. 1640-1706) and James Nokes (? -1696) played both men and women, and were the last players on the English stage to take important female parts in serious dramas. In France, men played women's parts in Molière's time [162] and André Herbert (c. 1634-1700) was famous for old women's parts. Laurence Olivier played Katharina in an all-male production of *The Taming of the Shrew* at Stratford in 1922, but the tradition of boy actors having been long lost the performance must have been improvised and not worth repeating.

If women did appear on the Elizabethan stage they must have been rare and probably not as actresses. [163] Almost as soon as actresses entered the English theatre (in 1660) [164] they distinguished themselves in men's parts. In 1672 an all-women production could be staged of Killigrew's comedy *The Parsons Wedding* at Lincoln's Inn Field. [165] Mrs. Bracegirdle (1663-1748) played in male roles in the early part of the eighteenth century. [166] Nell Gwynn (1650-87) was admired both as woman and as man and Peg Woffington (c. 1714-60) played the parts of Sir Harry Wildair and Lothario so well that actors dared not compete with her. Charlotte Cibber (? - c. 1760), Colley Cibber's daughter played indifferently in both men's

---

[156] "Maccus the Maiden" and "Maccus the Soldier" — Nicoll, *Masks Mimes and Miracles,* 73.

[157] P. L. Duchartre, *The Italian Comedy,* trans. R. T. Weaver (1929), 38.

[158] T. Komisarjevsky, *The Costume of the Theatre,* 55, *et. seq.*

[159] Smith, *The Commedia dell' arte,* 57 n.

[160] Smith, *The Commedia dell' arte,* 72 *infra.*

[161] Charles de Brosses (1709-77), *Letters,* trans. R. S. Gowen, 228.

[162] G. Freedley and J. A. Reeves, *A History of the Theatre* (1941), 81.

[163] Chambers, *Eliz. Stage,* I. 371 n; III. 297.

[164] W. R. Davies, *Shakespeare's Boy Actors* (1939), 198; or in 1656 according to T. Komisarjevsky, *The Costume of the Theatre,* 85. *Vide* H. W. Lanier, *The First English Actresses* (1930), 39-48.

[165] Summers, *The Playhouse of Pepys,* 331, note 72.

[166] Cibber, *An Apology for the Life of Mr. Colley Cibber* (1740), 143.

and women's parts, in the former probably because she was like a man in real life, but Dorothy Jordan (1761-1816) was really famous in male roles. Breeches parts were very common in the nineteenth century; Madame Vestris (1797-1856), wife of Charles Mathews, was, among others, well known for them, [167] and Marie Wilton (1839-1921), later Lady Bancroft, played Fleance to Macready's Macbeth — her Prince Arthur in *King John* was said to be admired by Charles Kean. Breeches parts can still be seen in the English Christmas pantomime where, by a tradition established in the eighteen-eighties, the Principal Boy, such as Prince Charming, is always played by a woman. [168]

In France, Jeanne A. Baron (1625-62) was admired in male roles, and within living memory, Sarah Bernhardt (1845-1923) scored one of her greatest successes in the title role of *Hamlet*. [169] Here great histrionic genius again transcends the limitations of sex.

The movement of women's emancipation was probably responsible for some male roles in this century. Edith Evans played the Bishop of Beauvais in *The Trial of Jeanne d'Arc* in 1913, and Captain Dumain in *All's Well That Ends Well* in 1919. In the latter production, Winifred Oughton played the other French Lord and Clare Greet was rehearsed for Parolles. [170] Poel is said to be indifferent to the sex of the player and chose women frequently for male parts. [171] During the First World War, Sybil Thorndike played in Old Vic male parts, including Puck, Lear's Fool, and Ferdinand in *Tempest*.

---

[167] Speaight, *Juvenile Drama*, 33.

[168] *Vide* A. E. Wilson, *Christmas Pantomime* (1934), especially Pls. facing pp. 220, 221.

[169] *Vide* S. Bernhardt, *The Art of the Theatre*, trans. H. J. Stenning, 137-45, "Why I have Played Male Parts".

[170] R. Speaight, *Wm. Poel and the Elizabethan Revival*, 222, 233.

[171] *Ibid.*, 101.

CHAPTER XLIV

HISTORIES OF THE CHINESE AND THE EUROPEAN THEATRE — III

(Attitude of the Audience — Sensuous Pleasures — Naturalism — Sense of Reality
— Western Classicism)

(13)

Sensuous delight and intellectual interest have equally laid claim on the theatre. The theatre of a nation can sometimes be without the latter, because those who can appreciate intellectual delights are always few and the demand may not be sufficient to create the supply, but it cannot be without the former, because all people can enjoy simple spectacles. Whether or not one style of theatre is sufficient for a country depends on whether that style can satisfy both needs: if a style of theatre pleases the mind alone another will rise up to please the eyes and the ears. In the later part of the history of Greek theatre dances were performed in the dramas even though they were not connected with the action. [1] At the present, outside the European drama, revue theatres and ballets satisfy the need for sensuous pleasures in the theatre. In China there has been, until recently, only one style of theatre because it has satisfied both the intellectual needs of the few and the simple taste of the many, but in Europe, there have been many types of theatre since the Renaissance, with different proportions of simple and sophisticated, sensuous and intellectual pleasures. To compare the Chinese drama with the European drama alone would be therefore to compare what represents the total of Chinese theatrical taste with what stands for only a part of the European theatrical taste. The high-minded aim of the Renaissance has clung to the European drama till the present, putting on it a bias towards intellectualism, consequently, throughout the history of modern European theatre light entertainment in one form after another rose outside the drama to meet the popular demand.

Appreciation of sensuous pleasures requires an atmosphere in the theatre

---

[1] Pickard-Cambridge, *The Theatre of Dionysus,* 71.

different from that for intellectual interests. Pleasures of the eyes and the ears can be taken casually and increase with concerted expressions of approval amid congenial company; but the pleasures of the mind are solitary pleasures, even in the theatre, and it is essential to eliminate distraction so that the audience can concentrate on and savour them. The Chinese theatre, which caters also for those who seek sensuous pleasure, is always a lively and sometimes a boisterous and even rowdy place, but the European theatre for the spoken drama has become a quiet and even solemn place. Dramatic illusion as the modern European audience understands it is assisted by suppressing the consciousness of the world of the audience so that that of the drama can predominate in their mind, hence the lights are turned off, all activities cease in the auditorium, and the stage becomes the only part of the theatre with life in it. This has brought about the complete passivity of the European audience. European theatres were, however, not always like this.

"Fifteen years ago our theatres were tumultuous places. The coldest heads became heated on entering, and sensible men more or less shared the transports of madmen. *Place aux dames!* was heard on one side; *Haut les bras, monsieur l'abbé!* on another; *A bas le chapeau!* elsewhere, and on all sides: *Paix-là, paiz la cabale!* There was movement, bustle, and pushing; the soul was beside itself; I know of no frame of mind more favourable to the poet. The play began with difficulties and was often interrupted. But when a fine passage arrived there was an incredible din; encores were demanded unceasingly, the actor and the actress aroused enthusiasm. The infatuation swept from the pit to the amphitheatre, and from the amphitheatre to the boxes. People had arrived heatedly, they went away in a state of drunkenness. Some went to the brothels, others went into polite society. That is enjoyment! To-day, they arrive coldly, they listen coldly, they leave coldly, and I do not know where they go afterward. I am singularly shocked by these insolent fusiliers posted to left and to right in order to moderate my transports of admiration, sensibility, and joy, and who turn our theatres into resorts more peaceful and more respectful than our churches". [2]

At about the same time as Diderot's bustling theatre, in Italian opera houses chattering continued throughout the performance and those in the pit went in and out all the time.

"Italian audiences listened to and applauded the big songs of their favourite singers, and in the intervening stretches of the performances, comfortably seated in their boxes, they were served with supper, or had little conversation parties, or played cards".

---

[2] Diderot, "Résponse à la lettre de Mme. Riccoboni" (1758), in *Diderot's Writings on the Theatre,* ed. F. C. Green (1936), 216.

Writing in 1739, Charles de Brosses also said,

> "Draughts are an admirable invention — just the thing to fill up the gaps whilst the long recitatives are being sung, as music itself is to relieve the pressure of a too great devotion to draughts". [3]

At this time spectators in the continental theatres for dramas also ate their meals in the boxes. In England, at the Theatre Royal,

> "The Pit is an Amphitheater, fill'd with Benches without Backboards, and adorn'd and cover'd with green Cloth. Men of Quality, particularly the younger Sort, some Ladies of Reputation and Virtue, and abundance of Damsels that haunt for Prey, sit all together in this Place, Higgledy-piggledy, chatter, toy, play, hear, hear not". [4]

Elsewhere in the English theatre:

> "Our Galleries too, were finely us'd of late,
> Where roosting Masques sat cackling for a Mate:
> They came not to see Plays but act their own,
> And had throng'd Audiences when we had none.
> Our Plays it was impossible to hear,
> The honest Country Men were forc't to swear:
> Confound you, give your bawdy prating o're,
> Or, Zounds, I'll fling you i' the Pitt, you bawling Whore". [5]

> "Last, some there are, who take their first Degrees
> Of Lewdness in our Middle Galleries:
> The Doughty Bullies enter Bloody Drunk,
> Invade and grubble one another's Punk:
> They Caterwaul and make a dismal Rout,
> Call Sons of Whores, and strike, but ne're lugg-out:
> Thus, while for Paultry Punk they roar and stickle,
> They make it Bawdier than a Conventicle". [6]

People went to the Restoration theatre as much to look at the ladies in the boxes, especially if they were connected with gossip, as to see the plays — if we do not count Pepys as an abnormal audience. [7] The attention paid to the audience was not entirely unrewarding, as Pepys found on February 18, 1667:

---

[3]   *Vide* P. A. Scholes, *Oxford Companion to Music* (1945), OPERA.

[4]   Henri Misson, *Misson's Memoirs and Observations in His Travels over England* (1719), 219 f.

[5]   Crowne, *Sir Courtly Nice,* Epilogue, quoted in Summers, *Restoration Theatre,* 89.

[6]   Dryden, *The Disappointment; or, The Mother in Fashion* (1684), Prologue, quoted in Summers, *Restoration Theatre,* 88 f.

[7]   See, for example, his *Diary,* 1 February, 1664 and 21 December, 1668.

"To the King's house to *The Mayd's Tragedy;* but vexed all the while with two talking ladies and Sir Charles Sedley, yet pleased to hear their discourse, he being a stranger. And one of the ladies would and did sit with her mask on, all the play, and, being exceedingly witty as ever I heard woman, did talk most pleasantly with him; but was, I believe, a virtuous woman and of quality. He would fain know who she was, but she would not tell; yet did give many pleasant hints of her knowledge of him, by that means setting his brains at work to find out who she was, and did give him leave to use all means to find out who she was but pulling off her mask. He was mighty witty, and she also making sport of him very inoffensively, that a more pleasant rencontre I never heard. By that means lost the pleasure of the play wholly''. [8]

In the Restoration theatre fruits and other refreshments were sold by female pedlars, and light women found the theatres a profitable haunt. Flirtations went on in most parts of the theatre aloud and quarrels and fights were by no means unknown. [9] In the mid-nineteenth century the expectant imagination pictured the scene in Drury Lane as follows:

"In less than an hour I should be at Drury Lane, seated in the pit, dazed with the chatter of 'Orange, apples, ginger-beer, bills of the play', monotonously delivered by the women who were then permitted to drag their heavy baskets through the pit benches, and waiting anxiously for the curtain to be drawn up and show me *The Lady of Lyons* to be followed by Rodwell's pantomime of *Harlequin and Good Queen Bess; or, Merrie England in the Olden Time''.* [10]

These passages can become, with a few modifications, a happy description of the Chinese tea-house theatre.

When the theatregoers are without good manners they are a mob, as Diderot's description clearly shows, and among a mob feelings are contagious. "Certainly it is most true, and one of the greatest secrets of nature, that the minds of men are more open to impressions and affections when many are gathered together than when they are alone''. [11] To stop this contagiousness and eliminate other mob-characteristics of the audience one has only to isolate them from each other. With the nineteenth century, gas lighting came to the theatre. It was first introduced into it in 1815 and first used in London in 1823 to dim the lights in the auditorium during the performance. It was not, however, until Henry Irving that the audience were left in complete darkness during the play. Even after the introduction of gas lighting theatre-going was essentially a social instead of an artistic activity and space had to

---

[8]   Pepys, *Diary.*

[9]   Summers, *Restoration Theatre,* Ch. III.

[10]   S. McKechnie, *Popular Entertainment through the Ages,* 123, quoting Clement Scott.

[11]   Bacon, *De Augmentis,* quoted in Lawrence, *Old Theatre Days and Ways,* 198.

be provided for those who wanted to enjoy first themselves and each other and secondly, the play. In the *Observations on the Design for the Theatre Royal, Drury Lane* (1813), Benjamin Wyatt gave particular consideration to the "social rooms", such as coffee rooms, saloons, lobbies and rotundas, so that there were places in the theatre for both undisturbed seclusion and the parade of fashion.

Meanwhile those who preferred uninterrupted lively atmosphere repaired to the music-halls, where amid drinks and friends they could mix the pleasures of conversation and eating with those of spectacles and songs. English music-halls had started in small taverns in the early eighteenth century and had already developed into "musick-houses" like the Sadler's Wells where among dance, song and acrobatics, performances which were dramas in every way except in name were given in defiance of the law of stage monopoly. The lack of street lighting, which made the long distance travel at night irksome, restricted the size of most of these establishments. In the early nineteenth century, as gas lighting spread, the larger ones became prosperous and improved in surface appearance, the smaller ones grew and, under the augmented public demand, every tavern had a music-room. Apart from the inevitable comic songs, there were clowning, acrobatics, juggling, conjuring, dancing, drama, and, early in this century, to meet the competition of the moving picture, Wild West Rodeo, symphony orchestra, ballet, tennis matches, boxing and other acts were added. By then, however, except for the bar in the auditorium, they were run very much like theatres. [12]

The music-hall of nineteenth century England was a tavern-theatre and had many common characteristics with the Chinese tea-house theatre. In both the audience drank and laughed and talked and joined in the shouts and boos. Nothing was restrained; all were in good spirits. As in Chinese theatres in the early part of this century, some music-halls in London in the last century did not charge for admission, but made profits in the drinks sold. At the Canterbury in London the stage was a platform stage and patrons sat around it at small tables. At this theatre and at the Oxford food was served if desired. Although the programme in the English music-hall never acquired a definite form, the quality of the entertainment was not always low; Sir Herbert Tree, Sir Henry Wood, Sarah Bernhardt, Grock and Pavlova appeared in them. The best days of music-halls are over, but they are still holding their own in England and France.

(14)

No period in European theatrical history is as dominated by sensuous delights as the Roman theatre. Dramatic and quasi-dramatic performances were part of the *ludi,* or games, which also included gladiators, chariot races, beast

---

[12] *Vide* A. J. Park, *The Variety Stage* (1895).

baiting, boxing matches and circuses. [13] Naturally, vendors of refreshments could be found inside and around the theatres. [14] Acrobatics was mixed with theatrical performances as early as the third century B.C. [15] and probably came from the strolling players of the Graeco-Roman world. Xenophon described one girl who was a mime and an acrobat. Mime and pantomime, the distinctive types of theatre in this period, came from popular entertainment [16] and the interest in them was not purely dramatic in nature. There were, in the mime, *paegnia,* performances of slight and trivial nature, and *hypotheses,* which had some plot; but in all types the appeal of licentious action and naked actresses was exploited. Ventriloquism and dog performances were also part of the mime. [17] Even when tragedies were performed, the mime was played in the intermission and as after-piece. [18] The delights were not only sensuous but also sensual, consequently those who ministered them, the *mimi,* were of the lowest social status. [19] It was against a similar background that the Chinese drama was developed in the Sung dynasty.

When theatre was revived in the Italian Renaissance, spectacle was preferred to drama. From the last part of the fifteenth to the middle of the sixteenth century, drama was almost buried in the decorative *intermedii,* with songs and dances predominating. [20] In the seventeenth century the opera was entirely a display of scenery, machines and vocal skill. [21] In 1690, the Teatro Farnese was flooded for spectacles on water. [22]

Dance and music entered the European theatre in one form or another, sometimes as part of the drama and sometimes in a separate form of entertainment. Music and poetry were listed by Aristotle among the "pleasurable accessories" of tragedy (*Poetics,* 6). [23] Recitation of dramatic passages in Roman times was accompanied by music; [24] the Englishmen had their Elizabethan jig; [25] the Germans had their *Singspiel;* the French, the *ballet de cour;* the Spaniards, the *zarzuela*

---

[13] Beare, *Roman Stage,* 10 f.

[14] *Ibid.,* 166.

[15] Nicoll, *Masks Mimes and Miracles,* 35 et seq.

[16] Beare, *op. cit.,* 141 f.

[17] *Ibid.,* 142 f.

[18] Bieber, *History of the Greek and Roman Theatre,* 313.

[19] Beare, *op. cit.,* 158.

[20] Chambers, *Eliz. Stage,* I. 185.

[21] G. Craig, *Books and Theatres* (1925), 26 f.

[22] Craig, *op. cit.,* 122.

[23] The reason for this is that music is an effective means of expression. Even to-day we instinctively feel that ceremonies such as weddings and memorial services are not complete without music.

[24] Beare, *Roman Stage,* 19.

[25] For the influence of dumb shows on the spectacular elements in the Elizabethan theatre see Chambers, *Eliz. Stage,* I. 185.

and the Italians, the pastoral and the opera. [26] The *Singspiel* played an important part in the development of the German opera, and the English jig was the predecessor of the *ballad opera* of the eighteenth century which, like the Chinese dramas of Yüan dynasty, consisted partly of spoken dialogue and partly of songs sung to existing popular tunes. Had there been no other forms of theatrical entertainment in England to compete with the ballad opera and had a flexible form of adapting music to words been found it would probably have also developed into a national theatre. Early Spanish dramas were closely associated with music; sometimes whole plays had musical settings. [27] In Spain Lope de Vega and Calderón were among those who wrote *zarzuelas* and a *Teatro de la Zarzuela* was opened in Madrid in 1856 for this type of entertainment alone. In eighteenth century Italy, plays in which music and words were of equal importance were developed, called *melodramma*. At the present there is musical comedy in the European theatre and music has also become a regular element of the motion picture.

Of music outside the drama, one can point to the "private" theatres in Elizabethan England in which plays were cut in the early seventeenth century in order that inter-act music could be played. [28] In the eighteenth century it was the custom for the audience to call for the tunes they liked to hear and the musicians would have to oblige, even with conflicting demands. In one instance the custom of calling for a specific piece of histrionics even extended to a passage in the play: Garrick, playing in a masque called *Britannia* in 1755, wrote and delivered a topically patriotic prologue in the character of a drunken sailor which was so well liked that he was called to deliver it in costume even on nights when he was not announced to act. [29] In America the custom of calling for tunes persisted into the nineteenth century, and verbal demands were reinforced by "throwing apples, stones, etc., into the orchestra" and "stamping, hissing, roaring, whistling, and when the musicians were refractory, groaning in cadence". [30]

In France, Addison reported, the audience joined the singers in the operas:

"The chorus in which that opera abounds gives the *parterre* frequent opportunities of joining in consort with the stage. This inclination of the audience to sing along with the actor so prevails with them, that I have sometimes known the performer on the stage do no more in a celebrated song than the clerk of a parish church, who serves only to raise the Psalm, and is afterwards drown'd in the musick of the congregation". [31]

---

[26] And outside the drama the *intermedii* were inserted between the acts of a drama. Chambers, *Eliz. Stage,* I. 185.

[27] *Oxford Companion to the Theatre* (1951), SPAIN 2.

[28] Lawrence, *Old Theatre Days and Ways,* 114 f.

[29] *Ibid.,* 116.

[30] *Vide ibid.,* 119.

[31] *The Spectator,* No. 29.

The practice must have started in the seventeenth century, and appears to include some degree of gesticulation:

> "In France the oldest man is always young,
> Sees operas daily, learns the tunes so long,
> Till foot, hand, head, keep time with every song.
> Each sings his part, echoing from pit to box,
> With his hoarse voice, half harmony, half pox;" [32]

Hogarth records in his *Memoirs of the Musical Drama* (1838) that

> "Towards the end of the seventeenth century a species of entertainment was introduced at Venice which was for a short time in great vogue. It consisted of little dramas, in which the actors appeared on the stage without speaking. Scrolls descended from the roof upon their heads in succession, in which were written, in large letters, verses of songs, the airs of which were played by the orchestra, while the words were sung by the spectators; the performers on the stage, meanwhile, carrying on the action in dumb show. The spectators found it very amusing to sing in this manner the dialogue of the piece, but soon began, doubtless, to think it somewhat childish, for the scroll-pieces did not long remain in fashion". [33]

The custom of singing audiences faded out in the eighteenth century but in the English Christmas pantomime, the players leading the audience in songs is still regularly done. The audience in the Chinese theatre do not sing aloud, but a low hum is sometimes heard which spoils the enjoyment of some of the best passages of an aria.

Of scenic spectacle in drama, there were the "machine plays" of seventeenth century France, the pantomime of eighteenth century England (in which the Transformation Scene was a regular feature) and the melodrama of the nineteenth century. In 1804 at Sadler's Wells theatre in London a gigantic tank was constructed and filled from the New River and naval battles were staged with heroines rescued by heroes and children by Newfoundland dogs. This was called the Aquatic Drama and its vogue lasted some years, extending its influence also to the Covent Garden. [34] At the Amphitheatre, from 1770 onwards theatrical performances were mixed with displays of horsemanship and in the nineteenth century, at the Royal Circus, Equine or Wild Beast Spectacles were shown in the

---

[32] Dryden, Preface to *Albion and Albanius* (1685), quoted in Lawrence, *Old Theatre Days and Ways*, 195, where an anecdote is related of how when Mathew Prior was tormented at the opera by a persistent singing person next to him, he hissed and booed the singer on the stage and when asked the reason for his disapproval answered, "Every reason in the world, my good sir, the fellow makes so much noise that I actually cannot hear you sing".

[33] *Vide* Lawrence, *op. cit.*, 197 f.

[34] Nicoll, *Development of the Theatre*, 190.

arena in the early part of the evening's programme, after which half-price seats filled the arena and plays started on the stage. [35] Horses were worked into a new type of drama, the Equestrian Drama, which entered even Drury Lane and Covent Garden. [36] There was also the Dog Drama of which the most famous example was Pixerécourt's *The Dog of Montargis, or The Forest of Boudy*. It is said that the Duke of Weimar's insistence on seeing it caused Goethe's retirement from the court theatre. Melodramas were supplemented with farce and burlesque and drama mixed with extravaganzas and harlequinades. Extravaganzas were based on classical stories but were tagged with topical allusions, puns and absurdities and harlequinades were farce, sometimes with conjuring acts, called tricks. [37] Phantoms which could be walked through and stabbed with impunity were brought to the stage by mirrors and sheets of glass, actors could jump through apparently solid objects by means of the Vamp Trap which sprang open or be shot up suddenly to the stage through the Star Trap, or rise slowly as ghost, as if through the floor, by means of the Bristle Trap, or drift across the stage while rising by means of the Ghost Glide. Acrobatic performers flourished, for instance, "Don Jumpedo" who jumped "down his own throat" and the "extortillationists", known as the Hanlon-Lees, who exhibited "zampillerostation". In the early nineteenth century the "Looking Glass Curtain", in which the audience could see themselves and than which few things could be more detrimental to the dramatic illusion, was very much in fashion [38]

In any theatre, dramatic illusion has only a precarious hold on the mind, because the ultimate sanity of most people resists mental efforts towards delusion. Distractions, on stage as well as in the auditorium, undo the cultivated suspension of disbelief. Therefore European drama is now usually played in a single-bill programme and the audience see it from start to finish. Yet multiple bill has been, until the rise of naturalism, the rule of the dramatic performances in Europe, as it still is in China. The Elizabethan theatre was essentially single-billed but several popular plays were sometimes given in the same performance, written on the same theme with very different treatments, such as tragedy, farce or comedy, or sometimes loosely connected together by a thread of plot, as, for example,

---

[35] *Vide Stages of the World* (Theatre Arts, Inc.), Pl. 26.

[36] *Vide* Speaight, *Juvenile Drama*, 31. It is to be noticed that even at the beginning of the nineteenth century there were only two theatres in London licensed to produce legitimate dramas, hence, the smaller theatres had special reasons for producing musical plays which were dramas thinly disguised with songs and dances. The licensed theatres were the Theatre Royal (Drury Lane) and Covent Garden.

[37] For the nature of burlesque plays in the early nineteenth century see V. C. Clinton-Baddeley, *The Burlesque Tradition in the English Theatre After 1660*, 107-117.

[38] *Vide* H. Hobson, *Theatre*, Plate facing p. 114.

Fletcher's *Four Plays in One*, [39] and composite plays were common in many European countries in the seventeenth and eighteenth centuries. [40] Elizabethan dramas were interrupted by dances in the "private" theatres and followed by jigs in the public theatres, and in the latter the audience could call for the particular jigs they liked.[41] On special occasions multiple-bill performances, very similar to those of the Chinese theatre, were forced on the players:

"I have known upon one of these *Festivals* [holidays], but especially at Shrove-tide, where the Players have been appointed notwithstanding their bills to the contrary, to act what the major part of the company had a mind; sometimes *Tamerlane,* sometimes *Jugurth,* sometimes the *Jew of Malta,* and sometimes parts of all these, and at last, none of three taking, they were forc'd to undresse and put off their Tragick habits, and conclude the day with *The Merry Milkmaids.* And unlesse this were done, and the popular humour satisfied, as sometimes it so fortun'd, that the Players were refractory; the benches, the tiles, the laths, the stones, oranges, apples, nuts flew about most liberally, and as there were Mechanicks of all professions, who fell every one to his trade, and dissolved a house in an instant, and made a ruine of a stately Fabrick". [42]

In the seventeenth and eighteenth centuries evening performances started at five or five-thirty [43] and acrobatics and dances were sandwiched between the acts. Late comers who saw only the last two or three acts of the play paid part of the price of admission. [44] After the main drama came the "after-piece", a comedy lasting about an hour, often adapted from a full length comedy but sometimes written specially for relieving the gloom and horror of the tragedy. [45] The audience, it appears, did not go to the theatre to learn the story, but to be entertained by whatever histrionic and other theatrical display there was. Probably to attract latecomers, the programme was eventually broken up into separate items; a Covent Garden playbill of 1758 shows a programme, which started at six o'clock, consisting of a tragedy, a comic dance and farce. [46] The theatre-going habits of nineteenth century Europe were very much the same as those in China until recently: in the Chinese theatre performances started early in the evening, at or before seven, and patrons could go

---

[39] W. Smith, *The Commedia dell' arte,* 120 f.

[40] Lawrence, *Pre-Restoration Stage Studies,* Ch. VIII. Early Composite Plays.

[41] Lawrence, *Pre-Restoration Stage Studies,* 91, 94 f.

[42] Edmund Gayton, *Pleasant Notes upon Don Quixote,* quoted in Lawrence, *Old Theatre Days and Ways,* 113.

[43] Summers, *Restoration Theatre,* 20.

[44] Lawrence, *Old Theatre Days and Ways,* 181 *et seq.*

[45] Garrick, Murphy and Foote had all written these. Japanese Noh plays, on serious subjects, are also interspersed with farcial pieces.

[46] *Vide* K. Macgowan and W. Melnitz, *The Living Stage* (1955), 239.

to the theatre at any time between the beginning and nine o'clock, or later. [47] A playbill for Theatre Royal, Drury Lane, in 1827 shows a melodrama, a farce and a one-act play; another shows that at the Olympic in 1831, Madame Vestris offered a "comic burletta", "an entirley new burletta", another "comic burletta", and "a Grand Allegorical Burlesque Burletta;" and in another for Old Vic in 1835 are, besides Shakespeare's *Coriolanus,* dances, "a Classical Scene", "third act of another play" and "a new original play". [48] The "curtain-raiser" of this period, a one-act farce which opened the programme, subsisted in the English theatre into the early years of this century. In Spain, the inter-act song-and-dance was called the *entremés* and in France, *entremets*. In the theatres of Italy, pyrotechnics, as in the Elizabethan theatres, was an attraction. "I was amazed to find", said Charles de Brosses (1709-77) after his visit to Lucca, "that the performance ended in a huge firework display all along the theatre, right across the stage and the boxes, without causing any alarm to the audience, myself excepted". [49]

The fact that single acts could be played in a multiple-bill programme suggests that European audiences in the past, like Chinese audiences now, were sometimes more appreciative of the technical skill of the actors than of the emotional effects intended by the dramatists. This was at least the case in eighteenth century Venice:

"The spectators who liked to follow the recital in the book, carried a bit of candle in their pockets, holding it on or near the book that was often burnt or soiled with the drippings. There was a space some three yards wide between the orchestra and the first row of seats, in which people walked about. The audience was generally very noisy; it was considered fashionable to talk aloud even during the play". [50]

The concentration on technical skill was probably why interruptions did not seem to spoil the enjoyment:

"Imagine my surprise when, at the comedy for the first time, a church bell having suddenly been rung, I heard a noise behind me which made me think the whole building was collapsing around me; the actors and actresses also rushed from the stage, although one of the latter had, in playing her part, just swooned away. The cause of all this commotion was the 'Angelus', which had been rung, and on hearing which all the audience had fallen on their knees facing towards the east, while at the same moment actors and actresses ran off into the side

---

[47] *Vide* Lawrence, *Old Theatre Days and Ways,* 49 for conditions in Madrid, and Speaight, *Juvenile Drama,* 27 for those in London.

[48] Macgowan and Melnitz, *op. cit.,* 328, 334, 342.

[49] Charles de Brosses, *Letters,* trans. R. S. Gower (1897), 91, from Florence to Livorna, to M. de Blancey.

[50] J. S. Kennard, *The Italian Theatre* (1932), II. 32. cf. Chinese audience reading the libretto at the performance mentioned in Ch. XXVIII.

scenes. The Ave Maria was well sung, after which the actress who had to swoon re-swooned, having made her curtsey at the close of the Angelus, and the play recommenced afresh''. [51]

(15)

By taking the whole histories of the theatre into account it has been shown that most if not all of the characteristics of the Chinese theatre can be found in the European theatre; and *vice versa*. [52] The history of a national theatre may be considered to be the trace of the wandering theatrical taste of the people. That wandering theatrical taste of the peoples of different cultures has, throughout the long histories, covered more or less the same area, and given more time can be expected to exhibit even greater similarity. The history of the European theatre is about 2,500 years and that of naturalism, counting from the *Théâtre Libre,* less than seventy years. If we consider the Greek theatre to end at the beginning of the Christian era, it still covered a period longer than that of the European theatre from the Renaissance, say 1500, till to-day. Considered in this way, the dissimilarities between the Chinese and European theatre dwindle to negligible proportions.

There is however one notable difference, that is, the general lack of realism in the Chinese theatre, and the elements of realism in almost all forms of the European theatre. In the Chinese cities concessions are made in the commercial theatres to the taste for gruesome effects and erotic sensationalism and in the country spectacular and awe-inspiring purgatory scenes are sometimes indulged in at religious festivals, but the systematic cultivation of the realistic stage is lacking. The difference is one of degree, but it is a real difference.

There are two aspects of the realism in the European theatre: one, the streak of realism which runs through its history and which produced a gradual drift towards naturalism after music and dance became dissociated from drama and two, the culmination of that process in naturalism at the end of the last century and its wide-spread and apparently irradicable influence on the European drama of to-day. [53]

The aim to affect the audience of the theatre in the same way as they would be affected by real events was served in the Roman theatre by exhibiting the physical charms of the actress, [54] by parading real animals and slaves across the stage and by substituting a condemned criminal for the actor in real execution scenes. [55] Europeans in the Middle Ages relished such scenes as a St. Peter's head that could

---

[51] Charles de Brosses, *Letters,* trans. Gower, 15.

[52] The only difference is that some of the characteristics appeared in the European theatre in extreme forms, for instance, the amount of spectators on the Restoration stage and the symbolism in the costume of English court masques.

[53] *Vide* H. S. Davies, *Realism in the Drama* (1934), especially p. 120.

[54] *Vide* T. Komisarjevsky, *The Costume of the Theatre* (1931), 48 f.

[55] *Vide* Beare, *The Roman Stage,* 230, 232, 143; Bieber, *History of the Greek and Roman Theatre,* 422.

jump, heavens and monuments that opened, flaming swords and burning altars, earthquakes and thunder, hell, smoke and floods, devils and squibs, [56] and the sudden appearance and disappearance of Jesus and the Devil. [57] The gruesome "hell mouth" — a large monster's head from which devils issued — was indispensable. [58] Though some machinery and trap doors were used, these scenes could scarcely have been truly realistic, considering the limited stage equipment at the disposal of medieval producers. In acting, however, greater success was possible: in 1437 in Metz, France, a priest, who played the victim of crucifixion, "fainted and would have died had he not been rescued", and in the same district one priest who played Judas hung too long and had to be "sprinkled with vinegar and other things to bring him round". [59] Scenes of martyrdom, with tortures such as pulling out tongues, were, judging by contemporary pictures, very realistically staged. [60] Dummies were used for execution scenes with the heads carefully modelled to the likeness of the actor and skilfully coloured. This part of the medieval taste survived in the Elizabethan theatre where dummies were used in scenes of violence such as in *Selimus* (1594) in which a man was hurled from an eminence and landed on a circle of spears, [61] in *Sir John Oldcastle,* where MacShane entered with the body of his murdered master and proceeded to rifle it of all its possessions, [62] in Peele's *The Battle of Alcazar* in which mutilation was acted with real blood and the internal organs of an animal [63] and in *The Duchess of Malfi,* in which the bodies of several strangled children were shown. [64] In the early seventeenth century decapitation scenes were in vogue and dummy heads, which bled, were used. [65] Later in the century, in Dryden and Lee's *Oedipus, King of Thebes,* the king threw himself from a balcony and fell on the stage — a dummy was here used — and as the Thebans surrounded it, the stage trap opened and the actor substituted for the dummy, so that later the audience saw real flesh and blood. [66] In 1850, at the Olympic, in *Ariadne,* a play adapted from Corneille, a human double and a dummy were used in conjunction with the leading actress in the scene where Ariadne leaps from the rock.

[56] Nicoll, *Development of the Theatre,* 73 *infra;* Nicoll, *Masks Mimes and Miracles,* 206 f.

[57] *Vide* Lawrence, *Pre-Restoration Stage Studies,* 148, quoting L. Petit de Julleville, *Les Mystères.*

[58] G. Cohen, *Le Théâtre en France au Moyen Age,* I. (1928), Pl. XX; H. H. Borcherdt, *Das europäische Theater im Mittelalter und in der Renaissance* (1935), 24-25, 27, 35, 45.

[59] Nicoll, *Development of the Theatre,* 80; Nicoll, *Masks Mimes and Miracles,* 206 f.

[60] *Vide* Gustav Cohen, *Histoire de la Mise en Scène dans la Théâtre Religieux Français du Moyen Age* (1926), Pl. III facing p. 86.

[61] Lawrence, *Speeding Up Shakespeare,* 130.

[62] Lawrence, *op. cit.,* 132.

[63] Lawrence, *Pre-Restoration Stage Studies,* 236 f.

[64] Lawrence, *Speeding Up Shakespeare,* 132.

[65] Hodges, *Globe Restored,* 75.

[66] Lawrence, *Speeding Up Shakespeare,* 134.

The illusion was so complete that spectators went to it night after night with powerful opera glasses in the hope of discovering the secret. According to the *Autobiography* of Anna C. Mowatt (1819-70), who played the heroine, on the first night a man started up in the pit and, in a tone of genuine horror, cried, "Good God! she has killed herself". [67] Direct emotional agitation rather than detached contemplation is suggested by an anonymous eighteenth century description of Betterton:

> When Betterton as Hamlet met the Ghost his countenance, "thro' the violent and sudden Emotions of Amazement and Horror, turned instantly on the Sight of his Father's Spirit, as pale as his Neckcloth, when every Article of his Body seem'd to be affected with a Tremor inexpressible; so that, had his Father's Ghost actually risen before him, he could not have been seized with more real Agonies; and this was felt so strongly by the Audience, that the Blood seemed to shudder in their Veins likewise, and they in some Measure partook of the Astonishment and Horror, with which they saw this excellent Actor affected". [68]

With dance and music dissociated from the drama and after verse had also fizzled out in it, the scenery in the European theatre, which started as a toy in the court theatre and became an indispensable adjunct in all theatres, was bound to engender, some time or other, the ideal of the stage as an oversized doll-house. What was decoration and spectacle became a habit which lasted for two or three centuries, till the *new* possibility of its being lifelike was discovered and exploited, and the function of scenery was changed. Realistic scenery, as distinguished from the spectacular or decorative, was first used by Kemble in his "historically correct" productions and by the Duke of Saxe-Meiningen's players for their productions which were almost museum exhibits, [69] and later by Antoine in the *Théâtre Libre*. Strindberg scorned the painted pans and kettles and the canvas doors which "swung back and forth at the lightest touch" and which made the house "sway" when they were slammed, his ideal being the "real room, with the fourth wall missing, and a part of the furniture placed back towards the audience". Antoine, the father of the naturalistic theatre, wanted "expression based on familiar and real props: a returned pencil or an overturned cup". [70]

All reformers thrive on the real and imaginary evils of the *status quo,* and in most cases sweep away the old merits as well as old evils. Antoine could not see the

---

[67] Lawrence, *Speeding Up Shakespeare,* 138 f.

[68] (Anonymous), *The Laureat, or the Right Side of Colley Cibber* (1740), quoted in Nagler, *Sources of Theatrical History,* 219.

[69] cf. "I am anxious to make the theatre a school as well as a recreation" — Kean's farewell speech before his retirement from the theatre in 1859, quoted in Nagler, *Sources of Theatrical History,* 488.

[70] *Vide* André Antoine, *Le Théâtre Libre* (1890), 72-90; Preface to *Miss Julia,* in *Plays by August Strindberg,* trans E. Björkmann (1912).

possibility of sincerity and élan in any style of acting except the naturalistic, which was to him the only cure for the "yelling" of actors and their "striking poses". The change in actors from "playing *at* the public" to "playing *for* the public" was considered by Strindberg as "highly desirable". [71] The truth is, the appreciation of art which is a language more powerful than that used in the daily life requires initiation and effort. All art consists of formal and intellectual elements and for the formal element there are rules to guide the artist. Those who ostensibly flout the rules are merely following them in an unrecognized way, and those who really work without any rules whatsoever are no artists, they can only produce something bizarre which attracts attention for a while through its novelty and is soon forgotten. Architects, musicians, dancers, poets and painters all have their rules even though the rules may be constantly changing or sometimes disguised. Naturalism *in the performance* has hardly any rules, because it is not art in the sense that architecture, music and poetry are arts. [72] That is why there is no virtuosity in the players; of the two qualifications of an artist, techniques and inspiration, the former is lacking. [73] As the theatre was brought within the financial reach of wider and wider public it had to cater for less and less intelligence and taste. The cult of "simple gestures and natural movements of a modern man living our everyday life" [74] had the strength of numbers — "the drama's laws the drama's patrons give", the men in the street can understand vernacular prose, but not poetry — only a low ebb in the theatrical tradition was needed to start the popular movement. "Does not the uncultivated amateur", asked Goethe, referring to 'natural' taste, "just in the same way, desire a work to be natural, that he may be able to enjoy it in a natural, which is often a vulgar and common way?" [75] From the real room and real props it is only one step to the real scenes of adultery and real execution which the plebeian crowd of Roman times enjoyed.

If "the actor's supreme endeavour is so to interpret real life that his audience shall feel that they are actually present and participating in some event which is happening before their very eyes", [76] to be completely successful he should not only act the event but *do* it; good appearance is not enough, the efforts should also be genuine, for the audience always can tell which it is. In connection with the demand for the actor's real emotions, Nicoll asked of the actor playing Othello,

---

[71] Strindberg, *op. cit.*

[72] cf. Craig, *The Theatre Advancing*, 156.

[73] Craig's ideal was an art of directing which bore the same relation to dramatic action as poetry does to language, music to delivery and dance to movements. cf. "The greatest work of art is that which expresses the deepest thoughts most beautifully".

[74] Antoine, *op. cit.*

[75] "On Truth and Probability in Works of Art", in *Goethe's Literary Essays*, Ed. J. E. Spingarn (1921), 56.

[76] J. S. Kennard, *The Italian Theatre*, I. 21.

"Why does he not kill a new Desdemona each night? Or, rather, why does he not kill his particular Desdemona at a special matinee, forthwith put an end to himself, and let a companion reproduce the same bloody process the following evening?" [77]

Whatever the reason may be, it is not the lack of thoroughness in the demands for realism — witness Strindberg's real room even though he could not have the fourth wall — and the Romans did have actual killing as part of their theatrical attraction. The similarity between Roman and modern European theatrical taste has been stated by historians of the theatre — for example, in Bieber's *History of the Greek and Roman Theatre,* p. 391. Social conditions and moral conventions do not allow the same type of programme, but whereas the Romans had their gladiators, animal baiting, naked actresses and parades of slaves and animals, [78] the modern world has boxing matches, auto races and the American striptease. [79] "The passionate tussle between the elephant and the tiger gives us all the excitement that we can get from the modern stage, and can give it us unalloyed". [80] In 1935 Verdi's *Aida* was produced in Yankee Stadium with 1,000 supers, numerous camels, horses and elephants and the production was repeated in 1937 in Madison Square Garden and in 1938 on Randalls Island Stage.[81] These spectacles differ in no way except in size from Mr. Crummles' "real pump and splendid tubs" which Nicholas had to work into a play. [82] Most people, however, have to be satisfied with the reasonable substitutes in the moving picture for which a "cast of thousands" and "actual locality" are badges of merit, or else indulge in games and contests which are real but less spectacular and exciting.

As for the missing fourth wall, Evreinov sarcastically suggested supplying it at all costs. "For Chekhov's *Three Sisters*", he said, "a small two-storey house would be rented somewhere in the suburbs of Moscow" to which the spectators would come to watch the action through keyholes under the pretext of looking for apartments, a few trips being required to see the complete play and in the evening a real fire would burn the house down. [83] The suggestion is less fantastic than perhaps the theorist meant it to be, for conflagration and falling buildings are the constantly advertised attractions of the moving pictures, and the audience who watched the gigantic parade of camels and elephants in *Aida* should require no encouragement to see a real fire.

---

[77] Nicoll, *Development of the Theatre,* 196.

[78] *Ibid.,* 424.

[79] *Ibid.,* 391.

[80] G. Craig, *On the Art of the Theatre* (1911), 58.

[81] Bieber, *op. cit.,* 412.

[82] Dickens (1812-70), *Nicholas Nickleby,* Ch. XXII.

[83] N. Evreinov, *The Theatre in Life,* trans. A. I. Nazaroff (1927), 137.

The question whether a good actor feels the emotions he portrays concerns mainly the actors themselves as a problem of training and technique, but from the point of view of the audience, the idea that they should feel the emotions is probably subconsciously connected with the thrill in real events, hence the disappointment when a pretty woman on the stage is found to be played by a man. The problem, considered from the actor's point of view has little meaning, if any, to the Chinese actor, and the long-standing controversy in Europe, from Diderot's *Le Paradoxe sur le comédien* (written in 1700s) to William Archer's *Masks or Faces? A Study in the Psychology of Acting* (1880), is a sign of an element of naturalism in European acting from at least Diderot's time till now. Archer starts with the categorical statement; "Acting *is* imitation". [84] which may well be true of the European style of acting but the Chinese style is precisely what imitation is not. The Chinese player who has to sing at the most emotional moments and sing the most demanding arias under the strongest presumed emotions, cannot afford to lose the "disinterestedness" of Diderot's description [85] and even if he could control his expressions through what Archer calls "double strata of mental activity", his self-excited illusion of emotions would be to no purpose, because the "true ring" of great acting, for which the "intervention of imaginative sympathy" is said to be necessary, concerns the apparent sincerity of the expressions which is required for the dramatic illusion that the characters are real people, but the Chinese audience do not seek that kind of illusion.

The Romans, in spite of their love for real blood, knew the beauties of stylish acting. Quintilian praised the comic actor Demetrius for his "unique gifts in the movements of his hands", his "power to charm his audience by the long drawn sweetness of his exclamations", the "skill with which he would make his dress seem to puff out with wind as he walked" and the "expressive movement of the right side which he sometimes introduced with effect". [86] Miming was then cultivated to a standard probably never reached in the European theatre since, and versatility was valued for its own sake. The same writer mentioned a comic actor who was "best in the roles of gods, young men, good fathers, slaves, matrons and respectable old women", and another who "excelled in sharp-tempered old men, cunning slaves, parasites and pimps". [87]

The problem of feeling the simulated emotions also occurred to "an actor of repute" whom Lucian saw.

"He was acting the madness of Ajax, just after he has been worsted by

---

[84] Italics his.

[85] cf. ". . . the unassailable poise of the Oriental actor, who is cool and impersonal in the midst of the most passionate action". Stella Bloch, *Dancing and the Drama East and West* (1922), 8.

[86] Quintilian, *Institutio Oratoria,* trans. H. E. Butler (1936), IV. 345-7.

[87] *Ibid.*

Odysseus; and so lost control of himself, that one might have been excused for thinking his madness was something more than feigned. He tore the clothes from the back of one of the iron-shod time-beaters, snatched a flute from the player's hands, and brought it down in such trenchant sort upon the head of Odysseus, who was standing by enjoying his triumph, that, had not his cap held good, and borne the weight of the blow, poor Odysseus must have fallen a victim to histrionic frenzy. The house ran mad for company, leaping, yelling, tearing their clothes. For the illiterate riff-raff, who knew not good from bad, and had no idea of decency, regarded it as a supreme piece of acting; and the more intelligent part of the audience, realizing how things stood, concealed their disgust, and instead of reproaching the actor's folly by silence, smothered it under their plaudits; they saw only too clearly that it was not Ajax but the pantomime who was mad. Nor was our spirited friend content till he had distinguished himself yet further: descending from the stage, he seated himself in the senatorial benches between two consulars, who trembled lest he should take one of them for a ram and apply the lash. The spectators were divided between wonder and amusement; and some there were who suspected that his ultrarealism had culminated in reality. However, it seems that when he came to his senses again he bitterly repented of this exploit, and was quite ill from grief, regarding his conduct as that of a veritable madman, as is clear from his own words. For when his partisans begged him to repeat the performance, he recommended another actor for the part of Ajax, saying that 'it was enough for him to have been mad once'. His mortification was increased by the success of his rival, who, though a similar part had been written for him, played it with admirable judgement and discretion, and was complimented on his observance of decorum, and of the proper bounds of his art''. [88]

Perhaps the unfortunate player was tempted to the extravagance by the groundlings who relished real emotions as well as real fights. In any case, the ideal that "his audience shall feel that they are actually present and participating in some event which is happening before their very eyes" was undoubtedly attained, and the riff- raff did regard it as supreme achievement.

The tradition of both the real spectacles and the skilful pantomime of the Roman theatre was broken and has hardly any effect on the modern European theatre. Naturalism as we know it now has been a general tendency since the Renaissance, a tendency in which the replacement of the boy actors by actresses in the Restoration theatre, the decay of the poetic drama in the eighteenth century, the elimination of the boxes on the stage and the innovation of the box-set in the mid-nineteenth century are but conspicuous steps in the gradual change. The banners and slogans of

---

[88] *Works of Lucian,* H. W. Fowler and F. G. Fowler, Vol. II, 262 f.

Antoine's *Théâtre Libre,* which marked the culmination of the process and which has been taken as a monument of the naturalistic movement, were among the many liberties enjoyed by ambitious intellects in an age when tradition was weak enough and artists bold enough for excursions into striking unorthodoxy. [89] A few years after Antoine founded the *Théâtre Libre* in 1887, the banner of symbolism was raised in Paul Fort's *Théâtre Mixte,* later *Théâtre d'Art,* in which plays by Maeterlinck and others were produced with the decor of Vuillard, Bonnard, Maurice Dennis and others. Since then many novel methods of production have been proposed and experimented on, for example, formalism, constructivism, bio-mechanics (or *Über-Marionette*) and expressionism. Among those who have deviated from or reacted against naturalism are Gordon Craig (1872-1966), V. E. Meyerhold (1874-1940), M. Maeterlinck (1862-1949), N. K. Evreinov (1879-1953), Terence Gray (Festival Theatre in Cambridge, 1926-1933), J. Copeau (1878-1949), Max Reinhardt (1873-1943) and A. Appia (1862-1928). In the International Exhibition of Theatrical Arts (1922) in Amsterdam, there were about three hundred books written in the previous twenty-five years most of which concerned new ideas. [90] Many producers were not satisfied with naturalism and some of them exploited single aspects of the theatre such as lighting, scenery, dance, and so on, to achieve something new [91] but the standard of value among the general public has scarcely been changed and will probably, by its large inertia, perpetuate naturalism for some time yet. The creed of ordinary European theatregoers is well represented by Lawrence's criterion of theatrical progress:

"From the days of Thespis to our own the whole directing-force in dramatic representation has been towards higher and higher illusion, though progress has been made by slow and almost infinitesimal increments". "In the age-long history of the theatre the highest, because the most illusive, form of histrionic art has been attained under the rule of the law of the invisible fourth

---

[89] Theorists connect André Antoine's theatrical innovations with the literary movement of naturalism advocated by Zola, but naturalistic theatre and naturalistic writing are two entirely different things, notwithstanding Zola's dramatic efforts. In literature images can only be introduced into the reader's mind in succession and the process of writing is *ipso facto* a highly selective one. On the stage, however, all the sights and sounds are *simultaneously* arrayed and if naturalism is served, all the irrelevancies in the scenes of real life have to be included in detail, hence the baseness and crudity as of a photographic style of painting. In dramatic writing the dramatist cannot make good use of "a slice of life" because the physical endurance of the theatre-audience limits the size of the "slice" and, unlike the novel, drama, if it is not to be shapeless, must involve compression and concentration of action. cf. M. C. Bradbrook, *Themes and Conventions of Elizabethan Tragedy,* 43 f.

[90] E. Rose, *Gordon Craig and the Theatre* (1928), 145.

[91] *Vide* Craig, *The Theatre Advancing,* 82.

wall, and to nullify that law would be to enter upon an era of inferiority". [92]

This type of illusion, long since deprecated in the graphic arts, is bought in the theatre at a very high price: the modern Europe stage has become a language without rhetoric, it lacks the formal elements which give expressions power and beauty. [93] The language in dramas becomes arid and poor [94] and imagination is atrophied in the aural and visual aspects of the theatre, till poetry, in the wider sense, is gone out of it and only "consistency in characterization and plot, a reproduction of colloquial speech with the consequent prevention of any delicate or precise use of words are the requisites of most contemporary plays". [95] Drama becomes "the desert of exact likeness to the reality which is perceived by the most commonplace mind". [96] Colloquial language is feeble because it is developed by and for the petty needs of daily life in which strong emotions are few and far between and when they occur their expressions are suppressed. Its expression has a very narrow range beyond which it is ineffective, for it never needs to be very expressive. Poetic form imposed on language liberates it from the restrictiveness of colloquial usage.

On the visual side of the stage P. Fitzgerald said,

"Of course it may be said that mere spectacular display is all that is now desired, and a brilliant gaudy show; but if *illusion* be sought, it can only be repeated that too much light, too much colour, and the principles of 'set scenes' are destructive of it". [97]

In other words a stage that serves illusion is drab.

Crudeness follows lack of rhetoric and the more sensitive artists find "nothing more outrageous than that men and women should be let loose on a platform, so that they may expose that which artists refuse to show except veiled". [98] "It is bad art", said Craig, "to make so personal, so emotional an appeal that the beholder forgets the thing itself while swamped by the personality, the emotion, of its maker", [99] and he referred to Jonson, Lessing, Edmund Scherer, Lamb, Goethe, George Sand, Coleridge, Anatole France, Ruskin and Pater for protests against reproduction of nature "with its photographic and weak actuality". [100] This type

---

[92] W. J. Lawrence, *Old Theatre Days and Ways* (1935), 25, 249. cf. ". . . an outrage upon the best principles of theatrical usage" — which the proscenium picture frame was supposed to be by a Manchester journalist when it was installed in Queen's Theatre, Manchester, in March 1846. See Lawrence, *Elizabethan Playhouse and Other Studies, First series,* 184 n.

[93] In Japan, where both conventional and more or less naturalistic theatre, *Noh* and *Kabuki* respectively, are native, the latter is considered to be the inferior form.

[94] Thorndike, *Shakespeare's Theatre,* 401.

[95] Bradbrook, *Elizabethan Stage Conditions* (1932), 126.

[96] Eliot, Four Elizabethan Dramatists, *Selected Essays* (1950), 93.

[97] P. Fitzgerald, *The World Behind the Scenes* (1881), 7. His italics.

[98] G. Craig, *On the Art of the Theatre,* 58.

[99] *Ibid.,* 79.

[100] *Ibid.,* 81.

of bad art, in the form of the cinema, is now bringing up new generations of theatre audience by shaping their taste. Richard Wagner (*Über die Bestimmung der Oper*) mentioned singers who got in difficulty because they imagined a situation too realistically, as when Schröder-Devrient, playing in Fidelio, did not sing, but "positively *spoke* — and with a terrible accent of despair — that last word of the phrase: 'another step — and — thou art — DEAD'." Here weak actuality invaded even a form of expression which has been divorced from everyday life — singing — and the incongruity is obvious, but in less conspicuous ways, all artistic expression requires some detachment and alertness. "Naturalism destroys the critical awareness for appreciation", said one Shakespearean critic, and he added "it is hardly surprising that a method thus divided against itself has produced little of permanent value". [101]

Unless one considers the appeal of street fights and real fires as the essence of drama, one must conclude that all drama is pretence and that a willingness to cooperate is the condition for its appreciation. The minimum amount and the type of accessories required to win the cooperation of the audience vary with time and locality: the audience in Restoration times required more scenery than those of the Elizabethan period, the European audience of to-day more than the Chinese, and so forth. At one time the audience demanded consistency in motivation — as in the "well made" plays — in others they wanted unity of place and time, and in still others, naturalistic diction and delivery or historical accuracy in costume. When children play at keeping shop they use the stool for counter and the odds and ends among their toys for whatever goods they pretend to be selling and buying. Evreinov's hypothetical fastidious audience corresponds to children who refuse to play shop-keeping unless they are given a real shop, an attitude of withheld cooperation also represented by the Chinese saying: "Those who play in dramas are lunatics; those who watch them are fools". [102] Absolute sobriety is incompatible with dramatic appreciation.

(16)

The sense of reality in the drama is much more a matter of mental habit and less a matter of lifelike representation than is apparent in the appreciation of the naturalistic theatre. It is significant that in the book of critical miscellanies by Wang Meng-Sheng, who was familiar with the traditional Chinese theatre but was also appreciative of the then newly imported naturalistic dramas, there is no indication that the naturalistic style struck him as more "real"; the distinction he noticed was that it was "easier to understand".

"Its merit lies in that even old women can understand it . . . its appeal lies

---

[101] S. L. Bethell, *Shakespeare and the Popular Dramatic Tradition* (1944), 31.

[102] 做戲的是瘋子；看戲的是傻子.

in the plot such as sad events and exciting situations; for ordinary scenes it has nothing of interest . . . it cannot be repeatedly enjoyed . . . it is half of the theatrical art, not the whole". [103]

The ancient Greeks, who had a permanent building of stone and timber for their "set", and whose actors were among natural surroundings, would undoubtedly, if they could see the modern European theatre, be struck by the falsity of the canvas however lifelike that may be. In the Roman comedies action took place in front of houses and the audience could, in the original theatre, be taken as a street crowd, which is more realistic than the audience in modern theatres. [104] "The modern convention which enables our theatre-going audience to see into the interior of a house would have startled the Greeks and the Romans". [105] When the Greek *skene* represented a temple approached by some characters in a drama, the audience would be similar to a large crowd watching a wedding party at a church. The artificial lighting of the modern stage, if nothing else, makes it into an exhibition window which one cannot watch without the feeling of artificiality. Europeans of the Middle Ages who were used to all the localities involved in a drama being laid out at once before them in different places in the church or the market place would, however conventional their *mise-en-scène* may appear to us, be baffled by the successive localities represented by the same stage. [106] The modern Europeans have consented to forget about the missing fourth wall and hardly notice it is missing, but to people of other periods the absurdity would appear glaring. It is not convention, but a mixture of convention and naturalism that is difficult to comprehend. In the opera, the orchestra is now accompaniment to the singing, now a musical stage-effect and now the expression of the emotional tone of the action. The dialogue is in verse and is sung but the manners and actions are realistic; vocal expression is minutely specified and carefully trained but acting is left to the natural capabilities of the players. Even in the modern European dramas incongruities abound: scenery is made to look natural but lighting is entirely artificial; the faces are disguised by make-up, but movements are supposed to be natural and costume to be "correct". In W. J. Lawrence's criterion of good theatre quoted above, a matter of mental habit is taken to be a matter of principle.

The sense of reality in the drama can exist on different levels. To the Chinese their drama is real because it is a real dramatic dance, the action is fictitious but the dance is real, the characters are not real but the actors are. [107] The imagination of

---

[103] 王夢生, 梨園佳話, 四章, "新戲".

[104] Beare, *Roman Stage*, 170, 174.

[105] Beare, *Roman Stage*, 170.

[106] G. Cohen, *Histoire de la Mise en Scène dans le Théâtre Religieux Français du Moyen Age* (1926), Planche 1. (pp. 70-1); Planche IV. (p. 100).

[107] cf. Wm. Poel on the Elizabethan, *Bulletin of John Rylands Library*, Vol. 3. No. 1. p. 223.

the Elizabethan and Chinese audience is not trained to see in their mind's eye the pictorial stage, because they have no idea what the pictorial stage is like. Some dialogue must have conjured up visual images, as some of the descriptive lines of Shakespeare were bound to do, for example, Ophelia's death report and the description of the cliffs at Dover in *King Lear,* but they would be the images of a poetic world, not of canvas and paint. The audience saw the action not as a convincing copy of the events but as an event in its own right: players acting a drama. There is no suspension of disbelief, because there is no disbelief to be suspended — they believe the stage is a platform; the players, players; the drama, a performance. It is in the same sense that marionettes are real: they cannot pretend to be anything else. [108] There are reasons for believing that, outside naturalism, European audiences also saw and still see the theatre in this way.

"When the opera is good, it creates a little world of its own, in which all proceeds according to fixed laws, which must be judged by its own laws, felt according to its own spirit". [109]

In the naturalistic theatre the sense of reality is shifted to what is represented, the audience try hard to think that there are no actors but only people in the story — and they never really succeed.

If the highest achievement of naturalistic acting is *literally* "the feeling of being present at and participating in some event" then the appreciation of the riff-raff in the Roman theatre was exemplary and the momentarily deranged player of Ajax was one of the best actors that ever lived. In that case for an actor to play a drunkard he need only drink till he is drunk and the best stage waitresses and domestic servants are those hired through the employment agent. Or else, if naturalistic acting is selective imitation, recognizably different from real events, then the ideal of feeling "being at an event" is a fallacy. All styles appear natural to those who like them.

"The Kembles and their grand artificiality had to make room for Edmund Kean, who in thirty years from then was looked on as anything but natural, for was not Macready 'more natural'? And in a few years' time all these actors seemed to us stilted and artificial when Henry Irving appeared. And now we talk of Irving's artificiality by the side of Antoine's natural acting. 'It is Nature itself', cried the critics, and soon Antoine's natural acting is to become mere artifice by the side of Stanislavsky.

"What, then, are all these manifestations of this 'Nature'? I find them one and all to be merely examples of a new artificiality — the artificiality of naturalism". [110]

---

[108] cf. G. Craig, *The Theatre Advancing,* 111 f.

[109] Goethe, "On Truth and Probability in Works of Art", *Goethe's Literary Essays,* Ed. J. E. Spingarn (1921), 56.

[110] Craig, *On the Art of the Theatre,* 290.

There might have been gradual stylization in the acting which was counteracted by the reforms towards greater sincerity, but obviously no serious critic could conceive of the "natural" style as that which approaches the actual manners of the common people. The difference between Irving and Macready might be a difference in degree — of stylization — but it was also a difference in kind. The public was under the illusion that they were seeing something more "natural" when they saw something merely more moving to them.

> "A hundred years ago Clarkson Stanfield in England was painting scenery which amazed the critics by its 'natural' appearance, and that, too, after they had known the work of de Loutherbourg; and soon Stanfield was looked on as unnatural, for Telbin the Elder gave them what they asserted was very Nature itself; and yet hardly have they said so before they eat their words, turn their backs on Telbin, and find true Nature in Hawes Craven, only to put him away a little later for Harker, who 'at last paints Nature for us'." [111]

The criterion of naturalism can have a meaning, but only in a way which outrages all artistic sensibility, as in the case of the stage waitresses from the employment agent, or else it is meaningless, as Craig points out. For most modern European audiences, it is probably a little bit of both.

The comparative conventionalism of the Chinese stage cannot be entirely explained by the European invention of scenery and the dissociation of music and dance from the European drama, because even in the Elizabethan theatre, where the facility of realistic setting was comparable to that prevailing in China, there was some degree of realistic representation, and on the Chinese stage properties which can, without much ado, be realistic were conventionalized. Despite the settings and properties "the normal state of mind of the Elizabethan audience was one of absolute vagueness and carelessness as to the particular locality the stage was supposed to represent", [112] but on the Chinese stage, which is a bare platform, there is never any ambiguity of locality except in short unlocated scenes. The locality of *Macbeth* I. ii. and iii. is not indicated and *Othello*, IV. ii. begins with the painful "closet, lock and key" scene between Othello and Desdemona and ends with conversation between Iago and Roderigo, and IV. iii. of the same play begins in some hall or corridor in the castle but ends in Desdemona's apartment. The uncanny memory of the Chinese audience in assumed localities is shown when the forgetful novice "Walks through the wall" or "gets downstairs without ladder", which is so unusual that it invariably causes involuntary, and often visibly unkind, merriment among the audience. The memory is not visual in nature, as at least one Chinese theatregoer can testify here, because the stage does not have and has never had any scenery, rather, it is akin to children's ability to keep in mind all the details

---

(111) *Ibid.*, 289 f.

(112) W. Archer, *The Old Drama and the New*, 36.

of a story and to question and correct inconsistencies which the story-teller's improvision, necessitated by defective memory, brings into the narrative, or a mathematician's ability to make an assumption and to carry out a series of calculations consistent with it. This precision of their imagination may also be called a sense of reality.

The significance of the Chinese conventionalism is twofold: the lack of the taste for emotionally disturbing sights and the ability to dispense with visual aids in dramatic representation.

The problem arises as to whether the psychology is the cause and the practice the effect, or *vice versa*. It may be argued that the Chinese, owing to racial characteristics, are particularly sensitive to representations of suffering and also have a strong imagination, and their psychological needs and capacities determined their stage conventions, or it may be thought that conventionalism was started sometime in the history of the Chinese theatre and has since then trained the sensibility and imagination which perpetuate the conventions. The plausibility of grafting realism onto the Chinese theatre and the prospect of the European theatre becoming conventional again depend on the answer to the above question. If, for example, the practice is the cause and the psychology the effect, then by injecting realism into the Chinese drama the imagination of the audience may be expected to weaken for lack of exercise which in turn will demand more scenery and machinery, and a reverse process may be initiated in the western theatre; otherwise such movements cannot bear results. Any conclusive failure to start such processes in the future or in the past would be evidence that the difference in oriental and occidental mental make-up causes the difference in the theatre, not *vice versa*. Comparative study of the theatrical histories of other races, especially those showing unequal imagination in other fields, should shed some light on the problem. It is difficult to maintain that the Chinese are naturally more sensitive than other races to cruelty and violence, and this suggests that they could lose their present theatrical taste and acquire one for realistic effects.

The ability to dispense with the stage set has kept scenery and its many far-reaching influences from being introduced into the Chinese drama. This, together with other reasons for the lack of a drift towards naturalism, has produced a tradition of acting more continuous and stable than that of the European actors. The result of this longer [113] and more stable tradition is the achievement of a highly developed *style*. That art of acting is not, as a western dancer puts it, "one man deep, but behind the Asiatic craftsman stands the race" [114] and the "great historical

---

[113] The first players' troupe established in a permanent European theatre was the *Confrérie de la Passion*, 1402 — See Nicoll, *Development of the Theatre*, 77. The Chinese public theatre started in the twelfth century, if not earlier.

[114] Stella Bloch, *Dancing and the Drama East and West* (1922), Introduction, also pp. 4, 9.

roles have been chiselled and polished for generations". [115] Acting, conventional and sophisticated, has, in the Chinese theatre, become an artistic medium, not of everyday usage, but, like poetry, only for the trained audience and therefore has to be learned.

(17)

The quality and style of a theatre can also be seen through its critics. The Chinese are known, in contrast to the Europeans, for the detachment and contemplation in their appreciation of the fine arts, including the drama, yet European theatrical practice and dramatic criticism before the advent of naturalism show attitudes and standards similar to those of the Chinese audience.

Owing to the comparatively stable tradition in the Chinese theatre since the beginnings of the Chinese drama, dramatic criticism has not suffered as much change as it has in the West. European stage has been now the dramatist's art, now the actor's; at one time it was the machinist's show-place, and at another it was the demagogue's platform; at the present there is agitation to make it the director's art. No wonder then that one can only find among the many schools of European criticism a few that apply to the oriental theatrical taste. [116]

In the use of verse the Elizabethan dramatists appear to work under the same principles as the Chinese, that is, "when the dramatist wished to *lower the level* of action or expression from romantic to humorous, from ideal to colloquial, or (less frequently) from emotional to merely intellectual, he introduced prose, and when he wished to lift the action or expression again to the normally idealized plane of the dramatic form, he returned to verse". [117]

In the Chinese theatre music is used in the same way, so that when the "level" of action or emotions is raised both the diction and the mode of delivery are changed. [118] Verse, like music and dance, is the natural tool of all early dramatists: the Greeks, the Romans, the Elizabethans, the early Spaniards all wrote their dramas in verse and even under the restrictions of the scripture, some medieval

---

[115] Harold Acton, *Oxford Companion to the Theatre,* CHINA.

[116] The oscillation between extreme unbalanced forms of theatre is a characteristic which cannot be found in the oriental theatres; for example, the costume and scenery of the sixteenth and seventeenth century court masques, the machines in the seventeenth century machine plays, the music in the opera, the dance in the ballet, the farce in the *commedia dell' arte,* the intellectual interests of the problem plays, the dramatic construction in "well-made plays", and the mime in the Roman pantomime. See Bieber, *History of the Greek and Roman Theatre,* 315; Beare, *The Roman Stage,* 226 f; Haigh, *The Attic Theatre,* 312.

[117] R. M. Alden, The Development of the Use of Prose in the English Drama, 1600-1800. *Mod. Phil.* Vol. VII. 1909-12. I. His italics. For Shakespeare's use of prose see M. Crane, *Shakespeare's Prose* (1951).

[118] *Vide* section on the use of singing in 齊如山, 中國劇之組織, 一章, 歌唱.

650

dramas were also versified. [119] The early French farces of the sixteenth and seventeenth centuries were in verse. [120] The general decline of verse in the European drama which occurred in the eighteenth century suggests a parallel change in the style of delivery: the tone, perhaps became more naturalistic first and then poetry became incongruous with it. In England, by the middle of the eighteenth century verse was entirely estranged from comedy and tragedies were written in a mixture of verse and prose, the prose being highly stylized and, to the modern ear, bombastic. [121] By the nineteenth century dramas on the English stage, mainly comedies, were entirely in prose; tragedies in verse were still written but only to be read — that is, poetry was still an effective means of dramatic expression but the tone and manners of the actors had fallen below the poetic level. [122] Tragedy, with verse, left the stage then because "it is very clear to all who understand poetry, that serious play ought not to imitate conversation too nearly". [123]

"All who love poetry love it because in poetry the profoundest interests of life are spoken of directly, nakedly and sincerely. No such habitual intimacy of expression is possible in daily speech. In poetry it is possible, because the forms and convention and restraints of art give dignity and quiet to the turbulent feelings on which they are imposed, and make passion tolerable. Without the passion there is no poetry; to recognize great poetry is to hear the authentic voice. Poetry is a touchstone for insincerity; if anyone does not feel that which he desires to express, he may make a passable oration, he will never make a great poem". [124]

Colloquial diction and naturalistic action show us what men say and do, but not, at least not directly, what they feel. If feelings are shown in the ordinary way on the stage, the expressions are as unseemly as in real life. In contrast to the reluctance with which one reviews the distressful parts of *Clarissa Harlowe* or *The Gamester,* Wordsworth spoke of Shakespeare's dramas which even "in the most pathetic scenes, never act upon us as pathetic beyond the bounds of pleasure — an effect which, in a much greater degree than might at first be imagined, is to be ascribed to small, but continual and regular impulses of pleasurable surprise from the metrical arrangement". [125] This function of the musical aspect of verse is served in the Chinese theatre by music itself, which dissolves the bitterness of pain and suffering and gives them glorious colours.

---

[119] *Vide* K. Young, *The Drama of the Medieval Church* (1933), II. 317 f; I. 499 f.

[120] B. Swain, *Fools and Folly During the Middle Ages and the Renaissance* (1932), Ch. VI.

[121] For examples see Alden, *op. cit.,* 8 f.

[122] cf. Alden, *op. cit.,* 6-8.

[123] Dryden, Of Heroic Plays, *Dramatic Essays,* Ed. Everyman Library, p. 87.

[124] Raleigh, *Shakespeare,* 88.

[125] Wordsworth, Preface to *Lyrical Ballads,* 24th para.

At the beginning of the nineteenth century poetry, which guarded the mind of the audience against emotional agitation, had left the stage and serenity was threatened, hence Schiller's warning shown in the following was appropriate.

> "The mind of the spectator ought to maintain its freedom through the most impassioned scenes; it should not be the mere prey of impressions, but calmly and severely detach itself from the emotions which it suffers. The commonplace objection made to the chorus, that it disturbs the illusion, and blunts the edge of the feelings, is what constitutes its highest recommendation; for it is this blind force of the affections which the true artist deprecates — this illusion is what he disdains to excite. If the strokes which tragedy inflicts on our bosoms followed without respite, the passion would overpower the action. We should mix ourselves up with the subject-matter and no longer stand above it. It is by holding asunder the different parts, and stepping between the passions with its composing views, that the chorus restores to us our freedom, which would else be lost in the tempest". [126]

This injunction loses much of its force on the Chinese, and is probably wellnigh meaningless to the modern European audience.

> "The highest problem of any art", said Goethe, "is to produce by appearance the illusion of a higher reality. But it is a false endeavour to realize the appearance until at last only something commonly real remains". [127]

In the best of theatrical art, East or West, the vision of a higher reality is achieved not only on the literary level but on the histrionic level also — gesture and voice, as well as language, become revealing.

---

[126] Preface to *Die Braut von Messina,* 1803. 23rd para.

[127] *Autobiography of Goethe together with his Annals,* trans. J. Oxenford (1894), I. 422.

CHAPTER XLV

SOME OBSERVATIONS ON THE EVOLUTION OF THE THEATRE

(Roots of the Theatre — Farce and Dramatic Dance — Drama)

(1)

General conclusions on the genesis and evolution of world theatre acquire validity in proportion to the scope of the information on which such conclusions are based, and the validity reaches its maximum only when the theatres of all the races in the world have been investigated. Such a synthesis of historical data is, at the present, far from being completed: even the theatres of the more cultured peoples such as Indian and Japanese theatre, have not been studied in this light. Of all the theatres in the world, however, the Chinese and the European are probably the only two of which reasonably full records can be found. The study of the theatres of the other races may not be as informative as these two, because in some of them as among primitive races the development is only beginning, in others, like the Indian theatre, the history may be hard to trace, and in still others, like those in South America, European influence makes the data less valuable for the present purpose. The histories of the Chinese and the European civilizations are sufficiently long for the development of theatre and drama to work itself out fully, and they are, at least in theatre, completely independent of each other, so that conclusions based on their comparative study acquire, if not general, at least augmented validity. The fact that the development of the European theatre was interrupted in the Middle Ages for several hundred years and that the Chinese drama came more than sixteen centuries later than Greek drama shows how important the length of civilizations is if all the potentialities of the mimetic instinct in man are to be fully realized, and the deep-rooted differences between the development of the Chinese and the European theatre shows the limitation of the conclusions drawn from one line of development alone.

From the two long histories emerges the following picture of the theatre as an anthropological phenomenon, in so far as one can trace it in the available data.

653

There are two ultimate sources of theatre and drama: the *mimetic instinct* and the *exhibitionistic trait*. They are distinct, as shown by the fact that separately they have fathered many types of activities other than drama.

Exhibitionism, in mild form, is universal: few men, if any, do not try to make good impressions on others. Although in adults it is usually disguised to conform with social conventions, children make overt efforts to attract attention, often by creating annoyance if other methods fail, for they do not understand modesty and take conspicuous pleasure in showing newly acquired skill and receiving approbation for it. Some adults, who retain more of the trait than others, would venture to entertain, and sometimes bore, their companions with their impromptu performances, such as conjuring tricks, ventriloquism, or funny stories, especially in jovial company. In these efforts lies the germ of the theatre. [1]

The mimetic instinct, which is also innate, may or may not be associated with the exhibitionistic trait. In their recreation, children, without being taught, invent little dramas and play in them, often without any audience and sometimes one child plays it all by himself. Children's mimetic play, though prompted by the instinct to imitate, which is evident also in some animals, may also be their attempt to gain wider experience by living the life of adults. It is not without significance that in many languages "play" means both "sport" and "dramatic performance", for example, *giuoco, joueur* (actor), *Schauspiel, hsi* (戲) — they are both unprofitable but enjoyable activities. Thespis, when asked by Solon whether he was not ashamed to utter and act such lies in the presence of so large a company, answered that there was no harm to speak and act thus *in sport*. [2] The Elizabethan jig, a primitive form of theatre, resembles children's games very closely. [3] Medieval merry-making included sports, contests, dances, mummers' plays, and comic speeches, all of which were called "games". [4] Under special circumstances some adults also enjoyed mimetic play like children:

> "Emperor Ling Ti (reigned A.D. 168-189) often played with his court ladies in his private park. He would ask the ladies to play inn-keepers, and, dressed like a merchant, would come and dine with them for the fun of the pretence". [5]

---

(1) Some people possess natural histrionic talents to an amazing degree. It was said of Sir Thomas More that "would he at Christmas tyd sodenly sometymes stepp in among the players, and never stydinge for the matter, make a parte of his owne there presently amonge them". Roper, *Life and Death of Sir Thomas More,* quoted in Chambers, *Med. Stage,* II. 193.

(2) Plutarch, *Lives* (Solon), Everyman Edition (1910), I. 142.

(3) *Vide* Baskerville, *The Elizabethan Jig,* Ch. VIII.

(4) *Ibid.,* 36 f.

(5) 後漢書, 卷二十三, 五行志, 靈帝. cf. similar activities in the eighteenth century French court.

The desire to show off and the desire to imitate, both dormant in adults, attach themselves to and find expression in many a social and religious activity. Exhibitionism lies behind dress and personal ornaments, it causes the change of manners in different levels of social intercourse, it works through instinct and produces the characteristic behaviour of the sexes in front of each other, it motivates dancing and athletic displays, it lies behind the preacher's affected tone and the messenger's animated gestures, and it expresses itself in all parades and ceremonies. The mimetic instinct shows itself when we imitate the tone and facial expressions of a speaker whom we quote. We unconsciously imitate those whom we love and admire, in fact a large part of the life of a growing child consists of imitating his elders. Among primitive people the mimetic instinct finds outlet in sympathetic magic and similar rituals, which may not have an audience; at least one religion among civilized peoples still has a ritual of a mock sacrificial feast. [6]

One sees the exhibitionistic trait and the mimetic instinct as two different forces ready to come to the surface. The activities listed above, however, all have some social or religious purpose, they are not pure expressions of the desires to show off, which is the ultimate source of the theatre, or of that to imitate, the germ of drama. Pure expressions of the mimetic instinct in daily life are found in, for example, experimenting on pulling faces in front of a mirror and practising caricatures behind the back of those who mortify us unreasonably, and those of the exhibitionistic trait, in display of musical talents, demonstration of skill with toys, teaching card tricks and so forth.

Theatre, in the widest sense, consists of the effort to entertain and the readiness to be entertained. Whenever there is a performance aimed at producing pleasure and an audience to receive it there is theatre: neither the commercialization that ensures constant supply, nor the professionalism that brings specialized cultivation is the differentia of theatre; it is the psychological purpose and the cooperation of performers and spectators that constitute its essence.

Events which are essentially theatrical in nature have been diffused throughout the world in all stages of civilization, before as well as after theatre became an institution, with or without mimetic or dramatic elements, and in conjunction with social and religious activities or independently. It was from this thinly dispersed ''energy'' that the organized theatre first took shape and it is from this that when a theatrical tradition is lost a new birth can take place. The exact time and manner of

---

[6] *Vide* B. Hunninger, *The Origin of the Theatre* (1955), 18-28. In primitive religion, hysteria induced by dance and incantation could make the change of identity a reality to those officiating at the ritual, especially if it was connected with hypnotism and mental derangement. The behaviour of primitive people is said to resemble that of children; hence they may have stronger and less inhibited mimetic desires.

the rise of organized theatre depend on social and cultural conditions and even on historical accidents, but the potentiality is ever present and shows itself in rudimentary manifestations. The mimetic instinct may first find outlet in rituals and grow, inside the religion, into drama, as in the Greek and the medieval theatre, or the exhibitionistic trait may bring about stable forms of pure entertainment first and then the mimetic part of the entertainment grows into drama later, as in the Chinese theatre. [7] It can be noticed that in both the Greek and the medieval religious drama the performance soon became entertainment — the amusement dominating over the element of religion.

Of the early theatrical activities which changed from the diffused to the specific, from the spontaneous and improvised to the deliberate and commercialized, from the connection with social functions to independence, from the amateur to the professional and from the sporadic to the continuous, it is difficult to say at which stage it qualifies for the name of theatre. [8] When a form of entertainment was so often repeated that it acquired a name, it might leave some traces in books and archaeological objects and historians can point to it as a form of theatre, but for one form that acquired a name there might be dozens or hundreds which were nameless [9] and passed unrecorded in history — in harvest festivities, in the formulae of magic charms, in the improvised entertainment for special events,[10] in the itinerant showmen, [11] and in the amusements of the fair ground. [12] The history of the theatre is not like that of a single living thing, growing from seed to embryo and from infancy to maturity, each stage following the preceding one in a definite sequence, it is rather like the volcanic vein which comes to the surface in

---

(7) Since even in the Greek theatre, there were separate origins for Tragedy and Comedy (Bieber, *History of the Greek and Roman Theatre, 7 et seq, 65et seq*) it is futile to look for a universal genesis of the drama. cf. W. Ridgeway, *The Dramas and Dramatic Dances of Non-European Races in Special Reference to the Origin of Greek Tragedy* (1915); and C. Niessen, *Ursprung des asiatischen und griechischen Dramas aus dem Toten- und Ahnenkult* (1953).

(8) The expressions of the exhibitionistic trait in village festivals, which are one source of theatre and drama, are still visible in many parts of Italy, the country of natural actors, although the commercialized theatre and religious ceremonies have had influence on their form. *Vide* J. S. Kennard, *The Italian Theatre*, II. Ch. XV.

(9) Early English dramatic efforts in masques and kindred performances were called "devices" or 'disguise" or "mumming". Chambers, *Elizabethan Stage*, I. 162, 190; III. 279, 256; I. 155. Opera originally meant "works".

(10) e.g. the special play staged in T'ang dynasty for a converted rebel, before the rise of the Chinese drama. See Ch. XXII.

(11) e.g. the troupe described in Xenophon's *Symposium*.

(12) In revelry the mind of the participants is well disposed to entertainment, hence theatrical activities readily arise. The humble efforts at rustic festivities are difficult to trace, but those of the court are well recorded. In the tilts, tournament mixed with impersonations and speeches, in the masque, dance mixed with masquerade and pageant (and sometimes interludes were added). (Chambers,

eruptions at different places and different times, and causes hot springs and geysers besides. [13]

The exhibitionistic trait, without the mimetic instinct, gives rise to various types of non-dramatic shows. The showman sometimes exploits the fascination of danger, as in wild animals and other circus acts, or that of violence, as in cock-fights, animal baiting and gladiators; [14] sometimes he exploits natural curiosity and the sense of wonder, as in story-telling, riddles, puppets, conjuring, ventriloquism, shadow plays, display of scenery, and so on; or he appeals to the appreciation of virtuosity, in difficulty for its own sake, as in acrobatics, juggling, improvised verse, [15] and in the skill of the crippled, or to the sense of beauty, as in instrumental music, ballad singing, fireworks and dancing, or to erotic sensibility, as in nude shows and suggestive songs and dances, or to the interest in contests, as in the exhibition of ball games, wrestling, fencing, and boxing, or to the sense of humour, as in jokes, clowning and nonsensical interpretation of well known books. [16] The variety of his fare is endless.

Drama is a type of "show". It is the most fully developed product of the mimetic instinct, and is preceded by simpler manifestations of that instinct. At the lowest level, the mimetic instinct is satisfied by masquerade in which only substitution is involved and to which the audience is attracted by the mere spectacle. This stage is represented by the pageant. [17] On the next level, mimicry or imitation is

---

Elizabethan Stage, I. 142, 145, 150. III. 212 f). The City (London) also had pageants for its own festivities. (*Ibid.,* I. 135 f). These are in every way the same as rustic revelry except in their lavish ornaments. Medieval revelry, both in England and in Italy, also contained dramatic elements. See Baskerville, *The Elizabethan Jig,* Ch. I and Chambers, *Medieval Stage,* I. Chs. V-XVII for the broad theatrical background in folk festivities and merry-making.

[13] In medieval times, in spite of the suppression by the church, the theatrical demands of the people were expressed in numerous forms of entertainment or quasi-entertainment, such as the Feast of Fools, masques, minstrels, May-games, puppets, pageants, and so on. Chambers, *Med. Stage,* I. Chs. V-XVII *passim;* II. 175 f, 180; C. E. Baehrens, *The Origin of the Masque* (1929). Puppets might have had unrecorded influence on the folk drama of the Renaissance: western actors sometimes imitated puppets (Welsford, *The Fool,* 303 and Ill. facing p. 285). cf. the fascinating performance in the modern Chinese theatre of the actor Liu Pin-K'un 劉斌崑 who played paper-figures used in funerals coming to life.

[14] The sight of a fight stirs our subconscious aggressiveness and love for action and that of danger excites our sympathy and concern.

[15] Tarlton (-1588), the famous Elizabethan clown, was well known for his extempore verse — Baskerville, *The Elizabethan Jig,* 99; Chambers, *Eliz. Stage,* II. 553. For extempore verse-making in Sung dynasty see Ch. XXIV.

[16] cf. the nonsense songs in the Elizabethan jig (Baskerville, *The Elizabethan Jig,* 83) and the nonsense-talks of the Sung dynasty (Ch. XXIV).

[17] e.g. the pageants of Han dynasty. Masquerade was also a form of the Italian popular entertainment in the sixteenth century: in Morley's *Plaine and Easie Introduction to Practicall Musicke* (1597) is

involved and the spectators are amused because they are surprised by the likeness achieved. (18) This stage may be said to be represented by the pantomime. In the highest level — highest because it is the last stage of the development — the player assumes a new identity for a period of time, not only in appearance but also in expression: he acts. The mime copies the surface likeness, and he has to be clever; the actor reveals the heart of the role, and he must have insight.

The development of the Chinese drama from simple impersonation to action and plot was much slower than that of the Greek drama, hence it can serve as a picture of the process, as it were, in slow motion. Beyond pantomime we find three stages in the drama: farce, dramatic sketches and drama with plot.

(2)

Theatrical performances hold the attention of the audience either by immediate appeal or by sustained expectation. In the full-length dramas to which we are now accustomed real excitement does not come until near the end, but the audience, having confidence in the familiar scheme of the dramatists, willingly gather information in the first acts for the pleasures of the last ones. This, however, is not the case in primitive theatres. There the audience will not wait, their patience is not trained and they do not understand investing their mental efforts for long-term dividends. To succeed, the earliest players must excite pleasurable feelings in their audience without lengthy preparations and laughter is the obvious choice for the subject (19) — we can laugh at a funny person at first sight but we do not pity, admire or detest him without some degree of acquaintance. Note how the volunteering guest always chooses laughter for the theme of his improvised entertainment, and how sympathy or horror or hero-worship is hardly ever the subject of entertainment of short duration. The early Chinese farces were dramatized jokes and required one player to introduce the background of the joke, another to make a feint and a last one to surprise the audience with some absurdity or satire. (20) The audience were at

---

mentioned the Italian *mascaradoes* in which players sang and danced to galliards, but sometimes they used no instruments, instead "they haue Curtisans disguised in mens apparell, who sing and daunce to their owne songes". (Quoted in Baskerville, *The Elizabethan Jig,* 37). The European courtezans did not play as important a part as the Chinese sing-song girls in the development of the theatre but they too seem to have had some connection with it.

(18) e.g. the Roman pantomime and the Chinese theatrical representations in Chin dynasty (A.D. 265-419) — see Ch. XXII.

(19) Curiosity and the sense of physical danger can also be exploited in simple entertainment, as they are in the circus, but acrobatics has less dramatic potential than farce.

(20) See Ch. XXIII.

first informed, then baffled and finally tickled, but they did not have long to wait: the whole farce, judging by extant examples, was no longer than a few minutes, and the programme consisted of a series of farces. In the *commedia dell' arte,* which was farce grown to the dimensions of drama, there was continuous comic stage business, but the plot was a mere framework, of little dramatic interest, to hold together the performance of the specialized farce-players.

The psychology of the farce is a mild form of sadism, with unconscious rejoicing over one's own superiority — there is always a butt. [21] In caricatures, a common characteristic of primitive farce, [22] some type or profession is held up for derision, [23] in slap-stick action, a fool or clown receives the deserved violence from a bully, his assistant, [24] and where a cheat is outwitted or a thief swindled, the mirth is mixed with slight moral justification.

The early European farces were buried in the unrecorded history of antiquity, and what traces can be found of them are almost lost in the overwhelming shadow of the Greek dramas. One has to trace the farcical stage of the development of primitive drama in the several periods in which European drama rose entirely or partially anew from the mimetic instinct of the people, such as the Roman theatre and the European theatre in the Renaissance. It is known, however, that farce existed in Greece before the Old Comedy and that some form of popular entertainment involving impersonation existed before Tragedy. [25] Aristotle (*Poetics,* 3) said that the Megarians claimed the comedy as their invention when they became a democracy (about 600 B.C.). Susarion, a comic poet of Megara, who settled in Icaria, was said to have organized simple improvisations into a comic chorus and to have introduced it into Athens between 580 and 560 B.C. [26] Reference is made in Aristophanes' *Wasps* to "merriment filched from Megara". [27] Pre-dramatic and quasi-dramatic

---

[21]   *Vide* E. Welsford, *The Fool,* 314 ff. for the psychology of the Fool in the theatre. Welsford's theory that the audience identify themselves with the Fool who is "none the worse for his slapping" is no doubt true for modern clowns, but in primitive farces a more naive and direct brutality seems to be the dominant factor.

[22]   e.g. the *phlyakes,* in which the gods are caricatured — Bieber, *History of the Greek and Roman Theatre,* Ch. X; Nicoll, *Masks Mimes and Miracles,* 50.

[23]   e.g. the many names of professions in the farces of Sung dynasty, such as "soldiers", "physicians", "thieves", etc. — see Ch. XXIII — and similar names in the *atellanae* — see Nicoll, *Masks Mimes and Miracles,* 73.

[24]   e.g in *ts'an-chün-hsi* 參軍戲 the early Chinese conventionalized farce — see Ch. XXII — or horse-play in the *commedia dell' arte* — see K. M. Lea, *Italian Popular Comedy,* 184, 188 — or mental torments of which the *commedia dell' arte* contains ample examples — see Lea, *op. cit.,* Ch. III. *passim.* cf. *Punch and Judy;* and the definition of the Fool as "he who gets slapped" — E. Welsford, *The Fool,* 314.

[25]   J. T. Allen, *Stage Antiquities,* 8.

[26]   Flickinger, *The Greek Theatre and Its Drama,* 38; Haigh, *The Tragic Drama of the Greeks,* 27.

[27]   *Vide* Flickinger, *op. cit.,* 48.

performances by the *deikeliktai* apparently existed in Sparta. [28] Among the Dorian peoples, theatrical interests appeared to be well developed, for the choral lyrics, which might be religious or secular, and which were sung and danced to by a chorus, reached a high degree of perfection among the Dorian peoples of the Peloponnese, and the Dorian mime or farce, consisting of loosely connected burlesque scenes, abounding in stock characters and enlivened by obscenity and ribald jests, existed among them before Old Comedy. [29] Dramatic representation involving the "development of plot" did not start in Athens, the cradle of European drama, but was, according to Artistotle, "a Sicilian invention" *(Poetics, 5)*. Megarian farce and early impersonation in Corinth were found depicted on vases before the advent of the Old Comedy, with the Corinthian players shown in the phallic costume, heavily padded, similar to those in the Old Comedy. [30] Greek drama, as was developed in connection with the Dionysian cult in Athens, is therefore a sudden flowering rather than the first budding of the mimetic instinct and Comedy and Tragedy were not the earliest forms of dramatic representation; they were, as far as one can see, preceded by farce. Even in Tragedy the plot was at first "short and ludicrous and the language undignified" *(Poetics,* IV). It was the flow of the known dramatic elements of impersonations, farce and plot into the Dionysian Festivals in Athens which gave rise to the Attic drama. [31]

In the Chinese history, the earliest form of theatrical entertainment was court jesters, and there was, before the rise of drama, simple impersonation for many centuries, but it was only at the end of the Sung dynasty when the intensity of the vogue of popular entertainment reached a certain pitch that the drama emerged. In ancient Greece, as the contemporary references and archaeological evidence suggest, the diffused background of theatrical activities were also raised to a level sufficient to give birth to drama in Athens, the then cultural centre. [32] Mimetic ritual alone does not seem to be sufficient explanation for the rise of drama, but a certain degree of vigour is required in the general expression of the mimetic instinct, a minimum "energy-level" to excite a transformation, like the temperature of spontaneous combustion. Mimetic elements existed in the ceremonies of the cults at Eleusis and Delphi but they, like those in the ritual of many other religions, did not develop directly into drama. [33] A departure from the strictly religious interest and

---

[28] T. B. L. Webster, *Greek Theatre Production* (1956), 128.

[29] Flickinger, *op. cit.,* 47; F. M. Cornford, *The Origin of Attic Comedy* (1914), 180.

[30] Pickard-Cambridge, *Dramatic Festivals of Athens,* 194; Bieber, *History of the Greek and Roman Theatre,* 70 f.

[31] Flickinger, *op. cit.,* 51, 56.

[32] In China, the general exuberance in theatrical entertainment gave birth simultaneously or nearly simultaneously to the drama in the northern (Peking) and southern centres of culture (Wenchow).

[33] *Vide* Bieber, *The History of the Greek and Roman Theatre,* 24. Some information on the theatrical characteristics of Tibetan rituals can be found in B. Laufer, *Oriental Theatricals* (1923) published by the Field Museum, Chicago.

the admixture of entertainment is necessary. This shift of interest started early but continued in the Greek theatre till, in the fourth century, the religious and moral significance of Greek dramas was replaced by interest in histrionic technique. [34] This can explain why the mimetic elements in the shamans' rituals in ancient China never became drama in spite of the ornamented liturgy they had. [35] The Dionysian cult, a cult of joy and abandon, [36] and the fair ground and brothel of the late Sung dynasty, were in fact the points of least resistance for the outbreak of the drama. [37] One sees how in China centuries passed without any attempt to deepen the appeals of the topical farce and the dramatic dance by using longer plots: the interest in theatrical entertainment was then too weak to demand such improvements and the influence of other forms of entertainment was lacking to facilitate such a change. Thus the European drama originated in embellished religious ceremony, and the Chinese drama, in embellished pastime, both under the stimulation of general exuberance of theatricals.

To enhance immediate and continual appeal of an impersonating performance, dance and music can also be incorporated. In the farce, the interest of the audience is kept alive by frequent renewals of surprise and humour, but in the dramatic dance, it is the patterned movement that charms the spectators. We watch dances for the same reason as we do processions and marching soldiers; their orderliness appeals to us. The earliest Greek dramas were dances with mimetic elements added to them, hence they were essentially dramatic dances. The rise of the dramatic dance in China may be simultaneous with that of the farce or, owing to the technical development required, slightly later — it is difficult to determine, with the fragmentary information now available, which was the case. The exact origin of the dramatic dances was already obscure at the time when they became worth writing about: [38] the origin of the theme was confused with that of the form in the earliest performance. Of ancient Greek theatricals we learn from Xenophon (*Symposium*) of a boy and a girl from Syracuse who, by means of dance, gesture and words, represented the love of Dionysus and Ariadne at a banquet at which Socrates was a guest. It was then already a commercialized form of entertainment. Mime was also

---

(34) Pickard-Cambridge, *The Theatre of Dionysus in Athens,* 71, referring to Aristotle, *Rhetoric.* For the hedonistic nature of the Greek theatre in spite of the religious background see Flickinger, *op. cit.,* 122 f.

(35) Extra-religious interests caused some of the dances to be diverted into recreational purposes, e.g. the "rain-dance" called *yü* — see Ch. XXXII and 論語，先進（雩）.

(36) cf. Nietzsche, *Birth of Tragedy,* Section 2.

(37) As suitable birthplace of the drama, the fair ground has the advantage of hedonistic background, but the ritual has the advantage of pseudo-dramatic elements: the liturgical text became the dialogue (Aristotle, *Poetics,* 4) the vestment, the costume (Haigh, *The Attic Theatre,* 239) and the ritual formula, perhaps, the action.

(38) See Ch. XXII.

popular among the Dorians of Sicily "from an early period" and Herodas (third century B.C.) wrote mimes which are still extant. [39] The broad undercurrent of popular theatricals in the ancient world which produced the Greek dramas ran through the Republican into the Imperial period and tossed up various forms of primitive theatre that formed the medley of the Roman theatrical performance.

According to Livy, in the games organized in 364 B.C. to avert a pestilence there were dancers imported from Etruria whose graceful movements made a great impression. Native amateurs added banter and mime and the accompaniment by the flute, and a medley, called *Fabulae Saturae,* was evolved which continued to entertain Rome. [40] The mimetic element came from the *Fescennine* verses which were the bantering jests and abuse of clowns, in cork masks, at harvest time. [41] Some time in the third century before Christ, a form of rustic farce, called *Atellanae,* grew up in Campania and became connected in name with the small town of Atella. The present knowledge of *Atellanae* is mostly based on some titles and fragments by Pomponius and Novius, both of the early first century before Christ, but the genre had existed long before then. Even in the first century the farce appeared to have strong characteristics of the primitive theatre and in several ways resembled the early Chinese farces. Among the extant titles of the two types one finds many which suggest similar content:

Atellanae	*Chinese farces of Chin dynasty* (A.D. 1115-1234)
Maccus the Soldier	*Soldier* (卒子家門)
Maccus the Innkeeper	*Quarrel in the Wineshop* (一鬭酒店)
Maccus the Maiden	*Poor and Rich Maidens* (貧富旦)
Maccus in Exile	*Honourable Home-Coming* (衣錦還鄉)
Pappus the Farmer	*The Farmer* (禾下家門)
The Bride of Pappus	*Doctor as Go-Between* (醫作媒)
Inspector of Morals	*The Scheming Officer* (算計孤)
The Pimp	*Teacher's Wife* (師婆兒) [42]

These titles suggest caricature of types and professions and simple dramatization of ridiculous situations. [43] As in early Chinese farces, in *Atellanae* men played

[39] W. Beare, *Oxford Companion to the Theatre* (1951), 532.

[40] Beare, *Roman Stage,* 11.

[41] Beare, *op. cit.,* 9 f; Bieber, *History of the Greek and Roman Theatre,* 301.

[42] *Vide Oxford Companion to the Theatre,* FABULA 1; Nicoll, *Masks Mimes and Miracles,* 68 f; 陶宗儀 , 輟耕錄 , 卷二十五 (金院本名目).

[43] Caricature of people whose life and manners are remote from one's own is still a stock resource of the clown, as in the caricature of professors, landladies, and so on. The appearance of the fool in the rustic farce may have a basis in the personal ridicule of the village fool, who is represented on the stage by the clown. Baskerville (*The Elizabethan Jig,* 91) mentions him in the Elizabethan jig, and he also appeared in the Chinese drama of Yüan dynasty in a fragment called "The Country Clown Knows Not the Theatre" (太平樂府 , 卷九 , 杜善夫 , 莊家不識勾闌). An

women, and riddles and topical allusions were incorporated in the performance as extra attraction. [44] Acting, exaggerated in style, was improvised in the *Atellanae* and masks were used. By the time of Pomponius and Novius the type had grown into verse drama. [45] It did not become a school of literary drama probably because the social function of the theatre in Roman times prevented it from further development in that direction. *Phlyakes,* the type of theatre prevalent in the Dorian settlements in Italy, had also prominent farcical characteristics, but owing to the influence of the Greek theatre on its themes, it became burlesque on mythological characters. [46] This was primitive farce with the ready-made subject matter from a well developed theatre.

The rise of the more sumptuous and poetical forms among the different types of the Renaissance theatre was preluded by a growth of farce all over Europe. [47] Here again the native mimetic instinct was aroused and the resultant energy was tapped by the different rising forms of theatre. In England, for example, farce entered the short moralities which became interludes. [48] In the fifteenth century farce was played in France by many kinds of amateur associations and the development of farce was more complete than in the interludes of England. [49] The dramatic dance appeared in the English theatre in the form of the Elizabethan jig [50] in which the relation to the ballad can, as in early Chinese dramas, be traced, and the music was likewise based on existing tunes. [51] The *sotie* of medieval France was also farcical and included burlesque and clowning; in the fifteenth and sixteenth centuries farce with caricature mixed with dance. [52] Although the extant text of the Elizabethan jigs does not suggest high artistic quality in the literary sense, the actual performance was probably pleasant in its way. A Swiss traveller, Thomas Platter, who visited the Globe Theatre on 21 September, 1599, saw *Julius Caesar* followed by a "dance according to their custom, with extreme elegance. Two in men's clothes and two in women's gave this performance in wonderful combination with each other". [53] It can be noticed that the comic effects of the farce and the interest in

---

element of raillery also seems to be a common characteristic of early farce — as in early Greek comedy, see Flickinger, *The Greek Theatre and Its Drama,* 38 f.

[44] Beare, *op. cit.,* 132 f.

[45] *Ibid.,* 139.

[46] Beare, *op. cit.,* 15.

[47] Nicoll, *Masks Mimes and Miracles,* 172 et seq.

[48] Thorndike, *Shakespeare's Theatre,* 13.

[49] Chambers, *Medieval Stage,* II. 197, 202.

[50] *Vide* Lawrence, *Pre-Restoration Stage Studies,* Ch. IV. The Elizabethan Stage Jig.

[51] *Vide* Baskerville, *The Elizabethan Jig,* 4 f. English ballads in dialogue form could have been performed as jigs — *Ibid.,* 164 f.

[52] Nicoll, *Masks Mimes and Miracles,* 173.

[53] Lawrence, *Pre-Restoration Stage Studies,* 80.

dance and music are not diminished by the lack of illusion: clowns can excite laughter without representing any character and on a bare platform; dramatic illusion became important only when more complicated emotional response required a higher degree of personal sympathy. In fact, the grotesque costume and gestures, for example, in the *phlyakes* and the *commedia dell' arte,* kill rather than create illusion; but accentuation is necessary for the audience of primitive theatres.

(3)

Drama is the most important type of "show", because its interest is the most serious and lasting. [54] Its subject is life itself hence it touches the mainspring of human interest, the interest in emotions, fate and morals. [55] It has a stabilizing effect on the theatre because its deeper appeal brings to the theatre more earnest efforts which lead to professional cultivation, and because its connection with literature, through the script, makes it, at least partially, less perishable.

Much of the cruder interests which the showman exploits has been part of the dramatic interest. Danger and violence are perennially fascinating: wars between countries distant from our own make headlines and crimes and catastrophes attract readers. The motion picture, more frequently than is usually realized, has a chase in its story. The basic pattern of the drama includes the approach of a crisis, the outcome of which keeps the attention of the audience on the play until the end. In milder forms and mixed with some sense of moral superiority, this fascination of danger shows in the favourite subject of scandal in the drama. Whatever drama may be as a form of writing, in the theatre it is always a show and as a show it is often mixed with or incorporates non-dramatic elements, [56] and in the history of theatre and drama cases are not lacking in which after a heavy dose of literature in the drama, the public returned to a style of theatre with more sensuous pleasures in it. [57] All great movements of the theatre are motivated jointly by the invigorating popular appeal and the refinement of aristocratic taste, [58] without the latter the theatre is crude [59] and without the former drama becomes reading material. [60]

---

[54] The early Roman theatre had acrobatics, juggling, sword-swallowing, fire-spitting, fireworks, rope-dancing, trained animals and scenic display: — Nicoll, *Masks Mimes and Miracles,* 84 f. — and so did the spectacles of Han dynasty. These performances may be highly entertaining, but they cannot stir the audience deeply.

[55] It carries also the danger of excessive literary merits choking and ousting the theatrical interests. All art survives by its unique appeal; literature can wither the theatre by sapping the vigour of its sensuous elements.

[56] cf. the repertoire of the English actors in Germany in the seventeenth century; tragedies, comedies, histories, farce, jigs, songs, dances and acrobatics — see Baskerville, *The Elizabethan Jig,* 127.

[57] e.g. the Roman theatre and the modern Chinese theatre.

[58] e.g. the Chinese theatre in the Yüan dynasty and the Elizabethan theatre.

[59] e.g. the English interludes and the Chinese farce of the Sung dynasty.

[60] e.g. Chinese dramas of Ming dynasty and English poetic dramas of the nineteenth century.

With drama, the psychological and artistic purpose of the theatre is of course greatly extended. [61] It can bring excitement and agitation to exercise the psyche of those who live dull lives, [62] it can parade the virtuous and the successful for the audience to admire and to envy, it can teach the detached contemplation on life, it can reveal the depth and power of human emotions, it can criticize or moralize, [63] it can glorify refined sensibility, [64] and it can provide momentary and illusionary escape from and revolt against moral laws. [65] The European dramatic interest, for example, has been constantly shifting its centre: there have been classicism, *tragédie bourgeoise, comédie larmoyante,* romanticism, *pièces à thèse,* naturalism, and so on.

What are normally considered materials for the production of drama, such as scenery, stage lighting, dialogue, music, costume and so on, can enter the performance in various proportions and thearical elements not normally found in drama such as conjuring, acrobatics, trained animals, fireworks, and so forth can also become part of the performance. The variety of style in dramatic elements alone, for instance, in verse or decor, can already produce many different styles of dramatic production, but the relative emphasis on the different elements, [66] the

---

[61] This is why dramatic appreciation requires a connoisseurship of feelings — the ability to distinguish between shades, to comprehend complexities and to catch the elusive.

[62] It can hardly be overlooked that this is an important function of any popular theatre. The people in the audience identify themselves with the characters in the drama to share their excitement and yet remain secure from real dangers.

[63] When social medicine is sugar-coated with wit and humour, it becomes a matter of aesthetic allegiance whether the whole pill or the coating alone deserves the name of art. In any case all propaganda works encourage the confusion between ethical and aesthetic values. They also become obsolete soon and carry with them whatever art they contain to obscurity. From the intellectual point of view, theatre with a message is always suspect, because it is as unreliable a tool for criticism as it is effective for propaganda: particular cases instead of general truth sway the judgement of the sentimental through dramatic devices which can be, and have been used to make the audience sympathize even with the criminal. Theatre is not a place where clear thinking is taught. Besides, imaginative readers do not require the moving life-size book illustrations and specimens for lecture-room demonstration which actors in problem plays have become.

[64] There are only two psychological positions for the audience: to be emotionally involved and to remain mentally detached. One or the other is adopted by the audience according to the type of appreciation they seek. The two positions mark the difference between the Chinese and the modern European theatre.

[65] As in the medieval Feast of Fools and the stage clown. See Chambers, *Medieval Stage,* I. Chs. XIII- XIV; E. Welsford, *The Fool,* 317.

[66] Exclusive interest in one part of the theatre leads to forms of entertainment which are not theatre in the usual sense of the term, such as the display of scenery alone (in nineteenth century England), recital of dramatic passages (in ancient Rome) and closet dramas written to be read only. A curious combination is found in the monodrama, which consists of one actor or actress, supported by music and silent figures (or chorus); it was popular in Germany in the late eighteenth century.

incorporation of various non-dramatic material, [67] the success with which such material is worked into the dramatic purpose and the various psychological and artistic inclinations and aims give infinite variety to the potential styles of drama and supply the reforming spirit with endless opportunities for battle cries. The history of the theatre is the story of how the many interests of the theatre became at one time active and at another, latent, how they take turn to be deprecated, how their vogue and decline are influenced by social conditions and other forms of art and how the public, like a person without deep interest in any aspect of art, sought diversion along the line of least resistance, refusing to make conscious effort in the cultivation of taste, and getting tired of one toy after another. Since many theatrical ideals are mutually exclusive, for example, one cannot have realistic scenery and yet reap the advantage of the geometrical clarity of the bare platform stage, it is difficult to believe in the absolute superiority of one form over another, or in the existence of the "ideal theatre".

The claim that later forms are always better than earlier ones becomes meaningless when the sequence is found to be reversed in the theatrical history of other countries. The "advance" and "retrogression" of the theatre can have meaning only after it has been determined what historical changes are and what are not natural evolution. This problem, like that of progress and degeneration which is a matter of artistic or ethical value, lies outside the purpose of this book.

---

[67] For example, the chorus in the Greek drama, and the prologue in the Chinese southern dramas: they were carried over into drama from its antecedent forms, partly through the inertia of public taste and partly through conservation by the players in the period of transition.

BIBLIOGRAPHY

(The following list gives the titles of the Chinese works that provided the documentary basis for this book. Titles of books in European languages that are cited or that relate to particular topics covered in the text are given in the footnotes).

(A) Modern Chinese theatre.

聽花, 中國劇, 民一四 (日文：辻武雄, 支那芝居, 大正十三年).
(T'ing Hua, *Chung-kuo chü)*

齊如山, 中國劇之組織, 民十七.
(Ch'i Ju-shan, *Chung-kuo chü chih tsu-chih)*

齊如山, 京劇之變遷, 民二四.
(Ch'i Ju-shan, *Ching-chü chih pien ch'ien)*

齊如山, 國劇身段譜, 民二四.
(Ch'i Ju-shan, *Kuo-chü shen-tuan p'u)*

齊如山, 上下場, 民二四.
(Ch'i Ju-shan, *Shang hsia ch'ang)*

齊如山, 臉譜, 民二五.
(Ch'i Ju-shan, *Lien-p'u)*

齊如山, 戲班, 民二四.
(Ch'i Ju-shan, *Hsi pan)*

齊如山, 行頭盔頭, 民二四.
(Ch'i Ju-shan, *Hsing-t'ou k'uei-t'ou)*

齊如山, 戲劇脚色名詞考, 民二四.
(Ch'i Ju-shan, *Hsi-chü chiao-se ming-tz'u k'ao)*

齊如山, 國劇簡要圖案, 民二四.
(Ch'i Ju-shan, *Kuo-chü chien yao t'u-an)*

張笑俠, 臉譜大全, 民二七.
(Chang Hsiao-hsia, *Lien-p'u ta ch'üan)*

徐慕雲, 梨園影事, 民二二.
(Hsü Mu-yün, *Li-yüan ying shih)*

王大錯 (編), 戲考, 民十四.
(Wang Ta-ts'o, *Hsi k'ao)*

凌善清等, 戲學彙考, 民十四.
(Ling Shan-ch'ing, *Hsi hsüeh hui k'ao*)

中國戲曲研究院, 京劇叢刊（增編中）.
(Chung-kuo hsi-ch'ü yen-chiu, yüan, *Ching, chü ts'ung-k'an*)

李世忠, 梨園集成, 光緒六年.
(Li Shih-chung, *Li-yüan chi ch'eng*)

齊如山, 梅蘭芳藝術之一斑, 民二四.
(Ch'i Ju-shan, *Mei Lan-fang i-shu chih i-pan*)

王夢生, 梨園佳話, 民四.
(Wang Meng-sheng, *Li yüan chia hua*)

(Valuable information can also be found in:
北平國劇學會出版, 戲劇叢刊一至四期 . (Pei-p'ing kuo-chü hsüeh-hui, *Hsi-chü ts'ung-k'an*), especially in the following articles: 齊如山, 論戲詞 不怕典在事後（二期）. 尚和玉, 武工把子名詞（二期）. 張伯駒, 亂彈音韵輯要（二至四期）.   Articles of less importance are listed in: 國立北平圖書館, 文學論文索引, 民二一； 續編, 民二二； 三編, 民二五.   (Kuo li Pei-p'ing tu-shu-kuan, *Wen-hsüeh lun-wen so-yin*).

(B) History of the Chinese theatre.
王國維, 宋元戲曲史, 民二三. (First chapter translated by E. Erkes, Das chinesische Theater vor der T'ang Zeit, *Asia Major,* Vol. X (1935)). (Wang Kuo-wei, *Sung Yüan hsi ch'ü shih*)

王國維, 曲錄序（海寧王靜安先生遺書, 民二五）.
(Wang Kuo-wei, *Ch'ü lu hsü*)

王國維, 唐宋大曲考（見遺書中）.
(Wang Kuo-wei, *T'ang Sung ta-ch'ü k'ao*)

王國維, 戲曲考源（見遺書中）.
(Wang Kuo-wei, *Hsi-ch'ü k'ao yüan*)

王國維, 古劇脚色考（見遺書中）.
(Wang Kuo-wei, *Ku chü chiao-se k'ao*)

王國維, 優語錄（見遺書中）.
(Wang Kuo-wei, *Yu yü lu*)

王國維, 錄曲餘談（見遺書中）.
(Wang Kuo-wei, *Lu ch'ü yü t'an*)

青木正兒, 中國近世戲曲史（王古魯譯, 民二七）.
(Aoki Masaru, *Shina kinsei gikyoku shi*)

馮沅君, 古劇說彙, 民三六.
(Feng Yüan-chün, *Ku chü shuo hui*)

盧前，明清戲曲史，民二四．
(Lu Ch'ien, *Ming Ch'ing hsi-ch'ü shih*)

吳梅，中國戲曲概論，民十五．
(Wu Mei, *Chung-kuo hsi-ch'ü kai lun*)

鹿原學人，京戲二百年史，民二二．
(Lu-yüan hsüeh-jen, *Ching-hsi erh-pai nien shih*)

盧冀野，中國戲劇概論，民二三．
(Lu Chi-yeh, *Chung-kuo hsi-chü kai lun*)

青木正兒，元人雜劇序說（隋樹森譯，民三十）．
(Aoki Masaru, *Gennin zatsugeki josetsu*)

周貽白，中國戲劇小史，民三五．
(Chou I-pai, *Chung-kuo hsi-chü hsiao shih*)

周貽白，中國戲劇史，民四二．
(Chou I-pai, *Chung-kuo hsi-chü shih*)

姚燮，復道人今樂考證，民二五印．
(Yao Hsieh, *Fu tao-jen chin yüeh k'ao-cheng*)

焦循，劇說（清）．
(Chiao Hsün, *Chü shuo*)

李嘯倉，宋元伎藝雜考，一九五三．
(Li Hsiao-ts'ang, *Sung Yüan chi-i tsa k'ao*)

吳自牧，夢粱錄（宋）．
(Wu Tzu-mu, *Meng liang lu*)

周密，武林舊事（宋）．
(Chou Mi, *Wu-lin chiu shih*)

陶宗儀，輟耕錄（元）．
(T'ao Tsung-i, *Ch'o keng lu*)

孟元老，東京夢華錄（宋）．
(Meng Yüan-lao, *Tung-ching meng hua lu*)

耐得翁，都城紀勝（宋）．
(Nai Te-weng, *Tu-ch'eng chi sheng*)

崔令欽，敎坊記（唐）．
(Ts'ui Ling-ch'in, *Chiao-fang chi*)

段安節，樂府雜錄（唐）．
(Tuan An-chieh, *Yüeh-fu tsa lu*)

黃雪蓑，青樓集（元）．
(Huang Hsüeh-so, *Ch'ing lou chi*)

潘之恆，秦淮劇品（明）．
(P'an Chih-heng, *Ch'in-huai chü p'in*)

阿魯圖等, 宋史, 樂志.
(A Lu-t'u et al., "Yüeh chih", Sung shih)

歐陽修等, 新唐書, 禮樂志.
(Ou-yang Hsiu et al., "Li yüeh chih", Hsin T'ang shu)

劉昫等, 舊唐書, 音樂志.
(Liu Hsü et al., "Yin yüeh chih", Chiu T'ang shu)

魏徵等, 隋書, 音樂志.
(Wei Cheng et al., "Yin Yüeh chih", Sui shu)

房喬等, 晉書, 樂志.
(Fang Ch'iao et al., "Yüeh chih", Chin shu)

班固, 漢書, 禮樂志.
(Pan Ku et al., "Li yüeh chih", Han shu).

(Historical information on the musical aspects of the theatre can also be found in books on dramatic poetry — see list below in (E). Miscellaneous historical information and criticism in the later part of Ch'ing dynasty can be found in the convenient collection: 張江裁（編), 清代燕都梨園史料, 民二三. (Chang Chiang-ts'ai, Ch'ing tai Yen-tu Li-yüan shih liao) which contains: 燕蘭小譜, 夢華瑣簿, 燕臺花事錄, 日下看花記, 曇波, 鳳城品花記, 片羽集, 法嬰秘笈, 懷芳記, 聽春新詠, 明僮合錄, 側帽餘譚, 鶯花小譜, 增補菊部羣英, 菊臺集秀錄, 金臺殘淚記, 評花新譜, 新刊菊臺集秀錄, 燕臺鴻爪集, 菊部羣英, 瑤臺小錄, 辛壬癸甲錄, 羣英續集, 情天外史, 長安看花記, 宣南雜组, 越縵堂菊話, 丁年玉筍志, 擷華小錄, 異伶傳, 哭庵賞菊詩, 梨園舊話, 北京梨園掌故長編, 鞠部叢譚, 梨園軼聞, 北京梨園金石文字錄, 宣南零夢錄, 舊劇叢譚. Most of the writings, which cover the eighteenth and nineteenth centuries, are about favourite players. The authors are nearly all anonymous, or known only by pen names).

(C) Dramatic text of Yüan, Ming and Ch'ing dynasty.

（明）臧晉叔（編）, 元曲選
(Tsang Chin-shu, Yüan ch'ü hsüan)

東京帝國大學刊, 覆元槧古今雜劇三十種.
(Tung-Ching Ti-kuo-ta-hsüeh, Fu yüan-ch'ien ku chin tsa-chü san-shih chung)

北京古今小品書籍刊行會, 永樂大典本戲文殘本三種.
(Pei-Ching ku chin hsiao p'in shu-chi k'an hsing hui, Yung-lo Ta-tien pen hsi-wen ts'an-pen san chung)

上海涵芳樓刊印, 孤本元明雜劇.
(Shang-Hai Han-fang-lou, Ku pen Yüan Ming tsa-chü)

南京國學圖書館影印，元明雜劇．
(Nan-Ching kuo-hsüeh t'u-shu-kuan, *Yüan Ming tsa-chü*)

（明）毛晉（刊），六十種曲．
(Mao Chin, *Liu-shih chung ch'ü*)

（明）沈泰（刊），盛明雜劇．
(Shen T'ai, *Sheng Ming tsa-chü*)

（民國）劉世珩（編），暖紅室彙刻傳奇．
(Liu Shih-heng, *Nuan-hung-shih hui k'o ch'uan-ch'i*)

（民國）吳梅（編），奢摩他室曲叢．
(Wu Mei, *She-mo-t'a-shih ch'ü ts'ung*)

（明）周憲王（撰），雜劇十段錦．
(Chou Hsien-wang, *Tsa-chü shih tuan chin*)

（清）李漁（撰），笠翁十種曲．
(Li Yü, *Li-weng shih chung ch'ü*)

（民國）鄭振鐸（編），清人雜劇．
(Cheng chen-to, *Ch'ing jen tsa-chü*)

（清）錢沛思（編），綴白裘．
(Ch'ien P'ei-szu, *Chui pai ch'iu*)

（清）余治，庶幾堂全集．
(Yü Chih, *Shu-chi-t'ang ch'üan-chi*)

（清）李世忠，梨園集成．
(Li Shih-chung, *Li yüan chi ch'eng*)

(Many minor collections are not included in this list. Discoveries of hitherto unknown dramas are still being made; for bioliography see. 王國維，曲錄（海寧王靜安先生遺書）**(Wang Kuo-wei, *Ch'ü lu*),** 吉川幸次郎，元雜劇研究（昭和十九年），序說四；**(Yoshikawa Kojiro, Gen zatsugeki kenkyū),** 徐調孚，現存元人雜劇（一九五五），頁四至六）． **(Hsü T'iao-fu, *Hsien ts'un Yüan jen tsa-chü).***

(D) Dramatic text with musical score.

（清）葉堂（撰），納書楹曲譜，乾隆五十六年，一七九二．
(Yeh T'ang, *Na shu ying ch'ü p'u*)

（清）王季烈（編），集成曲譜，光緒三年，一八八一．
(Wang Chi-lieh, *Chi ch'eng ch'ü p'u*)

（清）張怡菴（撰），六也曲譜，光緒三十四年，一九〇九．
(Chang I-an, *Liu yeh ch'ü p'u*)

（清）莊親王（撰）九宮大成南北詞宮譜，乾隆殿刊本，乾隆七年，一七四三，始編． (Chuang Ch'in-wang, *Chiu kung ta ch'eng nan pei tz'u kung p'u*)

673

(E) Books on the theory of dramatic poetry (especially on its relation to music).

寧獻王，太和正音譜（明）．

(Ning Hsien-wang, *T'ai ho cheng yin p'u*)

沈璟，南九宮十三調曲譜（明）．

(Shen Ching, *Nan chiu kung shih-san tiao ch'ü p'u*)

康熙（勅撰），欽定曲譜（清）．

(K'ang Hsi (decreed comp.), *Ch'in ting ch'ü p'u*)

周德清，中原音韻（元）．

(Chou Te-ch'ing, *Chung-yüan yin-yün*)

范善溱，中州音韻（明）．

(Fan Shan-chen, *Chung-chou yin-yün*)

王驥德，曲律（明）．

(Wang Chi-te, *Ch'ü lü*)

吳梅，顧曲麈談（民國）．

(Wu Mei, *Ku ch'ü t'an*)

王季烈等，集成曲譜（附論）（清）．

(Wang Chi-lieh (ed.), *Chi ch'eng ch'ü p'u*)

魏良輔，曲律（明）．

(Wei Liang-fu, *Ch'ü lü*)

沈寵綏，度曲須知（明）．

(Shen Ch'ung-sui, *Tu ch'ü hsü chih*)

徐大椿，樂府傳聲（清）．

(Hsü Ta-ch'un, *Yüeh-fu ch'uan sheng*)

何良俊，曲論（明）．

(Ho Liang-chün, *Ch'ü lun*)

沈德符，顧曲雜言（明）．

(Shen Te-fu, *Ku ch'ü tsa yen*)

騷隱居士，衡曲麈談（明）．

(Sao Yin Chü Shih, *Heng ch'ü chu t'an*)

呂天成，曲品（明）．

(Lü T'ien-ch'eng, *Ch'ü p'in*)

李調元，雨村曲話（清）．

(Li T'iao-yüan, *Yü ts'un ch'ü hua*)

項衡方，曲韻探驪，民三三．

(Hsiang Heng-fang, *Ch'ü yün t'an li*)

李漁，李笠翁曲話（清）．

(Li Yü, *Li Li-weng ch'ü hua*)

INDEX

675